A Chronology of Conflict and Resolution, 1945–1985

A Chronology of
Conflict
and
Resolution,
1945–1985

John E. Jessup

Greenwood Press
New York • Westport, Connecticut • London

70

Library of Congress Cataloging-in-Publication Data

Jessup, John E.
  A chronology of conflict and resolution, 1945-1985 / John E.
Jessup.
    p. cm.
  Includes index.
  ISBN 0-313-24308-5 (lib. bdg. : alk. paper)
  1. Military history, Modern—20th century—Chronology. 2. World
politics—1945- —Chronology. I. Title.
  U42.J47 1989
  355'.02'0904—dc19   88-28974

British Library Cataloguing in Publication Data is available.

Ref

JES

Library of Congress Catalog Card Number: 88-28974
ISBN: 0-313-24308-5

First published in 1989

Greenwood Press, Inc.
88 Post Road West, Westport, Connecticut 06881

Printed in the United States of America

The paper used in this book complies with the
Permanent Paper Standard issued by the National
Information Standards Organization (Z39.48-1984).

10 9 8 7 6 5 4 3 2 1

Contents

vi   Contents

Preface

The history of conflict since the end of the Second
World War is a story that defies human understanding. When World
War I ended in 1918, the civilized world rejoiced that it had
"fought the war to end all wars," and that it could begin the
process of rebuilding a shattered Europe based upon principles
that transcended regional differences. That dream was short-
lived, however, and the very outcome of the war and the means
used to build the new Europe set into motion forces that plunged
the world into an even deeper abyss of misery and despair with
the onset of World War II.

Once again, the victory, in 1945, over the dark forces
was perceived as a sign that humanity had been given a "second
chance" to set the world right. It is a sad commentary on the
nature of man that we seem to have allowed this opportunity to
slip through our fingers. The United Nations, born of such high
hopes and lofty ideals, offered to many the very instrument of
restraint and conciliation that its predecessor, the League of
Nations, had failed to become. Some say the United Nations also
has failed in furnishing the authority to impel restraint and
that it continues to fail. The truth is, of course, that men and
nations have allowed it to fail. Ralph Waldo Emerson probably
said it best when he wrote, "A nation never fails but by
suicide." Certainly, the suicidal course upon which men and
nations seem to be embarked, if the content of this volume is to
be believed, gives every indication that man has learned nothing
from the past and that conflict will continue if not in volume
then at least in intensity.

It must be stated from the outset that this chronology
barely scratches the surface when taken as a record of the
misery that man has inflicted on his fellow man since 1945. If
it was purely a study of war and its consequences, then at least

some relatively clear lines of demarcation might be drawn. The
struggle in Viet Nam was a war, whether or not the politicians
were willing to   admit it, and, as such, it could be properly
categorized as to size, longevity, force ratios, etc. Such
parameters would make it relatively easy to choose what should
and what should not be included. This is a chronology of conflict rather than of war, however, and there are few, if any,
rules that can be applied to determine what qualifies for
cataloging and what does not. There are as many definitions of
conflict as there are people to ask and none of them seems
properly adequate when it comes to settling on standards for a
work of this type. Similarly, it is unclear how one determines
the onset of conflict or, for that matter, when it ends.

        As there are so few "rules," other than those that
could be applied based on my view of the world, and a lifetime
of experience in the military service and as a military
historian, the choice of entries took on a rational, yet totally
arbitrary, nature. If the event caused misery, or was brought
about by one man's struggle against another, it became a part of
the chronology. While this system probably works as well as any,
it does leave one exposed to the most serious charge that can be
made, that of failing to identify an event of great or significant importance. Almost certainly, some patriot or widow will
find fault with this book because a particular event of great
national or personal success or tragedy has been overlooked. For
this I apologize and hope the oversight does not create a
greater consternation than did the event itself.

        The intent behind the preparation of this book was
that it should be used as a research tool and not read as one
would read a text book on a single subject. There are some,
however, who claim that much can be gained from reading the book
from cover to cover and that such an idea be recommended to
industrious readers interested in better understanding the
course of events that has led us to the world as we see it
today. The work covers the period 1945 through 1985. The years
following have shown that little was learned from these four
decades, although the world appears to have become somewhat more
quiet. Let us hope the trend continues.

        The research for this work was conducted in two parts:
first, a group of dedicated students of military history at
George Mason University in Fairfax, Virginia, assisted me without remuneration and collected extracts from several of the
leading newspapers' indices. Concurrently, I attacked a lengthy
list of publications, such as <u>Strategic Survey</u>, <u>Naval Pro-
ceedings</u>, various official and unofficial chronologies on the
war in Viet Nam and the wars in the Middle East, chronologies I
had prepared for other projects on Afghanistan and Viet Nam, the
publications of the Department of State on terrorism, and the
Department's current policy papers produced by the Bureau of
Public Affairs. Other sources included the "Issue Briefs," published by the Congressional Research Service of the Library of

Congress, reference publications of the Department of Army, such as _Internal Defense Operations: A Case Study: Malaya 1948-60_, which was printed by the US Army Command and General Staff College, and the International Institute for Strategic Studies _Adelphi Papers_ and annual _Military Balance_ reports. In addition to this, only partially complete, list of sources, I relied on the various yearbooks of the _Encyclopedia Britannica_ and on R. Ernest and Trevor N. Dupuy's _Encyclopedia of Military History: From 3500 B.C. to the Present_ for the proper spellings of names and places and to confirm otherwise elusive dates.

The question of spelling was, in itself, quite a problem. Where variant spellings for place and other names existed, and were readily apparent, I included them parenthetically so as to insure proper identification by the reader. More of these were obviously missed than found, however, so there may be difficulty in identifying a few people and place names. I have relied heavily on acronyms and abbreviations to save space in the text and have included a rather lengthy glossary. Similarly, I have used a few basic identifiers, such as "Communist China," even though a more proper designation would be "The Peoples' Republic of China." I have taken one or two other, similar liberties in index headings, etc., but they should not distract from the overall value of the work.

Another major problem that had to be dealt with concerned the accurate placing of events geographically. This was accomplished by the use of a large collection of excellent maps acquired over the years as a subscriber to the _National Geographic_. In addition, the "Background Notes" series, published by the Department of State, were invaluable in locating obscure locations in some of the emerging countries, especially those on the Africa continent. Lastly, the gazetteers in at least one-half dozen world atlases assisted in both locating and spelling otherwise impossible to locate corners of the world.

As one can see, this work was produced in camera-ready copy for the publisher through the use of a word processer. It was not the way the project started, but forces beyond anyone's con- trol prevailed, and it is how the project was finally completed. Research and writing are fun; editing and formatting for publi- cation are not! As the events that caused this decision to be made were primarily of my doing, the responsibility for allowing that decision was largely mine also.

For the computer enthusiast, the actual work was accomplished on an enhanced Apple IIe computer with a 1.5MB RAM, a 10MB Apple Sider hard drive, and a 20MB streamer tape backup sub-system. The word-processing software utilized in the effort was Appleworks v.2.0 reinforced with Pinpoint Accessories. The final product was printed on a NEC 3530, letter-perfect printer. This printer utilized a Pica 10, Spinwriter thimble. I do not believe I could have manipulated the amount of data that found its way into this book without this computer configuration.

Lastly, and as is proper, I need to thank the number of
people who gave their support and assistance in the
preparationof this study. I must thank my students collectively
as fate dealt me a sad blow when my list of helpers
mysteriously disappeared, probably buried in one of the mounds
of paper that the use of computers has yet to overcome. They
will know who they are and that they have my heartfelt thanks.
My special gratitude goes to Marcia Markey who somehow managed
to find the time to index this work and to compile the
abbreviations and acronyms. All of this she accomplished in
between caring for her family and her own graduate studies. She
is a major contributer to this work and she, along with the two
dozen students who helped compile the data, deserves much of the
credit for any success this book may achieve. As to the book's
shortcomings, oversights, errors, confoundments, derelictions,
and blatant incongruities, these are my responsibility, and mine
alone.

Chronology

1945

2   JAPAN - Traditional date signifying the end of World War II.

2   JAPAN - US General of the Army Douglas MacArthur is designated Supreme Commander Allied Powers and is given the mission of establishing the occupation of Japan.

2   INDOCHINA - Having seized power on 25 August, the Viet Minh leader, Ho Chi Minh, proclaims the independence of Viet Nam and the establishment of the Democratic Republic of Viet Nam.

9   CHINA - Japanese occupation forces capitulate to Chiang Kai-shek's Nationalist government in Nanking. British forces reoccupy Shanghai.

10   NORWAY - Vidkun Quisling is sentenced to death as a Nazi collaborator. Sentence is carried out on 24 October.

12   SINGAPORE - The Japanese garrison formally surrenders to British forces.

13   IRAN - The Allied Command assures the Iranian government that all foreign troops will be withdrawn by 2 March 1946.

14   UNITED STATES - A Joint Congressional Committee is ap-
            pointed to look into the causes of the disaster that
            struck Pearl Harbor on 7 December 1941, when the Jap-
            anese disabled the American fleet.

20-23   INDIA - The All-India Congress rejects the 19 Septem-
            ber English offer of limited autonomy within the
            British Empire and demands Great Britain immediately
            leave India.

23   EGYPT - The Egyptian government demands a termination
            of British occupation through modification of the 1936
            Anglo-Egyptian Treaty. The Egyptians also demand the
            annexation of the Sudan.

29   INDONESIA - Anglo-Dutch forces arrive in Batavia to
            disarm and repatriate the Japanese garrison and to
            reestablish Dutch authority in the Netherlands East
            Indies.

30   CHINA - United States military forces, including the
            US 1st Marine Division, arrive in China to prevent
            further clashes between Communist and Nationalist
            forces in the civil war that reignited in August 1945.
            The Americans initially occupy the Shantung Peninsula
            and eastern Hopei province.

OCTOBER

            SOUTH AFRICA - The wartime coalition government breaks
            up as Labor and Dominion Party representatives with-
            draw. This leaves the United Party of Jan Smuts in
            complete control.

7   PORTUGAL - Opposition political parties are allowed
            for the first time by Premier Antonio Salazar.

9   FRANCE - Pierre Laval is sentenced to death for col-
            laborating with the Nazis.

9   INDOCHINA - An Anglo-French pact giving full recogni-
            tion to French rights in Indochina is signed in Lon-
            don.

11   MOROCCO - The Allies invoke a slightly modified 1924
            convention and reestablish the international adminis-
            tration of Tangiers.

12   INDONESIA - The Dutch government offers to negotiate
            with those Indonesians wishing an independent nation
            within the Kingdom of the Netherlands.

14   CZECHOSLOVAKIA - A new provisional national assembly is elected by indirect suffrage.

15   GREAT BRITAIN - Parliament votes to extend its wartime emergency powers for an additional five years.

18   VENEZUELA - A military-led coup overthrows the government of President Isaias Medina. A military ruling junta takes charge of the country.

19   INDONESIA - War begins when troops of the Indonesian People's Army attack the Anglo-Dutch occupation force.

20   MIDDLE EAST - Egypt, Iraq, Lebanon, and Syria warn the US that the establishment of a Jewish state in Palestine will mean war.

20   MONGOLIA - The Mongolian people overwhelmingly vote for independence from China.

22   VENEZUELA - Romulo Betancourt is named provisional president by the ruling military junta.

24   UNITED NATIONS - The United Nations Organization comes into formal existence when the 29th nation ratifies the pact.

25   BRAZIL - Because of popular unrest, President Getulio Vargas is forced to resign after a 15-year dictatorship. He is temporarily replaced by Chief Justice Jose Linhares

NOVEMBER

6   INDONESIA - A Dutch offer of autonomy and dominion status is rejected by Indonesian Republican Party leaders.

10   ALBANIA - The USSR and most western powers recognize the government of Premier Enver Hoxha.

11   YUGOSLAVIA - Marshal Tito's National Front wins a substantial majority in the constituent assembly elections.

13   INDONESIA - Achmed Sukarno becomes president of Indonesia.

15   UNITED NATIONS - The United States, Canada, and Great Britain offer to share scientific nuclear data with the United Nations.

15   UNITED STATES - The Pearl Harbor investigating commit-
           tee opens its formal hearing into the causes of the
           disaster.

15   CHINA - A Nationalist Chinese military offensive
           begins in southern Manchuria aimed at halting Commu-
           nist infiltration into region under the cover of the
           Chungking peace talks. The Soviet Union refuses per-
           mission for the Nationalists to traverse its treaty
           zone, but the United States allows them to land and
           pass through its occupation territory.

16   FRANCE - Charles DeGaulle is unaminously elected pres-
           ident by the provisional government.

18   IRAN - A revolt sponsored by the communist-inspired
           Tudeh Party begins in Azerbaijan Province. Soviet
           troops intervene and prevent Iranian government forces
           from quelling the uprising.

18   BULGARIA - The communist Fatherland Front wins in a
           single-list general election.

18   PORTUGAL - Salazar wins an easy victory when the oppo-
           sition parties boycott the first general election in
           20 years.

20   GERMANY - Twenty-two Nazi war criminals go on trial
           before an international tribunal at Nuremburg.

25   AUSTRIA - The first general elections since the war
           are held in Austria. The People's Party wins over the
           Socialists and Communists.

25   CHINA - Chinese Nationalist troops push as far as
           Chinchow easily defeating the forces of Mao Tse Tung.

26   CHINA - US Ambassador Patrick J. Hurley resigns after
           the failure of his peace-making mission.

29   INDONESIA - British forces capture the Indonesian
           rebel capital at Surabaya.

29   YUGOSLAVIA - The Federal People's Republic of Yugo-
           slavia is proclaimed.

30   CHINA - A Chinese Communist offensive seizes most of
           the Shantung Peninsula not in American hands.

DECEMBER

2   ALBANIA - A communist-style single-slate general
           election returns the Hoxha government.

2   BRAZIL - General Enrico Dutra is elected president.

4   UNITED STATES - American participation in the United
         Nations Organization is approved by the Senate.

5   CHINA - Former Ambassador Hurley accuses a number of
         Department of State Foreign Service Officers of sym-
         pathy for the Communists and complicity in the failure
         of his mission.

6   GREAT BRITAIN - The United States grants the British a
         loan of $3.75 billion. This is followed by an addi-
         tional loan of $1.25 billion given Great Britain by
         Canada.

12   GREAT BRITAIN - The British government announces the
         formation of the East African High Commission.

14   CHINA - US General of the Army George C. Marshall is
         appointed the personal representative of President
         Harry S. Truman and is sent to China to seek peace for
         that country.

18   SYRIA - An Anglo-French agreement pledges the with-
         drawal of their troops from Syria. The withdrawal is
         completed by 15 April 1946.

20   AUSTRIA - Karl Renner is unanimously elected president
         of the republic.

27   KOREA - The US, USSR, and Great Britain reach an
         agreement at the Moscow Conference to establish a pro-
         visional democratic government for Korea. The plan is
         to last for five years and includes China in the trus-
         teeship. The plan is doomed from the outset.

Notes

1946

INDIA - The month marks the beginning of a long period of serious clashes between Hindu and Muslim factions in which thousands will die on both sides.

1   ITALY - The Allies return control of the province of Balzano to the Italian government.

3   GREAT BRITAIN - William Joyce (Lord Haw Haw) is hanged for treason at London's Wandsworth Prison.

7   AUSTRIA - The Republic of Austria is recognized by the Allies and is restored to the borders it held in 1937 before the German "Anschluss."

10   UNITED NATIONS - The first UN General Assembly session is held in London.

10   CHINA - Ambassador George C. Marshall is successful in concluding a truce between Nationalist and Communist factions. The truce proves to be fragile and short-lived, however, and fighting will once again break out in several areas.

11   ALBANIA - The nation proclaims itself a People's Republic with close ties to the USSR.

11   HAITI - Led by Colonel Paul Magloire, a military junta overthrows the government of President Elie Lescot. Dumarsais Estime takes his place as the nation's leader.

12   UNITED NATIONS - The membership of the United Nations
            Security Council is finalized.

17   UNITED NATIONS - The Security Council meets in formal
            session for the first time in London.

20   FRANCE - President DeGaulle resigns because of Leftist
            opposition to his programs.

27   GERMANY - The first elections are held at the local
            level in the American occupation zone.

31   YUGOSLAVIA - A new constitution is adopted that
            closely resembles that of the USSR.

FEBRUARY

1   HUNGARY - Hungary proclaims itself a republic. Zoltan
            Tildy is elected president.

4   HUNGARY - Ference Nagy becomes premier.

17   CHINA - The Chinese Communists demand joint authority
            in Manchuria.

19   INDONESIA - Dutch and British forces continue to push
            back the rebel forces as negotiations get underway for
            a peaceful settlement to the dispute.

21   FINLAND - The ex-president, Risto Ryti, and a number
            of other former national leaders are sentenced to
            prison for involving the nation in the war as a Nazi
            ally.

24   ARGENTINA - Colonel Juan D. Peron is elected presi-
            dent.

27   MONGOLIA - The government signs a ten-year treaty of
            friendship with Moscow.

MARCH

1-9   CHINA - The Soviets begin withdrawal from Manchuria
            taking vast amounts of Japanese machinery and other
            military and civilian equipment with them. Much mili-
            tary equipment was left behind, however, for the ob-
            vious purpose of being collected by the Chinese Commu-
            nist forces moving into the region.

4   SPAIN - A number of western powers appeal to the Span-
            ish people to oust the Franco government.

5   UNITED STATES - British Prime Minister Winston S.
           Churchill makes his "Iron Curtain" speech at West-
           minister College in Fulton, Missouri. Churchill tells
           an audience that includes President Harry S. Truman
           that the activities of the Soviet Union have caused a
           decline in confidence in "the haggard world."

6   INDOCHINA - Under an agreement reached with the com-
           munists, France recognizes the Democratic Republic of
           Viet Nam as a "free state" within the French Union and
           the Indochinese Federation. French troops return to
           the northern provinces. Fighting continues, however,
           as the Vietnamese press for even greater freedom and
           hegemony over the rest of Indochina.

10   LEBANON - Great Britain and France agree to evacuate
           their forces.

10-15   CHINA - After the Battle of Mukden (Shenyang) in which
           Nationalists are victorious over Communist forces, the
           Nationalist Army begins a drive northward.

14   GREAT BRITAIN - The government offers India its full
           independence.

15   USSR - The Fourth Five-Year Plan is adopted by the
           Supreme Soviet.

17   CHINA - Battle of Szeping takes place in which Commu-
           nist forces counterattack and push Nationalists back
           from this important communications center.

19   IRAN - The government sends a formal protest to the
           United Nations concerning the continued Soviet
           presence and activity in Iran.

22   JORDAN - Great Britain grants independence to Trans-
           jordan which was formed earlier by a mandate from the
           League of Nations. The British also conclude an
           alliance with the new nation.

24   YUGOSLAVIA - The wartime foe of Marshal Tito and for-
           mer Chetnik leader, General Draja Mikhailovich, is
           captured and prepared for trail.

26   GERMANY - The Allied Control Commission limits German
           industrial production to one-half its 1938 level. The
           plan is short-lived, however, as the restrictions
           cripple the nation's recovery.

29   IRAQ - A treaty of friendship is concluded with Turkey
           that calls for joint control of the upper Tigris and
           Euphrates rivers.

APRIL

IRAQ - A Kurdish tribal uprising begins in the province of Kurdistan.

4   UNITED STATES - The US Army abandons the use of horse cavalry as a tactical formation.

5   IRAN - An agreement is reached with the USSR concerning the withdrawal of Soviet forces. Iran agrees to reforms in Azerbaijan.

10   JAPAN - The Allied Supreme Command orders a series of purges to remove the last vestiges of radical Japanese nationalism. Also, an international tribunal opens in Tokyo to hear the cases against major war criminals.

14-18   CHINA - Communist forces open an attack in which they drive Nationalist forces out of Ch'angch'un. All-out civil war resumes after the three-month truce, negotiated by US Ambassador Marshall, breaks down.

15   SYRIA - The British and French complete their military withdrawal.

16   CHINA - The Second Battle of Szeping is fought. In a fierce battle, a veteran Nationalist Chinese army force of 70,000 defeats 110,000 Communist troops. The battle ends on 20 May.

18   LEAGUE OF NATIONS - The League of Nations votes itself out of existence and transfers its responsibilities and assets to the United Nations.

21   GERMANY - The communist-inspired Socialist Union Party (SED) is formed in the Soviet occupation zone.

23   THE PHILIPPINES - Manuel Roxas is elected president.

25-28   CHINA - After the Soviet withdrawal, Communists occupy the important cities of Harbin and Tsitsihar.

29   PALESTINE - An Anglo-American investigating committee recommends against the partition of Palestine but does recommend the establishment of an independent state of Israel.

MAY

GREAT BRITAIN - Parliament begins a period of legislation passage that nationalizes the country.

GREECE - Greek Civil War begins when Communist rebels, led by General Markos Vafiades, seize control of key border installations. The Greek Communists are aided by Albania, Bulgaria, and Yugoslavia. The war lasts until October 1949.

1   CHINA - The Nationalist government moves from Chung-king to Nanking.

5   CHINA - Fighting breaks out around Hankow in the wake of the cease-fire breakdown.

5   FRANCE - The draft constitution of 19 April is rejected in a popular referendum.

9   ITALY - King Victor Emmanuel III abdicates in favor of his son, Umberto II.

9   GREAT BRITAIN - In the face of growing opposition to its continued occupation in Egypt, the British government announces its readiness to withdraw from its longtime colony.

9   IRAN - The Soviet withdrawal from Iranian territory is completed.

17   ROMANIA - Romania's wartime dictator, General Ion Antonescu, is sentenced to death.

17   UNITED STATES - Federal troops seize the railroads to prevent an imminent strike.

22   UNITED STATES - President Truman orders Federal troops to seize the mines to end a two-month old soft coal strike

22   CHINA - The Communists evacuate the city of Ch'ang-ch'un. Nationalist military forces continue their drive northward.

25   UNITED NATIONS - The USSR vetoes the admission of the newly independent Kingdom of Transjordan into the United Nations Organization (UNO).

26   CZECHOSLOVAKIA - Communist leader Klement Gottwald forms a new government based on the results of constituent assembly elections that gave the Communists nearly 40% of the popular vote.

26-30 SOUTHEAST ASIA - Clashes between Thai and French Indochinese forces along the Mekong River border lead to a Thai request to the UN to halt further French aggression in the region.

JUNE

1   CHINA - Nationalist forces continue their drive northward crossing the Sungari River and threatening Harbin. Communist resistance begins to stiffen.

1   INDOCHINA - The French proclaim an autonomous Republic of Cochin China at Saigon.

2   PORTUGAL - The US and Great Britain return their wartime bases in the Azores to Portuguese control.

2   ITALY - As a result of popular referendum Italy is declared a republic. Over 10 million vote to remain a monarchy, while slightly over 12 million vote for the republic.

6   FRANCE - The Fountainbleau Conference breaks up when two months of negotiation fail to achieve a reconciliation of French and Vietnamese positions on the future of Indochina.

7-30   CHINA - US Ambassador Marshall is able to bring about a cease-fire. Hostilities begin again, however, when peace talks break down. A period of stalemate follows that lasts until December.

9   SIAM - King Ananda (Rama VIII) dies of a gunshot wound and is replaced by his brother, Phumiphon Aduldet (Rama IX) (5 May 1950). Ananda's death is probably an assassination.

13   ITALY - King Umberto II, having refused to accept the popular decision to form a republic, leaves the country to avoid the outbreak of violence.

13   IRAN - The northwestern province of West Azerbaijan is returned to Iranian control.

14   UNITED NATIONS - US delegate Bernard Baruch presents to the UN Atomic Energy Commission a US plan to destroy its stockpile of nuclear weapons and to give all of its secrets to an international atomic energy authority.

19   UNITED NATIONS - The USSR presents a counter-plan to outlaw all nuclear weapons but demands a retention of a veto provision in the proposed agreement.

19   FRANCE - Georges Bidault is elected president of the provisional government.

19   CZECHOSLOVAKIA - Edward Benes is unanimously elected president.

25   UNITED STATES - Congress extends the Selective Service
            Act to 31 March 1947.

27   ITALY - The Allies strip Italy of sovereignty over the
            Dodecanese Islands and give over their control to
            Greece. Other parts of Italy's northern territories
            are given to France.

28   ITALY - Enrico de Nicola is elected first president of
            the new republic.

28   AUSTRIA - The Allies grant a substantial degree of au-
            tonomy to the government.

30   GERMANY - Elections are held in American occupation
            zone for the constituent assembly.

JULY

            CHINA - A major Nationalist offensive begins in north-
            ern China that lasts until November. Much of Kiansu
            and Hopeh provinces are cleared of the Communists.

1-25   UNITED STATES - The US government conducts a series of
            nuclear tests on Bikini Atoll in the Marshall Islands
            in the Pacific Ocean. These are the first peacetime
            tests ever conducted and include a series of under-
            water detonations and weapons tests against warships.

2   GERMANY - As a means of speeding up the denazification
            program the Allies announce a selective amnesty for
            certain groups of suspected war criminals.

4   UNITED STATES - The Philippines achieve their indepen-
            dence under the provisions of the McDuffie-Tydings Act
            of 1934.

6   AUSTRIA - The USSR claims the right to pack up and
            move substantial industrial facilities in Austria. The
            Soviets claim these plants and their equipment as re-
            parations, claiming they are German assets.

14   POLAND - In a pogrom in the city of Kielce a number of
            Jewish Holocaust survivors are killed.

15   UNITED STATES - President Truman signs a bill granting
            Great Britain $3.75 billion in credit.

17   YUGOSLAVIA - General Draja Mikhailovich is executed by
            a Tito firing squad amid violent protests from the
            West.

17-21   BOLIVIA - A popular revolution led by students, work-
           ers, and the military overthrows the government of
           President Gualberto Villaroel. Villaroel is killed in
           the fighting.

22   PALESTINE - Ninety-one people are killed when the King
           George Hotel in Jerusalem is blown up by a group of
           Zionist extremists.

24   USSR - The Soviet UN delegate, Andrei Gromyko, rejects
           the Baruch Plan for nuclear disarmament and states the
           Soviet Union would never allow inspection of its nuc-
           lear facilities.

29   UNITED STATES - Ambassador Marshall orders a halt to
           all military aid to the Nationalists as a result of
           renewed fighting across China.

29   WW II ALLIES - The Paris Peace Conference begins with
           the 21 allied nations meeting to discuss the draft
           peace treaties for Bulgaria, Finland, Hungary, Italy,
           and Romania.

AUGUST

16   HAITI - The military junta elects Dumarsais Estime as
           the new president.

27   LAOS - The French grant unity and independence to Laos
           as a part of the French Union.

31   LEBANON - The Anglo-French withdrawal of forces is
           completed.

SEPTEMBER

6   GERMANY - The US announces a new policy of leniency
           toward Germany and calls for a unified German
           economic program.

6   AUSTRIA - An Italo-Austrian agreement gives substan-
           tial autonomy to the southern Tyrol.

14   FRANCE - Ho Chi Minh signs a modus vivendi with the
           French Minister of Overseas Affairs, Marius Moutet, in
           Paris.

15   IRAN - An uprising of rebellious tribesmen breaks out
           in southern Iran. The issue is not settled until 22
           October 1946.

15   BULGARIA - A People's Republic is declared.

17   BRAZIL - A new constitution outlaws all "non-demo-
          cratic" parties.

18   YUGOSLAVIA - Wartime Croatian leader Alois Cardinal
          Stepinac is captured by Tito forces and is sentenced
          to 16 years imprisonment.

22   IRAN - A serious uprising begins in the province of
          Fars.

26   CHINA - US Marines begin their withdrawal from China.
          The move is interpreted in Nanking as US abandonment
          of the Nationalist government.

30   GERMANY - The International Tribunal at Nuremburg de-
          livers its verdict against the 22 Nazi war criminals.
          Three are acquitted, the remainder are sentenced to
          death or imprisonment.

OCTOBER

10   PORTUGAL - An attempted military coup is suppressed by
          loyal government troops. Unrest continues, however,
          until 1947.

10   CHINA - Chiang Kai-shek is re-elected president by the
          Kuomintang.

13   FRANCE - The revised draft constitution is adopted.
          France's overseas possessions become part of the
          French Union.

22   ALBANIA - The "Corfu Channel Incident" takes place in
          which two British destroyers are damaged by Albania
          mines which had been laid in the waters of the inter-
          national channel between Albania and the Greek island
          of Corfu (Coccyra, Kerkira, Kerkyra).

NOVEMBER

3   JAPAN - The Japanese nation adopts a new constitution
          that renounces war. The new constitution goes into
          effect on 3 May 1947.

4   CHINA - China and the US sign a treaty of friendship
          that includes commercial and navigational arrange-
          ments.

8   CHINA - The Nationalists order a cease-fire, but the
          Communists reject the gesture.

13   INDONESIA - Following a truce in the fighting between
            Indonesian rebels and Dutch and British forces, a pact
            (Cheribon Agreement) is negotiated and initialed. The
            Netherlands government recognizes the Indonesian Re-
            public composed of the islands of Java, Sumatra, and
            Madura, and the United States of Indonesia composed of
            the major islands of Borneo, Molucca, the Celebes, and
            Sunda.

18   USSR - Marshal Georgi Zhukov is succeeded as commander
            in chief of the Soviet armed forces by Marshal Ivan
            Konev.

19   UNITED NATIONS - Afghanistan, Iceland, and Sweden are
            admitted to the UNO.

19   ROMANIA - After a campaign punctuated by violence
            against the opposition, the communist-controlled gov-
            ernment wins a majority.

23   INDOCHINA - The French-Indochinese War breaks out in
            the northern port city of Haiphong after months of
            fruitless French-Viet Minh negotiations on the in-
            dependence of Viet Nam. More than 6,000 Vietnamese
            civilians are killed when the French open fire on
            demonstrators in Haiphong.

DECEMBER

2   GERMANY - The US and British zones are fused for the
            purpose of economic development. France and the USSR
            are invited to join.

10   GREECE - Continued border incursions into Greece from
            Albania, Bulgaria, and Yugoslavia necessitate the for-
            mation of a special UN investigative commission to
            study Greek charges.

11   UNITED NATIONS - Spain is barred from all UN activi-
            ties, and the General Assembly urges all its member
            nations to break diplomatic relations with Spain.

11   SOUTH KOREA - A legislative assembly is formed with
            one-half of its membership having been chosen by
            popular vote. Although largely advisory, it consti-
            tutes the product of the first free elections in Korea
            in decades.

14   UNITED NATIONS - The General Assembly unanimously
            passes a resolution calling for worldwide disarmament.

16   UNITED STATES - The President signs an executive order
            establishing Joint Commands in overseas theaters.

19   INDOCHINA - Viet Minh forces open a series of   attacks
            against the French in a number of areas thoughout   the
            country. (This   date   is   usually   designated   as   the
            official beginning of the French-Indochinese War   even
            though the   first military   action   took place   on   23
            November.)

25   CHINA - A new national constitution goes into effect.

30   UNITED NATIONS - The   Baruch Plan for nuclear   control
            and inspection is killed in the Security Council by   a
            Soviet veto.

Notes

1947

CHINA - The Nationalist government finds itself generally surrounded by the Communists who hold most of the
countryside by year's end.

EGYPT - A central bureau is established to coordinate
the activities of the various independence movements
in northern Africa.

MOROCCO - Nationalist discontent with the French
administration is supported by Sultan Mohammed V. This
unrest continues until 1953 when the French instigate
further trouble.

MADAGASCAR - Year-long, bloody uprisings by nationalist elements, especially along the east coast of the
island, are put down by French forces.

PHILIPPINES - The government of Manuel Roxas begins a
campaign to subdue the communist-inspired Hukbalahap
peasant uprising in central Luzon.

JANUARY

CHINA - Communist forces under Lin Piao open three offensives across the Sungari River in Manchuria. By the
end of March, all of these spearheads are driven back
by Nationalist forces.

INDOCHINA - Communist Viet Minh forces encircle and
lay siege to the city of Hue. The siege is not broken
until February when a French relief column enters the
city.

1   UNITED STATES - The Atomic Energy Commission is creat-
        ed on the same day that George C. Marshall is appoint-
        ed Secretary of State.

1   NIGERIA - The nation is granted limited self-govern-
        ment by Great Britain.

5   MIDDLE EAST - The Arab League accepts a British pro-
        posal to participate in a conference dealing with the
        Palestinian problem.

6   CHINA - General Marshall's request for relief from his
        peace mediation role is approved. He leaves China the
        next day amid criticism from both sides.

11   TRANSJORDAN - The Jordanian government signs an alli-
        ance with Turkey.

14   ALLIED POWERS - Talks begin in London on the settle-
        ment of the German and Austrian peace treaties.

19   POLAND - The US and Great Britain complain that the
        terms of the Yalta Agreement have been violated by
        excessive Communist interference in the first general
        elections to be held in Poland since before the war.

21   UNION OF SOUTH AFRICA - The Smuts government rejects
        the UN decision to place Southwest Africa under UN
        trusteeship.

25   GREAT BRITAIN - Egypt is informed of the British in-
        tention to ready the Sudan for self-government.

26   EGYPT - The government breaks off negotiation for a
        renewal of the 1936 treaty with Great Britain and re-
        fers the matter to the UN.

26   MIDDLE EAST - The British-sponsored conference on the
        Palestine problem begins.

28   GREAT BRITAIN - The government announces a plan for
        the independence of Burma.

29   CHINA - On the recommendation of Secretary of State
        Marshall, the United States officially abandons its
        role as mediator between the Chinese government and
        the Communists.

FEBRUARY

7   MIDDLE EAST - The final British proposal for the
        division of Palestine is rejected by both the Israelis
        and the Arabs.

9   SPAIN - Rodolfo Llopis forms an anti-Franco government-in-exile.

10   FRANCE - A Treaty of Peace is concluded in Paris between the Allies and Bulgaria, Finland, Hungary, Italy, and Romania, all of whom supported Nazi Germany during the Second World War.

12   CANADA - The government affirms its continued military cooperation with the US.

18   UNITED NATIONS - The Soviet Union begins a campaign to kill the nuclear control and inspection program.

20   GREAT BRITAIN - The government announces its intention to transfer control of India to native Indian hands by June 1948. As a gesture of friendship, Viscount Montgomery of Alamayn is named Governor General of India to serve in the interim.

25   HUNGARY - The arrest of Bela Kovacs, the Secretary General of the Smallholders' Party, for plotting against the Soviet occupation, signals the beginning of a general purge within Hungary.

MARCH

        INDOCHINA - The final attempts at negotiations between the government of Ho Chi Minh and the French fail.

3   NORWAY - A Soviet demand for military basing rights on Spitzbergen is categorically rejected by the government.

4   FRANCE - A treaty of alliance is signed at Dunkirk by Great Britain and France.

5   USSR - The UN Atomic Energy Agency's report on nuclear control is rejected by the Kremlin.

10   USSR - An Allied Council of Ministers' meeting opens in Moscow. After more than a month of deliberation, the council fails to resolve the problems arising over the language of the draft peace treaties for Germany and Austria. The failure reveals the widening rift between East and West. The only agreement reached is the one that deals with the abolition of the state of Prussia.

12   UNITED STATES - The President announces the details of a plan (Truman Doctrine) designed to give economic and military aid to Greece and Turkey.

14   THE PHILIPPINES - The government grants a series of
            99-year leases to the United States for the use of
            certain military and naval facilities. At the same
            time, the US establishes a sizeable military mission
            to help develop and train the Philippine armed forces.

16   CZECHOSLOVAKIA - The Benes government tries and exe-
            cutes the former president of Slovakia, Josef Tiso,
            for wartime crimes against the people.

19   CHINA - Nationalist Chinese forces culminate a suc-
            cessful campaign with the capture of the Communist
            capital city of Yenan in Shensi Province.

29   MADAGASCAR - A revolt against French rule begins. Re-
            inforcements must be sent from France before the up-
            rising is finally quelled in July.

30   PARAGUAY - An attempt to seize the government is made
            by the left-wing forces of former President Rafael
            Franco. A civil war ensues that lasts until 20 August.

31   UNITED STATES - The Selective Service Act expires.

31   SPAIN - Francisco Franco asserts his right to co-opt
            his successor who is to be crowned king.

31   GREECE - The Dodecanese Islands are returned to Greek
            control.

APRIL

1   GREECE - King George II dies and is succeeded to the
            throne by his brother Paul.

2   GREAT BRITAIN - The Palestine question is referred to
            the UN.

2   UNITED NATIONS - The United States is designated the
            trustee of those Pacific island groups formerly in
            Japanese hands.

14   TRANSJORDAN - The Jordanian government signs an alli-
            ance with Iraq.

MAY

            CHINA - A major Communist offensive cuts off the Man-
            churian cities of Kirin, Ch'angch'un, and Szeping.
            Nationalist forces are rushed to the region where a
            major campaign lasts into June.

INDONESIA - Beginning in May, there is growing evidence that the terms of the Cheribon Agreement are unworkable. A period of tension develops between the government of Indonesia and the Dutch.

1   BRAZIL - The Communist Party is outlawed.

3   JAPAN - The new constitution goes into effect.

4   INDONESIA - Independence is proclaimed by nationalists in western Java.

15   UNITED NATIONS - The UN forms a special commission to study the Palestine question.

31   HUNGARY - Ference Nagy is forced to resign as Premier after the Soviet Union accuses him of conspiracy to commit treason.

JUNE

5   UNITED STATES - Secretary of State George C. Marshall calls for a European Recovery Program (Marshall Plan) in a speech made at Harvard.

5   UNITED STATES - The Senate ratifies a series of peace treaties with Bulgaria, Hungary, Italy, and Romania.

5-8   MONGOLIA - Mongolian army forces carry out a raid into Sinkiang Province to repatriate Mongols taken by the Chinese in previous border skirmishes.

6   BULGARIA - The leader of the Bulgarian Agrarian Party is arrested, tried, and executed (23 September) for treason.

16   CHINA - Communist forces occupy the strategically important rail center of Szeping, but are driven off by Nationalist troops in a month-long battle.

26   INDONESIA - Amid growing numbers of violations of the cease-fire agreement, the Prime Minister resigns. His successor, Amir Sjarifoeddin, is equally unsuccessful in stopping the incidence of violence or breaking the negotiations deadlock.

JULY

6   UNITED STATES - Congress approves the Armed Services Unification Act. James V. Forrestal is designated the first Secretary of Defense.

7   CZECHOSLOVAKIA - Under intense pressure from the USSR, the Czechoslovakian government is forced to withdraw its acceptance to attend the Marshall Plan conference to be held in Paris.

7   USSR - The Kremlin categorically rejects the Marshall Plan.

12-15   FRANCE - The Marshall Plan is presented to 16 western European nations meeting in Paris. The Soviet Union had already refused, along with its new array of satellites, to participate. A committee is established to chart a European Recovery Program.

15   ROMANIA - The leader of the National Peasant Party, Julius Maniu, is arrested along with many others, and charged with treason. Maniu is subsequently sentenced to life in solitary confinement.

19   BURMA - The head of the majority party, the Anti-Fascist People's Freedom League (AFPFL), U Aung San, and a number of the members of the newly established provisional government are assassinated in Rangoon. The assassins, members of the opposition party of U Saw, are captured, tried, and executed (8 May 1948).

20   INDONESIA - Following an Indonesian suggestion for a joint military action against the dissidents, the Dutch launch a major operation into the eastern and central regions of Java.

26   UNITED STATES - President Truman signs the Armed Services Unification Act which, among other things, establishes a separate US Air Force.

28   ROMANIA - The government dissolves the National Peasant Party.

AUGUST

1   UNITED NATIONS - Although the UN ordered a cease-fire in Indonesia, both sides continue to violate the directive.

5   UNITED NATIONS - The dispute between Great Britain and Egypt is taken up by the Security Council but no decision is reached.

12   UNITED NATIONS - A UN commission on conventional weapons decides that the prevailing international situation prevents further discussion of reductions in this area.

15   INDIA - The Indian Independence Bill takes effect. The Dominion of India is proclaimed. The partition of India and Pakistan, which had been endorsed by the Muslim League and the All-India Congress, is accompanied by extreme violence especially in the Punjab. Pundit Jawaharlal Nehru becomes the first Prime Minister.

15   PAKISTAN - The Dominion of Pakistan is proclaimed. Mohammed Ali Jinnah becomes the Governor General.

23   ECUADOR - The Ibarra government is overthrown by a military revolt led by Colonel Carlos Mancheno.

26   BULGARIA - The Agrarian Party is dissolved after an extensive Communist campaign to discredit it.

26   UNITED NATIONS - A special "Good Offices" commission is formed to help settle the worsening Indonesian situation.

27   SPAIN - The Llopis government-in-exile fails. A new group forms under the leadership of Alvaro de Albornoz.

SEPTEMBER

        UNITED STATES - Sensing the futility in further negotiations with the Soviet Union over the future of Korea, the United States refers the question to the UN.

1   FRANCE - French citizenship is granted to all Algerians.

2   BRAZIL - A conference on Inter-American Maintenance of Peace and Security adopts the Inter-American Mutual Assistance Treaty (Treaty of Rio de Janeiro) and establishes an American defense zone stretching from Greenland to the Antarctic.

3   ECUADOR - After only 11 days in office, the government of Colonel Carlos Mancheno is ousted and is subsequently replaced by Carlos Arosemena

16   ITALY - When a Yugoslav army force threatens the city of Trieste, US military forces deploy to repel them in an incident that creates increased tensions throughout Europe.

20   CHINA - Communist forces open a campaign designed to isolate Mukden from northern China. This action is called the Liaosi Corridor Offensive.

21   INDIA - India and Pakistan issue a joint statement de-
            ploring the violence between Hindu and Muslim factions
            and move to stop the conflict.

OCTOBER

            CHINA - The Communists open a number of offensives in
            Manchuria which will eventually leave most of the
            country in their hands.

            CHILE - Because of continued communist-led agitation,
            which leads to severe rioting, Chile breaks diplomatic
            relations with the USSR and Czechoslovakia.

6   IRAN - A military assistance agreement is reached with
            the United States and a US Military Assistance Mission
            is formed.

10   CHINA - A Nationalist counteroffensive secures the
            Liaosi Corridor from further Communist onslaught.

13   SIAM - The government accepts a UN decision to return
            a number of its provinces to Indochina that were
            acquired in 1941, when the Thais were Japanese allies.

21   UNITED NATIONS - The UN General Assembly demands that
            peaceful means be found to settle the dispute among
            Albania, Bulgaria, and Yugoslavia and Greece.

22   IRAN - The parliament abrogates the Soviet oil agree-
            ment.

26   GREAT BRITAIN - The government announces its intention
            of withdrawing all but a few of its military forces in
            Iraq.

26   INDIA - The admission of the predominantly Muslim
            state of Kashmir into the Indian Union precipitates a
            clash with Pakistan. Joined by Afridi and Mahsud
            tribesmen from Pakistan, the Muslims marched on the
            capital. Indian troops are airlifted into the province
            on 27 October.

27   UNITED NATIONS - A special commission is formed to ob-
            serve the situation along the northern frontiers of
            Greece.

28-30   INDIA - There is heavy fighting between Indian ground
            and air units and rebellious Muslims in Kashmir which
            signals the beginning of an undeclared war that lasts
            until December 1949.

NOVEMBER

5   ROMANIA - The Communist Anna Pauker replaces the   non-
        Communist Jorge Tatarescu as premier.

8   SIAM - In a bloodless coup, the government of Prime
        Minister Pridi Phanomyong is overthrown by a military
        group headed by Marshal Luang Pibul Songgram.

14   UNITED NATIONS - The UN recognizes the independence of
        Korea and accepts a plan for the withdrawal of all
        occupation forces. The US and Soviet Union indicate
        they will comply with the plan.

25   UNITED KINGDOM - A Big Four conference opens in Lon-
        don. Although it lasts until 16 December, it once
        again fails to agree upon a solution to the German
        problem.

27   BULGARIA - A treaty of friendship and mutual assis-
        tance is signed with Yugoslavia.

29   UNITED NATIONS - After listening to the report of the
        Special Committee on Palestine, the UN General Assem-
        bly votes to partition Palestine into Arab and Jewish
        states with Jerusalem under UN trusteeship. There is
        an immediate Arab rejection of the plan.

29   INDONESIA - The last British troops are withdrawn.

DECEMBER

9   INDONESIA - Under the supervision of a UN committee,
        Dutch and Indonesian officials resume negotiations to
        end the fighting.

14   ITALY - Allied occupation forces withdraw from Italy
        although US and British forces remain in Trieste in
        view of Yugoslav threats to take the city.

15   BULGARIA - Soviet occupation forces are withdrawn.

17   MIDDLE EAST - The Arab League announces its intention
        to use military force to prevent a partition of
        Palestine and the subsequent establishment of a Jewish
        state.

24   GREECE - A rebel commander calling himself "General
        Markos" proclaims the "First Provisional Democratic
        Government of Free Greece." Some 20,000 insurgents
        follow Markos.

27   GREECE - The government outlaws the Communist Party.

30   INDIA - When no resolution to the fighting connected
            with the Kashmir dispute appears possible the govern-
            ment transfers the problem to the United Nations.

30   ROMANIA - After a seven-year reign, King Michael ab-
            dicates under Communist pressure.

Notes

1948

MALAYA - A communist-inspired uprising begins that lasts until 1960.

AUSTRIA - Soviet and Yugoslav demands block all Allied attempts at reaching a peace settlement with Austria. This impasse continues until 1950.

PALESTINE - As the Arabs and Israelis maneuver for favorable tactical advantages, a complex situation unfolds during the first quarter of the year. The British try to keep order while avoiding a major military confrontation with either side.

JANUARY

1   GREECE - Greek forces lift the siege of Konitsa and force the withdrawal of Communist rebel troops into neighboring Albania.

4   BURMA - An independent republic is proclaimed.

10 PALESTINE - An Arab raid on the Jewish settlement of Kafr Szold is repelled by British forces. The operation, which is launched in Syria, reveals the existence of the newly-organized Arab Liberation Army (ALA). The ALA is a confederation of volunteers from all over the Arab world, including Palestine, under the vaguely-defined leadership of Iraqi General Ismail Safwat. In another raid, this time at Kafr Etzion, south of Jerusalem, Palestinians of the "Army of Salvation" are beaten off by units of the Palmach, an elite unit of the Israeli Haganah.

12   HUNGARY - President Zoltan Tildy, an anti-Communist,
            is forced to resign and is replaced as president by
            the communist-controlled Arpad Szakasits.

17   INDONESIA - A truce agreement between the Dutch and
            Indonesians is signed aboard a US warship.

20   UNITED NATIONS - A UN mediation commission begins work
            to settle the Kashmir problem in India.

25   GREECE - A rebel attempt to take Konitsa is repulsed.

30   INDIA - Mahatma Gandhi is assassinated by a Hindu ter-
            rorist in New Delhi. A period of rioting breaks out
            between Hindus and Muslims.

FEBRUARY

            USSR - Beginning in February a number of treaties of
            friendship and mutual assistance are concluded with
            Balkan states.

1   MALAYSIA - The Federation of Malaysia is established.
            A Communist-inspired revolt begins among the new
            nation's Chinese population.

2   YEMEN - The Imam Yahya is overthrown and killed in a
            palace revolt that places Imam Ahmed in power.

2   UNITED STATES - A treaty of friendship, commerce, and
            navigation is signed with Italy.

4   CEYLON - The island becomes a self-governing dominion
            within the British Commonwealth.

8   COSTA RICA - A civil war follows the government's an-
            nouncement invalidating the results of an election
            that would have replaced the present regime with
            National Union candidates.

8   INDIA - Indian troops suppress a Pathan uprising in
            Kashmir.

8   PAKISTAN - Rioting breaks out in Karachi in the wake
            of economic failures and dissatisfaction with the
            government.

11   HAITI - The Communist Party is outlawed.

15   UNITED STATES - The final withdrawal of American
            troops from their wartime bases in Panama is
            announced.

25   GOLD COAST - A major nationalist uprising begins but
        is repressed by British forces.

25   CZECHOSLOVAKIA - In a bloodless coup, Soviet-inspired,
        Communist elements, who threaten violence, convince
        President Edward Benes to install Klement Gottwald as
        Prime Minister. This begins a period wherein Czecho-
        slovakia loses its independence and becomes a Soviet
        satellite.

MARCH

        BURMA - A communist-led insurrection begins.

4   ARGENTINA - An agreement is reached with Chile dealing
        with the defense of their rights in the Falklands and
        in Antarctica. This is done to counter British claims
        in these regions.

10   CZECHOSLOVAKIA - Jan Masaryk, the Foreign Minister,
        dies from a fall which is probably the result of
        Soviet treachery. The government announces his death
        as a suicide.

17   GREAT BRITAIN - A 50-year treaty of mutual assistance
        (Brussels Treaty) is signed by Belgium, France, Great
        Britain, Luxembourg, and The Netherlands.

18   YUGOSLAVIA - The Soviet Union recalls its military and
        technical missions.

20   GERMANY - The Soviets walk out of the Allied Control
        Commission after accusing the Western Powers of under-
        mining the Four-Power administration of Germany.

29   CHINA - The National Assembly severely criticizes the
        government for its military ineptitude against the
        Communists.

31   UNITED STATES - The Congress approves the Foreign As-
        sistance Act (Marshall Plan).

APRIL

1   GERMANY - The Soviets begin interfering with traffic
        flowing between Berlin and the Western Allied Zone of
        Germany.

3   UNITED STATES - The Marshall Plan is implemented when
        President Truman signs a $6.98 billion foreign aid
        appropriation bill.

6   USSR - A ten-year military assistance pact is con-
        cluded with Finland. This treaty is directed against
        Germany.

9   PALESTINE - In fierce fighting near Kastel on the Tel
        Aviv-Jerusalem road, Abdel Kader El-Husseini, an im-
        portant Palestinian Arab leader, is killed. On this
        same day, members of two Jewish terrorist groups, the
        Irgun Zvai Leumi (Irgun) and the Lohamut Herut Israel
        (Stern Gang), massacre more than 250 Arab civilian
        men, women, and children at Deir Yassin on the Tel
        Aviv-Jerusalem road.

9   COLOMBIA - The assassination of a left-wing liberal
        instigates widespread rioting which interrupts the Pan
        American Conference and causes more than 1,400 deaths.

16   FRANCE - The nations involved in the European Recovery
        Program meet in Paris to establish their permanent ap-
        paratus for economic cooperation.

18   PALESTINE - The Israelis are successful in the fight-
        ing around the town of Tiberias (Teverya) on the Sea
        of Galilee.

19   CHINA - General Chiang Kai-shek is reelected president
        and given dictatorial powers.

21-23   PALESTINE - After heavy fighting in the city and the
        surrounding countryside, the Arab population evacuates
        the important northern Israeli port of Haifa (Hefa).

23   UNITED NATIONS - A Palestine Truce Commission is es-
        tablished. Count Folke Bernadotte is named as its
        head.

25   PALESTINE - Heavy fighting begins in and around the
        predominantly Arab city of Jaffa.

25   MIDDLE EAST - Egypt, Iraq, Lebanon, Syria, and Trans-
        jordan decide to aid the Palestinians by attacking the
        Israelis. They open their offensive one day after the
        Israelis proclaim their independence (14 May 1948).

30   COLOMBIA - The Organization of American States (OAS)
        is organized at a meeting of the ninth Pan-American
        Conference held in Bogota. The OAS is placed under the
        UN. An Inter-American Defense Board is established.

MAY

1   NORTH KOREA - North Korean independence is proclaimed
        by the Soviets.

6-12   PALESTINE - The Arabs withdraw from the town of Safad (Zefat) under heavy Israeli pressure.

7   THE NETHERLANDS - The first session of the Congress of Europe convenes in The Hague to discuss plans for a European union.

8   COSTA RICA - The National Union Party's success in the civil war is demonstrated with the announcement of a military junta led by Jose Figueras. The Communist Party is outlawed.

13   PALESTINE - The Arabs evacuate Jaffa after three weeks of heavy fighting.

14   UNITED NATIONS - Sweden's Count Bernadotte is given command of the UN Palestine Mediation and Observer Group and is appointed chief mediator for the Middle East.

14   PALESTINE - The mandate ends when the British decide not to wait for the UN-established date of 1 October and begin an immediate withdrawal. The State of Israel is proclaimed, with Chaim Weizmann as president. A war between the new Israeli state and the Arab League, which will last until July 1949, begins when Lebanese and Syrian forces invade Israel. At the same time, Arab forces that have laid siege to four Jewish settlements in the Kfar Etzion area for weeks successfully overrun the settlements.

15   ISRAEL - Transjordanian Arab Legion forces, led by an English general, Sir John Bagot Glubb (Pasha), seize the southern and eastern portions of New Jerusalem and most of the old city. Thereafter, they lay siege to the Jewish Quarter. At the same time, Egyptian forces intervene on the side of the Arabs against the Israelis. At least two brigades under Major General Ahmed Ali el-Mawawi are involved with one brigade (main force) moving along the coast from El Arish on an axis of advance Nirim-Kfar Darom-Gaza-Ashdod. Gaza is taken on 16 May. There is much bitter fighting, such as at Yad Mordechai (19-24 May), Nitzanin (7 June), and Ashdod, which is captured on 29 May. The second column, made up primarily of ALA forces, moves through Gvulot and Beersheeba (Be'er Sheva') (taken 20 May), toward Hebron (taken 21 May). Local Arabs aid the invading troops. Egyptian patrols moving up the Beersheeba- Jerusalem road make contact with Arab Legion forces at Bethlehem (Bet Lehem) on 22 May.

16   ISRAEL - The United States and the Soviet Union recognize the new state.

16-22   ISRAEL - Iraqi forces attack on Geshir (Gesher), south of the Sea of Galilee, after crossing the Jordan River on 15 May but, after six days of fighting, fail to take the town.

18   ISRAEL - Israeli forces move out of Tel Aviv under the command of an American, David "Micky" Marcus, in an attempt to lift the siege of the Jewish Quarter in Jerusalem. To enter the city and avoid strong Arab positions, the Israelis build a new road through hilly terrain.

19   ISRAEL - The Syrian advance is checked along a general line from Degania to Zemach to Mishmar HaYardan. The Lebanese attack is stopped at Malkya.

20   UNITED NATIONS - Count Folke Bernadotte is appointed UN special mediator for Israel.

25   ISRAEL - Two battalions of poorly trained Israeli recruits open an ill-conceived and poorly executed attack on an Arab Legion battalion position at Latrun (Bab el Wed). All efforts at seizing the high ground (Mehlef Latrun) held by the Arabs are repulsed. The Israelis break contact on 30 May.

26   SOUTH AFRICA - The Nationalist Afrikander bloc, with its apartheid platform, wins the national elections.

28   ISRAEL - After several attempts fail to relieve the defenders of Jerusalem's Jewish Quarter, the besieged enclave is finally taken by Israeli forces.

30   ISRAEL - The town of Jenin, in north-central Israel, is occupied by Iraqi forces, and nearby Natania is threatened.

JUNE

1   GERMANY - Agreement is reached among the three Western Allied Powers and the three Benelux nations, on a formula for German participation in the Marshall Plan and the drafting of a West German constitution. This same meeting produces a call for international control of the Ruhr and the creation of an Allied Military Security Board.

1   ISRAEL - Israeli forces open a three-day operation to retake Jenin but are repulsed. The Iraqis, however, are forced to consolidate their positions in western Samaria behind a line from Shekhem (Nablus or Nabulus) to Jenin.

5   INDOCHINA - The State of Viet Nam is established by the Baie d'Along (Ha Long Bay) Agreement signed by Bao Dai, French High Commissioner Emile Bollaert, and General Nguyen Van Xuan. Bao Dai is designated chief of state within the French Union.

6   ISRAEL - The Lebanese and Syrians renew their offensives into Israel. By 10 June, the Lebanese, reinforced by ALA troops, take Matka (6 June), Ramat Naftali, and Kadesh (7 June). Much of the region north of the Sea of Galilee is now in Lebanese/ALA hands. On the Syrian front, Mishmar HaYarden is captured.

7   CZECHOSLOVAKIA - On the pretext of poor health, Edward Benes is forced to resign the presidency. One week later, on 14 June, the Communist Klement Gottwald is installed as president.

9   ISRAEL - In central Israel a new attack opens to dislodge the Arab Legion battalion at Latrun. This attack fails and contact is broken the next day (10 June).

10   UNITED NATIONS - A cease-fire is ordered in the Arab-Israeli fighting. The next day (11 June) both sides accept the terms of the cease-fire. The truce lasts for one month.

11   UNITED STATES - Senator Arthur H. Vandenberg proposes a resolution promising military aid, in return for defensive alliances, to the nations of the free world.

16   MALAYA - A national state of emergency is declared as Australian, New Zealand, and British troop reinforcements are ordered into the region.

16   WEST BERLIN - The Soviets walk out of the Four-Power Allied Kommandantura that theoretically controls both sectors of Berlin.

19   UNITED STATES - Congress passes a peacetime Selective Service Act.

19   GREECE - A government military offensive begins that is designed to clear the Mount Grammos region of Communist rebel forces. This campaign will last for several months and will be only partially successful.

20   ISRAEL - Forty-nine UN truce observers arrive to supervise the cease-fire.

22   EAST GERMANY - All rail traffic between West Germany and West Berlin is severed.

26   GERMANY - The Berlin Airlift, later called "Operation VITTLES," is initiated to offset the effects of the Soviet blockade.

28   USSR - The COMINFORM expels Yugoslavia for practices contradictory to Marxist-Leninist doctrine.

JULY

9   ISRAEL - Fighting is renewed when Israeli forces, now numbering about 50,000, attack Mishmar HaYardan in the north. Syrian forces occupying the town are successful in repelling the attack and, on 15 July, the Israelis are forced to withdraw. In the central region, Israeli forces attack Arab Legion positions in the Ramla (Ramle)-Lod (Lydda) sector, especially the tactically important airport (today, Ben Gurion Airport). All of these objectives are secured by the Israelis by 12 July.

12   ISRAEL - The Israelis open an offensive designed to clear the area north of Haifa (Hefa). The attackers then turn eastward and capture Nazareth (16 July), which lies halfway between Haifa and the Sea of Galilee.

14-16   ITALY - Communist-inspired rioting follows the assassination of the Communist leader Palmiro Togliatti. Order is restored after much bloodshed by military and police units.

14-18   ISRAEL - Repeated Israeli attacks on Jerusalem and in the Latrun area (Third Battle of Latrun) are repulsed by the Arab Legion.

15   SUDAN - Over strong Egyptian objections, the British begin a reform program.

18   ISRAEL - A second ceasefire is accepted by both sides.

21-29   YUGOSLAVIA - Speaking before a session of the Yugoslav Communist Party, President Tito refutes the Soviet COMINFORM charges of revisionism. After a vote of confidence the Yugoslav Party organization begins a purge of its COMINFORM supporters.

26-27   EAST GERMANY - Following a squabble over economic issues and recent currency reforms, the Soviets block all rail and road traffic between West Berlin and West Germany. In retaliation for the "Berlin Blockade," the Western Powers halt all trade with East Germany. The Western Allies institute a massive airlift to ferry needed supplies to Berlin.

30   YUGOSLAVIA - The Danube Conference convenes in Bel-
            grad. At the conference, the Soviet delegate submits a
            new plan for the Danube to replace the 1921 conven-
            tion.

AUGUST

            BURMA - In a drive to establish a separate state, the
            Karen tribe rises up against the government. With the
            support of the Communists, it soon controls much of
            central and southern Burma.

12   UNITED NATIONS - A special commission decides that ex-
            isting conditions prevent any type of control on con-
            ventional weapons.

13-14   ARGENTINA - The Peron government is granted extra-
            ordinary powers in time of emergency.

15   KOREA - The Republic of Korea is proclaimed with Syng-
            man Rhee as president. The US military government is
            officially terminated. The US agrees to train the ROK
            army.

23   UNITED STATES - The roles and missions of the US armed
            forces are revised in the Newport Agreement.

25   USSR - All consular activities with the US are sus-
            pended after an incident involving a Soviet female
            defector.

SEPTEMBER

1   CHINA - The Communists announce the formation of the
            North China People's Government.

2   CHILE - The Communist Party is outlawed.

7   INDIA - When the state of Hyderabad, located in the
            center of the Indian subcontinent, persists in its
            refusal to join the Dominion of India, Prime Minister
            Pandit Jawaharlal Nehru threatens war.

9   KOREA - A People's Democratic Republic is proclaimed
            in the north and announces its jurisdiction over the
            entire Korean peninsula. Kim Il Sung is named presi-
            dent.

11   HYDERABAD - In face of the Indian ultimatum of 7 Sep-
            tember, the Nizam of Hyderabad, Sir Osman Ali Khan
            Bahadur, appeals to the UN for assistance.

12   CHINA - Heavy fighting begins in the Liaosi Corridor
            area of Manchuria. When the Corridor is taken by the
            Communists, Chiang Kai-shek orders a general
            withdrawal of Nationalist forces southward.

13   HYDERABAD - Indian forces invade the state.

14-24   CHINA - More than 80,000 Nationalist troops defect or
            are captured as a result of the Battle of Tsinan in
            the Yellow River valley.

17   HYDERABAD - The state's government surrenders when
            Indian troops enter the capital city.

17   ISRAEL - Chief UN Mediator Count Folke Bernadotte is
            assassinated by three members of the Zionist extremist
            Stern Gang. He is replaced by Doctor Ralph Bunche.

18   INDONESIA - The Communists attempt to set up a Soviet-
            style government on Java. Subsequent action by the
            government forces the Communists back into the jungle.

20   SPAIN - The 1939 Treaty of Friendship and Non-Aggres-
            sion that Spain has with Portugal is extended for an-
            other ten years.

29   ISRAEL - The Israelis carry out a number of actions in
            the Faluja area to drive a wedge between the two chief
            Egyptian axes of advance into southern Israel.

OCTOBER

15-19   ISRAEL - Israeli attacks to dislodge Egyptian forces
            in the Ashdod-Gaza area are unsuccessful.

19   NORTH KOREA - Soviet occupation forces begin their
            withdrawal from North Korea. The operation is com-
            pleted on 25 December.

19-21   ISRAEL - Israeli forces seize Huleiqat separating the
            two Egyptian axes of advance. Beersheba is recaptured
            on 21 October. This isolates Egyptian forces in Hebron
            and Faluja.

20-27   SOUTH KOREA - A communist-inspired revolt begins in a
            number of ROK army units stationed in the southern
            part of South Korea. There are heavy casualties on
            both sides as loyal government forces put down the up-
            rising.

20-28   INDIA - French troops are employed to suppress a pro-
            Indian uprising in the French Indian province of Mahe.

20-31   ISRAEL - A major operation begins in which the Israeli army moves to clear the region north of the Sea of Galilee after Arab Liberation Army forces (ALA) take Manara (Menara) (22 October). The Israelis are initially thrown back at Tarshia (28 October), but drive the ALA out of Israel with the capture of Gish (28 October) and Sasa (Sesa) (29 October). Tarshia is occupied on 30 October and Manara on 31 October. The Israelis then discontinue operations and begin consolidating their positions, including those still held in Lebanese territory.

25   UNITED NATIONS - The USSR vetoes a UN Security Council resolution to settle the Berlin Blockade.

25   CZECHOSLOVAKIA - Penal labor camps are set up as a means of controlling dissidence.

27   ISRAEL - The Egyptians begin a withdrawal from positions inside Israel to more concentrated ones along the El Arish-Gaza corridor. Egyptian forces continue to hold out in pockets near Hebron and Faluja.

27-29   PERU - The government of President Jose Bustamonte is overthrown and replaced by a military junta led by General Manuel Odria.

27-30   CHINA - A Communist counteroffensive destroys a major portion of the withdrawing Nationalist Army near Mukden.

NOVEMBER

1   CHINA - Mukden falls after the Nationalist garrison surrenders. By the year's end the Communists hold all of Manchuria.

3   SOUTH KOREA - A communist-inspired uprising in Taegu in south-central South Korea is surpressed quickly.

12   JAPAN - General Hideki Tojo and six others are sentenced to death for war crimes. Sixteen other war criminals are given life sentences by the international military tribunal.

19   ISRAEL - A new Egyptian offensive begins which is designed to relieve the Faluja pocket. Initial gains are made in the area east of Gaza but by 7 December they have not yet reached Faluja.

24   VENEZUELA - The government is overthrown by a military junta led by Colonel Carlos Delgado Chalbaud.

27   UNITED NATIONS - The General Assembly votes to condemn
            Albania, Bulgaria, and Yugoslavia for their parts in
            supporting the Communist side of the on-going Greek
            Civil War.

30   ISRAEL - A cease-fire is arranged between Israel and
            Transjordan, and between Israel and Syrian and Leban-
            ese forces in the north.

DECEMBER

1   TRANSJORDAN - King Abdullah is named king of Palestine
            by the Palestine Arab Congress meeting in Jericho.
            This move creates more dissension among other Arab
            factions.

9-10   UNITED NATIONS - The General Assembly adopts the Con-
            vention on the Prevention and Punishment of Genocide,
            and the Universal Declaration of Human Rights.

10-12   COSTA RICA - Costa Rican rebel exiles invade the coun-
            try from Nicaragua. By 12 December, the invasion is
            repulsed by Costa Rican troops. Subsequent investi-
            gations by the OAS disprove the Costa Rican claims of
            Nicaraguan complicity. Strained relations between the
            two neighboring countries continue for some time.

11   UNITED NATIONS - A UN Conciliation Commission for
            Palestine is established.

12   UNITED NATIONS - The General Assembly endorses the
            government of the Republic of Korea (ROK). A commis-
            sion is establish to work toward reunification of the
            two Koreas.

13-20   COSTA RICA - The government of President Teodoro
            Picado is overthrown.

14   EL SALVADOR - President Salvador Castaneda is forced
            to resign in a bloodless coup. His government is
            replaced by a provisional revolutionary government
            which sets about restoring full constitutional
            liberties.

18   INDONESIA - The Dutch resume military operations after
            repeated violations of the truce agreement by the
            Indonesian rebels. Before the end of the year the
            Dutch occupy a number of important cities and capture
            Achmed Sukarno and his rebel government.

19   INDONESIA - Dutch paratroopers capture the important
            rebel stronghold of Jogjakarta.

20   ISRAEL - The Israelis concentrate their forces against
      the Egyptians and launch a major campaign designed   to
      force Egypt out of the war. Moving out of Beersheba
      the Israelis isolate Rafah (Rafiah) (22 December), and
      Asluj is taken on 25   December. While one force moves
      west to secure the Rafah crossing point, another force
      of Israelis, led by Colonel Yigil Allon, crosses   into
      the Sinai at Nizzana and captures the important   town
      of Abu Ageila (Abu Aweigila) on 28 December. Three
      columns then move on Bir Hama, Bir Hassaneh, and El
      Arish. At El Arish, after capturing the outlying   set-
      tlements and the airport, the Israelis order a gen-
      eral withdrawal because of overextension of their
      lines, increasing Egyptian resistance, and Anglo-
      American pressure.

21   INDONESIA - A cease-fire goes into effect.

25   USSR - The Soviet government announces the final with-
      drawal of its forces from North Korea.

25   INDONESIA - The Dutch effect control of the entire
      island of Java.

27   HUNGARY - Josef Cardinal Mindszenty, the Roman Catho-
      lic Primate of Hungary, is arrested and charged with
      conspiracy to overthrow the Communist government.

28   EGYPT - Premier Nokrashy Pasha is assassinated.

Notes

1949

PARAGUAY - Serious unrest and chaos continue.

LIBYA - A decade-long period of violent anticolonialism begins.

UGANDA - A decade-long period of anticolonialism begins.

BELGIAN CONGO - A decade-long period of anticolonialism begins.

CHINA - There are over 250,000 Nationalist casualties at the conclusion of the Battle of Hwai Hai.

AFGHANISTAN - Year-long border clashes flair up with Pakistan over provisions of the Durand Line Agreement of 1893.

JANUARY

BURMA - After a two-month drive, Karen rebels are on the outskirts of Rangoon and cut the rail line to Mandalay.

1   INDIA - The commission of the UN Security Council is successful in arranging an India-Pakistan cease-fire in Kashmir.

7   ISRAEL - Under UN supervision, an Egyptian-Israeli armistice goes into effect as Israeli forces prepare to attack Rafah, and after Egypt asks for a truce.

13   SOUTH AFRICA - Over 100   are killed and 1,000   injured
            in race riots between Indians and Zulus in Durban.

14   CHINA - The major Chinese city of Tientsin falls to
            the Communists.

17   GERMANY - An Allied Military Security Board is estab-
            lished by the Western powers to supervise occupied
            Germany's disarmament and demilitarization.

21   CHINA - Peking falls to the Communists after a long
            seige. Chiang Kai-shek resigns as President leaving
            the Vice President, Li Tsung-jen, to attempt a contin-
            uation of peace talks with the Communists.

28   UNITED NATIONS - The Security Council calls for an im-
            mediate end to the fighting in Indonesia. The Security
            Council also orders the Dutch to transfer the sover-
            eignty of the country to the United States of Indone-
            sia no later than 1 July 1950.

FEBRUARY

            CHINA - The last US combat forces withdraw from the
            Chinese mainland. This act is taken as US abandonment
            of the Nationalist Chinese cause.

8   IRELAND - The government declares it is impossible to
            participate in NATO as long as Eire remains divided.

21   COSTA RICA - A friendship pact is signed with Nicara-
            gua.

22   FRANCE - French Communists announce that they will re-
            fuse to fight an invading Soviet army.

26-27   THAILAND - There is extensive fighting between mili-
            tary units after a state of emergency is declared be-
            cause of Communist activity along the border with Ma-
            laysia. Each side accuses the other of plotting to
            overthrow the government.

MARCH

8   FRANCE - The Elysee Agreement, in the form of letters
            exchanged between the Emperor of Annam, Bao Dai, and
            French President Auriol, establishes the framework of
            French-Vietnamese relations. Paris recognizes Vietnam-
            ese independence while retaining the right to military
            bases in Viet Nam.

19   GERMANY - A "People's Council" approves an East German constitution for the Democratic Republic of Germany.

23   LEBANON - An armistice is concluded which ends the Israeli invasion.

26   UNITED STATES - The B-36 ten-engine intercontinental bomber is successfully test flown for the first time.

30   SYRIA - The government of Shukri al-Kuwatly is overthrown in a bloodless coup led by the army chief of staff, Husni Za'im.

APRIL

1   CHINA - The Nationalists propose dividing China along the Yangtze River. The Communists reject the plan and demand an immediate surrender.

3   COSTA RICA - An coup attempt fails to topple the government of Jose Figueres.

4   UNITED STATES - The North Atlantic Treaty is signed in Washington by the 12 member nations. Later, other free nations will join.

8   GERMANY - An "Occupation Statute" is approved by the Western Allies that ensures West Germany a certain amount of autonomy and eases industrial dismantling requirements.

9   UNITED NATIONS - The International Court of Justice in the Hague hands down its first decision and finds Albania guilty of causing the explosions that damaged British war- ships in the Corfu Channel in 1946. The Court awards damages to the British.

14   WEST GERMANY - The Nuremberg Trials come to an end.

18   IRELAND - The Republic of Ireland is proclaimed.

19   CHINA - The Nationalist capital is moved to Canton in southern China.

20   CHINA - Communist military operations begin again when the Nationalists balk at demands. Communist forces cross the Yangtze between Nanking and Wuhan, attacking two British warships in the process. The campaign will drive the Nationalists off the mainland before year's end.

22   CHINA - Nanking falls to the Communists.

23   UNITED STATES - In an economy move, the Secretary of
            Defense announces a halt in the construction of the
            65,000-ton aircraft carrier <u>USS United States.</u>

MAY

            BOLIVIA - Over a five-month period there are serious
            strikes and uprisings that center around workers in
            the country's tin mines. These revolts are put down by
            the army.

5   GREAT BRITAIN - The document of agreement on the es-
            tablishment of the Council of Europe is signed in Lon-
            don. Ten countries sign initially, three more will
            join later.

7   INDONESIA - A cease-fire goes into effect.

11   THAILAND - The name, "Thailand," is officially adopted
            to replace the country's historical title of Siam.

12   GERMANY - The Berlin Blockade is officially lifted by
            the Soviets. The airlift continues, however, until 30
            September. By the end of the blockade, 277,264 airlift
            sorties will have been flown. A total of 2,323,736
            tons of food, fuel, and raw materials will have been
            delivered to the 2.5 million inhabitants of the city
            of West Berlin.

14   UNITED NATIONS - The General Assembly votes to call a
            meeting of India, Pakistan, and South Africa to dis-
            cuss discrimination against persons of Indian origin.

17   GREAT BRITAIN - The British government affirms the in-
            dependence of Ireland but declares that Northern Ire-
            land (Ulster) will remain a part of the Empire. This
            move is almost immediately protested by Ireland.

JUNE

            FRANCE - The government approves limited independence
            for Viet Nam, Cambodia, and Laos under the terms of
            the Elysee Agreement.

            SOUTH AFRICA - The anti-black program of <u>aparthied</u> is
            put into effect.

2   TRANSJORDAN - The Hashemite Kingdom of Jordan composed
            of Transjordan and Arab Palestine is proclaimed at Am-
            man.

3   UNITED STATES - Presidential cabinet members are accused of collusion and fraud in what will become known as the "B-36 Controversy." This incident becomes one of the most overt examples of interservice rivalry in the postwar period.

10   ALBANIA - A number of high-ranking officials are convicted as Yugoslav spies and are executed the following day. A general roundup of dissidents begins forcing many to flee the country.

14   BURMA - Karen rebels proclaim an independent state to be called Toungoo.

16   HUNGARY - A wholesale purge follows the arrest of the Communist foreign minister, Laszlo Rajk, who is accused of crimes against the state.

25   UNITED NATIONS - The UN Special Committee on the Balkans charges Bulgaria with complicity in the Greek civil war. The Bulgarian government is accused of giving aid and sanctuary to the Communist-controlled Greek rebels.

25   BULGARIA - A party purge begins with the arrest of Deputy Premier Traicho Kostov. Along with ten others, he is subsequently found guilty of treason and executed (16 December).

27   AUSTRALIA - A Communist-inspired strike almost brings the nation to a standstill. It is settled by emergency measures and the use of troops.

29   SOUTH KOREA - The US completes the withdrawal of its occupation forces.

30   INDONESIA - Dutch troops withdraw from Jogjakarta and Djakarta.

JULY

1   INDOCHINA - Bao Dai issues a decree formally establishing the State of Viet Nam and the framework for its constitutional rule.

8   LEBANON - An antigovernment uprising is quickly suppressed.

13   THE VATICAN - A decree announces the excommunication of all Roman Catholics adhering to Communism.

16   CHINA - The Nationalists, under Chiang Kai-shek, organize for a withdrawal to Taiwan (Formosa).

16-19   GUATEMALA - A large-scale rebellion is put down by the government of Juan Jose Arevalo.

19   LAOS - The Indochinese nation of Laos becomes one of the Associated States within the French Union.

21   UNITED STATES - The Senate ratifies the North Atlantic Treaty.

29   UNITED NATIONS - The International Atomic Energy Agency votes to cease its functions until a basis can be found upon which some agreements as to its purpose and functions may be reached.

AUGUST

          FINLAND - Month-long Communist-instigated strikes are put down by strong government action supported by popular anti-Communist reaction.

2   UNITED STATES - The Congress approves a major restructuring of the Department of Defense.

3   THE NETHERLANDS - The North Atlantic Treaty is ratified.

3   NEW ZEALAND - There is overwhelming approval in a referendum of a plan for the establishment of peacetime military service.

4   UNITED STATES - The Senate refuses to extend Marshall Plan aid to Spain.

5   UNITED STATES - The US cuts off all aid to Nationalist China and denounces the Nationalist government in a State Department white paper.

14   SYRIA - Another, this time successful, coup d'etat overthrows the government. President Husni Za'im is arrested and executed.

25   UNITED STATES - Following two months of investigation, the House Armed Services Committee finds no fault with the B-36 acceptance decision.

25   PANAMA - An armed struggle for succession is touched off by the death of President Florencio Arosemena.

28   GREECE - The area around Mount Grammos is cleared of Communist rebels by Greek army forces.

29   UNITED STATES - The Senate approves the establishment of a 70-group Air Force.

SEPTEMBER

USSR - A nuclear detonation is reported to have taken place inside the Soviet Union.

2   UNITED NATIONS - The international commission appointed to mediate a reunification of the two Koreas cites its failure and warns of the possibility of civil war. Sporadic fighting is thereafter reported along the 38th Parallel.

7   WEST GERMANY - The Federal Republic of Germany is established.

19   WEST GERMANY - The US, Great Britain, and France guarantee the security of the new Federal Republic of Germany.

21   WEST GERMANY - The Allied occupation statute goes into effect. An Allied High Commission for Germany assumes authority from the occupation forces.

23   UNITED STATES - The President announces that there is clear evidence that the Soviet Union has detonated its first nuclear device.

27   USSR - After its East European satellites had broken off economic ties with Yugoslavia, the Soviet Union repudiates its treaty of friendship and cooperation with the Tito government.

30   WEST GERMANY - The Berlin airlift is officially concluded.

OCTOBER

1   CHINA - The People's Republic of China (PRC) is proclaimed with Mao Tse-tung as Chairman. The new state is immediately recognized by the USSR, the eastern bloc nations, Burma, and India. The US and other Western nations withhold recognition.

3   UNITED STATES - The so-called "Revolt of the Admirals" begins in a continuation of the long-standing interservice battle over shares in the defense budget. In this instance, the Navy accuses the Army and Air Force of working to destroy naval aviation. Before the rhetoric is finished, rash accusations fly in all directions.

6   UNITED STATES - President Truman signs the Mutual Defense Assistance Act which makes more than one-billion dollars available to NATO members.

7   UNITED STATES - The US Air Force announces that nuc-
        lear weapons are ready and available, if ordered to be
        used.

7   EAST GERMANY - The German Democratic Republic is es-
        tablished. The Soviet Union ends it occupation and
        sets up a Soviet Control Commission in its place.

14   UNITED STATES - A several leaders of the American Com-
        munist Party are convicted of conspiracy to advocate
        the violent overthrow of the government.

15   CHINA - Canton falls to the Communists.

16   GREECE - The three-year-old civil war ends in a vic-
        tory for the government.

27   UNITED STATES - As a result of an investigation, the
        Secretary of the Navy orders the relief of Admiral
        Louis Denfield, the Chief of Naval Operations. This
        effectively ends the "Revolt of the Admirals."

NOVEMBER

2   INDONESIA - An agreement is reached between Indonesian
        and Dutch officials over the transfer of sovereignty
        and future relations.

7   POLAND - Marshal of the Soviet Union Konstantin
        Rokossovsky is appointed to be the Polish Minister of
        Defense and Commander in Chief of the Polish armed
        forces.

8   UNITED STATES - The government announces stringent
        controls on strategic goods to prevent their shipment
        to the USSR.

11   YUGOSLAVIA - Over the strenuous objections of the US,
        France, and Great Britain, the Danube Conference ac-
        cepts a Soviet proposal to limit membership in the
        Danube River Commission to those states touched by its
        flow.

21   UNITED NATIONS - The General Assembly votes to approve
        the independence of Libya. The order is to take effect
        on 1 January 1952.

24   PANAMA - Aided by the national police, Arnulfo Arias
        emerges from the months-long succession fight as the
        head of government. He immediately begins a campaign
        to eradicate his opposition.

24   TIBET - The rival Tibetan leader, Panchen Lama, urges
        the Communist liberation of Tibet in a radio broadcast
        originating in Peking.

27   THE NETHERLANDS - The Dutch government formally trans-
        fers sovereignty of the Indonesian islands to the
        United States of Indonesia.

30   FRANCE - Sovereignty of the three states of Viet Nam
        is transferred to the Vietnamese government.

30   CHINA - Chungking falls to the Communists.

DECEMBER

5   UNITED NATIONS - The General Assembly approves a reso-
        lution of the Commission on Conventional Weapons that
        all nations report their armed forces and their wea-
        ponry to the UN.

7   UNITED STATES - Secretary of Defense Louis Johnson be-
        gins his "all fat and no muscle" cost-cutting program
        that nearly emasculates the US armed forces.

8   CHINA - The Nationalist withdrawal to Taiwan is com-
        pleted.

8   UNITED NATIONS - The General Assembly calls upon all
        nations to respect the rights of the Chinese people to
        choose their own form of government.

9   UNITED NATIONS - The General Assembly reiterates its
        desire to internationalize Jerusalem.

14   SYRIA - A new government is sworn in with Hashim al-
        Atasi as President.

14   ISRAEL - Defying the UN decision to internationalize
        Jerusalem, the government decides to establish its
        capital in the city.

15   WEST GERMANY - West Germany becomes a recipient of
        Marshall Plan aid.

16   INDONESIA - Achmed Sukarno is elected President.

16   INDOCHINA - Communist Chinese troops arrive on the
        North Vietnamese border.

19   SYRIA - A third coup attempt leads to the arrest of a
        number of government officials and others who are ac-
        cused of plotting the overthrow of the government and
        a union with Iraq.

28   HUNGARY - All major industries within the country are
          nationalized.

                              Notes

1950

INDONESIA - There are sporadic uprisings and incidents of guerrilla warfare in several parts of the country.

POLAND - There is a year-long deterioration of relations with the West. A number of foreign diplomats and newsmen are expelled.

CZECHOSLOVAKIA - A year-long series of trials purges many dissidents and Party non-conformists. Also, a large number of foreign diplomatic personnel are accused of spying and most Western newsmen are expelled.

JANUARY

1   COMMUNIST CHINA - The government announces it intends to intervene both politically and militarily in the affairs of Tibet.

3   UNITED NATIONS - After failing at several attempts to force an exclusion of Nationalist China, the USSR removes itself from all bodies within the United Nations Organization in which the Nationalist Chinese participate.

5   UNITED STATES - President Harry S. Truman announces his decision to continue military and economic aid to Nationalist China.

6   NATO - A NATO Master Defense Plan is approved.

12   USSR - The death penalty is restored in cases dealing with treason, espionage, and sabotage.

14   BOLIVIA - There is an unsuccessful attempt to over-throw the government.

16   WEST GERMANY - Rationing is ended in West Germany.

18   COMMUNIST CHINA - The government recognizes the Communist government in Hanoi.

25   UNITED STATES - Alger Hiss is found guilty of perjury after lying about his Communist affiliations. He is also convicted of espionage for his role in transferring classified information to Soviet hands.

25   INDIA - The former British colonial possession becomes a republic.

26   IRELAND - A treaty of friendship, commerce, and navigation is concluded with the United States.

29   UNITED STATES - The government enters a number of bilateral agreements through which it can provide arms to the 11 other NATO nations.

29   SOUTH AFRICA - Anti-apartheid rioting breaks out in Johannesburg.

30   USSR - The government recognizes the Communist government in Hanoi.

31   UNITED STATES - The President orders the Atomic Energy Commission to proceed with the development of a hydrogen bomb.

FEBRUARY

7   UNITED STATES - The US recognizes the Government of Viet Nam and dispatches a minister accredited to Viet Nam, Laos, and Cambodia. Great Britain also extends de jure recognition.

14   USSR - A 30-year Treaty of Friendship, Alliance, and Mutual Assistance is signed between the Soviet Union and the People's Republic of China.

19   SOUTH VIET NAM - The US Consulate General in Saigon is raised to Legation status.

21   BULGARIA - As a part of a general purge that began following the death of Premier Vassil Kolarov, the government accuses the US of complicity in the Kostov affair. The US and Bulgaria break diplomatic relations over the alleged incident.

23   UNITED STATES - The government signs a Mutual Defense
            Assistance Agreement with France, Viet Nam, Cambodia,
            and Laos which extends indirect military aid to the
            three Indochinese states.

MARCH

1   GREAT BRITAIN - Physicist Klaus Fuchs is found guilty
            of espionage for transferring nuclear information to
            Soviet agents.

1   TAIWAN - Chiang Kai-shek resumes the presidency of Na-
            tionalist China.

3   FRANCE - The government announces an agreement with
            the Saar in which the region will have autonomy and
            economic ties with France.

8   FRANCE - A strong anti-sabotage law is enacted that is
            directed against Communist-inspired activities.

8   USSR - Marshal of the Soviet Union Klementi Voroshilov
            announces the Soviet Union possesses nuclear weapons.

19   BURMA - Government forces capture the Karen enclave of
            Toungoo.

20   POLAND - The government confiscates church land in the
            continuing struggle between the church and Communist
            state.

24   TURKEY - A treaty of friendship and conciliation is
            signed with Italy.

29   GREAT BRITAIN - Prime Minister Churchill suggests the
            rearmament of Germany as a deterrent against Soviet
            aggression.

APRIL

            DENMARK - The parliament dissolves the union with Ice-
            land which had proclaimed its independence in 1944.

            CZECHOSLOVAKIA - The Czech armed forces begin reorgan-
            izing along Soviet lines.

3   INDIA - The Delhi Pact is signed as a means of easing
            the growing tension between India and Pakistan. This
            does not settle the deadlock over Kashmir, however,
            and any real progress toward friendly relations be-
            tween the two states appears impossible.

10   BOLIVIA - The Communist Party is outlawed.

23   COMMUNIST CHINA - The government completes the take-
          over of Hainan Island.

24   JORDAN - In spite of the protests of most members of
          the Arab League, Arab Palestine is incorporated into
          the recently (2 June 1949) renamed "Hashimite Kingdom
          of Jordan."

27   SOUTH AFRICA - The government implements a Group Areas
          Bill which further segregates the races. This leads to
          serious race riots.

MAY

          HUNGARY - The last anti-Soviet elements are purged
          from the government.

2   COMMUNIST CHINA - Communist forces complete their oc-
          cupation of Hainan Island that separates the Gulf of
          Tonkin from the South China Sea.

5   UNITED STATES - A Uniform Code of Military Justice
          that ensures equal justice for all members the armed
          forces is put into effect.

8   UNITED STATES - The government agrees to supply in-
          direct military aid to Indochina through France.

10   HAITI - A military junta, led by Colonel Paul
          Magliore, overthrows the government of President
          Dumarsais Estime, the man Magliore put into office in
          a similar move in 1946.

13   VENEZUELA - The Communist Party is outlawed.

18-19   BOLIVIA - There is an unsuccessful attempt to over-
          throw the government.

19   EGYPT - Egypt closes the Suez Canal to Israeli ship-
          ping.

19   BURMA - The important Communist town of Prome is taken
          by government forces. Rebel activity continues spo-
          radically until 1974.

25   ISRAEL - The US, Great Britain, and France guarantee
          the agreed-upon armistice lines to end the fighting in
          the recent Arab-Israeli conflict.

28   ALBANIA - A treaty of friendship with the USSR is con-
          cluded, and Albania joins the COMINFORM.

30   SOUTH VIET NAM - A US economic mission arrives in Saigon.

JUNE

5   NORTH KOREA - The government proposes negotiations leading to reunification, but it emphatically refuses to deal with the Syngman Rhee government.

6   EAST GERMANY - An agreement establishes the Oder-Neisse Line as the new Polish-East German border.

17   EGYPT - A Collective Security Pact is signed by Egypt, Lebanon, Saudi Arabia, Syria, and Yemen in Alexandria. A number of other Arab nations abstain.

25   SOUTH KOREA - North Korean troops begin an invasion of the Republic of Korea. They cross the 38th Parallel at 11 points. Approximately ten North Korean Army (NKA) divisions take part in the offensive.

25   UNITED NATIONS - The Security Council orders an immediate cease-fire in South Korea and the withdrawal of all North Korean forces.

25   NATIONALIST CHINA - Chiang Kai-shek offers military assistance to South Korea through the UN.

27   UNITED STATES - The US intervenes in South Korea when President Truman directs the Far East Command to furnish naval and air support to the Republic of Korea (ROK) armed forces. Also, although General of the Army Douglas MacArthur, the Supreme Allied Commander in the Far East, considers it a good idea, the President rejects the Nationalist Chinese offer of military aid for South Korea.

27   UNITED NATIONS - The Security Council votes to aid the South Koreans who have asked for assistance from the UN member nations.

30   SOUTH KOREA - US ground forces of the 24th US Infantry Division begin moving into the battle area by airlift from Japan where the division had been stationed on occupation duty. Also, the President authorizes air strikes into North Korea.

30   UNITED STATES - In light of the trouble in Korea, the Congress gives the President a bill calling for a partial mobilization of its armed forces. The same act authorizes an extension of Selective Service until July 1951.

JULY

4   SOUTH KOREA - US combat units join the ROK army (ROKA) at Osan.

5   SOUTH KOREA - Units of the US 24th Infantry Division (Task Force Smith) are attacked by numerically super-ior North Korean forces. When the ROK army forces desert their positions, the Americans have to stand alone and are eventually forced to abandon most of their equipment and fight their way out of the enemy encirclement often using only their bayonets.

6-21   SOUTH KOREA - The US 24th Infantry Division delays the North Korean thrust until elements of the US 25th In-fantry and 1st Cavalry Divisions begin to land. This action becomes known as the Battle of Taejon.

7   UNITED NATIONS - The United Nations Command is estab-lished in Korea.

8   UNITED NATIONS - General of the Army Douglas MacArthur is appointed Commander-in-Chief of United Nations Forces, Korea (UNC).

15   SOUTH VIET NAM - A US military mission arrives in Sai-gon.

20   UNITED STATES - The charges leveled by Senator Joseph McCarthy at numerous Americans, especially those made against officials within the Department of State, are found to be mostly fabrications.

20   SOUTH KOREA - The North Koreans launch a three-pronged attack on Taejon forcing the withdrawal of American troops of the US 24th Infantry Division. The division commander, Major General William F. Dean, is captured.

22   BELGIUM - Even though a referendum (12 March 1950) ap-proved his return, the arrival of King Leopold on Belgian soil, after six years in exile, is met with violent protest from leftists and Socialists. This issue is not settled until Leopold's abdication in July 1951.

22   SOUTH KOREA - Two US and several reconstituted ROK divisions blunt the North Korean Army (NKA) drive and begin organizing a defensive position known as the Pusan Perimeter.

24   NATIONALIST CHINA - The Communists begin a period of intense artillery fire on Nationalist Chinese Quemoy island.

AUGUST

5   SOUTH KOREA - For a period of six weeks the US Eighth Army, along with ROKA, holds off NKA attacks along a front of about 150 miles (Pusan Perimeter) while, at the same time, receiving replacements and building strength. This includes the arrival of the first of many forces from other UN sending nations. All through this period, US and Allied aircraft and naval units batter NKA positions.

6   FRANCE - The government announces a plan to create 15 new divisions for the French army.

17   INDONESIA - The Republic of Indonesia is proclaimed as a unitary state replacing the previous confederation.

SEPTEMBER

1   SOUTH AFRICA - Jan Christian Smuts dies.

5   SOUTH KOREA - The North Korean invasion reaches its high point as fresh UN forces are crowded into the Pusan Perimeter.

13   SOUTH KOREA - The breakout of the Pusan Perimeter begins when American, South Korean, and Allied forces take the offensive.

15   SOUTH KOREA - Amphibious forces of the US X Corps begin landing at Inchon gaining almost total strategic surprise.

15   SOUTH KOREA - After a period of heavy attacks across the Naktong by strategic bombers from as far away as Okinawa, The US Eighth Army begins its breakout of the Pusan Perimeter. After initially stiff resistance, the NKA forces begin to withdraw in confusion.

18   UNITED STATES - The Congress passes special legislation authorizing General George C. Marshall to be Secretary of Defense.

19   UNITED STATES - Along with the other Western powers, the US announces that it will consider any attack on West Germany or on Berlin as an attack upon itself. It is also announced that Allied military forces will be strengthened in Germany and that a revision of the Occupation Statute will be enacted to permit West Germany more latitude in diplomatic and economic affairs. West German security police forces were also authorized as a counter to an East German "police force" build-up.

20   TURKEY - A military force of 4,500 men is dispatched to join the United Nations Command in Korea.

26   SOUTH KOREA - At the same time that the capital city of Seoul is liberated, units of the US 1st Cavalry Division affect the US Eighth Army link-up with the Inchon landing force.

30   SOUTH KOREA - Having reached the 38th Parallel, the UN command demands the surrender of North Korean forces. The demand is ignored.

OCTOBER

COMMUNIST CHINA - The Mao Tse-tung government threatens retaliation if UN forces cross the 38th Parallel in Korea.

NORTH KOREA - Chinese forces are first detected opposing UN troops operating in North Korea.

INDOCHINA - The French suffer a series of setbacks in their struggle against the Viet Minh to retain domination.

1   SOUTH KOREA - Having received no reply to his surrender demand, MacArthur requests that the United Nations Command (UNC) be authorized to invade North Korea. Republic of Korea army units are already across the border.

3   BRAZIL - Former dictator Getulio Vargas is reelected president.

7   UNITED NATIONS - The General Assembly adopts a resolution calling for a unified Korea and establishes a commission to pursue the matter.

7   TIBET - The country is invaded by the Communist Chinese army. By November, the entire country is overrun and occupied. Widespread unrest continues for years, even though the Chinese ruthlessly attempt to suppress it.

9   SOUTH KOREA - The UN General Assembly authorizes United Nations forces to cross the 38th Parallel. Units of the US Eighth Army cross immediately and continue the attack northward.

9   INDOCHINA - The French are defeated at Fort Caobang, near the Chinese border.

15   FRANCE - The French defense minister, Jules Moch, an-
            nounces that the United States will furnish $2 billion
            for the French military buildup and that this money
            will be used to support French efforts in Indochina.

15   UNITED STATES - President Truman travels to Wake
            Island to meet with General MacArthur and discuss dif-
            ferences between official US policy and statements
            made by MacArthur.

19   AUSTRALIA - The Parliament moves to dissolve the Com-
            munist Party.

20-21   USSR - Along with its satellites, the Soviet Union de-
            nounces Western liberalization of the Allied policy on
            Germany and calls for the reunification of the two
            Germanies.

21   INDOCHINA - The French are forced to abandon most of
            northern Viet Nam.

26   FRANCE - Henri Pleven, the French premier, proposes
            the establishment of a European ministry of defense as
            an alternative to rearming Germany.

30   NORTH KOREA - United Nations forces approach the Yalu
            River at a number of points.

NOVEMBER

1   UNITED STATES - Puerto Rican nationalists attempt to
            kill the President of the United States.

1   NORTH KOREA - A North Korean counteroffensive stops UN
            forces and succeeds in dislodging them from a number
            of forward positions. The North Koreans do not take
            advantage of the successes. The first Chinese
            "volunteer" prisoners are captured by UN forces. The
            UN Command is forced to accept hitherto rejected in-
            telligence that Communist Chinese forces have crossed
            the Yalu into North Korea in large numbers.

2   UNITED NATIONS - The General Assembly changes its
            rules to allow for its being called into session on
            short notice in emergency situations when the Security
            Council fails to gain unanimity to settle the problem.

3   INDOCHINA - French forces withdraw from the northern
            frontier of Indochina.

7   NEPAL - A palace coup, led by Premier Mohan Shumshere,
            overthrows King Tribhubarra Bir Bikram.

7   IRAQ - The government   declares the Anglo-Iraqi   alliance obsolete.

8   NORTH KOREA - The first air-to-air combat between jet aircraft takes place when North Korean MiG-15 jets challenge USAF aircraft over North Korea.

10   TIBET - An appeal for a peaceful settlement of the Chinese invasion is sent to the United Nations.

10-12   AUSTRIA - The Western Allies protest indirect Soviet instigation of the rioting and strikes that have broken out in the country.

11-20   NEPAL - The deposed king leads an unsuccessful attempt to regain his throne. He is subsequentially asked by the government to again wear the crown.

13   VENEZUELA - The President, Carlos Delgado Chalbaud, is assassinated.

16   EGYPT - Prime Minister Mustafa el-Nahas Pasha demands a British withdrawal from the Suez Canal and from the Sudan.

18   UNITED NATIONS - The UN General Assembly condemns the Chinese invasion of Tibet.

19-26   WEST GERMANY - Political forces opposing the rearming of Germany gain significant strength following elections in the American zone.

20   GREAT BRITAIN - In opposition to Egyptian demands for its annexation, the British government reiterates its intent to establish the Sudan as a self-governing state.

20   INDIA - The government accepts the McMahon Line as the rightful boundary between India and Tibet and repudiates the Chinese version.

24   NORTH KOREA - United Nations forces launch a general offensive to end the war.

25-26   NORTH KOREA - Chinese Communist forces, now in North Korea in significant numbers, open a campaign that drives UN forces back to the 38th Parallel by the end of the year.

27   VENEZUELA - The ruling military junta appoints Suarez Flammerich to be President.

27   NORTH KOREA - MacArthur orders the withdrawal of the US Xth Corps through the ports of Wonsan and Hungnam.

27   NORTH KOREA (Cont'd) - More than 120,000 Chinese
            troops moving down both sides of the Chosin reservoir
            threaten to surround and destroy the American force.

DECEMBER

            INDOCHINA - The French establish a defensive enclave
            around the Red River Delta. During this month also,
            General De Lattre de Tassigny is given command of
            French forces in the region.

3   LIBYA - As the country prepares for independence in
            1952, Mohammed Idris ei-Senussi (Idris I) is pro-
            claimed king.

5   SOUTH KOREA - The US Eighth Army is finally able to
            stem the Communist counterattack but, before being
            able to do so, it is forced to withdraw nearly 150
            miles.

5-15   SOUTH KOREA - More than 100,000 US Army, Marine, and
            ROK forces and another 100,000 refugees are evacuated
            from the Wonsan-Hungnam perimeters under the protec-
            tion of the heaviest naval gunfire since World War II.

8   UNITED STATES - The British Prime Minister, Clement R.
            Attlee, meets with President Truman seeking assurances
            that the US will not initiate nuclear warfare in
            Korea. Both agree to support the UN resolution seeking
            peace.

16   UNITED STATES - A state of national emergency is de-
            clared following serious reversals in Korea.

18-19   NATO - General of the Army Dwight D. Eisenhower is
            appointed Supreme Allied Commander in Europe.

19   SOUTH KOREA - The first Canadian contingents arrive to
            join the United Nations Command.

20   NATO - The Brussels Treaty nations merge their armed
            forces with those of NATO.

23   UNITED STATES - The US signs the Pentalateral Agree-
            ment with France, Viet Nam, Laos, and Cambodia, pro-
            viding indirect US military assistance for use in
            Indochina. A US Military Assistance Advisory Group
            (USMAAG) is established with 128 personnel assigned
            under the command of Brigadier General Francis G.
            Brink.

23   INDOCHINA - Viet Nam is given sovereignty within the
            French Union.

28   SOUTH KOREA – Chinese forces cross the 38th Parallel
          into South Korea.

Notes

1951

JANUARY

1   SOUTH KOREA - A Communist Chinese-North Korean offen-
        sive force of more than one-half million troops breaks
        through the UN lines on the 38th Parallel.

3   SOUTH KOREA - Communist forces penetrate as far south
        as the Chongpyong reservoir south of Kapyong over-
        running a number of ROK units in the process. The UN
        command commits its reserve to extricate the trapped
        US 2nd Infantry Division.

4   UNITED STATES - President Truman informs the American
        people that there would be no bombing of China without
        a declaration of war by the Congress.

4   SOUTH KOREA - The capital city of Seoul falls to the
        Communist armies after being evacuated by UN and ROK
        forces.

6   UNITED STATES - The US reveals it is sending arms and
        other military supplies to the Nationalist Chinese on
        Taiwan (Formosa).

11   UNITED NATIONS - The special UN truce committee pro-
        poses a five-point plan for peace in the Far East.

15   SOUTH KOREA - The Communist advance is stopped and the
        front stabilizes along a general line from Pyongtaek,
        which is about 50 miles south of Seoul, to Samchok on
        the east coast.

17   COMMUNIST CHINA - When the government rejects the UN peace plan, the United States submits a motion to the UN to brand the Chinese as aggressors.

20   USSR - In notes to Great Britain and France, the government identifies the rearming of Germany as the chief threat to peace in Europe.

25   SOUTH KOREA - The UN Command begins a limited offensive near Seoul.

29   GREAT BRITAIN - The government announces a three-year armament program that will cost 4.7 billion pounds Sterling.

29   JAPAN - At the very moment that the US and Japan are conducting peace talks, the opposition party issues a demand for the return of the Soviet-controlled Kurile Islands and the US-controlled Ryukyus, including Okinawa, to Japanese authority.

30   UNITED STATES - A Military Assistance Group is established to support Nationalist China.

31   UNITED STATES - Talks with the USSR over the repayment of $11 billion dollars in Lend Lease are indefinitely suspended.

FEBRUARY

1   UNITED NATIONS - The General Assembly finds the People's Republic of China (Communist China) guilty of aggression in Korea.

8   UNITED STATES - The President orders the army to take over the railroads after a week-long strike has paralyzed the country.

8   UNITED NATIONS - The General Assembly orders an arms embargo on Communist China.

11-18   SOUTH KOREA - A Communist counteroffensive in the Wonju-Chipyong area blunts the UN drive northward although some UN units are close to Seoul.

12   GREAT BRITAIN - Even though United Kingdom forces are fighting in Korea, the Attlee government balks at sanctions against Red China as long as there is a possibility of finding a peaceful solution to the Korean problem.

15   GREECE - The government demands that the British allow the island of Cyprus to reunite with Greece.

MARCH

1   INDONESIA - The government sends 25,000 troops to Java to suppress <u>Darul Islam</u>, a fanatical Muslim group, and a number of Communist and other outlaw bands operating there.

2   CZECHOSLOVAKIA - There are reports of a major purge aimed primarily against "Titoist" elements in the Party.

5   COMMUNIST CHINA - An agreement is reached with Tibet whereby the Dalai Lama will control internal affairs while Peking will control defense and foreign affairs.

7   SOUTH KOREA - UN forces begin Operation RIPPER which is planned to retake Seoul while inflicting maximum casualties upon the enemy.

14   SOUTH KOREA - The UN Forces retakes Seoul after it was abandoned by the Communists. Enemy resistence soon increases.

23   SOUTH KOREA - A US airborne landing near Munsan, 25 miles north of Seoul, breaks Communist resistence and a general retirement begins toward the north.

24   SOUTH KOREA - General MacArthur declares his readiness to meet the Communist commanders in the field to seek a truce.

26   UNITED STATES - A meeting of the foreign ministers of 21 American republics begins in Washington. The purpose is to draw up a series of declarations (7 April) that provide for mutual assistance against international communism.

28   UNITED STATES - The commander of the US Seventh Fleet in the western Pacific states that the US Navy will fight if the Communist Chinese attempt any military actions against the Nationalist Chinese.

29   UNITED STATES - The US distributes copies of the draft peace treaty with Japan to the 14 Allied Powers.

29   COMMUNIST CHINA - The government rejects the MacArthur offer to end the fighting in Korea.

31   INDIA - The government urges a solution to the Korean problem.

31   SOUTH KOREA - The UN Command reoccupies positions along the 38th Parallel.

APRIL

2   NATO - General Eisenhower assumes command of all NATO forces in Europe.

2   GREAT BRITAIN - The British government joins India in urging a peaceful solution to the Korean problem.

3   SOUTH KOREA - After containing the last Communist offensive, the UN Command counterattacks north across the 38th Parallel.

4   UNITED STATES - After months of debate, the Senate approves a resolution approving the President's desire to send four additional divisions to Europe. Although the resolve had a 3:1 margin, the Senate held that additional deployments could only be accomplished with the approval of Congress.

5   ISRAEL - Israeli fighter-bombers attack Syrian positions in retaliation for Syrian border incursions into Israeli territory. These clashes continue until 15 April.

7   ICELAND - In response to a request from the government, the US sends troops to Iceland to help defend the country.

7   VIET NAM - Finding frontal assaults on French military positions too costly, Ho Chi Minh orders a return to the tactics of guerrilla warfare.

11   UNITED STATES - After a continuing conflict with the President over Far East policy, General MacArthur is relieved of his command and ordered to return to the United States.

12   SOUTH KOREA - United Nations forces resume the offensive to thwart an expected communist counter-blow designed to protect the strategically important "Iron Triangle" lying roughly in the Chorwon-Kumhwa-Pyonggang area.

13   ARGENTINA - President Juan Peron orders the closing of the newspaper La Prensa.

22   SOUTH KOREA - The Communists begin their expected counteroffensive. They break through the lines of the 6th ROK Infantry Division near the Chongpyong reservoir.

23   SPAIN - Over a quarter-million workers go on strike in protest against rising living costs.

25   UNITED STATES - The Secretary of State formally acknowledges that arms and equipment are being sent to Taiwan.

27   DENMARK - The government signs a 20-year treaty with the US for the defense of Greenland.

30   SOUTH KOREA - The Communist offensive loses momentum and stalls. Communist units eventually break contact and move northward to avoid further, continued subjection to intensive artillery fire.

MAY

1   GREAT BRITAIN - The armed forces of the United Kingdom are unified into a single service.

5   ICELAND - A US-Icelandic agreement is signed which provides for the use of defense bases in Iceland by the NATO allies.

8   ISRAEL - A cease-fire along the Israeli-Syrian border is reestablished.

9   PANAMA - The government of President Arnulfo Arias suspends the constitution and dissolves the assembly. There is rioting in Panama City.

9   UNITED NATIONS - The Security Council orders a cease-fire in the fighting that has broken out along the Israeli-Syrian border. Both sides comply with the order.

10   PANAMA - President Arias is impeached and replaced by Domingo Arosemena.

14   SOUTH KOREA - The Communists open their second spring offensive.

16   BOLIVIA - A military junta, led by General Hugo Ballivan, forces the resignation of President Mamerto Urriolagoita.

18   UNITED NATIONS - The General Assembly places an embargo on a wide assortment of military arms and supplies to Communist China.

19   UNITED STATES - The US formally rejects a Soviet counter-proposal that would give the People's Republic of China a voice in drafting the Japan peace treaty.

20   SOUTH KOREA - The Communist offensive stalls.

22   POLAND - The Soviets force the Polish government to
            cede the oil-rich Lublin valley to the USSR in return
            for less profitable territory. The transfer presumably
            decreases Poland's oil-producing capacity by one-
            fifth.

22   SOUTH KOREA - A major UN offensive begins.

24   ISRAEL - The government charges that Jordanian army
            units operated inside Israeli borders twice during the
            preceding week.

31   SOUTH KOREA - Even though the UN offensive is eminent-
            ly successful, the US Joint Chiefs of Staff (JCS) or-
            ders a halt in the face of Soviet threats to inter-
            vene. The decision is also tempered by a general dis-
            approval of the war elsewhere in the world.

JUNE

            UNITED STATES - The results of a Congressional inves-
            tigation into President Truman's policies on Korea and
            the relief of General MacArthur prove to be incon-
            clusive.

1   SOUTH KOREA - The UN begins consolidating its
            positions and "digs in."

19   UNITED STATES - President Truman signs a Military
            Manpower Bill which extends the draft until 1 July
            1955, and lowers the draft age to 18 1/2. The bill
            also establishes Universal Military Training to take
            effect sometime in the future.

21   FRANCE - After weeks of wrangling, the deputy foreign
            ministers of the US, Great Britain, France, and the
            USSR find themselves hopelessly deadlocked and end a
            conference that was to draw up an agenda for the
            forthcoming meeting of foreign ministers.

23   UNITED NATIONS - The Soviet representative, Jacob A.
            Malik, hints at the possibility of a cease-fire in
            Korea. The area around the town of Kaesong is neu-
            tralized as a possible meeting site for future negoti-
            ations.

25   UNITED STATES - The President states a willingness to
            engage in Korean truce talks.

26   GREAT BRITAIN - A meeting of Commonwealth defense
            ministers is called to discuss the Middle East situ-
            ation.

28   HUNGARY - A Catholic archbishop, Josef Groesz, is con-
        victed of conspiracy to overthrow the government.

29   SOUTH KOREA - The UN Command broadcasts an offer to
        the Communists to arrange a meeting to discuss a
        truce.

29   THAILAND - There is a uprising among naval personnel
        that is surpressed within 72 hours.

JULY

1   NORTH KOREA - The Communists agree to a meeting to
        discuss a truce.

3   INDIA - The Nehru government files a formal complaint
        against Pakistan with the UN charging repeated
        cease-fire violations in Kashmir.

4   CZECHOSLOVAKIA - An American journalist, William
        Oatis, is convicted of espionage.

8   SOUTH KOREA - Truce negotiations begin at Kaesong.

16   BELGIUM - King Leopold abdicates in favor of his son,
        Baudouin, who is crowned the following day.

20   JORDAN - King Abdullah is assassinated by a follower
        of the former Mufti of Jerusalem, Haj Amin al-Husaini.

21   CZECHOSLOVAKIA - An official US request for the re-
        lease of William Oatis is denied. The US prepares to
        initiate diplomatic reprisals.

21   HUNGARY - After two years of refusal, Hungary's Roman
        Catholic bishops swear allegiance to the state.

AUGUST

5   SOUTH KOREA - The UN Command breaks off truce talks
        after North Korea forces violate the demilitarized
        area around Kaesong. Limited military operations
        resume.

6   EGYPT - The foreign minister announces abrogation of
        the 1936 Anglo-Egyptian treaty.

10   SOUTH KOREA - The truce talks resume but soon become
        hopelessly deadlocked.

11   PERU – Fighting begins along the Peru-Ecuador border
            over the issue of access to the Amazon.

13   PERU – The US, Argentina, Brazil, and Chile are asked
            to investigate the border incidents involving Ecuador.

23   SOUTH KOREA – The Communists break off truce negoti-
            ations after alleging the UN Command bombed Kaesong.

30   THE PHILIPPINES – The government signs a mutual de-
            fense pact with the United States.

SEPTEMBER

1   AUSTRALIA – The US, New Zealand, and Australia sign a
            tripartite security pact (ANZUS Pact).

1   UNITED NATIONS – The Security Council votes to order
            Egypt to stop interfering with the movement of Israel-
            bound shipping through the Suez Canal. Egypt states
            the UN resolution was illegal and, therefore, not
            binding.

3   MIDDLE EAST – The Arab League appeals to its seven
            member nations to further restrict trade, especially
            in oil, with Israel. Israel is branded as a threat to
            peace in the region.

5   JORDAN – The mentally-ill Emir Talal is crowned King.

6   UNITED STATES – A US-Portuguese agreement brings the
            strategically-important Azores into NATO.

7   UNITED STATES – The government signs an agreement with
            South Viet Nam for direct economic assistance.

8   UNITED NATIONS – After four days of discussion during
            which a number of Soviet proposals were defeated, 48
            nations and Japan sign a peace treaty. The USSR and
            its satellites boycott the signing ceremonies. Also,
            delegates from Viet Nam, Laos, and Cambodia partici-
            pate in the signing of the Japanese peace treaty in
            San Francisco.

8   UNITED STATES – The US signs a Mutual Security Pact
            with Japan which permits the US to indefinitely
            station its military forces on Japanese soil (to the
            exclusion of all other nations not approved by the
            US.)

10   YUGOSLAVIA – Tito offers to settle all outstanding
            problems with Italy.

12   IRAN - The Mossadegh government sends an ultimatum to Great Britain ordering the British out of Abadan.

15   CANADA - The NATO council opens a conference in Ottawa to discuss the defense of western Europe.

20   CANADA - The NATO Council of Ministers recommends that Turkey and Greece be admitted into the organization.

23   SOUTH KOREA - The UN Command captures "Heartbreak Ridge" after 37 days of heavy fighting.

24   WEST GERMANY - The three Western powers inform Chancellor Adenauer that the occupation statute will be abrogated and the Allied High Commission abolished if Germany takes part in the defense of western Europe.

27   IRAN - Iranian forces occupy Abadan.

28   ARGENTINA - Government forces put down a military uprising led by General Benjamin Menendez. President Juan Peron blames the former US Ambassador, Spruille Braden, with inciting the revolt. Martial law is declared.

OCTOBER

2   AUSTRALIA - The British successfully detonate a nuclear device in a test at Monte Bello Island (near Australia).

4   GREAT BRITAIN - After an appeal to the UN fails the British evacuate Abadan.

8   SOUTH KOREA - An announcement is made that the Communists have agreed to resume peace talks at a newly chosen demilitarized site at Panmunjom.

10-22 SOUTH KOREA - Arrangements for the resumption of the truce talks begin between liaison officers at Panmunjom.

13   VENEZUELA - Government forces quell an uprising in Caracas that is said to have been inspired by the outlawed communists and other groups.

14   YUGOSLAVIA - The government signs an agreement with the US for the supply of arms and other military materiel and services.

15   PAKISTAN - Prime Minister Liaqat Ali Khan is assassinated.

19   UNITED STATES - The President signs a Joint Resolution
          of Congress formally ending the state of war with Ger-
          many.

22   NATO - Meeting in Lisbon, the NATO Council accepts the
          Greek and Turkish representatives into the organiza-
          tion.

25   SOUTH KOREA - Formal truce negotiations begin again at
          Panmunjom.

27   EGYPT - The Anglo-Egyptian Defense Treaty of 1936 is
          formally abrogated. At the same time, the 1899 con-
          dominium dealing with the Sudan is abrogated.

27   SUDAN - The Assembly rejects the Egyptian demand for
          unification.

29   CAMBODIA - The French High Commissioner, Jean de Ray-
          mond, is assassinated.

NOVEMBER

9   MIDDLE EAST - The US, France, Great Britain, and Tur-
          key announce plans for a Mid-East security program.

12   SOUTH KOREA - The UNC orders a halt to all offensive
          operations in Korea.

21   UNITED NATIONS - The Middle East conciliatory commis-
          sion ends its attempts at settling the Arab-Israeli
          problem in failure.

27   SOUTH KOREA - A provisional cease-fire line is agreed
          upon, on the proviso that all other truce arrangements
          can be made within 30 days.

29   SYRIA - The government of pro-Soviet Maarouf Dawalibi
          is overthrown the day after he takes office.

29   THAILAND - A military revolt is suppressed but the
          government is forced to make concessions.

DECEMBER

2   SYRIA - Colonel Adib Shishakli assumes the office of
          president.

3   HUNGARY - A US Air Force transport is forced down by
          Soviet fighters in Hungarian air space. The four-man
          crew is taken prisoner and held until 28 December when
          the US ransoms them for $120,000.

10   IRAN - After repeatedly denying that the court had any authority in the matter, the Iranian government finally decides to submit its oil nationalization problem to the International Court of Justice.

13   OAS - The charter of the Organization of American States goes into effect after Colombia ratifies the agreement.

24   LIBYA - The nation is declared independent.

27   SOUTH KOREA - The 30-day truce period ends. Neither side suggests an extension.

31   UNITED STATES - Marshall Plan aid ends as the plan expires.

Notes

1952

SAUDI ARABIA - Government forces seize Buraimi Oasis also claimed by the Sultan of Oman and Muscat.

KENYA - Four years of Mau Mau terrorism begins.

CYPRUS - Seven years of guerrilla warfare begins between Greek and Turkish nationalists.

JANUARY

1   LIBYA - The UN-mandated independence of Libya takes effect.

5   UNITED STATES - British Prime Minister Sir Winston Churchill begins a series of discussions with President Truman concerning the European Army Plan and strengthening the NATO Alliance.

11   UNITED NATIONS - A 12-nation disarmament commission is formed. It is composed of the 11 members of the UN Security Council and Canada.

12   IRAN - The government orders all British consulates in Iran closed.

13   GREAT BRITAIN - The British reject the Iranian demand to close its consulates.

14   TUNISIA - The government appeals to the UN for a hearing on its demands for autonomy. When the request is denied, there is wide-spread anti-French rioting in the country.

18   NATO - There is agreement that a US Supreme Commander
            should be named to head the NATO naval forces in the
            Atlantic.

18   EGYPT - British troops clash with Egyptian guerrillas
            in Port Said (Bur Sa'id) at the northern end of the
            Suez Canal. The British cruiser <u>HMS Liverpool</u> opens
            fire on the city in support of forces ashore.

20   EGYPT - British forces occupy Ismailia at the southern
            end of the Suez Canal.

24   NEPAL - There is a Communist-inspired but unsuccessful
            revolt against the government.

25   WEST GERMANY - The French government's decision to re-
            place the High Commissariat for the Saar with a diplo-
            matic mission creates a furor in Bonn.

26   EGYPT - Widespread rioting breaks out in Cairo. There
            is heavy destruction of foreign property, and a number
            of deaths are reported. King Farouk is forced to
            replace his Premier, Mustafa el-Nahas, with Ali Maher
            Pasha.

FEBRUARY

1   UNITED NATIONS - The General Assembly finds the Soviet
            Union guilty of obstructing Nationalist Chinese ef-
            forts to restore order on the mainland and with help-
            ing the Chinese Communists.

4   WEST GERMANY - Chancellor Adenauer demands the Western
            powers consult West Germany before any changes are
            made in the status of the Saar.

6   GREAT BRITAIN - King George VI dies. On his death, his
            daughter, Elizabeth II, becomes Queen.

7   MALAYA - The British begin a counter-insurgency cam-
            paign designed to destroy rebel forces. Over 45,000
            British and colonial forces are engaged in the offen-
            sive.

8   GREAT BRITAIN - Queen Elizabeth II formally assumes
            the throne.

22   NATO - The European Defense Plan is approved.

23   NATO - A plan is approved calling for a 50-division
            force to protect Western Europe from Soviet attack by
            the end of 1952.

25   JAPAN - Peacetalks between Japan and Nationalist China are deadlocked over Chinese demands that Japan acknowledge 1937 as the start of the war, and that Japan recognize Communist-held territory as rightfully belonging to Nationalist China.

26   GREAT BRITAIN - Winston Churchill officially announces that Great Britain has produced and detonated a nuclear weapon in tests near Australia on 2 October 1951.

MARCH

1   EGYPT - The Premier, Ali Maher Pasha, resigns.

1   GREAT BRITAIN - The government formally returns Helgoland Island to West Germany.

4   UNITED STATES - The Congress defeats a plan for Universal Military Training. At the same time, the government proposes a formal inquiry into the Chinese Communist accusations that the US is engaging in biological warfare in Korea.

10   USSR - The government calls for a Four-Power summit to discuss German reunification and rearmament.

10   CUBA - The elected government of Prio Socarrus is overthrown in a military coup led by General Fulgencio Batista y Zaldivar.

14   USSR - The Soviets repeat the Chinese Communist charge that the US is employing biological warfare in Korea.

14   THE PHILIPPINES - The Communist leader of the rebel Hukbalahaps, William J. Pomeroy, is captured.

15   TUNISIA - Bowing to heavy pressure from the French, the Bey of Tunis removes the pro-independence members of the government. The Bey asks the populace for a period of calm.

20   UNITED STATES - The Senate ratifies the peace treaty with Japan. It also approves a series of security agreements with Australia, Japan, New Zealand, and The Philippines.

20   ITALY - An anti-Allied uprising takes place in Trieste. The principal cause of the rioting is a protest against continued occupation by American and British forces.

20   SOUTH AFRICA - The Supreme Court voids the Apartheid Bill.

23   UNITED STATES - Along with Great Britain and France,
            the US responds to the Soviet note of 10 March stating
            it would endorse a reunified Germany only if free
            elections could be held under four-power supervision.

30   TANGIER - There are violent anti-French riots in the
            International Zone.

APRIL

            FRANCE - Jean Letourneau, the French Minister of State
            for the Associated States is named Minister-Resident
            for Indochina.

2   EGYPT - The government protests the British offer of
            limited self-government to Sudan.

7   SPAIN - The government formally demands police powers
            in the international zone of Tangier.

8   UNITED STATES - The President orders the seizure of
            the steel industry. This action was later ruled un-
            constitutional (29 April).

11   BOLIVIA - The Ballivan junta is ousted after a three
            day revolt led by the National Revolutionary Movement.

12   NATO - General Matthew Ridgeway is appointed to re-
            place General Eisenhower as Supreme Allied Commander,
            Europe.

15   GREAT BRITAIN - The government endorses the European
            Army Plan and states it is willing to agree to a
            mutual defense agreement with the European Defense
            Community.

22   SOUTH AFRICA - Prime Minister Daniel F. Malan intro-
            duces legislation making the Parliament the highest
            court in the land thereby bypassing the Supreme Court
            ruling of 20 March.

25   UNITED STATES - The US resumes arms shipments to Iran
            after a four month suspension.

28   JAPAN - A peace treaty is agreed upon with Nationalist
            China in which Japan renounces its claim to Taiwan
            (Formosa), the Pescadores, and all claims against
            China. With the exception of the Soviet Union, 49
            other nations, including the US, sign a peace treaty
            with the Japanese. The US also initials a bilateral
            defense treaty with Japan.

MAY

EGYPT - The month is spent in fruitless negotiations between Great Britain and the Egyptian government over the issues of the Suez Canal and the Sudan.

7   SOUTH KOREA - A well-organized revolt breaks out among Communist POWs in the UN prison camp on Koje Island at the southern tip of the Korean Peninsula. The US camp commander, Brigadier General Francis T. Dodd, carelessly allows himself to be taken prisoner and becomes the center of a propaganda coup for the Communists. Order is restored only after US troops, commanded by Brigadier General Haydon Boatner, sweep through the camp.

23   UNITED STATES - The government returned the railroads to private management after 21 months of federal operation.

26   WEST GERMANY - The internal independence of West Germany is approved by the US, Great Britain, and France after lengthy negotiation at Bonn.

26   EAST GERMANY - The government begins a campaign of pressure on the West Germans in response to the signing of the Bonn Agreement. The principal tool is curtailment of east-west communications.

27   FRANCE - A series of documents are signed that create a unified European Defense Community (EDC) of The Netherlands, Belgium, Luxemburg, France, and West Germany. The signatories also initial a treaty with Great Britain in which the British promise military aid to any of the five who are attacked. The US and Great Britain sign a treaty with France that states any attack will be considered a threat upon their security. Lastly, NATO guarantees are given to West Germany.

29   ROMANIA - Foreign Minister Ana Pauker, along with two other ministers, is removed from the Politburo.

29   SOUTH AFRICA - The Parliament approves a bill limiting the powers of the Supreme Court after it overturned a government-sponsored race law.

JUNE

6   CAMBODIA - Prince Sihanouk dismisses his cabinet and the National Assembly and decides to run the country himself. He promises elections in three years.

7   CZECHOSLOVAKIA - The government announces a major coal shortage and failure of the nation's agricultural system.

14   USSR - The government agrees to allow Austrian shipping to use the Danube through the Soviet zone after seven years of refusal.

23   TUNISIA - The nationalists reject the French offer of greater self-reliance in the French Union.

23   NORTH KOREA - US bombers attack hydroelectric plants in North Korea.

26   ARGENTINA - Eva Peron dies.

26   SOUTH AFRICA - A period of black disobedience to "unjust laws" begins with numerous acts of violence and many arrests.

JULY

           SOUTH VIET NAM - The US Legation in Saigon is raised to embassy status and an ambassador assigned. At the same time, a Vietnamese embassy is opened in Washington.

3   UNITED NATIONS - The USSR vetoes a proposal that the International Red Cross investigate the biological warfare charges leveled at the US.

6   YUGOSLAVIA - Tito rules out any alliances but states a willingness to cooperate with Austria, Greece, and Turkey.

13   UNITED STATES - The government announces a decision to equip the Yugoslav army with American arms and materiel.

17   IRAN - After Premier Mossadegh resigns he is replaced by Ahmad Ghavam.

22   IRAN - Mohammed Mossadegh is returned to power after bloody rioting forces the overthrow of the Ghavam government.

23   EGYPT - King Farouk I and his government are overthrown by a military coup led by General Mohammed Naguib Bey.

24   EGYPT - Ali Maher Pasha is reinstalled as the Premier. King Farouk abdicates in favor of his infant son, Fuad II.

AUGUST

4   UNITED STATES - The United States, Australia, and   New Zealand form the Pacific Council.

11   JORDAN - King Talal is declared unfit to rule by the Parliament because of mental illness (schizophrenia). Seventeen-year old Crown Prince Hussein (Husain Ibn Ralal) is designated his successor.

13   NEPAL - The king assumes dictatorial control of his country to end the violence.

13   CANADA - The government announces a decision to provide $150 million in a gift of aid to Great Britain.

15   UNITED STATES - The US announces it will not adhere to any conditions set down by the UN Disarmament Commission until verifiable international controls   are adopted.

SEPTEMBER

7   EGYPT - Forty-seven Egyptian leaders are imprisoned by General Naguib as he consolidates his power.

10   WEST GERMANY - The government agrees to pay the State of Israel over $820 million in reparations.

11   ETHIOPIA - The government formally accepts transfer of Eritrea from Great Britain and makes it a part of Ethiopia.

18   UNITED NATIONS - The USSR vetoes Japan's admission to the UNO.

18   LEBANON - In the face of mounting labor strikes and civil unrest in his country, Bisgara (Bishara) al-Khoury (Khuri) resigns as President.

19   UNITED NATIONS - The USSR exercises its veto power and blocks the admission of Vietnam, Laos, and Cambodia to the UNO.

23   LEBANON - Camille Chamoun (Sham'un) is elected President by Parliament.

OCTOBER

2   GREAT BRITAIN - The government formally rejects Iran's demands concerning the oil crisis.

3   USSR - When he comments that Western diplomats are
            isolated in Moscow, the Soviet government declares the
            US Ambassador, George F. Kennan, persona non grata
            (PNG) and demands that Washington immediately recall
            him.

3   GREAT BRITAIN - The government announces the detona-
            tion of a nuclear weapon in northwestern Australia.

8   SOUTH KOREA - The Communists break off truce negoti-
            ations.

12   SOUTH VIET NAM - On this day, the 200th ship carrying
            US military aid arrives in Saigon.

13   EGYPT - An agreement is signed with the Sudan over the
            use of the waters of the Nile.

20   GREAT BRITAIN - Unrest in Kenya, led by a secret or-
            ganization called "Mau Mau" (Hidden Ones), requires
            the British government to declare a state of emergency
            and to dispatch an infantry battalion and naval units
            to that country.

22   GREAT BRITAIN - The government approves the formation
            of a self-governing Anglo-Egyptian Sudan.

22   IRAN - The government breaks diplomatic relations with
            Great Britain.

24   SYRIA - Having abolished all other political parties
            in the country, the Syrian strongman, Adib Shishlaki
            proclaims his Arab Liberation Movement as the coun-
            try's sole political organization.

29   EGYPT - The government signs the final agreement on
            Sudanese independence.

NOVEMBER

            UNITED STATES - The US detonates a thermonuclear de-
            vice at Eniwetok Island.

7   ISRAEL - Chaim Weizmann dies in office.

12   UNITED STATES - The US lends Japan 18 frigates and a
            number of landing craft to begin its defensive rearm-
            ament.

14   SPAIN - The US, Great Britain, and France set aside
            the Tangier agreement and return control of the ter-
            ritory to Spain.

18   WEST GERMANY - The Bundestag rejects the entire con-
        cept of the Saar elections to be held on 30 November.

20   CZECHOSLOVAKIA - A major trial begins in which numbers
        of individuals, including former party secretary
        Rudolf Slansky and former foreign minister Vladimir
        Clementis, plead guilty to charges ranging from
        treason to espionage and sabotage.

23   IRAQ - There is an outbreak of anti-British and anti-
        American rioting. Martial law is declared.

24   IRAQ - All political parties are abolished, a ban is
        placed upon further demonstrations, and 12 newspapers
        are closed.

30   SAAR - The elections give a clear majority for auton-
        omy and for association with France.

DECEMBER

2   UNITED STATES - After winning the election, President-
        elect Dwight D. Eisenhower visits Korea where he dis-
        covers the solution to the problem of ending the
        fighting is more difficult than he orginally thought.

3   UNITED NATIONS - A Indian proposal for a Korean
        armistice is accepted by the General Assembly.

3   CZECHOSLOVAKIA - Rudolf Slansky and ten others are
        executed.

10   EGYPT - Egyptian strongman General Naguib abolishes
        the Constitution of 1923.

12   COMMUNIST CHINA - The government rejects the UN peace
        proposal for Korea.

17   YUGOSLAVIA - The governmment breaks diplomatic rela-
        tions with the Vatican when the Pope refuses to inter-
        vene in the struggle between the Catholic church in
        Yugoslavia and the state.

20   TUNISIA - Bowing under heavy French pressure, the Bey
        of Tunis issues a series of decrees dealing with
        governmental reform. These reforms are based upon
        French "guidance."

31   INDONESIA - The government announces its decision to
        participate in the Columbo Plan. It sets a number of
        restrictions on the decision, however, that include no
        obligation for military participation.

31   COMMUNIST CHINA – The Soviets relinguish their control
          of the Chinese Changchun Railroad and tranfer author-
          ity to the Communists.

Notes

1953

NEPAL - Indian troops are called in to help suppress a Communist-inspired revolt.

MIDDLE EAST - Three years of intermittent border fighting begins between Israel and Syria.

JANUARY

KENYA - The British government orders an increase in military activity designed to quell the Mau Mau uprising.

VIETNAM - The French step up their operations against the Viet Minh.

1   CZECHOSLOVAKIA - The government announces severe food shortages and a failure to meet industrial production goals.

5   GREAT BRITAIN - Winston Churchill announces British opposition of any extension of the Korean War into Communist China. He stresses that Western Europe is the real center of the struggle.

14   YUGOSLAVIA - Marshal Tito is elected President of Yugoslavia.

17   EGYPT - General Naguib's dictatorial powers are extended for one year and all opposition political parties are abolished.

19   IRAN - Despite strong political and popular opposition, Premier Mossadegh's dictatorial powers are extended for one year.

20   UNITED STATES - Dwight D. Eisenhower is inaugurated President. Richard Nixon becomes the Vice-President.

20   YUGOSLAVIA - The Turkish foreign minister arrives in Belgrad to open talks on a Balkan defense alliance.

24   SOUTH AFRICA - The Parliament votes to give Prime Minister Malan virtual dictatorial powers to enforce apartheid.

25   INDOCHINA - Pro-French candidates win in all areas except Hanoi in the Vietnamese nation's first national elections.

31   USSR - The exposure of the so-called "Doctors' Plot" is announced. Most observers view this as an opening move in a new purge, especially against the Jews.

FEBRUARY

        INDOCHINA - Negotiations with France over the transfer of defense and security to the Vietnamese government continue.

2   UNITED STATES - President Eisenhower announces that he has issued orders that the US Seventh Fleet is no longer responsible for "neutralizing" Nationalist China and is not to interfere in any Nationalist Chinese attack on the mainland.

6   AUSTRIA - The conference on the Austrian peace treaty is deadlocked.

12   SUDAN - A majority of the electorate votes for complete independence rather than union with Egypt.

13   BULGARIA - The government decrees all defectors will face execution and their families, internment.

21   HUNGARY - At the direction of the Soviets, about thirty Jewish Communists are purged from the Hungarian Communist Party.

24   NATIONALIST CHINA - The government abrogates the 1945 treaty with the USSR and threatens to sue for indemnities.

24   SOUTH AFRICA - The government assumes dictatorial powers in the continuation of its aparthied policies.

25   UNITED NATIONS – The US delegate affirms US approval of
            India's truce proposal for Korea.

MARCH

2   UNITED NATIONS – The Soviet delegate declares peace can
            come in Korea only on Communist terms.

3   BURMA – The army begins a campaign in northern Burma to
            uproot a Nationalist Chinese Army force operating there
            since 1949.

5   USSR – Premier Josef Stalin dies. A triumvirate of com-
            posed of Georgi Malenkov, Lavrenti Beria, and Nikita
            Khrushchev takes power.

6   USSR – Georgi Malenkov is named to head the government.

10   WEST GERMANY – A US fighter aircraft is shot down by
            Soviet fighters in West German air space. The US moves
            immediately to bolster its air strength in Europe with
            the newest Sabrejet fighters.

12   WEST GERMANY – A British bomber is shot down by Soviet
            fighters in West German air space.

14   CZECHOSLOVAKIA – Klement Gottwald dies.

16   UNITED NATIONS – Despite Soviet objections the life of
            the Collective Measures Committee is extended.

16   INDONESIA – Violence breaks out when the government
            attempts to implement its land reform program.

20   USSR – Nikita S. Khrushchev succeeds Georgi Malenkov as
            First Secretary of the Communist Party.

21   CZECHOSLOVAKIA – Premier Antonin Zapotocky is elected
            President.

25   BURMA – The government asks the UN to condemn National-
            ist China for aggression.

28   LIBYA – The government joins the Arab League.

28   SOUTH KOREA – The Communists agree to a prisoner ex-
            change and a resumption of truce talks.

31   YUGOSLAVIA – Marshal Tito announces that Great Britain
            has agreed to act as the protector of Yugoslavia in
            return for its assurances that Yugoslavia would fight
            any aggression.

31   GREAT BRITAIN - Secret mediation begins over the inci-
            dent involving the Soviet downing of a British bomber.
            The US and France are later invited to attend these
            meetings.

APRIL

            NATO - Nuclear weapons are disclosed as being the main-
            stay of the defense of Western Europe.

            SOUTH KOREA - Operation LITTLE SWITCH takes place in
            which sick and wounded UN prisoners of war are ex-
            changed for their Communist counterparts. The total ex-
            change involves only 213 UN personnel and slightly over
            470 ROK soldiers. Over 5,800 Communist troops are
            repatriated.

4   USSR - The physicans arrested in the "Doctors' Plot"
            are released.

8   KENYA - Jhomo Kenyatta (Kamau wa Ngengi) and five other
            rebel leaders are convicted for Mau Mau terrorist
            activities aimed at driving the whites out of Kenya.

14   LAOS - A Viet Minh invasion of Laotian territory be-
            gins.

20   LAOS - The Viet Minh, aided by Pathet Lao rebels, cap-
            ture the provincial capital town of Xieng Khoaung on
            the Tranninh Plateau in the area known as the Plaine
            des Jarres (Plain of Jars).

22   UNITED NATIONS - The Political Committee votes for the
            removal or internment of foreign troops operating in
            Burma.

23   UNITED NATIONS - The General Assembly votes to conduct
            an investigation of Communist charges that the US is
            using biological warfare in Korea.

26   SOUTH KOREA - After months of secret negotiation, the
            truce talks between the United Nations and Communist
            delegations resume at Panmunjom.

MAY

            SOUTH KOREA - President Syngman Rhee's refusal to abide
            by a decision to keep Korea divided results in a
            furtherance of the war.

2   JORDAN - The reign of King Hussein I begins.

9   CAMBODIA - France grants Cambodia full sovereignty in economic, judicial, and military affairs. Thereafter, Prince Norodom Sihanouk seizes all government buildings in the capital city of Phnom Penh in a bid for complete independence.

11   GREAT BRITAIN - Winston Churchill proposes a conference of the major powers to discuss world peace.

13   UNITED STATES - The State Department declares the US is not interested in a big-power conference until the USSR shows a sincere desire for peace.

20   FRANCE - A pact is agreed upon in which Germany and France agree to give the Saar autonomy, but ties it to France economically.

23-24   NATO - The Ministerial Council declares it sees no real change in Soviet intentions. The council also declares its intention to add six new divisions to the defense of Western Europe in 1953.

28   EAST GERMANY - The Soviet Control Commission is abolished and is replaced by a Soviet High Commissioner.

JUNE

1   YUGOSLAVIA - In another slap at the Soviet Union, Tito announces the removal of political commissars from the Yugoslav army.

7-8   CZECHOSLOVAKIA - An anti-inflationary currency reform bill causes rioting in several cities of the country.

8   AUSTRIA - The Soviets lift their control measures on the border between the east and west zones.

9   SOUTH KOREA - The government, in rejecting the proposed armistice agreement, declares itself ready to continue hostilities and to "march north."

10   SOUTH KOREA - Communist Chinese forces launch a series of attacks mostly against ROKA positions.

13   COLOMBIA - The government of President Laureano Gomez is overthrown by a military junta led by Lieutenant General Gustavo Rojas Pinilla.

14   YUGOSLAVIA - Tito announces that the Soviet Union has asked for a resumption of normal diplomatic relations.

15   CAMBODIA - Prince Norodom Sihanouk accepts voluntary exile in Thailand.

15   KENYA - The British win a major victory against the Mau
      Mau in the Aberdare Forest region of central Kenya.

16   EAST GERMANY - Immediately following a relaxation of
      rules against demonstrations, East German workers take
      to the streets demanding a general strike and shouting
      anti-government slogans.

17   EAST GERMANY - Martial law is declared and Soviet ar-
      mored units are sent into East Berlin to suppress an
      estimated 30,000 demonstrators.

18   SOUTH KOREA - President Rhee demands a resumption of
      hostilities after Communist forces attack ROK posi-
      tions.

18   EGYPT - Egypt is proclaimed a republic with strongman
      Mohammed Naguib Bey as its first President and Premier.

19   UNITED STATES - Julius and Ethel Rosenberg are executed
      for transmitting nuclear weapons information to the
      Soviet Union.

20   CAMBODIA - Prince Sihanouk returns after five days in
      exile. Cambodian army units seize control of all gov-
      ernment buildings in Phnom Penh.

22   USSR - Most travel restrictions for foreigners in the
      Soviet Union are lifted.

22   EAST GERMANY - The government offers improvements in
      working conditions to forestall further rioting. Ar-
      rests continue.

25   SOUTH KOREA - The Communists break off the truce talks
      and open a new series of attacks.

29   UNITED STATES - President Eisenhower informs Iran that
      there will be no additional aid granted until Iran
      settles its oil dispute with Great Britain.

30   USSR - The government announces it will pay its own oc-
      cupation costs in Austria after 5 August. (The US had
      been paying its own costs since 1947.)

JULY

3   FRANCE - The government proposes negotiations for more
      autonomy with each of the three Indochinese states.

4   HUNGARY - Prime Minister Matyas Rakosi resigns in favor
      of Imre Nagy.

6   INDOCHINA - Along with Laos, the Vietnamese agree to
           the French plan for greater autonomy.

7   UNITED STATES - As a result of the McCarthy anti-com-
           munist campaign, Doctor Robert Oppenheimer is denied
           future access to classified information.

9   EAST GERMANY - The East Berlin government lifts all
           restrictions on travel between east and west.

10   SOUTH KOREA - The truce talks resume.

10   USSR - Lavrenti Beria, the Soviet Minister of Internal
           Affairs, is dismissed.

10-14   UNITED STATES - The Foreign Ministers of the US, Great
           Britain, and France issue a call for an autumn meeting
           with the USSR on the issues of German reunification and
           the Austrian peace treaty. The meeting also produces a
           warning of renewed fighting if the Communists break the
           truce in Korea or commit aggression anywhere else in
           Asia.

11   SOUTH KOREA - After the US exerts pressure, the govern-
           ment declares it is ready to accept the armistice
           terms.

11   EAST GERMANY - The East Berlin government announces the
           lifting of the martial law order that was imposed on 17
           June.

15   KENYA - The Kenyan Supreme Court overturns the
           conviction of Jomo Kenyatta.

23   THE NETHERLANDS - The European Defense Community Treaty
           is approved.

23   COMMUNIST CHINA - The government announces the signing
           of a major economic aid program with the USSR. It is
           reported that the pact is designed to improve the
           potential of Communist Chinese heavy industry.

26   SOUTH KOREA - An armistice is signed at Panmunjom.

26-27   CUBA - A revolt led by Fidel Castro is crushed by the
           Batista government. Castro and his brother are impris-
           oned.

27   SOUTH KOREA - The terms of the armistice agreement go
           into effect. At the same time, the sixteen nations who
           have supplied combat forces as a part of the United
           Nations Command declare their willingness to resume the
           fighting should the Communists break the truce.

27   CAMBODIA - The government accepts the French plan but
            issues a list of demands that must be included in any
            final agreement and further demands that the meeting
            site be Phnom Penh instead of Paris as originally pro-
            posed.

29   GREAT BRITAIN - The government enters into a 20-year
            treaty with Libya that grants Britain military basing
            rights in the North African country in return for
            substantial economic investments.

AUGUST

            FRANCE - Months-long negotiations begin with Cambodia
            over the issue of greater autonomy.

6-28   FRANCE - Public service strikes almost cripple the
            nation.

8   USSR - Premier Malenkov announces that the Soviet Union
            has the hydrogen bomb.

11   IRAN - The Shah flees to Iraq after an unsuccessful at-
            tempt to depose Mossadegh.

12   USSR - The Soviet Union detonates its first thermo-
            nuclear (hydrogen) device.

14   MOROCCO - Sultan Sidi Mohammed is deposed in a French-
            inspired coup and, over French objections, Moulay
            Mohammed ben Arafa is enthroned.

16   MOROCCO - Berber tribesmen depose Moulay Mohammed ben
            Arafa. There is much rioting and bloodshed.

16   USSR - The Soviets propose a Big-Four conference on the
            German peace treaty. The conference is to be held with-
            in six months. The Soviets also recommend an advance
            meeting between East and West German representatives to
            set up a program for the reunification of the German
            state.

17   AUSTRIA - The Western Allies suggest a Four-Power meet-
            ing to be held in London on 31 August to settle the
            terms of the Austrian peace treaty.

19   IRAN - In a CIA-financed coup, troops loyal to the Shah
            depose Prime Minister Mossadegh.

20   INDIA - A plebiscite is decided upon as the means of
            settling the long-smoldering Kashmir question. The
            Indian government later withdraws its approval.

21   UNITED NATIONS - The USSR proposes a one-third reduc-
            tion in the armed forces of the super powers and a ban
            on nuclear weapons.

21   MOROCCO - Sidi Mohammed ben Arafa is proclaimed sultan.

22   IRAN - The Shah Mohammed Reza Pahlavi returns from his
            exile.

23   EAST GERMANY - The USSR relaxes its occupation of Ger-
            many including the release of POWs it still holds pri-
            soner since the end of the war.

26   SPAIN - The government announces a ten-year defensive
            agreement with the US.

28   FRANCE - President Auriol and Emperor Bao Dai affirm
            the decision granting Viet Nam independence within the
            French Union.

29   USSR - The Soviets reject the call for the London meet-
            ing on Austria.

29   ITALY - Emergency conferences are held among political
            and military leaders as fear of a Yugoslav takeover of
            Trieste grows.

29-31   ITALY - A series of Italo-Yugoslav border incidents
            occurs as both sides hold maneuvers near Trieste. Yugo-
            slav troops also open fire on Allied patrols along the
            border.

SEPTEMBER

            UNITED STATES - An allotment of $385 million in addi-
            tional aid for Indochina is authorized, and plans are
            laid to support a 40,000-man expansion of indigenous
            Indochinese troops in 1954.

OCTOBER

6   BRITISH GUIANA - British troops and warships are dis-
            patched to Guiana to forestall a suspected Communist
            takeover attempt.

8   UNITED STATES - In a decision that is coupled to the
            withdrawal of occupation forces from Trieste, the US
            and Great Britain announce that Zone "A" of Trieste
            will be returned to Italy, and that Zone "B" will be
            given to Yugoslavia. The Italians agree, but Yugoslavia
            denounces the plan.

11   YUGOSLAVIA - Tito threatens to send military forces in-
            to Zone "A" as soon as the Italians move to take over.

12-15   YUGOSLAVIA - Tito asks for a conference on the Trieste
            quetion while, at the same time, the USSR demands that
            the UN Security Council take action.

18   UNITED STATES - The United States and Great Britain
            propose an international meeting with Yugoslavia and
            Italy to settle the Trieste issue.

20   KENYA - Mau Mau leader Jomo Kenyatta is sentenced to
            seven years imprisonment by a military tribunal.

22   LAOS - Laos becomes a sovereign state within the French
            Union.

23   RHODESIA - The unification of Southern and Northern
            Rhodesia, and Nyasaland is accomplished.

25   SOUTH KOREA - Negotiations begin to arrange a location
            and time for the opening of peace talks on Korea.

NOVEMBER

1   YUGOSLAVIA - Tito agrees to the joint meeting on
            Trieste.

2   PAKISTAN - The Constituent Assembly votes to make
            Pakistan a republic within the British Commonwealth.

8   BOLIVIA - There is an unsuccessful attempt to overthrow
            the government of President Estenssoro.

11   UNITED NATIONS - The US charges Communist atrocities in
            the Korean War.

12   INDOCHINA - The French government announces it is not
            seeking the unconditional surrender of the Viet Minh.

14   JORDAN - The government rejects the US plan for ad-
            ministration of the Jordan Valley.

17   JORDAN - The US representative in Jordan reports that
            Syria, Israel, and Jordan have promised to give serious
            consideration to the US proposal.

20   INDOCHINA - The siege of the French stronghold at Dien
            Bien Phu begins.

21   ITALY - The government agrees to the joint meeting on
            Trieste.

DECEMBER

SYRIA - An uprising begins among Jebel Druze tribesman. This revolt will last for three months and will be put down by the Syrian army only after heavy fighting.

4-7   BERMUDA - A meeting of the leaders of the US, France, and Great Britain is held to discuss future relations with the USSR, free-world, defense, and the problems of Germany and Austria.

5   YUGOSLAVIA - Tito agrees to withdraw his forces from the area around Trieste. The Italians make a similar promise.

5   GREAT BRITAIN - The governments of Great Britain and Iran announce they will resume diplomatic relations and use negotiations to settle the oil dispute.

12   SOUTH KOREA - The US breaks off the Korean peace talks after being subjected to abusive diatribes by the Communist representatives.

18   POLAND - The government announces that the Catholic bishops of Poland have taken the oath of loyalty to the state.

19   UNITED STATES - The government enunciates a policy of defense through air power.

19   NATO - The US Secretary of State, John Foster Dulles, warns NATO to get the European Army Plan moving or risk the threat of the US undertaking "an agonizing reappraisal" of its commitment to the defense of Europe.

22   YUGOSLAVIA - Yugoslavia, Greece, and Turkey agree in principle on the terms of a Balkan alliance. It is agreed that, should any one of the three be attacked through or by Bulgaria, it would be considered an attack on all three.

22   ALBANIA - Diplomatic relations are resumed with Yugoslavia after a six-year break.

23   USSR - The execution of Lavrenti Beria is announced.

23   INDOCHINA - A Viet Minh offensive cuts Viet Nam in two near the 17th Parallel.

1954

TIBET - Chinese Communist forces suppress a six-month-long revolt with great bloodshed.

JANUARY

UNITED STATES - The President sends Lieutenant General John W. ("Iron Mike") O'Daniel (CINCUSARPAC) to Viet Nam to evaluate the US Military Assistance Program.

9   VENEZUELA - After charges of fraud in the elections held in November 1953, the National Assembly names Colonel Marcos Perez Jimenez to be its provisional president.

11   UNITED STATES - Work begins on the construction of "Texas Towers" to improve the nation's air defense capabilities.

12   UNITED STATES - Secretary of State John Foster Dulles announces a policy of massive retaliation against any would-be aggressor.

13   EGYPT - The fanatical Muslim Brotherhood is outlawed and 78 of its leaders are arrested for political interference.

19-22 SOUTH KOREA - About 22,000 North Korean and Chinese POWs, who refuse to be returned to Communist control, are freed despite the protests of the Neutral Nations Repatriation Commission.

21   MOROCCO - At a meeting at Tetuan, opposition leaders call for the separation of Spanish Morocco and condemn the French appointment of Sultan Sidi Mohammed ben Afara.

24   BERLIN - A conference of Big Four Foreign Ministers opens to discuss the Soviet proposed security plan for Europe.

26   UNITED STATES - The Senate ratifies a mutual security pact with the Republic of Korea.

28   SPAIN - Anti-British demonstrations over the Gibraltar question force the Spanish government to cancel scheduled British naval unit visits to Spanish ports.

29   GUATEMALA - The leftist government of Jacobo Arbenz Guzman declares that the US, Nicaragua and other Central American states are preparing to invade the country.

FEBRUARY

2   IRAN - Troops are employed to restore order after a new wave of antigovernment rioting breaks out in Tehran.

6   INDIA - Over Pakistani protests Kashmir accedes to annexation.

8   MALAYSIA - The Communist headquarters directing the Malay uprising moves to Sumatra to undertake the establishment of an Indonesian liberation movement.

18   BERLIN - Hopelessly deadlocked, the Big Four Foreign Minister's conference adjourns. A new conference is scheduled to be held in Geneva to discuss Far Eastern affairs. Communist China is scheduled to be invited.

20   IRAN - The government of General Fazollah Zahedi is overwhelmingly returned to office.

24   SYRIA - There is an army-led coup d'etat in Damascas that forces the resignation of President Adib Shishakli and the ouster of his Arab Liberation Movement. Former President Hashim al-Atasi, himself the victim of a coup in 1951, is reinstalled as the nation's leader.

25   EGYPT - Gamal Abdul Nasser begins his campaign to unseat Mohammed Naguib.

MARCH

1   INDIA - Premier Jawaharlal Nehru rejects a US offer of military aid and demands the removal of US observers in Kashmir.

3   UNITED STATES - The US detonates a hydrogen (thermo-nuclear) weapon in the Marshall Islands test area.

3   VENEZUELA - The Tenth Inter-American Conference opens in Caracus.

8   UNITED STATES - The government signs a mutual defense treaty with Japan.

9   FRANCE - The government is authorized to negotiate an Indochinese peace settlement.

14   INDOCHINA - The Viet Minh opens a 10,000-man offensive campaign against the French garrison at Dien Bien Phu.

16   UNITED STATES - The US declares that the NATO and Rio treaties authorize immediate retaliation if the country, or one of its western or hemispheric allies, is attacked.

17   UNITED STATES - The Department of State announces the government's grave concern over Communist arms shipments to Guatemala.

20   INDOCHINA - General Paul Ely, the French commander in Indochina, informs Washington that, unless the US intervenes directly and soon into the war in Southeast Asia, Indochina is lost.

21   GUATEMALA - Foreign Minister Guillermo Toriello states that the US military equipment boycott has left his country defenseless, and that it is forced to buy arms from the Communists.

22   UNITED STATES - French Chief of Staff General Paul Ely meets with President Dwight D. Eisenhower and Defense Department officials over the Indochinese situation.

23   UNITED STATES - The Secretaries of State and Defense are reported to have promised to deliver 25 B-26 bombers and other military assistance to relieve the pressure on Dien Bien Phu.

24   UNITED STATES - The President announces that the defense of South East Asia against Communism is crucial to US interests.

25   USSR - The government recognizes the sovereignty of
          East Germany and announces that, although the occu-
          pation has ended, Soviet troops would remain in East
          Germany for security reasons and to fulfill the terms
          of the Potsdam Agreement.

26   WEST GERMANY - A constitutional amendment is signed by
          President Theodor Heuss that allows the West German
          state to rearm as a member of the European Defense
          Community (EDC).

28   VENEZUELA - Having already called for a withdrawal of
          all European colonies in the western hemisphere (19
          March), the Caracas Conference declares that a Commu-
          nist takeover of any nation in the Western Hemisphere
          would be a threat to the security of all the member
          nations.

29   JORDAN - Israeli forces attack a Jordanian village.

30   JORDAN - The joint Israeli-Jordanian armistice commis-
          sion, with Israel absent, condemns the Israeli attack
          on Jordanian territory.

APRIL

1   UNITED STATES - A bill authorizing the creation of the
          Air Force Academy is signed into law.

2   PAKISTAN - A five-year mutual defense pact is signed
          with Turkey in Karachi.

5   UNITED STATES - Secretary of State John Foster Dulles
          erroneously reports that Communist Chinese forces are
          fighting at Dien Bien Phu. United States combat forces
          are put on alert for possible commitment in SEA.

12   UNITED STATES - The President names Lieutenant General
          John W. O'Daniel to be Chief of the Military Assis-
          tance and Advisory Group, Indochina (MAAGI).

13   GREAT BRITAIN - The government formally agrees to its
          association with the European Defense Community.

13   UNITED STATES - The US and Great Britain agree to the
          establishment of a ten-nation collective security or-
          ganization for the protection of South East Asia.

14   UNITED STATES - Along with Great Britain and France,
          the US informs the USSR that Communist China will not
          receive great power treatment at the upcoming Geneva
          Conference.

16   YUGOSLAVIA - The government announces a reaffirmation of the long-standing desire for a Balkan military alliance with Turkey and Greece.

16   UNITED STATES - The President assures European Defense Community premiers that American forces will remain in Europe as long as the Soviet threat continues. At the same time, Vice-President Richard M. Nixon writes that, unless other means are found by which the communists could save face in Indochina, the US must be prepared to commit combat troops into that theater, if it is to saved.

17   EGYPT - In a major reorganization, General Mohammed Naguib Bey is replaced by Colonel Gamal Abdul Nasser.

26   SWITZERLAND - A 19-member international conference on Indochina opens in Geneva. The plenary sessions of the conference will open on 8 May and the meeting will last until 21 July.

28   SPAIN - Anti-British demonstrations that focus on the Gibraltar question lead the British to cancel all future naval visits to Spanish ports.

29   INDIA - The government signs a non-aggression treaty with Communist China.

MAY

        BURMA - The last of the Chinese Nationalist guerrilla forces still remaining in Burma are evacuated to Formosa.

        YEMEN - There are intermittant military clashes along the borden with Aden.

2   JORDAN - The cabinet rejects an Anglo-American offer of peace talks with Israel and resigns in protest. A new, more moderate, government is installed the next day.

3   USSR - The government ratifies the Genocide Convention with only one reservation.

5   PARAGUAY - An army-led revolt ousts President Frederico Chaves, and a junta takes control of the government.

7   UNITED STATES - After consultation with Great Britain and France, the United States rejects a Soviet bid to join NATO.

7   UNITED STATES - Secretary of State John Foster Dulles
           announces the US may have to militarily intervene in
           Indochina.

7   INDOCHINA - The French fortress at Dien Bien Phu falls
           to the Viet Minh forces commanded by General Vo Nguyen
           Giap. French influence in Asia ends.

9   SWITZERLAND - The Western powers reject the Communist
           demand that Laos and Cambodia be represented at the
           Geneva talks by their respective "Liberation Fronts."

18   SWITZERLAND - The Geneva Conference is deadlocked when
           the Soviet's V.M. Molotov demands that the Laotian and
           Cambodian independence issues be set aside and that
           the conference concentrate on Viet Nam.

19   UNITED STATES - The government agrees to supply mili-
           tary aid to Pakistan after the Pakistani government
           declares the materiel will be used solely for defen-
           sive purposes. India protests.

29   THAILAND - The government asks the UN Security Council
           for assistance to prevent the Indochinese conflict
           from speading into Thailand and to send UN observers
           to supervise the peace.

30   PAKISTAN - A major labor disturbance in East Pakistan
           is quelled by 10,000 government troops.

31   SWITZERLAND - The United States rejects a Soviet pro-
           posal to establish a truce supervisory commission com-
           posed of Czechoslovakia, Poland, and Pakistan.

JUNE

           UNITED STATES - The US moves to stop Communist arms
           shipments to Guatemala.

2   INDOCHINA - Cease-fire talks open in Viet Nam between
           the French and Viet Minh. The talks deadlock almost
           immediately over the issue of Communist representation
           on the truce supervision team.

3   UNITED STATES - A conference opens in Washington to
           establish a Southeast Asian alliance.

4   UNITED STATES - Thailand and the Philippines protest
           their exclusion from the Washington conference on
           Southeast Asian security.

4   FRANCE - The government announces that Viet Nam is
           completely independent within the French Union.

18   GUATEMALA - An anti-Communist army led by Lieutenant
        Colonel Carlos Castillo Armas invades the country to
        attempt the ouster of the leftist goverment of Jacobo
        Arbenz Guzman. The campaign is successful and the
        Guzman government is forced out of office.

18   UNITED NATIONS - The Soviet representative to the UN
        Security Council vetoes a proposal that would send
        observers to Thailand.

19   SWITZERLAND - The Geneva Conference calls on the gov-
        ernments of Laos and Cambodia to meet with the Viet
        Minh to arrange a truce.

20-29   UNITED STATES - After consultations with Britain's
        Prime Minister Churchill and Foreign Secretary Anthony
        Eden, the President announces the "Potomac Charter" in
        which Great Britain promises not to press for Commu-
        nist Chinese admission into the United Nations and not
        to endorse Communist victories in Indochina. Both
        sides agree (28 June) to seek alternatives for the
        defense of Southeast Asia if the Mendes-France initi-
        atives are unsuccessful.

23   SWITZERLAND - At a meeting in Berne, Premier Mendez-
        France and Communist China's Chou En-Lai decide on a
        political settlement for Indochina, providing the
        Geneva Conference arranges a cease-fire.

27   GUATEMALA - Arbenz Guzman, the ousted president, seeks
        political asylum in the Mexican Embassy in Guatemala
        City. The next day (28 June), the junta, headed by
        Carlos Castillo Armas, relinquishes control of the
        country to Colonel Elfego Monzon who immediately
        arranges for a cease-fire and the arrest of all known
        Communist leaders.

28   INDIA - An Indo-Communist Chinese agreement on the
        future of Indochina is announced in New Delhi after
        India's Prime Minister Nehru and China's Chou En-Lai
        meet.

JULY

1   JAPAN - After great debate, the Diet approves the re-
        arming of Japan and authorizes the establishment of
        national armed forces.

1   GUATEMALA - Carlos Castiilo Armas is declared Presi-
        dent of the country by the military junta which he
        heads.

6   MIDDLE EAST - A settlement is reported on sharing the
           waters of the Jordan River by Israel, Jordan, Syria,
           and Lebanon.

7   VIET NAM - Emperor Bao Dai appoints Ngo Dinh Diem his
           Prime Minister.

20-21   SWITZERLAND - The Geneva Accords are signed, ending
           hostilities in Indochina. Vietnam is partitioned at
           the 17th Parallel. President Eisenhower declares the
           US will not sign the treaty, nor be bound by its
           terms.

21   UNITED STATES - The authorized strength of US military
           personnel in Viet Nam is increased to 342.

22   GOA - Portuguese troops drive out bands of Indian na-
           tionalists who are intent upon seizing sections of the
           Portuguese colony.

23   GREAT BRITAIN - The government offers Cyprus limited
           self-rule but refuses to discuss a change in its
           sovereignty.

30   FRANCE - The government approves a proposal by Pierre
           Mendes-France and gives Tunisia autonomy.

30   UNITED STATES - The Senate unanimously authorizes the
           restoration of West German sovereignty, if France
           fails to ratify the EDC.

AUGUST

5   IRAN - The Anglo-Iranian Oil Company renews produc-
           tion of petroleum.

5   INDIA - An agreement is reached with the Pakistani
           government over use of water from the Indus River.

5   UNITED STATES - The first B-52A strategic bomber makes
           its maiden flight. It is destined to become the main-
           stay in America's airborne deterrent force during the
           next three decades.

7   TUNISIA - Following France's approval of full internal
           independence, a government is formed under Tahar ben
           Ammar.

8   BRAZIL - Widespread disorder leads President Getulio
           Vargas to resign. Vice-President Joao Cafe Filho is
           installed in his place.

9   YUGOSLAVIA - A 20-year treaty of political cooperation
        and military assistance is signed with Greece and
        Turkey.

10   THE NETHERLANDS - The union with Indonesia is dis-
        solved. The new Indonesian government sends the unre-
        solved issue of New Guinea to the UN.

13   COMMUNIST CHINA - Chou En-Lai calls for a drive on the
        Nationalist government on Taiwan.

15   INDIA - The government breaks off diplomatic relations
        with Portugal over the Goa issue.

15   PARAGUAY - The leader of the recent revolt, General
        Alfredo Stroessner, is made President.

17   UNITED STATES - The President announces the decision
        to employ the US Seventh Fleet, if Communist China
        attacks Formosa.

24   BRAZIL - The former president, Getulio Vargas, appar-
        ently commits suicide.

24   UNITED STATES - The President signs a bill outlawing
        the American Communist Party.

27   FRANCE - The National Assembly approves a plan that
        will grant Tunisia and Morocco greater autonomy.

30   FRANCE - The National Assembly rejects the 1952 Euro-
        pean Defense Community plan thereby jeopardizing plans
        to revitalize Europe and rearm Germany.

SEPTEMBER

3   TAIWAN - United States naval units take up positions
        as the Communist Chinese step up their bombardment of
        Quemoy island.

8   THE PHILIPPINES - The South East Asia Treaty Organi-
        zation (SEATO) is formed in Manila. The treaty will go
        into force in February 1955. The new organization's
        head- quarters is established in Bangkok.

9   LIBYA - A 20-year agreement is reached with the US
        over the use of airbases on Libyan territory. The US
        promises to pay $5 million the first year and $2 mil-
        lion each succeeding year.

30   UNITED STATES - The world's first nuclear-powered sub-
        marine, the USS Nautilus, is commissioned.

30   FRANCE - In a speech at Strasbourg, President Pierre
            Mendes-France proposes bringing West Germany into the
            Western Alliance, if Great Britain joins the pact.

OCTOBER

3   GREAT BRITAIN - Nine nations (United States, France,
            Great Britain, Canada, the Netherlands, Belgium, West
            Germany, Italy, and Luxembourg) meeting in London
            agree upon a formula that will economically and mili-
            tarily integrate West Germany into the Western Alli-
            ance and NATO as an alternative to the EDC.

4   PAKISTAN - The government issues a white paper that
            asks for UN settlement of the Kashmir situation.

5   JAPAN - The government announces that Japan has been
            admitted as a member of the Colombo Plan.

5   THAILAND - The government announces that Thailand has
            been admitted as a member of the Colombo Plan.

5   TRIESTE - A Yugoslav-Italian treaty that normalizes
            relations between the two countries and ends   a
            nine-year dispute over the Trieste issue is signed.
            The city of Trieste is given to Italy while Yugoslavia
            gets most of the eastern part of the territory.
            British and US forces are scheduled for early with-
            drawal.

6   USSR - Foreign Minister Molotov asks for Four-Power
            talks on the reunification and neutralization of Ger-
            many.

7   INDIA - The government signs a two-year trade agree-
            ment with Communist China.

11   NORTH VIET NAM - The Communist Viet Minh organization
            formally takes over control of Hanoi and North Viet
            Nam.

11   COMMUNIST CHINA - A Sino-Soviet treaty is announced
            that provides for Soviet evacuation of Port Arthur by
            June 1955 and provision of credit for the development
            of heavy industry. Both parties call for the rapid oc-
            cupation of Nationalist China.

12   FRANCE - The French government approves West Germany's
            admission into NATO.

12   JAPAN - The government rejects as propaganda a Commu-
            nist Chinese plan to normalize relations.

14   FINLAND - Premier Ralph Torngren is forced to resign
            to forestall   a   threatened general   strike   over   in-
            flation.

15   UNITED NATIONS - The USSR calls for condemnation of
            the US for its aggression against Communist China
            through its support of the Nationalist government on
            Formosa.

19   GREAT BRITAIN - The government signs a treaty with
            Egypt in which it agrees to give up and evacuate the
            Suez Canal within 20 months.

20-23   FRANCE - A ministerial conference held in Paris acts
            to   implement   the   3   October decisions reached in
            London. The occupation of West Germany is officially
            ended. Arrangements are made for the stationing of
            foreign troops on West German territory.

21   FRANCE - The government agrees to relinquish to India
            control of its four sub-continent colonies.

22   NORTH ATLANTIC COUNCIL - The North Atlantic Council
            approves West Germany's admittance into NATO.

22   UNITED STATES - President Eisenhower orders a crash
            program to strengthen the Diem regime in South Viet
            Nam.

23   FRANCE - The government recognizes West German sover-
            eignty after   settling   the Saar   issue. France   then
            joins   the   other   Western   Allies   in   bringing   West
            Germany into the alliance.

24   UNITED STATES - The President informs Prime Minister
            Ngo Dinh Diem that the US will furnish direct aid to
            Viet Nam on the basis of anticipated reforms in the
            country. This action bypasses France.

26   GREAT BRITAIN - Prime Minister Churchill rejects
            Soviet Foreign Minister Molotov's proposal for a
            meeting on the unification and neutralization of
            Germany.

31   ALGERIA - Open warfare begins over the issue of inde-
            pendence between the   French   and   the Front   de
            Liberation Nationale (FLN).

NOVEMBER

            SOUTH VIET NAM - The end of November witnesses the ar-
            rival of the last of nearly one million refugees from
            the north.

1   ALGERIA - At 1 AM (0100) 30 small, armed bands of
             Algerian Muslims simultaneously attack French army
             posts, settler's farms, lone motorists on isolated
             roads, and government buildings. Radio Cairo broad-
             casts news of the raids as they are occurring. This
             series of raids marks the beginning of the Algerian
             Revolution.

2   CUBA - General Fulgencio Batista is declared President
             after his only rival withdraws from the elections
             claiming that they are rigged.

5   BURMA - The signing of a peace treaty officially ends
             the war between Japan and Burma.

8   UNITED NATIONS - After months of fruitless negoti-
             ations the General Assembly unanimously approves a
             joint East-West proposal calling for the resumption of
             disarmament talks and a ban on the use of nuclear
             weapons.

13   USSR - The Soviet Union announces that a conference on
             European security will be held in Moscow beginning 29
             November. The USSR is joined by Poland and Czechoslo-
             vakia in inviting the United States and all European
             nations to the meeting. The US rejects the invitation
             as a propanganda ploy designed to thwart the Paris
             Accords.

23   COMMUNIST CHINA - Thirteen US airmen presumably forced
             down over the Chinese Communist mainland are sentenced
             to long prison terms for spying. On 26 November the US
             sends a note through the British diplomatic channels
             demanding the servicemen's immediate release.

DECEMBER

2   UNITED STATES - The government agrees to a mutual de-
             fense treaty with the Nationalist Chinese government
             on Taiwan following negotiations that dealt, among
             other things, with limiting Chiang's sphere of mili-
             tary operational authority.

10   UNITED NATIONS - The UN Security Council, in a lop-
             sided vote, condemns Communist China for imprisoning
             13 US airmen. The next day, Dag Hammerskjold, the UN
             Secretary General meets with Chou En-Lai in Peiping on
             the issue.

10   FRANCE - The government announces its opposition to
             the granting of full independence to any of its North
             African territories, including Tunisia.

13   UNITED STATES - The government announces the accep-
          tance of the Collins-Ely Agreements which provide for
          the return by the French forces in Indochina of Mutual
          Defense Assistance Program equipment furnished by the
          US.

14   GREECE - Anti-American rioting breaks out in Athens
          following a US refusal to support a Greek plan for
          self-determination in Cyprus.

15   THE NETHERLANDS - The Caribbean islands of Surinam and
          the Netherlands Antilles become autonomous as a result
          of a royal decree signed by Queen Juliana.

17   COMMUNIST CHINA - Chou En-Lai accepts the Hammerskjold
          proposal for the release of the American airmen.

20   UNITED STATES - The Defense Department announces an
          accelerated reduction in the size of the armed forces
          from 3.2 to 2.8 million men over the next 18 months.

28   PORTUGAL - The government reminds Great Britain of the
          terms of a 1937 treaty and demands support in the face
          of impending Indian moves against Portuguese enclaves
          on the sub-continent.

29   FRANCE - The French terminate the economic union with
          the three Indochinese states of Viet Nam, Laos, and
          Cambodia. This gives the Indochinese states virtual
          independence.

Notes

1955

CHINA - Throughout the months of January and February, Chinese Nationalist and Communist forces battle over the offshore islands in the Straits of Taiwan.

SUDAN - A major revolt begins in southern Sudan which lasts for 17 years. The chief cause is racial antagonism between the Arab-Muslims in the north and the black Sudanese in the south.

1   UNITED STATES - The US begins direct assistance to Viet Nam, based on the existing pentalateral agreement of December 1950. Lieutenant General John W. "Iron Mike" O'Daniel, the Chief of the US Military Assistance Advisory Group, Indochina (MAAGI), is assigned the responsibility of assisting SVN in organizing and training its armed forces.

2   PANAMA - President Jose A. Ramon-Guizado is dismissed by the National Assembly for his part in the assassination of the former president. The new president, Ricardo Arias Espinosa, is installed on 15 January.

11   COSTA RICA - When rebels seize the border town of Villa Quesada, President Jose (Pepe) Figueras accuses Nicaragua of aggression.

12   UNITED STATES - The government enunciates the policy of "massive retaliation."

15   SOVIET UNION - The Kremlin recognizes the sovereignty of West Germany.

20   GUATEMALA - A Communist-inspired revolt is suppressed
            by loyal military forces.

20   SOUTH VIET NAM - President Ngo Dinh Diem states he has
            asked the US to train the South Vietnamese army
            (ARVN).

25   UNITED STATES - President Eisenhower asks Congress for
            authority to use military forces to protect National-
            ist China positions in Taiwan and in the channel
            islands. These requests were granted almost immedi-
            ately by strong majorities.

FEBRUARY

            KENYA - A major campaign begins against the Mau Mau.
            Some 10,000 troops are employed against an estimated
            4,000 rebels in the Mount Kenya-Aberdare areas. By
            November, most of the rebels have been killed, cap-
            tured, or dispersed.

1   SOUTH VIET NAM - A US Army Training Relations and In-
            struction Mission is formed to undertake the training
            of ARVN.

3   COMMUNIST CHINA - Premier Chou En-Lai rejects a UN of-
            fer for a cease-fire in the fighting with Nationalist
            China.

5   FRANCE - The Mendes-France government is overthrown by
            the National Assembly because of its policies dealing
            with solving the insurgency in the French possessions
            in North Africa.

5   CHINA - US 7th Fleet naval units begin evacuation of
            more than 40,000 Chinese Nationalist forces and civil-
            ians on Tachen Island. Six days later (11 February),
            the island falls to the Communists.

8   USSR - Premier Georgi Malenkov resigns the Soviet
            leadership and is immediately replaced by Marshal
            Nikolae Bulganin.

9   SOVIET UNION - Marshal of the Soviet Union Georgi K.
            Zhukov is appointed Minister of Defense.

9   CAMBODIA - A two-day referendum confirms King Norodom
            Sihanouk as ruler.

11   SOUTH VIET NAM - The South Vietnamese government takes
            over control of the Vietnamese armed forces from the
            French.

12   SOUTH VIET NAM - The US formally takes over training
            of the South Vietnamese army.

19   SEATO - The South East Asia Collective Defense Treaty,
            with its protocol covering Viet Nam, Cambodia, and
            Laos goes into effect. Under its terms, member nations
            are obligated to aid protocol states in the event of
            aggression.

23   FRANCE - Edgar Faure is asked to form a new govern-
            ment.

23-25   THAILAND - SEATO holds its first meeting in Bangkok.

24   IRAQ - A five-year mutual defense treaty known as the
            "Baghdad Pact," (or Middle East Treaty Organization),
            is signed between Iraq and Turkey. Great Britain (5
            April), Pakistan (23 September), and Iran (12 Octo-
            ber) will all join later. Although the US is instru-
            mental in its establishment, it refuses to join. After
            Iraq withdraws (24 March 1959), the pact changes its
            name and becomes known as the Central Treaty Organi-
            zation (CENTO). Egypt and Saudi Arabia reject the
            treaty (11 June 1955) and agree to cooperate on
            defense matters and to place their armed forces under
            a joint unified command.

25   NATIONALIST CHINA - In light of the recent Communist
            victories on the off-shore islands, the government
            declares it will retreat no further.

MARCH

2   CAMBODIA - King Norodom Sihanouk abdicates in favor of
            his father, Norodom Suramarit.

3   NATIONALIST CHINA - A treaty is signed with the United
            States which deals with Nationalist territorial limits
            around the islands of Formosa and the Pescadores.

7   UNITED STATES - The United States and South Viet Nam
            sign additional economic agreements which supplement
            those cooperation protocols signed in September 1951.

21   VIET NAM - Militant religious groups (e.g. Cao Dai or
            Hoa Hao) give Premier Ngo Dinh Diem a five-day ulti-
            matum demanding a government reorganization. This is
            rejected on 24 March.

23   UNITED STATES - The President declares the US will not
            authorize the use of nuclear weapons in "police
            actions."

29   VIET NAM – Heavy fighting breaks out between govern-
            ment forces and the private armies of the Cao Dai and
            other dissident religious groups. A cease-fire is ar-
            ranged on 30 March.

APRIL

            ALGERIA – The French government declares a state of
            emergency in the Aures area of the mountainous Con-
            stantine in southeastern Algeria.

2-5   YEMEN – A military revolt led by Emir Seif al-Islam
            Abdullah is put down by troops loyal to Imam Seif
            el-Islam Ahmad and the Crown Prince, al-Badr Mohammed.

5   GREAT BRITAIN – When ill health forces Sir Winston
            Churchill to resign, Anthony Eden becomes Prime
            Minister.

11   AUSTRIA – At a meeting held in Moscow, the Austrians
            and Soviets decide upon a treaty (15 April) that al-
            lows for the withdrawal of Soviet troops by 31 Decem-
            ber.

13   UNITED STATES – President Eisenhower approves a plan
            for sharing nuclear weapons information with NATO.

21   FRANCE – The government announces that it has reached
            an agreement with the leader of the Tunisian national-
            ist movement, Habib Bourguiba, for the autonomy of
            Tunisia. A similar agreement is reached with Tunisian
            Premier Tahar ben Ammar on 3 June.

23   INDONESIA – Addressing the 29-nation Afro-Asian Ban-
            dung Conference (18-27 April), Communist Chinese Pre-
            mier Chou En-Lai disavows any desire for war with the
            United States.

23   CAMBODIA – Ex-King Prince Sihanouk is given assurances
            of "non-interference" by North Viet Nam and Communist
            China.

28   SOUTH VIET NAM – Heavy fighting breaks out in the
            Saigon suburbs as a result of Viet Cong (VC) activity
            in Binh Xuyen District.

MAY

1   SOUTH VIET NAM – In a test of strength, Ngo Dinh Diem
            wins control of the army from Bao Dai, the chief of
            state.

2   SOUTH VIET NAM - The VC rebels holding Binh Xuyen Dis-
        trict center are finally driven out of Saigon.

7   FRANCE - The organization of the new Western Europe
        Union is discussed at a meeting of the Foreign Minis-
        ters of France, West Germany, Great Britain, Italy,
        Belgium, Luxembourg, and The Netherlands.

7   USSR - The Supreme Soviet abrogates its treaties of
        friendship with Great Britain and France.

8   SOUTH VIET NAM - The Diem government rejects the
        French plan for the return of Emperor Bao Dai to South
        Viet Nam.

9   WEST GERMANY - The Federal Republic of Germany joins
        NATO four days after ratification of the peace trea-
        ties that ended World War II.

10   SOUTH VIET NAM - Ngo Dinh Diem begins his accumulation
        of power by forming a new cabinet composed largely of
        his own followers.

12   SOUTH VIET NAM - The government informs France that it
        must either move its troops into areas endangered by
        Viet Minh forces or withdraw entirely.

14   POLAND - A treaty ("Warsaw Pact") of mutual friendship
        and defense is signed in Warsaw by the USSR, East Ger-
        many, Bulgaria, Czechoslovakia, Poland, Hungary, Al-
        bania, and Romania. Yugoslavia refuses to join the new
        Soviet-inspired organization.

15   AUSTRIA - At a conference held in Vienna the Four-
        Power Foreign Ministers decide upon a peace treaty
        with Austria.

16   UNITED STATES - A direct military aid agreement is
        signed with Cambodia.

16   FRANCE - The government agrees with Vietnamese demands
        and orders its troops in Southeast Asia into the
        northern provinces of South Viet Nam to engage the
        Viet Minh.

JUNE

2   YUGOSLAVIA - At a reconciliation meeting held in Bel-
        grad between Tito and Khrushchev, the two leaders call
        for a ban on nuclear weapons, a European collective
        security treaty, and the admission of Communist China
        into the UN.

7   CHINA - An uneasy truce begins between Communist and
           Nationalist forces over the islands of Quemoy and
           Matsu.

13   CAMBODIA - A separate US Military Assistance and Advisory Group is formed in Cambodia. This group is
           assigned the mission of rendering military logistical
           support to the Cambodian armed forces.

15   UNITED STATES - The US and Great Britain sign an accord in Washington dealing with the peaceful uses of
           nuclear power.

16   ARGENTINA - After weeks of violence caused by a government edict against Roman Catholic interests in
           Argentina, Pope Pius XII excommunicates President Juan
           Peron.

22   SOVIET UNION - At the conclusion of a state visit to
           Moscow, India's Nehru announces the conclusion of an
           economic and technical assistance agreement between
           the two nations.

JULY

1   SOUTH VIET NAM - France formally relinquishes command
           authority over the Vietnamese navy.

7   NORTH VIET NAM - Ho Chi Minh signs a $338-million economic aid agreement with Communist Chinese representatives in Hanoi.

9   LAOS - The United States authorizes support of the
           Royal Laotian army.

16   SOUTH VIET NAM - Ngo Dinh Diem declares SVN will not
           take part in the elections prescribed in the Geneva
           Accords unless the signators of the Accords guarantee
           that they will be free.

18   ARGENTINA - Juan Peron is forced to give up most of
           his power.

18   NORTH VIET NAM - The USSR signs an aid agreement in
           with the NVN government in Hanoi.

18-23   SWITZERLAND - At a Big-Four Conference held in Geneva,
           President Eisenhower proposes a Soviet-American exchange of military information and aerial inspections
           as a means of controlling the nuclear arms race. Other
           topics include German reunification and European security.

20   SOUTH VIET NAM - The SVN government rejects a new NVN
            proposal to discuss the country-wide elections called
            for in the Geneva Accords. The SVN argument is that
            elections held in the north will not be "free."

22   WEST GERMANY - A rearmament bill is signed that pro-
            vides for a 6,000 man cadre to establish a half-mil-
            lion man army.

25   INDIA - The government orders the closing of the Por-
            tuguese legation in New Delhi because of that nation's
            refusal to allow its protectorate, Goa, to be absorbed
            into India.

27   AUSTRIA - The nation regains its sovereignty. Allied
            occupation forces begin withdrawing.

AUGUST

5   MOROCCO - Berber uprisings and terrorism embrace the
            country and do not subside until early November.

12   ROMANIA - Premier Gheorghe Ghiorghiu-Dej announces
            that Soviet forces will remain in Romania until NATO
            is abolished and all US forces are withdrawn from
            Europe.

12   SOVIET UNION - The government announces a 640,000-man
            reduction in its armed forces as a result of the "re-
            laxation of tensions" brought about by the Geneva Con-
            ference.

15   INDIA - Indian demonstrators surge across the border
            into Goa and Damoa where the police kill or wound
            about 150 before they are driven back across the bor-
            der.

16   SOUTH VIET NAM - The last French High Commissioner for
            Indochina departs.

16   SUDAN - Revolts which began during the month culminate
            in a demand from the Sudanese Parliament that Egyptian
            (500) and British (900) military forces be withdrawn
            within 90 days. Both parties agree.

19   INDIA - New Delhi breaks diplomatic relations with
            Portugal.

21   FRANCE - Premier Faure meets with Moroccan leaders at
            Aix-les-Bains in hopes of putting an end to the wide-
            spread violence in the French colony.

22   EGYPT - Fighting breaks out in the Gaza Strip   between
            Israel and Egypt.

27   FRANCE - The government announces the resignations   of
            the pro-French Sultan and the governor general   of
            Morocco as a part of the compromise reached at   Aix-
            les-Bains. Two days later, the Assembly accepts   the
            Faure program for peace in North Africa.

29   GREAT BRITAIN - A conference, called by the British at
            the end of June, begins in London to settle the Cyprus
            question. Turkish and Greek representatives   attend,
            but the meeting soon becomes hopelessly deadlocked.

30   MOROCCO - Sidi Mohammed ben Arafa, the   pro-French
            Sultan of Morocco, refuses to resign.

SEPTEMBER

1   TUNISIA - The nation becomes fully autonomous.

2   KENYA - The British government begins a reduction   in
            its military forces stationed in Kenya.

6   TURKEY - Anti-Greek rioting breaks out in Istanbul and
            elsewhere in the country over the Cyprus situation and
            in response to anti-Turkish rioting in Greece.

11   ARGENTINA - Peron declares a state of emergency.

13   WEST GERMANY - At the conclusion of a four day meeting
            in Moscow, Chancellor Adenauer and Soviet officials
            establish diplomatic relations between the USSR   and
            the Federal Republic of Germany.

16   ARGENTINA - A military junta ousts Juan Peron. Peron
            flees the country after nine years in power.

19   FINLAND - The USSR signs a treaty that restores the
            Porkkala naval base to Finland (completed 26 January
            1956) and allows free emigration of all Finns in
            Soviet territory. This includes Finnish prisoners of
            war held in the USSR since the end of the war.

20   EAST GERMANY - The USSR confers sovereignty upon the
            East Germans and grants them sole authority over ci-
            vilian traffic between Berlin and the West.

23   ARGENTINA -   Major General Eduardo Leonardi becomes
            President.

25   CAMBODIA - Cambodia leaves the French Union and be-
            comes an independent, sovereign state.

27   EGYPT - Gamal Abdul Nasser announces a trade agreement with Czechoslovakia that promises cotton and rice in return for arms. Nasser claims the West denied Egypt military aid although sales were being made to Israel.

OCTOBER

        ISRAEL - Over the next 14 months, increasing numbers of Arab terrorist raids on Israeli border settlements raise tensions in the Middle East.

1   FRANCE - France protests the UN discussion of the Algerian situation.

5   ARGENTINA - An anti-Peronista revolt begins following the ouster of the late dictator's followers in government.

10   SOVIET UNION - In advance of a state visit to Afghanistan, India, and Burma, the government begins agricultural and industrial aid to the Middle East and Asia.

11   CANADA - The government signs a treaty with the USSR granting economic "most-favored nation" status to the Soviets and promising cooperation in future Arctic research.

11   ISRAEL - An urgent appeal for arms is sent to the US in light of Soviet weapons shipments to Egypt.

12   SOVIET UNION - The Kremlin warns Iran about its plan to join the Baghdad Pact.

12   UNITED NATIONS - The General Assembly condemns South Africa because of its racial policies.

18   SOUTH VIET NAM - Bao Dai attempts to dismiss Ngo Dinh Diem but the Premier rejects the demand.

19   FRANCE - The government refuses suggested US intervention in Algeria claiming just-passed reform legislation will improve the situation.

20   EGYPT - Egypt signs defensive military alliances with Saudi Arabia and Syria.

23   SOUTH VIET NAM - A national referendum formally deposes the former emperor, Bao Dai, as chief of state (since 7 March 1949) in favor of Prime Minister Ngo Dinh Diem.

24   UNITED STATES - The President appoints Lieutenant Gen-
            eral Samuel T. Williams as Chief, MAAG, Vietnam, to
            replace Lieutenant General O'Daniel.

26   SOUTH VIET NAM - The nation is proclaimed a Republic
            with Ngo Dinh Diem as its President.

26   ARAB STATES - The Saudi Arabian forces that invaded
            the Buraimi Oasis claimed by Muscat and Oman are
            driven out by British-led troops.

28   SOUTH VIET NAM - The US MAAG, Indochina (MAAGI) is
            redesignated US MAAG, Vietnam (MAAGV).

30   MOROCCO - After two months of increasing tension, Sidi
            Mohammed ben Arafa abdicates in favor of Sidi Mohammed
            III who had been deposed as monarch by the French in
            1953.

NOVEMBER

            ISRAEL - Throughout the remainder of the year Israeli
            forces carry out a series of attacks along the Egyp-
            tian and Syrian borders.

5   FRANCE - The government recognizes Sidi Mohammed III
            as Sultan of Morocco.

9   SOUTH AFRICA - The government withdraws from the UN
            after being condemned by the world organization
            because of its racial policies.

11   BRAZIL - A military junta led by Lieutenant General
            H.B.D. Teixeira Lott seizes power in Brazil. The
            government overthrow is carried out when it becomes
            apparent that the acting president Carlos Coimbra da
            Luz is planning to prevent the assumption of the
            presidency by the duly elected Juscelino Kubitschek.
            Kubitschek is sworn in as scheduled, on 31 January
            1956.

13   ARGENTINA - A military coup replaces the Leonardi
            government with one led by Major General Pedro
            Arumburu.

21-22   IRAQ - The first formal meeting of the Baghdad Pact
            takes place.

29   FRANCE - The National Assembly ousts the Faure gov-
            ernment. As his last act, Faure dissolves the Assembly
            (30 November).

DECEMBER

SOUTH VIET NAM - US advisors begin being assigned to ARVN units other than the four field divisions.

12   UNITED STATES - The US closes its consulate offices in Hanoi.

14   UNITED NATIONS - Ireland and 13 other nations are admitted into the UN.

16   UNITED NATIONS - The General Assembly approves the Eisenhower Plan for aerial inspection of nuclear disarmament.

19   JORDAN - The government of Hazza al-Majali is forced to resign when rioting breaks out following the disclosure that Jordan intends to join the Baghdad Pact.

29   SOVIET UNION - Khrushchev denounces the American call for aerial inspection to insure a nuclear freeze calling it another indication of "western colonialism."

Notes

1956

CAMEROON - Widespread anticolonial unrest begins.

SIERRA LEONE - Widespread anticolonial unrest begins.

TIBET - A long period of unrest begins. It is fostered by increasing Communist Chinese incursions and repression in the country, primarily those incurred by the building of a military highway from Chungking to Lhasa.

SOUTH VIET NAM - Throughout the year the Viet Cong (VC) step up terrorist attacks against government officials in rural areas in the south.

JANUARY

SOUTH VIET NAM - When government troops occupy Tay Ninh Province, resistance by the militant religious Cao Dai order ceases.

1   SUDAN - With the end of Anglo-Egyptian control, the newly independent Sudanese nation forms a five-man council of state.

3   YUGOSLAVIA - The government reaches an agreement with the Soviet Union which will allow for the construction of a nuclear reactor in Yugoslavia.

3   ROMANIA - The government signs an economic agreement with Communist China.

4   CAMBODIA - A Communist-controlled government headed by
           Oun Cheeang Sun is installed.

9   JORDAN - After quelling a major disturbance, the   new
           Premier, Samir el-Rifai, reiterates his opposition to
           the Baghdad Pact and further de- clares that Arab
           unity is the cornerstone of his nation's security.

9   COSTA RICA - The government reaches an agreement with
           the government of Nicaragua over their long-simmering
           border dispute.

11   ALBANIA - The government announces an amnesty for all
           Albanian exiles. A deadline of 31 December 1957 is set
           for accepting the amnesty and returning to Albanian
           control.

13   SOUTH AFRICA - The government inaugurates a policy
           that will become known as __Apartheid__ by ordering the
           removal of the names of 60,000 "Coloreds" from the
           voting roles in Cape Province and by limiting the
           authority of the court system to intervene in racial
           problems.

13   MIDDLE EAST - As a result of Israeli military opera-
           tions against Syrian positions located along the Sea
           of Galilee (11 December 1955), Syria and Lebanon sign
           a military defense alliance guaranteeing mutual retal-
           iation if either is attacked by Israel.

18   EAST GERMANY - The rearming of East Germany becomes a
           reality after the Parliament authorizes the establish-
           ment of a defense ministry and armed forces.

19   SUDAN - The Sudanese government announces its decision
           to join the Arab League. This will bring the member-
           ship in the League to nine nations.

19   UNITED NATIONS - The Security Council votes unanimous-
           ly to censure Israel for its recent attack into Syrian
           territory.

24   FRANCE - After the resignation of the Faure govern-
           ment, a new Socialist government led by Guy Mollet is
           formed.

24   UNITED NATIONS - Jordan and Israel accept the UN truce
           proposals.

28   UNITED STATES - President Eisenhower rejects a Soviet
           bid to establish a treaty of friendship and cooper-
           ation.

FEBRUARY

1   UNITED STATES - In the Declaration of Washington President Eisenhower and British Prime Minister Anthony Eden reaffirm Anglo-American policy on the Middle East.

2   CYPRUS - Archbishop Makarios rejects a British proposal for gradual independence and demands immediate autonomy.

12   SOUTH VIET NAM - Although Tran Van Soai, the leader of the Hoa-Hao, surrenders to authorities, the private army of the religious sect continues to fight the government.

12   USSR - The government warns that any movement of American or British troops into the Middle East will violate the UN Charter.

14   USSR - At the opening session of the Twentieth Party Congress, Nikita Khrushchev denounces Stalin. The period of "De-Stalinization" begins. Khrushchev also announces that coexistence with the West is the nation's policy.

16-25   PERU - A military uprising at Iquilas is suppressed when support for the rebel cause from other military units fails to materialize.

17   UNITED STATES - The government announces it is suspending all military shipments to Israel and the Arab nations, but on the following day (18 February) specifically allows the shipment of tanks to Saudi Arabia.

18   CAMBODIA - Prince Sihanouk renounces SEATO protection for Cambodia.

26   CARIBBEAN - Delegates from Barbados, Jamaica, the Leeward Islands, Trinidad, Tobago, and the Windward Islands reach a preliminary agreement for the formation of a Caribbean Federation.

29   PAKISTAN - The nation becomes independent and is declared an Islamic republic, but stays within the British Commonwealth.

MARCH

ALGERIA - The Governor-General is granted extraordinary powers to deal with the growing insurgency.

1   UNITED STATES - The first aerial-deliverable thermo-
            nuclear (hydrogen) weapon (12-14 MT) is detonated at
            the US test range in the Pacific Ocean.

2   JORDAN - King Hussein dismisses the British commander
            of the Arab Legion, Lieutenant General John Bagot
            Glubb Pasha, for allegedly failing to prepare for an
            Israeli attack. Glubb returns to England.

2   MOROCCO - The nation's status as a French protectorate
            (Treaty of Fez, 1912) ceases by mutual consent.

3-11   ARAB LEAGUE - At a meeting held in Cairo, plans for
            joint military action against Israel are drawn up by
            Egypt, Syria, and Saudi Arabia. Jordan's Hussein re-
            fuses to take part for fear of losing his annual
            British subsidy.

4   UNITED STATES - The government reveals the opening of
            a new series of nuclear weapons tests at its nuclear
            test range in the South Pacific.

4   SOUTH VIET NAM - The first national elections give the
            National Revolutionary Movement and other pro-govern-
            mental political parties an overwhelming majority in
            the first national legislature, the National Constit-
            uent Assembly.

9   CYPRUS - The British arrest the Cypriot leader, Arch-
            bishop Makarios, and transport him into exile on the
            British island colony of Seychelles in the western
            Indian Ocean.

18   UNITED STATES - A long-simmering interservice conflict
            over national military policy is splashed across the
            Nation's newspaper headlines. An orchestrated program
            of demonstrating Defense Department harmony is pushed
            by Defense Secretary Charles E. Wilson, but the damage
            is already done.

20   FRANCE - A protocol granting Tunisia its independence
            is signed.

28   ICELAND - The government calls for the withdrawal of
            all foreign troops presently stationed on Icelandic
            soil.

APRIL

3   YEMEN - The government in San'a announces its claim to
            the British Protectorate of Aden. Sporadic border
            clashes follow.

6   SOUTH VIET NAM - The government announces it will con-
        tinue to cooperate with the International Control
        Commission (ICC). It also announces that country-wide
        elections can be held at any time the North Vietnamese
        will guarantee they will allow them to be freely held.

6   POLAND - Wladyslaw Gomulka is declared "rehabilitated"
        and is freed after having served five years in a
        Polish prison.

7   SPAIN - The independence of Morocco is recognized.
        Spain formally relinquishes control over its former
        colony of Spanish Morocco on 17 April.

9   UNITED STATES - The government announces a policy of
        complete support of the UN's role in Middle East af-
        fairs and, in doing so, denounces aggression in the
        region.

13   SOUTH VIET NAM - Ba Cut, another important leader of
        the Hoa Hao militant religious sect, is captured by
        the government. However, the Hoa Hao insurgency
        against the government in Saigon continues.

18   MIDDLE EAST - An Israeli-Egyptian cease-fire goes into
        effect following the efforts of UN General Secretary
        Dag Hammerskjold.

19   IRAN - A meeting of the Baghdad Pact ends with the US
        agreeing to establish economic and other ties with the
        organization.

23   USSR - On a state visit to Great Britain, Soviet Party
        Secretary Nikita Khrushchev announces that the USSR
        will build guided missiles armed with nuclear weapons.

24   SAUDI ARABIA - A tripartite military alliance of Saudi
        Arabia, Egypt, and Yemen is signed at Jidda.

28   SOUTH VIET NAM - The French Military High Command is
        dissolved and the French Expeditionary Force begins
        its departure. The USMAAGV assumes full responsibility
        for the training of the South Vietnamese army and be-
        comes the exclusive advisory agency for the South
        Vietnamese armed forces.

29   CUBA - An anti-Batista regime uprising in Matanzas is
        put down by government forces.

29   MIDDLE EAST - Dag Hammarskjold arranges a cease-fire
        between Israel and Jordan. On 1 May, he is able to
        also arrange a cease-fire between Israel and Lebanon.

MAY

12   ISRAEL - When the US lifts its objections, the French
            deliver the last twelve jet aircraft of a major arms
            sale to Israel.

14   USSR - The government announces a 1.2-million man re-
            duction in its armed forces.

18   USSR - The government establishes diplomatic relations
            with Cambodia.

20   POLAND - The government announces it will supply mili-
            tary arms and equipment to the United Arab Republic
            (Egypt).

21   JORDAN - After Premier Samir el-Rafai resigns and is
            replaced in office, the new Premier Said el-Mufti
            moves to renegotiate the Anglo-Jordanian defense
            treaty.

26   JORDAN - The Arab Legion is disbanded and is merged
            into the Jordan armed forces.

28   FRANCE - France gives up control of its territories
            (the enclaves of Pondicherry, Mahe, Chandernagore, and
            some smaller towns) on the Indian subcontinent which
            it has held since 1815.

JUNE

1   SOUTH VIET NAM - The Temporary Equipment Recovery Mis-
            sion (TERM) is activated to handle all logistic and
            maintenance matters in RVN. This action raises US
            strength in SVN to 740 men, 692 of whom are under
            MAAGV.

4   EGYPT - The government announces it will not renew the
            Suez Canal Company's concession when it expires in
            1968.

6   USSR - Premier Nikolae Bulganin demands a reduction in
            the number of Allied forces stationed in Western
            Europe.

10-14   ARGENTINA - A Peronist revolt is put down. Later, 26
            rebel leaders accused of being involved in the revolt
            are executed by the government.

13   EGYPT - British military occupation of the Suez Canal
            ends after 74 years. Egypt now has full responsibility
            for the defense of the canal.

15   CEYLON - Widespread rioting breaks out among Tamil
            tribesmen over the issue of whether Sinhalese, the
            majority tongue, should be accepted as the official
            language. This unrest will continue for five years
            before the issue is resolved.

23   EGYPT - Gamal Abdul Nasser is elected President under
            the newly adopted constitution.

28-29   POLAND - A demonstration for better working and social
            conditions begins in Poznan and soon turns into a
            riot. Over 100 people are killed; several hundred are
            wounded and over 1,000 are arrested.

30   USSR - The government recognizes Laos.

30   SOUTH VIET NAM - The reorganization of RVNAF to a 10-
            division structure is completed.

JULY

1   SOUTH VIET NAM - The US government agrees to support
            RVNAF which will have a ceiling of 150,000 men. The
            current ceiling on US military personnel does not
            allow advisors to be assigned to all battalions.
            USMAAGV's goal is to have two advisors for each
            battalion-sized unit.

2   TURKEY - The government rejects the British plan for
            the gradual independence of Cyprus.

4-26   ISRAEL - A period of increased tension begins as a
            series of border clashes occur along the Israel-Jordan
            and the Israel-Egypt border. Since 1954, and following
            Nasser's rise to power, the Sinai has been turned into
            a major Egyptian military base which is supplied prin-
            cipally by the Soviet Union. During this period the
            Egyptians also maintain a blockade of Israeli ports on
            the Gulf of Eilat. At the same time, several parties
            of Egyptian-trained terrorists (Fidayun/Fedaheen) raid
            settlements in Israel.

10   UNITED NATIONS - The North Koreans formally accuse the
            US of violating North Korean airspace. The US rejects
            the accusation.

18   EGYPT - When the US Secretary of State, John Foster
            Dulles, announces a withdrawal of financial aid in
            building the Aswan High Dam, President Nasser becomes
            furious. (He had recently announced publicly that the
            money to build the dam was coming from the US and
            Great Britain.)

20   SOUTH VIET NAM - The Viet Nam-wide elections, which
            were obligated under the terms of the Geneva Accords,
            fail to take place.

20   WEST GERMANY - Compulsary military training begins.

25   TUNISIA - The nation becomes independent.

26   EGYPT - Egypt's President Nasser seizes the Suez Canal
            under an edict outlawing the Suez Canal Company.

26   GREAT BRITAIN - The announcement of Egypt's Gamal
            Abdul Nasser's decision to nationalize the Suez Canal
            causes the British cabinet to consider military inter-
            vention.

30   SOUTH VIET NAM - A South Vietnamese liaison mission to
            the ICC is formed to assume the functions of the de-
            parting French liaison mission.

31   BURMA - Communist Chinese troops invade northern
            Burma.

AUGUST

            AFGHANISTAN - The government begins accepting Soviet
            military aid.

            ALGERIA - At a meeting in the Soummam Valley of the
            Kabyles, the leaders of the Army of National Liber-
            ation (ALN) decide to reorganize their various sepa-
            rate units into a formal military organization and
            divide Algeria into six rebel military regions.

1   GREAT BRITAIN - After the US, France, and Great
            Britain meet to discuss the Suez situation, a call
            goes out for a conference of most-interested nations.
            Thereafter the British and French begin secret plan-
            ning for military operations in the Canal Zone (3
            August).

2   EGYPT - Their respective governments order British and
            French nationals out of the country.

4   INDONESIA - President Sukarno repudiates a $1 billion
            debt owed to the government of the Netherlands.

7   UNITED STATES - President Eisenhower rejects recent
            Soviet demands for immediate force reductions in
            Europe.

9   EGYPT - British nationals are airlifted out of the
            country.

13   ARAB LEAGUE - The Arab League declares that an   attack
            on Egypt will be considered an attack on all of the
            nine member-nations.

14   UNITED STATES - The Middle-East Emergency Committee is
            established to insure a continuous flow of oil into
            Western Europe if events in the Middle East, especi-
            ally the Suez Crisis,   should interrupt petroleum
            shipments.

15   ARGENTINA - Another pro-Peronist revolt is quelled by
            government forces.

16   GREAT BRITAIN - The Suez Conference opens in London
            with 22 nations sending delegations. Egypt refuses to
            attend.

16   ISRAEL - New violence erupts along the Israeli borders
            with Egypt and Jordan.

25   ROMANIA - The government reestablishes diplomatic re-
            lations with Greece.

25   SOUTH AFRICA - The government orders the transporta-
            tion of over 100,000 non-whites from Johannesburg to
            make more room for whites.

SEPTEMBER

9-11   GREAT BRITAIN - After month-long negotiations with the
            Nasser government fail to resolve the Suez Crisis,
            France and Great Britain agree to apply economic
            pressure. The US declares its opposition to the use of
            military force to settle the issue.

12   EGYPT - President Nasser calls the US-Anglo-French ef-
            forts to establish international control over canal
            operations war provocations.

14   EGYPT - The Egyptian government takes over full oper-
            ation of the Suez Canal.

15   USSR - During a state visit of Indonesia's President
            Sukarno (12-17 September), the government announces a
            loan of $100 million.

21   GREAT BRITAIN - The Suez Conference ends with a plan
            to establish an "Association of Suez Canal Users." The
            plan is opposed by five members.

22   NICARAGUA - President Anastasio Somoza is shot and
            seriously wounded in an assassination attempt.

23   UNITED NATIONS - Over a three-day period, the Security
            Council listens to claims and counter-claims concern-
            ing the Suez Crisis.

24   NEPAL - The government announces an agreement with
            Communist China, giving the Chinese sovereignty in
            Tibet.

29   NICARAGUA - Somoza dies of his wounds. His son Luis
            replaces him as president until a scheduled election
            in May 1957.

OCTOBER

2   BURMA - The government announces that the Chinese Com-
            munist forces which had invaded the country in July
            would withdraw and the 1941 boundary between the two
            countries would be henceforth respected.

5   UNITED NATIONS - The UN Security Council begins debate
            over the Suez Crisis.

8   SOUTH VIET NAM - USMAAGV planners begin to participate
            with key RVNAF officers on the development of a master
            schooling plan for military personnel.

10   POLAND - In a surprise move, the trials of those ar-
            rested during the rioting in Poznan are suddenly ended
            without resolution.

13   UNITED NATIONS - The USSR vetoes a UN compromise reso-
            lution to the Suez Crisis.

15   UNITED STATES - The President announces the US will
            continue sending economic aid to the Tito government
            in Yugoslavia, but rules out military assistance for
            the moment.

15   UNITED NATIONS - Jordan accuses Israel of aggression
            before the Security Council.

16   POLAND - A number of Polish Communist leaders demand
            the removal of Soviet officers from the Polish army.

19   JAPAN - A peace treaty is finally agreed upon with the
            Soviet Union, but only after the Kurile Islands issue
            is settled.

20   POLAND - Wladyshlaw Gomulka is reinstated in the
            Central Committee of the Polish Communist Party after
            serving five years in prison. A number of Soviet
            officials, including Nikita Khrushchev, gather in
            Warsaw to convince Polish authorities to continue

20   POLAND (Cont'd) -   pro-Soviet policies. Warsaw Pact
            commander-in-chief, Marshal of the Soviet Union
            Konstantine K. Rokossovsky, orders a troop buildup
            around Warsaw. Soviet reinforcements are ordered into
            Poland from their garrisons in East Germany. A number
            of firefights erupt between Polish and Soviet forces.
            The next day, Gomulka is appointed First Secretary of
            the Polish Communist Party, at the same time rejecting
            the bid of Marshal Rokossovsky for membership in the
            Politburo.

20   MOROCCO - The territory of Tangiers becomes a part of
            an independent Morocco when a nine-power conference
            votes to end its international status. The transfer
            goes into effect on 29 October.

21-23   HUNGARY - Following months of growing unrest and
            political turmoil, the threat of a strike for freedom
            among university students quickly develops into a
            full-scale revolution. A major student demonstration
            (23 October) in Bem Square turns into a march to the
            Parliament Square. Nearly 100,000 students and workers
            participate. The demonstrators demand a return of Imre
            Nagy to power and the immediate release of Jozsef Car-
            dinal Mindszenty who has been held in solitary con-
            finement since 1948.

21   HONDURAS - A bloodless military coup forces the resig-
            nation of President Julio Lozano Dias. The next day a
            military junta led by Colonel Hector Caraccioli is in-
            stalled.

22   JORDAN - An anti-Western, pro-Egyptian government is
            elected to replace the caretaker one that assumed
            power when Said el-Mufti resigned on 30 June. Reaction
            to the continuing border clashes with Israel played a
            significant role in the election.

24   FRANCE - A secret agreement is reached wherein Great
            Britain, Israel, and France arrange for covert opera-
            tions against Egypt.

24   HUNGARY - Anti-Russian rioting in Budapest accompanies
            the installation of Imre Nagy as premier. Hungarian
            secret police (AVO) are unsuccessful in quelling the
            popular uprising. Soviet occupation forces move to
            suppress the disturbances.

24   POLAND - Soviet troops are ordered out of Poland. The
            move starts the next day but is never completed as at
            least three Soviet divisions remain on Polish terri-
            tory. A number of armed attacks are conducted against
            Soviet garrisons in Poland (as at Liegnitz). These are
            dispersed by Polish police and military forces.

25   HUNGARY - Gaining some concessions, the Hungarian
          "Freedom Fighters" demand more. The Stalinist Erno
          Gero is ousted as Communist Party secretary and is
          replaced by Janos Kadar.

25   ISRAEL - The government says it will abide by a UN
          resolution and never initiate a war, but it reserves
          the right to answer Arab aggression with force.

26   SOUTH VIET NAM - A constitution is promulgated, and
          the National Assembly is formed out of the National
          Constituent Assembly.

27   FRANCE - In an agreement with West Germany, the Saar
          Basin is returned to the German state. Before this
          plan is accomplished there will be much popular dis-
          sent.

27   HUNGARY - The revolt spreads throughout the country.
          Large numbers of Hungarian secret police (AVO) and
          their families flee into Austria to prevent being
          captured by the Freedom Fighters. Austria accepts the
          refugees without verification of their party affili-
          ations. At the same time, the Nagy government an-
          nounces its plan for the withdrawal of Soviet troops,
          restoration of order, and the appointment of formerly
          outlawed members of the Smallholder's Party to the
          cabinet. The following day, the Soviet High Command in
          Hungary announces it will start withdrawing its troops
          from Hungarian soil.

28   UNITED STATES - The President warns Israel over its
          provocative activities in the Middle East.

28   POLAND - After being dismissed as the Polish Minister
          of Defense, Soviet Marshal Konstantin K. Rokossovsky
          returns to the USSR. The next day (29 October) Stefan
          Cardinal Wyszinsky is released from his captivity.

28   UNITED NATIONS - The UN votes to discuss the Hungarian
          situation.

29   TANGIERS - The territory's international status comes
          to an end.

29   EGYPT - The Israelis open a full-scale attack on Egyp-
          tian positions in the Sinai and drive toward the Suez
          Canal. Israeli airborne units (the 1st Battalion,
          202nd Paratroop Brigade, commanded by Colonel Ariel
          Sharon) capture the eastern approach to the Mitla Pass
          deep in the Sinai. A land force, including the remain-
          der of the Paratroop brigade, attacks along an axis

29   EGYPT (Cont'd) - Kuntilla-Thamad to link up with this
            airhead. Another Israeli column (the 9th Infantry
            Brigade commanded by Colonel Avraham Yoffe) crosses
            the border near Eilat (Elat) and captures Ras el-Nagb
            in the Sinai. The Avraham force then begins an over-
            land march down the coast of the Gulf of Aqaba with
            the objective of taking Sharm esh Sheikh (Sharm el-
            Sheikh) at the southern tip of the Sinai peninsula.
            Egypt begins moves to reinforce its Sinai forces.

30-31   EUROPE - British and French governments threaten to
            intervene with military forces in the conflict between
            Egypt and Israel, if the opposing forces do not
            withdraw and allow for the occupation of key sites in
            the Canal Zone. The combatants both reject a US-USSR
            cease-fire appeal. After vetoing a UN resolution
            calling for restraint in the use of force (31 Octo-
            ber), British and French forces attack Cairo and
            various canal installations; Egyptian airfields are
            bombed.

30   HUNGARY - Soviet troops begin withdrawing from Buda-
            pest. Nagy promises the Freedom Fighters free elec-
            tions and an end to the Communist-imposed one-party
            system.

30   SINAI DESERT - The Israeli force out of Kuntilla cap-
            tures Thamad and links up with the airborne battalion
            holding the Mitla Pass. To the north, another Israeli
            division-size force drives along a general axis of
            Sabha-Kuseima-Abu Aweigila. Egypt orders an armored
            division into the Sinai to reinforce its positions
            around Bir Gifgafa and Bir Rud.

31   SINAI DESERT - The Egyptians block Israeli attempts to
            penetrate the Mitla Pass. The northern Israeli force
            captures part of the Abu Aweigila defensive positions
            but only after sustaining heavy casualties. Other ele-
            ments of this force, commanded by Colonel Jehuda
            Wallach, take Jebel Libni, Bir Hama, and Bir Hassnah
            (Bir Hassaneh).

31   ISRAEL - Following its bombardment of an oil refinery
            on the Israeli coast near Haifa, the Egyptian destroy-
            er Ibrahim al-Awal is chased down at sea, captured
            without a fight, and towed into port by Israeli naval
            units.

NOVEMBER

            WEST GERMANY - US occupation forces are put on alert
            preparatory to intervening in either Hungary or Egypt.

1   SINAI DESERT - An Israeli division-size force moves
         toward El Arish along the coastal road (known since
         Roman times as the Via Maris). Another Israeli as-
         sault is repulsed at Abu Aweigila (Abu Ageila) in the
         central sector. Before day's end, all Egyptian forces
         in the Sinai except those cut off at Gaza, and those
         with transport at Sharm esh-Shiekh, begin a general
         withdrawal.

2   HUNGARY - Premier Nagy repudiates the Warsaw Pact and
         requests the UN to take control of the situation.

2   UNITED NATIONS - The General Assembly orders an im-
         mediate cease-fire in the Suez Canal zone and condemns
         the USSR for the invasion of Hungary.

2   SINAI DESERT - The Israeli airborne forces now rein-
         forced by an infantry brigade, fight their way through
         the Mitla Pass and advance on the Gulf of Suez. Upon
         reaching the Gulf this force turns south and advances
         on Sharm esh-Shiekh moving down the western side of
         the Sinai Peninsula. In the central sector, the Egyp-
         tian forces evacuating Abu Aweigila are pursued to
         within ten miles of the Suez Canal near Kantara. In
         the north, El Arish is taken by an armored force com-
         manded by Colonel Haim Bar Lev, which then advances as
         far as Romani, approximately 30 miles from Port Said.
         To the rear, the city of Gaza and the northern half of
         the Egyptian enclave are captured.

3   SINAI DESERT - The two-pronged Israeli advance toward
         Sharm esh-Shiekh continues with a series of towns be-
         ing taken by each force. The western force takes Et
         Tur (El Tur) and is within 30 miles of Sharm esh-
         Shiekh. The local Egyptian commander orders a with-
         drawal of all outlying forces into their final defen-
         sive positions. In the rear, all of the Gaza Strip is
         captured by Israeli forces.

3   ISRAEL - Apparently under the assumption that Sharm
         esh-Shiekh would soon be taken, the government accepts
         the UN ceasefire. Yet, within twenty-four hours, and
         mostly because of Anglo-French opposition to the
         cease-fire, the Israelis create an impasse by making
         impossible demands and thereby delay the cessation of
         hostilities.

4   HUNGARY - Reinforced Soviet forces (16 divisions with
         2,000 tanks), now numbering more than 200,000 men, end
         their withdrawal and turn to crush the rebellion. Imre
         Nagy is ousted and Janos Kadar is appointed premier.
         Cardinal Mindszenty takes refuge in the US Embassy
         where he will be forced to remain for 15 years.

4   SINAI PENINSULA - The Israeli eastern force is within
         three miles of Sharm esh-Shiekh and is taken under
         fire by the Egyptians.

4   UNITED NATIONS - The General Assembly calls for an in-
         vestigation of Soviet activities in Hungary.

4   UNITED NATIONS - The General Assembly adopts a Canadi-
         an resolution to send an international force to the
         Middle East.

5   SINAI PENINSULA - Sharm esh-Shiekh is assaulted by
         Israeli forces shortly after midnight. Although de-
         layed by heavy fire and minefields, the Israelis, now
         reinforced with airborne troops from the western col-
         umn, breach the Egyptian defenses, and the Egyptian
         commander surrenders.

5   EGYPT - British and French airborne units are dropped
         on Gamil airport near Port Said at about 0830 hours.
         Another allied parachute contingent of about 600 men
         jumps into the area around Port Fuad. The Egyptian
         area commander arranges a brief cease-fire with the
         allies but fighting begins again before midnight.

5   HUNGARY - A wholesale flight begins as tens of
         thousands flee the reimposed Communist tyranny. Within
         three weeks more than 100,000 cross the border into
         Austria.

6   UNITED NATIONS - After the UN orders a cease-fire in
         the conflict in Egypt (2 November), the USSR threatens
         intervention to end the conflict. President Eisenhower
         puts US forces around the world on alert. First Great
         Britain, then France and Israel, accept the cease-
         fire. The UN creates a 6,000-man United Nations Emer-
         gency Force (UNEF) to supervise the cease-fire.

6   EGYPT - An amphibious assault is carried out at dawn
         with British and French forces landing in Port Said.
         Although the Egyptian sector commander is captured,
         the fighting continues until 1930 hours (7:30 PM) when
         the Allied commander receives the UN cease-fire order.
         As the cease-fire is being put into effect, Allied
         forces capture the important town of Et-Kap (El Kap).
         The cease-fire goes into effect, but not before the
         Egyptians have lost almost all of their Sinai equip-
         ment and have taken over 10,000 casualties killed or
         captured. The Israeli losses total 180 killed.

7   MIDDLE EAST - A general cease-fire begins. Great
         Britain says it will not withdraw its troops until the
         UN Emergency Force (UNEF) is in place.

11   YUGOSLAVIA - Relations with the USSR worsen as the re-
              sult of an inflammatory speech made by Tito before the
              Yugoslav Communist Party.

14   HUNGARY - The last defenses of the Freedom Fighters
              on Danubian Csepel Island are overrun by heavily
              reinforced Soviet forces.

15   SUEZ CANAL - The first UNEF elements arrive to super-
              vise the cease-fire. Among other strategic points,
              they occupy Sharm esh-Shiekh.

17   USSR - At a Moscow reception for Western diplomats,
              Premier Khrushchev announces that "History is on our
              side. We will bury you!"

22   ARGENTINA - Another pro-Peronist revolt is quelled by
              government forces.

22   HUNGARY - Imre Nagy is arrested by Hungarian author-
              ities as he leaves the Yugoslav Embassy in Budapest.

26   UNITED STATES - As a result of the doctrinal debates
              among the various armed services within the Pentagon,
              Secretary of Defense Charles Wilson curtails the
              Army's roles in missile employment and the use of
              aviation.

29   UNITED STATES - The US offers political asylum to Hun-
              gary's Freedom Fighters.

30   CUBA - An invasion led by Fidel Castro and mounted in
              Mexico is defeated in Oriente Province. Castro is sub-
              sequently reported dead (2 December).

DECEMBER

6   UNITED STATES - The government announces that Iceland
              has rescinded its request demanding the withdrawal of
              US forces from its territory.

12   SWITZERLAND - Foreign Minister Max Petitpierre reaf-
              firms his nation's neutrality stating that the Swiss
              will maintain their traditionally strong military
              posture.

12   UNITED NATIONS - The UN General Assembly condemns the
              Soviet Union for its aggression in Hungary and calls
              for an immediate withdrawal of Soviet troops from that
              country.

12   HUNGARY - A general strike in protest of the Kadar
              regime paralyzes the country.

12   HAITI – General unrest and chaos in the country forces
        the resignation of President Paul Magliore. There fol-
        lows a period of disorder in which a number of govern-
        ments rise and fall. In September 1957, an unusually
        large number of voters elect Francois Duvalier as
        their new President.

17   POLAND – An agreement limiting the role of Soviet
        military forces stationed on Polish soil is signed.

22   SUEZ CANAL – British and French forces complete their
        withdrawal.

26   USSR – The state of war that has existed with the Em-
        pire of Japan is ended.

27   SUEZ CANAL – Salvage crews begin the long-term task of
        clearing the canal of ships sunk by the Egyptians to
        block its use when the war started.

Notes

1957

JANUARY

SOUTH VIET NAM - The Viet Cong terror campaign against the South Vietnamese populace intensifies and spreads. Assassinations of rural area government officials and school teachers increase.

1   WEST GERMANY - The Bonn government accepts the return of the Saar which was agreed upon by the Franco-German Treaty of 27 October 1956.

3   SOUTHEAST ASIA - The ICC reports that between December 1955 and August 1956, neither North Viet Nam nor South Viet Nam fulfilled its obligations under the 1954 Geneva Armistice Agreement, and that both are guilty of violating the Accords.

9   GREAT BRITAIN - Anthony Eden is forced to resign as Prime Minister because of his handling of the Suez Crisis. The next day (10 January), (Maurice) Harold Macmillan accepts the Royal Summons and becomes Prime Minister.

9   USSR - A decree is signed which rehabilitates five minority groups in the Soviet Union that were accused of disloyalty during the Second World War and branded traitors. These are the Balkars, Chechens, Ingush, Kalmycks, and Karachais.

18   MIDDLE EAST - Both the USSR and Communist China announce that they have developed defense policies against Western aggression in the Middle East.

FEBRUARY

2   UNITED NATIONS - The General Assembly demands a withdrawal of Israeli troops from occupied Egyptian territory and issues new, broader instructions to the UNEF
which is to serve as a buffer between the opposing
forces. The following day (3 February) Israel refuses
compliance unless the United Nations can provide better guarantees against renewed attacks across its
borders.

5   UNITED STATES - The government announces its willingness to impose economic sanctions on Israel if the UN
demand is not accepted.

8   SAUDI ARABIA - On his departure from a state visit to
the US, King Saud announces an arms agreement that
includes a renewal of the US lease on the Dhahran air
base.

11   UNITED STATES - The government assures Israel that it
will support the Israeli's right to free passage
through the Gulf of Aqaba.

11   UNITED NATIONS - UN General Secretary Dag Hammarskjold
asks the General Assembly for new instructions following the breakdown of negotiations for an Israeli withdrawal from the occupied territories.

11   FRANCE - A Franco-Soviet trade pact is signed.

15   USSR - Andrei Gromyko becomes Foreign Minister replacing Dmitri T. Shepilov.

19   USSR - Premier Nikita Khrushchev announces in a speech
that Yugoslavia should not expect economic aid in the
future. This tends to confirm reports of the rift that
has been developing between the two countries since
last year.

MARCH

1   ISRAEL - The government announces its agreement to the
withdrawal of Israeli forces from the Gaza and Gulf of
Aqaba areas provided the Gaza demarcation line is pa-
trolled by UNEF and not by Egyptian forces, and that
free navigation in the Gulf of Aqaba is assured by the
United Nations.

1   SOUTH VIET NAM - The USMAAG and TERM are reorganized.
The total US strength in SVN is now 736, 535 of whom
are Army personnel.

2   INDONESIA - Following President Achmed Sukarno's de-
nunciation of western democratic ideals, a military
coup takes place in the eastern provinces (Celebes).
The junta demands complete autonomy.

5   UNITED STATES - The Senate authorizes the use of military force to repel any Communist aggression in the
Middle East. This comes in response to a presidential
request of 5 January. This will become known as the
Eisenhower Doctrine.

6   GOLD COAST - In accordance with the 1956 decision, the
Gold Coast becomes the independent nation of Ghana and
absorbs British Togoland into its structure.

9   UNITED STATES - The Congress authorizes the President
to spend up to $200 million in military and economic
support to any Middle East nation. This becomes a part
of the Eisenhower Doctrine.

9   INDONESIA - A second coup takes place; this one in the
area of southern Sumatra.

12   INDONESIA - Borneo repudiates the central government
and establishes its own independent leadership.

14   INDONESIA - Sukarno declares a state of siege and war
after the cabinet resigns.

17   THE PHILIPPINES - President Ramon Magsaysay is killed
in an airplane crash. Carlos Garcia becomes President.
(Garcia is later confirmed in a national election on
12 November.)

18   UNITED NATIONS - The subcommittee on disarmament opens
a meeting in London.

19   NATO - In a secret agreement, the NATO Foreign
Ministers reach a compromise over the British demand
that it be allowed to withdraw one-third of its 75,000
troops garrisoned on the continent.

20   YUGOSLAVIA - The Balkan Alliance is the topic of discussion at a meeting of representatives from Turkey,
Greece, and Yugoslavia.

21-24   BERMUDA - A fence-mending meeting takes place between
President Eisenhower and Secretary John Foster Dulles,
and Prime Minister Macmillan and his Foreign Secretary, Selwyn Lloyd. The US promises Great Britain intermediate-range guided missiles. The British announce
their decision to reduce their armed forces and to
rely on greater mechanization.

25   ITALY - The European Common Market is established by a
            treaty signed in Rome. A second treaty establishes the
            European Atomic Community (Euratom). Both treaties are
            to go into effect 1 January 1958.

28   CYPRUS - After his call for an end to terrorist activ-
            ities, Archbishop Makarios is released from detention
            in the Seychelles.

29   CYPRUS - Archbishop Makarios announces his determina-
            tion not to participate in any negotiations with the
            British until he is allowed to return to Cyprus.

29   ISRAEL - The government announces its agreement with a
            UN plan to erect a mined barrier fence along the Gaza
            border provided the UNEF continues its monitorship of
            the border area.

30   MOROCCO - The government signs a treaty of alliance
            and friendship with Tunisia.

APRIL

9   INDONESIA - Sukarno appoints a non-political cabinet.

10   JORDAN - King Hussein dismisses his pro-Egyptian Pre-
            mier, Sulaiman al-Nabulsi, as a first step in purging
            his government and armed forces of sympathizers of
            Egypt's Gamal Nasser.

11   GREAT BRITAIN - The government announces that Singa-
            pore will become self-governing on 1 January 1958.

11   CHILE - Amid growing economic unrest, the Chilean
            Congress authorizes sweeping dictatorial powers for
            the President.

25   UNITED STATES - The US Sixth Fleet is ordered to the
            eastern Mediterranean. This causes an anti-American
            outcry against US meddling in Jordanian affairs even
            though King Hussein denies any connection with Wash-
            ington.

28   UNITED NATIONS - The UN announces it has completed the
            task of clearing the Suez Canal of the sunken ships
            that had obstructed its use.

MAY

1   TURKEY - Turkey begins moving troops toward the Syrian
            border.

1   SOUTH VIET NAM - France's responsibility for naval and air force training terminates.

1   UNITED STATES - The US announces it has agreed to a $95 million aid package for Poland.

1   USSR - The Soviet Union ratifies the establishment of the International Atomic Energy Agency.

2   SOUTH VIET NAM - The President institutes conscription.

4   SOUTH VIET NAM - ARVN I Corps headquarters is established; the Vietnamese receive their first major tactical control headquarters.

5-19 UNITED STATES - President Ngo Dinh Diem of the Republic of Viet Nam pays a state visit to the US and addresses a joint session of Congress (9 May). The theme of the joint communique (issued 11 May) is the "peaceful reunification" of Viet Nam. The US pledges to continue aid to Viet Nam.

7   SYRIA - The government issues a warning against further Turkish troop movements toward their common border.

9   COLOMBIA - President Rojas Pinilla is forced to resign after the Roman Catholic church accuses him of authorizing murder in suppression of student riots. A military junta takes control of the country.

11   COMMUNIST CHINA - The government declares that the deployment of US Matador missiles on Taiwan will be considered an act of war.

13   GREAT BRITAIN - Although Israel refuses to accept the Egyptian decision to deny passage through the Suez Canal to Israeli ships, the British government accepts the general terms of the Egyptian canal usage plan. In another action, London agrees to terminate its 1948 alliance with Jordan.

15   GREAT BRITAIN - The government announces the successful detonation of a hydrogen weapon at Christmas Island in the Pacific. Additional tests follow on 31 May, 19 June, and from 14 September through 9 October. (The latter tests are conducted on the Australian mainland.)

20   CUBA - Rebel leader Fidel Castro appeals to the US to stop supplying military assistance to the Batista government.

20   SAUDI ARABIA - King Saud announces his support of
            Egypt's refusal to allow Israeli ships in the Gulf of
            Aqaba.

26   HAITI - A civil war breaks out over irregularities in
            the elections held earlier in the year. Army forces
            battle the followers of the provisional executive
            council who seized power on 26 April after the gov-
            ernment had resigned.

30   CUBA - The armed forces of the Batista government in-
            tensify their military operations in Oriente Province
            in hopes of putting an end to Castro's rebellion.

30   GREAT BRITAIN - Trade restrictions are eased with Com-
            munist China.

31   SOUTH VIET NAM - All French training assistance to the
            armed forces of the Republic of Viet Nam (RVNAF) is
            terminated.

JUNE

3   UNITED STATES - The US formally joins the Military
            Committee of the Baghdad Pact.

7   UNITED STATES - The administration announces it has
            granted Poland two loans in excess of $48 million.

14   HAITI - The army ousts the provisional leadership and
            declares a state of emergency.

21   UNITED STATES - An agreement is reached whereby the US
            promises to withdraw all its ground forces and to
            reduce the overall strength of US military forces in
            Japan.

21   UNITED STATES - The US declares that, because of re-
            peated violations of the truce agreement by the North
            Koreans, it is no longer bound by the 1953 Korean ar-
            mistice agreement provisions dealing with the intro-
            duction of forces and new-style weapons into the
            country.

27   INDONESIA - The North Celebes break away from the cen-
            tral government in the continuing internal political
            chaos that sweeps the country.

30   SOUTH VIET NAM - French naval and air force units,
            most of them former training cadres, are withdrawn
            from the country at the request of the South
            Vietnamese government.

JULY

1   WEST GERMANY - Three Bundeswehr divisions are turned
    over to NATO. Nine more are scheduled for later incor-
    poration into NATO ground forces in Europe.

1   SOUTH VIET NAM - An advance party of US Special Forces
    personnel arrives in South Viet Nam to organize a 16-
    week course at the Commando Training Center at Nha
    Trang.

3   USSR - A group of Stalinists, including Vyacheslav
    Molotov, Georgi Malenkov, Lazar Kaganovich, and (the
    next day) Dmitri Shepilov, are removed from the Cen-
    tral Committee of the Communist Party.

4   ROMANIA - Two Stalinists are removed from the Romanian
    Politburo.

6   INDONESIA - Local military commanders seize control of
    East Indonesia.

9   FRANCE - President Rene Coty restates his nation's
    categorical rejection of Algeria's bid for
    independence.

9   ISRAEL - A ten-hour battle between Israeli and Syrian
    forces is halted only by the arrival of the UNEF.

13 JORDAN - The last British troops depart.

16 ISRAEL - The government announces it will permit UNEF
    observation posts along the border with Syria for a
    one-month trial period.

18 FRANCE - The National Assembly votes extraordinary
    powers to Premier Bourges-Mannoury to surpress the
    Algerian rebel activities in France.

18 WESTERN HEMISPHERE - The Inter-American Defense Board
    approves a new joint military defense plan for hemi-
    spheric defense.

19 MUSCAT & OMAN - With British supervision, the Sultan's
    forces open a campaign to suppress a tribal uprising
    led by the Imam of Oman, Sheikh Ghalib bin Ali. The
    punitive action will continue until 26 August.

22 UNITED NATIONS - Israel charges Syria with truce
    agreement violations.

24 INDONESIA - Analysis indicates only Java remains in
    the hands of the Sukarno government.

25   WEST GERMANY - The United States, France, and West
            Germany sign the Berlin Declaration calling for the
            reunification of Germany.

25   TUNISIA - The Bey of Tunis, Sidi Mohammed el-Amin is
            ousted by the National Constituent Assembly. Habib
            Bourguiba is elected president.

26   GUATEMALA - President Castillo Almas is assassinated.
            The next day the Vice-President, Luis Arturo Gonzales
            is sworn in as provisional president.

26   COLOMBIA - Amid widespread rioting, the ruling junta
            dissolves the Constituent Assembly and promises elec-
            tions early in 1958.

29   USSR - The Soviet Union restores more than $250 mil-
            lion in aid to Yugoslavia following a conference aimed
            at reconciliation.

29   UNITED STATES - The US ratifies the International
            Atomic Energy Agency. This gives the necessary major-
            ity for the agency to begin its operation.

AUGUST

3   ROMANIA - A secret meeting is held between Yugoslav
            and Soviet officials to work out means for closer
            cooperation.

13   SYRIA - Three American diplomats are expelled for al-
            legedly plotting the overthrow of President Shukri al-
            Kuwatly.

13-21   UNITED STATES - President Eisenhower throws a number
            of Syrian diplomats out of the US and accuses the USSR
            of being the chief cause of unrest in the Middle East.

21   EGYPT - Syrian President Shukri al-Kuwatly meets in
            Cairo with President Nasser.

22   INDONESIA - In an attempt to end the crisis a meeting
            is held of all factions.

31   MALAYA - The British protectorship ends and Malaya be-
            comes independent.

SEPTEMBER

3   UNITED STATES - Arkansas governor Orval Faubus orders
            the National Guard to block black students attempting
            to enter Central High School in Little Rock.

5   UNITED STATES - The government announces plans to ac-
           celerate arms   shipments to Lebanon, Jordan, Turkey,
           and Iraq.

7   SYRIA - The government warns of retaliation if the US
           ships arms to Jordan.

9   TUNISIA - A state of emergency is declared after armed
           clashes take place between Tunisian troops and French
           and Algerian forces along the border with Algeria.

11   USSR - Moscow complains of Turkish troop concentra-
           tions along the Syrian border.

12   TUNISIA - President Bourguiba asks the US for military
           aid following border clashes with French and Algerian
           troops.

13   USSR - The Soviets issue a warning to Turkey to stop
           preparations for an attack on Syria.

19   JORDAN - The government accuses Syria of meddling in
           Jordanian affairs.

19   UNITED NATIONS - Secretary of State John Foster Dulles
           accuses the Soviet Union of building up   Syrian
           strength for an attack on Turkey.

20   UNITED STATES - A federal court order enjoins Arkansas
           Governor Orval Faubus from further   interference in
           school desegregation.

22   HAITI - Francois Duvalier is elected President.

24   UNITED STATES - The President orders federal troops
           into Little Rock, Arkansas, to prevent insurrection.
           The Arkansas National Guard is federalized and ordered
           to remain in its assembly areas to prevent interfering
           with the federal operations.

25   SYRIA - As a result of the al-Katwatly-Nasser meeting
           of 21 August, a conference opens in Damascus to estab-
           lish Arab solidarity. Iraq is represented by Premier
           Ali Jawdat; Saudi Arabia, by King Saud.

OCTOBER

3   UNITED NATIONS - President Nasser announces Egyptian
           support of Syria in the growing Turko-Syrian crisis.

5   USSR - The Soviet Union successfully places Sputnik I
           in an orbit around Earth.

7   YUGOSLAVIA - Apparently as a conciliatory gesture to
          the USSR, Tito recognizes East Germany.

10   SYRIA - Turkey is accused of aggression by the Syrian
          government.

11   LEBANON - The government announces its support of
          Syria in the growing crisis.

12   USSR - Nikita Khrushchev attempts to incite European
          labor unions against alleged US and Turkish aggression
          in the Middle East.

14   EGYPT - Egyptian troops are moved to Syria to rein-
          force the Syrian army.

14   UNITED STATES - The US informs the Soviet Union that
          an attack on Turkey would bring a swift military re-
          taliation.

16   UNITED NATIONS - The Syrian government asks the UN to
          investigate the border dispute with Turkey.

16   SYRIA - The government declares a state of emergency
          fearing a Turkish invasion.

20   SAUDI ARABIA - King Saud offers to mediate the Turko-
          Syrian crisis. Syria immediately rejects the offer.

22   SOUTH VIET NAM - American installations in Saigon, in-
          cluding the headquarters of USMAAG and USIS, are sub-
          jected to terrorist bombing attacks. Many American
          personnel are injured.

22   UNITED STATES - Following the beating death of a US
          citizen at the hands of Haitian police, the US govern-
          ment formally warns the newly elected Duvalier govern-
          ment of the seriousness of the situation.

24   GUATEMALA - A three-man military junta takes control
          of the country amid allegations that the elections
          held on 20 October were rigged. After three days (27
          October), Guillermo Flores Avendano is appointed pro-
          visional President.

26   USSR - Marshal Georgi K. Zhukov is arrested at the
          Moscow airport by the Commander of the Moscow Military
          District and is dismissed as Soviet Defense Minister.
          Marshal Rodion Y. Malinovsky is named as his replace-
          ment.

28   INDONESIA - Sukarno threatens to seize Dutch West New
          Guinea if the UN refuses to take up the Indonesian
          crisis.

31   MIDDLE EAST - The Arab League backs Syria in the Middle East crisis (which by this time has died down).

NOVEMBER

MOROCCO - The suppression of a major revolt led by the Ait Ba Amrane tribe in the Spanish Infi enclave in southern Morocco requires the use of army troops.

1   LAOS - The Communist Pathet Lao faction is taken into the government.

3   USSR - Sputnik II is successfully orbited with a live dog aboard.

8   VENEZUELA - The government announces an aid plan for Latin America.

11   USSR - Zhukov is stripped of his seat in the Presidium of the Supreme Soviet for fostering his own "cult of the personality."

14   TUNISIA - The government announces it will receive US and British small arms.

14   FRANCE - The government protests when it is learned that the US and Great Britain will supply arms to Tunisia.

15   PORTUGAL - The government announces that the 1951 Azores Common Defense Treaty with the US has been extended until 1962.

17   CZECHOSLOVAKIA - Upon the death of President Antonin Zapotocky, the First Secretary of the Czech Communist Party, Antonin Novotny, is elected president by the parliament.

18   TUNISIA - The government announces it has rejected a Soviet offer of military assistance.

DECEMBER

1   INDONESIA - Netherlands citizens are attacked and property destroyed during a 24-hour strike. Sukarno calls the strike after The Hague announces it will not give up Dutch New Guinea.

5   INDONESIA - The government orders all Dutch consular offices closed, except in Jakarta. Sukarno announces the expulsion of all Dutch citizens in Indonesia.

9   INDONESIA - The government seizes most Dutch property
         in the country, especially agricultural holdings.

19   NATO - NATO announces that missile bases will be es-
         tablished on European soil.

21   USSR - The government rejects a NATO proposal for dis-
         armament talks.

30   ISRAEL - A government crisis develops over the sale of
         arms to West Germany.

31   VENEZUELA - A major revolt starts against the policies
         of President Perez Jimenez.

31   SOUTH VIET NAM - The ARVN II Corps headquarters is ac-
         tivated.

Notes

1958

JANUARY

1-23   VENEZUELA - The government of President Marcos Perez
        Jiminez is able to crush early rioting but is eventu-
        ally overthrown by a military junta (22-23 January)
        led by Admiral Wolfgang Larrazabal. The junta assumes
        power on 23 January.

4   SOUTH VIET NAM - There is a large-scale VC attack 25
        miles north of Saigon on a rubber plantation operated
        by the French-owned Michelin Rubber Company.

8   INDONESIA - The government rejects a UN offer to medi-
        ate its West New Guinea territorial dispute with the
        Netherlands.

13   UNITED NATIONS - More than 9,000 scientists from 43
        countries petition the UN to establish an internation-
        al agreement halting all future nuclear weapons test-
        ing.

31   FRANCE - The National Assembly's plan for reform in
        Algeria is rebuked by the Algerians.

FEBRUARY

1   EGYPT - At a meeting in Cairo, Egyptian President
        Gamal Abdul Nasser and Syrian President Shukri al-
        Kuwatly proclaim the formation of the United Arab
        Republic (UAR) to be headed by Nasser.

8   ALBANIA - The government announces an agreement with the Greeks for a joint operation to clear the mines placed in the waters between Corfu and the Albanian coast.

8   TUNISIA - French planes bomb the village of Sakiet-Sidi-Youseff. Seventy-nine people are killed. This action causes the breakout of five months of sporadic conflict. The French carried out the retaliation raid against the Tunisian town because it was being used as a base for cross-border guerrilla operations in Algeria.

14   JORDAN - King Hussein announces in Amman the merger of Jordan and Iraq into an Arab Federation under Iraq's King Faisal.

22   UNITED STATES - The government announces it plans to supply Great Britain with 60 Thor intermediate-range ballistic missiles capable of delivering nuclear warheads.

MARCH

2   GUATEMALA - Ydigoras Fuentes is declared the elected president ending nearly nine months of political uncertainty.

16   CUBA - Rebel leader Fidel Castro declares "total war" against the Batista regime.

27   USSR - Nikolae Bulganin is replaced as Premier by Nikita S. Khrushchev.

28   WEST GERMANY - The government announces its decision to equip its armed forces with nuclear weapons while, at the same time, rejecting a Soviet plan for the reunification of the two Germanys.

31   USSR - The Soviet Foreign Minister, Andrei Gromyko, announces that his country has suspended the testing of nuclear weapons.

APRIL

8   UNITED STATES - The President proposes a system of mutual inspections to enforce a nuclear test ban.

14   LEBANON - A UAR-inspired uprising against the pro-Western Chamoun government breaks out throughout the countryside.

16   FRANCE - The government falls because of complications arising from the deadlock over its policy for the administration of its North African possessions.

28   UNITED STATES - The government announces the beginning of a series of nuclear tests at the Eniwetok test site in the Pacific.

MAY

9-13   LEBANON - Widespread antigovernment rioting, which is attributed to pro-Nasser groups, breaks out in the capital city of Beirut and the seaport town of Tripoli.

12   NORTH AMERICA - The North American Air Defense Command (NORAD) is jointly formed by Canada and the US.

13   FRANCE - A new cabinet is formed by Pierre Pflimlin. This ineffectual government lasts only two weeks.

13   VENEZUELA - The autocade carrying US Vice-President Richard M. Nixon is stoned by angry mobs in the Venezuelan capital city of Caracus. President Eisenhower alerts US forces for possible employment to protect the Vice-President.

15   ALGERIA - General Jacques Massu assumes the leadership of the Committee of Public Safety and uses the position to seize power in Algeria.

16-22   BOLIVIA - A military revolt is suppressed by loyal forces in Santa Cruz.

17   SOUTH VIET NAM - At the request of the South Vietnamese government, the North Vietnamese liaison mission to the ICC is withdrawn from its Saigon headquarters.

20   UNITED STATES - A force of 150,000 troops, including four divisions, is established as a strategic corps. This organization will be prepared to respond as the initial military force anywhere in the world.

24-25   TUNISIA - Army units clash with French military forces at Gabes and Remada.

27   USSR - At the conclusion of a Warsaw Pact meeting in Moscow, it is announced that Soviet forces will soon be withdrawn from Romania and that each member nation will reduce its armed forces by 119,000 troops. The Warsaw Pact also announces that the Soviet Union will withdraw one division from Hungary.

31   FRANCE - In the face of a possible civil war, President Rene Coty appoints General Charles DeGaulle Premier.

JUNE

1   FRANCE - Premier DeGaulle announces an offer of self-determination by referendum to Algeria. This is opposed by the French Algerian community.

6   UNITED NATIONS - The Lebanese government asks the Security Council to halt UAR aggression.

6   FRANCE - DeGaulle announces that General Raoul Salan is in complete control of Algeria and that Salan will maintain communications with Paris. Gaulist cabinet members continue to cause friction, however, throughout the remainder of the month.

11   UNITED NATIONS - The Security Council orders observers into Lebanon to determine whether the UAR is interfering in internal Lebanese affairs. Another team is ordered into Jordan. Both teams are to aid in the withdrawal of British and American forces.

13   UNITED NATIONS - It is announced that a six-nation conference will be held in Geneva to discuss technical problems in nuclear-test detection.

14   LEBANON - The continued fighting in Lebanon spreads to Beirut. UN Secretary General Dag Hammarskjold arrives with a team of UN observers.

17   HUNGARY - The government announces the execution of Imre Nagy, Pal Malater, and two others for their parts in the 1956 revolt. A number of others are sentenced to stiff prison terms.

17   FRANCE - The government announces an agreement with Tunisia whereby French troops will be withdrawn from all of Tunisia, except Bizerte.

JULY

UNITED NATIONS - During July and August the USSR vetoes all attempts to settle the crises in Lebanon and Jordan.

SOUTH VIET NAM - The army begins a major reorganization into seven standard-sized combat divisions.

10   CANADA - The US and Canada agree to the establishment
            of a Committee on Joint Defense when President Eisen-
            hower meets with Prime Minister John Diefenbaker in
            Ottawa.

11   SWITZERLAND - The government announces a decision to
            equip its armed forces with nuclear weapons.

14   IRAQ - A military coup, led by General Abdul Karim al-
            Kassem, seizes control of the country. King Faisal II
            is assassinated and a republic is proclaimed. Jordan's
            King Hussein becomes head of the Arab Federation.

14   JORDAN - Upon the assumption of the leadership of the
            Arab Federation, King Hussein asks for military aid
            from the US and Turkey. British troops (parachute
            units of the Red Devil Brigade) are committed to de-
            fend the country (17 July).

15-19   LEBANON - In response to Lebanese President Camille
            Chamoun's appeal for help in light of the Iraqi coup
            and because of the fear of civil war allegedly pro-
            voked by the UAR, more than 8,000 American Marines and
            Army troops are landed in Lebanon by units of the US
            Sixth Fleet and by air.

18   CAMBODIA - Premier Prince Norodom Sihanouk recognizes
            the Chinese Communists.

19   IRAQ - Iraq and the UAR agree to "stand together."

19   USSR - Premier Khrushchev calls for a five-power sum-
            mit conference to deal with the latest Middle-East
            crisis.

23   BURMA - More than 1,100 rebel Mon tribesmen surrender
            to the government, thus ending a decade-long rebel-
            lion.

23   VENEZUELA - An attempted coup is suppressed.

26   ROMANIA - The government announces the final departure
            of Soviet occupation forces.

30   ALBANIA - Along with the Greeks, the Albanian govern-
            ment certifies the Corfu Strait as being clear of
            mines.

AUGUST

2   JORDAN - King Hussein dissolves the Arab Federation.

3   COMMUNIST CHINA – At the conclusion of a four-day secret meeting in Peking, Mao Tse-tung and Soviet Premier Khrushchev call for the immediate withdrawal of American and British troops in Lebanon and Jordan and for a summit meeting on the Middle East.

4   CYPRUS – After year-long fighting, Greek Cypriot underground leader, Colonel George Grivas, declares a cease-fire which marks the beginning of the end of anti-British and anti-Turkish violence on the island.

5   CHILE – After ten years of official banishment, the Communist Party is reinstated.

8   UNITED NATIONS – In response to President Eisenhower's request, an emergency session of the UN Security Council is called to deal with the Lebanon crisis.

16   UNITED STATES – The US Navy announces that the nuclear submarine USS Nautilus successfully completed an undersea transit of the North Polar icecap.

21   UNITED NATIONS – The General Assembly passes a resolution that will allow the withdrawal of more than 14,300 US troops and a large contingent of British forces from Lebanon. This action is completed by November.

23   NATIONALIST CHINA – The Chinese Communists begin heavy shelling of Nationalist positions on the offshore islands of Quemoy and Matsu. This shelling is also designed to prevent the delivery of supplies to the offshore islands.

27   UNITED STATES – President Eisenhower declares Quemoy and Matsu islands are vital to the defense of Formosa (Taiwan). An aircraft carrier and four destroyers are transferred from the US Sixth Fleet in the Mediterranean to join the US Seventh Fleet guarding the Nationalist stronghold on Taiwan.

SEPTEMBER

     UNITED STATES – The US Seventh Fleet begins escorting supply ships to Quemoy and Matsu islands.

4   UNITED STATES – Secretary of State John Foster Dulles states that the US will defend the Taiwanese islands of Quemoy and Matsu and that the US rejects the 12-mile limit set by Communist China along its coastline.

7   VENEZUELA – Another coup attempt is suppressed.

10   FRANCE - The government signs an agreement with South
            Viet Nam providing 1,490 million francs for the South
            Vietnamese government's agrarian reform program.

11   UNITED STATES - President Eisenhower declares the US
            will fight to perserve Quemoy and Matsu, but goes on
            to state that negotiation would be a better course of
            action.

11   GREAT BRITAIN - The government declares it is not
            bound by the US decision to defend Quemoy and Matsu.

15   POLAND - Talks open in Warsaw between the US and Com-
            munist China at the ambassadorial level.

19   EGYPT - An Algerian provisional government-in-exile is
            established in Cairo by Algerian nationalist leaders.
            Ferhat Abbas is named Premier.

26   BURMA - The army takes over power at the request of
            Premier U Nu who resigns in favor of General Ne Win, a
            Communist sympathizer.

28   FRENCH SOMALILAND - The inhabitants decide to remain a
            French overseas territory rather than achieve indepen-
            dence. This is confirmed by the Territorial Assembly
            on 12 December.

30   UNITED STATES - Faced with serious opposition, the
            government announces it does not have a commitment to
            defend Quemoy and Matsu.

30   USSR - The Soviet Union resumes nuclear testing after
            a three-month suspension.

OCTOBER

            CUBA - Fidel Castro's rebel forces assume the offen-
            sive and move out of the Sierra Maestra mountains in
            Oriente Province.

1   MOROCCO - Morocco joins the Arab League.

1   TUNISIA - Tunisia joins the Arab League.

2   GUINEA - President Sekou Toure proclaims his nation an
            independent republic. Membership in the French Commu-
            nity is rejected.

6   COMMUNIST CHINA - The government declares a one-week
            cease-fire and calls for talks between the two Chinas.

7   PAKISTAN - After dismissing the premier and abrogating the constitution, President Iskander Mirza declares martial law. He appoints General Mohammed Ayub Khan to administer the martial law.

8   UNITED STATES - The Department of Defense announces it has halted convoy operations to Quemoy and Matsu but is ready to begin them again, if the Communist Chinese resume the shelling.

14   MADAGASCAR - The Malagasy Republic is proclaimed within the structure of the French Community.

17   NATIONALIST CHINA - Chiang Kai-shek announces his determination to maintain control over the offshore islands.

20   UNITED NATION - The French announce they will not be bound by any nuclear test-ban agreement that they have not signed.

20   JORDAN - British troops begin their withdrawal.

20   THAILAND - Military rule is established in Thailand when Field Marshal Sarit Thanarat leads a bloodless coup against the year-old government of Premier Pote Sarasin.

20   COMMUNIST CHINA - The Communists again begin shelling the Nationalist Chinese offshore islands of Quemoy and Matsu.

21   MOROCCO - An army revolt begins when forces loyal to King Mohammed V are attacked by central government forces. The revolt spreads to Rif tribesman who are dissatisfied with the Istiqlal Party's rule. The Rif uprising lasts into 1960.

21   BOLIVIA - A military revolt is suppressed.

22   COMMUNIST CHINA - The government announces the withdrawal of the last of its military forces from North Korea.

23   NATIONALIST CHINA - Generalissimo Chiang Kai-shek issues a communique in which he announces that his forces will not attempt a return to the mainland, and that his control over the offshore islands might be relaxed to reduce tensions.

24   FRANCE - DeGaulle offers to negotiate a cease-fire in Algeria. The rebels reject the offer the next day (25 October).

25   LEBANON - The last US forces are withdrawn from Leba-
        non after a new coalition government, led by General
        Fuad Shihad (Shehab/Chehab), takes control of the
        country.

27   PAKISTAN - President Mirza resigns and appoints Ayub
        Khan as his successor.

29   JORDAN - Withdrawal of British forces is completed.

31   UNITED NATIONS - The nuclear test-ban conference opens
        in Geneva. After two years the meetings accomplish
        nothing.

31   UNITED STATES - The State Department reveals that
        Chiang Kai-shek has reserved to himself the right to
        attack the mainland if a large-scale revolt starts
        against the Communist government.

31   UNITED STATES - The US unilaterally halts testing of
        nuclear weapons for one year.

NOVEMBER

        THAILAND - A number of clashes between Thai frontier
        forces and Cambodian army units occur over the next 60
        days.

4   UNITED STATES - A moratorium on nuclear testing goes
        into effect with Great Britain, the USSR, and the US
        agreeing.

17   SUDAN - The elected government is ousted by the Army's
        leader, Lieutenant General Ibrahim 'Abboud, who de-
        clares himself Premier and suspends the constitution.

23   GHANA - At Accra, Prime Minister Kwame Nkrumah of
        Ghana and Premier Sekou Toure of Guinea issue a joint
        declaration calling for the confederation of their two
        countries.

25   SENEGAL - The nation becomes independent within the
        French Community.

27   SOVIET UNION - Premier Khrushchev demands the Four-
        Power occupation of Berlin terminate immediately.

28   GABON - The nation becomes independent within the
        French Community.

28   REPUBLIC OF THE CONGO - The Middle Congo is proclaimed
        an independent republic within the French Community.

28   MAURITANIA - The nation becomes independent within the
            French Community.

28   MALI - The French Sudan is proclaimed to be the inde-
            pendent Republic of Mali within the French Community.

DECEMBER

            USSR - After completing the nuclear weapons test pro-
            gram it began in September, the Soviet Union quietly
            halts further testing.

            UNITED STATES - The government announces the existence
            of a military arms treaty between the USSR and Iraq.

1   NEW CENTRAL AFRICAN REPUBLIC - The nation is pro-
            claimed independent within the French Community.

4   DAHOMEY - The nation is declared independent within
            the French Community.

4   IVORY COAST - The former territory of French West
            Africa becomes autonomous.

6   USSR - The government announces an agreement to build
            a petroleum pipeline to link its oil fields with Po-
            land and East Germany.

10   FINLAND - President Kekkonen admits the chief goal of
            Finnish foreign policy is the maintenance of good re-
            lations with the USSR.

12   ALGERIA - DeGaulle replaces General Raoul Salan, as
            the French representative in Algeria, with Paul
            Delouvrier. Salan is named Inspector General of the
            French armed forces. Air Force General Maurice Challe
            is named military commander in Algeria.

14   UNITED STATES - Along with its British and French al-
            lies, the US states it has no intention of abandoning
            Berlin.

16   NATO - The NATO Council endorses Western determination
            to remain in Berlin.

21   FRANCE - Charles DeGaulle is elected President of
            France and the Fifth Republic is proclaimed.

1959

LAOS - Using recently furnished US military aid, Premier Phoui Sananikone begins a campaign to wipe out the Communist-inspired, and aided, Pathet Lao insurgency.

LAOS - North Vietnamese army units begin occupying key areas in the Laotian border territories to ensure safe passage of NVA military supplies into South Viet Nam. This marks the beginning of the development of the "Ho Chi Minh Trail."

ALGERIA - General Maurice Challe, French Air Force, assumes the duties of Commander in Chief of the French forces in Algeria.

MOROCCO - Rif tribesmen are dealt a series of defeats in their ongoing war against the central government.

1   CUBA - President Fulgencio Batista resigns his office and flees to the Dominican Republic and thence to Miami. Fidel Castro enters Santiago one day after taking Santa Clara.

3   CUBA - Castro's forces enter Havana.

4-5   BELGIAN CONGO - Seventy-one are killed when anti-European rioting breaks out in Leopoldville.

7   UNITED STATES - The Department of State announces that the US has granted recognition to the Castro government in Cuba.

10   USSR - The government rejects the West's proposal for
            a meeting on German reunification. As a counterplan,
            the Soviets propose a 28-nation conference aimed at
            demilitarizing Germany and continuing its division.
            They also propose giving East Germany control over ac-
            cess to Berlin.

13   BELGIUM - The government announces that the Belgian
            Congo will be granted independence at some indefinite
            time in the future.

17   GREAT BRITAIN - A financial settlement is reached with
            Egypt over the Egyptian seizure of the Suez Canal.

18   MALI - The Federal State of Mali is formed by the mer-
            ger of Senegal with Mali (French Sudan).

FEBRUARY

11   LAOS - Premier Phoui Sananikone abrogates Laotian ad-
            herence to the 1954 Geneva Accords stating his country
            would look to the UN to settle its disputes.

16   CUBA - Fidel Castro assumes the role of Premier.

19   GREAT BRITAIN - The government announces an agreement
            with Turkey and Greece dealing with the independence
            of Cyprus.

25   UNITED STATES - The President announces that Pakistan
            has accepted an offer of military aid. He also states
            that India has rejected a similiar offer.

25   INDIA - Prime Minister Nehru demands the immediate
            withdrawal of all Americans in the UN Ceasefire Ob-
            server Team in Kashmir because the US has supplied
            military assistance to Pakistan.

MARCH

2-3   NYASALAND - Rioting breaks out after the British gov-
            ernment outlaws the African National Congress and ar-
            rests nationalist leader Hastings Banda. Before the
            rioting ends at least 32 people are killed by security
            forces.

3   IRAN - The Shah announces his government no longer ad-
            heres to the 1921 agreement whereby Soviet forces can
            enter Iran if the USSR feels threatened by the pres-
            ence of foreign troops in that country.

3   UNITED STATES - The Chief of Naval Operations, Admiral
           Arleigh Burke warns of the increased danger posed to
           American naval vessels and merchant shipping by the
           growing Soviet submarine fleet.

5   UNITED STATES - The government announces bilateral
           defense treaties with Iran, Pakistan, and Turkey.

8-9   IRAQ - A revolt is suppressed in Mosul.

13   TIBET - Fighting breaks out in Lhasa between Communist
           Chinese troops and the native populace.

13   CYPRUS - Following agreements signed with Turkey and
           Greece, the British government reaches a settlement
           with the Greek and Turkish Cypriot communities, and a
           cease-fire is ordered, which ends years of fighting.

14   NATO - A crisis develops between the US and France
           when President DeGaulle refuses to allow the French
           Navy to put one-third of its Mediterranean fleet under
           NATO control.

19-20   USSR - In an exchange of heated remarks, Premier
           Khrushchev calls Egypt's President Nasser a "hot head"
           for his comments about a Communist attempt to cause a
           rift among the Arab states. Nasser responds by stating
           that the Soviet Union is meddling in Middle Eastern
           affairs.

24   IRAQ - Premier Karim al-Kassem announces Iraq's with-
           drawal from the Baghdad Pact.

26   UNITED STATES - The Western Allies invite the USSR to
           a conference of foreign ministers that will deal with
           the German peace treaty issue and with the status of
           Berlin.

28   TIBET - The Chinese Communists dissolve the Tibetan
           government headed by the Dalai Lama and replace it
           with a puppet government under the Panchen Lama. Three
           days later (31 March) the Dalai Lama flees into exile
           in India.

30   USSR - The Soviet government accepts the invitation to
           join in a conference of foreign ministers on the Ger-
           man situation.

31   TIBET - The Dalai Lama flees to India following an
           anti-Chinese uprising in Lhasa. The Indo-Tibetan
           border is closed as Chinese and Indian forces skir-
           mish.

APRIL

UNITED STATES - In response to Soviet demands, the US curtails flights in the corridors to Berlin to less than 10,000 feet, altitude.

SOUTH VIET NAM - VC terrorism and sabotage increase.

3　　INDIA - The Dalai Lama seeks the protection of the Indian government upon fleeing the Chinese Communists who have taken power in Tibet.

4　　ARAB LEAGUE - The League declares the pro-Communist government in Iraq to be a threat to peace in the Middle East even with several member nations, including Iraq, Jordan, Tunisia, and Libya, boycotting the meeting.

17　　UNITED STATES - On a visit to the US, Cuban leader Fidel Castro states his regime is not Communist.

19　　BOLIVIA - An uprising in La Paz is suppressed.

23　　TIBET - The puppet government claims it has defeated the rebels in southeastern Tibet and sealed the border with India.

24　　PANAMA - A Cuban-inspired "invasion" by about 100 men takes place and is crushed by the army. Almost all of the invaders are killed or captured by 1 May.

27　　COMMUNIST CHINA - Mao Tse-tung is replaced as head of state by Liu Shao-chi.

MAY

SOUTH VIET NAM - US advisors are assigned to regimental-level units of RVNAF.

NORTH VIET NAM - The Central Committee of the Communist Party calls for the overthrow of the Diem regime in SVN and the expulsion of the US.

1　　GUINEA - Premier Toure and Ghana's Prime Minister, Kwame Nkrumah, sign a draft agreement at Conakry, initiating the union of an independent Africa.

4　　MOSCOW - The Kremlin sends a note to Tokyo promising permanent neutrality. In return, the Soviets want Japan to order all US bases closed.

11   SWITZERLAND - The Conference of Foreign Ministers
        opens in Geneva. Little or no progress will be made by
        the time the conference closes on 5 August.

30   NICARAQUA - Loyal troops defeat a Communist Cuba-sup-
        ported rebel invasion. Mopping-up operations end on 14
        June.

JUNE

        UNITED STATES - The government announces that Iraq has
        spurned all US aid.

3   SINGAPORE - Singapore becomes an independent state.

4   GREECE - The government rejects the Soviet demand that
        no missile bases be established in Greek territory.

6   USSR - Premier Nikita Khrushchev demands the Western
        Allies accept a nuclear free zone in the Balkans or he
        will place Soviet missile bases in Albania, Bulgaria,
        and Romania.

12   EGYPT - Premier Ferhat Abbas, of the Algerian provi-
        sional government in Cairo, declares a willingness to
        negotiate an end to the fighting in Algeria.

20   SOUTH KOREA - The UN Command charges North Korea with
        building fortifications in the DMZ in violation of the
        truce agreement.

23   DOMINICAN REPUBLIC - A small Cuban-sponsored invasion
        is quickly squashed by Trujillo government forces.

26   BOLIVIA - A revolt in Santa Cruz is suppressed.

JULY

5   INDONESIA - The Constituent Assembly is dissolved by
        President Sukharno as his Communist Party (PKI) be-
        comes more powerful.

8   UNITED STATES - After France and the US fail to reach
        an agreement on nuclear weapons stockpiling, the US
        orders 200 combat aircraft redeployed from airfields
        in France to bases in West Germany and Great Britain.

8   SOUTH VIET NAM - Two US military advisors are killed
        near Bien Hoa. They are the first US casualties of the
        war.

14-20   IRAQ - An uprising against the government is put down, with heavy loss of life, by loyal military forces.

30-31   LAOS - Communist Pathet Lao forces carry out a series of attacks against Laotian military posts located in the northern provinces.

31   INDIA - The government of India takes over the Communist-run state of Kerala and bans the Communist Party there.

AUGUST

12   OAS - A week-long emergency meeting opens in Santiago, Chile, to deal with the problem of the Cuban-inspired tension that is seen developing in the Caribbean basin.

13   HAITI - A small, Cuban-inspired invasion force is defeated by the Haitian army.

18   OAS - The Declaration of Santiago is signed by 21 members in Santiago, Chile. The declaration condemns dictatorships, but also condemns other nations who attempt to overthrow them.

19   TURKEY - At a meeting in Ankara, the Central Treaty Organization (CENTO) is established. Its purpose is to replace the Baghdad Pact. Iraq does not join the new organization, nor does the United States who otherwise supports CENTO's aims.

20   OAS - Meeting in San Jose, Costa Rica, the Western Hemisphere Foreign Ministers issue a statement condemning the Dominican Republic for its aggression against Venezuela.

26   UNITED STATES - The government extends its unilateral nuclear test ban for two additional months.

27   UNITED STATES - The US agrees to increase military aid to Laos.

28   OAS - The Foreign Ministers Conference concludes with the signing of the Declaration of San Jose (Costa Rica). This declaration condemns Sino-Soviet attempts to import Communism into the Western Hemisphere.

28   INDIA - The government announces that Communist China has violated the Indian border where it joins China and Tibet.

SEPTEMBER

SOUTH VIET NAM - The military reorganization that began in 1958 is completed when the last of four field
and six light divisions are converted into seven
standard divisions.

2   LAOS - Pathet Lao forces reinforced by NVA regulars
open an offensive designed to secure control of
northwestern Laos.

4   LAOS - The government asks the UN for military assistance to halt the North Vietnamese aggression in
northwestern Laos.

7   UNITED NATIONS - The Security Council votes to investigate the charges that North Vietnamese has committed
aggression against Laos.

9   UNITED NATIONS - The UN receives a request from the
exiled Dalai Lama for action in settling the Tibetan
situation.

9   USSR - The government disavows any direct involvement
in the current Chinese-Indian border dispute.

13   AUSTRIA - Demonstrations break out protesting Italian
violations of the 1946 agreement dealing with the
Southern Tyrol.

16   UNITED NATIONS - A UN investigation team arrives in
Vientiane, Laos, to document the North Vietnamese aggression.

16   FRANCE - DeGaulle offers Algeria the right to choose
its future.

26   CEYLON - Prime Minister Sirimavo Bandaranaike dies of
wounds she receives in an assassination attempt.

28   UNITED STATES - Upon his departure from a visit to the
US, Premier Khrushchev promises President Eisenhower
that he will not insist on a deadline to settle the
issue of Berlin.

28   EGYPT - The Algerian provisional government in Cairo
offers to negotiate a cease-fire. France rejects the
offer.

29   COMMUNIST CHINA - On a visit to China, Soviet Premier
Khrushchev warns against testing Western resolve in
the Indian border dispute.

OCTOBER

7   UNITED STATES - The government warns that a Chinese
           Communist attack on Formosa could lead to "all-out
           war."

10   UNITED STATES - The government announces an agreement
           with Turkey that will allow the US to place inter-
           mediate-range ballistic missiles (IRBM) on Turkish
           soil.

21   USSR - Khrushchev notifies President Eisenhower of his
           support of the Chinese Communist position in the off-
           shore islands dispute with Nationalist China.

26   INDIA - Chinese Communist border troops and an Indian
           police patrol clash along the border in the Kashmiri
           province of Ladakh.

NOVEMBER

           RWANDA - A massive uprising of Hutu (Bahutu) tribesmen
           begins against the ruling Tutsi (Batutsi/Watusi) tri-
           bal aristocracy. Many of the Tutsi who are able flee
           into the Belgian Congo, Uganda, and Tanganyika.

3   UNITED STATES - The Department of State refuses to al-
           low the establishment of a Cuban government-in-exile
           in the US.

3   PANAMA - Anti-American rioting breaks out in Panama
           City.

6   UNITED NATIONS - The UN investigation team in Laos
           states it cannot identify clear evidence of North
           Vietnamese aggression.

10   SUDAN - A third attempt to overthrow the regime of
           General Ibrahim 'Abboud fails. Five officers are
           executed and five imprisoned as a result of their
           implication in the revolt.

22   MOROCCO - At a meeting in Casablanca, President Eisen-
           hower agrees to King Mohammed V's demand for the re-
           moval of all US military installations located in
           Morocco by the end of 1963.

30   HUNGARY - Hungarian Communist Party Secretary Janos
           Kadar announces that Soviet troops will remain in
           Hungary as long as the international situation re-
           quires their presence.

DECEMBER

PARAGUAY - An Argentina-based rebel force invades Paraguay and is crushed. Over the next year, several more such incursions are defeated.

1   ANTARCTICA - A 12-nation treaty is signed declaring the continent a region for peaceful research.

3   PAKISTAN - The government protests the possible partition, by the Indian government, of Ladakh Province, which it also claims.

10   ICELAND - The US withdraws the last of its troops ending a US military presence that has been in Iceland since the beginning of WWII.

14   CYPRUS - Archbishop Makarios is elected the island nation's first President.

15   LAOS - King Savang Vathana accepts the resignation of Premier Sananikone and places the army in control of the country. General Phoumi Nosavan is named to head the military government.

19   COMMUNIST CHINA - Quemoy is again shelled by artillery located on the Chinese mainland, and Chinese Communist MiG fighters fly over the island.

30   UNITED STATES - The first Polaris-class submarine, the USS George Washington, is commissioned.

31   UNITED STATES - When nuclear test ban talks in Geneva fail to produce a treaty, the government announces it is no longer bound to its unilateral test ban.

Notes

1960

VENEZUELA - A long period of Communist-inspired insurgency begins.

JANUARY

2   NICARAGUA - A long period of border raiding begins along Nicaragua's borders with Honduras and Costa Rica.

14   USSR - Premier Nikita Khrushchev announces a plan to reduce the size of the Soviet armed forces by one-third over the next two years.

19   UNITED STATES - A mutual security pact is signed with Japan.

19   UNITED STATES - The Defense Department admits that the previously reported "missile gap," which seemingly put the USSR ahead of the US in strategic weapons delivery systems, was erroneous.

20   USSR - The government announces the successful launch of a ballistic missile and claims it travelled more than 7,750 nautical miles and struck within 1.25 miles of its expected impact point in the Pacific Ocean.

25   ALGERIA - French ultra-nationalists stage a one-week uprising to protest French actions in dealing with the Algerians.

28   BURMA - The government signs a ten-year non-aggression pact with Communist China.

FEBRUARY

5   SOUTH VIET NAM - The government requests that the US
         double the size of its military assistance and advi-
         sory group from 342 to 685 American personnel.

6   BURMA - National elections are held in Burma, and
         power is returned to civilian authorities. U Nu is re-
         elected Premier.

13   FRANCE - The French detonate a nuclear weapon in the
         Sahara Desert in southwestern Algeria.

13   CUBA - Fidel Castro receives $100 million in credit
         from the Soviet Union.

16   GREAT BRITAIN - The government announces a new strate-
         gic policy that emphasizes submarine-launched and air-
         launched ballistic missiles rather than depending upon
         land-based nuclear missiles.

17   PAKISTAN - Ayub Khan is elected president.

MARCH

         UNITED STATES - The US Army Chief of Staff, General
         Lyman L. Lemnitzer, reports to the Joint Chiefs of
         Staff (JCS) that the situation in SVN has deteriorated
         markedly during the past months. Lemnitzer recommends
         to the JCS that ARVN change the emphasis in its train-
         ing toward the development of an anti-guerrilla capa-
         bility.

6   MOROCCO - US forces begin the promised withdrawal from
         military bases in Morocco by evacuating American per-
         sonnel from Ben Slimane.

15   SWITZERLAND - A ten-nation conference on disarmament
         opens in Geneva.

16   BELGIUM - The government declares that a decision has
         been reached to grant independence to the Belgian
         Congo on 30 June 1960, and to allow general elections
         in the Congo before that date.

16   UNITED STATES - The Defense Department claims the US
         has a nuclear weapons capability several times that of
         the USSR.

19   BOLIVIA - An uprising, led by the National Police, is
         suppressed by loyal army forces.

21   UNITED STATES – A formal protest is presented to the representatives of the Union of South Africa following the news of a massacre of black civilians at Sharpburg, near Johannesburg. Some 72 are killed and many more are wounded in the incident when South African police open fire on demonstrators.

21   COMMUNIST CHINA – An agreement is signed with Nepal to set up a commission to determine the border between the two states.

30   UNITED STATES – In a joint communique issued at the end of a visit to Washington, British Prime Minister Macmillan announces Anglo-American willingness to stop testing small-scale nuclear weapons as soon as a strategic nuclear arms agreement is signed.

APRIL

      MOROCCO – The Rif uprising is finally quelled.

13   GREAT BRITAIN – The British government announces it has stopped all development of new ballistic missiles in favor of US-developed weapons.

17   SOUTH VIET NAM – The ICC is reported to have agreed to the doubling of the size of the USMAAGV, even though the North Vietnamese protest.

19   SOUTH KOREA – After being re-elected president (15 March), Syngman Rhee is faced with massive student demonstrations (beginning 6 April) caused by the charge of "election rigging." When troops and police open fire on the crowds, over 125 are killed.

25   USSR – Premier Khrushchev threatens to cut off Allied access to Berlin by signing a separate peace treaty with East Germany, a threat he said he would back up with Soviet military power.

26   UNITED STATES – The US Commander in Chief, Pacific (CINCPAC) submits a study on combating insurgency in SVN and recommends an RVN national emergency organization and a coordinated national plan.

26   COMMUNIST CHINA – Premier Chou En-Lai refuses to accept the McMahon Line as his country's border with India.

27   UNITED STATES – President Eisenhower declares that US forces will not evacuate West Berlin.

27   SOUTH KOREA - Syngman Rhee is forced to resign the presidency and leave the country. Chung Huh, the Foreign Minister, is appointed Provisional President.

27   TOGOLAND - After two years of autonomous rule, Togo is granted full independence by France.

28   TURKEY - A month of student rioting begins. Military Academy cadets soon join in. By 21 May, martial law is declared and the widespread unrest is put down by military and police units with heavy loss of life.

MAY

1   USSR - Near Sverdlovsk, deep in the Soviet Union, an American U-2 high-altitude reconnaisance plane is shot down by a Soviet SA-2 surface-to-air missile. The aircraft's pilot, Francis Gary Powers, is captured alive.

2   UNITED STATES - The Defense Department authorizes the Chief, MAAGV, to assign military advisors to armored, artillery, and separate Marine battalion-level organizations.

2   SOUTH VIET NAM - The MAAG and TERM are consolidated. The total authorized US military strength in SVN now stands at 685.

5   UNITED STATES - The government pledges increased military aid to SVN and authorizes the increase in advisor strength to 685.

7   USSR - Premier Khrushchev informs the Supreme Soviet that an American spy plane has been shot down over Soviet territory.

7   UNITED STATES - The government announces plans to resume its underground testing program for nuclear weapons.

14   COMMUNIST CHINA - The rift between Communist China and the Soviet Union becomes more apparent when Mao Tse-Tung criticizes Khrushchev for his handling of the U-2 incident.

16   FRANCE - Soviet Premier Khrushchev wrecks the summit meeting with Eisenhower because the US President refuses to apologize for the U-2 incident.

25   UNITED STATES - The President informs the nation of the loss of a U-2 reconnaisance plane over the Soviet Union and tells of the aborted summit conference.

27   TURKEY - Premier Adnan Menderes and his cabinet are ousted by a military coup led by General Jemal Gursel. The junta, called the Turkish National Union Committee, begins preparations to hold free elections.

30   USSR - The Soviet government announces that any base, anywhere in the world, from which spy planes take off to fly over Soviet territory will be attacked by rockets.

30   SOUTH VIET NAM - Thirty members of the US Special Forces arrive in the RVN to conduct training in counterinsurgency for the ARVN.

JUNE

1-2   UNITED STATES - A top-level policy conference on Southeast Asia is held in Hawaii.

3   TIBET - Anti-Communist rioting breaks out in several locations.

6   UNITED STATES - The US enters an agreement with Great Britain dealing with British procurement of US ballistic missiles.

6   SOUTH VIET NAM - The Chief, MAAGV, Lieutenant General Sam Williams, institutes the planning for a full-scale counterinsurgency training program.

10   TIBET - Heavy fighting breaks out between the populace and Communist Chinese troops.

10   INDIA - The government claims heavy fighting between Indian and Chinese Communist forces on the Indian side of the frontier.

13   CAMBODIA - Prince Sihanouk becomes Chief of State.

13   ARGENTINA - A mutinous army unit in San Luis surrenders without bloodshed when the uprising it began is not supported by other army elements.

16   JAPAN - Widespread anti-American demonstrations over the last three weeks forces the Japanese government to request President Eisenhower postpone his proposed visit.

20   MALI - The former French colony of Sudan, which as the Sudanese Republic has been self-governing since 1958, is granted full independence by France. The union with Senegal continues.

20   SENEGAL - The former French colony is declared independent.

21   USSR - Khrushchev publicly attacks Mao Tse-Tung in a letter circulated at a Communist Party meeting held in Bucharest, Romania.

23   CUBA - Castro threatens to seize all American-owned property in Cuba.

24   VENEZUELA - An attempt is made on the life of President Romulo Betancourt.

25   FRANCE - Seeking an end to the Algerian crisis, French and Algerian officials open secret talks in Paris.

25   MADAGASCAR - The French island colony becomes the independent Malagasy Republic, and a part of the French community of nations.

28   COMMUNIST CHINA - The government claims Nepalese troops were fired on when they strayed into Tibetan territory.

29   NEPAL - The government reports increased tension along the border with Communist China.

30   BELGIAN CONGO - The nation is declared independent and assumes the name Democratic Congo Republic. President Joseph Kasavubu appoints Patrice Lumumba to be his Premier. Widespread rioting breaks out throughout the countryside.

30   UNITED STATES - CINCPAC submits a draft counterinsurgency operations plan for the RVN to Washington.

JULY

            RHODESIA - A period of violence begins in the southern part of the country.

1   SOMALIA - The two colonial provinces of British and Italian Somalia are combined and made independent.

6   UNITED STATES - President Eisenhower cuts Cuban sugar imports by 95%.

9   USSR - Premier Khrushchev threatens the use of Soviet missiles if the US intervenes militarily in Cuba.

12   USSR - According to Premier Khrushchev, the US Monroe Doctrine (1823) has died a "natural death."

14   DEMOCRATIC CONGO REPUBLIC - Premier Patrice Lumumba asks the UN for aid following severe troop mutinies and separatist-inspired unrest in several regions of the country. Katanga and Kasai Provinces break away from the central government in Leopoldville (11 July).

14   UNITED NATIONS - The Security Council votes to send a UN Emergency Force (UNEF) into the former Belgian Congo and orders the withdrawal of Belgian forces. The UNEF will reach 20,000, mostly from African nations including Tunisia, and will be under the command of Swedish Major General Karl Von Horn and will remain in the Congo until August, 1964.

14   UNITED STATES - The US State Department declares the nation will adhere to the Monroe Doctrine and that the Soviet Union is bent upon world-wide expansion.

20   UNITED STATES - The first successful submerged launch of a Polaris ballistic missile is accomplished.

22   UNITED NATIONS - The UN begins implementing the Belgian troop withdrawal for the Congo.

27   SWITZERLAND - Without warning, the Soviet Union breaks up the Geneva disarmament conference.

28   ARAB LEAGUE - When Iran recognizes Israel, the League imposes an economic boycott on the Tehran government.

31   MALAYA - The state of emergency which has gripped the country since 1948 is lifted.

AUGUST

SOUTH VIET NAM - MAAGV issues a comprehensive study on the tactics and techniques of counterinsurgency operations. Counterinsurgency training for ARVN begins. To accomplish this goal, MAAGV reorganizes to allow for a greater number of American personnel to be assigned to field duties.

1   DAHOMEY - France declares the new nation's independence.

3   DOMINICAN REPUBLIC - Popular unrest continues as Joaquin Balaguer is sworn in as President.

3   NIGER - The former French colony is declared independent.

5   UPPER VOLTA - The former French colony achieves full independence.

7   IVORY COAST - After ten years of sporadic disorder, the Ivory Coast is granted its full independence by France. (Ivory Coast had gained its autonomy on 4 December 1958.)

9   LAOS - A military coup, led by Captain Kong Le, overthrows the pro-western government of Tiao Samsonith. Samsonith is replaced by Prince Souvanna Phouma as Premier.

11   CHAD - The former autonomous French colony is declared independent.

12   DEMOCRATIC CONGO REPUBLIC - UN Secretary General Dag Hammarakjold leads a contingent of about 250 Swedish UN forces into Katanga Province. This creates a major crisis; the breakaway government of Moise Tshombe at first refuses the force's landing request at Elizabethville. They are finally allowed to land.

13   CENTRAL AFRICAN REPUBLIC - The former French colony is declared independent.

14   SOMALIA - A series of border clashes with Ethiopia are reported.

15   REPUBLIC OF CONGO - Called Congo (Brazzaville), this former French colony is declared independent.

15   OAS - A five-nation investigatory committee reports that the attempted assassination of Venezuelan President, Romulo Betancourt, was instigated by Dominican Republic officials.

15   LAOS - Neutralist Prince Souvanna Phouma is named to head the new government.

16   CYPRUS - Cyprus is declared independent. Great Britain, Greece, and Turkey agree to leave forces on the island to protect it.

17   USSR - Pilot Francis Gary Powers pleads guilty to flying a spy mission for the US over Soviet territory. Two days later (19 August) he is sentenced to ten years in prison.

17   GABON - This former French colony is declared independent.

20   MALI - The union of the former Sudanese Republic with Senegal breaks down after just two months of total independence.

24   DEMOCRATIC CONGO REPUBLIC - The central government
            under Patrice Lumumba sends troops into Kasai Province
            to put down the revolt.

29   JORDAN - Along with 11 others, Premier Hazza al-Majali
            is killed in a bombing.

31   BELGIUM - The government announces it has completed
            the withdrawal of almost all of its troops stationed
            in the Congo.

SEPTEMBER

1   SOUTH VIET NAM - Lieutenant General Lionel C. McGarr
            succeeds Lieutenant General Sam Williams as Chief,
            MAAGV.

2   LAOS - Civil war breaks out over makeup of the gov-
            ernment. The Pathet Lao, Prince Souvanna Phouma's
            Neutralist Party, and right-wing anti-Communist groups
            all are involved.

5   DEMOCRATIC CONGO REPUBLIC - President Joseph Kasa-
            vubu removes Patrice Lumumba from office. Lumumba re-
            fuses to relinquish the premiership and calls his cab-
            inet into session.

8   EAST GERMANY - The government announces that hence-
            forth all West Germans traveling into East Berlin will
            have to obtain an East German police pass. The Allies
            state this is a most serious violation of the Four-
            Power Agreement on access to Berlin.

11   DEMOCRATIC CONGO REPUBLIC - United Nations forces
            prevent Lumumba's attempt to seize the Leopoldville
            radio station.

12   DEMOCRATIC CONGO REPUBLIC - Congo army troops arrest
            Patrice Lumumba. The following day (13 September)
            Lumumba is voted extraordinary powers by both houses
            of Parliament.

14   DEMOCRATIC CONGO REPUBLIC - Control of the government
            is seized by Colonel Joseph Mobutu. President Kasavubu
            remains in power although Lumumba is ousted. Kasavubu
            appoints Joseph Ileo as premier. Both Kasavubu and
            Lumumba send delegations to the UN which refuses to
            accept either of them.

16   DEMOCRATIC CONGO REPUBLIC - President Kasavubu orders
            the departure of the Soviet and Czech diplomatic mis-
            sions for their sponsorship of Patrice Lumumba.

20   UNITED NATIONS - The General Assembly passes a vote of confidence in Secretary General Dag Hammerskjold after a bitter attack on his Congo policy by the Soviet Union.

21   UNITED NATIONS - The Austrian Foreign Minister, Bruno Kreisky, asks the General Assembly to investigate the status of the German-speaking minority in the Southern Tyrol.

22   MALI - Mali declares itself the Republic of Mali.

23   UNITED NATIONS - After an unsuccessful attempt to unseat Secretary General Dag Hammarskjold (20 September), Soviet Premier Khrushchev demands his replacement by a _troika_ that would consist of an eastern, western, and neutral member.

23   NATO - NATO headquarters announces the establishment of a unified air defense command for Europe.

27   UNITED NATIONS - In a speech before the 15th session of the General Assembly, the Secretary of the Romanian Communist Party, Gheorghe Gheorghe-Dej, affirms the possibility of the creation of a neutral buffer zone in the Balkans that would be composed of Romania, Hungary, Bulgaria, Albania, Yugoslavia, Greece, and Turkey.

OCTOBER

            DEMOCRATIC CONGO REPUBLIC - Widespread misbehavior by Congolese army troops causes considerable suffering throughout the country. Many die. There are several major clashes with UN forces.

16   CUBA - The government nationalizes all banks and large industries.

19   UNITED STATES - The government orders an almost total embargo on all goods to Cuba. Medical supplies and food are exempted from the order.

26   UNITED STATES - President Eisenhower assures South Vietnamese President Diem that the US will continue assistance to the RVN.

26   EL SALVADOR - President Jose Maria Lemus is overthrown by a military junta led by Colonel Cesar Yanes Urias.

28   OAS - The US charges that Cuba is receiving massive military aid from the Soviet Union and its allies.

NOVEMBER

SOUTH VIET NAM - The training of ARVN Rangers begins.

EL SALVADOR - A military junta overthrows the government.

1   GREAT BRITAIN - The government announces an agreement with the US that allows for the establishment of a US naval base at Holy Loch on the Firth of Clyde to be used for nuclear-powered and nuclear-armed submarines.

1   UNITED STATES - President Eisenhower warns the Castro government in Cuba that the US will take whatever steps are necessary to prevent a threatened Cuban takeover of the US naval base at Guantanamo Bay.

9-10   COSTA RICA - Costa Rican army units attack a group of Nicaraguan insurgents that has been assembling in the border area.

10   SOUTH VIET NAM - The government informs the ICC that the October Communist attacks in Kontum and Pleiku involved regular NVA troops sent through Laos and commanded by high-ranking NVA officers. This, they claim, constitutes open aggression.

11-12   SOUTH VIET NAM - Members of the Vietnamese airborne forces led by Colonel Thi attempt to depose President Ngo Dinh Diem. Diem is restored to power by loyal army troops.

11-15   NICARAGUA - The rebel force that has been engaged by the Costa Rican army invades Nicaragua where it is attacked by Nicaraguan regulars.

13   UNITED STATES - The Department of State expresses satisfaction at the failure of the coup attempt against South Vietnamese President Diem's government.

16   UNITED STATES - US Naval units are dispatched to the waters off Nicaragua and Guatemala to thwart an expected invasion of the two countries from Communist-controlled Cuba.

22   UNITED NATIONS - The General Assembly decides to seat the Kasavubu delegation from the Democratic Congo Republic.

22   HAITI - President Duvalier declares martial law as a means of controlling the rioting at the University of Haiti.

22   SOUTH VIET NAM - President Diem orders the transfer of
            the Civil Guard (Rural Police Constabulary) from the
            Interior Ministry to the Defense Ministry and attaches
            the Self Defense Force (Rural Militia) to the Director
            General of the Civil Guard.

25   DEMOCRATIC CONGO REPUBLIC - Patrice Lumumba escapes
            house arrest but is later captured by troops loyal to
            Colonel Mobutu.

28   MAURITANIA - The former French colony is declared in-
            dependent.

DECEMBER

            SOUTH VIET NAM - Intelligence reports estimate that
            over 4,500 former South Vietnamese, who have been in-
            doctrinated in NVN, have been infiltrated into SVN
            during the past year. There is an overall increase in
            VC attacks, some of which are conducted by
            battalion-size units.

1   DEMOCRATIC CONGO REPUBLIC - Patrice Lumumba is once
            again arrested.

5   USSR - In an affront to the Chinese, 81 Communist
            Parties sign a manifesto supporting Moscow's goal of a
            worldwide Communist victory by "peaceful means."

6   FRANCE - DeGaulle announces plans for the creation of
            a French nuclear strike force that will be independent
            of the US.

7   UNITED STATES - The US withdraws the naval units that
            had been sent into the Caribbean on 16 November to
            protect against expected Communist-inspired invasions
            of Nicaragua and Guatemala.

7   UNITED NATIONS - Ceylon, Yugoslavia, and the UAR with-
            draw their military contingents from the UN peace-
            keeping force in the Congo. Guinea and Morocco soon
            follow the lead and withdraw their forces.

11   ALGERIA - French paratroopers clash with European
            Algerians in Algiers. Sixty are killed.

14   ETHIOPIA - There is an attempted coup in Addis Ababa
            during the absence of Emperor Haile Selassie. Imperial
            troops seize the capital and proclaim Crown Prince
            Asfa-Wossen as king. After three days of fighting
            Haile Salassie is able to restore order.

14   DEMOCRATIC CONGO REPUBLIC - There is a pro-Communist attempt to gain control of the country. Led by Lumumba colleague Antoine Gizenga, the rebellious group expands its power base to large areas of the country.

15   NEPAL - Premier B.P. Kirala is ousted in a coup led by King Mahendra bir Bikham.

16   UNITED STATES - The government offers NATO five SSBNs equipped with 80 Polaris nuclear missiles provided the European NATO countries agree to purchase 100 additional Polaris missiles, and agree to a multinational system for controlling the weapons.

16   LAOS - General Nosavan defeats Kong Le and installs a pro-Western government. Souvanna Phouma flees the country. Kong Le joins the Communist Pathet Lao. Right-wing forces continue to battle the Pathet Lao.

16   EGYPT - The Algerian provisional government calls on all Algerian Muslims to reject the DeGaulle proposal for settlement of the Algerian crisis.

20   BELGIUM - An outbreak of Socialist-led strikes begins that protest the nation's austerity program.

20   NORTH VIET NAM - The Communist Party of NVN forms the National Front for the Liberation of SVN (NLFSV) to reunite the two Viet Nams.

21   UNITED NATIONS - The General Assembly becomes hopelessly deadlocked over what to do next in the Congo.

24   GUINEA - The presidents of Guinea, Ghana, and Mali sign an agreement at Conakry signifying the union of the three nations.

Notes

1961

ANGOLA - An insurrection against Portuguese rule begins that will last until 1974.

NIGER - A long period of unrest begins.

JANUARY

3   UNITED STATES - The government breaks diplomatic relations with Cuba after Castro demands that the number of personnel at the US Embassy in Havana be cut to eleven.

4-7   ANGOLA - Rioting breaks out throughout the country.

6   FRANCE - During a two-day referendum French voters voice their support of DeGaulle's Algerian plan.

7   MOROCCO - Based on the NATO formula, an organization of African states is agreed upon by Ghana, Guinea, Mali, Morocco, and the United Arab Republic (UAR). This becomes known as the Charter of Casablanca.

11   URUGUAY - Castro-inspired antigovernment rioting begins.

22   PORTUGAL - The Portuguese liner S.S. Santa Maria, with its over 600 passengers and crew, is seized by followers of the former (1958) presidential candidate, Lieutenant General Humberto da Silva Delgado. The hijackers, led by a former Portuguese naval captain, Henrique Malta Galvao, sail the ship into the Atlantic.

26   EL SALVADOR - A new junta, composed of military per-
            sonnel and civilians, takes over the government.

27   HONDURAS - A group of exiled Honduran insurgents in-
            vade Honduras from Nicaragua. It is quickly crushed.

27   PORTUGAL -The Portuguese government asks for American
            and British naval support in locating and capturing
            the Santa Maria.

29   NORTH VIET NAM - Radio Hanoi states the NLFSV has the
            "sacred task" of overthrowing the US-Diem clique and
            liberating the south.

31   UNITED STATES - CINCPAC authorizes Chief, MAAGV, to
            detail American advisors down to ARVN infantry
            battalion headquarters and to command posts at lower
            levels, as required.

FEBRUARY

1   ARAB LEAGUE - At a meeting in Baghdad, the League
            votes to supply military aid to the Algerian rebels
            fighting the French.

2   GREAT BRITAIN - Parliament receives a petition signed
            by nearly 50,000 citizens demanding a halt to the
            acquisition of nuclear weapons.

2   BRAZIL - The Portuguese liner Santa Maria sails into
            Recife where the passengers and crew are released. The
            next day the pirates surrender to authorities and are
            given political asylum.

8   FRANCE - A national referendum approves a plan that
            will eventually give Algeria its independence.

12   INDIA - The government claims the Chinese Communists
            have illegally occupied 12,000 square miles of Indian
            territory.

13   DEMOCRATIC CONGO REPUBLIC - The government in Katanga
            Province announces that Patrice Lumumba has been
            killed while trying to escape. Lumumba may have been
            assassinated as early as 17 January. It is almost
            certain that Moise Tshombe is responsible for ap-
            proving the killing.

14   USSR - The Soviet government accuses UN Secretary Gen-
            eral Dag Hammarskjold of complicity in the murder of
            Patrice Lumumba and demands the immediate withdrawal
            of UN forces in the Congo.

15   UNITED STATES - The new US President, John F. Kennedy,
            warns the USSR of the grave consequences to any uni-
            lateral action in the Congo.

16   USSR - The government announces it has withdrawn re-
            cognition of Dag Hammarskjold as UN Secretary General.

21   NORTHERN RHODESIA - The British propose a new formula
            that would allow for black rule. This plan is immedi-
            ately rejected by the white-dominated provincial
            government.

21   UNITED NATIONS - The Security Council orders the UN
            troops in the Congo to use force, if necessary, to
            prevent further violence.

21   DEMOCRATIC CONGO REPUBLIC - Following the UN decision
            to use force, Moise Tshombe orders a mobilization in
            Katanga Province.

22   DEMOCRATIC CONGO REPUBLIC - The government protests
            the 21 February UN decision as a violation of Congo-
            lese sovereignty.

24   DEMOCRATIC CONGO REPUBLIC - Premier Ileo asks the UN
            for the use of UN force to quell the revolt in Katanga
            Province.

28   DEMOCRATIC CONGO REPUBLIC - The warring factions agree
            to cooperate to prevent further Communist "tyranny"
            and UN "tutelage."

MARCH

            DEMOCRATIC CONGO REPUBLIC - Beginning in March, at-
            tempts to gain a confederation of the provincial
            states that make up the Congo are blocked by Stan-
            leyville forces under the leadership of Antoine
            Gizenga.

            NEPAL - A civil war begins that lasts throughout the
            remainder of the year.

12   MALAGASY - At a meeting in Tananarive, Congolese
            President Kasavubu, Premier Ileo, and all other
            provincial leaders except Antoine Gizenga, agree to
            reorganize the Congo into a confederation.

14   INDIA - The government announces it has volunteered
            forces to participate in the UNEF being sent to the
            Congo.

15   SOUTH AFRICA - The government announces it will not seek admission to the British Commonwealth when it is granted its independence on 31 May.

18   PORTUGUESE ANGOLA - The Portuguese government sends in troops to put down a native uprising.

19   NATIONALIST CHINA - An operation (Operation HURRICANE) is launched to evacuate a large number of Chinese troops who fled China during the Communist takeover and who have been causing trouble while living in northern Thailand, Laos, and Burma.

21   SWITZERLAND - Disarmament talks resume in Geneva.

22   UNITED STATES - Cuban exile groups in the US combine to form a revolutionary council to better fight Castro.

23   UNITED STATES - President Kennedy announces that the US will not allow a Communist takeover in Laos.

24   SOUTH VIET NAM - President Diem orders the call-up of all enlisted reserves because of the increased Communist threat.

28   UNITED STATES - After a reappraisal of the nation's defense posture that was begun at the first of the year, the President requests an increase of more than $1.9 billion over the already presented defense bill of $41.8 billion.

31   LAOS - Laotian Prince Souvanna Phouma states that if the US will stop supplying arms to the right-wing forces, he will ask the USSR to stop supporting the Pathet Lao.

APRIL

USSR - The Soviet government begins the withdrawal of its technicans working in Albania. Economic aid is cut off to that country, and the Soviet naval installion at Vlore is closed. It is announced that these actions are a result of Albanian support of Communist China.

UNITED STATES - There is considerable evidence that the US is sponsoring the training of anti-Castro military forces is the southern United States and in Latin America.

3   SOUTH VIET NAM - The US and RVN sign a Treaty of Amity and Economic Relations in Saigon.

3   LAOS - A cease-fire is arranged between the government
         and the Pathet Lao.

4   CEYLON - A campaign of disobedience sponsored by   the
         separatist Tamil-speaking Federal Party sparks   vio-
         lence. This brings about a   state of martial law   that
         will last almost two years.

4   SOUTH VIET NAM - President Diem appeals to the ICC for
         an energetic investigation of growing Communist   sub-
         version and terrorism in SVN.

9   UNITED STATES - The newly formed Cuban Revolutionary
         Council urges a revolt against Castro.

9   SOUTH VIET NAM - Ngo Dinh Diem wins a large   majority
         in the country's first presidential elections.

11   FRANCE - President DeGaulle discloses that France will
         not pay its share of the costs of the UN peacekeeping
         force in the Congo, and that his government is   no
         longer willing to participate in UN activities.

11   ISRAEL - Nazi war criminal Adolf Eichmann is put   on
         trial.

12   USSR - Piloting <u>Vostok I</u>, Major Yuri Gargarin becomes
         the first human to successfully orbit the earth.

13   UNITED NATIONS - The General Assembly condemns South
         Africa's apartheid policies.

14   SOUTH VIET NAM - President Ngo Dinh Diem divides   the
         country into three Corps Tactical Zones and individual
         Division Tactical Zones   for better   command   and
         control.

15   UNITED NATIONS - The Cuban foreign minister, Raul Roa,
         accuses the United States and several Latin American
         states of preparing an invasion of Cuba.

17-20   CUBA - A US government-sponsored invasion force   of
         about 1,600 anti-Castro Cubans lands in southern Cuba
         near Bahia de los Cochinos (Bay of Pigs). The invaders
         are driven out after three days when the US fails to
         provide military and naval support for the beachhead.

17   DEMOCRATIC CONGO REPUBLIC - Gizenga recognizes Joseph
         Mobutu as his commander in chief. This ends the stale-
         mate that has existed in consolidating the number of
         separate provinces into a single state and   allows
         President Kasavubu, with UN aid, to begin a reorgani-
         zation of the Congolese armed forces.

18   USSR - The Soviet Union demands the US immediately
            withdraw the invasion force in Cuba. If not, Premier
            Khrushchev declares, the USSR will come to Castro's
            aid.

18   UNITED STATES - In replying to the Soviet demand,
            President Kennedy declares that the United States will
            not allow outside intervention into the Western Hemi-
            sphere.

19   LAOS - The government announces the establishment of a
            US Military Assistance Advisory Group that will give
            tactical training and logistical support to the Royal
            Laotian armed forces.

20   UNITED STATES - President Kennedy states the US will
            take steps to protect the security of the country and
            its neighbors in the Western Hemisphere.

21-22   ALGERIA - French army units, led by Generals Maurice
            Challe and Raoul Salan, mutiny and seize control of
            Algiers. Four days later most, including Challe, are
            captured by loyal French forces as Algiers is retaken.
            Salan escapes to lead a new wave of OAS resistance
            against the French government.

23   FRANCE - The fear of an invasion by rightest elements
            in Algeria allows DeGualle to assume almost dictato-
            rial power in France.

24   DEMOCRATIC CONGO REPUBLIC - A month-long meeting opens
            at Coquilhatville. Moise Tshombe withdraws the
            Katangan delegation and is arrested and accused of
            treason. The conference reaches a decision to form a
            federal republic consisting of 20 states. The meeting
            closes on 31 May.

24   LAOS - Great Britain and the Soviet Union issue a
            joint appeal for a cease-fire.

26   DEMOCRATIC CONGO REPUBLIC - Moshe Tshombe's arrest is
            confirmed. He is to be held until he promises to bring
            Katanga back into the confederation.

27   SIERRA LEONE - Sierra Leone is granted its indepen-
            dence as a British Dominion.

MAY

1   CUBA - Fidel Castro proclaims Cuba a "Socialist Re-
            public."

2 INDIA - The government claims Chinese Communist military forces have made another border crossing into
Indian territory.

2 UNITED STATES - The Department of State announces that
Cuba has become a full-fledged Communist state under
Soviet control.

3 LAOS - A cease-fire goes into effect two weeks before
the opening of a 14-nation conference on the Laotian
situation. The conference is due to open in Geneva on
16 May.

5 UNITED STATES - President John F. Kennedy states at a
news conference that consideration is being given to
the employment of US combat forces in SVN and that
Vice-President Lyndon Johnson will discuss the matter
with President Diem during his forthcoming visit to
SVN. At the same time, the Joint Chiefs of Staff
authorize US advisors to accompany ARVN infantry battalions and companies on combat operations, but stipulates they are not to engage in combat except in self-
defense.

11 SOUTH VIET NAM - US Vice-President Lyndon B. Johnson
arrives in Saigon.

12 UNITED STATES OF THE CONGO - A new nation is founded
with its capital in Leopoldville.

13 SOUTH VIET NAM - US Vice President Johnson announces,
in Saigon, that additional US military and economic
aid is on the way.

16 SOUTH KOREA - An anti-Communist military junta, led by
General Park Chung Hee, seizes control of the government and arrests its President, Yun Po Sun.

16 SWITZERLAND - A fourteen-nation conference on Laos
convenes in Geneva. In June, the US and USSR will reaffirm their support of Laotian neutrality.

17 CUBA - Castro offers to exchange those personnel captured at the Bay of Pigs for 500 US tractors. The deal
is never consumated.

19 SOUTH VIET NAM - General McGarr, the Chief, MAAGV,
proposes an augmentation of RVNAF to the equivalent of
15 divisions composed 278,000 men.

20 UNITED STATES - President Kennedy sends his action
program for SVN to CINCPAC. The total authorized US
strength in SVN is raised to 929, 785 of them in
MAAGV.

20   FRANCE - Peace talks on Algeria begin at Evian-les-
            Bains.

30   DOMINICAN REPUBLIC - Generalissimo Rafael Leonidas
            Trujillo is assassinated at Ciudad Trujillo after 31
            years in power.

31   SOUTH AFRICA - Upon becoming a republic, the govern-
            ment severs its ties with the British Commonwealth.

JUNE

            UNITED STATES - The government officially announces
            its agreement to increase the size of the USMAAGV
            beyond the 785-man authorized level. American advisors
            officially enter field duty. (In both cases, implemen-
            tation has already taken place.)

3-4   AUSTRIA - US President Kennedy meets with Soviet Pre-
            mier Khrushchev in Vienna. The meeting concludes with-
            out any agreements being reached.

4   USSR - The government issues a memorandun calling for
            an immediate German peace that would make Berlin a
            "free" city.

6   SOUTH KOREA - An absolute, military dictatorship is
            declared by the ruling junta.

12   COMMUNIST CHINA - Premier Chou En-lai and NVN Premier
            Pham Van Dong meet in Peking and accuse the US of ag-
            gression and intervention in SVN.

15   USSR - Premier Khrushchev states that a separate peace
            treaty will be signed with East Germany before the end
            of the year. He reiterates his threat to use Soviet
            military power if the West attempts to force its way
            into West Berlin.

16   UNITED STATES - At a conference in Washington, US and
            RVN officials conclude an agreement whereby the US
            agrees to increase the size of the military assistance
            group in South Viet Nam, to send US personnel into the
            field to observe ARVN units in action, and to pay the
            salaries of an additional 20,000 troops.

22   DEMOCRATIC CONGO REPUBLIC - Tshombe is released from
            arrest and agrees to cooperate in the confederation
            process.

26   VENEZUELA - A military uprising is suppressed.

JULY

1   KUWAIT - In accordance with a defense treaty signed at the time of Kuwait's independence (19 June 1961), British military forces move into Kuwait at the request of the government to protect the realm after Iraq claims the territory as theirs.

3   SOUTH KOREA - Park Chung Hee is established as the leader of the junta.

4   DEMOCRATIC CONGO REPUBLIC - The Katangan Parliament decides to boycott the National Parliament which is to meet in Leopoldville.

5   ALGERIA - The Muslim population carries out a general strike to protest French plans to partition the country.

6   NORTH KOREA - The government signs a military and economic treaty with the USSR.

8   USSR - Using the Berlin Crisis as a reason, Premier Khrushchev cancels the planned armed forces reduction and announces an increase in defense expenditures instead.

11 ALGERIA - The leaders of the French army mutiny are tried and convicted.

17 UNITED STATES - Rejecting (along with Great Britain and France) the Soviet peace plan for Berlin, the US reinforces its Berlin garrison with an additional infantry battle group and artillery. Four US National Guard divisions are mobilized.

17 OAS - The OAS determines to continue its sanctions against the Dominican Republic.

19-20   TUNISIA - Tunisian army units lay siege to the French fortress at Bizerte. They are defeated when French reinforcements arrive. Tunisia breaks diplomatic relations with France.

20 ARAB LEAGUE - When the League accepts Kuwait into membership, Iraq walks out claiming the League is helping "British imperialism."

21 TUNISIA - Both sides in the Franco-Tunisian dispute accept a UN-mandated cease-fire.

24 DEMOCRATIC CONGO REPUBLIC - It is announced that the USSR has offered assistance to Katanga.

25   UNITED STATES - President John F. Kennedy states the
            US is prepared for any eventuality in the rising Ber-
            lin Crisis. To bolster US military strength he pro-
            poses a military manpower increase of 217,000, and a
            substantial increase in defense spending.

28   DEMOCRATIC CONGO REPUBLIC - Tshombe states he will
            fight to preserve Katangan independence. He does, how-
            ever, agree to send a delegation to the National Par-
            liament

AUGUST

1   DEMOCRATIC CONGO REPUBLIC - The Parliament recon-
            venes and names Cyrille Adoula to be Premier.

2   UNITED STATES - President John F. Kennedy declares the
            US will do all it can to save South Viet Nam from a
            Communist takeover.

11   SOUTH VIET NAM - The manpower strength of the RVNAF is
            increased to 200,000 troops. All men between 25 and 35
            years of age are ordered to report for military duty.

12-13   BERLIN - The East Germans prohibit all access from the
            west into East Berlin.

15-17   BERLIN - At dawn, on 15 August, the East German army
            begins the construction of a wall along the East-West
            Berlin border. The apparent purpose of the "Berlin
            Wall" is to stop the wholesale flight of East Germans
            to the West.

21   KENYA - The leader of the Kenya African National Union
            (KANU), Jomo Kenyatta, is released after nine years
            imprisonment.

21   DEMOCRATIC CONGO REPUBLIC - UN forces capture the
            radio station in Elizabethville, Katanga, hoping to
            compel Moise Tshombe to remove white mercenary troops
            in his payroll. Tshombe complies.

25   BRAZIL - The government of Janio Quadros is forced to
            resign by the military after less than seven months
            in office. The country verges of the brink of civil
            war.

31   USSR - The Soviets announce a resumption in nuclear
            weapons testing.

31   MOROCCO - Spanish forces evacuate their last base in
            Morocco.

SEPTEMBER

SOUTH VIET NAM - ARVN headquarters announces that there were 41 engagements between RVNAF and Communist forces in SVN in August.

1   USSR - The Soviet Union resumes atmospheric testing of nuclear weapons.

1-4   SOUTH VIET NAM - A series of attacks occurs in Kontum Province in which more than 1,000 Viet Cong take part. The RVNAF announces an increase in Communist aggression.

1-6   YUGOSLAVIA - A conference of 25 nonaligned nations meets in Belgrade and issues a communique calling on the superpowers to hold talks to halt the arms race and to avert war.

5   UNITED STATES - After joining with Great Britain in proposing to the USSR a halt to atmospheric testing of nuclear weapons (3 September), President Kennedy resumes US atmospheric testing of new types of weapons that can be detonated safely without fallout.

11   USSR - The Soviets reject Western protests against the Berlin Wall.

12   TURKEY - Former Premier Adnan Menderes is executed for violating the Turkish constitution.

13   DEMOCRATIC CONGO REPUBLIC - After a period in which the Kasavubu government receives UN assurances that the central government is the only authority in the Congo, fighting breaks out when UN forces attempt to disarm the Katangans. The UNEF is nearly defeated in fierce fighting.

17   IRAQ - A long-smoldering hostility over the Iraqi government's refusal to grant the Kurds autonomy erupts a civil war that will last for the remainder of the decade.

17   GREAT BRITAIN - Sir Robert K. G. Thompson, the architect of the British victory over the Communists in Malaya when he was the colony's Permanent Defense Secretary, leaves for SVN as the head of an advisory mission on administrative and policy matters.

18   DEMOCRATIC CONGO REPUBLIC - While flying to meet Moise Tshombe at Elizabethville, UN Secretary General Dag Hammarskjold is killed in an air crash near Ndola, in Northern Rhodesia.

18   FRANCE - The government announces an agreement to withdraw its garrison at Bizerte in Tunisia.

18   SOUTH VIET NAM - Phouc Vinh (Ap Son Thuy or Song Be), the capital of Phouc Long Province, 60 miles north of Saigon, is captured by a Viet Cong force estimated at 1,500.

20   DEMOCRATIC CONGO REPUBLIC - A cease-fire is arranged in the Katanga Crisis.

25   UNITED NATIONS - US President John F. Kennedy announces in a speech that SVN is "under attack."

26   UNITED STATES - The Arms Control and Disarmament Agency is established.

28-29   SYRIA - There is a revolt among Syrian army units. A junta establishes a civilian government to rule the country with Mahmoun al-Kuzbarti at its head. He is also to control national defense and foreign affairs.

28   EGYPT - President Nasser prepares to send Egyptian troops to quell the revolt in Syria, but quickly withdraws the order in the face of the fait accompli there.

29   SYRIA - The government announces its withdrawal from the UAR.

30   MOROCCO - The French base at Marrakesh is turned over to Moroccan control thus ending French hegemony in the region.

OCTOBER

            USSR - At the 22nd Party Congress, Khrushchev attacks Albania calling for the overthrow of the Hoxha government. The speech is in retaliation for Albania's support of Communist China. Premier Khrushchev also reopens the campaign of vilification against Josef Stalin.

            SOUTH VIET NAM - The Communists establish the Central Office of South Vietnam (COSVN) to replace the Nambo Regional Committee which has directed Communist affairs in SVN since the early 1950s.

1   PANAMA - President Roberto F. Chiari demands the US revise the Panama Canal Treaty and turn the canal over to Panamanian authority.

1   SEATO - Military experts gather to discuss guerrilla
        warfare in SVN. The US considers sending combat units
        to SVN although Admiral Harry D. Felt, CINCPAC, de-
        clares there is no immediate prospect of such an
        action.

1   CAMEROON - The East and West Cameroons are joined into
        the Federal Republic of Cameroon.

2   SOUTH VIET NAM - President Ngo Dinh Diem tells the
        National Assemby that their country "is no longer
        fighting a guerrilla war ... It is a war waged by an
        enemy who attacks us with regular units fully and
        heavily equipped...." The President also says that the
        US committee, headed by Eugene Staley, will recommend
        an increase in both economic and military aid.

11   UNITED STATES - President Kennedy announces he is
        sending General Maxwell D. Taylor, his military
        advisor, to SVN to study the situation there.

13   UNITED STATES - The government confirms that a mili-
        tary assistance agreement has been reached with Yugo-
        slavia. The US will supply 130 fighter aircraft and
        the necessary training for Yugoslav pilots.

16   MALAYSIA - Prime Minister Abdul Rahman announces that,
        when Singapore and Malaysia merge, Singapore may no
        longer be used as a SEATO base by Britain.

17   USSR - Premier Khrushchev opens the 22nd Party Con-
        gress by announcing a further delay in signing a sep-
        arate peace treaty with East Germany. He also states
        that the Soviet Union would soon test a hydrogen wea-
        pon with a yield probably in the range of 50 megatons.
        Khrushchev goes on to again attack Albania for its
        Stalinist form of government.

18   SOUTH VIET NAM - President Ngo Dinh Diem signs a
        decree proclaiming a state of emergency throughout
        RVN. This order gives the Chief of State special
        powers for one year. Diem also asks the US for combat
        troops.

23   USSR - The beginning of the Sino-Soviet rift occurs
        when Premier Chou En-lai walks out of a Soviet Party
        Congress session.

26   BERLIN - A military confrontation develops when East
        German authorities state that US civilians must pre-
        sent their travel documents to authorities at the
        East-West Berlin border. Soviet and US tanks face each
        other for two days while US diplomatic personnel cross

26   BERLIN (Cont'd) - and recross the border to prove the
            validity of the Four-Power agreement on travel through
            the city.

26   UNITED STATES - President Kennedy sends a personal
            message to South Vietnamese President Diem assuring
            him of continued US support.

27   UNITED NATIONS - The UN asks the Soviet Union not to
            detonate the 50 megaton hydrogen weapon it has
            announced it is about to test.

30   USSR - The Soviets detonate a 50 megaton hydrogen
            weapon near the Arctic Circle.

30   USSR - The Soviet government informs Finland that the
            threat of aggression posed by West Germany demands
            consultations leading to the implementation of the
            Finno-Soviet Mutual Defense Treaty of 1948.

30   SOUTH VIET NAM - MAAGV is augmented to a strength of
            972, 948 of whom are US Army personnel.

NOVEMBER

            DOMINICAN REPUBLIC - Leaders of the Trujillo regime
            flee the country in the face of an expected coup.
            United States warships patrol the waters around the
            country.

            DEMOCRATIC CONGO REPUBLIC - Fighting breaks out again
            in Katanga Province. Thirteen Italian members of the
            UN force are killed when Congolese troops mutiny in
            the eastern Congo region. The UN orders the use of
            force to restore order.

6   ECUADOR - Rioting begins forcing the resignation of
            the government of President Jose Maria Velasco Ibarra.
            Three days later (9 November) Carlos Julio Arosemena
            Monroy is installed as President.

7   USSR - Premier Khrushchev indicates a willingness to
            postpone talks on Berlin.

16   UNITED STATES - Accepting some of the recommendations
            in the Taylor-Rostow report, President Kennedy decides
            to increase the number of advisors in SVN, but not to
            commit combat troops at this time.

25   USSR - Following a two-day meeting at Novosibirsk in
            Siberia, Premier Khrushchev and Finnish President Urho
            K. Kekkonen issue a communique stating an indefinite
            postponement of military talks. The following day,

25   USSR (Cont'd) - Kekkonen reports to his nation that
            all anti-Soviet politicians will have to leave the
            government.

DECEMBER

            SOUTH VIET NAM - The Civil Irregular Defense Group
            (CIDG) program is put into effect. This paramilitary
            force will serve as a special guerrilla force in a
            number of areas in SVN.

2   CUBA - Castro declares himself a Marxist-Leninist, and
            states that he is setting up a Communist state in
            Cuba.

8   UNITED STATES - The State Department publishes a white
            paper outlining the NVN effort to take over SVN.

9   USSR - Khrushchev announces that the Soviet Union has
            nuclear weapons more powerful than 100 megatons.

9   TANGANYIKA - The nation is declared an independent
            member of the British Commonwealth.

10   USSR - The government recalls its diplomats from
            Albania and orders the Albanian legation in Moscow
            closed.

11   SOMALIA - There is an unsuccessful army revolt.

11   SOUTH VIET NAM - Two companies of US military heli-
            copters (8th and 57th Transportation Companies) arrive
            in the country. These are the first complete US mili-
            tary units to be deployed in SVN.

14   UNITED STATES - In a letter to President Diem, Presi-
            dent Kennedy pledges increased aid to SVN.

15   ISRAEL - Adolf Eichmann is found guilty and sentenced
            to death.

16   SOUTH VIET NAM - USMAAGV receives authorization from
            the Defense Department to provide an advisor to each
            province chief and a five-man advisory team to each
            operational RVNAF battalion.

17   SOUTH VIET NAM - A US logistic support team from the
            9th Logistical Command in Okinawa arrives in SVN.

18   DEMOCRATIC CONGO REPUBLIC - UN forces capture Eliza-
            bethville in Katanga Province.

18-19   INDIA - Indian forces seize the Portuguese territories of Goa, Damao, and Diu.

19   ALBANIA - The government breaks diplomatic relations with the Soviet Union.

19-20   DOMINICAN REPUBLIC - The government settles most of its difference with the opposition and establishes a plan to end the OAS boycott and the internal unrest that has beset the country.

21   DEMOCRATIC CONGO REPUBLIC - A cease-fire is arranged.

26   UAR - The government breaks relations with Yemen. Long-term support of subversive activities in North Yemen begins.

27   GREAT BRITAIN - The government announces it has dispatched additional naval units to the Persian Gulf to protect Kuwait against an unwanted annexation by Iraq.

31   LEBANON - A right-wing coup attempt led by the Parti Populaire Syrien is suppressed by the army.

31   SOUTH VIET NAM - US strength in SVN reaches 3,200. The enemy's strength is estimated at 26,700. This is a five-fold increase in NVA/VC strength during the year.

Notes

1962

PORTUGUESE-GUINEA - A 12-year rebellion begins which is led by the African Party for the Independence of Guinea and Cape Verde (PAIGC). It culminates in the colony gaining its independence in 1974 as Guinea-Bissau.

MOZAMBIQUE - A twelve-year rebellion, led primarily by the Frente de Liberatacao de Mocambique (FRELIMO), begins against the Portuguese colonial government.

GUYANA - A long period of racial and political violence begins which is caused by factions already vying for position before independence is declared in 1966.

JANUARY

DEMOCRATIC CONGO REPUBLIC - Antoine Gizenga, the Vice Premier of the central government, attempts to force the breakaway of Kasai Province. Congolese troops capture Stanleyville, and Gizenga is dismissed.

CAMEROON - A Communist-inspired insurrection begins that will last until 1971.

SOUTH VIET NAM - The US installs a tactical air control system in SVN and furnishes aircraft for combat and logistic airlift support.

1   PORTUGAL - There is an unsuccessful uprising in Beja. The small garrison that is involved in the revolt is quickly overwhelmed by loyal troops.

3   PORTUGAL - Premier Antonio de Oliviera Salazar lashes
           out at the US and Great Britain for failing to support
           Portuguese demands in the UN when India seized three
           colonies on the sub-continent.

3   UNITED STATES - The Department of Defense announces a
           two division increase in the size of the active army.

4   DOMINICAN REPUBLIC - The OAS lifts its sanctions after
           a Council of State is inaugurated to rule the country
           until an election can be held in mid-August.

4   SOUTH VIET NAM - A joint US-RVN communique announces a
           program of aid for economic and social development, as
           well as a program to stengthen RVN military defenses.

9   SOUTH VIET NAM - The strength of RVNAF is increased
           from 170,000 to 200,000 men.

12   SOUTH VIET NAM - The first herbicide defoliation mis-
           sion is carried out by the USAF. The principal chemi-
           cal substance used in this program, designed to strip
           away foliage around known VC hideouts, is Agent
           Orange. This marks the beginning of the defoliation
           program known as "Operation RANCH HAND." This campaign
           will continue until the end of the war.

13   DEMOCRATIC CONGO REPUBLIC - Fighting erupts in the
           city of Stanleyville. The UN orders its troops to take
           whatever steps necessary to prevent civil war.

13   DOMINICAN REPUBLIC - There is an unsuccessful attempt
           to overthrow the government.

15   DEMOCRATIC CONGO REPUBLIC - For leading the attempt to
           capture Stanleyville, Vice-President Antoine Gizenga
           is stripped of his title and office.

16   DOMINICAN REPUBLIC - A military coup overthrows the
           Council of State.

16   DUTCH EAST INDIES - Dutch forces engage an Indonesian
           motor torpedo boat off the coast of Dutch (West) New
           Guinea. This is the latest episode in a long-standing
           dispute in which Indonesia claims West New Guinea as
           its territory.

18   DOMINICAN REPUBLIC - A second coup takes place which
           restore the Council of State to power.

19   LAOS - A coalition government is announced, but the
           plan falls through when the right wing pulls out.

20   DEMOCRATIC CONGO REPUBLIC - UN forces arrest Antoine Gizenga and turn him over to Congolese authorities on 23 January.

22   UNITED STATES - The government warns Communist China to stay away from Quemoy and Matsu islands.

29   SWITZERLAND - The Big Power test ban conference comes to a close after 39 months of fruitless negotiation.

30   NIGERIA - At a six-day conference held in Lagos, the leaders of twenty African states agree to establish an organization of African states not associated with that proposed at Casablanca on 30 January 1961. Ghana, Guinea, Mali, Morocco, and the UAR boycott the meeting in protest over the exclusion of Algeria.

30   UNITED NATIONS - The General Assembly asks Portugal to cease its repressive practices in Angola.

FEBRUARY

        SOUTH VIET NAM - The government begins planning the Strategic Hamlet Program which will involve the forced relocation of the civilian populace into. secure areas.

1   SOUTH VIET NAM - US Special Forces personnel undertake the training the CIDG.

3   UNITED STATES - President Kennedy imposes an embargo on trade with Cuba.

7   SOUTH VIET NAM - Two more US Army helicopter companies totaling about 300 men arrive in country. The US military strength in SVN in now 4,000.

8   ARGENTINA - The government severs diplomatic relations with Cuba.

8   SOUTH VIET NAM - The US command in SVN is reorganized into the US Military Assistance Command, Vietnam (MACV). Lieutenant General Paul D. Harkins is given command and promoted to General. In addition, a Logistic Support Group is organized to provide administrative and logistical support to US Army units in SVN.

10   UNITED STATES - In an exchange of spies, the US and the USSR swap Francis Gary Powers for the convicted Soviet agent, Colonel Rudolf Abel, who has been in an American federal prison since 1957.

14   OAS - The OAS votes to exclude Cuba from the organization.

14   UNITED STATES - A White House order allows US forces
            in SVN to fight back in self-defense.

15   DEMOCRATIC CONGO REPUBLIC - The Katangan Assembly
            votes to reunite the province with the central gov-
            ernment.

20   NIGERIA - The Organization of African States is formed
            in Lagos. Twenty African states attend the meeting;
            Algeria is not invited.

20   INDONESIA - The Indonesians launch a guerrilla cam-
            paign against the Dutch in West New Guinea.

23   UNITED STATES - The size of the Strategic Army Corps
            is more than doubled from three to eight divisions.

24   COMMUNIST CHINA - The government demands the withdraw-
            al of US military forces and all US military equipment
            in SVN   claiming Chinese   security is   seriously
            threatened by the "undeclared war."

27   TURKEY - A mutiny at the Military Academy is put down
            without bloodshed.

27   SOUTH VIET NAM - Two VNAF fighters bomb and strafe the
            Presidential Palace in Saigon. Madame Ngo Dinh Nhu is
            slightly injured in the attack.

MARCH

2   BURMA - The U Nu government is deposed by a military
            coup led by General Ne Win.

5   FRANCE - The government announces it will not be rep-
            resented at the forthcoming disarmament conference to
            be held in Geneva.

7   FRANCE - A cease-fire is announced for Algeria.

14   SWITZERLAND - A 17-nation disarmament conference opens
            in Geneva.

17   USSR - The Soviet press publishes a note sent to all
            of the signatories of the Geneva Accords demanding an
            immediate withdrawal of American forces in SEA claim-
            ing they constitute a "serious danger to peace."

18   FRANCE - A peace agreement is concluded with the Al-
            gerian rebels.

21   UNITED STATES - The USSR agrees to cooperate in the
            peaceful exploration of outer space.

22   SOUTH VIET NAM - ARVN forces begin "Operation SUNRISE"
            which is planned to destroy VC guerrilla activity in
            Binh Duong Province. Six hundred troops of the ARVN
            5th Division, reinforced with Rangers, Civil Guards,
            and psychological operations personnel participate.
            The VC disperse, but are not beaten.

23   FRANCE - When new fighting breaks out in Algeria,
            President DeGaulle orders a full-scale offensive
            against Salan-led resistance.

24   NATIONALIST CHINA - Chinese Nationalist aircraft shoot
            down a number of Communist Chinese planes over Quemoy
            and Matsu Islands as the threat of a Communist inva-
            sion grows.

28   ARGENTINA - A military coup seizes control of the gov-
            ernment and ousts President Arturo Frondizi.

28   SYRIA - In a bloodless coup the Syrian government,
            elected as a result of the coup of September 1960, is
            ousted by a group of army officers.

30   ARGENTINA - The armed forces put Senate leader Jose
            Maria Guido into the presidency.

APRIL

1   SYRIA - There is an unsuccessful revolt at Aleppo.

1   MAURITANIA - A rebel army, seeking union with Morocco
            and based in that country, invades Mauritania but is
            driven out.

13   SYRIA - The government of President Nazem el-Kodsi,
            which was ousted in March, is returned to power after
            promising to work for a union of "Liberated Arab
            States."

16   BOLIVIA - The government breaks diplomatic relations
            with Chile over navigation rights on the Lauca River.
            This fight has been going on for 23 years. Four days
            later (20 April) the dispute is given to the OAS.

20   ALGERIA - Raoul Salan is captured by French army
            forces. Fighting continues for several more months.

20   SOUTH VIET NAM - The National Assembly approves a
            presidential plan (proposed 3 February) to establish a
            system of "strategic hamlets" in the Mekong River Del-
            ta area in which the Vietnamese people will be able to
            live free of harassment by the VC.

25   UNITED STATES - The US undertakes a series of nuclear
            weapons tests at Christmas Island in the Pacific.

MAY

            UNITED STATES - There are a total of 124 US aircraft
            in SVN, including two USAF C-123 transport squadrons
            and four companies of US Army helicopters.

4   VENEZUELA - A military uprising is suppressed.

6   UNITED STATES - When Pathet Lao forces capture the
            northern Laotian village of Nam Tha, the US asks for
            an investigation by the ICC to determine whether there
            has been a violation of the May 1961 cease-fire agree-
            ment.

6   UNITED STATES - When no agreement can be reached by
            the European NATO nations regarding the US offer of 16
            December 1960, the US assigns the five SSBNs to NATO
            on the provision they remain under US control.

8   UNITED STATES - The government announces the success-
            ful firing and detonation of a nuclear-armed Polaris
            missile from a submerged nuclear submarine (<u>USS Ethan
            Allen</u>) near Christmas Island in the Pacific.

11   LAOS - Intelligence reports indicate Pathet Lao forces
            have penetrated 100 miles beyond the cease-fire line.
            Thousands of Royal Laotian Army troops flee into Thai-
            land.

12   UNITED STATES - In reaction to repeated cease-fire
            violations by the Communist Pathet Lao in Laos, the US
            sends a naval task force, with an 1,800-man Marine
            Battalion Landing Team (BLT), into the Gulf of Siam.

15   UNITED STATES - President Kennedy orders 2,000 US Army
            combat troops, currently based in Hawaii, to be de-
            ployed to Thailand because of the weakening position
            in Laos.

19   THAILAND - The first of what will become a total of
            5,000 US troops arrive in Thailand to forestall any
            threats posed by the Pathet Lao forces across the
            border in Laos.

20   ALGERIA - A French operation is begun to airlift all
            Europeans out of the country.

21   ISRAEL - Adolf Eichmann is executed by hanging.

23   FRANCE - As OAS terrorist activity reaches a high
        point, Raoul Salan is tried in Paris by a court
        martial and sentenced to life imprisonment.

26   INDONESIA - As heavy fighting continues between the
        Dutch troops and the Indonesian forces and guerrillas,
        the Netherlands' government accepts a US plan for
        settling the dispute.

29   UNITED NATIONS - The UN calls for an immediate cease-
        fire in the Dutch-Indonesian conflict.

JUNE

        TUNISIA - With the exception of the retention of
        several airbases, the French complete the evacuation
        of their forces from Tunisian territory.

2   SOUTH VIET NAM - The International Control Commission
        (ICC) composed of Canada, India, and Poland reports
        that North Viet Nam is actively supporting and supply-
        ing Viet Cong forces operating in South Viet Nam.
        Poland refuses to sign the report.

4   VENEZUELA - A military uprising is suppressed.

10   COMMUNIST CHINA - A build-up of military strength is
        reported in the area facing Nationalist China on
        Formosa.

16   EGYPT - At a meeting of the "Casablanca States," held
        in Cairo, a military command structure is developed
        with an Egyptian in command and a headquarters in
        Ghana.

22   THE PHILIPPINES - Based on the contention of prior
        ownership dating from the 19th century, the government
        claims sovereignty over Sabah Province in British
        North Borneo and asks for talks to settle the matter.

22   LAOS - A coalition government is installed after ex-
        haustive negotiations. Premier Souvanna Phouma an-
        nounces that Laos refuses further association with
        SEATO.

26   SOUTH VIET NAM - The National Assembly votes to extend
        its tenure by one year claiming the insurgency prob-
        lem makes free elections impossible.

27   UNITED STATES - In response to the Chinese Communist
        build-up in Fukien Province, the President reiterates
        the warning that an attack on Quemoy or Matsu that
        threatens Taiwan will not go unanswered.

JULY

1   FRANCE - The government announces the full independence of Algeria.

1   ALGERIA - Achmed Ben Bella is confirmed as Premier. His presence raises widespread dissatisfaction with the government which is pro-Egypt and pro-Soviet. This unrest continues until his overthrow in 1965.

1   RWANDA - The former German colony becomes an independent republic.

1   BURUNDI - The nation is declared independent under the rule of King Mwami Mwambutsa.

6   UNITED STATES - Secretary of State Robert McNamara declares that, while victory in SVN is still years away, the increased US aid is having its effect.

13   USSR - Premier Khrushchev states the Soviet Union has an antiballistic missile (ABM).

17   UNITED STATES - On orders from President Kennedy, the DOD and CIA agree that the DOD will take over the control of overt operations of the CIDG program (Operation SWITCHBACK).

18   PERU - A military coup overthrows the government of President Manuel Prado Ugarteche. The new military government of General Ricardo Perez Godoy suppresses most democratic institutions in the country.

19   UNITED STATES - The US suspends diplomatic relations with Peru and, on 20 July, halts all military and economic aid.

20   SOUTH VIET NAM - On the occasion of the eighth anniversary of the signing of the Geneva Accords, the VC call for the establishment of a "neutral zone" composed of South Viet Nam, Cambodia, and Laos.

23   SWITZERLAND - The 14-member Geneva Conference on Laos publishes agreements on Laotian independence and neutrality (Geneva Accords of 1962).

24   ARGENTINA - The government bans the Peronist and Communist Parties.

30   UNITED STATES - The government announces it has withdrawn nearly 5,000 US Army forces and Marines recently sent into Thailand.

31   UNITED STATES - Meeting in Washington, Dutch and Indo-
          nesian delegations are able to agree upon the trans-
          fer of West New Guinea to UN supervision. This agree-
          ment is initialed on 15 August, and goes into effect
          on 1 October. A second provision transfers the terri-
          tory to Indonesia on 1 May 1963.

AUGUST

          SOUTH VIET NAM - US Special Forces establish a CIDG
          camp at Khe Sanh on Route 9 in Quang Tri Province.

5   USSR - The USSR detonates an apparent 40-megaton hy-
          drogen weapon in a high-air test.

7   GREAT BRITAIN - The government rejects the Philippine
          claim of sovereignty over British North Borneo and re-
          fuses to meet to discuss the subject.

8   WEST GERMANY - The government announces it will break
          diplomatic relations with any nation supporting the
          Soviet peace plan.

8-11   ARGENTINA - An army mutiny forces changes in the cabi-
          net of President Jose Maria Guido.

9   CUBA - Castro announces the collectivization of agri-
          culture.

15   THE NETHERLANDS - The government announces that it has
          made a decision to give up West New Guinea.

16   ARAB LEAGUE - Algeria is admitted to membership.

17   UNITED STATES - The US restores diplomatic relations
          with Peru.

20   CAMBODIA - Prince Sihanouk asks President Kennedy to
          organize an international conference that will guar-
          antee Cambodian neutrality and threatens to seek the
          protection of Communist China if the guarantees are
          not forthcoming.

22   SWITZERLAND - After five months of meetings the dis-
          armament conference finds itself hopelessly deadlocked
          and calls a recess.

22   BERLIN - The Soviet closing of its Berlin Kommandan-
          tura office is rebuffed by the Allies who state the
          Soviet action will, in no way, affect the Four-Power
          agreement on Berlin.

29   JORDAN - In a joint communique, King Ibn Saud of Saudi
            Arabia and King Hussein announce the merger of their
            military forces and economic policies.

31   TRINIDAD-TABAGO - The former British colony is granted
            independence.

SEPTEMBER

2   USSR - The government announces it will supply mili-
            tary aid and technical personnel to Cuba.

4   UNITED STATES - President Kennedy announces a signif-
            icant buildup of Soviet military equipment in Cuba
            even though there is no specific evidence of offen-
            sive weapons being supplied to the Castro regime.

11   USSR - Premier Khrushchev accuses the US of preparing
            for aggression against Cuba and that such an act would
            mean war. He goes on to state that the arms being sent
            to Castro are for defensive purposes only.

12   UNITED STATES - In the face of growing Congressional
            pressure for direct action against Cuba, President
            Kennedy states he is opposed to taking any offensive
            action against Castro.

13   UNITED STATES - President Kennedy responds to Premier
            Khrushchev's accusations by stating that the US does
            not feel military action is called for at the moment
            but that the US will act when its security is in
            peril.

13   ALGERIA - A cease-fire is arranged.

15   SOUTH VIET NAM - A provisional US Special Forces Group
            is established.

17   LAOS - The US begins withdrawing its military advisory
            personnel in accordance with the Geneva Agreements.

18   ARGENTINA - Following the ouster of the Secretary of
            War and a number of generals, an army-led revolt
            breaks out. Within five days (23 September) Buenos
            Aires is under military control.

19   YEMEN - A military coup follows the death of Imam
            Ahmed and the elevation of Prince Saif al-Islam Moham-
            med al Badr.

21   UNITED NATIONS - A UN security force is established to
            supervise the orderly transfer of western New Guinea
            from The Netherlands to Indonesian control.

26   UNITED STATES - The State Department announces it has reached agreement over the sale of missiles to Israel for defensive purposes.

27   NORTH YEMEN - The Free Yemeni Republic is proclaimed with Colonel Abdullah al-Salal as its leader (31 October). A civil war begins between pro- and anti-Communist forces that will last until 1965. Egyptian forces will support the rebels, while Saudi Arabia supports the royalist faction.

OCTOBER

            SAUDI ARABIA - Loyal Yemeni troops who were able to escape from North Yemen establish a government-in-exile in Saudi Arabia.

            SOUTH VIET NAM - An Australian counter-guerrilla expert, Colonel F. P. Serong, tells General Paul Harkins that the ARVN is poorly trained and led.

7   LAOS - In accordance with the Geneva Agreement on Laos, the last of about 800 US military advisors and technicans with the Royal Laotian Army are withdrawn.

8   UNITED NATIONS - Algeria is admitted to membership.

8   SOUTH VIET NAM - The US Second Air Division is established in country.

9   UGANDA - The Kingdom of Uganda, headed by King Mutesa II, is granted independence by Great Britain.

10   UNITED STATES - The government agrees to pay Castro $60 million in ransom for 1,113 prisoners taken at the Bay of Pigs.

15   SOUTH VIET NAM - US helicopters are authorized to "fire first" on established enemy targets.

17   USSR - At the 22nd Congress of the Communist Party, Khrushchev acknowledges that an ideological rift has developed between the Soviet Union and Communist China. He does this by attacking Albania, an ideological ally of China.

20   INDIA - Major fighting breaks out along the disputed border when the Chinese Communists attack Indian forces. The Chinese are successful in all of the affected areas.

20   DEMOCRATIC CONGO REPUBLIC - Fighting breaks out between central government forces and the Katangans.

22   UNITED STATES - President Kennedy announces an air and naval "quarantine" of Cuba following the establishment of firm evidence of the emplacement of Soviet offensive missiles and bomber bases on the island.

22   CUBA - An American U-2 reconnaissance aircraft is shot down by a Soviet-built SA-2 surface-to-air missile while on a mission over eastern Cuba .

23   OAS - The OAS authorizes the use of force to impose the quarantine on Cuba.

23   USSR - The Soviet Union puts its armed forces on alert because of the Cuban Missile Crisis.

24   CUBA - The American naval blockade of Cuba goes into effect.

25   UNITED NATIONS - The US and USSR agree to negotiation in the Cuban crisis. Secret negotiations begin.

26   SOUTH VIET NAM - The National Assembly extends, for one year, the extraordinary powers granted President Diem under the state of emergency edict.

27   UNITED STATES - Intelligence sources report that the first Cuban missile site will be operational on Tuesday, 1 November. This sets plans in motion for the first US air strikes to begin on 31 October.

28   UNITED STATES - The US and the USSR reach an agreement on Cuba in which the USSR agrees to withdraw its offensive weapons, and the US agrees not to invade Cuba after the Soviets have withdrawn.

29   INDIA - Prime Minister Nehru asks the US for military aid to assist in fighting the Chinese Communists.

30   UNITED NATIONS - Acting Secretary General U Thant proposes a UN inspection of the missile bases in Cuba to ensure compliance.

NOVEMBER

1   CUBA - Castro rejects the UN proposal for inspection of the Soviet missile sites.

6   SAUDI ARABIA - The government charges that UAR aircraft bombed a number of Saudi villages near the Yemeni border. Saudi Arabia breaks diplomatic relations with Egypt.

7   UNITED STATES - After Castro's rejection of the UN inspection plan, the US reveals an agreement with the Soviets in which the missiles will be counted at sea on the return to the USSR.

8   UNITED STATES - The US announces that all known Soviet missiles bases in Cuba have been dismantled.

8   SOUTH VIET NAM - The government breaks off diplomatic relations with Laos as a result of the Laotian action estabishing diplomatic relations with North Viet Nam.

11   EGYPT - The UAR and the Yemen Republic conclude a military alliance.

14   ERITREA - The National Assembly votes for permanent union with Ethiopia. A long period of unrest follows as pro-Communist and other elements fight the union.

15   CUBA - Castro threatens to shoot down US reconnaissance aircraft that continue to fly over Cuba.

16   UNITED STATES - The US declares its intention to continue Cuban overflights and to use force, if necessary, to protect them.

19   INDIA - Prime Minister Nehru asks the US for more military aid as the Chinese Communists push back the Indian Army.

20   UNITED STATES - President Kennedy lifts the Cuban blockade after the USSR agrees to remove all bomber aircraft in Cuba within thirty days.

20   SOUTH VIET NAM - As a result of his acceptance of the concept of a nationwide counterinsurgency plan, President Diem reorganizes RVNAF into four Corps Tactical Zones and the Capital Military District. A Joint General Staff and Army, Navy, Air Force, and Special Forces headquarters are established.

21   USSR - Soviet armed forces relax the state of alert imposed during the Cuban Missile Crisis.

21   UNITED STATES - The US answers India's call for assistance by dispatching US-manned cargo transports to India.

21   INDIA - The Chinese Communists offer a cease-fire and a reestablishment of the November 1959 border. The fighting ends within 24 hours even though the Indian government rejects the terms of the truce.

24   UNITED STATES - The US begins withdrawing the 2,300 US troops that had been sent to Thailand.

DECEMBER

            SOUTH VIET NAM - Intelligence reports indicate that VC terrorism is causing 1,000 murders or abductions of local leaders each month.

            INDONESIA - The Indonesian government instigates a rebellion in the British enclave of Brunei on Borneo. The revolt is put down by British troops.

3   USSR - Premier Khrushchev pledges the removal of Soviet-supplied jet bombers from Cuba.

6   SOUTH VIET NAM - The government protests the Communist introduction of Chinese-made weapons and ammunition into SVN.

8   MALAYA - An Indonesian-supported uprising in Borneo is quickly suppressed.

11-12   ARGENTINA - A military revolt is suppressed by loyal government troops.

14   INDIA - Even though the Indian government rejects the terms of the cease-fire, Chinese Communist forces begin a withdrawal from northeast India.

17   SENEGAL - There is an unsuccessful coup attempt.

20   DOMINICAN REPUBLIC - Juan D. Bosch is elected President.

21   GREAT BRITAIN - After returning from a meeting with President Kennedy in the Bahamas, Prime Minister Macmillan announces the US decision to scrap the "Skybolt" missile program in favor of the adoption of the US Polaris missile and the NATO multinational nuclear force concept.

22   TUNISIA - A coup attempt is put down.

23   CUBA - Repatriation of the 1,113 Bay of Pigs prisoners of war is begun. The US pays $53 million in foodstuffs and medical supplies as ransom for their release.

29   DEMOCRATIC CONGO REPUBLIC - Tshombe once again violates the truce agreement and defies the UN. United Nations forces open an offensive against Katanga.

31   SOUTH VIET NAM – There are now nearly 11,000 US
            advisors and support personnel in SVN, including 29
            Special Forces detachments.

Notes

1963

SOMALIA - A five-year period of border conflict begins with Kenya.

JANUARY

UNITED STATES - The government signs a nuclear weapons agreement with the Italians.

2   SOUTH VIET NAM - The ARVN 7th Division attacks the VC-held village of Ap Bac and is decisively beaten. The failure of the operation clearly demonstrates the inefficiency and poor training of South Viet Nam's military forces.

7   UNITED STATES - In a joint announcement, the US and the USSR declare that negotiations dealing with the Cuban Missile Crisis are at an end, and that the matter is closed.

13   TOGO - A military coup, led by a group of noncommissioned officers, seizes the government and kills President Sylvanus Olympio.

14   UNITED STATES - In his State of the Union address, President Kennedy over-optimistically reports that, "The spear point of aggression has been blunted in Vietnam."

14   FRANCE - President DeGaulle rejects French participation in a NATO multilateral nuclear force. At the same time, he states his categorical opposition to British admission into the EEC.

15   DEMOCRATIC CONGO REPUBLIC - In fear of being captured by UN forces, Moise Tshombe announces an end to Katanga's independence. He subsequently flees the country.

21   TURKEY - The government announces it has reached agreement with the US for the removal of the 30 "Jupiter," liquid-fueled ICBM missiles that have been based on Turkish soil, but which never became operational.

21   ITALY - The government announces it has reached an agreement with the US for the removal of the 30 operational "Jupiter" ICBM missiles which have been based on Italian soil.

21   UNITED STATES - The government announces it will deploy Polaris submarines into the Mediterranean to replace the Jupiter missiles it has agreed to remove from Turkish and Italian soil.

22   FRANCE - In Paris, West German Chancellor Conrad Adenauer and President DeGaulle sign a treaty of reconciliation.

31   CANADA - Prime Minister John Diefenbaker voices displeasure over the US State Department's criticism (30 January) of Canada's lack of progress in arming its forces with nuclear weapons.

FEBRUARY

5   CANADA - The Diefenbaker government is defeated because of its nuclear policies.

5   LIBERIA - There is an unsuccessful coup attempt.

6   UNITED STATES - The Defense Department states that the Soviets have completed the withdrawal of offensive weapons from Cuba.

8   IRAQ - An air force-led coup topples the government. Premier Kassem is killed. A pro-Nasser group led by Colonel Abdel Salam Arif takes control and Arif becomes the de facto ruler.

12   SWITZERLAND - The disarmament conference resumes its deliberations.

13   VENEZUELA - In a bizarre act of piracy, nine Communists seize a Venezuelan freighter and sail it to Brazil in protest against the Betancourt government. Brazil grants the highjackers asylum.

13   INDONESIA – President Sukarno voices opposition to the
            British plan for a Malay Federation.

16   IRAQ – Army units round up Communists in accordance
            with the government's decision to eradicate the Party.

18   USSR – The government announces the withdrawal, by 15
            March, of several thousand of the approximately 17,000
            Soviet troops in Cuba.

22   UNITED STATES – The Defense Department declares that
            many US pilots are flying VNAF operational missions in
            SVN and that they are authorized to make tactical air
            strikes against enemy targets.

27   COMMUNIST CHINA – The Chinese Communist Party criti-
            cizes the Soviet Union for supplying arms to India and
            for having stopped military and economic aid to China
            (1960).

MARCH

            LAOS – Fighting breaks out between Pathet Lao and
            neutralist forces. Sporadic incidents occur into May.

            KENYA – A series of border clashes takes place with
            Somalia over disputed areas.

1   IRAQ – Kurdish tribesmen, led by Mustafa al-Barzani,
            threaten war if the government does not honor its
            promise of an autonomous Kurdish state.

2   UNITED NATIONS – The UN dispatches Ralph Bunche to
            Yemen to investigate charges that the UAR and Saudi
            Arabia are involved in the Yemeni civil war.

3   PERU – A military coup overthrows the government of
            President Ricardo Perez Godoy after a long period of
            unrest. General Nicholas Lindley Lopez becomes Presi-
            dent.

5   SOUTH VIET NAM – The MACV commander, General Paul D.
            Harkins, asserts that the RVNAF has reached a level of
            training and experience along with having the
            necessary equipment to achieve victory.

8   SYRIA – Having dissolved Parliament and ruled by
            decree from 20 September 1962, the government is over-
            thrown by a pro-Egyptian group supported by Syrian
            Baath Party members. Egypt and Iraq threaten war with
            anyone offering any outside interference. A new, pre-
            dominently Baath party, pro-Nasser government is in-
            stalled the next day (9 March).

8   SOUTH VIET NAM - Rioting erupts in the ancient capital
           city of Hue. Twelve are killed. The Buddhists blame
           the government; the government blames the Communists.

13   UNITED STATES - The JCS approves a plan to increase
           the SVN Military Assistance Pact (MAP)-supported Civil
           Guard strength from 81,000 to 86,000, and the Self-
           Defense Force strength from 80,000 to 104,000.

14   SOMALIA - The government breaks diplomatic relations
           with Great Britain.

15   UNITED NATIONS - US representatives at the 17-nation
           Disarmament Committee recommend the installation of
           direct communications between Moscow and Washington to
           reduce the possibility of war as the result of an
           accident which could occur in a crisis such as the
           recent Cuban Missile incident.

19   COSTA RICA - The Declaration of San Jose is signed by
           the US and six Latin American states. This agreement
           establishes US economic aid for the region and is de-
           signed to thwart Soviet aggression.

19   ALGERIA - The government protests French plans for
           nuclear weapons testing in the Sahara and demands (20
           March) that France negotiate with them a test ban for
           the Sahara region.

22-26   SOUTH KOREA - Massive protests develop over Park Chung
           Hee's announcement cancelling promised elections.

30   UNITED STATES - The government announces that steps
           are being taken to ensure that US territory is not
           used as bases for the training of anti-Castro Cuban
           rebels.

31   GUATEMALA - A right-wing military coup, led by Defense
           Minister Colonel Enrique Peralta Azurdia, overthrows
           the government of President Ydigores Fuentes.

APRIL

           SOUTH VIET NAM - President Diem hestitates in accept-
           ing more American advisors because he feels the United
           States has made unwarranted criticism of his regime.

           LAOS - A period of fighting breaks out between govern-
           ment and Pathet Lao forces.

2-5   ARGENTINA - A military revolt is suppressed.

5   UNITED STATES - The US and USSR are linked together by
           a direct communications system (Hot Line). This action
           was agreed upon through the UN Disarmament Committee
           after the US proposed such a plan to reduce the
           possibility of an accident such as might have occurred
           during the recent Cuban Missile Crisis.

6   SOUTH KOREA - Faced by almost insurmountable opposi-
           tion, Park Chung Hee announces public elections to be
           held in the fall.

11   GREAT BRITAIN - The government rejects the white-
           dominated Southern Rhodesia request for independence.

17   UAR - The UAR, Syria, and Iraq announce the formula-
           tion of a new tripartite Arab state.

17   SOUTH VIET NAM - After delaying for more than twelve
           months, President Diem inaugurates the "Open Arms"
           (Chieu Hoi) program designed to induce Viet Cong guer-
           rillas to return to government control.

22   UNITED STATES - Secretary of State Dean Rusk calls the
           situation in SVN "difficult and dangerous," and de-
           clares the US role is one of supporting the RVN gov-
           ernment.

27-30   HAITI - Haitian police violate diplomatic immunity and
           break into the Dominican Republic Embassy in Port au
           Prince.

MAY

1   CEYLON - Emergency rule is ended.

1   INDONESIA - The government formally accepts West New
           Guinea from the Dutch.

2   HAITI - A further crisis develops when Haitian army
           troops surround the Embassy of the Dominican Republic
           where some two dozen opponents of the Duvalier regime
           have taken refuge.

8   SYRIA - Pro-Nasser rioting breaks out in Damascus and
           several other locations after the Baathist and pro-
           Nasser government coalition breaks up.

8   SOUTH VIET NAM - Rioting breaks out in Hue after the
           government forbids flying religious flags and holding
           processions on Buddha's birthday. Nine Buddhist monks
           are killed when government troops open fire on the
           demonstrators.

9   SOUTH VIET NAM - At an expected cost of $17 million to the government, the Strategic Hamlet Program goes into effect. The plan is similar to the one used successfully in Malaya.

9   UNITED STATES - The Defense Department states that intelligence sources have reason to believe that about 17,500 Soviets, of whom 5,000 are combat troops, still remain in Cuba.

11   CANADA - The government of Prime Minister Lester B. Pearson agrees with US proposals to equip the Canadian armed forces with US-supplied nuclear weapons.

17   UNITED STATES - The US suspends diplomatic relations with Haiti.

18   INDONESIA - Achmed Sukarno is named "President for Life."

20   TURKEY - A mutiny is suppressed at the Military Academy with some loss of life.

22   NATO - The NATO Council approves the formation of a Multi-Lateral Nuclear Striking Force.

25   ETHIOPIA - The leaders of thirty African states sign the charter of the Organization of African Unity (OAU) in Addis Ababa.

28   SOUTH VIET NAM - The head of the Buddhist church in SVN, Thich Tinh Khiet, calls for a nationwide hunger strike to protest governmental repression.

JUNE

1   UNITED NATIONS - The UN Security Council establishes a 200-man Observer Force under Swedish Major General Karl Von Horn to go to Yemen for two months. The force's tour of duty in Yemen is extended on 1 August. Von Horn soon resigns (27 August) and is replaced by Indian Lieutenant General Prem Singh Gyani.

1   KENYA - Jomo Kenyatta becomes Prime Minister.

2-3   SOUTH VIET NAM - Police quell a Buddhist demonstration in Hue using police dogs and tear-gas. The government places a dawn-to-dusk curfew on the city.

10   IRAQ - The government "declares war" on the rebellious Kurds.

11 SOUTH VIET NAM - Police use clubs against a group of 1,000 Buddhist priests, nuns, women, and children in a procession protesting religious discrimination held in front of a pagoda in Saigon. A Buddhist priest, Venerable Quang Duc, burns himself to death.

16 SOUTH VIET NAM - The government accedes to many of the Buddhist demands, but still refuses to accept responsibility for the inflamatory statements made by President Diem's wife, Madame Nhu, in which she calls the Buddhists "Communists," and insists the best thing they could do for the country was to "barbecue a monk."

17 BOLIVIA - The government withdraws from the OAS following what it considers to be the mishandling of Bolivia's dispute with Chile.

21 FRANCE - President DeGaulle announces that France will withdraw most of its available Channel and Atlantic naval forces from NATO control.

24-26 WEST GERMANY - During a visit to West Germany, President Kennedy pledges to defend the city of Berlin stating that any attack by East German or Soviet forces would be considered an attack on the United States. He electrifies a Berlin crowd by stating, "I am a Berliner."

27 UNITED STATES - The appointment of Henry Cabot Lodge to succeed Frederick E. Nolting, Jr. as US Ambassador to the RVN is announced. The changeover is to take place in September.

JULY

11 SOUTH VIET NAM - The American Ambassador, Frederick Nolting, upon returning to SVN from home leave, warns President Diem of growing US impatience with his repressive policies.

11-12 ECUADOR - A military coup overthrows the government of President Carlos Arosemena. The ruling junta promises a strong anti-Communist policy, especially against Cuba.

15 USSR - A Big Power nuclear test-ban treaty conference opens in Moscow.

18 SYRIA - Several attempts to form a new government fail and the Baathists return to power (10 July); a pro-Nasser coup attempt fails.

19   SOUTH VIET NAM - President Diem grudgingly   authorizes
            the flying of Buddhist flags. Even as he speaks,
            however, ARVN units are sealing off the pagodas with
            barbed wire.

24   GUATEMALA - The government breaks diplomatic relations
            with Great Britain because London announces (22 July)
            it is giving autonomy to British Honduras, which is
            claimed by Guatemala.

29   FRANCE - President DeGaulle announces France's re-
            jection of the limited nuclear test ban treaty.

31   UNITED NATIONS - The Security Council votes to ask all
            nations to stop all military and other aid to Portugal
            that could be used to maintain its colonies.

AUGUST

5   USSR - A limited nuclear test-ban agreement is signed
            by Great Britain, the Soviet Union, and the United
            States. This treaty goes into effect on 10 October
            1963, and will be signed by most of the nations of the
            world.

5   SOUTH VIET NAM - A series of self-immolations begins
            when a 21-year old Buddhist monk named Nguyen Huong
            burns himself to death in Phan Thiet.

5-7   HAITI - Government forces disperse a small force of
            Haitian exiles who land on Haiti to overthrow the
            Duvalier regime.

7   UNITED NATIONS - The Security Council votes unanimous-
            ly to ban all military aid to South Africa because of
            its racial policies.

15   REPUBLIC OF CONGO - The government of President Fubert
            Youlou is ousted after labor rioting breaks out in the
            city of Brazzaville. Youlou is put into prison. A pro-
            Chinese Communist, Alphonse Massamba-Debat, is made
            President.

20   ISRAEL - An emergency request for a cease-fire is sent
            to the UN Security Council after a pitched battle is
            fought along the Syrian border in the demilitarized
            zone north of the Sea of Galilee.

20   SOUTH VIET NAM - Senior army officers ask President
            Diem for a declaration of martial law to allow them to
            quell the growing Buddhist unrest that is spreading
            into the army itself.

21   SOUTH VIET NAM - In a crackdown on "dissident" ele-
            ments, ARVN forces occupy a number of pagodas, in-
            cluding the main Buddhist Xa Loi Pagoda in Saigon.
            Police and army troops arrest a large number of Bud-
            dhist priests. Martial law is declared throughout RVN.
            A curfew and censorship are proclaimed. There are
            wholesale arrests of Buddhists throughout the country.

26   UNITED STATES - The State Department announces that
            Henry Cabot Lodge has assumed the duties of Ambassador
            to RVN. Lodge, in SVN since 22 August, has been ad-
            vised (23 August) that a group of senior ARVN officers
            is ready to seize control from the Diem government.

27   CAMBODIA - The government breaks diplomatic relations
            with RVN.

29   SWITZERLAND - The disarmament conference adjourns
            without any success.

31   SOUTH VIET NAM - General Duong Van ("Big") Minh in-
            forms Ambassador Lodge that the coup has been called
            off because of a number of internal problems, not the
            least of which is fear among the generals as to US
            resolve.

SEPTEMBER

2   SOUTH VIET NAM - The Times of Viet Nam newspaper ac-
            cuses the CIA of having planned a coup against Presi-
            dent Diem that was supposed to have occurred on 28
            August.

9   UNITED STATES - The National Security Council (NSC)
            orders Ambassador Lodge to inform South Viet Nam's
            President Ngo Dinh Diem that it regards the removal of
            his brother, Ngo Dinh Nhu, as vital to continued US-
            RVN relations. The warning includes the threat of a
            halt in US aid to SVN.

12   BRAZIL - A military revolt is suppressed by loyal
            troops.

12   UNITED STATES - Senator Frank Church introduces a res-
            olution calling for withdrawal of US troops in SVN and
            an end to all aid unless the Diem regime abandons its
            present policies of religious and political repres-
            sion.

13   UNITED STATES - The Washington Post reports that reli-
            able sources in the American leadership in SVN claim a
            victory against the VC is possible in nine months.

14   SOUTH VIET NAM - The government announces an end to
            martial law effective on 16 September.

15   ALGERIA - Premier Ahmed Ben Bella is elected President
            and begins a program of Socialist-oriented reforms.

16   MALAYSIA - A Confederation of Malaysia is formed amid
            controversy between Indonesia and Malaya over claims
            to the territories of North Borneo and Sarawak.

16   INDONESIA - Refusing to accept the formation of the
            Federation of Malaysia, President Sukarno opens a dip-
            lomatic and guerrilla campaign to "destroy it."

16   UNITED NATIONS - Fourteen Afro-Asian nations demand a
            debate in the General Assembly on the "ruthless" sup-
            pression of Buddhist rights in RVN.

21   UNITED STATES - President Kennedy orders Secretary of
            Defense Robert McNamara and General Maxwell Taylor to
            Saigon to review the military campaign against the VC.

25   DOMINICAN REPUBLIC - The government of Juan Bosch is
            overthrown by a military coup.

27   SOUTH VIET NAM - Elections are held for the 123-member
            National Assembly. All candidates are approved in ad-
            vance by the government; many run unopposed, including
            President Diem's brother and his wife.

OCTOBER

            ALGERIA - Fighting that lasts for more than a month
            breaks out along the Algerian-Moroccan border. Egyp-
            tian forces support the Algerians.

2   UNITED STATES - Upon returning to the US after their
            fact-finding mission to SVN, McNamara and Taylor re-
            port that the US role in SVN can be ended by 1965, and
            that at least 1,000 training advisors can be withdrawn
            by the end of this year (1963).

3   HONDURAS - Ten days before the scheduled presidential
            elections, the government of President Ramon Villeda
            Morales is overthrown by a military coup led by Colo-
            nel Osvaldo Lopez Arellano.

4   UNITED STATES - Because of recent military coups in
            the two countries, the US announces its decision to
            withdraw all economic and military aid from Honduras
            and the Dominican Republic.

4   SOUTH VIET NAM - President Diem suggests the UN send a
           delegation to SVN to investigate the charges that his
           government is suppressing the Buddhists.

5   SOUTH VIET NAM - A Buddhist priest burns himself to
           death in Saigon. This is the sixth such incident since
           11 June. Ambassador Lodge delivers a formal protest to
           the government.

6-8   ALGERIA - A Berber uprising, led by Colonel Mohand ou
           el Hadj, begins in the Kabylien Mountain region. This
           revolt is put down by loyal troops.

7   SOUTH VIET NAM - Officials of the US Aid for Interna-
           tional Development (USAID) admit the program in SVN is
           at a virtual standstill.

8   UNITED NATIONS - The General Assembly orders a fact-
           finding commission to SVN to investigate charges of
           GVN repression of Buddhists.

9   UGANDA - The kingdom is declared a republic with King
           Mutesa II elected as its first president.

10   UNITED NATIONS - The General Assembly votes to ban the
           use of nuclear weapons in space.

10-28   SOUTH VIET NAM - US CIA agents meet with ARVN General
           Duong Van ("Big") Minh and learn some of the details
           of the new coup that is being planned against the Diem
           regime.

11   NATO - The US, Great Britain, West Germany, Belgium,
           Italy, Greece, and Turkey open discussions on the de-
           velopment of an integrated nuclear fleet.

13   ALGERIA - The government announces a border war with
           Morocco, which the Algerians claim is tied to the re-
           cent Berber uprising. Heavy fighting is reported along
           sections of the disputed border in the Atlas Mountains
           and in the Sahara Desert.

15   SOUTH KOREA - Park Chung Hee is formally elected Pres-
           ident.

17   UNITED NATIONS - The General Assembly votes to confirm
           earlier national renunciations of the use of outer
           space for military purposes.

21   UNITED STATES - The Defense Department orders a halt
           in financial aid to the ARVN Special Forces program
           until it is employed to fight the VC.

22   UNITED STATES - The US begins "Operation BIG LIFT" in which 15,000 combat troops are airlifted to West Germany in less than 64 hours.

28   DAHOMEY - A military coup overthrows the government of President Hubert Maga. A new ruling junta, led by General Christophe Soglo, promptly installs a civilian government.

NOVEMBER

            VENEZUELA - In a series of raids conducted throughout the month, government forces break up a Castro-supported plot to overthrow the government.

            SOUTH VIET NAM - Implementation is ordered of the 1,000-man reduction in US troop strength in SVN that was a part of the 11 September "Model Plan" for fighting Communist insurgency.

1   USSR - The government announces the successful testing of an unmanned, maneuverable, space satellite.

1   SOUTH VIET NAM - US General Paul Harkins estimates that victory over the Viet Cong "is just months away and that the reduction of American advisors can begin any time now."

1-2   SOUTH VIET NAM - Major General Duong Van ("Big") Minh leads a successful coup against the government after the US clearly indicates that it will not interfere in the overthrow of the Ngo Dinh Diem regime. Diem and others are later murdered. Former Vice-President Nguyen Ngoc Tho is named to head a provisional government. The constitution is suspended, and the National Assembly is dissolved.

4   ALGERIA - A cease-fire is arranged in the Algerian-Morocco border war. Emperor Haile Selassie of Ethiopia and President Modibo Keita of Mali are instrumental in affecting the truce.

7   UNITED STATES - The US recognizes the Military Revolutionary Council ruling SVN and the new "Provisional Government."

11   UNITED NATIONS - The General Assembly warns South Africa that it will be guilty of aggression if it attempts to annex Basutoland, Bechuanaland, or Swaziland.

12   CAMBODIA - The government refuses US offers of military assistance.

15   SOUTH VIET NAM - The US command announces that 1,000
        US servicemen will be sent home by 3 December.

18   IRAQ - The government is overthrown in a coup led by
        President Abdul Salam Arif.

19   CAMBODIA - Prince Sihanouk orders the US to stop all
        military and economic aid to his country.

20   UNITED STATES - Ambassador Lodge and General Harkins
        fly to Honolulu for a conference with Secretary of
        State Dean Rusk and Secretary of Defense Robert S.
        McNamara.

21   CYPRUS - Widespread fighting breaks out between Greek
        and Turkish factions on the island. The Turkish Cyp-
        riots claim the Greek Cypriots, led by President
        Makarios, are moving to change the constitution in
        favor of the Greeks. Britain reinforces its garrison
        in Cyprus.

22   UNITED STATES - President John F. Kennedy is assassin-
        ated by Lee Harvey Oswald in Dallas, Texas. Vice Pres-
        ident Lyndon B. Johnson is immediately sworn in as
        President of the United States. US military forces are
        placed on alert.

24   UNITED STATES - President Lyndon B. Johnson reaffirms
        the US commitment to SVN.

24   UNITED STATES - Jack Ruby murders Lee Harvey Oswald on
        national television.

DECEMBER

6   SOUTH VIET NAM - The government issues a formal pro-
        test to the ICC against the introduction of Chinese
        weapons and equipment in SVN.

10   ZANZIBAR - The nation is declared an independent mem-
        ber of the British Commonwealth.

12   CAMBODIA - The government withdraws its Embassy in
        Washington.

12   GREAT BRITAIN - The government announces the indepen-
        dence of Kenya within the British Commonwealth.

19   SOUTH VIET NAM - Defense Secretary McNamara and CIA
        Director John A. McCone arrive in Saigon to evaluate
        the military junta's performance against the VC.

29   SOUTH VIET NAM - The government announces that 4,077
          strategic hamlets have been completed, of the 11,182
          that are to be built. Thirty-nine percent of the popu-
          lation now reside in these "protected areas."

                            Notes

1964

GREECE - Tensions increase between Greece and Turkey during the spring and summer as the crisis on the island of Cyprus once again heats up.

THAILAND - A series of border clashes with Cambodia punctuate the next several years. A decade of Communist terrorism begins.

PERU - A year-long Cuban-sponsored revolt begins in the Andes region of the country.

SOUTH VIET NAM - Because of maladministration and the difficulties encountered in providing security, the "Strategic Hamlet" Program is declared a failure and scrapped.

JANUARY

EAST AFRICA - At the request of the individual governments, British forces are dispatched to Kenya, Uganda, and Tanganyika to suppress Communist-inspired, antigovernment revolts.

1   CYPRUS - President (Archbishop) Makarios abrogates the treaties of guarantee with Great Britain, Greece, and Turkey.

2   SOUTH VIET NAM - Two hundred VC troops hold off 2,000 ARVN troops supported by helicopters, aircraft, and tanks at the village of Ap Bac in the Mekong Delta. Five helicopters are shot down and three Americans killed. This is the first time the VC stand and fight.

2   UNITED STATES - Secretary of State Dean Rusk   reports
           that ARVN forces operating in the   Delta area in SVN
           have captured a large cache of enemy arms and   ammuni-
           tion of Chinese manufacture.

3   DEMOCRATIC CONGO REPUBLIC - The Angolan "government-
           in-exile," headed by Hastings Roberts, which is based
           in Leopoldville, decides to accept aid from Communist
           China and other Communist countries.

4   SOUTH VIET NAM - The Civil Guard Directorate is redes-
           ignated the Civil Guard Command and placed under the
           RVNAF Joint General Staff. The Civil Guard regional
           commanders are placed under the cognizant corps tacti-
           cal zone commander.

5   CAMBODIA - Meeting in Phnom Penh, Prince Sihanouk re-
           ceives an offer of military aid from French Defense
           Minister Pierre Messmer.

6   SOUTH VIET NAM - Three generals, Duong Van Minh, Tran
           Van Don, and Le Van Kim, assume the leadership of the
           country.

9-11   SOUTH VIET NAM - Admiral Harry D. Felt, CINCPAC, con-
           fers with General Paul D. Harkins, MACV, and declares
           that the VC are certain to be defeated.

10   PANAMA - The government breaks diplomatic relations
           with the US the day after rioting erupts when US stu-
           dents in the Canal Zone fail to fly the Panamanian
           flag alongside the US colors. President Chiari also
           denounces the Panama Canal Treaty.

10   TUNISIA - The government recognizes Communist China.

12   ZANZIBAR - The government of Mohammed Shamte is over-
           thrown by a leftist-led revolution. A Communist-domi-
           nated government, led by Abdullah Kassim Hanga, takes
           over on 14 January.

13-17   ARAB LEAGUE - An emergency meeting of the heads of
           state of 13 Arab League member nations is called to
           discuss a strategy, and to set up a joint military
           command against Israel's plan to divert the Jordan
           River.

14   CAMBODIA - Prince Sihanouk wishes good fortune to the
           Philippines in their mediation attempts to heal the
           rift in US-Cambodian relations.

15   GREAT BRITAIN - A meeting opens in London among all
           concerned parties in the growing Cyprus crisis.

17   JAPAN - US Attorney General Robert F. Kennedy advises Indonesian President Sukarno to halt guerrilla activities in Malaysia.

17   SOUTH VIET NAM - A joint US-SVN survey of the Strategic Hamlet Program indicates serious flaws. The report indicates that it is safe to live in only about one-fifth of the hamlets. There is growing evidence that the VC control more than half of SVN.

20   PAKISTAN - The government calls for an emergency session of the UN Security Council because of the worsening situation in Kashmir.

21   SWITZERLAND - The disarmament conference reconvenes.

22   ZAMBIA - The country is declared independent.

23   UNITED STATES - After first refusing, President Johnson agrees to open discussions on the Panama Canal Treaty.

23   INDONESIA - The government announces that Indonesian President Sukarno has agreed to the US request and has ordered a halt to fighting with Malaysia.

24   GREAT BRITAIN - The government announces its determination to uphold its commitments to Malaysia even if it requires military force.

24   INDIA - The government claims Pakistan is the cause of the unrest in Kashmir and asks for direct negotiations.

24   KENYA - There is an army mutiny over pay. The Prime Minister, Jomo Kenyatta, requests and receives British military assistance to put down the Communist-inspired unrest.

25   GREAT BRITAIN - In addition to supplying troops to Kenya to help suppress insurrection, London responds to similar requests from Tanganyika and Uganda.

25   SOUTH VIET NAM - When the French present a plan for ending the war in SEA to a governmental civilian advisory committee, the committee recommends that the GVN break diplomatic relations with France.

27   FRANCE - The DeGaulle government establishes diplomatic relations with Communist China. DeGaulle also calls for the neutralization of Indochina. The next day (28 January) relations with Nationalist China on Taiwan are severed. (Nationalist China retaliates on 10 February by breaking diplomatic relations.)

27   UNITED STATES - Defense Secretary McNamara indicates in testimony before the House Armed Services Committee that VC strength and activities were already increasing in September 1963, and that they continue to increase. McNamara adds that the situation in SVN "continues grave."

28   EAST GERMANY - After becoming lost on a training mission, a USAF jet trainer is shot down over East Germany.

28   FRANCE - A five-year trade treaty is concluded with the USSR.

29-30   SOUTH VIET NAM - Faced with a possible French plot to neutralize Viet Nam, Major General Nguyen Khanh leads a bloodless pre-dawn coup deposing Duong Van Minh, and establishes himself as the country's leader. The new leader's first act is to break diplomatic relations with France (30 January). Generals Le Van Kim, Tran Van Don, and Mai Huu Xuan of the ousted Military Revolutionary Council are arrested as French collaborators. General Ton That Dinh is arrested for crimes committed when Ngo Dinh Diem was in power.

31   FRANCE - DeGaulle suggests that France and Communist China neutralize the former French possessions in Indochina.

31   UNITED STATES - After Secretary of State Dean Rusk reports a failure of peace negotiations, President Johnson announces the resumption of US air strikes over NVN, after a 37-day halt in the bombing (from 24 December 1963).

FEBRUARY

            CYPRUS - Fighting escalates between Greek and Turkish Cypriots. American and British attempts at mediating the dispute have thus far failed. President Makarios is known to be increasing his Greek-oriented armed forces.

3   UNITED STATES - Four Cuban fishing vessels are seized in US waters.

3-7   SOUTH VIET NAM - Viet Cong forces launch major offensives in Tay Ninh Province and the Mekong Delta. The RVNAF suffers heavy casualties. Terrorist bombing attacks begin in Saigon.

4   FRANCE - The DeGaulle government recognizes East Germany.

4   OAS - The OAS agrees to   act as mediator   in the   US-
         Panama crisis and   appoints a 17-member committee (7
         February) to investigate the various charges leveled
         by Panama against the US.

4   GHANA - A major anti-American demonstration takes
         place for which the government apologizes (7 February)
         but refuses to accept responsibility.

6   THAILAND - During a meeting on the Malaysian situa-
         tion, the Foreign Ministers of Indonesia, Malaysia,
         and the Philippines announce that Thailand has been
         asked to   commit forces to patrol a cease-fire line
         along the Malaysia-Indonesia border. The UN Secretary
         General is notified of this action.

6   CUBA - In retaliation for the seizure of its fishing
         vessels, the Cubans cut the water supply to the US
         Naval Base at Guantanamo Bay to one hour a day.

6   GREAT BRITAIN - An agreement is reached with France
         for the construction of a railroad tunnel under the
         English Channel.

6   RWANDA - The nation is invaded by 6,000 Watusi tribes-
         men from the Congo. The attack is beaten back with
         heavy losses by Rwandan army troops.

7   UNITED STATES - The US reacts to Cuba's actions at
         Guantanamo by curtailing Cuban worker's access to the
         base.

7   CONGO - Supporters of former President Youlou attempt
         to break him out of prison. Rioting spreads through
         Brazzaville.

7   USSR - Krushchev warns of the grave consequences in-
         volved in outside interference in the Cyprus crisis.

8   SOUTH VIET NAM - Major General Khanh announces the
         formation of a new government with himself as Premier,
         Duong Van Minh as nominal Chief of State, and a mixed
         civilian-military cabinet.

8   UNITED STATES - The government recognizes the Khanh
         regime in SVN.

8   CAMBODIA - Prince Sihanouk charges the US with respon-
         sibility for a South Vietnamese attack on a Cambodian
         border village on 4 February, and demands that the US
         finance a border-truce observation program.

8   SOMALIA - There is a renewal of fighting with Ethiopia
         even though an OAU-sanctioned truce was in place.

9   UNITED NATIONS - Ethiopia and Somalia submit their
           border dispute for mediation after Somalia's President
           Aden Abdullah Osman declares a state of national emer-
           gency.

10   IRAQ - The government announces a cease-fire in its
           conflict with the Kurds and promises to recognize
           Kurdish national rights.

11   CAMBODIA - Prince Sihanouk seeks international assur-
           ances of his country's neutrality.

12-14   OAU - An emergency meeting is held in Tanganyika to
           discuss the Ethiopia-Somalia border dispute. The fol-
           lowing day (13 February) the organization votes to
           replace British forces with African ones. On 14 Febru-
           ary, the OAU calls for a cease-fire, which is not ef-
           fective.

13   GREAT BRITAIN - The government announces a policy to
           maintain an independent nuclear deterrant capability.

13   UNITED STATES - The US and British governments endorse
           each other's policies in Southeast Asia.

14   UNITED NATIONS - Great Britain, with US support, asks
           for a meeting of the Security Council to establish a
           UN peacekeeping force on Cyprus.

17   UNITED NATIONS - Pakistan requests a suspension of the
           discussions on Kashmir.

17   INDONESIA - Foreign Minister Raden Subandrio announces
           that Indonesia has infiltrated specially-trained guer-
           rilla forces into the Malaysian territories of Saba
           and Sarawak where they are expected to operate until
           the Malaysian situation is corrected.

17-18   GABON - The government of President Leon Mba is over-
           thrown, but is restored the following day (19 Febru-
           ary) by French troops flown in to suppress the insur-
           rection.

18   UNITED NATIONS - Cyprus asks the UN for protection and
           guarantees for its independence.

18   UNITED STATES - The JCS recommends to the Secretary of
           Defense that the US Country Team in RVN be directed to
           induce RVNAF to accept US military advisors at all
           levels considered necessary by MACV. At the same time,
           McNamara is telling Congress that the bulk of American
           advisors can be withdrawn from SVN by 1965.

19   CAMBODIA - Prince Sihanouk asks the US, RVN, and Thailand to guarantee Cambodian independence.

20   ALGERIA - A cease-fire is arranged in the fighting along the Algerian-Moroccan border.

23   PAKISTAN - At the end of an eight-day visit, Chinese Communist Premier Chou En-lai states his government supports the Pakistani proposal that Kashmir be allowed to choose its allegiance by referendum.

25   USSR - The Soviet Union warns the US not to carry the war in Vietnam into the north.

27   SUDAN - The government deports over 300 missionaries accused of inciting trouble in southern Sudan.

27   LAOS - The Pathet Lao capture a number of strategic locations in the Plaine des Jarres.

28   SAUDI ARABIA - King Saud II is stripped of much of his power by the Royal Council. Prince Faisal, who led the bloodless coup, takes over most of the country's leadership.

MARCH

SOUTH VIET NAM - The US Army Support Command is established in SVN.

4   UNITED NATIONS - A peacekeeking force is ordered to Cyprus. Forces from Canada, Ireland, and Sweden are volunteered for the UN force.

5   SWITZERLAND - After rejecting a Soviet plan to scrap ballistic missile submarines (11 February), the US states it will allow international inspection of one of its nuclear reactors (Rowe, Massachusetts), if the Soviet Union will reciprocate.

10   EAST GERMANY - Soviet fighters shoot down an unarmed US reconnaisance aircraft near the East-West German border.

10   CAMBODIA - Prince Sihanouk sends a delegation to Moscow to buy arms.

11   CAMBODIA - The US and British Embassies are attacked by Cambodians. Prince Sihanouk offers his apologies and withdraws his demands for US guarantees of his neutrality.

12   SOUTH VIET NAM - After completing a four-day tour of
            SVN, US Secretary of Defense Robert McNamara declares
            the US will support RVN for as long as necessary.

16   LIBYA - The government votes unanimously to order the
            removal of US and British bases in Libya.

16   LAOS - Neutralist and Communist representatives agree
            to end fighting in the Plaine des Jarres.

17   UNITED STATES - National Security Action Memorandum
            288 is issued. It accepts the McNamara position call-
            ing for "graduated overt military pressure" against
            NVN. At the same time, President Johnson notifies Am-
            bassador Lodge in Saigon "to prepare contingency re-
            commendations for specific tit-for-tat actions." The
            White House also approves the RVN National Pacifica-
            tion Plan that, among other things, calls for the ex-
            pansion of ARVN by 50,000 men.

18   SOUTH VIET NAM - Premier Nguyen Khanh begins the
            process of restoring diplomatic relations with Laos,
            and of ending the border dispute with Cambodia.

19   SWITZERLAND - At the disarmament conference, the US
            offers to scrap 480 B-47 strategic bombers if the USSR
            will destroy an equal number of TU-16 "Badger" medium
            bombers.

25   CYPRUS - The UN peacekeeping force takes up its posi-
            tions on the island.

25   GREAT BRITAIN - The government rejects a Soviet plan
            to sponsor a conference on Cambodian neutrality.

25   FRANCE - DeGaulle promises to use his good offices
            with the US and Great Britain to set up a conference
            aimed at the neutralization of Indochina.

26   UNITED STATES - The US outlines its goals in Viet Nam
            and rejects the French plan of neutralization as
            playing into Communist hands. Secretary of Defense
            Robert McNamara reports the war will end within "the
            first thousand days of the Johnson Administration."

28   YEMEN - In retaliation for an attack on Saudi Arabian
            (South Arabian Federation) positions, British aircraft
            attack and destroy a Yemeni fortification.

31   UNITED STATES - After the release of three US airmen
            shot down on 10 March along the East-West German
            border, the US Air Force announces a 70-mile buffer
            zone along the border to prevent future incidents.

31   BRAZIL - A major revolt begins that is aimed at the land reform policies of President Joao Goulart.

APRIL

            CYPRUS - Heavy fighting takes place in northern Cyprus.

            UNITED STATES - President Johnson calls for third country support in the effort to keep SVN free.

1   OAU - After a month of sporadic fighting the OAU is able to arrange an Ethopian-Somalian cease-fire.

1   BRAZIL - The government of President Joao Goulart is overthrown by a military coup. Goulart flees to Uruguay (2 April). US naval forces assemble in the Caribbean in case there is an attempt at a Communist takeover. The ruling junta begins an anti-Communist purge in the Brazilian government, and the US Ambassador, Lincoln Gordon, requests the US naval task force be withdrawn.

1   SOUTH VIET NAM - Testing of the value of a two-man American advisory team at sub-sector (district) level begins in 13 areas. The trial employment will last until August.

3   PANAMA - Diplomatic relations are resumed with the US after President Johnson agrees (21 March) to review the Panama Canal issue.

4   CYPRUS - Makarios abrogates a 1960 treaty with Cyprus, Greece, and Turkey.

8   INDIA - Sheikh Mohammed Abdullah, known as the "Lion of Kashmir," is released after six years in prison. He denounces Indian policy toward Kashmir, also claimed by Pakistan.

8   SOUTH VIET NAM - Because of the deteriorating situation in SVN, the US suspends five-year planning and abandons the Accelerated Model Plan adopted in 1963.

11   BRAZIL - General Humberto Castelo Branco is elected to serve out the remainder of Joao Goulart's term as President.

13-15   SYRIA - An unsuccessful revolt takes place at Hama. Loyal troops put down the uprising with heavy loss of life.

15   SEATO - The French representative to the SEATO con-
            ference in Manila (13-15 April), Foreign Minister
            Couve de Murville, refuses to sign the final communi-
            que in support of South Vietnamese war against the
            Viet Cong.

16   FRANCE - President DeGaulle announces that France will
            build its own nuclear force and that it intends to of-
            fer the Third World an alternative to US or Soviet
            support.

19   LAOS - Premier Souvanna Phouma is thrown out of office
            by a right-wing military coup.

20   UNITED STATES - President Johnson announces an agree-
            ment with the USSR to reduce the production of fis-
            sionable material for nuclear weapons.

24   BRITISH GUIANA - British reinforcements are landed to
            help quell the growing disorder among the Indian and
            Negro populace.

25   UNITED STATES - The President announces that General
            William C. Westmoreland will replace General Paul
            Harkins as the senior US military officer in South
            Viet Nam.

26   TANZANIA - The new nation of Tanzania comes into being
            as the result of the union of Tanganyika and Zanzibar.

27   SOUTH VIET NAM - Intelligence reports now carry the VC
            strength in SVN at 45 battalions.

28   FRANCE - President DeGaulle orders the removal of
            French naval officers from the NATO commands in the
            English Channel and the Mediterranean.

MAY

2   LAOS - Souvanna Phouma is restored to office after he
            agrees to a number of reforms demanded by the right-
            wing military leadership.

2   SOUTH VIET NAM - An explosion in Saigon Harbor sinks a
            US aircraft transport ship.

3   INDONESIA - President Achmed Sukarno announces his in-
            tention to crush Malaysia.

4   FRANCE - France withdraws its naval personnel in all
            NATO commands.

7   SOUTH VIET NAM - The Defense Minister, Major General
        Tran Thien Khiem, publishes a decree reorganizing the
        Civil Guard into Regional Forces (RF). A second decree
        issued on 12 May reorganizes the Self-Defense Corps
        into the Popular Forces (PF).

12   UNITED STATES - Secretary of State Dean Rusk asks the
        NATO members for greater support in SVN.

14   UNITED STATES - Upon his return from SVN (with General
        Taylor, 12-13 May), Defense Secretary Robert McNamara
        recommends to President Johnson that RVNAF be drasti-
        cally increased in numbers, and states that at least
        twice the number of VNAF pilots are needed than pre-
        sently exist.

15   SOUTH VIET NAM - USMACV assumes all of the remaining
        functions of USMAAGV, and the two organizations are
        combined. MACV now has 3,580 personnel assigned to it,
        of which 3,000 are US Army.

16-24   LAOS - Supported by NVA regular army forces, the Com-
        munist Pathet Lao open a major offensive in the Plaine
        des Jarres. The neutralist forces of General Kong Le
        are defeated in this battle. This Communist victory
        marks the beginning of a decade of almost constant
        warfare.

18   UNITED STATES - The President asks Congress for an
        additional $125 million in economic and military aid
        for SVN.

20   FRANCE - President DeGaulle proposes reconvening the
        14-nation Geneva conference on Laos. The US and Great
        Britain quickly reject the proposal although the
        Soviet Union, Communist China, and India endorse the
        plan.

21   LAOS - The US initiates a program of continuous recon-
        naissance flights over Laos.

25   UNITED STATES - The US rejects a Soviet bid for a
        full-scale conference on Laos.

26   COMMUNIST CHINA - The government proposes a foreign
        ministers' conference on Laos.

26   UAR - President Nasser and Iraqi President Abdul Salam
        Arif sign an agreement establishing a joint military
        command to be activated in time of war.

27   INDIA - Pundit Jawaharlal Nehru dies.

JUNE

SOUTH VIET NAM - Viet Cong guerrilla activities increase throughout the month.

NORTH VIET NAM - Sometime during the summer NVN decides to begin sending NVA forces into SVN.

DEMOCRATIC CONGO REPUBLIC - Fighting breaks out when Communist-backed rebels threaten to throw the country into chaos.

1   LAOS - The Pathet Lao withdraw from the coalition government in Vientiane.

1-2   UNITED STATES - US leaders meeting in Hawaii agree to increase the number of advisors supporting RVN pacification efforts.

3   SOUTH KOREA - President Park closes all the country's universities and declares martial law in Seoul in response to massive student demonstrations against his regime.

11   GREECE - The government rejects direct talks with Turkey on the Cyprus crisis.

12   EAST GERMANY - The announced treaty of friendship with the Soviet Union falls short of the promised peace treaty.

12   SOUTH AFRICA - Nelson Mandela and seven other black leaders are sentenced to life imprisonment for sabotage and subversion.

12   FRANCE - President DeGaulle calls for a halt to all foreign intervention in SEA.

14   BRITISH GUIANA - The governor, Sir Richard Luyt, assumes emergency powers when faced with race rioting among Indians and Negroes. Much of the trouble is blamed on Prime Minister Cheddi Jagan who refuses to resign.

15   COMMUNIST CHINA - The government signs a treaty of friendship with Yemen.

16   UNITED STATES - The State Department admits US citizens have participated in the Congolese government's campaign against native tribesmen in eastern Kivu Province.

17   ALGERIA - The last French troop units in Algeria are withdrawn.

20   SOUTH VIET NAM - General Willian C. Westmoreland as-
          sumes command of USMACV, replacing the retiring Gen-
          eral Paul Harkins.

20   MALAYSIA - When a special conference in Tokyo fails to
          settle the Malaysia situation, Indonesian guerrillas
          step up their activities in Sarawak.

22-25   UNITED STATES - In light of the fighting in Cyprus
          during the last several months, President Johnson
          meets with Greek Premier George Papandreou and Turkish
          Premier Ismet Inonu in an attempt to defuse the situ-
          ation.

23   UNITED STATES - President Johnson announces the ap-
          pointment of General Maxwell D. Taylor to replace
          Henry Cabot Lodge as Ambassador to RVN.

29   SOUTH VIET NAM - A 295-man increase in US Army per-
          sonnel is authorized, 211 of whom are scheduled for
          field duty.

30   DEMOCRATIC CONGO REPUBLIC - The last UN troops leave
          the country. Almost immediately the rebellion flares
          up again.

JULY

          SOUTH VIET NAM - Viet Cong activities continue to in-
          crease through the month. At the same time, senior
          diplomatic and military officials of the US Mission
          begin meeting formally as the Mission Council.

          CYPRUS - Fighting continues on Cyprus with both Greece
          and Turkey furnishing arms and support to their native
          Cypriot factions.

3   UNITED NATIONS - The UN Observer Force in Yemen has
          its charter extended until 4 September to facilitate
          the withdrawal of UAR and Saudi forces.

4   GREAT BRITAIN - At a conference held in London the
          government announces its plans to make the Federation
          of South Arabia independent by 1968.

4-9   SOUTH VIET NAM - Three Special Forces camps in the
          Central Highlands are attacked by VC/NVA forces.

6   NYASALAND - The country is declared independent and
          named Malawi. Malawi becomes part of the British Com-
          monwealth.

9   SOUTH VIET NAM - MACV asks for an additional 700 advisors (689 Army and 11 Marines). Of the 689 Army personnel requested, 226 are to be sub-sector advisors and 463 battalion advisors.

10   DEMOCRATIC CONGO REPUBLIC - Moise Tshombe returns from exile and is appointed premier. His first task is to stop the insurgency in the Kivu Province that is led by the Chinese-Communist inspired Comite National de Liberation.

18   UNITED STATES - Race rioting breaks out in the Harlem district of New York City.

21   OAU - At a conference in Cairo, the leaders of the member nations of the Organization of African Unity declare the denuclearization of Africa.

21-23   SINGAPORE - Serious rioting breaks out among the Chinese community in a Communist-inspired demonstration against Malaysia.

22   UNITED STATES - The government pledges its support of the new Malaysian state.

26   OAS - The OAS votes diplomatic and economic sanctions against Cuba because of its interference in Venezuelan internal affairs.

27   SOUTH VIET NAM - As the efficiency of RVNAF units deteriorates sharply, US advisory and logistics support increases at a rapid rate. In Washington the Pentagon orders 5,000 additional military personnel to SVN as advisors. This will raise the US strength in SVN to 25,000.

30   NORTH VIET NAM - Without notifying their American counterparts, the South Vietnamese Navy carries out a series of surface attacks against radar and naval installations on Hon Mat (Hon Matt) (in the estuary of the Giang River near Vinh) and Hon Ngu Islands.

30-31   NORTH VIET NAM - North Vietnamese motor torpedo boats carry out a series of attacks along the South Vietnamese coast.

AUGUST

2   NORTH VIET NAM - At least three NVN motor torpedo boats (MTB) attack the destroyer USS Maddox in international waters off North Viet Nam in the Gulf of Tonkin. With the support of aircraft from the carrier USS Ticonderoga, one enemy MTB is damaged.

3   MEXICO - The government announces it will not join   in
           the OAS sanctions   against Cuba. It   becomes the   only
           state in the Western Hemisphere to maintain any diplo-
           matic status with the Castro regime.

4   NORTH VIET NAM - The destroyers <u>USS Maddox</u> and <u>USS C.</u>
           <u>Turner Joy</u> are attacked by North Vietnamese MTBs.   Two
           of the MTBs are sunk.

5   NORTH VIET NAM - United States aircraft carry out   re-
           taliatory raids   against petroleum   and naval   instal-
           lations along the North   Vietnamese coast. The UN   Se-
           curity Council calls an   emergency session to   discuss
           the incident and asks both North and South Viet Nam to
           present evidence. US naval   strength in   the Gulf   of
           Tonkin is increased.

7   UNITED STATES - A Joint Congressional Resolution   on
           Southeast Asia (Gulf of   Tonkin Resolution, signed   11
           August [PL 88-408]) affirms that the US is prepared to
           assist any SEATO member   or protocol state   requesting
           defense assistance.

7   SOUTH VIET NAM - General   Khanh declares   a state   of
           emergency, taking   into his   own hands the   power   to
           impose censorship, military   justice, travel   restric-
           tions, arrest without   appeal, and   the death   penalty
           for "speculators, terrorists and saboteurs."

7-9   CYPRUS - Turkish Air Force units attack western Cyprus
           in support of Turkish Cypriot settlement operations in
           the region.   This   creates a   dangerous   situation   in
           which Greece and Turkey come close to war. Finally,   a
           UN ceasefire is arranged between Cyprus and Turkey.

8   SOUTH VIET NAM - An   additional 273 US Army   personnel
           are approved for MACV for staff and field   assignments
           with ARVN combat   units. Another 339   are assigned   to
           sub-sectors.

9   UNITED NATIONS - The Security Council orders a   cease-
           fire on Cyprus.

15   SOUTH VIET NAM - General Khanh assumes the   presidency
           in a government shake-up designed to consolidate power
           into his   hands. Duong   Van (Big)   Minh is   ousted   as
           Chief of State. A new constitution is approved by   the
           Military Revolutionary Council. Massive civil protests
           follow.

17   GREECE - The government   withdraws its military   units
           from NATO.

27   SOUTH VIET NAM - General Khanh resigns as President
            following demands by students and Buddhists for an end
            to dictatorial rule. Khahn retains command of the army
            and becomes part of the three-man group seeking to
            find a new government. The new constitution is with-
            drawn.

28   UNITED STATES - Race rioting breaks out in Philadel-
            phia, Pennsylvania.

29   SOUTH VIET NAM - At the behest of the triumvirate, a
            civilian economist, Dr. Nguyen Xuan Oanh, takes con-
            trol of the government stating he will hold office for
            two months. General Khanh is reported to be suffer-
            ing from a mental and physical breakdown.

30   SOUTH VIET NAM - The state of emergency order is ex-
            tended for one week. Some 50,000 Roman Catholics hold
            a funeral procession in Saigon for six demonstrators
            killed on 27 August. Five battalions of troops keep
            order.

30   DEMOCRATIC CONGO REPUBLIC - Congolese forces retake
            Albertville in Kivu Province.

SEPTEMBER

            DEMOCRATIC CONGO REPUBLIC - With Soviet and UAR
            assistance filtered into the country through Uganda
            and the Sudan, Communist-inspired elements in east
            central Congo grow dangerously stronger.

1   SOUTH VIET NAM - Total US strength in MACV now numbers
            4,739 of which 3,908 are Army personnel.

3   SOUTH VIET NAM - General Khanh, "rested and recover-
            ed," resumes control of the government when the civil-
            ian governnmment fails to make any gains. Duong Van
            Minh is reinstalled as Chief of State. The following
            day Khanh announces he will hold power for two months
            at which point control will be returned to a civilian
            government.

13   USSR - Nikita Khrushchev is stripped of power in a
            bloodless coup d'etat in the Kremlin.

13   SOUTH VIET NAM - A bloodless military revolt, led by
            Brigadier General Lam Van Phat and supported by a
            group of young officers, including Air Force commander
            Nguyen Cao Ky, is suppressed in Saigon.

15   CAMBODIA - The government indefinitely postpones the
            presentation of credentials by the US Ambassador.

18   NORTH VIET NAM – Several North Vietnamese MTBs harass
            the destroyers <u>USS Edwards</u> and <u>USS Morton</u>.

20   SOUTH VIET NAM – Montagnard tribesmen, serving with
            the ARVN Special Forces, mutiny against their Viet-
            namese officers at the Bong Sai Pa SF camp in the
            Quang Duc Province and demand autonomy for the
            mountain areas.

21   MALTA – The island nation becomes independent but
            remains in the British Commonwealth. The British are
            guaranteed the use of their military bases for ten
            years.

26   SOUTH VIET NAM – General Khanh leaves office to make
            way for a civilian government. A High National Council
            composed of 17 civilians is inaugurated and is given
            the task of preparing a new constitution for the
            country.

30   SOUTH VIET NAM – A number of senior military officers
            are sent into diplomatic exile in Europe.

OCTOBER

            SOUTH VIET NAM – The US charges that Cambodian troops
            have entered SVN. Probably at the same time, the first
            full NVA regiment crosses into SVN.

1   SOUTH VIET NAM – Elements of the 1,297-man US 5th
            Special Forces Group arrive in SVN. The unit will be
            completely moved into SVN on 5 April 1965.

14-15   USSR – Nikita Khrushchev is replaced in the Soviet
            hierarchy by Alexei N. Kosygin and Leonid I. Brezhnev.

16   COMMUNIST CHINA – The Chinese detonate a nuclear
            device.

20   SOUTH VIET NAM – A new constitution is presented. Pre-
            mier Nguyen Khanh and his caretaker government (since
            26 September) resign to clear the way for the
            appointment of a new constitutional government.

21   SOUTH VIET NAM – The US charges that Cambodian troops
            have crossed the border into SVN and have seized an
            American officer.

25   SOUTH VIET NAM – The US charges Cambodian forces have
            fired on a US helicopter that was searching for the
            missing American officer.

26   SOUTH VIET NAM - Phan Khac Suu becomes Chief of State
            ending nearly a year of military rule.

27   CAMBODIA - The government claims it has shot down a
            USAF C-123 over its territory. The US Command in Sai-
            gon later confirms the loss and blames the overflight
            on a navigational error.

30   SOUTH VIET NAM - Tran Van Houng, the Mayor of Saigon,
            is appointed Prime Minister.

NOVEMBER

            DEMOCRATIC CONGO REPUBLIC - The government prepares to
            retake Stanleyville where 2,000 whites are   held
            hostage.

1   SOUTH VIET NAM - The major US airbase at Bien Hoa
            north of Saigon is attacked by the VC. At least four
            American personnel at the base are killed, 12 wounded,
            and significant damage to helicopters is reported.

2   SAUDI ARABIA - Faisal is proclaimed King after Saud
            ibn Abdel Aziz is deposed.

2   CAMBODIA - The USSR delivers a large shipment of mili-
            tary equipment to the Cambodian government to replace
            the loss of American military aid.

3-4   BOLIVIA - A military coup overthrows the government of
            President Paz Estenssoro.

15   SUDAN - President Ibraham 'Abboud is forced to resign
            in the face of mounting unrest. Sirr al-Khatim, a
            civil servant, (Khalifa) is installed as   Prime
            Minister.

25-27   DEMOCRATIC CONGO REPUBLIC - Belgian   paratroopers
            flying in US Air Force planes are air dropped over
            Stanleyville. Having flown from Belgium by way of
            Ascension Island, the airborne forces are successful
            and rescue some 1,700 white prisoners. Several hundred
            more whites are massacred, however, while a storm of
            Communist rhetoric forces an early withdrawal of the
            Belgians.

DECEMBER

11   UNITED STATES - A massive increase in aid to South
            Viet Nam is announced.

16   UNITED STATES - The major increase in the size of RVNAF that was recommended by General Westmoreland is approved by the JCS. This increase of 30,309 will bring RVNAF to 273,908 with an concomitant increase in paramilitary strength to 322,187. An additional 446 US advisors will be assigned to SVN.

18   UNITED NATIONS - The UN Security Council extends its mandate (of 9 August) on Cyprus.

19   SOUTH VIET NAM - Leaders of the armed forces carry out a swift purge dissolving the High National Council (formed on 8 September). They arrest many political figures. The government is not disturbed, however, and continues its leadership.

24   SOUTH VIET NAM - Viet Cong terrorists bomb the Brink's Hotel, a US officers' military billet, in Saigon. Two Americans are killed and over 100 Americans and Viet-namese are wounded.

27   SOUTH VIET NAM - In an operation that lasts until 1 January 1965, two ARVN battalions are destroyed by the 9th VC Division at Binh Gia, east of Saigon.

31   SOUTH VIET NAM - US military strength now exceeds 23,000.

Notes

1965

SOUTH VIET NAM - Based on a decision made last summer, Hanoi begins steadily introducing NVA regulars into SVN via the Ho Chi Minh Trail. These forces use Laos and Cambodia as sanctuaries even though it is a violation of the Geneva Accords. By the end of February at least four NVA regiments are identified in SVN.

YEMEN - More than 60,000 Egyptian troops are in Yemen supporting the pro-Communist rebel government in its war against royalist forces.

JANUARY

1   SOUTH VIET NAM - Three battalions of the 9th Viet Cong Division attack and defeat an ARVN two-battalion force at Binh Gia east of Saigon.

3   BOLIVIA - Army units smash a federal police plot to overthrow the government of President Rene Barientos Ortuno.

7   UNITED STATES - Robert Glenn Thompson of Bay Shore, New York, is arrested on charges of spying for the USSR during and after his service in the US Air Force.

14   SOUTH VIET NAM - US Air Force planes destroy a vital bridge in Laos that served as a link between North Vietnamese and Pathet Lao forces. The US Command reports that a total of 28 US Army helicopters have been lost in combat since 1 January 1962. At least 58 more have been destroyed in accidents.

15   BURUNDI - Premier Pierre Ngendandumwe is assassinated.

21   UNITED NATIONS - Indonesia formally notifies the UN of
            its determination to withdraw after Malaysia is ac-
            cepted as a member.

22   SOUTH VIET NAM - Hundreds of Saigon Buddhists demon-
            strate at the US Embassy and stone the USIS library.
            This is the precursor to four days of rioting against
            the government.

24   COMMUNIST CHINA - Chou En-lai proposes the establish-
            ment of a new United Nations free of "the manipulation
            of United States imperialism."

26   IRAN - Premier Hassan Ali Mansour dies of wounds in-
            flicted by an assassin on 21 January.

27   SOUTH VIET NAM - A military coup, led by Lieutenant
            General Nguyen Khanh, seizes power in Saigon. The
            government of Tran Van Houng is ousted. Doctor Phan
            Khac Suu resigns, but consents to stay on as caretaker
            during the transition.

28   SOUTH VIET NAM - General Khanh is empowered by the
            military to find a solution to the political crisis
            touched off by violent Buddhist opposition to the
            government of Tran Van Houng. Nguyen Xuan Oanh, a
            Harvard-trained economist, is appointed Premier.

30   WEST GERMANY - Some $80 million dollars worth of US-
            produced military supplies are prepared to be shipped
            to Israel by West Germany. The shipments include US-
            made M48 "Patton" tanks, submarines, and helicopters.
            Protests from a number of Arab countries eventually
            force a termination of the shipments before they are
            completed.

31   LAOS - A coup attempt by right-wing army factions led
            by General Phoumi Nosavan fails.

FEBRUARY

2   UNITED STATES - The President sends White House ad-
            visor McGeorge Bundy to Viet Nam to survey the in-
            creasingly critical political and military situations
            there.

4   FRANCE - President DeGaulle calls for a five-power
            conference (US, Great Britain, France, USSR, Communist
            China) to reorganize the UN.

6 NORTH VIET NAM - Soviet Premier Alexei Kosygin is given a warm welcome upon his arrival in Hanoi.

7 SOUTH VIET NAM - A US support base near Pleiku is attacked by at least 100 Viet Cong. Twenty-six Americans are killed and 62 wounded. The US retaliates by sending carrier-based aircraft against the North Vietnamese base at Dong Hoi above the so-called Demilitarized Zone (DMZ). A second attack, which includes South Vietnamese aircraft, is carried out on 8 February against the North Vietnamese communications center at Vin Linh.

8 UNITED STATES - The White House orders the 1,800 US government-sponsored dependents still in country out of SVN and announces the dispatch of a Hawk air defense battalion to SVN.

9 SOUTH VIET NAM - A USMC Hawk (SAM) battalion arrives at Da Nang, a major US installation on the coast in the northern I Corps Tactical Zone (CTZ).

9 NORTH VIET NAM - Soviet Premier Kosygin promises increased military aid to NVN.

9 UNITED STATES - The government makes a billion-dollar arms sale to Great Britain and Australia.

9 GREAT BRITAIN - The government announces that budgetary considerations dictate the necessity to cooperate with foreign powers, especially the US, in future weapons developmental programs.

10 SOUTH VIET NAM - Viet Cong sappers (demolitions teams) blow up the US enlisted barracks at Qui Nhon killing 23 Americans and injuring 13 more.

10 WEST GERMANY - The government orders a temporary halt to arms shipments to Israel because of protests from the UAR.

11 SOUTH VIET NAM - In reprisal for the terrorist bombing attack on the US barracks at Qui Nhon, in which 23 are killed, 160 US and South Vietnamese aircraft carry out a massive attack against military bases in North Viet Nam.

13 HUNGARY - The US Embassy is attacked by African and Asian students protesting US policy in Southeast Asia.

15 INDONESIA - The USIS Library is seized by a mob protesting against the US air raids into North Viet Nam.

15   COMMUNIST CHINA - The government threatens to enter the war if the US sends combat units into SVN.

15   NORTH VIET NAM - The government asks for the withdrawal of the ICC field teams in NVN.

15   SOUTH VIET NAM - The US advisory effort is increased by the addition of another 446 personnel.

16   UNITED STATES - Members of the FBI, the New York City Police, and the Royal Canadian Mounted Police, working together, break up an extremist-group plot to blow up the Statue of Liberty.

16   UGANDA - US support of the Congolese government of Premier Moise Tshombe leads to anti-US rioting.

16   SOUTH VIET NAM - A new government is formed by Dr. Phan Van Quat. A new legislative council is also formed. Nguyen Khanh still holds the power.

18   GAMBIA - This former colony is declared independent and named "The Gambia" as a Dominion of the British Empire.

18   UNITED STATES - Secretary of Defense Robert McNamara declares the US has no other choice but to continue the struggle in SVN.

19   VENEZUELA - Mistaking him and his companions for terrorists, Venezulean police kill Peace Corps volunteer Joseph R. Rupley.

19   SOUTH VIET NAM - Claiming Nguyen Khanh has become a dictator, Colonel Pham Ngoc Thao and a group of officers, including Brigadier General Lam Van Phat, carry out a successful coup. As most of the military group are Roman Catholics, a Buddhist upheaval is predicted. At the same time, US military jet aircraft are employed for the first time in SVN when they carry out a raid in Binh Dinh Province in II CTZ.

20   INDIA - Prime Minister Lal Bahadur Shastri proposes a new plan that would guarantee the neutrality of the two Viet Nams.

20-21   SOUTH VIET NAM - Lieutenant General Nguyen Khanh is returned to power when his loyal troops recapture Saigon without firing a shot. Lam Van Phat surrenders to General Khanh claiming his group has "capitulated." Another more powerful group of officers forces Nguyen Khanh to yield to Major General Tran Van Minh who replaces him as Commander in Chief of RVNAF.

21   SOUTH VIET NAM - Intelligence reports indicate most
        North Vietnamese supplies enter SVN by sea rather than
        down the Ho Chi Minh Trail through Laos.

24   WEST GERMANY - After accusing Egyptian President Gamal
        Nasser of meddling in German affairs by inviting East
        German President Walter Ulbricht to Cairo (17 Febru-
        ary), the Bonn government cuts off all economic aid to
        Egypt.

24   UNITED STATES - The government announces that it is
        using jet aircraft against the North Vietnamese and
        Viet Cong in SVN.

25   SOUTH VIET NAM - A 600-man Republic of Korea Army
        (ROKA) engineer battalion arrives in the country. This
        is the first element of what will be a 41,000-man ROK
        force by October 1966.

26   INDONESIA - American-owned rubber plantations in North
        Sumatra are seized by the government.

27   UNITED STATES - The State Department issues a White
        Paper accusing the North Vietnamese of increasing ag-
        gression against South Viet Nam.

28   UNITED STATES - President Johnson announces continuous
        limited air strikes against NVN to force a negotiated
        settlement to the war.

MARCH

2   UNITED STATES - The US inaugurates "Operation ROLLING
        THUNDER," a major bombing campaign against NVN. Some
        160 US planes take part in the first day's operations
        against the north.

4   USSR - The US Embassy is the scene of a riot by about
        2,000 students, primarily Asian, who are protesting US
        involvement in Southeast Asia. Several hundred Soviet
        troops and mounted police finally break up the demon-
        stration.

6   UNITED STATES - The government announces the dispatch
        of about 3,500 Marines to South Viet Nam to increase
        security around the Da Nang air base. It also gives
        permission for US aircraft to act independently of
        VNAF.

6   COMMUNIST CHINA - Students protest in front of the
        Soviet Embassy. The principal reason for the demon-
        stration is denunciation of the Soviet use of force in
        quelling anti-US riots in the USSR.

8   SOUTH VIET NAM - The 3rd Battalion, 9th US Marine Ex-
        peditionary Brigade (approximately 3,500 men) lands at
        Da Nang in Quang Nam Province. This event marks the
        beginning of the US role in the ground war in South
        Viet Nam. Total US strength in SVN now stands at
        27,000.

10   UNITED STATES - The US Navy begins the "MARKET TIME"
        coastal barrier interdiction campaign designed to
        prevent the over-water delivery of men and materiel
        from NVN to SVN.

15   NORTH VIET NAM - US Air Force and Navy planes attack a
        munitions depot 100 miles from Hanoi.

19   INDONESIA - The government seizes four foreign oil
        companies, three of which are American. By 24 April
        all foreign-owned properties in Indonesia will be
        seized.

19   SOUTH VIET NAM - The first US Army ground battalion,
        the 716th Military Police Battalion, arrives in
        country.

24   COMMUNIST CHINA - The government announces its will-
        ingness to supply troops to aid the North Vietnamese,
        if they are requested.

24   UNITED STATES - Secretary of State Dean Rusk answers
        critics by declaring that the use of a riot-control
        agent (tear gas) against the enemy in SVN does not
        constitute "gas warfare" as claimed in some sources.

28   SOUTH CHINA SEA - The US Seventh Fleet begins coastal
        surveillance operations off SVN.

28-30   LAOS - A military coup fails without bloodshed.

30   SOUTH VIET NAM - A bomb explodes in the US Embassy in
        Saigon. Twenty are killed, 175 injured.

31   SOUTH VIET NAM - A huge incendiary raid is carried out
        against a Viet Cong stronghold 25 miles from Saigon.

APRIL

1   SOUTH VIET NAM - The US Army 1st Logistics Command is
        activated.

2   UNITED STATES - The government announces its intention
        to send several thousand more troops to SVN.

4	NORTH VIET NAM - North Vietnamese MiG fighters shoot down the first two US jets in a dogfight over NVN.

7   UNITED STATES - President Johnson, in a speech at Johns Hopkins University, offers unconditional discussions on settling the Viet Nam conflict and suggests a $1 billion aid program for SEA.

8   NORTH VIET NAM - The government proposes its own four-point formula for peace which includes US withdrawal from SEA.

8   COMMUNIST CHINA - The government denounces the US proposals of 7 April.

8   CUBA - Fifty-three members of an alleged spy ring are rounded up by the Castro government. A number of Americans are among them.

8   EAST GERMANY - An American convoy challenges the Communist closing of the autobahn between the West and Berlin.

9   NORTH VIET NAM - In an air duel fought over the Gulf of Tonkin a US jet and a MiG are shot down.

10   SOUTH VIET NAM - The headquarters elements of the US Third Marine Division arrive in the I CTZ. They are followed by the arrival of the 1st Marine Air Wing.

13   NORTH VIET NAM - A radar station is wrecked, and a bridge is destroyed in a US-SVN raid into NVN.

14   NORTH VIET NAM - In a joint statement, Soviet Premier Kosygin and NVN Premier Pham Van Dong outline their four-point program for peace. Foreign forces withdrawal is the key issue.

15   NORTH VIET NAM - Over 230 US and SVN aircraft take part in the largest raid to date into NVN. Military targets along the Red River are hit.

16   NORTH VIET NAM - The first surface-to-air missile (SAM) site is identified as being under construction near Hanoi.

16   SOUTH KOREA - After a riot in which scores are injured and arrested, the government closes four Seoul universities.

16-30   LAOS - Another army revolt, led by the supporters of Phoumi Nosavan, fails.

17   UNITED STATES - Over 12,000 people, protesting the war
            in Southeast Asia, demonstrate in front of the White
            House.

17   NORTH VIET NAM - Intelligence reports showing that the
            NVA is building Soviet-style surface-to-air missile
            (SAM) sites near Hanoi are confirmed by the US State
            Department.

19   NORTH VIET NAM - The government rejects peace talk
            proposals from 17 third world leaders.

19   UNITED STATES - A conference is held in Honolulu to
            develop US plans for SVN.

19   USSR - Premier Kosygin warns the US that its stepped-
            up participation in the war in Southeast Asia is mov-
            ing the world toward a "dangerous deadline."

21   UNITED STATES - The government announces an increase
            in aid to RVN, from $207 million to $330 million,
            raising the total aid package to $630 million.

24   INDIA - Renewed large-scale fighting breaks out along
            the Pakastani border in the Rann of Kutch region. The
            fighting lasts for two weeks without result.

24-25   DOMINICAN REPUBLIC - There is a military coup which
            overthrows the civilian triumvirate government. Civil
            war begins across the country.

25   UNITED STATES - The Department of State announces that
            the US is willing to participate in the nine-nation
            conference on the neutrality of Cambodia.

28   SOUTH VIET NAM - An additional 716 advisor spaces are
            authorized, 482 of which are designated for field
            activities.

28   TUNISIA - The government announces it will boycott the
            Arab League meeting because of recent Arab League mem-
            ber objections to President Bourguiba's peace plan for
            Israel.

29   OAS - The organization appeals for a cease-fire in the
            fighting in the Dominican Republic.

30   DOMINICAN REPUBLIC - The United States begins an major
            airborne operation to protect American interests in
            the country. Over 20,000 airborne troops and Marines
            participate in creating a nine-mile protective zone
            where Americans can seek refuge.

MAY

1   OAS - Five delegates are chosen to seek ways of ending the strife in the Dominican Republic.

1   SOUTH VIET NAM - The total American military advisory strength is reported to be 5,240; 5,054 are Army personnel.

3   CAMBODIA - The government breaks diplomatic relations with the US.

4   UNITED STATES - President Johnson asks Congress for an additional $700 million for SVN.

5   SOUTH VIET NAM - Two battalions of the US 173rd Airborne Brigade arrive from Okinawa. These are the first US Army ground combat units to arrive in the country. They are assigned the mission of protecting the huge US military complex at Bien Hoa, 25 miles north of Saigon.

5   DOMINICAN REPUBLIC - A cease-fire is arranged by the OAS and the US.

6   OAS - The organization agrees to establish an Inter-American Peacekeeping Force made up of contingents from Brazil, Costa Rica, Guatamala, Honduras, Paraguay, the US, and Venezuela.

6   SOUTH VIET NAM - The powerful Armed Forces Council (MRC) bows out of politics with a formal vote of confidence in the government of Prime Minister Phan Van Quat.

7   SOUTH VIET NAM - The US III Marine Amphibious Force (MAF) is activated in SVN.

13   UNITED STATES - Accused Soviet spy Robert Glenn Thompson is found guilty and is sentenced to 30 years imprisonment.

13   ARAB LEAGUE - Ten member nations sever diplomatic relations with West Germany because of its recognition of Israel. Libya, Morocco, and Tunisia do not join in the action.

13-19   UNITED STATES - The first pause in the bombing of NVN takes place.

13-19   DOMINICAN REPUBLIC - Renewed heavy fighting breaks out around the American Security Zone. US pressure finally brings about a new cease-fire.

14   SOUTH VIET NAM - The US government authorizes the use
            of naval gun fire in support of friendly operations.

19   NORTH VIET NAM - US bombing of targets in NVN resumes
            after a five-day pause.

23   DOMINICAN REPUBLIC - The Inter-American Peace Keeping
            Force moves into the country and becomes operational.
            Although large numbers (6,000) of US forces remain in
            the country, the bulk of the more than 20,000 US
            troops begin their withdrawal. Nineteen Americans are
            reported as having been killed in action during the
            operation.

JUNE

2   SOUTH VIET NAM - The first Australian combat forces,
            the 1st Battalion, Royal Australian Regiment, arrive
            in SVN.

7   SOUTH VIET NAM - US forces in SVN surpass 54,000;
            24,500 are Army personnel. There are 9,500 Air Force
            and 3,500 Navy personnel also in country. This does
            not include the personnel of the US Seventh Fleet at
            sea off the coast.

8   UNITED STATES - The State Department announces that
            MACV has been authorized to commit US troops into
            combat alongside the Vietnamese, if requested. The
            next day, when US involvement in ground actions is
            reported, the White House denies this constitutes a
            change in US policy.

9   SOUTH VIET NAM - Construction begins at Cam Rahn Bay,
            which is destined to become the largest port complex
            in SEA. The first US combat forces are committed in a
            ground combat role in SVN.

10   SOUTH VIET NAM - A major battle begins in the vicinity
            of Dong Xoai.

11   SOUTH VIET NAM - Prime Minister Quat resigns and re-
            turns power to the military.

14   SOUTH VIET NAM - A new military National Leadership
            Committee is formed by Major General Nguyen Van Thieu.

17   NORTH VIET NAM - Several enemy MiGs are shot down in
            dogfights over NVN.

18   SOUTH VIET NAM - USAF B-52s based on Guam make their
            first strike in SVN in an area 40 miles northeast of
            Saigon. This begins the "ARC LIGHT" campaign.

19   SOUTH VIET NAM - A new government is formed with Air Force Vice Marshal Nguyen Cao Ky as premier following a bloodless coup which began on 12 June.

19   ALGERIA - The government of Achmed Ben Bella is overthrown by Colonel Houari Boumedienne.

24   USSR - The Soviet government refuses to meet with a mission made up of British Commonwealth members sent to Moscow to help get Viet Nam peace talks started.

25   COMMUNIST CHINA - The Communist Chinese government (and, subsequently, the North Vietnamese) refuses an audience with the Commonwealth peace mission.

25   SOUTH VIET NAM - VC sappers float mines down the Saigon River and blow up the My Canh floating restaurant.

27   SOUTH VIET NAM - US combat troops participate in their first major combat action as the 173rd Airborne Brigade (2 battalions of the 503rd Airborne) and two Vietnamese battalions begin an operation in "War Zone D" in Bien Hoa Province, a known VC stronghold in the III CTZ, 20 miles north of Saigon.

28   SOUTH VIET NAM - Some 125,000 US combat troops are reported to be in SVN.

JULY

5   ALGERIA - Houari Boumedienne becomes President.

7   SOUTH VIET NAM - An additional 8,000 US Marines arrive in the I CTZ.

8   SOUTH VIET NAM - General Maxwell Taylor resigns as the US Ambassador and is replaced by Henry Cabot Lodge.

10   SOUTH VIET NAM - The US 1st Logistics Command is enlarged and begins a major logistical buildup.

11   UNITED STATES - Secretary of State Rusk comments that the North Vietnamese concept "of sanctuary is dead."

12   SOUTH VIET NAM - Elements of the 2nd Brigade, 1st US Infantry Division begin landing in SVN and are deployed to protect the major US base at Long Binh, 25 miles north of Saigon.

15   SOUTH VIET NAM - MACV asks the press corps to apply "voluntary censorship." At the same time, MACV confirms the presence of the NVA 101st Regiment in SVN.

16   SOUTH VIET NAM - US Defense Secretary Robert McNamara
            arrives for a five-day visit. He finds that "in many
            respects, there has been a deterioration" in the war
            effort since his last visit.

20   SOUTH VIET NAM - The US Army Support Command, Vietnam
            is redesignated the US Army, Vietnam (USARV). The new
            headquarters, located at Long Binh, 25 miles north of
            Saigon, is established to act as the major Army
            command and control element in SVN.

21   SOUTH VIET NAM - The first New Zealand combat element,
            a field artillery battery, arrives in SVN.

24   NORTH VIET NAM - The first US fighter-bomber aircraft
            is shot down by a Soviet-built SA-2 "Guideline" air
            defense missile near Hanoi. In retaliation, air
            strikes are carried out against targets in the Hanoi
            area (27 July).

25   UNITED STATES - The President announces US strength in
            SVN will rise to 125,000.

29   SOUTH VIET NAM - The 1st Brigade, US 101st Airborne
            Division arrives in country and is deployed near Cam
            Rahn Bay.

AUGUST

1   SOUTH VIET NAM - The US Command forms the US Army Task
            Force Alpha as the first US Army field force headquar-
            ters in SVN.

2   UNITED STATES - A conference held in Honolulu discuss
            US troop deployments to SVN.

4   SOUTH VIET NAM - A plan is approved to upgrade SEA
            long-line communications. This becomes the forerunner
            to the Integrated Communications System (ICS).

5-23   KASHMIR - Both Pakistani and Indian forces cross the
            cease-fire line and fighting breaks out. Clashes also
            occur in the Punjab.

9   SINGAPORE - The island that comprises Singapore is
            declared independent of Malaysia.

12   UNITED STATES - A major racial disturbance takes place
            in the Watts district of Los Angeles. Some 15,000
            police and National Guardsmen are required to restore
            order.

13   UNITED STATES - The government announces its adherence
            to the 1949 Geneva Convention concerning the treatment
            of prisoners of war (POW).

14   SOUTH VIET NAM - The 7th Marine Regimental Landing
            Team (RLT), 1st US Marine Division, arrives in SVN.

14   UNITED STATES - The Department of State closes the US
            Embassy in Brazzaville, in the People's Republic of
            Congo. This action follows repeated incidents of
            harassment of US diplomatic officials.

16   UNITED STATES - The US announces it will no longer de-
            mand the Soviet Union lose its UN General Assembly
            vote despite its refusal to pay its share of peace-
            keeping costs.

18   UNITED STATES - The Senate approves a $1.7 billion
            supplemental appropriation for military operations in
            South Viet Nam. At the same time, military intelli-
            gence sources confirm the presence of the NVA 325th
            Division in SVN.

18-21   SOUTH VIET NAM - In an operation codenamed STAR LIGHT,
            the US Marines count their first victory against the
            1st VC Regiment in a battle on the coast below the new
            USMC base at Chu Lai, Quang Ngai Pro- vince in the I
            CTZ. The VC stronghold at Van Tuong is destroyed after
            a fierce battle.

20   SOUTH VIET NAM - Henry Cabot Lodge arrives in SVN for
            his second tour as US Ambassador replacing Maxwell
            Taylor.

24   YEMEN - A cease-fire is agreed upon between Saudi
            Arabia's King Faisal and Egypt's President Abdul Gamal
            Nasser. Both agree to stop their support of the war,
            while the Yemeni factions agree to stop the fighting.
            This is the third such cease-fire agreement in two
            years.

24   KASHMIR - A large Indian force crosses the cease-fire
            line and fighting intensifies. The UN Cease-fire Ob-
            server Team in Kashmir is finally able to restore the
            truce.

28   GREECE - The Greek Parliament votes "no confidence" in
            the Royalist-backed government of Premier Elias
            Tsirmokos.

31   DOMINICAN REPUBLIC - A provisional government headed
            by Hector Garcia-Godoy is put in place.

SEPTEMBER

INDONESIA - The army defeats a Communist takeover attempt late in the month after the Army Chief of Staff and other senior officers are kidnapped by the Communists.

1
SOUTH VIET NAM - The senior American commander in each CTZ is named the senior tactical advisor to the Vietnamese Corps Commander.

1-25
KASHMIR - Renewed fighting erupts when Pakistani forces invade Kashmir in reprisal for the Indian raid of 24 August. Karachi and New Delhi are bombed. The "war" ends in a stalemate.

4
UNITED NATIONS - The Security Council calls for an immediate cease-fire in the Kashmir crisis.

4
UNITED STATES - The government recognizes the new provisional government established in the Dominican Republic.

6
PAKISTAN - Indian infantry and tank units cross the border into West Pakistan near Lahore. The Indian Prime Minister Lal Badahur Shastri calls the affair a "full-fledged war."

8
UNITED STATES - The government announces the suspension of military aid to India and Pakistan. Great Britain and Australia make similar announcements on 9 September.

9
COMMUNIST CHINA - Communist Chinese forces mass near the Indian border as a threat against continued Indian operations in the Himalayas.

10
FRANCE - President DeGaulle threatens to pull France out of NATO unless specific changes are made in the treaty organization.

10
SOUTH VIET NAM - The US Marines complete a sweep of the Batangan Peninsula, killing 138 VC and capturing 38.

11
PAKISTAN - The government formally rejects the United Nations cease-fire request aimed at stopping the fighting along its border with India.

12
SOUTH VIET NAM - The first elements of the 1st US Cavalry Division (Airmobile) arrive in SVN. US strength in SVN is now in excess of 128,500.

16   COMMUNIST CHINA - The government, siding with Paki-
          stan, warns India that "grave consequences" can be
          expected if India does not change its policy of
          maintaining military outposts in a northeast border
          area claimed by China.

17   GREECE - King Constantine swears in Stephanos
          Stephanopolous as the country's new Premier.

17   IRAQ - After putting down a coup attempt against his
          brother, President Abdul Salam Arif, General Abdul
          Rahman Arif seizes power for himself.

21   COMMUNIST CHINA - The government announces that India
          has complied with its ultimatum and has withdrawn its
          outposts from the contested border area.

21   UNITED STATES - The Defense Department recommends a
          new strength ceiling of 200,000 US servicemen men for
          SVN.

22   UNITED NATIONS - A UN-proposed cease-fire goes into
          effect between Pakistan and India. Fighting soon re-
          sumes, however, and the truce does not finally take
          effect until 27 September.

24   UNITED STATES - President Johnson announces that the
          US will enter into negotiations with Panama over the
          future of the Panama Canal.

25   SOUTH VIET NAM - Task Force Alpha is redesignated
          Field Forces, Vietnam.

27   SOUTH VIET NAM - Two US servicemen who were captured
          in South Viet Nam are executed by a Viet Cong firing
          squad.

28   UNITED STATES - Another conference on US troop deploy-
          ments in SVN is held in Honolulu.

29   NORTH VIET NAM - The government announces that US and
          Vietnamese airmen captured in NVN would henceforth be
          treated as war criminals.

OCTOBER

1   INDONESIA - An abortive Communist-inspired coup
          d'etat, led by Central Javanese army and some air
          force units against the Sukarno government, is de-
          feated by the Army's Strategic Reserve headed by
          General Suharto.

8   INDONESIA - A massive eradication of the Indonesian
             Communist Party (PKI) begins. Estimates run as high as
             400,000 killed in the purge, but not all are Commu-
             nists. A number are Chinese who have dominated society
             in the island nation. The massacre of innocent and
             guilty alike continues into December. It is estimated
             that more than 100,000 PKI members are killed. This
             loss diminishes Sukarno's hold on the country as the
             PKI had supported him in the past.

12   GREAT BRITAIN   - Prime Minister Harold Wilson asks
             Rhodesia to receive a Commonwealth Commission to help
             avert the possiblity of a racial war.

13   DEMOCRATIC CONGO REPUBLIC - Premier Moise Tshombe is
             ousted by President Kasavubu.

14   UNITED STATES - The Defense Department orders a mili-
             tary draft call-up of 45,224 for December. This is the
             largest draft call since the Korean War.

15-16   UNITED STATES - Thousands of students demonstrate all
             across the country to end the war in SEA.

17   NORTH VIET NAM - The first mobile SAM site is destroy-
             ed by US aircraft in a raid into NVN.

18   SOUTH VIET NAM - A major battle begins near Plei Me in
             Pleiku Province in the Central Highlands.

22   SOUTH VIET NAM - Initial elements of the ROK Capital
             (Tiger) Division arrive in country.

23   SOUTH VIET NAM - An NVN-initiated battle begins in the
             Ia Drang Valley in Pleiku Province with the objective
             of cutting SVN in half. The battle goes on into Novem-
             ber when the newly arrived 1st Cavalry Division (Air-
             mobile) defeats the NVA in the western part of Pleiku
             Province. Heavy casualties are taken by both sides.

25   SOUTH VIET NAM - An ARVN regiment relieves the outpost
             at Plei Me, which has been under siege for seven days.

27   BRAZIL - President Humberto Castello Branco's govern-
             ment orders the abolishment of all political parties
             and announces that sweeping authority has been granted
             to the military tribunals.

28   NORTH VIET NAM - US aircraft make the first propaganda
             leaflet drop over Hanoi.

30   UNITED STATES - An estimated 25,000 marchers demon-
             strate on New York City's Fifth Avenue against the war
             in SEA.

31   SOUTH VIET NAM - Following an investigation, the crew
            of an American B-52 is exonerated of responsibility
            for the accidental bombing of a South Vietnamese vil-
            lage in which 48 civilians were killed and at least 55
            wounded.

NOVEMBER

2   UNITED STATES - A 31-year-old Quaker, Norman Morrison,
            commits suicide by fire in front of the Pentagon in
            protest to the war in SEA.

4   SOUTH VIET NAM - The last elements of the ROK Capital
            Division arrive in country and are deployed to protect
            the strategically important Binh Dinh Province capital
            city of Qui Nhon, 400 miles north of Saigon in the II
            CTZ.

6   CUBA - The government permits those wishing to do so
            to leave Cuba by air for the US. The program continues
            until August 1971, by which time nearly 250,000 have
            fled the Castro regime.

7   USSR - At the annual parade celebrating the Bolshevik
            Revolution, the Soviets display four new missile sys-
            tems.

7   SOUTH VIET NAM - Elements of the US 1st Cavalry Div-
            ision successfully defend their positions and scatter
            a NVN force that had them outnumbered two to one. At
            the same time, US intelligence sources confirm the
            presence of at least five NVA regiments in SVN.

10   UNITED NATIONS - Roger LaPorte, a 22-year-old Paci-
            fist, burns himself to death in front of the UN Build-
            ing in New York City as a protest against the war in
            SEA.

11   RHODESIA - The all-white government of Ian D. Smith
            announces its Unilateral Declaration of Independence
            (UDI) from the British Commonwealth.

12   UNITED NATIONS - The Security Council calls on all
            nations to withhold recognition of the new Rhodesian
            government.

14   SOUTH VIET NAM - The final battle of the Ia Drang Val-
            ley campaign begins.

15   GUINEA - The government severs relations with France
            after the discovery of a plot to assassinate President
            Sekou Toure and overthrow the government.

22   SOUTH VIET NAM - In an attempt to take a Vietnamese
            Ranger base north of Saigon, the VC suffer very heavy
            casualties and are forced to retreat.

24   SOUTH VIET NAM - The US military forces in SVN suffer
            240 killed in action (KIA) during the week ending 20
            November; the highest weekly toll of the war to date.

24-25   DEMOCRATIC CONGO REPUBLIC - The government of
            President Joseph Kasavubu is ousted in a bloodless
            coup led by Lieutenant General Joseph D. Mobutu.

27   UNITED STATES - About 25,000 demonstrators march in
            Washington, DC, for peace in SEA.

28   SOUTH VIET NAM - The 2,000-man 7th ARVN Regiment is
            destroyed in a fierce battle on a Michelin rubber
            plantation in Loc Ninh Province north of Saigon and
            near the Cambodian border.

29   UNITED STATES - After spending only two days in SVN,
            Secretary of Defense Robert McNamara declares "we have
            stopped losing the war."

DECEMBER

            UNITED STATES - The US opens a two-month campaign in
            the world's capitals to achieve peace in SEA.

2   SOUTHEAST ASIA - The nuclear-powered aircraft carrier
            USS Enterprise arrives in the waters off Viet Nam.

2   UNITED STATES - The government announces it will take
            part in the proposed Southeast Asia Conference to end
            the fighting in SVN.

3   SOUTH VIET NAM - The Hotel Metropole, which is used as
            an American enlisted man's barracks in Saigon, is
            blown up by VC sappers. Eight US personnel are killed
            and 172 Americans and Vietnamese are wounded.

3   GHANA - The government severs relations with Great
            Britain over the Rhodesian issue.

5   AFRICA - The Organization of African Unity threatens
            to break relations with Great Britain unless a solu-
            tion is found to the racist policies of the Rhodesian
            government.

10   UNITED STATES - Yet another military planning confer-
            ence on SVN is held in Honolulu.

15   NORTH VIET NAM - The thermal power station at Uongbi, 14 miles north of Haiphong, is bombed by US aircraft in the first attack on a major North Vietnamese industrial target.

17   GREAT BRITAIN - Following a rebuke in the UN, the government announces a ban on oil shipments to Rhodesia.

18   NORTH VIET NAM - The government denies it is seeking to open peace talks on the war.

19   DOMINICAN REPUBLIC - Fighting breaks out after an attempt on the life of rebel leader Francisco Caamano Deno fails.

21   UNITED STATES - Following a two-day meeting in Washington, President Johnson and West German Chancellor Ludwig Erhard issue a joint communique announcing a future German role in nuclear defense.

22   DAHOMEY - A military coup led by General Christophe Soglo ousts the government he helped install in 1963. This time Soglo retains the presidency.

24-26   SOUTH VIET NAM - The scheduled one-day Christmas truce is extended through 26 December, at which time the VC resume heavy attacks. The concurrent bombing pause in NVN continues until 31 January 1966.

28   USSR - Amid increasing talk of peace in SEA, the Soviets send troubleshooter Alexander Shelepin to Hanoi for consultations.

28   UNITED NATIONS - The President of the General Assembly, Amantori Fanfani, announces his resignation as Italian Foreign Minister in the midst of a storm of protest over his handling of a NVN peace feeler.

29   SOUTH VIET NAM - Lead elements of the 3rd Brigade, US 25th Infantry Division begin arriving in country.

31   SOUTH VIET NAM - US military strength in SVN is now 154,000, plus numerous other "sending nation" contingents, including 20,620 ROK personnel. (The total is in excess of 184,000.) US combat losses since 1 January 1961 are listed as 1,636 KIA; 1,075 of this number have died since 16 August 1965. VC losses for 1965 are reported by the US Command as 25,000. The US also lost 351 aircraft (including helicopters) this year.

1966

WORLD - International Days of Protest against the US role in SEA take place in cities around the world.

BOLIVIA - Che Guevara is reported to have arrived in Bolivia. Insurgency increases.

SOUTHEAST ASIA - Intelligence reports indicate the total NVA/VC strength to be about 230,000. The Allied to NVA/VC troop ratio is about 3.5:1 during 1966.

SOUTH VIET NAM - Fifty-nine new airfields will be built in SVN during 1966.

JANUARY

1   CENTRAL AFRICAN REPUBLIC - The government of President David Dacko is overthrown in a military coup led by Colonel Jean Bedel Bokassa. The junta immediately breaks its ties with Communist China.

1-8   SOUTH VIET NAM - The US 173rd Airborne Brigade attacks and destroys a VC battalion in "Operation MARAUDER" in the Mekong Delta in the IV CTZ. A second VC battalion is routed and its headquarters destroyed in the Plain of Reeds sector.

3   UPPER VOLTA - A military coup, led by Lieutenant Colonel Sangoule Lamizana, overthrows the government of President Maurice Yameogo.

3   CAMBODIA - The government informs the US that it will use force to repel any invasion by US or SVN forces.

7   UNITED STATES - The Department of State issues a
            14-point peace proposal for SVN.

10   INDIA - The government announces it has signed a
            treaty with Pakistan (Treaty of Tashkent) that re-
            quires both sides to withdraw their forces from for-
            ward areas so as to prevent further confrontations.

11   INDIA - Prime Minister Lal Bahadur Shastri dies of a
            heart attack and is replaced by Mrs. Indira Gandhi
            (elected 18 January).

16   NIGERIA - A violent military coup overthrows the
            government of Prime Minister Sir Abudakar Tafawa
            Balewa who is killed. A fight among the military for
            control of the country ensues. General Johnson Aguyi-
            Ironsi finally emerges the victor and establishes a
            provisional government.

19   SOUTH VIET NAM - A force composed of the 1st Brigade,
            101st US Airborne Division, the 2nd ROK Marine Brig-
            ade, and the 4th ARVN Regiment takes part in a month-
            long operation called VAN BUREN in which Phu Yen
            Province in the II CTZ is secured from VC control.

20-23   SOUTH VIET NAM - A temporary cease-fire is arranged
            for the celebration of the Lunar New Year (Tet).

24   SOUTH VIET NAM - In an operation called MASHER WHITE
            WING, a combined force of 20,000 US, ROK, and ARVN
            troops sweep through Binh Dinh Province in II CTZ. The
            enemy main forces are composed of two VC and two NVA
            regiments.

25   JAPAN - Prime Minister Eisaku Sato announces an inter-
            national peace mission for Viet Nam.

28   UNITED STATES - Senate Foreign Relations Committee
            Chairman J. William Fullbright challenges the US
            military's role in Viet Nam.

31   UNITED STATES - The President announces the resumption
            of air strikes over NVN after a 37-day halt. This
            comes in response to the failure of peace negotia-
            tions.

FEBRUARY

            SAUDI ARABIA - In the wake of renewed fighting in
            North Yemen, the government accuses Egypt of bombing
            Saudi villages along the Saudi-Yemen border.

5   UNITED STATES - The US takes over the West German ob-
        ligation for supplying military equipment to Israel.

6   CUBA - Fidel Castro denounces Communist China for "be-
        traying" the Cuban revolution.

6-8   UNITED STATES - The periodic Honolulu conference on
        SEA is attended by President Johnson, SVN's Prime
        Minister Ky and Chief of State Thieu. The two gov-
        ernments pledge to defend against Communist aggres-
        sion, to bring about social reform, and to strive for
        free self-government and peace.

19   SOUTH KOREA - The government announces it will in-
        crease its troop strength in SVN to 46,000 by mid-
        June.

21   INDONESIA - President Sukarno dismisses the anti-
        Communist members of his government.

22   UGANDA - Prime Minister Milton Obote assumes full
        power.

22   NORTH YEMEN - Fighting commences again when UAR air-
        craft support a rebel attack on a royalist tribal
        camp.

22   EGYPT - Rejecting a Saudi appeal to withdraw from
        North Yemen, President Nasser states Egyptian forces
        will remain in that country until an election is held
        to determine the form of government that is to
        prevail.

23   SYRIA - The Baath government of Premier Salal al Bitar
        is overthrown in a coup, and is replaced by a radical
        left-wing party led by Major General Salal Jedid.

24   GHANA - A military coup, led by Lieutenant Colonel
        Joseph Ankrah and supported by the police, ousts
        President Kwame Nkrumah while he is on a state visit
        to Communist China.

24   INDONESIA - Antigovernment rioting breaks out in a
        number of regions throughout the country.

25   INDIA - India and Pakistan complete the withdrawals
        called for in the Treaty of Tashkent.

MARCH

        SOUTH VIET NAM - A number of Buddhist demonstrations
        take place in Saigon, Da Nang, and Hue urging an end
        to the military government.

1   UNITED STATES - President Johnson renews his appeal
           for peace in SEA and reiterates his offer of aid for
           NVN.

           DEMOCRATIC CONGO REPUBLIC - President Joseph Mobutu
           (Mobutu Sese Seho) assumes all legislative powers from
           the Parliament.

2   UGANDA - Prime Minister Obote deposes President Sir
           Edward Mutesa. Mutesa flees to Kampala in Buganda
           Province where he still rules. He demands the immedi-
           ate withdrawal of Ugandan forces from his territory.

8   AUSTRALIA - The government's decision to triple its
           force in SVN from 1,500 to 4,500 men and the adoption
           of the nation's first peacetime draft to support man-
           power requirements for the war cause widespread anti-
           government demonstrations.

10   GUINEA - Former President Kwame Nkrumah of Ghana is
           named co-president of Guinea and is give asylum by
           Guinea's President Sekou Toure who then threatens to
           invade Ghana and its ally, the Ivory Coast. Ivory
           Coast president, Felix Houphonet-Boigny mobilizes his
           army and forces Toure to back down.

11   FRANCE - Having already proposed his plan for a "Euro-
           peanized Europe" free of American and Soviet influ-
           ence, President DeGaulle announces France's withdrawal
           from the integrated NATO command. Further, he directs
           all NATO bases, including NATO headquarters, be re-
           moved from French soil by 1 April.

11   INDONESIA - A military junta, led by Lieutenant Gen-
           eral Suharto, seizes control of the government. Presi-
           dent Sukarno becomes a figurehead, the PKI is out-
           lawed, and a new purge of Communists in government
           begins.

14   ARAB LEAGUE - A conference of the League is held in
           Cairo. Tunisia refuses to attend because it feels that
           no peaceful solutions will be sought to settle the
           Israeli problem. Among the matters agreed upon is con-
           tinued withholding of diplomatic relations with West
           Germany, informing the US that its continued support
           of Israel threatens Arab-American relations, and de-
           velopment of it own plans to divert the Jordan away
           from Israel.

18   UNITED STATES - The government imposes economic sanc-
           tions on Rhodesia.

29   SOUTH VIET NAM - The last units of the 1st US Marine
           Division arrive in country.

29   ECUADOR - Antigovernment antimilitary rioting in Quito
        forces the resignations of the military junta that has
        ruled the country since July 1963.

31   SOUTH VIET NAM - US troop strength in SVN is now over
        215,000.

APRIL

        SOUTH VIET NAM - Buddhist demonstrations continue in
        Saigon, Da Nang, and Hue urging an end to the military
        government. At the same time, the 1st Battalion, First
        US Marines, sweep the Khe Sanh Plateau (Operation
        VIRGINIA), in Quang Tri Province, .

        NATO - NATO's headquarters is moved from Paris to
        Casteau, Belgium.

1   SOUTH VIET NAM - The US Seventh Air Force (7AF) is
        established in Saigon by changing the title of the
        Second Air Division (formed in 1962). At the same
        time, US Naval Forces, Vietnam (NAVFORV) is also
        established in Saigon.

10   SOUTH VIET NAM - US naval patrols become operational
        on the waterways near Saigon. These patrols will
        become a part of Operation GAME WARDEN in May.

12   NORTH VIET NAM - For the first time, B-52 bombers
        strike NVA infiltration routes in the Mugia Pass on
        the North Viet Nam-Laotian border.

30   SOUTH VIET NAM - US officials in Saigon estimate the
        NVA infiltration rate into SVN to be 5,500 men per
        month.

MAY

        SOUTH VIET NAM - Four months of continuous operations
        begin in Pleiku Province in the Central Highlands to
        prevent infiltration from NVN and Cambodia. The 25th
        US Infantry Division, the 1st Cavalry Division (Air-
        mobile), and ARVN forces take part in these opera-
        tions. At the same time, the elements of the 101st
        Airborne Division are heavily engaged in Kontum Pro-
        vince to the north.

        SOUTH VIET NAM - "Operation GAME WARDEN" begins in
        which air, sea, and ground units patrol coastal areas
        to prevent VC infiltration of the Mekong Delta region
        and area (Rung Sat) below Saigon.

1   SOUTH VIET NAM - Artillery units of the 1st US Cavalry
        Division (Airmobile) return fire on VC positions on
        the Cambodian side of the Caibac River.

10   ROMANIA   - Following Romanian suggestions that the
        Warsaw Pact be modified, Soviet leader Brezhnev visits
        Bucharest. The Romanians tone down their talk of inde-
        pendent policy making.

18   UNITED STATES - The government protests to Cambodia
        concerning VC use of its territory.

20   UNITED STATES - The government announces it will sup-
        ply A-4 "Skyhawk" aircraft to Israel.

23-24   UGANDA - Federal troops capture the Ugandan capital of
        Kampala. King Mutesa flees to England.

        DEMOCRATIC CONGO REPUBLIC - There is an unsuccessful
        coup attempt against the Mobutu government.

26   GUYANA - The former British colony is declared inde-
        pendent, but it remains within the British Common-
        wealth.

JUNE

        SOUTH VIET NAM - Two months of military operations
        begin in Binh Long Province, in the III CTZ, 70 miles
        north of Saigon. Forces involved include the 1st US
        Infantry Division and 5th ARVN Division.

1   THAILAND - Following a four-day conference a peace
        settlement between Indonesia and Malaysia is announced
        in Bangkok.

3   DOMINICAN REPUBLIC - Joaquin Balaguer is elected Pres-
        ident.

23   UNITED STATES - Month-long racial unrest breaks out in
        Cleveland, Ohio.

28   DOMINICAN REPUBLIC - The 8,200-man OAS Inter-American
        Peacekeeping Force begins leaving the country.

28   ARGENTINA - The government of President Arturo Illia
        is ousted by a military coup. Lieutenant General Juan
        Carlos Ongania is appointed Provisional President.

28-29   REPUBLIC OF CONGO (Brazzaville) - There is a success-
        ful coup against the government.

29   NORTH VIET NAM - Heavy air attacks are carried out on
          petroleum installation targets near Hanoi and the har-
          bor area of Haiphong.

JULY

          SOUTH VIET NAM - An existing chain of surveillance
          posts along the Laotian border is expanded, starting
          with the construction of a new camp at Dak Seang in
          the Central Highlands.

          INDONESIA - The month sees the end of the confronta-
          tion with Malaysia.

          JORDAN - The government suspends relations with the
          Palestine Liberation Organization (PLO).

1   SOUTH VIET NAM - The US Military Airlift Command init-
          iates its first direct medical evacuation flight from
          SVN to the US.

2   FRANCE - Ignoring protests from a number of nearby
          countries, the government begins a series of nuclear
          weapons tests in the Mururoa Atoll in the Pacific, 750
          miles southeast of Tahiti. Five shots will be made be-
          fore the tests are terminated on 4 October.

2   UNITED STATES - The Department of State estimates that
          at least 40,000 Communist Chinese workers are in NVN
          repairing bombed-out facilities.

4-6   ROMANIA - At a Warsaw Pact meeting held in Bucharest,
          Premier Nicolae Ceaucescu proposes a dissolution of
          both NATO and the Warsaw Pact. Ceaucescu also recom-
          mends the withdrawal of all foreign troops from all
          other nation's territories.

6   UNITED STATES - A number of captured American pilots
          are paraded through the streets of Hanoi.

7   WARSAW PACT - The Warsaw Pact nations announce they
          are ready to send "volunteers" to help support NVN, if
          the North Vietnamese government asks for help.

8   BURUNDI - King Mwami Mwambutsa is overthrown by his
          son, Prince Charles Ndizeye, who takes the throne for
          himself.

10   UNITED STATES - The Defense Department announces that
          US strength in SVN will expand to 375,000 by the end
          of 1966, and to 425,000 by the spring of 1967.

11   LAOS - There are reports that the US is carrying out
            over 100 air strikes a day on Communist supply routes
            in Laos.

20   UNITED STATES - President Johnson warns North Viet Nam
            that the US will   react strongly to any war-crimes
            trials of American prisoners of war held by the NVN.

23   NORTH VIET NAM - Ho Chi Minh states that there are "no
            trials in view."

29   NIGERIA - A second coup takes place when the army mu-
            tinies. President Aguyi-Ironsi is killed by opposition
            Muslim Hausa tribesmen. A Hausa officer, Colonel
            Yakubu Gowon takes the presidency and a long reign of
            terror begins against the southern Christian Ibo
            tribesmen who had achieved status in the preceding
            government. A great dislocation of the Ibo Tribe be-
            gins.

30   SOUTH VIET NAM - US bombers attack NVA facilities
            within the DMZ for the first time. The ICC says it
            will act to keep the DMZ free of any military activ-
            ities by either side.

AUGUST

            CYPRUS - After the UN intervenes to prevent a Turkish
            invasion, Cypriot President Makarios lifts some of the
            restrictions that were placed on Turkish Cypriots.

3   SOUTH VIET NAM - "Operation PRAIRIE" begins. This op-
            eration will last until the end of January 1967 and
            will involve the 3rd US Marine Division near the DMZ
            in Gio Linh and Con Thien Districts of Quang Tri Pro-
            vince.

7   UNITED STATES - Former Vice-President Richard Nixon
            suggests US forces in SVN be increased to 500,000 as a
            means of shortening the war.

9   SOUTH VIET NAM - The advance elements of the Republic
            of Korea Army's 9th (White Horse) Infantry Division
            ar- rive in country.

11   INDONESIA - A peace treaty with Malaysia is signed at
            Djakarta.

15   SOUTH VIET NAM - With the arrival of the US Army's
            196th Light Infantry Brigade, the total US strength in
            SVN rises to over 300,000.

15   ISRAEL – Two Syrian MiG fighters are shot down in a
          dogfight with Israeli jets over Lake Tiberias in
          northern Israel.

26   SOUTH VIET NAM – In operations that will last   until
          February 1968, the 1st US Cavalry Division begins a
          series of battalion-size search and destroy missions
          in Binh Dinh and Binh Thuan Provinces in the   Central
          Coastal Region.

SEPTEMBER

          SOUTH VIET NAM – The ROKA 9th (Whitehorse) Infantry
          Division completes its deployment to SVN and is now
          settled into its base camps.

          DEMOCRATIC CONGO REPUBLIC – A mutiny is reported among
          2,500 Katangan Gendarmes in Stanleyville (Kisangani).
          The revolt is crushed by government troops.

4   SOUTH VIET NAM – The US Army's Transportation Terminal
          Command, Vietnam arrives in SVN to help unclog the
          nearly hopelessly snarled port of Saigon.

5   UNITED STATES – President Johnson states he will offer
          a timetable for the withdrawal of US troops from SEA
          when the Communists present their timetable.

6   SOUTH AFRICA – Prime Minister Henrik F. Verwoerd is
          assassinated. One week later, Balthazar J. Vorster is
          named to replace him.

7   SOUTH VIET NAM – The US 11th Armored Cavalry Regiment
          (ACR) arrives at Vung Tau (Cap-Sainte Jacques), 40
          miles south of Saigon.

11   SOUTH VIET NAM – About 80% of the voters turn out to
          elect a constituent assembly.

14   SOUTH VIET NAM – "Operation ATTLEBORO" begins in "War
          Zone C" in Tay Ninh Province in the III CTZ. Over
          22,000 troops, including the 25th US Infantry Divi-
          sion, engage VC and NVA forces attempting to mass for
          an offensive. This is the largest US operation to date
          and lasts until 24 November.

16   THE PHILIPPINES – The government announces that it has
          reached an agreement with the US to reduce the US bas-
          ing rights from 99 to 25 years.

22   UNITED NATIONS – The US proposes to the General Assem-
          bly a step-by-step plan for the de-escalation of the
          war in SEA.

25   SOUTH VIET NAM - The first Filipino combat troops
                (engineers) arrive in country. This is the first ele-
                ment of a 2,000-man Civic Action Group which will be
                fully deployed by mid-October, and which will operate
                in Tay Ninh Province.

28   UNITED NATIONS - Indonesia resumes its membership in
                the UNO.

28   UNITED STATES - The government announces it is resum-
                ing economic aid to Indonesia.

30   BECHUANALAND - The former British colony proclaims its
                independence within the Commonwealth as Botswana.

OCTOBER

                DOMINICAN REPUBLIC - After Joaquin Balaguer is elected
                President, the OAS Inter-American peacekeeping force
                is withdrawn.

                SOUTH VIET NAM - The USAF 834th Air Division arrives
                in country. The 1st Battalion, Third US Marines,
                occupies the ground base at Khe Sanh (known as KSCB)
                relieving the CIDG.

3   TUNISIA - The government breaks diplomatic relations
                with the UAR.

4   BASUTOLAND - The former British protectorate in the
                middle of South Africa is declared independent under
                the name of Lesotho.

12   SOUTH VIET NAM - The last elements of the 4th US In-
                fantry Division arrive in country.

18   SOUTH VIET NAM - Operations aimed at disrupting the
                flow of enemy manpower and materiel continue in the
                Central Highlands in Pleiku Province. Elements of the
                4th US and 25th US Infantry Divisions, plus elements
                of the 1st US Cavalry Division (Airmobile) participate
                in these operations that last until 30 December.

24-25   THE PHILIPPINES - US President Lyndon Johnson extracts
                promises of support from Asian leaders at a conference
                held in Manila and attended by the Chiefs of State of
                six nations with forces in SVN. The conference atten-
                dees offer to withdraw their troops from SVN within
                six months of a North Vietnamese disengagement.

27   NORTH VIET NAM - The government rejects the Manila
                disengagement offer.

27   COMMUNIST CHINA - A nuclear warhead is detonated during the flight of a guided missile.

27   UNITED NATIONS - The UN abrogates a League of Nations mandate granting South Africa control over the former German colony of South West Africa. The South African government rebukes the UN resolution.

NOVEMBER

SOUTH VIET NAM - The government announces that, in 1967, the war against the enemy's main forces will be conducted by the US and its Allies, while the war to pacify the countryside will be conducted by RVNAF.

2   SOUTH KOREA - Six Americans and one South Korean soldier are killed in a skirmish with North Korean troops on the DMZ.

10   NORTH VIET NAM - The government announces that the USSR, Communist China, and other Communist countries have pledged increased military and economic aid.

11   JORDAN - The village of Sammu (Es Samu) is attacked by Israeli air and ground forces in reprisal for PLO attacks on Israeli border settlements. Fifteen Jordanians and one Israeli are killed. The town is heavily damaged.

25   NORTH VIET NAM - The government offers to observe a 48-hour truce at Christmas and New Years. With US consent, on 30 November, the RVN accepts the NVN holiday truce offer and suggests a four-day truce for the Lunar New Year (Tet) celebration.

28   BURUNDI - Charles Ndizeye, who ruled as King Mwami Ntare V, is overthrown by his prime minister, Michael Micombero, who proclaims a republic with himself as President.

28   SOUTH VIET NAM - The advance elements of the US Army's 199th Light Infantry Brigade arrive in SVN.

30   SOUTH VIET NAM - US forces begin operations to clear VC strongholds near Saigon. This phase of the war will continue for more than a year and will initially involve battalion-size elements of the 1st US, 4th US, and 25th US Infantry Divisions. Later, the US 199th Light Infantry Brigade and ARVN forces will take over responsibility for the area and will clear and secure it by 14 December 1967.

DECEMBER

ANGOLA - Seven Portuguese soldiers are killed in fighting between Angola and Congo-Kinshasa.

2-5   NORTH VIET NAM - US bombers stage heavy raids on depots and rail yards in Hanoi. The US government does not acknowledge these raids until 14 December.

3   GREAT BRITAIN - The government dispatches Royal Air Force units to Zambia at the request of Zambian President Kenneth Kaunda who fears a Rhodesian attack on the Kariba Dam.

5   RHODESIA - The government in Salisbury rejects an agreement reached by British Prime Minister Harold Wilson and Rhodesia's President Ian Smith which would have established majority rule in 10 years.

8   THE VATICAN - Pope Paul VI urges that the Christmas truce in SEA be extended into an armistice and that peace talks begin immediately.

9   SOUTH VIET NAM - The advance elements of the US 9th Infantry Division arrive in SVN.

10   JORDAN - The government agrees to an Arab League plan to station Saudi and Iraqi troops in Jordan as a means of strengthening its defenses against Israel. Syrian and PLO troops are barred from joining the Jordanian force and the entire plan is to be predicated upon UAR withdrawal from North Yemen and the replacement of UNEF in the Gaza and Sinai with UAR forces.

19   UNITED STATES - The government asks UN Secretary General U Thant to take steps to bring about cease-fire talks for SVN.

28   SUDAN - There is an unsuccessful coup attempt.

31   UNITED NATIONS - Secretary General U Thant urges the US to unconditionally halt its bombing of NVN.

31   UNITED STATES - President Johnson indicates he is more than willing to meet the North Vietnamese halfway in cease-fire or peace negotiations.

31   SOUTH VIET NAM - More than 389,000 US troops (about 6,900 of whom are advisors) are in country. This is an increase of 206,000 since the first of the year. At least 52,000 Allied troops are also in country. US losses now number 4,771 dead. The RVNAF strength is 623,000. At least 600,000 tons of supplies arrive every month.

1967

UNITED STATES - Major protests against the war in Viet Nam occur throughout the year.

URUGUAY - A long period of terrorist activity by a leftist organization known as Tupamaros begins.

JANUARY

MIDDLE EAST - There are sporadic exchanges of gunfire along the Israeli-Syrian border.

MACAO - Communist Chinese gunboats enter Macao Harbor in support of Chinese protests following the shooting of Communist demonstrators in a December 1966 riot.

NICARAGUA - There are reports of troops opening fire on demonstrators during the election campaign.

1   SOUTH VIET NAM - As a part of the Defense Department's "Key West Agreement," all 140 US Army Aviation CV-2 "Caribou" troop support aircraft are transferred to the USAF and renamed the C-7A. All of the aircraft are assigned to the 834th Air Division.

5   NORTH VIET NAM - The government indicates a willingness to examine and study US proposals for negotiations, if the US will definitely and unconditionally halt the bombing of Hanoi.

6   SOUTH VIET NAM - The 9th US Infantry Division and US Marines enter Long An Province in the III CTZ for the first time after establishing a base in Dinh Tuong Province in the Mekong Delta in IV CTZ.

8-26   SOUTH VIET NAM - "Operation CEDAR FALLS" begins in the
            "Iron Triangle" region of III CTZ, about 25 miles
            north of Saigon. It is an area called "a dagger point-
            ed at the heart of Saigon." Troops from the 1st and
            25th US Infantry Divisions, the US 173rd Airborne
            Brigade, the US 11th Armored Cavalry Regiment, and
            ARVN forces conduct operations against major VC head-
            quarters and supply bases.

11   BORNEO - The last British troops depart leaving only a
            single battalion in the British enclave at Brunei.

13   TOGO - A military coup d'etat, led by Lieutenant
            Colonel Etienne Eyadema, overthrows the government of
            President Nicholas Grunitzky.

18   UNITED STATES - The Defense Department announces it is
            sending an additional 10,000 troops to SVN. This will
            bring the total number in that theater to 405,000.

22-23   NICARAGUA - An attempted right-wing coup is crushed.

23   UNITED STATES - The Defense Department reports there
            are 275,000 enemy troops in SVN, including 45,000 NVA
            regulars.

27   GREAT BRITAIN - The government announces a new Anglo-
            South African Naval Defense Agreement that reappor-
            tions responsibility for the defense of the Cape of
            Good Hope sea route and removes the British Naval
            Commander in Chief, South Atlantic, from Simonstown.

27   UNITED NATIONS - The treaty on the peaceful use of
            outer space is signed in London, Washington, and
            Moscow.

FEBRUARY

            SOUTH VIET NAM - For an eight-month period the 3rd US
            Marine Division continues operations in Quang Tri Pro-
            vince along the DMZ. The 1st US Marine Division con-
            ducts its operations in Quang Tin and Quang Nam
            provinces.

            COMMUNIST CHINA - There are reports that Maoist Red
            Guards units are fighting troops from some People's
            Liberation Army (PLA) units.

8   SIERRA LEONE - A military coup attempt fails.

8   SOUTH VIET NAM - A seven-day truce to celebrate Tet
            goes into effect.

8   UNITED STATES - President Johnson addresses a letter
         to Ho Chi Minh in which he calls for peace talks and
         offers to halt the bombing of NVN and the US troop
         buildup, but only if the infiltration of SVN is
         halted.

14   LATIN AMERICA - At a meeting held in Mexico City the
         representatives of 14 Latin American countries sign a
         Treaty on the Denuclearization of Latin America.

14   NORTH VIET NAM - The US bombing of NVN resumes.

19   USSR - The government announces that Iran has placed a
         $110 million order for arms and military equipment.

20   INDONESIA - Sukarno is obliged to relinguish the last
         of his powers to Suharto.

22   SOUTH VIET NAM - The largest operation of 1967, "Oper-
         ation JUNCTION CITY," begins. The operation employs 22
         US battalions (two division equivalents) and 4 ARVN
         battalions (in all about 25,000 troops) in "War Zone
         C" in Tay Ninh Province, in the III CTZ, northwest of
         Saigon. It seeks to eliminate the major VC headquar-
         ters (COSVN) in SVN. The operation lasts until 14 May.

24   SOUTH VIET NAM - For the first time, US Marine artil-
         lery units fire into North Viet Nam as they shell NVA
         antiaircraft positions.

27   NORTH VIET NAM - US aircraft begin dropping mines in a
         number of NVN rivers. At the same time, US warships
         begin shelling coastal targets.

28   SOUTH VIET NAM - US Naval Task Force 117 is activated
         as a Riverine Assault Force. Later in the year it will
         become the Mobile Riverine Force for joint Army- Navy
         operations in the Mekong Delta.

MARCH

         BOLIVIA - Seven soldiers are killed in attacks by
         anti-government rebels during the month.

5   OAU - The use of force to topple the Rhodesian and
         South African governments is urged at a five-day meet-
         ing of the OAU.

9   UNITED STATES - The Defense Department announces that
         it is using its bases in Thailand to bomb NVN.

9   UAR - The UAR-Syrian Defense Agreement goes into
         effect.

10   NORTH VIET NAM - US bombers begin attacking North
          Vietnamese iron and steel works.

13   DEMOCRATIC CONGO REPUBLIC - A military tribunal
          sentences former Premier Moise Tshombe, in absentia,
          to death. The charges include inciting rebellion.
          Tshombe has already fled the country.

15   NORTH VIET NAM - Ho Chi Minh demands the bombing be
          halted and US forces withdrawn from South Viet Nam
          before any peace negotiations can go forward.

15   BELGIUM - Headquarters, Armed Forces, Central Europe
          (AFCENT), which has moved from France, opens its new
          facilities at Brunssum.

16   UNITED STATES - President Johnson signs a $4.5 billion
          FY67 supplemental fund appropriation in which Congress
          states support for the war in South East Asia.

20   RWANDA - Rwanda and Burundi affect a reconciliation
          after four years of border warfare.

20   UNITED STATES - President Johnson attends a conference
          held on Guam that is also attended by Secretary of
          Defense McNamara; the Chairman of the Joint Chiefs of
          Staff, General Wheeler; the South Vietnamese Chief of
          State, Nguyen Van Thieu; and the SVN Prime Minister,
          Nguyen Kao Ky. A joint communique is issued stressing
          a determination for freedom in SVN and a continued
          search for an honorable peace.

21   NORTH VIET NAM - Ho Chi Minh rejects the US proposal
          for talks to halt the bombing.

22   UNITED STATES - The government announces it has re-
          ceived permission from Thailand to station US B-52
          bombers (formerly stationed on Guam) on Thai soil. The
          US will initially base its B-52 operations at U Tapao
          Airbase.

23   SIERRA LEONE - A military coup, led by Lieutenant
          Colonel Andrew T. Juxton-Smith and Major Charles
          Smith, successfully overthrows the government.

28   UNITED NATIONS - Secretary General U Thant reveals the
          North Vietnamese rejection of his "stand still" truce
          proposal which was designed as a first step toward
          peace talks.

30   FRANCE - The last elements of Supreme Headquarters,
          Allied Powers Europe (SHAPE) leave the country.

31   BELGIUM - SHAPE opens its new headquarters in Casteau.

APRIL

1   UNITED STATES - The government announces it has signed
        an agreement with Great Britain on the joint use of
        the British Indian Ocean Territory on the Indian sub-
        continent.

1   SOUTH VIET NAM - The government promulgates a new con-
        stitution.

4   UNITED STATES - Martin Luther King calls the US the
        "greatest purveyor of violence in the world." He goes
        on to encourage draft evasion and a merger of civil
        rights and anti-war activities.

6   INDIA - The government protests the planned use of the
        British Indian Ocean Territory for joint US-UK opera-
        tions.

7   ISRAEL - The Israelis shoot down six Syrian MiGs in
        dogfights over the Golan Heights. This action follows
        an artillery exchange near the border at Lake
        Tiberias.

10   THAILAND - The first US B-52s arrive at the U Tapao
        Airbase.

15   UNITED STATES - Over 100,000 protesters in New York
        and 50,000 more in San Francisco march against the war
        in SEA.

19   SOUTH AFRICA - The government announces it has pur-
        chased three submarines from France.

20   NORTH VIET NAM - US bombers strike two power plants
        inside the city limits of the strategically important
        seaport of Haiphong.

20   SOUTH VIET NAM - The Third US Marines begin "Operation
        PRAIRIE IV" in the Khe Sanh area.

21   GREECE - A right-wing coup, led by Colonel George
        Papadopoulos and Brigadier General Styliano Patakos,
        establishes a military dictatorship. Four of the new
        ministers are army officers. Prime Minister George
        Papandreou is arrested. King Constantine II is eventu-
        ally forced to flee (14 December).

24   SOUTH VIET NAM - Contact is made with a large enemy
        force north of Hill 861, in Quang Tri Province. This
        triggers a premature NVA attack on the Marine base at
        Khe Sanh.

25   SOUTH VIET NAM - Khe Sanh is reinforced with two
            battalions of US Marines in anticipation of a major
            VC/NVA drive into the area. In the days following, the
            Marines expand their base of operations strengthening
            the base.

25   SOUTH VIET NAM - Ellsworth Bunker becomes the US Am-
            bassador succeeding Henry Cabot Lodge.

28   UNITED STATES - In addressing a joint session of Con-
            gress, the MACV commander, General William Westmore-
            land, states that the main North Vietnamese strategy
            for winning the war is the weakening of American
            resolve.

MAY

            HONG KONG - There is sporadic rioting in the Crown
            Colony throughout the month.

1   NORTH VIET NAM - US bombers attack MiG fighter bases
            for the first time.

1   UNITED STATES - Secretary of State Dean Rusk describes
            28 peace proposals the North Vietnamese have rejected.

2   GREAT BRITAIN - The government announces that, based
            on an agreement with the US and West Germany, it will
            reduce its forces in the British Army on the Rhine
            (BAOR) by 5,000 men.

2   UNITED STATES - The Defense Department announces US
            troop strength in Western Europe will be reduced by
            35,000 in 1968.

3-5   SOUTH VIET NAM - The Third US Marines seize the domi-
            nant terrain (Hill 881N) northwest of Khe Sanh. This
            cuts off a major infiltration route from Laos into
            Quang Tri Province in I CTZ. Hill 881S was taken on 1
            May. Heavy NVA counterattacks follow but are unsuc-
            cessful.

11-13   SOUTH VIET NAM - In a series of actions that began on
            24 April around Khe Sanh (called the "Hill Fights"),
            940 NVA and 155 US Marines are killed. The US Third
            Marine Regimental Landing Team, relieved at Khe Sanh
            by the 26th Marines, moves to Dong Ha. "Operation
            CROCKETT" begins.

13   NIGERIA - The Eastern Province declares itself free of
            Nigerian rule. Tribal warfare follows.

14   SOUTH VIET NAM - The 25th US Infantry Division begins search and destroy operations in Hua Nghia Province in the III CTZ west of Saigon. These operations will continue until 7 December.

14   EGYPT - Egyptian forces move into the Sinai.

14-16   MIDDLE EAST - The governments of Egypt and Syria order mobilization.

16   EGYPT - President Gamal Nasser accuses Israel of planning aggression and promises aid to Syria if it is attacked. He then declares a state of emergency, mobilizes, and asks for a withdrawal of the UNEF.

17   EGYPT - The Egyptian government, along with the Syrians, announce they are ready to fight.

17   JORDAN - The government announces mobilization.

18   UNITED NATIONS - Secretary General U Thant agrees to Egyptian President Nasser's demand to withdraw the UNEF in the Sinai. The force begins moving out on 19 May.

18   EGYPT - The Egyptians and Syrians go on full military alert.

18   IRAQ - The government orders full mobilization.

18   KUWAIT - The government orders full mobilization.

19   UNITED NATIONS - The UNEF begins its withdrawal from the Gaza Strip and Sharm esh-Sheikh.

20   ISRAEL - The government orders partial mobilization.

21   EGYPT - The government announces that the Palestine Liberation Organization has been put under the Arab Military Command.

22   EGYPT - Egyptian military forces occupy Sharm esh-Sheikh. President Nasser announces a blockade of the Tiran Strait.

23   SAUDI ARABIA - The Saudi military forces go on full alert.

23   SOUTH VIET NAM - Allied forces observe Buddha's birthday.

24   JORDAN - The armed forces complete their mobilization. Saudi Arabian forces are reported in Jordan.

24   EGYPT - The Gulf of Aqaba is claimed in the name of the UAR.

28   SUDAN - The Sudanese armed forces mobilize.

28   EGYPT - President Nasser warns of a possible closing of the Suez Canal.

28   SOUTH VIET NAM - Civil and military responsibility for support of the pacification effort are integrated under COMUSMACV. Ambassador Robert Komer is assigned as Deputy to COMUSMACV for CORDS (Civil Operations and Revolutionary Development Support).

29   ALGERIA - The Algerian government moves military forces into Egypt and pledges other military support to the UAR.

30   BIAFRA - The Republic of Biafra is proclaimed in the southeastern region of Nigeria. Ibo leader Colonel Chukwuemeka Odumegwu Ojukwu establishes the new capital at Enugu. The Nigerian government calls the whole affair a rebellion and heavy fighting follows.

30   UAR - A mutual security pact is signed with Jordan.

30   JORDAN - Egyptian General Abdul Moneim Riadh takes command of Arab forces in Jordan.

30   MOROCCO - The government pledges military support to the UAR.

31   IRAQ - The government begins moving its troops into Jordan.

JUNE

            UNITED STATES - Racial unrest breaks into violence during June and July. More than 75 are killed as rioting affects 127 cities.

            DEMOCRATIC CONGO REPUBLIC - A long-term uprising of foreign mercenaries and Katangans begins.

3-4   ISRAEL - Israel practices an elaborate deception by ostensibly moving military amphibious assault units and equipment, especially landing craft, from northern parts of the country to Elat (Eilat), on the Gulf of Aqaba.

3-4   EGYPT - Egyptian intelligence reports that almost half of Israel's landing craft have been sent to the Gulf of Aqaba.

4   IRAQ - Iraq joins the UAR-Jordan defense pact.

4   EGYPT - President Nasser rejects a worldwide plea to
         allow freedom of shipping in the Gulf of Aqaba.

4-5   EGYPT - The Egyptian Navy dispatches a number of
         surface combatants from the Mediterranean to rein-
         force Arab naval strength in the Gulf of Aqaba.

5   EGYPT - Two Soviet-built, OSA-class, guided-missile
         patrol boats engage an Israeli destroyer and several
         motor torpedo boats (MTBs) outside Port Said. Although
         a brief fight ensues, neither side is seriously dam-
         aged, and the Egyptians withdraw into the port's har-
         bor. Israeli frogmen, who were landed in Port Said and
         Alexandria Harbors under cover of the diversion, in-
         flict some damage but all are captured.

5   ISRAEL - The Six Day War begins when Israeli aircraft
         strike almost all Egyptian air fields destroying most
         of Egypt's military aircraft. Similar raids are car-
         ried out later in the day against Jordanian, Iraqi,
         and Syrian military airfields. At the same time,
         ground units begin moving into the Gaza Strip along
         three axes: in the north, along the coastal road
         (known since Roman times as the Via Maris), on the
         axis Gaza-Khan Yunis-Rafa (Rafah)-El Arish, in the
         center, toward the strategically important town of Abu
         Aweigila (Abu Ageila), and, in the south, into the
         Sinai to cut Egyptian lines.
            On the Jordanian front, the Israeli Central Com-
         mand (Brigadier General Uzi Narkiss commanding) begins
         an offensive aimed at taking the Arab sector of Jeru-
         salem. At the same time, elements of the Northern Com-
         mand, led by Major General David Elazar, move to seize
         Jenin (Janin), and Nablus (Nabulus or Shekhem) in the
         Shomeron region, preparatory to moving on to the
         Jordan River.

5   EGYPT - Naval units in the Eastern Mediterranean, un-
         der heavy Israeli air attack, are withdrawn to Port
         Said.

5   ARAB LEAGUE - At an emergency meeting in Baghdad, the
         11-nation league agrees to cut off oil to any nation
         suspected of attacking an Arab state. The US, Great
         Britain, West Germany, and Israel are thus affected.
         Egypt accuses the US of participating in the first
         bombing raids of the war.

5   SUDAN - The government declares war on Israel. Sudan-
         ese troops are sent to the UAR.

6   ISRAEL – The government releases the tape of an inter-
          cepted telephone conversation between Egypt's Presi-
          dent Nasser and Jordan's King Hussein in which they
          agree to blame the Middle Eastern situation on the
          United States as the collaborator of Israel. Hussein
          immediately halts his accusations, but Nasser and many
          other Arab leaders break relations with the US.

6   ISRAEL – On the afternoon of the second day of fight-
          ing, Gaza surrenders to the forces of a reinforced
          mechanized brigade commanded by Colonel Yehuda
          Resheff. Major General Israel Tal's mechanized divi-
          sion captures Rafah and El Arish, and sends a task
          force ahead toward Romani (on the coast, approximately
          20 miles from the Suez Canal). With the remainder of
          the division, Tal turns southwest to link up with
          Major General Avraham Yoffe's armored division that
          was operating in the desert between El Arish and Abu
          Aweigila. In Abu Aweigila, Major General Ariel
          Sharon's mechanized division is divided with part
          going north to help secure the Rafah-El Arish sector,
          while the remainder drives southward toward Nakhl and
          the Mitla Pass. Yoffe's forces capture the main
          Egyptian positions in the Sinai at Jebel Libni in a
          night attack. The Egyptian High Command orders the
          withdrawal of all forces in the Sinai to positions
          behind the Suez Canal.
                  The Israeli advance against the Walled City of
          Jerusalem is slowed by the stubborn resistance of the
          Jordanian garrison brigade commanded by Brigadier Ata
          Ali. Israeli forces receive reinforcements and encir-
          cle the city cutting off Jordanian relief efforts. An
          Israeli tank brigade captures the town of Ramallah to
          the north of Jerusalem. A second brigade captures Lat-
          run, the scene of bitter fighting in 1948. The Tel
          Aviv-Jerusalem Road is opened for the first time since
          1947.
                  A reinforced division from Elazar's Northern Com-
          mand takes Jenin after heavy fighting. The drive
          toward Nablus continues in the face of stiffening re-
          sistance and repeated Jordanian counterattacks.
                  Several Egyptian submarines shell the Mediter-
          ranean coastal town of Ashdod, about 20 miles south of
          Tel Aviv-Yafo. Other naval bombardments take place to
          the north along the coast north and south of Haifa
          (Hefa).

6   FRANCE – The French carry out a nuclear test in the
          South Pacific.

7   ISRAEL – Romani is captured on the third day of fight-
          ing, and the northern task force from Tal's division
          continues its advance toward the Suez Canal and, to
          the south, Tal's main force nears Bir Gifgafa. Yoffe's

7   ISRAEL (Cont'd) - forces enter the eastern approach to
        the Mitla Pass, but severe shortages of fuel and ammu-
        nition quickly put this Israeli group in danger of
        being overrun by retreating Egyptians. A relief column
        moves to extricate Yoffe. Sharon's forces prepare to
        attack Nakhl.
            Sharm esh Sheikh (Sharm el-Sheikh) is captured
        from the sea by three motor torpedo boats. Israeli
        airborne forces arrive to take over the occupation of
        the strategic Red Sea port. The MTBs then move north
        through the Strait of Tiran to Elat.
            Israeli forces take Arab Jerusalem by storm. Soon
        afterward, Bethlehem, Hebron, and Etzion are taken by
        the Israelis.
            Nablus falls just before dark as Jordanian forces
        withdraw across the Jordan River.

7   ISRAEL - The Israeli and Jordanian governments agree
        upon a cease-fire at 2000 hours (8 PM).

7   BIAFRA - A civil war begins when Nigerian troops enter
        the rebellious province. In the three years of fight-
        ing that follow, the Biafrans beat back the initial
        Nigerian attacks and seize the initiative by invading
        Nigeria.

8   ISRAEL - Tal's forces sweep aside an Egyptian armored
        force screen, that was thrown up to cover the
        withdrawal of Egyptian forces still in the Sinai,
        outside the important Suez town of Ismailiya. Tal then
        moves forward interdicting the Suez Canal between
        Ismailiya and Kantara. Yoffe, having relieved his
        force at the Mitla Pass, proceeds through the pass and
        comes upon the Suez, north of Port Tewfik and opposite
        Port Suez on the Egyptian side. Sharon successfully
        attacks Nakhl, and then follows Yoffe through the
        Mitla Pass.

8   ISRAEL - A UN-arranged cease-fire goes into effect on
        the Israeli-Syrian front where the main activity has
        been long-range artillery duelling. This truce is
        broken during the night when both sides resume heavy
        artillery firing.

8   MEDITERRANEAN SEA - An American naval electronics sur-
        veillance ship, (USS Liberty) operating in inter-
        national waters off the Egyptian coast, is attacked by
        Israeli fighter-bombers and MTBs. The ship is severely
        damaged before the attack is broken off. The Israeli
        government will subsequently apologize for the inci-
        dent. Thirty-four US personnel are killed in the
        attack

9   ISRAEL - The Northern Command's available forces begin a two-pronged offensive into the Golan Heights, one in the north in the Dan-Banyas area, and the other along the northern coast of the Sea of Galilee. The latter force is composed of elements released from the Jenin-Nablus sector.

10   ISRAEL - The two columns operating in the Golan converge on the strategically important city of Kuneitra (Quneitra) on the Damascus Road. Another column, which had moved north through the Yarmuk Valley from the Jordanian front, approaches Kuneitra from the south. As the city is surrounded, a new cease-fire goes into effect.

10   USSR - The government severs diplomatic relations with Israel.

12   SOUTH VIET NAM - Thirty-nine sick NVA prisoners of war are released at the border. This action is reported as a result of US concern over treatment of US POWs held in the north.

16   YEMEN - The UAR begins the withdrawal of substantial numbers of its armed forces that have been deployed in Yemen.

17   COMMUNIST CHINA - The Chinese detonate a hydrogen device near Lop Nor, in Sinkiang Province, but the government announces a "no first use" policy in the employment of nuclear weapons.

17   SOUTH VIET NAM - US troop strength in SVN is 463,000. Combat deaths to date number 11,099. RVNAF strength is over 600,000, with RVNAF losses numbering at 47,695. Communist strength in SVN is estimated to be 294,000, including about 50,000 NVA regulars.

20   SOUTH ARABIAN FEDERATION - Seventeen British soldiers are killed when rioting breaks out among members of the South Arabian Federation constabulary and police.

23   UNITED STATES - President Johnson meets with Soviet Premier Kosygin in a private home in Glassboro, New Jersey, to seek ways of ending the war in SEA. No solution is found.

27   ISRAEL - Arab Jerusalem is incorporated into the remainder of the city already in Israeli hands.

27   FRANCE - The government holds its second nuclear test of the month in the South Pacific.

30   ALGERIA - An airplane carrying Moise Tshombe is hi-
          jacked over the Mediterranean and flown to Algeria
          where Tshombe is taken into custody.

JULY

          DEMOCRATIC CONGO REPUBLIC - Pro-Tshombe foreign mer-
          cenaries revolt at Kisangani (Stanleyville). They are
          eventually driven across the border into Rwanda.

          HONG KONG - Two months of serious rioting and violence
          begin. British troops finally quell the trouble but
          only after many are killed.

          MACAO - Communist-inspired violence erupts in Portu-
          guese Macao following the rioting in Hong Kong. Order
          is quickly restored once British troops quell the
          trouble in Hong Kong across the bay.

2   FRANCE - The French conduct the third nuclear test of
          the current series.

5   DEMOCRATIC CONGO REPUBLIC - Anti-Mobutu rioting breaks
          out among the mercenary forces.

6   NIGERIA - Federal forces blockade Port Harcourt in the
          first "official" action of the war with Biafra.

7   NIGERIA - Troops of the Nigerian Federal Army cross
          the northern border of the secessionist Eastern Region
          (Biafra). Heavy fighting is reported.

10   UNITED NATIONS - A UN Observer Team is established to
          oversee the Suez Canal cease-fire.

11   ANGUILLA - After withdrawing from its association with
          St. Kitts and Nevis, and vainly seeking reunion with
          Great Britain or association with the US or Canada,
          the tiny island becomes independent.

11   UNITED STATES - The government announces it has turned
          down a request for military aid from Nigeria.

12   UNITED STATES - Five days of rioting follow the beat-
          ing of a black man for a minor traffic offense in
          Newark, New Jersey. National Guardsmen and police open
          fire without cause on a crowd of people, and 24 blacks
          are killed (two whites also die). Over 1,500 are
          injured.

12   HONG KONG - British troops are used for the first time
          in quelling the disturbances in the Crown Colony.

13   BIAFRA - A major battle takes place at Nsukka between Nigerian and Biafran forces. The Nigerian government claims 2,000 Biafrans are killed.

14   ISRAEL - The government rejects a UN request to withdraw and states it will retain the Golan Heights facing Syria and the West Bank facing Jordan.

15   SOUTH VIET NAM - In the waters of the coast of Chu Lai in Quang Tin Province, naval vessels employed in "Operation MARKET TIME" capture a North Vietnamese trawler carrying arms and ammunition to the Viet Cong. At the same time, the VC carry out a massive mortar attack on the US air base at Da Nang, 60 miles to the north. There are heavy casualties and the loss of numerous aircraft.

16   SOUTH VIET NAM - The US Marines terminate "Operation CROCKETT" in Quang Tri and begin "Operation ARDMORE." At least 200 NVA have been killed since 13 May; but 52 Marines have also died.

18   GREAT BRITAIN - The government announces sweeping reductions in troop strengths throughout the Empire. Overall troop strength is to be reduced by 37,000 by 1971 and an additional 38,000 by the mid-1970s. All forces are to be withdrawn from Aden and South Arabia by January 1968. By the mid-1970s, complete withdrawal of British forces from Malaysia and Singapore is also scheduled.

23   UNITED STATES - Seven days of racial rioting begins in Detroit, Michigan, following a raid on a black, after-hours club. Federal troops are called in as both blacks and whites loot large areas of the city. Forty-three are killed, 2,000 injured; damage runs into the tens of millions.

23   UNITED STATES - A Black Power Conference held in Newark, New Jersey, votes an anti-white, anti-Christian, anti-draft platform.

25   CANADA - On a state visit, France's President DeGaulle openly calls for a free Quebec promising his government's support. After the Canadian government rebukes him for his discourtesy, DeGaulle goes back to Paris.

25   UNITED STATES - One of the leaders of the militant Student National Coordinating Committee (SNCC), H. "Rap" Brown (Hubert Gerold Brown) is arrested for inciting to riot when he calls for the burning of Cambridge, Maryland.

AUGUST

SOUTH VIET NAM - The VC lay siege to US Marine positions at Con Thien in Quang Tri Province near the DMZ. The siege is finally broken in September.

1   UNITED STATES - Press reports greatly distort the facts when minor scuffles between demonstrators and police are termed "rioting" in Washington, DC.

3   UNITED STATES - The Defense Department announces that President Johnson has authorized an increase in the troop strength in SVN by 45,000. This will bring the total US troop strength to 525,000.

9   DEMOCRATIC CONGO REPUBLIC - Katangan rebels supported by white foreign mercenaries capture the capital of Kivu Province.

9   NIGERIA - Biafran forces capture the important province capital of Benia.

9   GREAT BRITAIN - The government announces it has sold a "small purchase in arms" to Nigeria.

10   NIGERIA - Heavy fighting is reported in the ongoing civil war.

12   UNITED STATES - A spokesman reveals that the US has been bombing Communist targets in Laos, at the request of the Royal Laotian government, since May 1964.

13   UNITED STATES - CINCPAC headquarters in Hawaii reports that Chinese Communist gunners are manning some anti-aircraft sites in North Viet Nam.

15   UNITED STATES - Martin Luther King calls for "massive disobedience" to foster black demands.

15   NIGERIA - Intelligence reports indicate at least 20 Soviet military jet aircraft are in country.

17   UNITED STATES - SNCC leader Stokley Carmichael calls upon all blacks to arm themselves for "total revolution."

22   COMMUNIST CHINA - Members of the Red Guard burn down the British Diplomatic Mission in Peking.

24   EGYPT - A joint communique issued by Egypt and Saudi Arab announces an acceptance of proposals to stop the war in Yemen.

24   UNITED STATES - Two brigades of US airborne troops are
            ordered into Detroit, Michigan, to restore order dur-
            ing rioting in that city.

30-31   COMMUNIST CHINA - Parachute troops are reported to
            have been dropped into Wuhan Province following anti-
            government rioting in the region.

SEPTEMBER

            SOUTH VIET NAM - For the first time, Thai troops are
            committed to the fighting.

            NIGERIA - The central government opens a new military
            campaign against Biafra. Biafran forces at first with-
            draw but stop the Nigerian forces before the Biafran
            capital of Enugu. The fighting in this phase of the
            war will continue into May 1968.

3   SOUTH VIET NAM - Lieutenant General Nguyen Van Thieu
            is elected President and Air Marshal Nguyen Cao Ky
            Vice President in national elections in which 81% of
            the electorate vote.

7   UNITED STATES - Defense Secretary McNamara announces
            the building of a strong-point obstacle system as an
            anti-infiltration barrier on the South Vietnamese side
            of the DMZ that cuts Viet Nam in half at the 17th
            Parallel.

11-14   INDIA - The government reports a number of skirmishes
            with Communist Chinese forces along the Sikkim-Tibetan
            border.

15   EGYPT - Field Marshal Abdal Hakim Amer, the Minister
            of War and Commander in Chief of the Armed Forces,
            commits suicide following his arrest on charges stem-
            ming from the Arab defeat in the recent war with
            Israel.

21   SOUTH VIET NAM - The first elements (1,200 troops) of
            the Royal Thai Volunteer Regiment arrive for duty near
            Saigon. The regiment completes its deployment to SVN
            on 29 September.

23   SOUTH VIET NAM - Task Force Oregon is resdesignated
            the US 23rd (Americal) Division.

23   USSR - In connection with the signing of a new aid
            agreement with NVN, Premier Kosygin promises support
            "till total victory" is achieved.

27   SOUTH VIET NAM - The siege of the US Marine base at Con Thien near the DMZ is lifted after 49 days. A build-up of massive firepower is credited for the enemy withdrawal.

28   UNITED STATES - Speaking in San Antonio, Texas, President Johnson declares a US willingness to halt the bombing of NVN when there is any indication that such an act will lead to fruitful peace negotiations.

OCTOBER

KENYA - A peace accord is negotiated with Somalia.

3   NORTH VIET NAM - The government rejects the latest US peace initiative.

4   BIAFRA - The capital city of Enugu is captured by Nigerian troops. The war will continue, however, until 1970.

5   AUSTRALIA - The government announces an additional 20 million Australian dollars in aid to Malaysia and Singapore following Britain's decision to withdraw from the region.

9   BOLIVIA - Army troops kill Che Guevara who is leading Bolivian guerrillas. Most of Guevara's men also are killed or captured in the firefight.

13   FRANCE - The NATO Council moves from Paris to Brussels where it is joined by the Military Committee which has sat in Washington.

17   AUSTRALIA - The government announces an increase in military support to SVN. New Zealand makes a similar announcement.

21   UNITED STATES - A massive anti-war demonstration takes place at the Pentagon. Federal troops surround the building. Of about 50,000 demonstrators, 647 are arrested.

21   EGYPT - The government announces it has sunk the Israeli destroyer Eilat.

24   SINAI - The Israelis shell an oil refinery across the Suez Canal.

25   NORTH VIET NAM - For the first time, US warplanes attack the major North Vietnamese air base at Phuc Yen.

28   TANZANIA - In the Declaration of Arusha, Kenya and Somalia agree to end their border conflict.

31   SOUTH VIET NAM - Enemy activity around Khe Sanh in
            Quang Tri Province, I CTZ has reduced significantly.
            "Operation ARDMORE" is terminated. Enemy losses number
            113 killed. Ten US Marines are also listed as KIA.

NOVEMBER

            CYPRUS - The Greek Army begins a gradual withdrawal of
            its forces from Cyprus following US mediation which
            reduces some of the tension.

1   SOUTH VIET NAM - The 3rd US Marine Division begins a
            new series of probing operations (Operation SCOTLAND
            I) around Khe Sanh. These will continue until the end
            of March 1968.

2   UNITED STATES - The US tells the UN it is willing to
            participate in a reconvened Geneva Conference on Viet
            Nam peace discussions in the UN Security Council.

2   GREAT BRITAIN - The government announces it plans to
            give up its colonial empire in Arabia.

3   UNITED STATES - The Secretary of Defense announces
            that the Soviet Union has developed a Fractional Or-
            bital Bombardment System (FOBS) which would permit it
            to launch an attack from an orbiting position in
            space.

5   NORTH YEMEN - The republican government of Abdullah
            al-Salal is overthrown by a dissident faction led by
            Rahman al-Iryani. Although the new government seeks
            accommodation with the royalists, the fighting
            continues.

5   DEMOCRATIC CONGO REPUBLIC - As central government
            forces push forward in all areas, the uprisings in
            Kivu and Katanga Provinces are crushed. Most of the
            French and Belgian mercenaries who participated are
            pursued into neighboring Rwanda.

6   JORDAN - King Hussein announces he is ready to recog-
            nize Israel if the boundary questions can be settled.

8   SOUTH VIET NAM - ARVN forces reinforced with US ground
            units rout an enemy force in a battle near the Cam-
            bodian border at Loc Ninh, in Tay Ninh Province, in
            III CTZ.

11   UNITED STATES - The government claims that 67% of the
            South Vietnamese population live in areas under GVN,
            while 17% live under Communist control. The remaining
            16% live in contested areas.

15   CYPRUS - Fighting breaks out between Greek and Turkish
            Cyriots.

16-17   CENTRAL AFRICAN REPUBLIC - The French send forces into
            the country to support the Bokassa government during
            an uprising.

19   SOUTH VIET NAM - The VC announce a holiday cease-fire
            and a seven-day truce for Tet.

22   UNITED NATIONS - The Security Council unanimously
            votes (Resolution 242) to ask Israel to withdraw its
            forces from the occupied territories.

23   SOUTH VIET NAM - In a major battle to take Dak To near
            the triborder area in Kontum Province in the Central
            Highlands, a large Communist force is defeated.

29   ADEN - The British complete their troop withdrawal.

30   SOUTH YEMEN - The nation becomes independent as the
            The People's Democratic Republic of Yemen.

DECEMBER

1   THAILAND - Increased Communist activity, which began
            in 1964, requires that a total of 12 provinces be put
            under martial law.

3   CYPRUS - With UN and US assistance, an agreement is
            reached which ends the fighting.

5   UNITED NATIONS - The General Assembly approves the
            Latin American Denuclearization Treaty.

5   SOUTH VIET NAM - In a Montagnard village in Phouc Long
            Province in III CTZ, VC forces systematically murder
            200 civilians and kidnap 400 others.

8-18   SOUTH VIET NAM - The US 101st Air Cavalry Division,
            with 10,024 men and almost 5,500 tons of equipment is
            airlifted from Fort Campbell, Kentucky to SVN.   There
            are 369 C-141 Starlifters and 22 C-133 Cargomasters
            used in the largest and longest airlift to date.

10   UNITED STATES - The US carries out a nuclear test de-
            signed to study the peaceful uses of nuclear fission
            (Operation GAS BUGGY).

12   CAMBODIA - The government acknowledges that the Viet
            Cong use Cambodia as a sanctuary but denies they gave
            permission to North Viet Nam to do so.

13   SOUTH VIET NAM - The 101st Airborne Division arrives in Saigon with its last two brigades.

13   ALGERIA - A coup attempt against the Boumedienne government fails.

13-14   GREECE - When a radio plea to his people fails to bring about the overthrow of the junta, King Constantine II is forced to flee to Italy.

17   DAHOMEY - President Soglo is ousted by a military coup led by Major Maurice Kouandete. Kouandete promotes himself to Lieutenant Colonel and assumes the presidency.

22   THE VATICAN - Pope Paul VI asks for a peace without victory in SVN, and for the US to halt its bombing of NVN.

26   SOUTH VIET NAM - The government threatens to pursue fleeing VC forces into Cambodia if that country does not prevent use of border areas as VC bases.

29   COMMUNIST CHINA - The government promises Cambodia military support if US or SVN forces enter that country.

31   SOUTH VIET NAM - US military strength in SVN exceeds 480,000, 315,000 of whom are US Army personnel. Combat losses since 1 January 1961 are 16,106, including 9,699 killed in 1967.

Notes

1968

OMAN - A revolt lasting eight years breaks out in Dhofar when separatists supported by Marxists and South Yemeni open a guerrilla campaign against the province. British-officered Omani troops, supported by Iran forces (1973), finally quell the disturbances.

1   WEST GERMANY - Great Britain begins withdrawing 5,000 troops from the British Army on the Rhine (BAOR).

2   INDIA - The former Prime Minister of Kashmir, Sheikh Mohammed Abdullah, "The Lion of Kashmir," is released from internment.

2   SOUTH VIET NAM - The bombing of NVN resumes after the Allied forces observe a 24-hour cease-fire that was extended to 36 hours in response to an appeal by Pope Paul. Over 200 enemy initiated incidents are reported during the cease-fire period. One of these incidents is the detection and engagement of a reconnaisance patrol of the western edge of the US Marine base at Khe Sanh's main perimeter. Five NVA officers are killed. An intelligence report covers another incident in which two NVA divisions, and possibly a third, have infiltrated into the Khe Sanh base's tactical area of operations (TAOR).

5   CZECHOSLOVAKIA - Stalinist party chief Antonin Novotny is removed from power. He is replaced by progressive Alexander Dubcek.

8   JORDAN - Israeli jets attack Jordanian artillery
           positions that have been shelling Israeli targets.

9   UNITED STATES - The government agrees to furnish Hawk
           surface-to-air missiles to Thailand. In return, Thai-
           land consents to send additional troops to SVN and in-
           crease the Thai commitment to 7,400 men.

10   FRANCE - The government announces the withdrawal of
           5,000 French troops from West Germany.

12   UNITED STATES - The US renews its assurance of respect
           for Cambodian neutrality and territorial integrity.

15   JAPAN - Violent clashes between police and a radical
           left-wing students' organization Zengakuren take place
           in the port city of Sasebo on the island of Kyushu.
           The protest is against the expected visit of the
           aircraft carrier USS Enterprise.

16   CYPRUS - The last Greek troops are withdrawn from the
           island.

16   TURKEY - The government begins demobilizing the troops
           prepared to invade Cyprus.

16-20   SOUTH VIET NAM - The US Marine base at Khe Sanh is
           reinforced with one additional battalion of Marines
           (17 January). During the next several days, Marine
           patrols are brought under increasingly heavy enemy
           fire. On 20 January, for instance, "I" Company, 26th
           Marines, supported by air and artillery, badly mauls
           an NVA battalion dug in on the southern slopes of Hill
           881N. Seven Marines are killed, but enemy losses num-
           ber 103. One NVA lieutenant is captured; he confesses
           that an attack on Khe Sanh is imminent.

19   YEMEN - Peace talks, which began on 12 January, break
           down.

20-21   SOUTH VIET NAM - An estimated NVA battalion attacks
           the Marine company dug in on Hill 861N on the outer
           perimeter of Khe Sanh.

21   SOUTH VIET NAM - Some 40,000 NVA begin an attack and
           eventually lay siege to the 8,000-man Marine base at
           Khe Sanh in Quang Tri Province. The base, wedged be-
           tween the DMZ and the Laotian border on Route 9 in I
           CTZ blocks an important NVA resupply route into SVN.
           The siege, supported by heavy mortar, artillery, and
           rocket fire, lasts until April, but the long-awaited
           final blow never materializes. The base is relieved by
           an Allied forces on 6-8 April and abandoned at the end
           of June. From 21 January through 31 March, 75,631 tons

21   SOUTH VIET NAM (Cont'd) - of bombs are dropped in B-52 "ARC LIGHT" air strikes around the fort. The general scheme to provide massive air support to Khe Sanh is called "Operation NIAGARA" (begun 22 January).

21   GREENLAND - A US B-52 bomber carrying four hydrogen weapons on airborne alert suffers difficulties and attempts a landing at Thule AFB in North West Greenland. The aircraft crashes on the ice in Baffin Bay. A frantic search for the fusion weapons fails to produce more than fragments. Because of this incident, the Social Democratic government of Denmark loses its bid for reelection.

21   SOUTH KOREA - A group of North Korean commandos carry out a raid in Seoul.

23   NORTH KOREA - North Korean motor torpedo boats (MTB) operating in international waters in the Sea of Japan capture an American electronic surveillance ship, the USS Pueblo, off the coast of North Korea. The ship is taken to Wonsan Harbor. The crew of 83 American service personnel is taken into custody. Faulty communications, poor contingency planning, and lax leadership all are described as causes for a lack of American reaction other than a vocal outcry. A later display of American military strength fails to dissuade the North Koreans, and the American crew is held in beastly conditions for 11 months. The ensuing negotiations for the release of the crew lead to a straining of South Korean-American relations as the Seoul government views the US as weak.

23   UNITED STATES - President Johnson orders a call-up of 14,000 Air Force and 600 Navy reservists in response to the Pueblo Incident in Korea.

23-28   SOUTH VIET NAM - To protect them from hostile fire, a large number of Montagnard tribesmen and South Vietnamese civilians are evacuated from the Khe Sanh area.

25   SIERRA LEONE - A new military coup overthrows the ruling junta. The new government is headed by Andrew T. Juxton-Smith who helped lead the first coup in March 1967.

26   ISRAEL - The government agrees to the Egyptian plan for clearing the Suez Canal.

27   SOUTH VIET NAM - The Communist forces begin their declared seven-day Tet truce. At the same time, the 37th ARVN Ranger Battalion reinforces the Khe Sanh Marine base.

29   SOUTH VIET NAM - The Allies begin their 36-hour cease-
            fire for Tet in all areas except I CTZ and north of
            the DMZ. The threat of large scale attacks and the
            Communist buildup around Khe Sanh preclude a general
            truce.

30   SOUTH VIET NAM - The NVN begin their largest offensive
            in SVN, coinciding the attack with the beginning of
            the Lunar New Year (Tet). More than 50,000 NVA and VC
            troops take part in the surprise attack which centers
            on the five northern provinces in SVN, but affects all
            locales, including Saigon, where the fighting reaches
            the American Embassy grounds. In the ancient capital
            of Hue, street-to-street fighting continues until 24
            February. The Allies cancel the Tet standdown.

30   SUEZ CANAL - Work is halted on clearing the canal
            after an exchange of gunfire between Israeli and
            Egyptian forces.

31   KENYA - A peace accord is signed with Somalia.

31   SOUTH VIET NAM - Martial law is declared throughout
            SVN in view of the widespread enemy attacks which now
            include 120 cities and towns.

31   ADEN - The British Royal Navy discontinues its sur-
            veillance in the waters off Aden.

31   ALGERIA - The French evacuate Mers el-Kebir.

31   YUGOSLAVIA - The government opens diplomatic relations
            with West Germany.

FEBRUARY

4   CENTRAL AFRICA - The Union of Central African States
            is created. Those initialing the charter include Chad,
            Congo-Kinshasa, and the Central African Republic. The
            formal signing takes place on 2 April.

7   SOUTH VIET NAM - The US Special Forces camp at Lang
            Vei in Quang Tri Province is overrun by an NVA bat-
            talion supported by Soviet-built PT-76 tanks. This is
            the first use of enemy tanks in SVN. Most of the mili-
            tary personnel and about 3,000 civilians filter into
            the Marine positions at Khe Sanh where most are
            evacuated.

9-10   SOUTH VIET NAM - President Thieu orders a partial
            mobilization and calls up the reserves.

10   NORTH VIET NAM - The US renews its attacks on the port
            city of Haiphong.

12   SUDAN - The government announces it has concluded mil-
            itary aid agreements with Bulgaria, Yugoslavia, and
            the Soviet Union.

13   UNITED STATES - The Pentagon announces the movement of
            an additional 10,500 troops into SVN to counter an ex-
            pected second Communist offensive.

14   UNITED STATES - The Secretary of Defense orders   an
            increase in the B-52 sortie rate to 1,800 per month.
            This level of intensity is maintained until 15 July
            1969.

19   SOUTH YEMEN   - The government announces that it has
            entered the war in North Yemen on the side of the
            Republicans.

20   EGYPT - Those military officers held responsible for
            the Arab defeat in the 1967 Arab-Israeli War are tried
            and sentenced by courts-martial after four months of
            secret trails. None are sentenced to be executed but
            some are sentenced to life at hard labor.   The
            "leniency" of the sentences causes widespread rioting
            which forces the government to cancel the sentences
            and order new trials.

21   SOUTH VIET NAM - The first elements of the 3rd   Bri-
            gade, US 82nd Airborne Division arrive by air at   Chu
            Lai (I CTZ) from Fort Bragg, North Carolina. This   is
            the longest distance, large unit, combat deployment in
            history. The brigade is closed into its bases in SVN
            by 26 February.

23   SOUTH VIET NAM - The US Marine's 27th Regimental Land-
            ing Team (RLT) arrives by air in I CTZ from Califor-
            nia. The unit is closed in by 29 February and immedi-
            ately begins relieving other USMC units who move from
            Da Nang to Hue.

24   UNITED NATIONS - Secretary General   U Thant declares
            that if the US stops bombing the north meaningful
            talks can begin with Hanoi.

24   SOUTH VIET NAM - US troop strength in SVN is 495,000.
            ARVN strength is 600,000. The enemy's strength is
            estimated at 223,000-248,000.

24   NORTH VIET NAM - Naval attack aircraft from the USS
            Enterprise strike the port of Hanoi.

25   SOUTH VIET NAM - South Vietnamese forces recapture the citadel at Hue. By November 1969 the bodies of 2,810 persons murdered by the VC during the Communist control of the city will be found. More than 2,000 additional civilians, suspected victims of Communist atrocities, remain unaccounted for.

28   SAUDI ARABIA - The government announces that it has renewed military aid to the Royalist forces fighting in North Yemen.

29   SOUTH VIET NAM - Casualty figures from the Communist Tet Offensive (29 January-29 February) include 45,000 enemy KIA and 7,417 taken prisoner. US losses include 1,825 killed; ARVN losses are 3,557 KIA; and of the Free World Military Forces, 92 KIA, for a total of 5,474 killed. Almost 600,000 South Vietnamese find themselves refugees.

MARCH

            CAMBODIA - The intensity of Communist activity increases.

6   CZECHOSLOVAKIA - A group of liberal Communists take control of the government.

6-13   POLAND - Major student demonstrations break out in Warsaw. By 13 March they spread to Cracow (Kracow).

8   SOUTH VIET NAM - The US MACV Deputy Commander for Air (Commander, Seventh Air Force) becomes the single manager for air, assuming operational control of all strike aircraft in the theater.

9   SOUTH VIET NAM - General Westmoreland asks for an additional 206,000 troops, an increase of 40% over present force ceilings.

10   SOUTH VIET NAM - A Provisional Corps, Vietnam, is formed in the Hue-Phu Bai area to control US units in northern I CTZ.

12   ITALY - Students fight a violent street battle with police in Rome. The incident was provoked by "Chinese" students seeking to impose Maoist philosophy as the cure of all ills.

12   MAURITIUS - The former British possession in the Indian Ocean becomes independent and signs a defensive agreement with Great Britain.

12   NORTH YEMEN - Yemeni Republican forces break the
        Royalist siege of San'a.

15   CHAD - A revolt begins in the Tibesti Desert region
        among the Arabs. This uprising will continue until
        1971 when it will be suppressed with the aid of French
        troops.

15   SOUTH VIET NAM - US intelligence detects a withdrawal
        of major NVA units from the Khe Sanh area in Quang Tri
        Province, I CTZ.

16   SOUTH VIET NAM - Troops of "C" Company, 1st Battalion,
        20th Infantry of the 23rd (Americal) Division rape,
        sodomize, and massacre the inhabitants of the South
        Vietnamese village of My Lai 4 (Song My) in Quang Ngai
        Province. A massive attempt to suppress the informa-
        tion fails as, after 20 months, the details of the
        massacre become known. The most junior officer in the
        chain of command, Second Lieutenant William L. Calley,
        is ultimately tried and convicted of the crime. Five
        other participants will be tried. Thirteen others, in-
        cluding the division commander, Lieutenant General
        Samuel W. Koster (later the Commandant at the USMA,
        West Point), are accused of a cover-up. Koster is
        eventually forced to resign. None of the more senior
        officers are tried either for complicity in the crime,
        or for the attempted cover-up.

17   GREAT BRITAIN - The biggest anti-American demonstra-
        tion in history takes place in London's Trafalgar
        Square. The issue is US policy in SEA.

18   GUATEMALA - A state of siege is declared following a
        wave of terrorist activity. The order is lifted on 20
        June.

20   SOUTH YEMEN - A coup attempt, led by the army, fails.

21   ISRAEL - When warnings to Jordan's King Hussein failed
        to stop terrorist activity by Al-Fatah, Israeli mili-
        tary forces, in a massive retaliatory operation, at-
        tack the terrorist training bases near the town of
        Kerama (Karameh) in the Jordan Valley. Jordan claims a
        victory by forcing the Israelis to withdraw after 15
        hours of heavy fighting.

21   SOUTH VIET NAM - Black market stalls in Saigon are
        closed by the GVN at the request of USMACV. At the
        same time, President Thieu announces that RVNAF will
        be increased by 135,000 men. The actual current
        strength of RVNAF is listed as 677,600.

24   UNITED NATIONS - The Security Council unaminously con-
            demns Israel for its raid into Jordanian territory.

27   INDONESIA - The Consultative Assembly names Suharto
            President. This effectively ends Sukarno's role in the
            rule of the country.

30   SOUTH VIET NAM - "Operation SCOTLAND I" terminates in
            Quang Tri Province with 1,062 NVA and 205 US Marines
            confirmed as killed. It is probable that enemy dead
            number between 10,000 and 15,000. A diversionary at-
            tack (Task Force Kilo) is launched in the Gio Linh
            area on the coast near the DMZ in Quang Tri Province
            to divert NVA attention from Khe Sanh.

30   UNITED STATES - The government announces Canada has
            agreed to a five-year extension of the NORAD agree-
            ment.

31   UNITED STATES - Faced with mounting public resistance
            to the war in SEA, President Johnson announces he will
            not run for reelection. He also announces a call-up of
            some 50,000 reservists and authorizes a 13,500-man in-
            crease in the troop strength in SVN. This brings US
            strength to 538,500. Lastly, the President halts all
            bombing and naval gunfire attacks over most of NVN
            (above the 19th parallel).

APRIL

            SOUTH VIET NAM - Mobile Riverine Force operations be-
            gin in the Mekong Delta. Also during the month, the
            Popular Self Defense Force (PSDF) is inaugurated. This
            force will constitute a "town militia" in each village
            and hamlet in SVN.

1   SOUTH VIET NAM - The ICC "temporarily suspends" all
            fixed and mobile team operations outside Saigon and
            Hanoi.

1   SOUTH KOREA - The government calls up a reserve corps.

1-15   SOUTH VIET NAM - "Operation PEGASUS" (Lam Son 207a)
            begins. The task force, composed of some 30,000 troops
            including elements of the First Marines, the 1st US
            Cavalry (Airmobile) Division and ARVN units, attacks
            to relieve the US Marine garrison at Khe Sanh. When
            the attack begins NVA forces begin withdrawing into
            Laos. Aerial resupply of Khe Sanh is halted on 8
            April, when Route 9 is reopened. The area is declared
            "secured" on 15 April.

2   WESTERN EUROPE – The Pentagon orders the withdrawal of 35,000 US troops from Western Europe.

3   UNITED STATES – President Lyndon B. Johnson and the North Vietnamese government exchange public statements in which they agree to establish contacts between their representatives for the purpose of negotiating an end to the war.

4   UNITED STATES – Martin Luther King is assassinated in Memphis, Tennessee by prison escapee James Earl Ray. King's death sparks massive racial rioting throughout the country, which claims 46 lives. More than 55,000 federal troops and National Guardsmen are employed in quelling the disturbances.

5   UNITED STATES – The US agrees to return the Bonin Islands to Japan.

6   PAKISTAN – The government informs Washington that it will not renew the lease on the American communications facility at Peshawar when it expires in July 1969.

8   SOUTH VIET NAM – "Operation COMPLETE VICTORY" begins. This operation includes the employment of over 100,000 troops from 42 US and 37 ARVN battalions who seek to rid the 11 provinces in the III CTZ of the presence of the Viet Cong.

11   WEST BERLIN – Violent demonstrations follow the attempted assassination of Rudi Dutschke, the leader of the Socialist Students League (SDS). The rioting spreads to West Germany and the situation remains serious until after 17 April.

11   UNITED STATES – Secretary of Defense Clark Clifford announces a new force ceiling of 549,000 for SVN and declares a policy of gradually shifting the responsibility for fighting the war to the South Vietnamese. At the same time, 24,500 reservists are called, 10,000 of whom are scheduled for service in SVN.

13   GREAT BRITAIN – After an exchange of notes the government ends its defense pact with Kuwait.

13   TANZANIA – The government recognizes the breakaway state of Biafra which was formerly a province of Nigeria.

15   NORTH KOREA – A US reconnaisance aircraft is shot down 90 miles off the North Korean coast.

15   SOUTH VIET NAM - "Operation SCOTLAND II" begins in the
            Khe Sanh TAOR. Most of the relief forces are withdrawn
            from the Khe Sanh area to Quang Tri City in prepara-
            tion for "Operation DELAWARE."

15   UNITED STATES - The government cuts off all develop-
            mental aid to Peru after the Peruvian government or-
            ders Mirage fighter-bombers from France.

16   SOUTH VIET NAM - There are 110 US combat battalions in
            SVN. Of this number, 24 are US Marine battalions.

18   SIERRA LEONE - The government of Andrew Juxton-Smith
            is overthrown by a group of noncommissioned officers
            (Sergeant's Coup) who install in his place Colonel
            John Bangura, who is in exile. Siaka Stevens is ap-
            pointed Prime Minister.

18   SOUTH VIET NAM - As a result of the recent VC/NVA
            spring offensive, the GVN loses control over more than
            1.1 million civilians.

19   SOUTH VIET NAM - "Operation DELAWARE" begins in the A
            Shau Valley and in Quang Tri and Thua Thien provinces
            in the I CTZ to break up preparations for an expected
            NVA/VC attack on Hue. Elements of the 1st Cavalry
            Division (Airmobile), 101st Air Cavalry Division,
            196th Light Infantry Brigade, 1st ARVN Division, and
            Task Force Bravo, ARVN Airborne Division participate.

24   CZECHOSLOVAKIA - The government suspends the shipment
            of arms to Nigeria.

25   ALGERIA - An assassination attempt on the life of
            Houari Boumedienne fails.

25   DEMOCRATIC CONGO REPUBLIC - A group of 137 foreign
            mercenaries who had been interned for their part in
            the unsuccessful rebellion against President Mobutu
            are turned over to the International Red Cross.

29   LIBYA - The government negotiates a contract to buy
            "Thunderbird" and "Rapier" surface-to-air missiles
            from Great Britain.

MAY

1   SOUTH VIET NAM - To curb profiteering, new currency is
            issued, and a black market control system is imple-
            mented by MACV. Also, the USAF 120th Tactical Fighter
            Wing arrives at Phan Rang Air Base in II CTZ. This is
            the first Air National Guard unit to be deployed to a
            war zone since WWII.

1-7   UNITED STATES - Student demonstrations against the war
         in SVN take place on the Columbia University campus in
         upper New York City. They soon spread into the streets
         of Harlem and elsewhere in the city.

2-3   FRANCE - Student protests at Nanterre turn unrest into
         nationwide violence against the DeGaulle government.

5   SPAIN - The government closes its border with British-
         controlled Gibraltar.

5-13   SOUTH VIET NAM - NVA and VC forces launch new attacks
         (Mini-Tet) on more than 120 towns, military posts, and
         airfields throughout SVN. Ground fighting con- tinues
         in and around Saigon until 9 May. At least 2,500 enemy
         troops are killed in this fighting.

6   OAS - The OAS establishes a peacekeeping force to be
         sent to the Dominican Republic.

8   GABON - The government recognizes Biafra.

9   UNITED NATIONS - The Security Council orders a trade
         embargo against Rhodesia after it refuses to negotiate
         with Great Britain over civil rights issues involved
         in the all-white government's control of 5.4 million
         native blacks.

10   GREAT BRITAIN - The government announces a 40% in-
         crease in troop commitments to NATO.

13   FRANCE - US-NVN peace negotiations to end the fighting
         in Southeast Asia open in Paris. An unrelated nation-
         wide strike begins in France. On 14 May, students for-
         cibly occupy the Sorbonne in Paris where they remain
         until 16 June.

13-16   SOUTH YEMEN - A revolt against the central government
         is unsuccessful.

19   SOUTH VIET NAM - The VC begin a month-long program of
         nightly rocket barrage attacks on Saigon. Consider-
         able damage is done and over 100,000 are left homeless
         before the attacks end on 21 June.

20   ZAMBIA - The government recognizes Biafra.

21   UNITED NATIONS - The Security Council declares invalid
         Israeli expropriation of Arab land and property in
         Jerusalem.

23-31   UGANDA - Nigerian peace talks are held in Kampala.

24   FRANCE - President DeGaulle calls for a restoration of
            order in France as communist-inspired student demon-
            strations grow in intensity.

29   UNITED NATIONS - The Security Council imposes compre-
            hensive mandatory sanctions against Rhodesia.

30   FRANCE - The French Parliament is dissolved.

JUNE

            MALAYSIA - Communist guerrilla activity resumes after
            a long period of quiet.

            FRANCE - New elections give the Gaulists a clear ma-
            jority, while the Communists and other radical parties
            lose seats.

3   YUGOSLAVIA - A student demonstration is forcibly sup-
            pressed by the police.

5   UNITED STATES - Presidential hopeful, Senator Robert
            F. Kennedy, is assassinated in a Los Angelos hotel
            kitchen by Sirhan Bishara Sirhan.

6   THE NETHERLANDS - The government suspends arms ship-
            ments to Nigeria.

6   PAKISTAN - The government announces its   gradual
            withdrawal from SEATO and CENTO.

9   SOUTH VIET NAM - General William Westmoreland leaves
            SVN to become Army Chief of Staff. He is to be re-
            placed by General Creighton W. Abrams as COMUSMACV on
            3 July.

12   FRANCE - The government halts all arms shipments to
            Nigeria.

15   SOUTH VIET NAM - The government orders a general mobi-
            lization of all manpower between 18-38 years of age
            (some reports say 17-43).

23   SOUTH VIET NAM - The Marine base at Khe Sanh is dis-
            mantled and abandoned.

28   PAKISTAN - Foreign Minister Arshad Husain abrogates
            the 10-year-old mutual security pact with the US.

29   SOUTH VIET NAM - The US has had 10,503 soldiers killed
            in action in the first six months of 1968. Enemy
            losses are listed as 170,000. The present US strength
            in SVN is 528,840.

JULY

1   UNITED STATES - A Nuclear Non-Proliferation Treaty is signed simultaneously in Washington, Moscow, and London by most nations of the world. France, Communist China, Israel, Argentina, Brazil, India, Pakistan, South Africa, and Spain refuse to sign.

1   USSR - The government circulates a nine-point memorandum on disarmament.

3   UNITED STATES - General William Westmoreland, former COMUSMACV, is made Army Chief of Staff. Army General Creighton W. Abrams assumes command of American forces in SVN.

5   BELGIUM - The government suspends all arms shipments to Nigeria.

7   FRANCE - The government starts a new series of nuclear tests at its test facilities in the South Pacific.

14-18   NORTH VIET NAM - An intensified bombing of NVN begins with attacks on targets north of the DMZ and, for the first time, B-52 attacks on NVA SAM sites.

15   CZECHOSLOVAKIA - The government of Prime Minister Alexander Dubcek demands a revision in the Warsaw Pact to prevent its use for political purposes.

15   EGYPT - Leaders of various Palestinian Arab "commando" factions meet in Cairo to map out new coordinated strategies for attacking Israel.

17   IRAQ - A Baath-led revolt compels President Abdel Rahman Arif to give up his office. Major General Ahmed Hassan al-Bakr takes over the title of President.

17   SOUTH VIET NAM - A US Command announces that Cambodian forces have seized a US riverine patrol craft in the Mekong Delta.

17   DAHOMEY - The government is returned to civilian control after nearly three years of military leadership.

19   UNITED STATES - At a conference held in Honolulu, President Johnson promises SVN President Thieu that the US will continue the war at the present level, unless the North Vietnamese agree to some form of mutual restraint.

20   NIGER - Preliminary Nigerian peace talks, held under OAU sponsorship, open in Niamey.

23   USSR - Reservists are called up to participate in military exercises along the western frontier, primarily in the vicinity of the Czechoslovakian border.

26   SOUTH YEMEN - A rebellion against the central government is quelled after heavy fighting.

26   THAILAND - The first Communist raid against a Thai military installation is reported.

26   MEXICO - A long period of student unrest begins which is centered mostly around the National University.

29   CZECHOSLOVAKIA - The entire Soviet Politburo travels to the Czech border town of Cierna nad Tisou for talks with 16 members of the Czech Presidium.

29   SOUTH VIET NAM - Elements of the Thai "Black Panther" Division arrive in Saigon. This brings the Thai military strength in country to 3,300 of a programmed 12,000.

AUGUST

1   RHODESIA - Police and security forces conduct a number of widespread antiguerrilla raids throughout the country.

2   INDIA - The government announces it has sealed its border with Burma to prevent Naga rebels from crossing into India on their return from China.

3   CZECHOSLOVAKIA - A one-day meeting in Bratislava takes place between the Soviet and Czech leaders attempting to settle the rift between the two states. The Czech government reports the departure of the last Soviet troops.

5   ETHIOPIA - Nigerian peace talks are resumed in Addis Ababa.

9   CZECHOSLOVAKIA - Yugoslav President Tito arrives in Prague and receives a hero's welcome.

15   SOUTH VIET NAM - US troop strength is reported at 534,000.

16   CZECHOSLOVAKIA - President Nicolae Ceaucescu arrives in Prague to an enthusiastic welcome. Before his departure a treaty of friendship and cooperation is signed.

16   UNITED NATIONS - The Security Council accuses Israel of flagrant violation of the Charter and repeatedly ignoring UN resolutions banning further reprisal raids into Jordan.

17   SOUTH VIET NAM - The Communists open a new series of attacks against US, Allied, and ARVN bases throughout the I, II, and III CTZs.

17   USSR - Probably on this date the Politburo, after much debate, reaches a concensus on the decision to invade Czechoslovakia.

18   UNITED STATES - A Pentagon spokesman reports there have been 100,000 bombing missions over NVN since July 1965.

20-21   CZECHOSLOVAKIA - More than 200,000 soldiers (some estimates are as high as 500,000 men) in Soviet, East German, Polish, Hungarian, and Bulgarian military units invade Czechoslovakia. (Romania does not participate, and probably was not informed about the plan.) The "Prague Spring" ends. Soviet strength in Czechoslovakia will eventually reach over 650,000 troops.

21   SOUTH VIET NAM - Nightly rocket attacks on Saigon resume.

21   UNITED NATIONS - The Security Council orders an immediate withdrawal of Warsaw Pact forces from Czechoslovakia.

24   FRANCE - The government detonates a two-megaton thermonuclear device at Mururoa Atoll, 750 miles southeast of Tahiti.

27   CZECHOSLOVAKIA - Czech leaders are forced to abrogate a series of reforms that were part of a program instituted by Communist Party Secretary Alexander Dubcek.

28   GUATEMALA - The US Ambassador to Guatemala, John Gordon Mein, is killed by Communist guerrillas during an apparent kidnap attempt.

28   CHAD - Chad asks the French for assistance in putting down an insurrection in northwest Chad. France sends a battalion of paratroopers.

28   ROMANIA - The government implements a plan to develop an armed militia.

29   UNITED STATES - During the Democratic Party Convention
          in Chicago, National Guardsmen are used to break up a
          massive demonstration against the nomination of Hubert
          Humphrey. Five thousand Guardsmen plus 12,000 police
          are required to maintain order.

SEPTEMBER

3   CZECHOSLOVAKIA - East German troops begin their with-
          drawal from Czechoslovakia.

4   REPUBLIC OF CONGO (Brazzaville) - There is a bloody
          military coup in which Congolese army forces battle
          Cuban-trained   rebels   in   Brazzaville.   President
          Massema-Debat resigns. Major Marien Ngoubai becomes
          president on 6 September, and maintains a pro-Chinese
          Communist outlook.

4   NIGERIA - In a renewal of the civil war with Biafra,
          Nigerian forces capture the important town of Aba on
          the country's main road to the coast.

6   CZECHOSLOVAKIA - Political clubs are banned.

6   SWAZILAND - The South African province of Swaziland
          becomes independent.

8   FRANCE - A second thermonuclear device is detonated by
          the French at Mururoa Atoll.

10   SOUTH VIET NAM - The US Marine's 27th RLT, ordered
          temporarily to SVN in February, is returned to the US.

11-12   CZECHOSLOVAKIA - Soviet tanks begin withdrawing from
          Prague and other cities.

12   ALBANIA - Albania withdraws from the Warsaw Pact and
          accuses the Soviet Union of planning an invasion of
          its borders.

13   CZECHOSLOVAKIA - A censorship program is installed.

16   NIGERIA - The Biafran town of Owerri is captured. The
          occupation of Owerri means the Biafran state is now
          cut off from access to the sea.

18   THE PHILIPPINES - The government reasserts its claim
          to the Saba District of Borneo following a breakdown
          in negotiations being conducted with Malaysia. Malay-
          sia immediately breaks diplomatic relations with the
          Philippines.

18-24   MEXICO - Army troops and police seize the National University in a bloody battle to put an end to disorders that began in July. Over 50 students are killed.

19   CZECHOSLOVAKIA - The Foreign Minister is forced to resign because of his involvement in Dubcek's reform program.

20   SOMALIA - An agreement ends Somalian incursions into the French protectorates of Afars and Issas.

26   TUNISIA - The government announces it will boycott all future Arab League meetings.

30   SOUTH VIET NAM - The battleship <u>USS New Jersey</u> joins the US naval task force off the Vietnamese coast near the DMZ. This is the first use of battleships since June 1953 (Korean War).

OCTOBER

1   SOUTH VIET NAM - As a means of controlling NVA/VC infiltration the government orders all SVN citizens to register and henceforth carry ID cards.

2   MEXICO - Student rioting in Mexico City reaches its peak just ten days before the opening of the XIX Olympic Games. The students are armed with automatic weapons and Molotov cocktails. Police and army units finally put down the rioting with heavy losses, including the army force commander, General Hernandez Toledo, who is killed in the fighting.

3   PERU - President Fernando Belaunde Terry is deposed in a bloodless coup led by General Juan Velasco Alvarado, the Army Chief of Staff.

4   CAMBODIA - The government indirectly concedes that VC/NVA forces have been launching attacks against SVN from Cambodian sanctuaries since June 1965.

5   NORTHERN IRELAND - The Roman Catholic minority begins a campaign of protests claiming discrimination by the Protestants. Rioting breaks out in Londonderry where demonstrators clash with police.

7   UNITED NATIONS - Speaking before the General Assembly, the Finnish Foreign Minister, A. Karjalainen, demands the withdrawal of all foreign troops from Czechoslovakia.

10   GIBRALTAR - After five days of meetings aboard a war-
            ship (HMS Fearless), Ian Smith, the Rhodesian Prime
            Minister, again rejects British demands for a settle-
            ment to the Rhodesian crisis.

11   PANAMA - A military coup d'etat, led by the Panamanian
            National Guard, ousts the recently seated government
            of President Arnulfo Arias. A military junta elects
            Colonel Bolivar Urrutia as the country's new Presi-
            dent.

12   EQUATORIAL GUINEA - The former Spanish Colony becomes
            independent.

15   SOUTH VIET NAM - There is a lull in fighting amid re-
            ports of NVA/VC withdrawals.

16   CZECHOSLOVAKIA - Soviet Premier Alexei Kosygin and
            Czech Prime Minister Oldrich Cernik sign an agreement
            in Prague that will allow 70,000 Soviet troops to be
            stationed on Czech soil. All other foreign troops cur-
            rently in Czechoslovakia are to be withdrawn within
            two months.

18   SOUTH VIET NAM - Allied naval units begin "Operation
            SEA LORDS." Three task forces coordinate moves to
            halt maritime resupply from Cambodia of VC and NVA
            forces in the Mekong Delta.

25   UNITED STATES - Secretary of Defense Clark Clifford
            announces the withdrawal of an estimated 30,000-40,000
            NVA/VC troops from SVN.

31   SOUTH VIET NAM - The US Command announces a cessation
            of all bombardment fires north of the 20th parallel
            effective at 0800 (8 AM EST) on 1 November.

NOVEMBER

1   SOUTH VIET NAM - The inauguration of the "Accelerated
            Pacification Campaign" is announced. This campaign is
            designed to bring more of the civilian population un-
            der government control by eradicating local VC opera-
            tions around hamlets and villages.

4   SOUTH VIET NAM - President Thieu announces his govern-
            ment will boycott the Paris Peace Negotiations if the
            National Liberation Front (Viet Cong) representatives
            are allowed to attend.

5   NORTH VIET NAM - The government issues a five-point
            program for peace which calls for the immediate with-
            drawal of all US troops.

5   EGYPT - Israeli commandos attack the Qena (Qina) Dam
        and the Nag Hammadi (Naj Hammadi) hydroelectric plant
        at the confluence of the Nile and Wadi Qena rivers.

7   UNITED NATIONS - The Security Council votes to extend
        the sanctions imposed against Rhodesia. It also orders
        Great Britain to use force to end the regime in
        Rhodesia.

14   UNITED STATES - Anti-war groups call this "Turn in
        Your Draft Card Day." Numerous demonstrations take
        place throughout the nation.

16   SOUTH VIET NAM - Reconnaissance pilots report that
        enemy troop and supply movements along the Ho Chi Minh
        Trail in Laos have increased fourfold since the bomb-
        ing halt.

19   MALI - A military coup overthrows the socialist gov-
        ernment of President Modibo Keita. The government is
        taken over by a junta calling itself the National
        Military Liberation Committee.

23   INDIA - Pro-Chinese Naxalite extremists begin a series
        of disturbances in Kerala Province and elsewhere.

27   UNITED STATES - The US announces that the South Viet-
        namese government agrees to send delegates to the
        peace talks in Paris, and that the GVN representative
        will take the lead and be the chief spokesman in all
        matters of principle dealing with SVN.

28   WEST GERMANY - The government announces the purchase
        of 88 US F-4 fighters and 50 additional F-104 "Star-
        fighters."

DECEMBER

2   ALBANIA - During a visit to Tirana, Chinese Communist
        General Huang Yung-sheng signs a defense agreement
        with the Albanian government.

8   SOUTH YEMEN - The Gulf Liberation Front, a new Arab
        nationalist organization, is formed in Aden.

9   MALI - Lieutenant Moussa Traore, one of the leaders of
        the November coup, is proclaimed President.

10   UNITED NATIONS - The maintenance of UN forces in Cyp-
        rus is extended six more months by the Security Coun-
        cil.

13   BRAZIL - A coup takes place in which President Costa e Silva seizes absolute power.

13   CENTRAL AFRICAN REPUBLIC - The government announces it is withdrawing from the Union of Central African States.

17   EGYPT - The government announces it has placed commando forces in the Sinai.

18   UNITED NATIONS - The General Assembly votes to order Great Britain to return Gibraltar to Spain by 1 October 1969.

20   UNITED STATES - The government suspends military and economic aid to Brazil.

21-25   SIERRA LEONE - Violence breaks out, which is finally surpressed by government troops.

23   SOUTH KOREA - Eleven months after their capture, 82 members of the crew of the USS Pueblo are released to American authorities at Panmunjon.

24   SOUTH VIET NAM - A 24-hour cease-fire goes into effect. The VC announce a 72-hour truce. At least 113 enemy-instigated incidents are reported during the period.

26   GREECE - Two terrorists from the Popular Front for the Liberation of Palestine (PFLP) attack an El Al Boeing 707 as it is about to take off from Athens airport.

27   UNITED STATES - The Department of State announces approval of the sale of 50 F-4 Phantom jets to Israel.

27   COMMUNIST CHINA - The Chinese explode their second thermonuclear device.

27   UNITED STATES - The US sells 50 F-4 "Phanthom" jet fighters to Israel.

28   LEBANON - Israeli commandos in four helicopters conduct a nighttime raid on Beirut airport in reprisal for terrorist activities. Thirteen airliners belonging to Arab nations are destroyed.

31   SOUTH VIET NAM - US troop strength nears 540,000. US casualties exceed 30,500 killed, with 14,592 KIA in 1968. RVNAF losses include 17,486 killed in action. Enemy losses are listed as 191,307 confirmed killed, 21,050 captured, and 17,597 defected.

1969

NORTHERN IRELAND - Year long violence sparked by enmity between Catholics and Protestants requires major troop commitments by the British.

IRAQ - A yearlong dispute breaks out with Iran. Border clashes punctuate the verbal battle over navigation rights in the Strait of Shatt al-Arab and over Iranian support of the Kurds.

JANUARY

1   SOUTH VIET NAM - The VC free three American (US Army) prisoners of war.

1   NIGERIA - Biafran leader Colonel Chukwuemeka Odumegwu Ojukwu calls for a truce to allow much needed emergency supplies to reach civilian victims of the civil war.

2   ISRAEL - Israeli forces open fire on three Lebanese border positions.

2-4   GUYANA - A major uprising in the Rupununi District is crushed by army and security forces. The uprising had been supported by Brazilian and Venezuelan factions. Security forces complete the mopping-up by 12 January.

4   NORTHERN IRELAND - Violence breaks out between Roman Catholic marchers and Protestants during a four-day civil rights march from Belfast to Londonderry.

5   UNITED STATES - President Nixon names Henry Cabot
           Lodge to replace W. Averell Harriman as chief US
           negotiator at the Paris peace talks on Viet Nam.

6   KENYA - The government begins a program to oust Indian
           merchants in the country.

7   UNITED STATES - San Francisco State College reopens
           after a long period of student violence and teacher
           strikes against the war in SEA.

7   FRANCE - The government announces a ban on the sale of
           military equipment to Israel. At the same time, it an-
           nounces an agreement with the USSR to double trade
           over the next five years.

7   CZECHOSLOVAKIA - The Presidium of the Communist Party
           ousts National Assembly chairman, Josef Smrkovsky.

7   SOUTH VIET NAM - The government protests continued NVN
           violations of the DMZ to the International Commission
           of Control and Supervision (ICC).

8   NORWAY - Norwegian naval units capture three Soviet
           and two East German trawlers operating in "military
           waters."

8   FRANCE - The government extends its embargo to cover
           all arms shipments to Israel, Jordan, Libya, and the
           UAR.

14   FRANCE - The government pledges to help Lebanon if
           Israel attacks it.

14   SOUTH VIET NAM - The government proposes that the US
           begin a gradual withdrawal of its forces.

16   CZECHOSLOVAKIA - Protesting the Soviet occupation of
           his country, a student, Jan Palach, burns himself to
           death in Prague.

17   COMMUNIST CHINA - There are reports of unrest in the
           Sinkiang Uighur Autonomous Region.

17   FRANCE - The government proposes Four-Power talks on
           the continuing Middle East crisis.

18-19   JAPAN - Fighting breaks out at Tokyo University be-
           tween police and left-wing student groups.

18   BOLIVIA - A state of siege is declared following
           reports of a plot against the government.

20   USSR - The Foreign Ministry indicates a willingness to enter into Strategic Arms Limitation Treaty (SALT) discussions.

20   EAST PAKISTAN - Antigovernment rioting breaks out in Dacca. Prolonged violence follows that quickly spreads throughout East and West Pakistan and eventually leads to military intervention.

23   INDIA - Serious rioting breaks out in the state of Andhra Pradesh.

25   FRANCE - Peace talks on SEA begin in Paris.

27   NORTH VIET NAM - The government accuses the US of bombing north of the DMZ. The US immediately denies the charges.

29   NIGERIA - The government launches what it calls the "final offensive" against Biafra.

30   CZECHOSLOVAKIA - Prime Minister Oldrich Cernik announces plans to increase his country's contribution to the Warsaw Pact.

30   SOUTH VIET NAM - The Accelerated Pacification Campaign terminates. At least 5,000 VC have accepted the "Chieu Hoi Plan" and have returned to the government's side. The 1969 Pacification Plan begins 1 February.

FEBRUARY

            NIGERIA - Biafran forces open a counter-offensive designed to open a supply route to the sea.

1-2   ROMANIA - A joint communique marking the completion of meetings between Yugoslavia's Marshal Tito and Romania's Party Secretary Nicholae Ceaucescu denounces the "Brezhnev Doctrine."

3   MIDDLE EAST - The Al Fatah leader, Yasser Arafat, is elected chairman of the executive committee of the Palestine Liberation Organization (PLO).

3   ISRAEL - The Arab population of Gaza begins two days of demonstrations and violence.

3   TANZANIA - The leader of the Mozambique Liberation Front (FRELIMO), Eduardo Chivambo Mondlane, is assassinated in Dar-es-Salaam.

5   UNITED NATIONS - Big-Four representatives open discussions on the Middle East.

6   SOUTH VIET NAM - A   joint US-RVNAF staff is formed   to
         facilitate the "Vietnamization" of the war.

6   MIDDLE EAST - PLO leader Yasser Arafat announces he is
         shifting his guerrilla army from bases in Syria and
         the UAR to Jordan.

6   INDIA - Five days of rioting begin that will leave 43
         dead.

7   ROMANIA - Party Secretary Nicolae Ceaucescu   reaffirms
         his country's independence and sovereignty.

7   USSR - The Soviet Union warns West Germany not to hold
         presidential elections in West Berlin.

7   ANGUILLA - The population votes to establish an   inde-
         pendent republic.

7-8   INDIA - Politically-motivated rioting, which involves
         the Marathi nationalist (Shiv Sena)   paramilitary
         group, breaks out in Bombay. More than 50 are killed.

8-16   TURKEY - Violent demonstrations in Istanbul attend the
         visit of the US Sixth Fleet. Rioting spreads to
         Ankara, Izmir, and Trabzon.

9   EAST GERMANY - The government announces that West
         German Federal Assembly members will not be permitted
         to cross East Germany on their way to the presidential
         elections being held in West Berlin.

9   SOUTH YEMEN - Upon his return from Moscow, President
         Qahtan al-Shaabi announces that the USSR will supply
         arms and materiel to South Yemen to help strengthen
         its defenses.

10   SWITZERLAND - An Israeli El Al airliner is attacked by
         Arab terrorists at Zurich Airport.

10   MALAYSIA - The first contingents of British troops
         leave the country.

11   CANADA - Student rioting breaks out at Sir George
         Williams University in Montreal.

12   RHODESIA - Nationalist leader, Ndabaningi Sithole, is
         convicted of planning to assassinate Prime Minister
         Ian D. Smith.

12   SOUTH VIET NAM - The South Vietnamese Navy begins ac-
         ceptance of US Naval "brown water" craft and respon-
         sibility for riverine and delta operations.

13   GREAT BRITAIN - The government reaffirms the Anglo-Malaysian Defense Agreement.

14   PERU - Peruvian gunboats fire on two American tuna-fishing trawlers within its claimed territorial waters. In retaliation, the US orders a halt to all arms shipments to Peru.

14   SOUTH VIET NAM - The last elements of the Thai Black Panther Division arrive in SVN. There are now about 11,250 Thai troops in country.

14-15   PERU - The US Embassy in Lima is attacked with bombs and Molotov Cocktails.

15   SOUTH VIET NAM - The VC begin a seven-day truce for Tet. The GVN orders a 24-hour cease-fire on 16 February. Ninety-three enemy-instigated incidents are reported.

16   TURKEY - A major riot, involving some 20,000 people, breaks out in Istanbul during a left-wing demonstration protesting a visit by US Sixth Fleet units. One man is killed in the rioting. A US fleet visit to Izmir is cancelled as a result of the violence.

17   PAKISTAN - Following more than two weeks of political disorders, President Ayub Khan releases a number of political prisoners including former Foreign Minister Zulfikar Ali Bhutto.

18   SWITZERLAND - Arab terrorists from the Popular Front for the Liberation of Palestine (PFLP) attack an El Al airliner at Kloten Airport in Zurich. The Israeli pilot and one terrorist are killed.

21   ISRAEL - Arab terrorists explode a bomb in a Jerusalem supermarket.

23   SOUTH VIET NAM - The Communist "Second Tet Offensive" begins. Over 100 towns, military posts and airfields are hit with mortar and rocket fire. The expected attack on Saigon is thwarted by shifting the 1st Cavalry Division (Airmobile) south in III CTZ. This move is largely made using the division's organic airlift capability.

24   SYRIA - Israeli jets bomb two sites on a road allegedly used by Palestinian terrorists for raids into Israel.

24   UAR - A state of emergency is declared in response to the Israeli attack on Syria.

25   AUSTRALIA - The government announces that it will
          maintain military forces in Malaysia and Singapore
          after the withdrawal of Great Britain. New Zealand
          makes a similar announcement.

25   ISRAEL - Arab terrorists bomb the British Consulate in
          East Jerusalem.

26   UAR - President Nasser warns that a new Middle East
          war is probable if Israel does not withdraw from the
          occupied territories.

28   SYRIA - There is a coup in which the defense minister,
          Lieutenant General Hafez al-Assad, seizes much of the
          power from President al-Attassi and the head of the
          Baath Party, General Salah Jadid.

28   EQUATORIAL GUINEA - The government requests the UN
          assign a peace-keeping force to help counter Spanish
          aggression.

28   SOUTH VIET NAM - The NVA/VC offensive is terminated.

MARCH

          COMMUNIST CHINA - There is a major clash between Chi-
          nese and Soviet troops at Sui-fenho. The date cannot
          be fixed with certainty.

1   EAST GERMANY - Routes to West Berlin are blocked by
          the East Germans apparently in response to heavy road
          use by Soviet and East German armored units partici-
          pating in an exercise.

2   LAOS - The Pathet Lao reject a government offer to
          negotiate a peace in the civil war.

2   USSR - The government announces it will not guarantee
          air safety in the flight corridors between West Berlin
          and Western Europe.

2-15   COMMUNIST CHINA - A series of border clashes (3-4, 14-
          15 March) take place between Communist Chinese and
          Soviet forces along the disputed border at Chen-pao
          (Damanski) Island on the Ussuri River in Manchuria.
          Major anti-Soviet demonstrations are held in Peking (7
          March).

3   NIGERIA - The Biafran counter-offensive stalls short
          of Aba, but not before Biafran forces surround the
          town of Owerri.

3   EQUATORIAL GUINEA - A state of emergency is declared.

3   COMMUNIST CHINA - Throngs of Chinese begin a two-day
        seige of the Soviet Embassy in Peking protesting the
        Sino-Soviet border clash on the Ussuri River.

4   PAKISTAN - After a two week respite, a new wave of
        violence breaks out.

5   EQUATORIAL GUINEA - There is an unsuccessful coup
        attempt against the government of President Francisco
        Macias Nguma. The leader of the coup attempt, Foreign
        Minister Atanasio N'Dongo, and others, is reported
        executed. The President then assumes dictatorial
        powers as unrest spreads.

6   SOUTH VIET NAM - US troop strength is reported at
        541,000, with another 72,000 Allied troops also in
        country. Saigon comes under a very heavy rocket and
        mortar attack.

6   ISRAEL - Arab terrorists explode a bomb in the cafe-
        teria of the Hebrew University in Jerusalem. In re-
        sponse, Israeli security forces level five Arab homes
        in East Jerusalem.

7   SOUTH VIET NAM - The new Communist offensive begins to
        stall as US forces throw back the NVA and VC attackers
        at a number of points throughout the country.

7   USSR - A major anti-Chinese demonstration is staged in
        front of the Chinese Embassy in Moscow.

8   LAOS - A US Marine task force crosses the border into
        Laos. It is also reported that a revised estimate in-
        dicates over 452 tons of enemy weapons and ammunition
        have been captured by the 9th US Marine RLT in the A
        Shau Valley in I CTZ since 21 February.

8   UNITED NATIONS - Secretary General U Thant announces
        he is sending a personal representative to Equatorial
        Guinea.

9   UAR - The Army Chief of Staff, Lieutenant Abdel Moneim
        Riadh, is killed while observing an artillery duel be-
        tween Egyptian and Israeli forces along the Suez
        Canal. He is replaced (13 March) by Major General
        Ahmed Ismail.

10   GUINEA - There is an unsuccessful coup attempt against
        the government of President Sekou Toure.

11   SOUTH KOREA - The US Command announces that a fire-
        fight has taken place between US and North Korean
        forces in the DMZ.

11   FRANCE - The country is hit by widespread strikes.

11   WEST GERMANY - An Ethiopian airliner is blown up at
            Frankfurt Airport by terrorists representing the Arab
            Liberation Front for Eritrea.

12   ANGUILLA - A British Minister is expelled.

13   UNITED STATES - The Senate ratifies the Non-Prolifer-
            ation Treaty (NPT).

13   NIGERIA - The government rejects a Biafran call for a
            one-month truce to allow for peace negotiations.

13   FRANCE - In Paris, US Ambassador Henry Cabot Lodge ac-
            cuses NVN of attempting to terrorize SVN into accept-
            ing Communist terms for a truce with the continuance
            of its present offensive.

14   ISRAEL - Israel announces it will send its jets
            against Palestinian guerrilla bases in retaliation for
            recent raids against Israeli settlements. The first
            Israeli attack is against a base east of the Jordan
            River.

14   UNITED STATES - President Nixon announces he has no
            plans to reduce US troop strength in SVN.

14   COMMUNIST CHINA - Communist China stops all Soviet
            shipments bound for North Viet Nam from transiting its
            territory.

14   COLOMBIA - Martial law is declared in three towns in
            northern Colombia following rioting.

15   SOUTH VIET NAM - US Marines move into the DMZ for the
            first time in a year to prevent further NVA encroach-
            ments.

15   URUGUAY - President Jorge Pacheco Areco begins lifting
            some of the restrictions imposed in June 1968 during
            the state of emergency.

15   COMMUNIST CHINA - New Sino-Soviet armed border clashes
            are reported in the Ussuri River region.

16   INDIA - Indian forces capture General Angami, the re-
            puted leader of the rebel Naga National Army.

17   WARSAW PACT - At its annual meeting in Budapest, Hun-
            gary, the WPO announces it has established a joint
            command for its combined forces.

17   JORDAN - King Hussein announces the establishment of the Arab Eastern Command, comprising military forces from Iraq, Jordan, and Syria.

17   ISRAEL - Golda Mier becomes Prime Minister replacing Levi Eshkol who suffered a fatal heart attack (26 February).

19   ANGUILLA - A force of about 100 British Marines, paratroopers, and police are landed on the tiny Caribbean island to restore order after a long period of criminally-inspired unrest. There is no resistance.

20   SOUTH VIET NAM - MACV reports that 1,140 US troops have been killed in the three weeks of the latest enemy offensive.

21   GUINEA - President Sekou Toure announces he has thwarted a coup attempt against his government by arresting two of his cabinet ministers.

23   SOUTH VIET NAM - The US and SVN commands confirm that their forces have been engaged in two major drives into the A Shau Valley.

25   PAKISTAN - To forestall further internal unrest that is growing in the country, Ayub Khan resigns the presidency. The government is placed in the hands of General Agha Mohammed Yahya Khan. As his first act, the new President declares martial law.

25   SOUTH VIET NAM - President Thieu offers to negotiate directly and privately with the NVN without preconditions. The NVN reject the offer on 26 March.

28   CZECHOSLOVAKIA - The recent Czech victory over the USSR in the hockey world championships touches off anti-Soviet rioting throughout the country.

30   ISRAEL - The government rejects all peace proposals, including those proposed by the Big Four, that are contrary to the nation's best interests.

APRIL

            LAOS - Army forces, supported by US air strikes, open a successful campaign to free the Plaine des Jarres from Communist control.

1   UNITED NATIONS - The Security Council votes to censure Israel for its recent air attack against the Jordanian city of Salt.

1   THAILAND - A joint Thai-Malaysian campaign opens against insurgents operating in southern Thailand.

1   UNITED STATES - The Defense Department announces a curtailment of B-52 (ARCLIGHT) strikes in SVN.

2   IRAN - The government severs diplomatic relations with Lebanon.

2   UNITED STATES - Twenty-one members of the Black Panther movement are charged with planning to place bombs in five New York stores.

3   UNITED STATES - As of this date, combat deaths in the war in SEA exceed those of the Korean War.

3   UNITED NATIONS - Representatives of the Big Four Powers meet to discuss the Middle East.

3   CANADA - The government announces a decision to withdraw all of its 10,000 troops in the NATO forces in Europe.

6   EQUATORIAL GUINEA - The Spanish complete their evacuation of the former colony.

7   SOUTH VIET NAM - The government announces a six-point plan to end the war that, among other things, calls upon NVN to stop its attempt to conquer SVN and its use of Laos and Cambodia as sanctuaries.

8   ISRAEL - An artillery duel across the Suez Canal takes place between UAR and Israeli gunners. Major clashes occur between Israeli forces and Arab guerrillas in Aqaba (Al Aqabah) and Elat (Eilat, Elath) at the head of the Gulf of Aqaba.

9   UNITED STATES - Three hundred students seize University Hall at Harvard.

11   USSR - To settle the long-standing border dispute, the government proposes the resumption of negotiations with Communist China.

11   CENTRAL AFRICAN REPUBLIC - President Jean Bedel Bokassa announces he has crushed a move to topple his government.

12   UNITED STATES - For the first time since 1965 the US formally recognizes the government of Cambodia.

12   SOUTH VIET NAM - The government agrees to open talks with Cambodia over their long-standing border dispute.

14   COMMUNIST CHINA - Vice-Chairman Lin Piao calls for
            preparations for war with the Soviet Union.

15   UNITED STATES - The Defense Department announces that
            a US EC-121 reconnaisance aircraft was shot down by
            two North Korean fighters 100 miles off the North
            Korean coast over the Sea of Japan. The 31-man crew
            was killed. The US will protest the attack to the UN
            Truce Commission at Panmunjom (18 April) and will
            continue flying reconnaissance missions.

15   CHAD - French reinforcements are flown into Chad in
            the face of new Muslim uprisings.

16-17   COMMUNIST CHINA - Clashes are reported between Chinese
            and Soviet troops at Chuguchak (T'ach'eng) in Sinkiang
            Province.

17   USSR - The Soviets begin a two-month series of missile
            testing in the Pacific. Among the missiles tested is a
            multiple re-entry weapons system for the SS-9 surface-
            to-surface missile.

19   IRAN - The government abrogates the 1937 Navigation of
            Shatt-al-Arab (Arand-Rud) Treaty claiming numerous
            violations by Iraq. Both sides begin massing forces
            along their common border.

19   SINAI - UAR commandos attack Israeli positions on the
            east bank of the Suez Canal.

20   LIBERIA - The OAU meeting in Monrovia fails to reach
            an accord on the Nigerian crisis.

20   NORTHERN IRELAND - A weekend of violence culminates in
            the terrorist bombings of nine post offices and a bus
            station.

20   IRAN - Iranian military forces in the Persian Gulf
            area go on alert because of a dispute with Iraq over
            navigation rights in the Shatt-al-Arab River.

21   NORTHERN IRELAND - Over 1,000 British troops occupy
            key installations throughout the country.

21   SEA OF JAPAN - A US naval task force enters the Sea of
            Japan in a demonstration of strength following the
            North Korean attack on an unarmed reconnaissance air-
            craft on 15 April.

21   LIBYA - The government announces a decision to pur-
            chase tanks and artillery from Great Britain.

22   UNITED NATIONS - The Secretary General, U Thant, re-
            ports that a state of war exists between Israel and
            the UAR.

23   BIAFRA - Nigerian forces claim the capture of Umuahia,
            the adminstrative capital of the province.

23   UAR - The government announces it considers the 1967
            cease-fire agreement void.

23   LEBANON - A state of emergency is declared in the wake
            of violent demonstrations favoring the Palestinian
            guerrillas.

24   SOUTH VIET NAM - Almost 100 B-52s carry out the heavi-
            est bombing attacks of the war near the Cambodian bor-
            der in Tay Ninh Province, III CTZ.

24   LEBANON - The Prime Minister, Rashid Karami, is forced
            to resign amid growing criticism of the restrictions
            he has placed upon Palestinian guerrillas who use the
            country as a base of operations in their terrorist
            campaign against Israel.

24   BIAFRA - Biafran troops recapture Owerri.

25   COMMUNIST CHINA - An armed clash takes place between
            Chinese and Soviet forces at Chuguchak in Sinkiang
            Province.

25   BARBADOS - The ratification of the Treaty of
            Tlatelolco by the Barbados Assembly puts into force
            the agreement on the denuclearization of Latin
            America.

26   SOUTH VIET NAM - In the first "Vietnamization" action,
            the US 6th Battalion, 77th Field Artillery turns over
            its equipment to the 213th ARVN Artillery Battalion,
            at Can Tho in Phong Dinh Province, IV CTZ.

26   UNITED STATES - The government orders the withdrawal
            of its naval task force in the Sea of Japan after the
            Japanese and Soviet governments express their concerns
            over the antagonistic act.

27   BOLIVIA - President Ortuvo Barrientos is killed in a
            helicopter crash. Vice-President Luis Adolfo Siles
            Salinas is appointed President.

28   JAPAN - Anti-American rioting breaks out in Tokyo
            during a demonstration celebrating "Okinawa Reversion
            Day."

29   UAR - An Israeli raiding party destroys   installations
            and bridges deep in the Egyptian interior.

29   UNITED STATES - After three nights of racial violence,
            the governor orders the National Guard into Cairo,
            Illinois.

30   SOUTH VIET NAM - US troop strength reachs 543,482.
            Hereafter, US troop strength in SVN will decline.

30   CAMBODIA - Prince Norodom Sihanouk reverses his
            position and claims he is no longer interested in
            resuming normal relations with the US.

MAY

            SOUTH VIET NAM - The heavy losses suffered by Viet
            Cong forces in the Delta require the North Vietnamese
            to use NVA regulars to keep VC units up to strength.

1-6   LEBANON - Fighting breaks out between government
            forces and Palestinian commandos.

2   COMMUNIST CHINA - An armed clash between Chinese and
            Soviet troops is reported at Yu-min.

3   INDIA - President Zakir Husain dies suddenly in New
            Delhi.

3   UNITED STATES - Defense Secretary Melvin Laird states
            that US withdrawal from SVN could begin at any time
            given certain conditions, which include improvement in
            RVNAF effectiveness, a lessening in enemy offensive
            activity, or progress at the Paris peace talks.

5   SYRIA - President al-Attassi announces a delay in his
            planned trip to Moscow apparently in a show of dissat-
            isfaction with the slow delivery of Soviet military
            equipment. At the same time, the Syrian Chief of
            Staff, General Mustafa Tlass visits Peking and reports
            that the Chinese are willing to build missile sites in
            Syria.

5   YUGOSLAVIA - The government announces it has signed an
            agreement to build a naval base in Sudan.

5   SOUTH AFRICA - The government announces it is develop-
            ing a new surface-to-air missile system with the help
            of France.

6   NORTHERN IRELAND - An amnesty is declared for all per-
            sons charged in incidents between Catholics and Pro-
            testants.

7   JORDAN - Israeli jets carry out the second air strike
            in four days against a Palestinian guerrilla base.

8   USSR - The government announces its armed forces are
            holding maneuvers along the Chinese border.

8   FRANCE - The Viet Cong delegation at the Paris peace
            talks puts forth a ten-point plan to end the war in
            SVN. The proposal calls for immediate US withdrawal
            and a coalition government in SVN without foreign
            interference.

8-20   SOUTH VIET NAM - US troops take Ap Bia Mountain (Hill
            937) (20 May) on the eleventh attempt. This cuts a
            major infiltration route through the A Shau Valley
            into Quang Tri Province. The action becomes known as
            the Battle of Hamburger Hill.

9   ISRAEL - A government spokesman reports that Israeli
            commandos have been regularly crossing the Jordan
            River to carry out raids against Palestinian guerrilla
            bases in Jordan.

11-14   SOUTH VIET NAM - The Communists carry out their summer
            offensive with ground and rocket attacks on US and
            RVNAF bases throughout SVN.

12   LEBANON - The government refuses Palestinian demands
            for passage of Syria-based guerrillas moving to attack
            Israel.

12-15   COMMUNIST CHINA - Fighting breaks out between Chinese
            and Soviet troops near Hu-ma (12-15 May) and near
            Ai-hui (14 May) on the Amur River.

14   UNITED STATES - President Nixon announces a plan for
            the mutual withdrawal of all outside forces, including
            NVA, from SVN.

15   UNITED STATES - A serious "counter-institution" riot
            breaks out in "People's Park" on University of Cali-
            fornia property in Berkeley. After an initial battle
            with police, the dissidents holding the park are
            forced out by National Guard troops.

16   MALAYSIA - A state of emergency is declared following
            four days of inter-communal clashes between Chinese
            and Malay factions. At least 196 have been killed in
            the violence.

17   ISRAEL - Al Fatah guerrillas attack a fortified Is-
            raeli position.

18   USSR - The government offers to normalize relations with Yugoslavia if the Yugoslav government muzzles its press.

19   UNITED STATES - The Defense Department announces that, of the 1,303 US service personnel listed as missing in action, only 336 are reported as being prisoners of war. Secretary Laird criticizes the North Vietnamese for their handling of the prisoner situation.

20   LAOS - Prince Souvanna Phouma informs NVN that he will halt US and South Vietnamese air attacks on the Pathet Lao if NVA forces are withdrawn from Laos.

20   COMMUNIST CHINA - Fighting breaks out along the Sino-Soviet border north of the Irtysh River in Sinkiang Province. An armed clash also occurs near Chuguchak.

21   MALAYSIA - The government appeals to Great Britain, Australia, and India for military aid.

22   BIAFRA - Biafran aircraft attack the government-held airfield at Port Harcourt.

22   THAILAND - At a Bangkok-held conference of Allied nations with troops in SVN, the participants agree on the principles of mutual withdrawal and regional security.

22   ARGENTINA - Martial law is declared in Rosario following serious student rioting. The following day (23 May) trade unions vote a general strike in support of the students. As the violence spreads, martial law is imposed in a widening circle of towns. By 28 May a limited state of siege is declared throughout the country.

23   IRAQ - The government offers the Kurdish tribes self-determination.

23   PERU - The government expels the US military mission.

24   COMMUNIST CHINA - The government demands a Soviet admission that the 19th century border treaties that are to be renegotiated to settle the current dispute were originally "unequal" when signed.

25   ROMANIA - President Ceaucescu proposes a dismantling of both NATO and the Warsaw Pact.

25   SUDAN - The government of Prime Minister Mohammed Ahmed Mahgoub is overthrown by a left-wing military coup led by Colonel Mohammed Gafaar al-Nimeiry. Abibakr Awadallah becomes Prime Minister.

25   COMMUNIST CHINA - An armed clash takes place along the
            Sino-Soviet border near the Siberian town of Blago-
            veshchensk on the Amur River.

25   SOUTH VIET NAM - A coalition of six political groups
            known as the National Social Democratic Front gives
            its support to President Thieu.

26   LAOS - In a deep penetration of Pathet Lao territory,
            Royal Laotian forces capture a key objective close to
            the North Vietnamese border.

27   ISRAEL - Palestinian guerrillas shell the city of
            Jericho (Ariha, Yeriho) for the first time since the
            1967 war.

28   ARGENTINA - The government imposes a limited state of
            siege in the wake of student violence and the threat
            of a general strike.

28   SOUTH VIET NAM - US forces abandon "Hamburger Hill"
            (Ap Bia Mountain).

28   NATO - The NATO military command establishes a
            multi-national naval force in the Mediterranean.

28   COMMUNIST CHINA - Fighting breaks out between Chinese
            and Soviet forces on the Amur River island of Pa-ch'a
            (Goldinsky).

29   NIGERIA - Biafran forces attack the Shell Oil refinery
            at Ugheli.

29   ARGENTINA - A strike by workers in Cordoba leads to a
            major clash with the military.

29   ECUADOR - Major violence breaks out as a result of
            anti-American student demonstrations in Quito pro-
            testing the visit of Governor Nelson Rockefeller of
            New York.

29   SOUTH VIET NAM - The VC proclaim a 48-hour cease-fire
            to celebrate the birthday of Buddha. The South Viet-
            namese government grants a 24-hour truce on 30 May.
            Only 15 Viet Cong instigated incidents are reported.

30   NETHERLANDS ANTILLES - Rioting and political disturb-
            ances in Curacao follow a labor demonstration by the
            Federation of Workers for better wages. The strike
            goes on for ten days. Dutch Marines are airlifted from
            the Netherlands to help local security forces in
            quelling the violence.

31   SOUTH VIET NAM - "Operation SPEEDY EXPRESS" is termin-
       ated in the Delta. In the six months the operation was
       underway, 19,899 enemy were killed and 2,579 captured.
       Friendly losses include 242 combat deaths, 2,385
       wounded in action, and 10 missing.

JUNE

       NIGERIA - Central government forces begin a new of-
       fensive against the breakaway Biafran regions.

       SAUDI ARABIA - A plot to assassinate King Faisal is
       uncovered.

1   SINGAPORE - Two days of clashes between Malays and
       Chinese factions are reported.

2   SOUTH VIET NAM - The government reports that the
       number of VC/NVA defectors (Hoi Chanh) thus far in
       1969 is 18,748. This number exceeds the total of
       18,171 who surrendered in all of 1968.

2   CANADA - The Minister of Defense, Leo Cadieux, an-
       nounces plans to withdraw the mechanized brigade
       stationed in Europe and replace it with a highly
       mobile force stationed in Canada.

4   SYRIA - The government recognizes East Germany.

4   HAITI - The capital city of Port-au-Prince is bombed
       by an unidentified cargo aircraft. Three people are
       killed by the six homemade bombs that are dropped.
       Cuba is suspected of being behind the raid.

5   NORTH VIET NAM - When NVA antiaircraft guns shoot down
       an unarmed US reconnaissance aircraft, US warplanes
       resume bombing the north. This breaks a pause that has
       extended from November 1968.

5   ARGENTINA - The limited state of siege is lifted.

7   SPAIN - In retaliation for British publication of a
       new constitution for the colony following the 1968
       constitutional conference, the Spanish government
       imposes a land blockade along the Lan Linea frontier
       on the British stronghold at Gibraltar.

8   MIDWAY ISLAND - President Nixon meets with Vietnamese
       President Nguyen Van Thieu and announces the start of
       US troop withdrawals from South Viet Nam. Twenty-five
       thousand troops are to be withdrawn by 31 August.

10   NORTH VIET NAM - The National Liberation Front an-
            nounces the formation of the Provisional Revolutionary
            Government of South Viet Nam. Twenty-five nations,
            including the Soviet Union, Communist China, UAR,
            Algiers, and Cambodia will subsequently recognize it
            as the legitimate government.

10   UNITED NATIONS - The Security Council votes to extend
            the UNEF in Cyprus for an additional six months.

10   COMMUNIST CHINA - Reports reach the west that Soviet
            armored forces have crossed the Chinese border near
            Yu-min in Sinkiang Province.

12-13   SOUTH VIET NAM - Two brigades of the 9th US Infantry
            Division and a USMC RLT receive orders transferring
            them out of SVN as a part of the 25,000-man force
            reduction announced by President Nixon. The first unit
            of the 9th US Division departs for Fort Lewis, Wash-
            ington on 8 July (Operation KEYSTONE EAGLE). The 9th
            USMC RLT departs for Okinawa on 13 July. The entire
            movement of all 25,000 troops (Phase I Redeployment)
            is completed on 28 August.

15   HONDURAS - Anti-Salvadoran rioting breaks out in the
            wake of World Cup soccer matches held in El Salvador.

15   EL SALVADOR - A state of emergency is declared and the
            armed forces mobilized in response to the situation in
            Honduras.

17   SOUTH VIET NAM - Communist forces retake "Hamburger
            Hill."

17   SOUTH KOREA - A North Korean commando force attempting
            to infiltrate into the ROK is wiped out by South
            Korean forces.

18   PAKISTAN - An Ethiopian airliner is blown up at
            Karachi Airport by Arab Liberation Front for Eritrea
            terrorists.

19   PARAGUAY - Serious student rioting precedes the visit
            of Governor Rockefeller.

20   SPAIN - The government announces it has signed a
            mutual assistance agreement with the US that will
            permit the retention of US bases on Spanish soil for
            an additional 15 months (September 1970).

20   ISRAEL - Three terrorist bombs explode near the
            Wailing Wall in Jerusalem.

20   ECUADOR - Ecuadoran naval units capture two American
            and three Japanese tuna boats fishing within 200 miles
            of their coast.

22   SOUTH YEMEN - A bloodless coup forces the resignation
            of the government of President Qahtan al-Shaabi. He is
            replaced by a leftist-oriented five-man Presidential
            Council led by Salem Ali Rubayyi.

23   JORDAN - Israeli commandos wreck the East Ghor Canal
            irrigation project.

23   CANADA - The Defense Ministry announces plans to cut
            military forces over the next three years to a total
            of 80,000-85,000 personnel.

23   SOUTH VIET NAM - The US Special Forces camp at Ben Het
            in Kontum Province, II CTZ, undergoes an enemy ground
            attack after two months of heavy mortar and rocket
            fire. RVNAF relieves the siege on 1 July when it opens
            the road between Ben Het and Dak To.

23   ROMANIA - The government announces it has established
            diplomatic relations with Communist China.

24   ISRAEL - Arab commandos blow up a petroleum pipeline
            in Haifa Bay (Mifraz Hefa).

24   LEBANON - President Charles Helou orders all Pales-
            tinian guerrilla forces to leave Lebanon.

24   URUGUAY - Faced with new student violence, President
            Jorge Pacheco Areco reimposes the limited state of
            seige which had been lifted in March.

24   CANADA - What starts as a peaceful parade celebrating
            St. Jean Baptiste Day turns into a bloody riot in
            Montreal.

24   GREAT BRITAIN - The government severs diplomatic
            relations with Rhodesia after the former colony passes
            a "white supremacy" constitution.

24-28   HONDURAS - El Salvadoran troops invade Honduras after
            bitter rioting breaks out as the result of a soccer
            game. OAS intervention brings an end to the fighting.

25   INDIA - The government protests the building of a
            military road between Kashmir (Pakistan) and Tibet
            (Communist China).

25   SOUTH VIET NAM - The US Navy turns over 64 river gun-
            boats to the South Vietnamese Navy in the largest
            single turnover of US military equipment to date.

25   NEPAL – Prime Minister Kirti Nidhi Bista announces his government's cancellation of an arms agreement with India in effect since 1965. Indian troops stationed in Nepal had already been asked to leave.

26   EL SALVADOR – The government severs diplomatic relations with Honduras following Honduras' expulsion of Salvadoran settlers. The entire incident was exacerbated by the results of the play-offs in the World Soccer Cup competition.

26   SOUTH VIET NAM – President Thieu orders a new Accelerated Pacification Campaign to last from 1 July to 31 October. The principal thrust will be security, administration, and law and order in the villages.

27   SOUTH KOREA – Students riot in an attempt to force the ouster of President Park Chung Hee.

27   GREECE – The President of the Greek Council, Michael Stasinopoulis, is ousted following his dismissal of charges against 21 magistrates.

27   SPAIN – The government suspends the ferry service between the Spanish mainland and British-controlled Gibraltar.

28   CAMBODIA – US intelligence sources in SVN report heavy fighting in Cambodia as government troops try to drive out NVA and VC forces from their border sanctuary areas.

29   LAOS – Pathet Lao and NVA forces capture the important town of Muong Soui in the northern province of Sam Neua. Other Royal Laotian government sources indicate the NVA holds most of the strategically important Plaine des Jarres (Plain of Jars).

30   EGYPT – Israeli commandos destroy the power line between the Aswan Dam and the city of Cairo.

30   SPAIN – The government cedes the colony of Ifni to Morocco.

30   ARGENTINA – The limited state of siege is reinstituted following the assassination of Augusto Vandor, a labor leader, who was shot during violence surrounding the Rockefeller visit.

30   SOUTH VIET NAM – The move of over 12,000 US forces out of Saigon (Operation MOOSE) is completed. US military strength in SVN is down to 538,714.

JULY

1   UNITED NATIONS - The Big Four representatives suspend their Middle East talks.

3   UNITED NATIONS - The Security Council censures Israel for its plans to change the status of Jerusalem by taking over control of the Arab section.

3   UNITED STATES - The Department of State lifts the ban on credit arms sales to Ecuador (imposed in December 1968) and to Peru (imposed in February 1969).

3   UNITED STATES - A new US-Turkish agreement is signed which extends US rights to bases on Turkish soil.

4   OAS - The organization meets in emergency session to hear charges of aggression by both El Salvador and Honduras against each other.

5   KENYA - Tribal fighting follows the assassination of the Minister of Economic Affairs, Tom Mboya.

5   BERMUDA - British Royal Marines are landed on the island to provide security for an upcoming Black Power conference.

6   SOUTH VIET NAM - A large group (231) of VC accepts the Chieu Hoi program and "rally" (surrender) to SVN of-ficials in Chau Doc Province, IV CTZ.

7   UNITED STATES - A secret agreement with Thailand is revealed by Senator J. William Fullbright. By its terms, 47,000 US troops are authorized to be stationed in Thailand.

7   UNITED NATIONS - Secretary General U Thant informs the Security Council that general warfare has resumed along the Suez Canal.

8   SOUTH VIET NAM - The 3rd Battalion, 60th Infantry, 9th US Infantry Division becomes the first unit (800 men) withdrawn from SVN when it departs Tan Son Nhut air-base in Saigon for a flight to Fort Lewis, Washington.

8   ISRAEL - There is a Syrian-Israeli air battle over the Golan Heights.

8   COMMUNIST CHINA - The government accuses the USSR of carrying out an air and ground attack across the Amur River into Manchuria. There is a ground battle at Pa-ch'a (Goldinsky) Island.

9 UNITED STATES - The Defense Department announces a worldwide reduction of more than 20,000 troops by 1 July 1970.

10 UNITED STATES - The Department of State confirms that a secret "contingency" treaty was signed with Thailand in 1965.

10 FRANCE - The government reaffirms its embargo on arms shipments to Israel, Jordan, Syria, and the UAR.

11 SOUTH VIET NAM - President Thieu presents a six-point proposal for free elections, calling for a national vote to settle the war and offering conditions for the participation of all political parties.

11 UNITED STATES - President Nixon calls upon NVN to accept the Thieu proposal.

12 DAHOMEY - A coup attempt by a group of military officers, including the former head of state, Lieutenant Colonel Alphonse Alley, is thwarted when President Emile Derlin Zinsou has them all arrested.

12 NORTHERN IRELAND - A new outbreak of violence follows Protestant celebration of the victory at the Battle of the Boyne.

14 HONDURAS - The government charges El Salvador with a 40-mile-deep military invasion of its borders. Honduran towns are attacked by El Salvadoran fighters.

14 WEST IRIAN - The populace votes overwhelmingly to remain a part of Indonesia.

16 EL SALVADOR - The government claims the capture of several towns in Honduras and calls for a surrender of the Honduran army.

17 PAKISTAN - A government refusal to renew a lease (up for renewal in 1968) forces the US to abandon an important electronic intercept site in Peshawar.

18 UNITED NATIONS - The Security Council hears complaints of Portuguese raids into Zambian territory.

19 CHAD - President Francois Tombalbaye acknowledges France's military support of Chad in fighting Arab guerrillas.

20 UAR - Iraeli jets attack Egyptian installations on the west bank of the Suez Canal.

20   NORTH VIET NAM - Ho Chi Minh states there can be no
            free elections in Viet Nam as long as US troops remain
            in SVN.

22   EL SALVADOR - The government refuses an OAS order to
            remove its troops from Honduras unless five conditions
            are met.

22   UNITED STATES - The Defense Department acknowledges
            that chemical nerve agents have been sent to US forces
            overseas.

23   UAR - President Gamal Abdul Nasser calls an Arab sum-
            mit to discuss plans for the "elimination" of the
            areas occupied by Israel.

23   SWEDEN - The government orders a halt to the further
            export of aircraft of the type (MFI-9) used by Biafra.

24   UAR - In the heaviest fighting since the 1967 war, UAR
            and Israeli forces clash along the Suez Canal.

24   FRANCE - US Ambassador Henry Cabot Lodge, Jr., denies
            a North Vietnamese charge that US forces have invaded
            Laos.

25   LAOS - Prime Minister Prince Souvanna Phouma announces
            that there are 60,000 NVA fighting in his country, and
            that he has authorized US aircraft to bomb Communist
            targets within the boundaries of the country, especi-
            ally along the Ho Chi Minh Trail.

27   NORTH VIET NAM - The government vehemently denies that
            60,000 NVA troops are operating in Laos as charged by
            Premier Prince Souvanna Phouma.

28   UNITED NATIONS - The Security Council censures Portu-
            gal for its recent incursions into Zambia.

29   EL SALVADOR - In the face of implied OAS sanctions, El
            Salvador agrees to withdraw its troops in Honduras.

30   SOUTH VIET NAM - US President Richard Nixon pays an
            unannounced brief visit to SVN.

30   SYRIA - A Syrian-Iraqi defense agreement is signed.

30   OAS - The OAS approves a peace argreement ending the
            El Salvador-Honduras War.

31   FRANCE - The government announces it has signed an
            agreement to furnish military aircraft to Algeria.

AUGUST

1 UNITED STATES - The government reestablishes diplomatic relations with Cambodia.

2 JORDAN - Lebanese sources report that Syrian troops have moved into Jordan.

2 NORTHERN IRELAND - A new round of violence breaks out between Roman Catholics and Protestants in Belfast.

3 ISRAEL - The government announces its intention to retain portions of the territory it seized during the 1967 war.

4 NORTH VIET NAM - The government releases three American prisoners of war.

5 EL SALVADOR - The government announces it has completed the withdrawal of all its forces from Honduras.

8 UNITED STATES - A "Hot Line" is established between Washington and the government of the Federal Republic in Bonn, West Germany.

8 COMMUNIST CHINA - An agreement on navigation of border lakes and rivers is signed with the USSR.

10 LAOS - Pathet Lao and NVA forces capture the important stonghold at Xieng Dat.

10 LEBANON - Israeli jets attack Palestinian guerrilla bases.

11 CHAD - President Francois Tombalbaye asks France to restore order in his country.

12 SOUTH VIET NAM - The NVA summer offensive begins. This ends an eight-week lull in the war. Heavy attacks are reported on more than 100 cities, towns, and military installations. At the same time, US officials approve RVNAF and National Police manpower increases to speed up the "Vietnamization" process.

12 UNITED NATIONS - The Security Council orders South Africa to surrender its mandate over Namibia (South West Africa) by 4 October.

12 UNITED STATES - The US Senate places a $2.5 billion limit on military assistance to SEA.

12 BRAZIL - The government opens a military campaign against rebels in the Atlantic coastal region.

13   COMMUNIST CHINA – A new clash takes place on the Sino-Soviet border near Yu-min in Sinkiang Province.

14   NORTHERN IRELAND – At the request of the Northern Ireland government, British troops are employed in Londonderry to separate rioting Catholic and Protestant factions.

15   IRISH FREE STATE – The government mobilizes its army and occupies positions along the border with Ulster (Northern Ireland) when Great Britain rejects a plan for a joint UK-Irish peacekeeping force for the province.

17   NORTH KOREA – The government announces that a US helicopter has been shot down over North Korea.

18-25   CZECHOSLOVAKIA – Joint Soviet-Czech maneuvers are held coinciding with the first anniversary of the Soviet invasion.

19   NORTHERN IRELAND – As the violence continues and grows, the British Army takes over responsibility for security throughout Ulster.

19   GUYANA – Dutch forces stationed in Surinam occupy a disputed region along the border that is claimed by Guyana. Fighting breaks out between Guyana forces and Surinam police and continues until 10 September when Dutch forces withdraw.

22   UNITED STATES – The government announces it will open talks with the Thai government for the reduction of US troop strength in Thailand.

22   NORTHERN IRELAND – The British command begins disarming a part of the Ulster Constabulary (B Special Constabulary) to allay Catholic fears.

22   ISRAEL – An Australian Christian, Michael Rohan, is arrested and charged with arson in the fire that damaged the Muslim Al Aqsa Mosque in the Old City of Jerusalem on 21 August.

22   CZECHOSLOVAKIA – The government tightens its security controls in the wake of four days of orderly but massive demonstrations marking the first anniversary of the Soviet invasion.

23   SOUTH VIET NAM – Announcement of further US troop withdrawals is postponed in light of increased enemy activity throughout the country since 11-12 August.

24   SOUTH VIET NAM - A US rifle company refuses to make
            any further attempts to salvage a helicopter in the
            Que Son Valley after five previous attempts have
            failed.

25   SAUDI ARABIA - King Faisal calls an Islamic summit to
            discuss protection of the Holy Places.

25   ZAMBIA - President Kenneth Kaunda declares a state of
            emergency in the face of growing political unrest
            stemming from tribal rivalries.

25   SOUTH VIET NAM - The US Mobile Riverine Force is dis-
            established, and the South Vietnamese Naval Amphibious
            Task Force 211 assumes its missions and responsibili-
            ties (effective 1 September).

25-26   ARAB LEAGUE - A meeting of foreign ministers in Cairo
            considers the calling of a Jihad (holy war) against
            Israel.

26   UNITED NATIONS - The Security Council condemns Israel
            for its 11 August air raid on Lebanon.

28   COMMUNIST CHINA - The Central Committee of the Commu-
            nist Party issues a directive ordering the population
            to prepare for war.

28   USSR - The government warns Communist China of the
            dangers of nuclear war.

28   SOUTH VIET NAM - The withdrawal of the first 25,000 US
            troops from SVN is completed.

29   MIDDLE EAST - Two Arab terrorists hijack a US airliner
            bound from Athens to Tel Aviv and divert the plane to
            Damascus, Syria.

31   BRAZIL - President Artur da Costa e Silva suffers a
            stroke. A military junta takes control of the country.

31   NORTHERN IRELAND - Roman Catholics erect barricades
            around the Bogside district of Londonderry and refuse
            to remove them until convinced the civil rights re-
            forms proposed by the British and Northern Ireland
            governments will work.

31   SOUTH VIET NAM - US strength in SVN is now 509,618,
            which is well below the goal set by President Nixon.
            Also, RVNAF is to assume responsibility for the IV CTZ
            battle area effective 1 September. The 7th ARVN
            Division takes over the US 9th Division's base camp at
            Dong Tam, in Dinh Tuong Province.

SEPTEMBER

IRAN - A series of border clashes with Iraq takes place.

1   LIBYA - King Idris I is overthrown by a military coup led by Colonel Muammar al-Qaddafi.

1   SOUTH VIET NAM - RVNAF assumes responsibility for the defense of the Mekong Delta region of SVN.

2   UNITED STATES - Two US Navy pilots, who were North Vietnamese prisoners of war, describe the brutality of their captors.

2   MIDDLE EAST - A summit meeting of Arab leaders is called to coordinate military activities against Israel.

3   LEBANON - Israeli military forces carry out a series of large-scale raids against suspected Palestinian guerrilla bases in southern Lebanon.

3   NORTH VIET NAM - Ho Chi Minh dies in Hanoi at age 79.

4   BRAZIL - US Ambassador C. Burke Elbrick is kidnapped on the street in Rio de Janeiro by the revolutionary group MR8. The terrorists demand the release of 15 political prisoners held in Brazilian jails.

6   NORTH VIET NAM - A collective leadership assumes the power left by Ho Chi Minh.

6   YEMEN - Republican forces capture Sa'dah, the last Royalist stronghold in Yemen.

7   BRAZIL - US Ambassador C. Burke Elbrick is released when the ransom demands are met.

7   ISRAEL - The first of a shipment of US-built F-4 "Phantom" aircraft begin to arrive.

8   WESTERN EUROPE - Israeli Embassies in Bonn and the Hague, and the El Al airline office in Brussels, are attacked by Palestinian Front for the Liberation of Palestine (PFLP) terrorists.

8   SOUTH VIET NAM - A three-day cease-fire is ordered by the VC/NVA in commemoration of the death of Ho Chi Minh. RVN rejects the cease-fire because of a new round of enemy attacks.

9   CZECHOSLOVAKIA - The Presidium rescinds the 1968 condemnation of the Soviet invasion.

9   UAR - Israeli armored forces cross the Gulf of Suez
        and wage a ten-hour battle against Egyptian positions
        along the coast.

10   OAU - A meeting of the OAU heads of state, held in
        Addis Ababa, Ethiopia, adjourns, having failed to do
        more than call for an end to the fighting in Nigeria
        and immediate peace negotiations.

11   ISRAEL - The government reports its fighters have shot
        down 11 UAR aircraft over the Gulf of Suez in some of
        the heaviest aerial combat since the 1967 war.

12   UNITED STATES - As a new peace initiative, the US
        suspends all B-52 missions in SVN for 36 hours.

15   ANGUILLA - The British forces sent to Anguilla in
        March to restore order are withdrawn.

15   UNITED NATIONS - Secretary General U Thant recommends
        Communist China be included in future arms talks.
        Also, the Security Council passes a resolution de-
        manding that Israel halt plans to alter the status of
        Jerusalem.

15   SOUTH VIET NAM - The government reports there are now
        2.1 million members in the PSDF. They are not com-
        pletely armed, however, having only 346,162 weapons
        among them.

16   UNITED STATES - The President announces the withdrawal
        of an additional 35,000 troops from SVN by the end of
        1969 (Phase II Redeployment).

16   NORTH VIET NAM - The Hanoi government reiterates its
        demand for an immediate, total, and unconditional US
        troop withdrawal.

17   LAOS - Government forces are reported to have recap-
        tured two long-time Pathet Lao strongholds in the
        Plaine des Jarres.

18   UNITED NATIONS - In an address before the General
        Assembly, US President Nixon appeals for inter-
        national support in getting the North Vietnamese to
        negotiate a settlement.

18   INDIA - Rioting breaks out between Hindus and Muslims
        in Ahmedabad.

18   ARGENTINA - Argentine troops occupy Rosario as new
        violence breaks out in the city.

19   CANADA - The government announces it will cut the overall strength of its forces in Europe from 9,800 to 5,000 by the fall of 1970.

19   SOUTH VIET NAM - President Thieu refuses to agree to a cease-fire without follow-on arrangements.

21   SOUTH VIET NAM - The Phase II redeployment of 35,000 US service personnel begins (Operation KEYSTONE CARDINAL).

22   NORTHERN IRELAND - The barricades around the Roman Catholic Bogside district in Londonderry are taken down.

22   MOROCCO - Representatives of 25 Islamic countries meet in Rabat to consider the consequences of the Al Aqsa Mosque fire.

22   UNITED STATES - The Defense Department announces a military manpower cut of 77,500 spaces as a means of saving $356 million.

22   COMMUNIST CHINA - A nuclear device, with a yield of approximately 25 kilotons, is detonated underground in the ninth test of the current series.

26   UNITED STATES - Fighting breaks out between police and white construction workers protesting plans to desegregate the building trade unions.

26   BOLIVIA - The government of President Luis Adolfo Siles Salinas is overthrown by a military coup, led by General Alfredo Ovando Candia. Candia appoints himself President.

27   SOUTH VIET NAM - President Thieu says the US withdrawal of forces will not succeed because his country does not have the ambition or will to take over the war.

29   UNITED STATES - Murder charges against eight Special Forces personnel are dropped by the Secretary of the Army, Stanley Resor, because CIA personnel refuse to testify.

29   GIBRALTAR - Spanish warships anchor in Gibraltan waters.

29   COMMUNIST CHINA - A three megaton hydrogen bomb is detonated in the tenth shot of the current test series.

30   UNITED STATES - In a joint statement, the US and Thai governments announce the withdrawal, within the next ten months, of 6,000 of the 48,000 US service person-nel stationed in Thailand.

30   COMMUNIST CHINA - The government indicates a willing-ness to negotiate the border dispute with the USSR.

OCTOBER

1   SOUTH VIET NAM - RVNAF assumes responsibility for the defense of the Capital Military District (Saigon). Also, President Thieu makes public information about the heretofore, highly-classified, Phung Hoang (Phoenix) Program which deals with the elimination of the VC infrastructure.

1   GIBRALTAR - Spain severs all telephone and cable links from the Spanish mainland to the British protectorate and later stations warships near its harbor.

1   COMMUNIST CHINA - In a speech celebrating the twen-tieth anniversary of the founding of the Communist Party in China, Lin Piao, designated to be Chairman Mao's successor, speaks of need to prepare for war against the USSR and the US.

2   SOUTH VIET NAM - The lowest casualty figures in more than two years are reported for the past week.

3   ISRAEL - UAR commandos conduct a large-scale raid against Israeli positions on the east bank of the Suez Canal.

3   LEBANON - Israel forces level a group of buildings in two villages presumed to house Palestinian guerrillas.

4   THE PHILIPPINES - President Marcos announces his nation will begin a slow withdrawal of its 1,500-man non-combat force from SVN.

4   UNITED STATES - A national poll indicates more than half the people polled (58%) feel the US made a mis-take going into SEA.

7   SWITZERLAND - The US and the USSR present a joint draft treaty banning nuclear weapons from the seabed at the Geneva Disarmament Conference.

8   URUGUAY - Tupamaro rebels take control of Pando. Gov-ernment forces quickly eject them from the town.

10   ISRAEL - The government announces it has successfully
            defended itself against a UAR summer offensive.

12   UNITED STATES - President Nixon predicts the war in
            SEA will be over in three years.

12   NORTHERN IRELAND - British troops are sent into Bel-
            fast to halt serious rioting following a report call-
            ing for reforms within the national police forces.

14   THE PHILIPPINES - The government asks the US to re-
            negotiate its basing agreements.

14   CAMBODIA - The government orders the ICC out of the
            country by 31 December when its authority will cease.

15   UNITED STATES - Hundreds of thousands march in Wash-
            ington, DC, and elsewhere around the country to end
            the war in SEA, in what becomes known as the "Vietnam
            Moratorium."

15   SOMALIA - During a visit to a drought-stricken part of
            the country, President . Abdi Rashid Ali Shermarke is
            assassinated by a national policeman.

15   BIAFRA - Biafran leader C. Odumegwu Ojukwu signals a
            desire to negotiate a peace settlement with Nigeria
            through the good offices of Gabon President Albert
            Bongo.

15   USSR - North Viet Nam signs new military and economic
            agreements with the government in Moscow.

18-19   LEBANON - Fighting breaks out in southern Lebanon be-
            tween the Lebanese army and the PLO. Before the end of
            the month the PLO takes charge of more than a dozen
            refugee centers run by the UN.

19-20   COMMUNIST CHINA - In Peking, the government opens for-
            mal discussions with the USSR about the border crisis.

21   SOMALIA - Army and police units carry out a successful
            coup which leads to a military-controlled government.

21   DAHOMEY - There is an unsuccessful coup attempt.

21   SYRIA - The government orders the country's border
            with Lebanon closed as a means of halting Lebanon's
            growing anti-guerrilla campaign.

21   JAPAN - Serious rioting accompanies demonstrations
            marking "International Anti-War Day" in Tokyo and
            other cities.

21   CHILE - A state of emergency is declared following a
          mutiny in a Chilean army regiment in Santiago. The
          state of emergency is lifted on 23 October.

22   SINAI PENINSULA - UAR jets attack Israeli positions in
          the Sinai after intelligence reports an Israeli mili-
          tary buildup.

22   FRANCE - The government announces that nuclear test-
          ing, which had been halted for economic reasons, will
          resume in 1970.

24   LEBANON - More clashes are reported between government
          troops and Palestinian guerrillas.

24   LIBYA - Rebel forces seize Tripoli.

25   UNITED STATES - The government announces jointly with
          the USSR that SALT discussions will begin on 17 Novem-
          ber, in Helsinki, Finland.

25   LEBANON - Syrian commandos occupy a Lebanese village
          near the border.

26   LAOS - A US press report states the US has a 40,000-
          man army of Meo tribesmen operating in Laos.

28   UNITED STATES - The Department of State says that the
          US has no defense agreement with Laos.

29   LIBYA - The government asks the US and Great Britain
          to remove their bases on Libyan soil.

30   SOUTH VIET NAM - For the first time in five weeks, US
          combat deaths exceed 100.

30   KENYA - The government outlaws and declares subversive
          the Kenya People's Union, a party in opposition to the
          rule of Jomo Kenyatta.

31   SOUTH VIET NAM - A major RVNAF operation (Codename
          TOAN THANG Phase III) terminates in III CTZ. The
          operation has been going on since 16 February. Almost
          42,000 enemy have been killed and 3,299 captured.
          Thousands of tons of enemy arms, food, and equipment
          have been captured.

NOVEMBER

3   EGYPT - A cease-fire agreement for Lebanon is signed
          in Cairo. Lebanon is forced to accept a de facto
          recognition of the PLO as an extraterritorial govern-
          ment within its boundaries.

3	UNITED STATES - The President indicates that the latest secret US peace proposals have been rejected by NVN. President Nixon goes on to reject any immediate withdrawal of all US forces, but states that US forces in SVN will be reduced on a secret schedule and that the process of "Vietnamization" is well underway.
4	SOUTH VIET NAM - A major battle is fought at Duc Lap.
4	BRAZIL - In a gun battle, Sao Paulo police kill Carlos Marighela, the reputed leader of the terrorist group, National Liberation Action.
5	SOUTH VIET NAM - Communist troops release three American prisoners. This brings to 27 the number of US personnel released by the enemy since February 1967. Also, the US Naval Coastal Surveillance Center at Qui Nhon (Binh Dinh Province, II CTZ) is turned over to the South Vietnamese Navy.
6	UAR - President Nasser rejects US-USSR peace proposals for the Middle East by stating that the Arab world has no alternative but to fight Israel.
6	FRANCE - North Vietnamese delegate Xuan Thuy criticizes President Nixon for disclosing the secret peace negotiations, even though his country rejected them.
7	LIBYA - The government offers military training and support for the PLO.
7	SOUTH VIET NAM - Increased VC/NVA-initiated attacks mark the beginning of the enemy winter offensive.
7-10	PAKISTAN - Troops are sent into Dacca to restore order following a long period of violence.
8	SINAI PENINSULA - A UAR gunboat shells an Israeli position in the northern Sinai.
10	ISRAEL - The government announces that all UAR surface-to-air missile sites along the east bank of the Suez Canal have been attacked and destroyed.
10	ARAB LEAGUE - The Arab League conference, held in Cairo, closes with an accusation that the US is blocking peace efforts, and that they will support PLO military organizations. Only Tunisia fails to attend the meeting.
11	UNITED STATES - A nationwide Veteran's Day rally supports the President's Viet Nam policy.

11   UNITED NATIONS - The General Assembly refuses admis-
            sion to Communist China. Also, the US asks for   inter-
            national pressure to force NVN to abide by the   Geneva
            Conventions concerning the treatment of prisoners of
            war.

11   THAILAND - A joint command is established with Malay-
            sia to combat insurgents operating in the border area.

12   UNITED STATES - The Department of Army charges 1st
            Lieutenant William L. Calley, Jr., with murder in
            connection with the alleged massacre at My Lai, Quang
            Ngai Province in SVN.

12   ISRAEL - The government announces new harsher rules
            for Arab residents of the occupied zones because of
            increased PLO activity.

13   SOUTH VIET NAM - US forces in the DMZ come under the
            heaviest attacks in a year.

13-15   UNITED STATES - Three days of Vietnam Moritorium
            demonstrations to halt the war in Vietnam end with
            nearly 250,000 marching peacefully in Washington.

15   COMMUNIST CHINA - The government announces it has
            signed an agreement to build a 1,042-mile railroad
            between Tanzania and Zambia.

15   SOUTH VIET NAM - President Thieu repudiates the use of
            the term "Vietnamization" and directs that "Ba Tu"
            (Three Selves) be used in its place.

16   ISRAEL - Two Israeli ships are damaged at Elat (Elath)
            by limpet mines placed against their hulls by Arab
            frogmen.

16   CAMBODIA - US and Allied forces shell and attack NVA
            positions in Cambodia.

17   FINLAND - US and Soviet representatives meet in
            Helsinki for the opening round of talks leading to the
            Strategic Arms Limitation Treaty (SALT).

17   JORDAN - Israeli jets carry out a heavy and sustained
            air raid against a number of targets in Jordan.

17   GREECE - The government introduces new censorship re-
            strictions against the press.

17   JAPAN - Announcement of Prime Minister Eisako Sato's
            planned trip to the US to discuss the return of Oki-
            nawa to Japanese control causes major demonstrations
            in which 1,200 are arrested.

17   CAMBODIA - US bombers strike NVA artillery positions in Cambodia in an "inherent right of self-defense against enemy attacks." These guns had been firing on the US Special Forces camp at Bu Prang on the Mnong Plateau, Quang Duc Province, II CTZ.

20   LEBANON - Three PLO guerrillas are killed and six wounded in a clash with Lebanese troops. This breaks the truce put into effect 3 November.

20   CHILE - A new state of emergency is declared in Santiago Province following a new wave of unrest in the army.

20   SOUTH VIET NAM - The last US National Guard unit leaves SVN. Phase II of the US troop withdrawal is completed prior to the 15 December deadline.

20   UNITED STATES - The resignation of Henry Cabot Lodge as US Chief Negotiator at the Paris peace talks is announced. The resignation is effective 8 December.

21   UNITED STATES - In a meeting with Japan's Prime Minister Sato, the US announces retention of the US-Japan Mutual Security Treaty and that Okinawa and the US-held Ryukyu Islands will be turned over to Japan in 1972.

21   UNITED NATIONS - The General Assembly orders Great Britain to use force against Rhodesia.

23   CONGO (BRAZZAVILLE) - The government puts its army on alert following President Joseph Mobutu's (Congo Kinshasa) threats to invade and occupy Brazzaville.

23   UAR - Israeli jets attack Egyptian positions between the cities of Qantara (Al Qantarah) and Suez (As Suways) in retaliation for UAR commando raids on Israeli positions on the east bank of the Suez Canal.

24   UNITED STATES - The US and USSR simultaneously sign, but do not deposit, the Nuclear Non-Proliferation Treaty.

24   SOUTH VIET NAM - Captured enemy documents reveal that during the 1968 Tet Offensive the NVA and VC eliminated 2,900 South Vietnamese considered by them to be politically undesirable.

25   OKINAWA - The 3rd US Marine Division completes its redeployment to Okinawa after nearly five years of combat in SVN.

25   UNITED STATES - President Nixon states the US has re-
          nounced first-use chemical weapons, and any use of
          biological weapons. Nixon further states he will ask
          the US Senate to ratify the 1925 Geneva Protocol out-
          lawing the use of chemical warfare, and that he has
          ordered the destruction of all stocks of biological
          weapons.

26   SAUDI ARABIA - A series of border clashes takes place
          along the Yemeni border. The fighting centers around
          the oasis at Al Wadeiah.

26   SWITZERLAND - The government confirms that Biafran
          leader, Colonel C. Odumegwu Ojukwu, has asked them to
          mediate an end to the Nigerian civil war.

27   WARSAW PACT - All Warsaw Pact members except Romania
          pledge support for the Arabs in the current Middle
          East crisis.

29   SOUTH VIET NAM - Thirty-eight former senior govern-
          ment officials are found guilty of treason and other
          lesser offenses.

30   ITALY - An agreement is signed with Austria settling
          the South Tyrol controversy.

30   SOUTH VIET NAM - US strength in SVN is now 478,701.

DECEMBER

1   SOUTH VIET NAM - The US command announces that the
          60,000 US troops that were to have been withdrawn from
          SVN by 15 December have already left the country.

3   NORTH KOREA - Three US helicopter crewmen, who were
          shot down over North Korea in August, are released.

3   LEBANON - Israeli forces attack a village in Lebanon
          after an Israeli patrol is ambushed in the Golan
          Heights.

3   BIAFRA - Nigerian forces open a two-pronged offensive
          against Biafran positions.

3   CAMBODIA - US bombers begin a two-day bombing attack
          on NVA positions in Cambodia.

6   ISRAEL - The government announces that a prisoner ex-
          change with Syria and the UAR has been successfully
          completed.

6   BRAZIL - Military officials ban publication of all accounts about the unwarranted killing of Brazilian native Indians and the torture of political prisoners.

7   SAUDI ARABIA - The government resumes military aid to the Yemeni Royalists.

9   UNITED STATES - The Secretary of State calls upon Israel to withdraw from the occupied territories in return for a permanent peace settlement.

10   DAHOMEY - A military coup overthrows the governmment of President Emile Derlin Zinsou. Lieutenant Colonel Maurice Kouandete assumes the presidency.

10   CHILE - A group of army officers is arrested in connection with an alleged plot to overthrow the government.

10   USSR - Premier Kosygin expresses support for Arab guerrilla organizations during the course of Soviet-UAR talks in Moscow.

11   SYRIA - Israeli jets shoot down three Syrian MiGs near Damascus.

12   GREECE - The government withdraws from the Council of Europe in advance of its being ousted for civil rights violations.

12   ITALY - A terrorist bomb explosion in Milan's Bank of Agriculture kills 14 and injures over 90. Three more bombs explode in Rome.

12   SOUTH VIET NAM - Filipino forces in SVN begin their withdrawal.

13   GREAT BRITAIN - The government agrees to remove its bases from Libya by March 1970.

14   CYPRUS - Terrorists attack and bomb British bases on the island.

15   UNITED NATIONS - The General Assembly endorses the US-USSR Seabed Treaty.

15   UNITED STATES - The President announces the withdrawal of an additional 50,000 troops (Phase III) from SVN to be completed by 15 April 1970. This brings the total reductions authorized since 20 January to more than 115,000. (The 1968 closing strength in SVN was 549,500.)

15   PANAMA – A plot by military officers to overthrow the
            government fails.

16   AUSTRALIA – The government announces it is preparing
            plans for the withdrawal of Australian forces from SVN
            after the US completes its Phase III redeployment.

16   FRANCE – The government announces it has restored
            diplomatic relations with Morocco which were broken in
            1965.

17   PANAMA – General Omar Turrijos returns as the central
            figure in the ruling junta after his ouster on 15
            December.

18   FRANCE – The government agrees to sell 50 Mirage
            fighters to Libya.

19   UGANDA – A would-be assassin wounds President Milton
            Obote as he leaves a rally in Kampala. A state of
            emergency is declared the following day (20 December).

20   SOUTH VIET NAM – US bombers attack NVA positions in
            the A Shau Valley.

20   COMMUNIST CHINA – Little or no progress is reported in
            the Sino-Soviet border discussions.

21   JORDAN – Israeli jets attack Arab military positions
            in Jordan in a five-hour raid.

21   CANADA – The Defense Ministry announces plans to cut
            militia strength from 23,000 to 19,000 by the end of
            1970.

23   UNITED STATES – The US agrees to withdraw all its
            assets from Wheelus Air Base in Libya by 30 June 1970.

23   MOROCCO – An Arab summit conference ends in a dispute
            over financing military operations against Israel.

23   NIGERIA – Federal troops open a four-pronged attack
            into Biafra.

23   SOUTH VIET NAM – A major threat to the Special Forces'
            camps at Bu Prang and Duc Lap in Quang Duc Province is
            reduced when NVA forces withdraw.

24   SOUTH VIET NAM – A 24-hour Christmas truce is ordered.
            About 115 enemy-instigated incidents occur.

25   FRANCE – Israeli commandos seize five missile frigates
            that were built for Israel but impounded by Presi-
            dent DeGaulle, and escape from Cherbourg Harbor.

25   SOUTH VIET NAM - The government and Thai officials
            begin negotiations on the withdrawal of 12,000 Thai
            troops fighting in SVN.

26   EGYPT - Israeli commandos capture and haul off a
            Soviet-built radar station culminating two days of
            raids along the coast of the Gulf of Suez.

27   FRANCE - The government launches an investigation into
            the mysterious theft of the five Israeli missile
            frigates on 25 December. A Norwegian firm is believed
            implicated.

28   SOUTH VIET NAM - An investigation team headed by
            Lieutenant General William R. Peers arrives in SVN to
            lead a full-scale investigation into the allegations
            of a massacre committed by US forces operating in the
            village of My Lai (Pinkville) in March 1968.

29   GREAT BRITAIN - The British Aircraft Corporation can-
            cels a contract to supply Libya with a 135-million
            Pound-Sterling surface-to-air missile system.

31   FRANCE - A number of French officials are suspended
            and a number of Israeli Embassy personnel are ordered
            out of the country as a result of the Israeli missile
            frigate theft.

31   ISRAEL - The five missile frigates stolen in France
            arrive at Haifa.

31   SOUTH VIET NAM - US troop strength in SVN is 484,326.
            US combat losses in 1969 total 6,727 dead. US combat
            deaths, since 1 January 1961, number 37,270. There are
            also more than 67,000 Allied troops and 969,256 RVNAF
            personnel in SVN. VC terrorists have killed 19,157
            civilians since 1965, and an estimated 7,400 killed
            during the Tet 1968 offensive.

Notes

1970

IRAN - The modernization of the Iranian army begins.

THE PHILIPPINES - A Muslim-inspired insurgency begins in the southern Philippine Islands.

JANUARY

1   JORDAN - Israeli jets attack and damage the East Ghor Canal for the third time in 12 months.

1   PAKISTAN - Restrictions on political activity are lifted by President Yahya Khan.

2   NIGERIA - The government claims its forces have cut Biafra into three segments.

2   SOUTHEAST ASIA - The New Year's cease-fire ends.

3   RHODESIA - Zambia-based African nationalist guerrillas carry out a raid into Rhodesia.

3   UNITED NATIONS - Lebanon files a complaint with the Security Council against Israel for what it calls "aggression and kidnapping" in Israeli raids against suspected terrorist camps.

4   COMMUNIST CHINA - The New China News Agency accuses the Soviet Union of preparing to attack mainland China.

5   UNITED NATIONS - UN Secretary General U Thant urges Biafra to accede to the negotiation offer of the OAU.

5   ISRAEL - The government files a formal complaint with
the UN Security Council claiming that in the last ten
days 19 guerrilla raids on border towns have come from
Lebanon.

5   SOUTH VIET NAM - The VC announce a four-day truce for
Tet.

6   USSR - The Soviet newspaper *Pravda* accused Communist
China of preparing for war.

6   SOUTH VIET NAM - Intelligence reports indicate about
110,000 NVA infiltrated into SVN during 1969. There
are about 240,000 enemy troops in country at this
time.

6   ALGERIA - President Houari Boumedienne calls for the
removal of all foreign (non-Mediterranean) naval
forces from the Mediterranean Sea.

7   ISRAEL - The government begins a campaign of deep
penetration air attacks into Egypt's Nile Delta and
the area around Cairo.

8   UNITED STATES - Two more army personnel are charged
with murder in the My Lai massacre investigation.

9   FRANCE - The government announces the sale of military
aircraft to Libya. Israel formally protests the
action.

9   SOUTH VIET NAM - In response to reports of the impending withdrawal of US troops from RVN, President Nguyen
Van Thieu announces that such a plan is "impossible
and impractical."

11   LAOS - The NVA uses Soviet-built SAMs for the first
time against US aircraft operating in Laotian air
space.

12   NIGERIA - Following the capture of Owerri, the last
Biafran bastion, and the capitulation of Biafran
leader Brigadier Philip Effiong (who assumed
leadership when C. Odumegwu Ojukwu fled to the Ivory
Coast), the two and one-half year civil war ends. Two
million have died.

13   COMMUNIST CHINA - Border talks resume between the
Soviet Union and China in Peking.

13-14   SAUDI ARABIA - Yemenite rebels attack the border town
of Nahuga. Saudi jets retaliate by attacking a Yemeni
border post.

14   NIGERIA - Major General Yakubu Gowon refuses outside aid from all countries who supported Biafra during the civil war.

14   AUSTRALIA - In response to the growing Soviet naval threat in the Indian Ocean, the government orders the strengthening of its western coastal defenses.

15   NIGERIA - A formal surrender is arranged with the government of the break-away province of Biafra.

16   LIBYA - Twenty-seven-year-old Colonel Muammar al Qaddafi assumes control of the country four and one-half months after the old government has toppled.

16   EGYPT - Israeli commandos carry out a raid within 37 miles of Cairo destroying transmission towers along the road to Port Said.

18   EAST PAKISTAN - Fighting breaks out between right- and left-wing factions in Dacca.

18   EGYPT - Israeli jets attack and bomb military targets near Cairo.

20   UNITED STATES - The government asks the International Red Cross to investigate the circumstances surrounding the apparent executions of two US prisoners of war whose graves were discovered on 17 January. Immediate evidence indicates the murders of the two captured servicemen took place on 20 September, in Thua Thien Province, in I CTZ.

20   IRAQ - The government smashes a right-wing, Iranian-sponsored coup.

20   JORDAN - Israeli armored units, supported by jet aircraft, carry out a raid-in-force against Arab guerrilla bases in Jordan.

20   USSR - The Soviet military newspaper Krasnaya Zvezda accuses Communist Chinese leaders of creating a "mass war psychosis" over a "threat from the North."

21   FRANCE - The government promises the Qaddafi regime in Libya 100 Mirage III aircraft, instead of the original 50, after Qaddafi promises an end to support of rebel forces in Chad.

21   NORTH VIET NAM - Declaring them "criminals" and not prisoners of war, the government refuses to publish a list of captured US airmen.

21.-28   EAST GERMANY - The East German government periodically stops traffic between West Germany and Berlin to protest a Berlin meeting of a committee of the West German **Bundestag**.

22   WEST GERMANY - Chancellor Willy Brandt informs East Germany that his government is prepared to open negotiations to settle the East-West German issue.

22   USSR - Egypt's President Gamal Nasser visits Moscow and receives assurances of increased military aid against Israel.

22   EGYPT - Israeli forces are airlanded on Shadwan Island in the Gulf of Suez where they neutralize a UAR military installation and occupy the island.

24   SOUTH VIET NAM - The government protests to the ICC about Communist terrorism. In 1969, Communist terrorists killed 4,619 civilians and injured 14,412. In addition, 1,879 civilians were kidnapped.

26   THE PHILIPPINES - Anti-Marcos rioting breaks out following charges of voting irregularities in the November 1969 elections.

26   COSTA RICA - Talks open between El Salvador and Honduras aimed at ending the border conflict that has been going on since last year.

28   CZECHOSLOVAKIA - Lubomir Strougal succeeds Oldrich Cernik as Premier.

28   UNITED STATES - The Department of Air Force announces that by the end of 1971 RVNAF will take over one-half of the air operations in the war in Viet Nam.

28   NORTH VIET NAM - US aircraft bomb an antiaircraft missile site in NVN.

30   LESOTHO - King Moshoeshoe II is overthrown by his Prime Minister Chief Leabua Jonathan who also arrests his principal parliamentary opponent, Ntsu Mokhehle. The king goes into exile (31 March), returning 4 December 1971. He is reinstated after promising to avoid further political interference in parliamentary elections.

30   UNITED NATIONS - The Security Council condemns South Africa's presence in South West Africa.

30   SOUTH VIET NAM - MACV announces that eight unarmed US reconnaissance aircraft have been shot down over NVN since the November 1968 bombing halt began.

30   GUATEMALA - A state of siege is declared following the
            assassination of an anti-Communist newspaper editor,
            and an attempt on the life of the Christian Democratic
            Party's (PDC) presidential candidate, Jorge Lucas
            Cabelleros.

31   USSR - Premier Aleksei N. Kosygin warns his country
            will increase arms shipments to the UAR if the US
            continues to give military aid to Israel.

31   LAOS - Prime Minister Souvanna Phouma offers to negot-
            iate the neutralization of the Plaine des Jarres with
            the Communists.

FEBRUARY

            USSR - Before the end of the month the Soviet govern-
            ment begins shipping military equipment formerly re-
            served only for Warsaw Pact members to Egypt. This new
            equipment includes the latest antiaircraft cannon (ZSU
            23-4 "Shilka"), improved SA-2 "Guideline" SAMs, and
            SA-4 "Ganef" SAMs. This is in addition to already pro-
            mised MiG 21 "Fishbed" fighter interceptors, and SA-3
            "Goa" SAMs.

            LAOS - Communist activity increases with NVA troops
            seizing an important objective in the Plaine de
            Jarres. US forces move into Laos to establish a fire
            base and to mine the Ho Chi Minh Trail.

1   ISRAEL - A two-hour pitched battle between Israeli and
            Syrian tank and artillery units takes place in the
            Golan Heights.

1   COMMUNIST CHINA - The government pledges support of
            the Arab cause against Israel.

1   NORTH VIET NAM - The government warns its people to be
            prepared for a long war.

2   LAOS - Premier Prince Souvanna Phouma's suggestion
            that the Plaine des Jarres be neutralized is rejected
            by the Pathet Lao and North Viet Nam.

3   SOUTH VIET NAM - An Allied spokeman in Saigon reports
            that North Vietnamese infiltration of arms and sup-
            plies over the Ho Chi Minh Trail has increased about
            50% over last year.

5   SOUTH VIET NAM - One of the largest caches of   VC/NVA
            weapons and equipment uncovered in the war is discov-
            ered in the vicinity of Rang Rang in Phouc Thanh Pro-
            vince, approximately 45 miles northeast of Saigon, in

5   SOUTH VIET NAM (Cont'd) - III CTZ. When the cache is
               finally cleared on 12 February, 169 tons of munitions
               are collected. Also, a fragmentation grenade is deto-
               nated in the US Enlisted Man's Club in Da Nang. One
               person is killed and 62 injured. The incident is not
               blamed on enemy action.

5   NORTH VIET NAM - US aircraft attack SAM sites in NVN
               in retaliation for attacks on unarmed US reconnais-
               sance aircraft.

6   ISRAEL - UAR frogmen sink an Israeli supply vessel in
               the harbor at Eilat. In retaliation, Israeli jets sink
               a UAR mine-laying vessel in the Gulf of Suez.

7-9   EGYPT - A five-nation Arab conference in Cairo plans
               strategy against Israel and threatens the US with an
               oil embargo if it continues its support of the Israeli
               state.

8   LAOS - The US reports 150 US service personnel are
               listed as missing or captured in Laos.

8   UNITED STATES - Former Alabama Governor George C.
               Wallace urges Southern governors to defy the federal
               government's integration orders.

10   WEST GERMANY - A terrorist hand grenade attack kills
               one and wounds 11 at Munich's airport.

10-12   JORDAN - Serious fighting breaks out in and around
               Amman between Jordanian army forces and Palestinian
               "comman- dos" when the Palestinians refuse to obey a
               government order requiring them to surrender their
               arms and ammu- nition. The fighting is halted only
               when other Arab nations threaten intervention.

11   THAILAND - About 4,200 troops depart Thailand as the
               US begins withdrawing its 48,000 man force from the
               country.

11   CAMBODIA - US bombers attack artillery positions in
               Cambodia.

12   UNITED STATES - The government urges the Big Four to
               adopt a program to slow arms shipments to the Middle
               East.

12   LAOS - NVA forces open a new major offensive in the
               northeastern section of the country.

12   EGYPT - Israeli jets attack a scrap metal processing
               plant near Cairo killing 70.

13   SOUTH VIET NAM - Completing an inspection trip to SVN, Secretary of Defense Laird indicates the US will continue to withdraw its troops from SVN despite the deadlocked Paris peace talks.

14   UNITED STATES - The US bans toxins as a part of its renunciation of the use of biological weapons.

16   USSR - The Kremlin pledges support to the Arab nations but indicates it still hopes for a negotiated settlement to the Middle East question.

17   SWITZERLAND - The Disarmament Conference reconvenes in Geneva.

18   THE PHILIPPINES - The US Embassy in Manila is attacked by about 2,000 rioters.

19   CANADA - The Ministry of External Affairs asserts Canada's jurisdiction over the Northwest Passage and other Arctic regions.

20   CHILE - In spite of the OAS economic embargo against Cuba, Chile decides to sell $11 million in foodstuffs to the Castro government.

21   LAOS - Pathet Lao forces successfully complete the recapture of the Plaine des Jarres by taking the last government stronghold there.

21   PORTUGAL - There are massive student demonstrations protesting a plan to allow conscription for military service in the Portuguese African colonies.

25   UNITED STATES - Senator Charles Mathias of Maryland denounces US policy in Laos stating it violates Congressional measures to limit US activities in SEA. At the same time, CINCPAC announces concern over Laos stating at least 50,000 NVA are presently deployed there.

26   UNITED STATES - Secretary of Defense Melvin Laird denies that any US combat forces are engaged in Laos.

26   SOUTH VIET NAM - The US Command charges five Marines with the murder of 16 Vietnamese women and children while on patrol south of Da Nang.

26   LAOS - Communist Pathet Lao and NVA forces overrun the Plaine des Jarres.

26   ISRAEL - The government announces its fighters, after attacking missile bases near Cairo, have shot down three UAR MiG-21 fighters.

27   UNITED STATES - The government announces the Western Allies have accepted a Soviet proposal for talks on the future of Berlin.

27   GUATEMALA - Foreign Minister Alberto Fuentes Mohr is kidnapped in Guatemala City by members of the Rebel (or Revolutionary) Armed Forces (FAR). He is exchanged for an imprisoned rebel leader the next day (28 February).

MARCH

1   LAOS - The government formally asks the USSR and Great Britain to convene a conference of the signatories to the 1962 Geneva Accords.

2   RHODESIA - The British colony unilaterally declares its independence.

5   WORLD - The Nuclear Non-Proliferation Treaty goes into effect even though a number of powers still refuse to sign it.

6   UNITED STATES - An explosion in New York City's Greenwich Village district completely levels a house where Weather Underground faction members of the Students for a Democratic Society (SDS) were making bombs. Three are killed.

6   GUATEMALA - A US Embassy official, Sean M. Holly, is kidnapped in Guatemala City.

7   THAILAND - Thailand and Malaysia sign an agreement allowing each to battle guerrillas on the other's territory.

7   LAOS - A Pathet Lao broadcast from Hanoi proposes a five-point peace formula that calls for the strict neutrality of Laos.

7   SOUTH VIET NAM - "Operation SEA LORDS" is transferred from US Navy control to that of the South Vietnamese Navy. The operation establishes an infiltration barrier between Cambodia and SVN in IV CTZ.

8   CYPRUS - An attempted assassination of President Makarios fails in Nicosia.

9-12   LAOS - Prince Souvanna Phouma agrees to meet with the Pathet Lao to discuss peace. On 12 March, he states NVA must withdraw from Laos before the US bombing will be halted.

10   FRANCE - On a visit to Paris, Camdodian Prince
         Sihanouk acknowledges that NVA/VC forces are using
         Cambodia as a sanctuary.

11   UNITED STATES - Senator J. William Fullbright accuses
         President Nixon of fighting a secret war in Laos.

11   IRAQ - The government announces it will institute con-
         stitutional reforms granting the Kurds autonomy and a
         greater voice in the central government as a means of
         ending eight years of warfare. The Kurdish rebellion
         is officially ended.

11   BRAZIL - Revolutionaries kidnap the Japanese Consul
         General, Nobuo Okuchi, in Sao Paulo.

11   CAMBODIA - The embassies of North Viet Nam and the
         Provisional Revolutionary Government of South Viet Nam
         (Viet Cong) are sacked on the third day of anti-Com-
         munist rioting. The Cambodian government demands that
         all VC/NVA forces be withdrawn from Cambodian soil by
         dawn, 15 March.

14   CAMBODIA - A cargo ship, the SS Columbia Eagle, loaded
         with American ammunition, is highjacked by two
         mutineers and taken into a Cambodian port. The ship
         will later be released (29 March) by the Cambodian
         government.

15   CAMBODIA - Premier Lon Nol demands the immediate
         withdrawal of NVN and VC forces operating in his
         country.

15   SYRIA - Israeli forces carry out a number of raids on
         Syrian military installations as a "self-defense
         measure."

16   INDIA - The Chief Minister of West Bengal resigns in
         protest of the tactics of violence practiced by the
         Marxist Communists Party of India.

17   UNITED STATES - The Department of Army accuses 14 of-
         ficers, including two generals, of complicity in the
         1968 My Lai massacre and the conspiracy to cover it
         up.

17   UNITED NATIONS - The US exercises its first veto and
         stops a resolution condemning Great Britain for not
         forcibly ejecting the white-minority government in
         Rhodesia.

17   CAMBODIA - Government troops, supported by ARVN artil-
         lery, launch an attack against VC/NVA forces along the
         Cambodian-SVN border.

17   TURKEY - Anti-American protests, organized by the
            Federation of Revolutionary Youth at a number of
            universities, erupt into violence. They are supported
            by militant workers led by the minority Confederation
            of Reformist Workers' Unions (DISK).

17   INDIA - Rioting breaks out in West Bengal during a
            Marxist-inspired strike.

18   UNITED NATIONS - The Security Council condemns Rho-
            desia for its policies toward blacks.

18   CAMBODIA - Prince Narodom Sihanouk is overthrown while
            on a state visit to Moscow. National Assembly chairman
            Cheng Heng assumes the provisional title of Head of
            State. Premier Lon Nol begins an almost unprecedented
            reign of terror primarily aimed at Cambodia's 400,000
            Vietnamese residents. Sihanouk goes to Peking for
            sanctuary, where he is publicly received by Chairman
            Mao.

19   UNITED STATES - The government confirms that it has
            agreed to sell eight jet fighters to Libya.

19   EGYPT - The arrival of Soviet SA-3 surface-to-air mis-
            siles in the UAR is confirmed.

19   CAMBODIA - The Lon Nol government closes the port of
            Sihanoukville to NVN supply ships. The port is renamed
            Kompong Som.

19   INDIA - The central government imposes direct rule
            over West Bengal in an effort to stop the violence.

19   VENEZUELA - Defense Minister Garcia Villasmil an-
            nounces his government will integrate its defense
            system with that of Colombia.

22   CAMBODIA - The government asks Great Britain and the
            Soviet Union to reactivate the ICC and peacefully ex-
            pel the VC/NVA from Cambodian territory.

22   THAILAND - Amid reports that at least two Thai bat-
            talions are fighting in Laos, the government admits
            there may be some "volunteers" there.

23   UNITED STATES - The Department of State announces a
            postponement in the decision on the sale of 125 A-4
            and F-4 jet aircraft to Israel.

23   SAUDI ARABIA - A 24-nation Islamic conference opens in
            Jidda. The principal topic of the meeting is support
            to the Palestinians.

23   COMMUNIST CHINA - Ousted Cambodian leader Prince
      Sihanouk declares he will establish a government and
      an army-in-exile. The Pathet Lao, VC, and NVN offer
      him their support.

24   DOMINICAN REPUBLIC - The US Air Attache, Lieutenant
      Colonel Donald J. Crowley, is kidnapped by terrorists.

25   UNITED STATES - After a three-month lapse, the US re-
      turns to the bargaining table with the USSR over Mid-
      dle East issues.

25   LEBANON - Clashes break out between Palestinian com-
      mandos and anti-PLO Lebanese civilians.

26   DOMINICAN REPUBLIC - The government releases 20 po-
      litical prisoners to obtain the freedom of the kid-
      napped American Air Attache, Lieutenant Colonel Donald
      J. Crowley.

27   ISRAEL - The government reports its jets have shot
      down five UAR MiG-21s while conducting air raids on
      Soviet-built SA-2 sites along the Suez Canal.

27   UNITED STATES - Washington reaffirms its policy not to
      expand the war in SEA and states it had no prior
      knowledge of the US support given to the recent ARVN
      incursion into Cambodia.

27   SOUTH VIET NAM - RVNAF, with heavy US helicopter sup-
      port, launches a major offensive against VC/NVA bases
      in Cambodia.

27   SUDAN - An attempt by followers of Imam al-Hadi al-
      Mahdi to assassinate President Gafaar Muhammad al-
      Nimeiry fails. The Imam is killed as he trys to escape
      to Ethiopia (31 March).

28   ARGENTINA - The Paraguayan Consul in Ituzaingo is re-
      leased by his kidnappers when the Argentine government
      refuses their ransom demands.

28   DAHOMEY - Because of continuing unrest, the ruling
      military junta suspends the forthcoming public
      elections.

28   CAMBODIA - The government orders a call-up of all
      veterans to face an expected VC drive on Phnom Penh.

28   NORTHERN IRELAND - Rioting breaks out in several areas
      in Northern Ireland following Protestant and Catholic
      Easter parades.

28   BURMA - Communist guerrilla forces capture the Burmese
            border town of Kyugok.

28   GREAT BRITAIN - The government announces it has com-
            pleted its military withdrawal from Libya in accord-
            ance with the terms of the 1969 agreement.

29-30   SOUTH VIET NAM - Heavy mortar, rocket, and ground
            attacks on two successive days on the Chi Lang
            Training Center result in more than 200 ARVN killed
            and wounded. Enemy losses are reported as 52 killed.

30   LAOS - Government troops recapture from NVA troops the
            strategically important hamlet of Sam Thong.

31   GUATEMALA - The German Ambassador, Count Karl von
            Spreti, is kidnapped in Guatemala City. When the
            demands of FAR are not met, he is murdered (5 April).

APRIL

1   SOUTH VIET NAM - The Communists launch their annual
            spring offensive with attacks on more than 130 towns
            and military bases, including the Cam Ranh Bay fuel
            storage facility, throughout SVN. This offensive ends
            a six-month lull in the fighting. At the same time,
            VC/NVA forces lay siege to the CIDG camp at Dak Seang
            in Kontum Province. Attacks on nearby camps at Dak Pek
            and Ben Het continue into May.

1   CAMBODIA - The government reports that several thou-
            sand VC are battling government forces near the Cam-
            bodian-SVN border.

1   FRANCE - The government proposes an international
            conference on SEA.

2   ISRAEL - An eight-hour firefight is reported between
            Israeli and Syrian forces.

4   SOUTH KOREA - A North Korean ship is sunk by ROK naval
            units as it attempts to land North Korean agents along
            the ROK coast.

4   GREAT BRITAIN - The government dispatches 500 addi-
            tional troops to Northern Ireland because of increased
            unrest.

4   UNITED STATES - An estimated 50,000 people march in
            Washington, DC, in support of the war in SEA. On the
            other side, this date marks the beginning of two weeks
            of anti-war demonstrations throughout the country.

5   ISRAEL - The government rejects a proposal for peace negotiations allegedly made by UAR President Nasser to the World Jewish Congress.

5   CAMBODIA - Two ARVN battalions located in Tay Ninh Province, III CTZ cross into Cambodia and attack VC sanctuaries ten miles inside the border.

7   SOUTH VIET NAM - The last detachment of the US 1st Infantry Division departs SVN marking the end of nearly five years of combat.

7   INDIA - The government announces the Soviet Union will help it produce an improved model of the Soviet MiG-21 aircraft.

8   CAMBODIA - The SS Columbia Eagle is released to American authorities.

8   UAR - An elementary school is reportedly bombed by Israeli warplanes, killing 30 children.

9   LAOS - The government indicates its unwillingness to halt the bombing of the Ho Chi Minh Trail, even though it is willing to hold peace talks with the Pathet Lao under a ground cease-fire.

11   SOUTH VIET NAM - Bodies of Vietnamese residents of Cambodia are found floating in the Mekong River.

12   ISRAEL - The government reports increased Arab violence in the Gaza Strip.

12   GUYANA - The government agrees to the demilitarization of its border with Surinam on the upper Courantyne River.

13   SOUTH VIET NAM - The VC/NVA begin a new round of sporadic rocket attacks on Saigon.

14   SAUDI ARABIA - King Faisal announces the recognition of the republican government in North Yemen based upon an agreement to include royalists in the government. This effectively ends the long-standing civil war.

15   CAMBODIA - The Lon Nol government announces its willingness to accept unconditional military aid from anyone interested in their assisting in the defeat of the Communists.

15   SOUTH VIET NAM - US military strength in SVN is listed as 425,500.

15   UNITED STATES - The Defense Department announces it
            has stopped using the herbicide "Agent Orange" as a
            defoliant in SVN.

15   EUROPE - The Council of Europe Committee of Ministers
            condemns Greece for numerous civil rights violations.

16   AUSTRIA - The US and USSR reopen SALT negotiations in
            Vienna.

16   CAMBODIA - NVA/VC strength in Cambodia is estimated to
            be 54,000, with most of them deployed in the northern
            provinces.

16   JORDAN - King Hussein acknowledges the presence of
            Pakistani troops in Jordan.

17   JORDAN - Following violent anti-American demonstra-
            tions in Amman, and the US' decision to cut Jordan
            from the itinerary of Assistant Secretary of State
            Joseph J. Sisco, the government asks the US to recall
            its Ambassador in Amman.

17   SOUTH VIET NAM - After reports of the mass killing of
            Vietnamese in Cambodia, the GVN offers to repatriate
            all of those remaining in Cambodia. On 26 April, the
            Cambodian government allows the RVN Red Cross to enter
            Phnom Penh and begin the process.

19   UNITED STATES - The White House acknowledges that US
            forces are operating in Laos. This revelation was
            first made when a Senate subcommittee released clas-
            sified information to the press. It was further ac-
            knowledged that more than 100 Americans had been
            killed in Laos since 1962.

19   CAMBODIA - Communist forces capture the important town
            of Saang about 20 miles south of Phnom Penh.

20   UNITED STATES - President Nixon announces the planned
            withdrawal of 150,000 troops from SVN by Spring 1971,
            and again appeals the to NVN to enter into meaningful
            negotiations.

20   SOUTH VIET NAM - For the third time in a week, ARVN
            forces cross into Cambodian territory to attack VC/NVA
            sanctuaries.

20   CAMBODIA - Lon Nol makes a personal appeal to Presi-
            dent Nixon to extend military assistance.

21   COLOMBIA - Martial law is declared following serious
            disorders during the presidential election.

21-25   TRINIDAD-TABAGO - Four days of rioting begins between blacks and East Indians. British and US warships arrive off the coast (22 April). About one-quarter (200 men) of the army mutinies. The remainder puts down the uprising (25 April).

22   AUSTRALIA - Prime Minister John Gorton announces the withdrawal of one of his country's three infantry battalions (1,000 men) in SVN.

23   SOUTH VIET NAM - Captured Communist weapons and munitions are sent to Cambodia.

23   THE GAMBIA - The former British colony is proclaimed a republic within the Commonwealth.

23   PAKISTAN - The government acknowledges that it has troops in Jordan under the terms of a formal agreement in which Pakistan pledged to help Jordan fight Israel.

24   UNITED STATES - A Taiwanese national fails in an attempt on the life of Nationalist Chinese Deputy Premier Chiang Ching-kuo, visiting in New York City.

24   HAITI - A mutiny breaks out among 120 Haitian Coast Guardsmen. The mutineers, who are aboard three vessels, shell Port-au-Prince, but they are quickly subdued.

27   SOMALIA - The government announces it has thwarted a coup attempt (21 April) led by Major General Jama Ali Qorshel.

28   GREAT BRITAIN - A British warship is sent to Grand Cayman Island, in the West Indies, following anti-administration demonstrations.

28   INDONESIA - Foreign Minister Adam Malik announces that an Asian conference on Cambodia will be held despite the opposition of Communist China, the USSR, and NVN.

28   UAR - The government claims it has inflicted heavy casualties on Israeli forces near the Suez Canal.

29   SOUTH VIET NAM - A massive Allied offensive into Cambodia, north of Tay Ninh Province in III CTZ, begins under the direction of South Vietnamese Lieutenant General Do Cao Tri. General Tri, one of the few able senior field commanders in ARVN, is killed in the campaign. US forces support the invasion aimed at the destruction of North Vietnamese supply and communication bases inside Cambodia.

29   ISRAEL - The government confirms that Soviet pilots
            are flying operational combat missions over the Suez
            Canal.

29-30   LAOS - NVN troops capture Attopeu (Attapu) (Muang Mai)
            in southern Laos, near the triborder area. This impor-
            tant town, lying at the junction of Routes 16 and 18,
            marks the farthest NVA advance into Laotian territory
            thus far in the war.

30   UNITED STATES - President Nixon announces he has or-
            dered US forces to support the invasion into Cambodia.
            The areas known as the "Parrot's Beak" and the "Fish-
            hook" are occupied by the 1st US Cavalry Division
            (Airmobile), which is operating with the support of
            the ARVN Airborne Division.

MAY

1   CAMBODIA - Lon Nol states that, although the Communist
            penetration into Cambodia poses a major threat to
            Phnom Penh, he was given no advance warning, nor was
            he consulted, about the US-RVNAF offensive into his
            country.

1-2   NORTH VIET NAM - The US carries out intensive retali-
            atory bombing raids in NVN. These are the first air
            strikes since November 1968.

1-2   UNITED STATES - Demonstrations are held in many uni-
            versities across the country protesting the US role in
            the Cambodian invasion.

3   ISRAEL - Twenty-one Al Fatah guerrillas are killed at-
            tempting to infiltrate Israeli lines along the Jordan
            River.

4   SOUTH VIET NAM - The US command announces that the
            bombing of NVN has been halted.

4   UNITED STATES - Frustrated, tired, and poorly-led,
            Ohio National Guardsmen open fire on demonstrators at
            Kent State University protesting the Cambodian in-
            vasion. The Guard had been sent to the campus to re-
            store order. Four students are killed, eight wounded.
            At the same time, the US Senate Foreign Relations
            Committee charges that the White House has been con-
            ducting a constitutionally unauthorized war in Indo-
            china.

4   USSR - Premier Aleksei Kosygin denounces the US for
            its participation in the invasion of Cambodia and for
            the resumption of the bombing of NVN.

4   CAMBODIA - NVA and VC forces cut the road between Sai-
        gon and Phnom Penh at a point 29 miles from the Cam-
        bodian capital. At the same time, about 2,000 US
        Special Forces-trained Cambodians arrive in Phnom Penh
        to assist in the defense of the city.

5   UNITED STATES - The President announces that US forces
        operating in Cambodia have been ordered not to pene-
        trate more than 21.7 miles, and that all US forces
        will be withdrawn from Cambodia by 30 June.

5   COMMUNIST CHINA - Prince Sihanouk, the deposed ruler
        of Cambodia, announces the formation of a government-
        in-exile (Kampuchea) in Peking. The Chinese government
        immediately recognizes it.

5   REPUBLIC OF IRELAND - Two Cabinet Ministers are dis-
        missed by Prime Minister John Lynch for conspiring to
        ship weapons to Roman Catholic factions in Northern
        Ireland.

6   SOUTH VIET NAM - The South Vietnamese Navy assumes re-
        sponsibility for "Operation GIANT SLINGSHOT" which is
        designed to prevent VC/NVA river traffic from the Cam-
        bodian area known as the "Parrot's Beak" from reaching
        the Saigon area. At the same time, US troops open two
        new operations into Cambodia, increasing US-RVNAF
        cross-border fronts to six, with about 50,000 Allied
        troops now in Cambodia.

6   FRANCE - The NVN and VC representatives refuse to at-
        tend the Paris Peace Talks because of the renewed
        bombing of NVN.

6   CAMBODIA - On this day Communist China, North Viet
        Nam, and North Korea break diplomatic relations with
        Cambodia.

6   CZECHOSLOVAKIA - The government signs a 20-year treaty
        of friendship with the Soviet Union.

6   TANZANIA - The government announces that Communist
        China will assist in the construction of a naval base
        at Dar-es-Salaam.

7   UNITED STATES - The White House announces the capture
        of major Communist supply bases during the Cambodian
        incursion.

7   UNITED STATES - The House of Representatives rejects a
        move to cut off funds for US troops operating in Cam-
        bodia as of 1 July.

7   INDIA - Violent clashes break out between Hindus and Muslims in Bhiwandi, Bombay.

8   UNITED STATES - Construction workers (Hard Hatters) in New York City break up an antiwar demonstration then march on City Hall where they force officials to raise the flag to full-staff. It had been flown at half-staff in honor of those killed at Kent State.

8   SOUTH VIET NAM - The government announces that a major NVA offensive in the DMZ has been beaten back, and that more than 69 SVN villages were shelled overnight. Also, President Thieu announces that SVN will not be bound by any 30 June deadline, set by the US Congress, for withdrawal from Cambodia.

9   UNITED STATES - A major anti-war demonstration in Washington, DC, attracts about 100,000 youthful marchers.

11   SAUDI ARABIA - The government accuses Syria of sabotaging the Trans-Arabian Pipeline.

12   SOUTH VIET NAM - Vice President Ky announces that Allied naval vessels, including US Navy ships, have begun a blockade along 100 miles of Cambodia's coastline, from Kompong Som to the RVN border.

12   UNITED STATES - Racial unrest in Augusta, Georgia, claims the lives of six blacks. Sixty more are injured.

13   UNITED STATES - The Department of State declares that the US will not become involved in the defense of Cambodia.

13   LAOS - NVA troops, apparently operating out of bases in northern Cambodia, are said to have attacked Laotian positions on the Bolovens Plateau in southern Laos.

16   UAR - Following the sinking of an Israeli fishing boat by a UAR missile boat off the Sinai, Israeli aircraft conduct a reprisal raid on the UAR Red Sea naval base at Ras Banat and sink a UAR destroyer and a missile ship.

16   INDONESIA - A conference of Asian Foreign Ministers, held in Djakarta, calls for the immediate withdrawal of all foreign troops in Cambodia.

16   FRANCE - Paris is rocked by a series of bomb blasts at police stations, public buildings, and politicans' homes.

17   CAMBODIA - US forces operating in Cambodia capture part of the VC Central Office of South Viet Nam (COSVN). Cambodian government forces retake Kompong Cham which was taken yesterday by the NVA.

17   INDONESIA - In Jakarta, an 11-member Asian conference on SEA, recommends a new international conference on Indochina. It also recommends that the UN establish an international peacekeeping apparatus (ICC) for Cambodia.

17   EL SALVADOR - Fighting breaks out between Salvadoran and Honduran forces near Chalatanango.

17   ISRAEL - The government admits it has stepped up air and artillery attacks along the Suez Canal to thwart further UAR reinforcement of its missile sites in the area.

18   COMMUNIST CHINA - The government announces it has cancelled scheduled ambassadorial talks with the US that were set to begin in two days in Warsaw, Poland.

18   SOUTH VIET NAM - Allied forces observe a 24-hour truce to celebrate the birth of Buddha. Over 200 enemy-instigated incidents occur.

19   UNITED NATIONS - The Security Council condemns Israel for its recent raids into Lebanon.

19   SOUTH VIET NAM - Enemy shelling hits more than 60 towns in celebration of Ho Chi Minh's birthday while the US and its allies end a 24-hour truce celebrating Buddha's birthday.

20   SOUTH VIET NAM - RVNAF goes on the offensive.

20   UNITED STATES - A pro-Viet Nam demonstration takes place in New York. About 150,000 participate.

20   UAR - President Nasser announces Soviet pilots are flying combat missions against Israel.

21   COMMUNIST CHINA - Mao Tse-tung calls for a world revolution to defeat "US imperialism."

21   UNITED STATES - Intelligence sources confirm that COSVN headquarters has been moved deeper into Cambodia to avoid further US attacks.

22   ISRAEL - Twelve persons are killed when Arab terrorist infiltrators ambush a school bus near the Israeli-Lebanese border.

22   SOUTH VIET NAM - The government decides to halt the
            mass evacuation of Vietnamese from Cambodia as the
            immediate threat to their safety appears over. About
            70,000 Vietnamese remain in Cambodia. At the same
            time, the government announces there are about 40,000
            RVNAF operating in Cambodia as a result of an expanded
            campaign plan.

23   ANGOLA - Portuguese forces open an offensive against
            rebel forces in southern Angola.

24   LAOS - Government troops open a new offensive against
            NVA and Pathet Lao forward positions.

24   NORTH VIET NAM - A military and economic assistance
            pact is concluded with Communist China.

27   LEBANON - The government agrees to taking action to
            curb Palistinian activities against Israel.

27   SOUTH VIET NAM - A treaty is concluded with Cambodia
            by which SVN can supply direct military assistance to
            the Phnom Penh government. The two nations' foreign
            ministers renew diplomatic relations after a seven-
            year break. At the same time, the ARVN fire base
            "O'Reilly" located west of Hue in I CTZ is attacked by
            an estimated battalion of VC/NVA.

27   CAMBODIA - A decision is made by the SVN government to
            continue operations in Cambodia after the Americans
            withdraw.

27   NATO - The Council of Ministers invites the Warsaw
            Pact to enter negotiations to achieve a mutual, bal-
            anced, reduction of conventional forces in Central
            Europe.

28   THAILAND - The government resumes diplomatic relations
            with Cambodia but rejects a request for military
            forces, promising only limited aid.

28   ANGOLA - Portuguese military headquarters claims the
            destruction of a major rebel base in southern Angola.

29   SOUTH VIET NAM - The important town of Dalat in Tuyen
            Duc Province in the Central Highlands, II CTZ, is at-
            tacked by an unknown-size force. The VC/NVA are forced
            to withdraw after three days of heavy fighting.

29   ARGENTINA - Former President Pedro Eugenio Aramburu is
            kidnapped on this date and is murdered (c.1 June) by
            members of the National Command for National Liber-
            ation (Peronist). His body is not discovered until 16
            July.

31   UAR - Defense Minister Mohammad Fawzi states that UAR forces training for the "war of liberation" have been withdrawn from the Suez area to lessen the impact of incessant Israeli attacks.

JUNE

1-7   SOUTH VIET NAM - The Communists begin an intensive shelling of the US base at Da Nang, in Quang Tri Province.

2   UNITED STATES - The US and Soviet Union resume Middle East talks in Washington, DC.

2   THAILAND - The government decides to furnish large-scale military aid, including troops (of Cambodian descent), to Cambodia.

3   UNITED STATES - A US Congressional delegation leaves for South Viet Nam for a firsthand look at the war.

4   TONGA - The former British colony becomes an independent member of the Commonwealth.

4   EL SALVADOR - A 1.8-mile-wide demilitarized buffer zone is agreed upon along the border with Honduras.

5   USSR - Moscow accuses Communist China of meddling in the internal affairs of SEA nations.

5   NORTH KOREA - The government claims its naval vessels sank a US "spy ship" within North Korean territorial waters.

5   SOUTH KOREA - The government announces one of its naval vessels was attacked and captured by North Korea naval units while it was escorting fishing vessels.

7-11   JORDAN - Fighting is renewed between the Jordanian Army and Palestinians. Both sustain heavy losses before the two sides bow to Arab pressure and the entreaties of their leaders, including Yasser Arafat, the commander of Al Fatah.

8   ARGENTINA - President Juan Carlos Ongania is forced to resign following a military-led coup. Brigadier General Roberto Marcelo Levingston becomes President.

8   SOUTH VIET NAM - Intelligence exploitation of captured enemy documents requires MACV to revise upward its estimates of NVA/VC strengths in SVN and Cambodia.

9   NORTH KOREA - The government announces a five-point program for the reunification of Korea.

9   MIDDLE EAST - A Central Committee is formed to coordinate the activities of ten Palestinian groups.

9   JORDAN - An assassination attempt near Amman fails against King Hussein. Palestinian commandos battle Jordanian troops nearby.

9   LAOS - After almost five years of being surrounded by Communist troops, the town of Saravane (Saravan), on Route 16 north of the Bolovens Plateau, is captured by NVA forces.

9   EAST AFRICA - Kenya and Ethiopia sign a treaty formally establishing the border between the two countries.

10   JORDAN - The US Military Attache to Amman, Major Robert Perry, is assassinated by Palestinian terrorists as a truce goes into effect between the Palestinians and Jordan.

10   MOZAMBIQUE - Portuguese forces open a major offensive in northern Mozambique against rebels who operate out of base areas in Tanzania.

11   CAMBODIA - Communist forces capture the ancient city of Angkor Wat.

11   UNITED STATES - The US Senate defeats a resolution authorizing the President to maintain US forces in Cambodia.

11   SOUTH VIET NAM - Viet Cong forces attack and destroy the hamlet of Thanh My, south of Da Nang in I CTZ. At least 74 civilians are massacred; 68 are wounded.

11   BRAZIL - The West German Ambassador, Ehrenfried von Hollenben, is kidnapped in Rio de Janeiro. His kidnappers, terrorists of the Popular Revolutionary Vanguard and the National Liberation Alliance, set a ransom of the release of 40 political prisoners.

11   LIBYA - The last US service personnel leave Libya under the terms of the 1969 agreement.

12   UAR - Israeli commandos carry out two raids on UAR positions on the Gulf of Suez and the Suez Canal.

14   CEYLON - The newly seated left-wing government recognizes North Korea, North Viet Nam, Communist China, and East Germany.

16   TURKEY - Following outbreaks of labor violence in Istanbul and in Kocaeli Province, the government declares martial law.

18   CAMBODIA - Communist forces cut the strategically important Route 1 between Phnom Penh and Saigon at Koki Thom on the Mekong River.

18   VENEZUELA - A twelve year moritorium on the border dispute is delared between Venezuela and Guyana.

19   UNITED STATES - The government announces that multiple warheads are being deployed on some of the nation's ICBMs.

20   COMMUNIST CHINA - The government announces it has further deferred consideration of resuming ambassadorial-level talks with the US that were to be held in Warsaw.

22   SOUTH VIET NAM - MACV announces a decision to halt the nine-year-old program of spraying chemical defoliants (Operation RANCH HAND) in SVN.

22   JAPAN - Amid violent protests, the government declares its intention to allow the security pact with the US to be automatically extended.

22   ECUADOR - President Jose Maria Velasco Ibarra states he is assuming dictatorial powers following major rioting in the universities in Quito and Guayaquil.

24   CAMBODIA - A government operation begins that is aimed at removing about 8,000 civilians from the endangered northern provinces.

25   UNITED STATES - The government calls for a 90-day cease-fire in the Middle East as it presents a new peace proposal for the region.

25   CAMBODIA - The government orders a general mobilization of all citizens between 18 and 60.

25   NORTH VIET NAM - The government produces a list of 334 American service personnel it is holding prisoner. The US immediately disputes the low number and demands a full list.

26   UNITED STATES - The Defense Department reports the loss of more than 7,000 military aircraft from all causes in connection with the war in SEA.

26   ITALY - Serious rioting breaks out in Pescara over the choice of a new regional capital.

27 CAMBODIA - The Communists push government forces out of the last of the four northern provinces. At the same time, Lon Nol assumes full wartime powers.

27 CHILE - President Eduardo Frei Montalva declares a six-month state of emergency in Santiago Province.

29 ISRAEL - Prime Minister Golda Meir announces her opposition to the cease-fire proposal presented by the US.

30 CAMBODIA - US forces withdraw from Cambodia on schedule and report the capture of 155 tons of enemy weapons and equipment, 1,786 tons of ammunition, and 6,877 tons of rice. They also report 388 US KIA, 1,525 WIA, and 4,766 enemy killed.

30 UNITED STATES - The Senate passes legislation barring further US incursions into Cambodia without Congressional approval.

30 OAS - The General Assembly adopts a resolution condemning terrorism and political kidnapping.

30 SOUTH VIET NAM - US strength in SVN is 412,675.

JULY

1 TURKEY - The martial law edict is lifted.

4 NORTHERN IRELAND - British forces carry out a house to house search of the Falls Roads district of Belfast following the killing of five civilians.

6 ISRAEL - Israeli Defense Forces Chief of Staff Major General Haim Bar-Lev announces the loss of three Israeli jets to Soviet-built and manned SAMS in the last six days.

9 UNITED STATES - The Defense Department announces that the USSR has continued to deploy ICBMs during the SALT negotiations.

9 COLOMBIA - Former Foreign Minister Londono y Londono is kidnapped by members of the National Liberation Army. He is subsequently released on 19 July.

10 JORDAN - In Amman, the government signs a new accord with the Palestinian commandos.

14 ITALY - Rioting breaks out in Reggio Calabria when a new regional capital is chosen.

15   SOUTH VIET NAM - RVNAF opens a new offensive.

19   COLOMBIA - As one of his last acts in office, retiring
          President Carlos Lleras Restrepo imposes a state of
          siege because of the violence that followed the elec-
          tion that unseated him.

20   FINLAND - The government extends its treaty of friend-
          ship with the USSR to 1990. The treaty was originally
          due to expire in 1975.

21   SOUTH VIET NAM - President Thieu announces his opposi-
          tion to any form of coalition government.

22   UNITED STATES - The government announces it has agreed
          to strengthen the ROK armed forces and industrial base
          before any substantial US force withdrawals will be
          contemplated.

22   GREECE - Palestinian terrorists hijack a Greek air-
          liner and demand the release of seven Arab terrorists
          held in Greek jails.

23   UAR - President Nasser announces the acceptance of the
          US 90-day cease-fire plan for the Middle East.

23   OMAN - Sultan Sa'id bin Taimur is overthrown by his
          son, Prince Qabus bin Said, in a palace coup at
          Salalah.

23   UNITED NATIONS - The Security Council approves an
          Afro-Asian resolution that extends the 1963 arms
          embargo on South Africa.

23   THAILAND - The government refuses a Cambodian request
          to station Thai troops in northern Cambodia to block
          the use of the region by the Communists.

24   EGYPT - President Nasser accepts the US peace proposal
          to end hostilities in the Middle East.

24   UNITED STATES - The government announces that about
          6,000 US troops will be withdrawn from the Philippines
          within one year.

26   JORDAN - King Hussein accepts the US peace proposal to
          end the hostilities in the Middle East. Other Arab
          nations, such as Iraq and Syria, reject the proposal.

27   USSR - In Moscow the government begins renunciation of
          force negotations with West Germany.

30   ISRAEL - The government claims it destroyed four UAR
          fighters over the Suez Canal.

31   COMMUNIST CHINA - The government accuses the USSR of
            massing troops along the common border.

31   ISRAEL - After a lengthy debate, the government ac-
            cepts the US peace proposal to end hostilities in the
            Middle East. At the same time, in Amman, Jordan, a
            meeting of Palestinian leaders rejects the cease-fire
            proposal.

31   URUGUAY - US diplomat Dan A. Mitrione, along with the
            Brazilian Consul, are kidnapped in Montevideo by
            Tupamaro terrorists.

AUGUST

1   MIDDLE EAST - A cease-fire is arranged between Egypt
            and Israel. Each side is required to remain at a
            standstill and to maintain any of the positions it
            holds within 32 miles of the Suez Canal.

1   NORTHERN IRELAND - British military authorities impose
            new security rules in the troubled areas.

1   CAMBODIA - US aircraft are reported to be furnishing
            close air support for the Royal Cambodian Army.

2   MIDDLE EAST - Arab and Israeli forces clash on three
            fronts.

3   UNITED STATES - The Navy successfully launches a
            Poseidon missile from a submerged platform as the crew
            of a nearby Soviet intelligence ship watches.

4   ISRAEL - Right-wing (Gahal) members of the Cabinet
            resign because of Israeli acceptance of the US peace
            proposal.

5-6   EGYPT - At a meeting in Cairo, the Arab defense minis-
            ters agree to establish northern, eastern, and western
            military fronts against Israel.

7   MIDDLE EAST - A 90-day cease-fire and "stand still"
            agreement goes into effect although PLO leaders in
            Amman say they will ignore it.

8   SPAIN - The government announces it has renewed its
            basing agreements with the US in return for $153
            million in military and economic aid, which includes
            the leasing of 12 naval vessels.

9   LEBANON - Israeli jets attack PLO bases in Lebanon.

10 URUGUAY - The body of US diplomat Dan A. Mitrione is found in Montevideo after the government refused to negotiate with the terrorists for his release.

12 USSR - West German Chancellor Willy Brandt signs a non-aggression pact with Soviet Premier Alexei Kosygin.

12 NORTHERN IRELAND - British security forces seal off the Catholic section of Londonderry to quell an outbreak of violence.

14 JORDAN - Israeli military aircraft break the 7-day-old truce by attacking Jordanian army positions in repri-sal for Arab guerrilla raids into Israel that were al-legedly supported by the Jordanians.

14 AUSTRIA - The SALT negotiations are adjourned with an announcement that they will be reconvened in Helsinki, Finland.

15 PARAGUAY - An attempt to assassinate President Alfredo Stroessner fails. Over 100 students are arrested as a part of the plot.

17 LAOS - The Pathet Lao announce that the peace talks with the government have broken down.

19 ISRAEL - Government sources publish photographs to support the contention that the UAR is emplacing Soviet-built missile bases in the Suez Canal truce zone.

20 CAMBODIA - Government troops engage Communist forces only seven miles from Phnom Penh.

20 NEW ZEALAND - Prime Minister Sir Keith J. Holyoake an-nounces that one-half of the New Zealand military contingent in SVN will be withdrawn before the end of 1971.

21 WARSAW PACT - The Warsaw Pact officially endorses the USSR-West German Treaty renouncing the use of force.

22 NORTH KOREA - The government rejects a South Korean proposal aimed at reunification.

24 UNITED STATES - In one of many incidents, student dem-onstrators, protesting the University of Wisconsin's participation in defense research, blow up a labor-atory killing a graduate student and destroying mil-lions of dollars worth of school equipment.

25   UNITED NATIONS - Middle East peace talks begin.

27   UAR - The UAR files its first formal protest against
            an Israeli truce violation.

28   THAILAND - The government announces its decision to
            withdraw its forces from SVN.

30   JORDAN - Serious fighting breaks out in Amman between
            Jordanian army forces and Palestinian guerrillas.

30   SOUTH VIET NAM - The VC/NVA systematically destroy a
            Buddhist orphanage at An Hoa, MR 1. Fifteen civilians
            are killed, 45 wounded; most are children. At the same
            time, sappers infiltrate and blow up the USAF POL farm
            at Cam Ranh Bay, MR 2. More than 400,000 gallons of
            aviation fuel are destroyed.

31   THE NETHERLANDS - Indonesian Amboinese separatists
            seize the Indonesian Embassy in the The Hague.

SEPTEMBER

            SOUTH VIET NAM - Intensive B-52 bombing takes place
            along the Laotian border to thwart an expected attack
            by 40,000 NVA massed in the area.

1   JORDAN - King Hussein escapes an assassination attempt
            in Amman.

1   UNITED STATES - The Senate rejects the McGovern-Hat-
            field Amendment that would have required the with-
            drawal of all US forces in Southeast Asia by the end
            of 1971.

2   SOUTH VIET NAM - The South Vietnamese Navy assumes re-
            sponsibility for the inner barrier of coastal "Oper-
            ation MARKET TIME." The outer barrier remains under US
            Navy control.

3   UNITED STATES - US intelligence sources report numer-
            ous UAR and USSR truce violations in the Middle East.

3   PANAMA - The government rejects three draft treaties
            on the Panama Canal Zone.

3   UNITED NATIONS - The Committee on Disarmament approves
            a draft treaty banning nuclear weapons on the seabed.

4   UAR - The government rejects US and Israeli charges
            that it is violating the truce.

4   CHILE - The Marxist candidate, Doctor Salvador Allende Gossens, is elected President. He assumes office on 4 November.

5   UNITED NATIONS - The Security Council condemns Israel for its attacks on Palestinian guerrilla bases in Lebanon.

5   JORDAN - A cease-fire is arranged between government forces and Palestinian commandos after four days of fighting.

6   ISRAEL - The government announces it is withdrawing from the Middle East peace talks.

6   UNITED STATES - Arab terrorists hijack three passenger aircraft (2 US, 1 Swiss) bound for Europe. A fourth attempt, against an Israeli airliner, fails. The terrorists demand the release of Arab prisoners held in a number of countries including Israel. One of the US aircraft is blown up (7 September) after landing in Egypt. The other two aircraft are flown to Dawson's Field in Jordan. The passengers are declared "prisoners of war" by the hijackers.

7   UNITED STATES - The Defense Department announces US military strength in SVN is below 400,000 for the first time since January, 1967.

7   THAILAND - Joint US-Thai announcements forecast the withdrawal of 9,800 US troops from Thailand, and the withdrawal of 12,000 Thai troops from SVN.

8   JORDAN - A second cease-fire is ordered by both sides.

8   UNITED STATES - The Defense Department announces that rather than the imposing higher draft call-ups in future emergencies, reservists and the National Guard will be mobilized.

9   JORDAN - A British airliner is hijacked and brought to Jordan where it joins two others held in the desert at Dawson's Field.

10   JORDAN - A third cease-fire is announced.

11   UNITED STATES - Federal marshals are placed on US aircraft to prevent further hijackings.

12   JORDAN - Palestinian terrorists blow up all three hijacked aircraft in the Jordanian desert. All but 54 of the crews and passengers are released.

14   SIERRA LEONE - A state of siege is declared after two
            senior ministers resign protesting the policies of
            Prime Minister Siaka Stevens.

14-15   JORDAN - Palestinian guerrilla forces take control of
            the towns of Irbid, Zarqa (Az Zarqa), Jerash (Jarash),
            and Salt (As Salt) in northern Jordan. They are driven
            out the next day.

15   JORDAN - King Hussein announces the formation of a
            military government headed by a new Prime Minister,
            Brigadier General Muhammed Daoud. The Palestine or-
            ganization rejects the new government and fortifies
            its positions.

16   JORDAN - Martial law is declared.

17   FRANCE - The VC present an eight-point peace proposal
            at the SEA peace talks in Paris.

17-27   JORDAN - King Hussein, tiring of Palestinian resis-
            tance to his authority, orders an all-out attack
            against their bases in his country. Syria, in support
            of the Palestinians, invades Jordan (19 September)
            under heavy artillery fire from across the border. The
            Syrian armored attack is initially successful and,
            with Palestinian support, captures the strategically
            important city of Irbid (20-21 September), and Ramtha.
            In a classic tank battle fought near Irbid on 22 Sep-
            tember, the Syrian army is defeated and withdraws
            across its own border (23 September). In a continua-
            tion of its campaign against the Palestinians, Jordan
            inflicts very heavy casualties. Complete destruction
            is averted only when an Arab-mandated cease-fire goes
            into effect of 27 September. Casualties may be as high
            as 5,000 killed and 10,000 injured.

20   UNITED STATES - The State Department warns Syria of
            the serious consequences of its invasion of Jordan.

21   YUGOSLAVIA - Tito announces he will be succeeded by a
            collective leadership when he leaves office.

22   UAR - An emergency meeting of the Arab League heads of
            state, to be held in Cairo, is postponed when Jordan
            and the Palestinians refuse to attend.

22   UNITED STATES - The government announces a decision to
            resume arms shipments to Greece.

23   SOUTH VIET NAM - VC sappers blow up an ammunition ship
            being unloaded at Cam Ranh Bay, MR 1.

23   JORDAN - Jordanian forces rout a large commando force
        supported by Syrian tanks.

24   JORDAN - Prime Minister Daoud resigns and disappears
        into Egypt.

25   UNITED STATES - The government warns the USSR against
        the construction of a strategic submarine base in
        Cuba, following a Defense Department report that such
        a facility is already under construction.

25   JORDAN - A new cease-fire is put into effect as Jor-
        danian forces surround Palestinian positions.

26   NORTHERN IRELAND - Fighting breaks out in the streets
        of Belfast following a soccer game.

26   JORDAN - King Hussein appoints a new military-civilian
        government headed by Shmed Toukan.

28   EGYPT - President Gamal Abdul Nasser dies of a heart
        attack in Cairo after attending the arrival ceremonies
        for the Arab League conference, which had been re-
        scheduled to this date.

28   UNITED STATES - The President cancels naval manuevers
        in the Mediterranean that had been designed to demon-
        strate the US presence.

29   JORDAN - The last passengers from the hijacked air-
        liners are released after some of the demanded terror-
        ists are released from European jails.

29   INDIA - Heavy fighting between government troops and
        rebels breaks out in the Khasi Hills in the
        northeastern state of Nagaland.

30   USSR - The government denies the US allegation that it
        is building a submarine base in Cuba.

OCTOBER

5   SIERRA LEONE - Prime Minister Siaka Stevens announces
        the discovery of an army plot to overthrow the govern-
        ment. A state of emergency is declared.

5   CANADA - French-Canadian terrorists kidnap British
        diplomat James R. Cross in Montreal.

5   SOUTH VIET NAM - RVNAF announces that the siege at
        Fire Base O'Reilly has been lifted. The onset of the
        monsoon season has caused a VC/NVA withdrawal from the
        area.

6   BOLIVIA - President Alfredo Ovando Candia is forced to
            resign by a right-wing military junta led by Chief of
            Staff General Rogelio Miranda. During the confusion of
            the next 24 hours a left-wing coup, led by recently
            dismissed Commander-in-Chief of the Armed Forces Gen-
            eral Juan Jose Torres Gonzales, takes over the
            presidency.

7   EGYPT - The National Assembly designates Anwar el
            Sadat, a loyal Nasserite, as President.

7   UNITED STATES - President Nixon proposes a peace plan
            for SEA which includes a standstill cease-fire and a
            new Indochina peace conference.

7   COMMUNIST CHINA - The government announces the signing
            of a military assistance pact with North Viet Nam.

7-18   ITALY - Serious rioting breaks out again in Reggio
            Calabria when the regional seat of government is moved
            to the rival city of Catanzaro.

8   USSR - The government denies any complicity in the
            Middle East truce violations.

9   CAMBODIA - The Legislature votes to end the monarchy
            and declares itself the Khmer Republic.

10   FIJI - The former British island colony is declared
            independent.

10   CANADA - French-Canadian terrorists kidnap the Quebec
            Minister of Labor, Pierre Laporte, from his Montreal
            home.

10   COMMUNIST CHINA - The arrival of a new Soviet Ambassa-
            dor, Vasily S. Tolstikov, marks the resumption of full
            diplomatic relations between China and the USSR. A
            Chinese Ambassador arrives in Moscow on 22 November.

11   SOUTH VIET NAM - The US military strength ceiling of
            384,000 set for 15 October is attained.

11   CHAD - Heavy fighting is reported between French
            troops and rebel forces.

11   BERMUDA - Government troops are called out to put down
            the increasingly serious violence fostered by Black
            Power advocates.

12   UNITED STATES - President Nixon announces the
            withdrawal (Phase V) of 40,000 troops from SVN by
            Christmas.

13   UNITED STATES - Sir Robert Thompson reports to President Nixon that, in his opinion, the VC infrastructure has not been destroyed, and that the basic political problem in SVN remains unsolved.

13   CANADA - The government recognizes Communist China.

14   EGYPT - Anwar el Sadat is formally elected President.

14   NORTH VIET NAM - The government formally rejects the latest US peace proposal.

16   ITALY - Italian troops are sent to Reggio Calabria to put down a months-long period of violence stemming from the unpopular selection of a capital (Catazano) for the region.

16   FRANCE - The government announces that all French troops will be withdrawn from Chad during 1971.

17   JORDAN - Heavy fighting erupts between government troops and Palestinian commandos.

17   UNITED STATES - The government admits it has been arming and training Ethiopian forces since 1960.

18   CANADA - The body of kidnapped Labor Minister Pierre Laporte is found near Montreal.

19   BURUNDI - An unsuccessful military coup attempt by Hutu (Bahutu) tribesmen leads to a bloody conflict between the Hutu and Watusis. Almost all Hutu leaders are subsequently killed.

21   JORDAN - The government announces that Iraqi troops have begun a withdrawal from Jordanian territory.

22   CHILE - The government declares a state of emergency following the assassination of the army commander, General Rene Schneider Chereau.

26   BURMA - Heavy fighting is reported in northern Burma as Communist rebel forces open a major offensive in the region.

28   GREAT BRITAIN - The government announces it will keep military forces in SEA and will increase its military commitment to NATO.

29   LAOS - The government accepts a Pathet Lao peace proposal.

30   NORTHERN IRELAND - A four-hour street battle in Belfast marks the beginning of a new wave of violence.

30   USSR - A Soviet airliner is hijacked at Smolny Airport
            and diverted to Turkey.

31   SOUTH VIET NAM - President Thieu reiterates his rejec-
            tion of the concept of a coalition government with the
            Communists.

NOVEMBER

1   CAMBODIA - Cambodia becomes the Khmer Republic (GKR)
            when the National Assembly ends a 2,000-year-old
            monarchy.

2   INDIA - Security forces in West Bengal are given
            authority to use deadly force to help suppress the
            pro-Communist Naxalite violence in that state.

2   FINLAND - The SALT talks resume in Helsinki.

4   CHILE - Salvador Allende Gossens, an avowed Marxist,
            becomes President.

4   UNITED NATIONS - The General Assembly adopts a reso-
            lution calling for a 90-day extension of the Middle
            East truce.

4   UNITED STATES - The Defense Department announces a
            decision to withdraw the US infantry division deployed
            along the DMZ in Korea.

5   SOUTH VIET NAM - US intelligence sources report a mas-
            sive supply build-up in southern NVN.

6   ISRAEL - Two Arab terrorists bombs explode in the Tel
            Aviv central bus station. One person is killed.

8   UAR - Along with Libya and the Sudan, the UAR pledges
            to work for a tripartite confederation.

8   SOUTH VIET NAM - A combined RVNAF-Cambodian offensive
            begins which is aimed at opening the road to Phnom
            Penh.

8   EAST GERMANY - The government offers to negotiate a
            Berlin access treaty with West Germany, if the Allies
            leave the city.

9   FRANCE - Charles DeGaulle dies.

9   KHMER REPUBLIC - NVN and VC troops open an offensive
            to take the important Mekong River ferry crossing at
            Kompong Cham north of Phnom Penh.

12   CHILE - The government of President Salvador Allende Gossens announces its decision to resume diplomatic relations with Cuba.

13   SYRIA - A military coup ousts the civilian government of Nureddin al-Attassi and places Lieutenant General Hafez al-Assad, the Defense Minister, in power as Prime Minister on 19 November.

13   GUATEMALA - President Carlos Arana Osorio declares a 30-day state of emergency to halt a wave of terrorism sweeping his country.

14   GUATEMALA - Guatemalan naval units open fire on Salvadoran fishing boats off Guatemala's Pacific coast.

16   JORDAN - King Hussein rejects bilateral peace talks with Israel amid rumors that the talks are being held in secret.

17   SOUTH VIET NAM - The huge US Air Base at Bien Hoa, just north of Saigon, is hit with rocket fire. Four are killed, 30 wounded. Many aircraft and buildings are damaged.

18   WEST GERMANY - The government normalizes relations with Poland and recognizes the "Oder-Neisse Line" as Poland's western boundary.

18   THAILAND - The government announces that it will withdraw all of its forces in SVN by 1972.

19   INDIA - The government expresses its opposition to the construction of US, Soviet, and British naval bases in the Indian Ocean.

20   UNITED STATES - Staff Sergeant David Mitchell is acquitted of murder charges growing out of the My Lai Massacre.

21   NORTH VIET NAM - A daring US helicopter-borne raid is carried out to free those held in a POW enclosure at Son Tay, 23 miles from Hanoi. Although the raid is successful in its execution, the camp is found to be empty.

21   SOUTH VIET NAM - A NVN trawler attempting to infiltrate Kien Hoa Province in MR 4 is challenged by "Operation MARKET TIME" naval units. The trawler attempts to ram USS Endurance and then attempts to evade capture. It is finally sunk in shallow water where it is determined that it is carrying a large quantity of ammunition.

22   SOUTH VIET NAM - MACV confirms that the US 23rd
            (America) Division employed the herbicide "Agent
            Orange" during May-August 1970, in violation of DOD
            instructions.

22-24   GUINEA - A Portuguese-organized seaborne attack by
            about 350 men on the capital city of Conakry takes
            place. Two army camps are occupied, and the city's
            main jail is emptied. About 100 Guineans are killed
            and 100 of the invaders are captured when government
            forces retake the city. President Sekou Toure accuses
            (8 December) the Portuguese of masterminding the
            attack.

23   UNITED STATES - The government announces that a Soviet
            Lithuanian defector who jumped from his vessel to the
            deck of the US Coast Guard Cutter Vigilant off
            Martha's Vineyard, Massachusetts, was returned to
            Soviet control. President Nixon orders an immediate
            investigation that subsequently accuses the cutter's
            skipper, Commander Ralph W. Eustis, the Commandant of
            the First Coast Guard District, and his Chief of Staff
            of dereliction. Eustis is relieved of command and the
            two others are retired (21 December).

25-26   MALAYSIA - Government aircraft attack and bomb rebel
            guerrilla bases in Sarawak, East Malaysia, close to
            the Indonesian border.

27   SYRIA - The government announces it is joining the
            UAR, Sudan, and Libya in forming a new Arab con-
            federation.

28   ISRAEL - The government announces that one of its
            patrol boats sank a UAR launch in the Gulf of Suez.

29   UNITED STATES - Along with Great Britain and France,
            the US warns the Soviet Union that further East German
            interruptions of traffic between West Germany and
            Berlin will jeopardize the planned talks on Berlin.

30   SOUTH YEMEN - The country changes its name to the
            People's Democratic Republic of Yemen.

DECEMBER

1   SPAIN - The West German Honorary Consul in San Sabas-
            tian, Eugen Beihl, is kidnapped by Basque terrorists
            of the ETA group who demand the release of 16 ETA mem-
            bers who are to be tried by a military court on 3
            December.

1   ETHIOPIA - The government recognizes Communist China.

2   SOUTH VIET NAM - The VC clandestine radio station an-
         nounces that VC/NVA forces will observe an eight-day
         Christmas-New Year truce, and a four-day truce at Tet.

3   CANADA - British diplomat, James R. Cross, who was
         kidnapped 5 October, is released by French Canadian
         terrorists as they are being flown to Cuba.

7   WEST GERMANY - The government formally signs
         (initialed 18 October) a treaty with Poland that re-
         cognizes the "Oder-Neisse Line" as the demarcation
         between Germany and Poland. This effectively cedes
         40,000 square miles (or approximately one-quarter of
         the landmass) of German territory to Poland.

7   BRAZIL - The Swiss Ambassador in Rio de Janeiro,
         Giovanni Enrico Bucher, is kidnapped by terrorists of
         the National Liberation Alliance (ALN). He is released
         on 16 January 1971.

8   SOUTH VIET NAM - Violent anti-American demonstrations
         take place in Qui Nhon City in MR 2 following the
         shooting of a Vietnamese youth on 7 December. The city
         is put off-limits to US personnel.

10   FRANCE - The two sides in the SEA peace talks call for
         an immediate prisoner exchange.

10   UNITED STATES - President Nixon warns of more bombings
         of NVN if US forces in SEA are endangered by the
         buildup of NVA/VC forces during the withdrawal period.

11   UNITED STATES - Secretary of Defense Laird says US
         forces will remain in SVN until all PWs are released
         by NVN.

12   NORTH VIET NAM - The government condemns President
         Nixon's bombing threats.

14   POLAND - Rioting over food shortages begins in Gdansk
         (formerly Danzig) and quickly spreads to other cities.
         The unrest is finally put down by the police and army
         with great loss of life.

14   SPAIN - The government authorizes the police emergency
         powers as tension grows over the trial of 16 Basque
         terrorists.

14-19   POLAND - Severe rioting over food prices breaks out
         among workers in Gdansk, Gdynia, Szczecin, and other
         towns. Security forces are used to restore order.

15   KHMER REPUBLIC - ARVN forces are airlifted to Kompong
            Cham to help thwart the NVA offensive.

16   THE NETHERLANDS - Fifty nations sign a convention
            calling for severe punishments for those convicted of
            hijacking civilian airliners.

16   ETHIOPIA - The government declares a state of emer-
            gency in the Eritrean provincial area in the face of
            growing guerrilla activity.

17   FRANCE - The North Vietnamese delegation asks the US
            for a reasonable deadline for the withdrawal of its
            forces from SEA.

18   FINLAND - The Helsinki SALT talks recess.

19   UNITED NATIONS - Guinean President Sekou Toure asks
            the UN to investigate his charges that Portugal is
            massing troops on the Guinean border.

19   EAST GERMANY - Authorities again impede travel between
            West Germany and Berlin.

20   OKINAWA - Serious fighting breaks out at Koza between
            US forces stationed on Okinawa and anti-American
            rioters. This rioting continues sporadically until 31
            December.

20   POLAND - Wladyslaw Gomulka and other members of the
            Polish Politburo are forced to resign. Edvard Gierek
            is named the new Party Secretary.

21   CAMBODIA - Government forces begin an offensive to
            open the main supply route between Phnom Penh and the
            Gulf of Siam.

21   UNITED STATES - The Defense Department announces that
            12,000 US troops will be withdrawn from Japan by
            mid-1971.

22   EAST GERMANY - The road between West Berlin and West
            Germany is opened after four days.

22   NORTH VIET NAM - The government releases a "defini-
            tive" number of US prisoners of war.

24   SPAIN - The West German Consul to San Sabastian is
            released by his kidnappers.

28   CANADA - Three French Canadians are arrested near
            Montreal in connection with the kidnap and murder of
            Labor Minister Laporte.

28   SPAIN - All 16 Basques accused of terrorist activities
        are found guilty; six are sentenced to death.

29   UAR - President Anwar Sadat orders a state of war-
        readiness as Arab guerrillas in Jordan, Lebanon, and
        Syria step up terrorist attacks against Israel.

31   EGYPT - There are 200 Soviet pilots, about 15,000
        Soviet troops at SAM sites, and about 4,000 other
        Soviet military personnel in Egypt. More than 85
        Soviet-manned SAM sites exist along with about 150
        Soviet-manned MiG-21J fighters at six Soviet-
        controlled airfields.

31   SOUTH VIET NAM - Phase V of the Redeployment Program
        is reported completed (30 December). US troop strength
        is 335,794. Other Allied forces number 67,444. Losses
        for 1970 include 7,171 US dead. Total US deaths is now
        44,441.

Notes

1971

ETHIOPIA - The Eritrean Liberation Front (ELF) takes over leadership of the struggle against the central government in Addis Ababa in the protracted insurgency that began in 1964.

RHODESIA - A long period of black insurgency begins against the white government.

JANUARY

2   UNITED STATES - President Nixon states that, although the US will continue winding down its involvement in SVN, 25,000 American troops will remain there until all US prisoners of war are released.

4   CANADA - Four French-Canadian separatists are charged in the assassination of Quebec Labor Minister Pierre Laporte.

4   SOUTH VIET NAM - The last US Special Forces border camp in the Central Highlands is turned over to ARVN Special Forces control.

5   CHILE - The government recognizes Communist China.

5-7   USSR - A Soviet military court in Leningrad sentences Vulf Zalmanson to ten years imprisonment for his part in the Smolny Airport hijacking incident.

6   SOUTH VIET NAM - A VC/NVA mortar attack on Qui Nhon destroys an estimated 6,300 tons of ARVN ammunition.

7   JORDAN - Heavy fighting is reported between Jordanian army units and Palestinian commandos.

8   URUGUAY - Tupamaro terrorists kidnap the British Ambassador, Geoffrey Jackson, in Montevideo. The kidnappers demand the release of 150 political prisoners held by the Uruguayan government.

8   UNITED STATES - A bomb explodes outside the USSR Cultural Building in Washington, DC.

9   SOUTH VIET NAM - USMACV announces that US aircraft have attacked a missile site in NVN after the site's radar locked on to an American reconnaissance aircraft.

11   BOLIVIA - President Torres announces he has crushed a right-wing coup d'etat attempt by the army.

12   SOUTH VIET NAM - South Vietnamese naval units begin convoying supply ships up the Mekong River to the Cambodian capital city of Phnom Penh.

13-25   CAMBODIA - A joint Cambodian-ARVN operation begins to reopen the road between Phnom Penh and Kompong Som. The operation has heavy US air support.

14   JORDAN - A cease-fire agreement ends fighting between Jordanian forces and Palestinian commandos.

14   LEBANON - Israeli forces carry out a heliborne attack on a Palestinian commando base 28 miles inside the Lebanese border.

16   BRAZIL - Brazilian terrorists release kidnapped Swiss Ambassador Giovanni Enrico Bucher after forty days captivity.

18   UNITED STATES - The government announces it is suspending aid to Ecuador because of its continued violations of freedom of seas in the seizure of US tuna boats outside the 12-mile limit. Ecuador has claimed a 200-mile limit.

21   SIERRA LEONE - There is an unsuccessful coup attempt carried out by the army against the government of Prime Minister Siaka Stevens.

22   CAMBODIA - South Vietnamese and Cambodian forces successfully complete the operation clearing Route 4 between Kompong Som (Sihanoukville) on the Gulf of Thailand coast and Phnom Penh when they link up at Pich Nil Pass (Col de Pich Nil). At the same time, however, guerrilla forces (possibly Viet Cong) attack the air-

22   CAMBODIA (Cont'd) - field at Phnom Penh destroying
        nearly 95% of the Cambodian Air Force's aircraft. Also
        on this date, Communist artillery shells Phnom Penh
        airport for the first time.

23   EGYPT - The government announces it has rejected a US
        proposal to extend the Suez cease-fire past the 5 Feb-
        ruary deadline.

25   UGANDA - While visiting Singapore, President Milton
        Obote is overthrown by a military coup led by Major
        General Idi Amin. Amin begins an immediate campaign of
        liquidating his opposition.

26   UNITED STATES - The Defense Department admits that a
        special undercover team has been landed in Phnom Penh,
        Cambodia, to recover a number a damaged helicopters.

26   SOUTH KOREA - The government reports it is in full ac-
        cord with the planned reduction of 20,000 US troops
        stationed in South Korea. A modernization of ROKAF is
        an expected part of the plan.

27   UNITED STATES - In response to Senator Frank Church's
        unfounded charge, made in a letter to President Nixon
        (22 January 1971), that the US was planning to expand
        its biological warfare (BW) testing facility at Fort
        Douglas, Deseret, Utah, the White House announces the
        closing of the BW Development Center at Pine Bluff,
        Arkansas. All BW weapons are to be destroyed.

27   CAMBODIA - Cambodian forces open an offensive in the
        region west and northwest of Phnom Penh.

27   OAS - Ecuador files a formal protest charging the US
        violated its established fishing limits.

30   SOUTH VIET NAM - "Operation DEWEY CANYON" begins. This
        operation is designed to clear the area just south of
        the DMZ so as to establish the necessary bases and
        lines of communication for an anticipated ARVN drive
        into Laos.

FEBRUARY

1   ECUADOR - The government orders the withdrawal of the
        US Military Mission because of deadlocked negotiations
        over fishing rights.

2   OAS - The OAS Foreign Ministers sign a convention
        denying sanctuary and asylum to kidnappers of foreign
        representatives.

3   SOUTH VIET NAM - The RVNAF renews its offensive in
         Cambodia. The US Command announces it is furnishing
         full air support for the operations in the "Parrot's
         Beak" and "Fishhook" near the border.

3   FINLAND - The USSR accuses the US of negotiating in
         bad faith at the SALT discussions in Helsinki because
         they refuse to include fighter-bombers in the talks.

3   NORTHERN IRELAND - Roman Catholic civilians battle
         British troops in Belfast.

4   EGYPT - President Sadat accepts a 30-day extension of
         the Suez truce and offers to reopen the Suez Canal if
         the Israelis withdraw from its east bank.

6   NORTHERN IRELAND - In an incident in Belfast, the
         first British soldier is killed. This is the first
         fatality since British forces were moved into Ulster
         in 1969.

8   SOUTH VIET NAM - "Operation LAM SON 719" begins. The
         ARVN 1st Infantry Division and 1st Armored Brigade
         cross into Laos with American support to cut NVA lo-
         gistics lines along the Ho Chi Minh Trail. Although no
         US troops cross the border, the operation achieves
         some success in the eventual capture of Tchepone
         (Xenon) (6 March), an important supply depot for the
         NVA. The gross incompetence and personal cowardice of
         the senior South Vietnamese commander limits the ef-
         fectiveness of the operation. When the operation term-
         inates on 8 April, however, ARVN claims 13,462 enemy
         are killed and 56 captured. Tons of supplies are
         taken, including 106 tanks, 425 trucks, 5,066 individ-
         ual and 1,935 crew-served weapons. ARVN loses 1,531
         killed, 5,400 wounded, and 650 missing. US losses
         include 176 killed, 1,042 wounded, and 42 missing.

9   ISRAEL - The government rejects the latest Egyptian
         offer.

10   CAMBODIA - Lon Nol suffers a stroke and is paralyzed.

11   UNITED STATES - The US joins more than 60 other coun-
         tries in signing a treaty prohibiting the emplacement
         of nuclear weapons "on the seabed and the ocean floor
         and in the subsoil thereof."

11   JORDAN - Clashes are reported near Amman between Jor-
         danian forces and Palestinian commandos.

11   SOUTH KOREA - The ROKAF assumes responsibility for the
         protection of the armistice border after the reduction
         of US troop strength.

13   SOUTH VIET NAM - The US Command imposes a 24-hour cur-
            few for American personnel in Qui Nhon following two
            days of anti-American demonstrations that were caused
            by an accidental shooting of a student by an American.

15   ISRAEL - Defying world opinion, Israel prepares to
            open new settlements in lands captured during the 1967
            war.

17   ITALY - There is renewed violence in Reggio Calabria
            after the move of the regional capital to Catanzaro is
            confirmed by the Regional Council.

17   ISRAEL - Foreign Minister Abba Eben states that re-
            tention of some of the lands captured in the 1967 war
            was a precondition to any peace settlement.

17   LAOS - Heavy fighting is reported in "Operation LAM
            SON 719."

17   SYRIA - The government resumes diplomatic relations
            with Tunisia.

18   EGYPT - The government states it is willing to sign a
            peace treaty with Israel if Israel withdraws from all
            captured Arab land.

20   LAOS - South Vietnamese advances in "Operation LAM SON
            719" are stalled. US air support is hampered by in-
            creasingly heavy enemy antiaircraft fire.

20   SOUTH VIET NAM - USMACV announces that herbicides will
            no longer be used in SVN. The only exceptions will be
            the clearing of areas around Allied firebases.

21   URUGUAY - Tupamaro terrorists release Brazilian diplo-
            mat Aloysio Dias Gomide. The Brazilian has been held
            captive for seven months and is released only after a
            ransom of about one-half million dollars is paid to
            the kidnappers.

21   PAKISTAN - President Yahya Khan dissolves his civilian
            cabinet because of a dispute arising from the question
            of East Pakistani autonomy.

22   EGYPT - The government warns that Israel's refusal to
            withdraw from the occupied Arab territories creates a
            "dangerous situation."

23   UNITED STATES - The Defense Department reports that
            recent ARVN operations in Laos have failed to stem the
            flow of supplies from NVN into the south.

23   UNITED NATIONS - The Conference on Disarmament recon-
            venes in Geneva, Switzerland. The USSR urges a ban on
            all NBC weapons. The US supports a British proposal to
            ban only biological weapons.

26   COLOMBIA - A state of siege is declared as rioting in
            the city of Cali begins to spread to other locales.

28   SOUTH VIET NAM - US armor moves into forward positions
            along the SVN-Laotian border to stop an expected NVA
            tank attack.

29   SOUTH VIET NAM - At least 50 "protective reaction"
            strikes are reported against missile sites in NVN over
            the past week.

MARCH

1   UNITED STATES - A bomb explodes in the Senate wing of
            the US Capitol. The blast causes extensive damage.

1   SOUTH VIET NAM - The last elements of the US 5th
            Special Forces Group leave SVN.

1   SYRIA - The government resumes diplomatic relations
            with Morocco.

1-5   PAKISTAN - Widespread rioting breaks out when it is
            announced that the recently elected National Assembly
            will not be convened. By 5 March the rioting is de-
            clared a popular uprising in East Pakistan by the
            government.

2-3   WARSAW PACT - At a defense ministers meeting in
            Budapest a decision is reached to strengthen the WP
            armies because of the "unceasing strengthening of the
            aggressive NATO bloc."

3   SOUTH VIET NAM - For the first time in the war NVA
            antiaircraft bases in NVN begin firing on US aircraft
            flying over SVN.

4   TURKEY - Four US airmen are kidnapped by Turkish
            terrorists.

5   EGYPT - At the close of an eight-day conference, the
            Palestinian National Council agrees to place all revo-
            lutionary forces under a single command.

6   LAOS - ARVN forces committed to "Operation LAM SON
            719" capture the strategically important town of
            Tchepone (Xenon) on Route 9.

6   THE PHILIPPINES - New government military operations
         against the Muslim insurgents in Mindinao are ordered
         by President Marcos.

7   EGYPT - President Sadat states the cease-fire will not
         be extended.

8   TURKEY - The four American airmen, who were kidnapped
         on 4 March by Turkish leftists, are released unharmed.

8   UNITED STATES - Captain Ernest L. Medina is ordered to
         stand trial for his part in the My Lai Massacre of
         March 1968.

8   PORTUGAL - Members of the Revolutionary Armed Action,
         an urban guerrilla group, sabotage Portuguese aircraft
         at a military base near Lisbon in a protest of govern-
         ment policies in Africa.

10   USSR - About 100 Soviet Jews occupy the Supreme Soviet
         office building in Moscow demanding the right to
         emigrate.

10   URUGUAY - Attorney General Berro Oribe is kidnapped by
         Tupamaro terrorists who interrogate him concerning the
         upcoming prosecution of Tupamaro leaders currently
         held by the police. He is released unharmed on 23
         March.

11   LAOS - ARVN forces are reported to be withdrawing from
         Tchepone in the face of growing numbers of NVA forces.

11   MIDDLE EAST - The PLO rejects hijacking as an allow-
         able political action.

12   TURKEY - The government of Prime Minister Suleyman
         Demirel falls when the military issues a series of
         reform demands.

12   ISRAEL - Prime Minister Golda Mier announces that her
         government will demand retention of some occupied
         territory and the demilitarization of the Sinai as a
         part of any peace settlement.

12   SYRIA - Hafez al-Assad is elected to a seven-year term
         as president after having assumed the powers of that
         office on 22 February.

15   EAST PAKISTAN - Local officials assume administrative
         contol of their province. Pakistani President Agha
         Mohammed Yahya Khan opens talks on self-rule in Dacca.

15   SOUTH VIET NAM - Khe Sanh, the support base for the
            incursion into Laos, comes under heavy mortar and
            rocket attack.

15   AUSTRIA - The fourth round of SALT discussions opens
            in Vienna.

15   MEXICO - The government announces that a group known
            as Movimiento de Accion Revolucionaria (MAR) is plot-
            ting the overthrow of the government. It is further
            charged that Moscow recruited the group and sent it to
            North Korea for training in Marxist terror tactics.

15   UNITED STATES - Intelligence sources report that the
            Soviet forces stationed in Egypt have been withdrawn
            from forward positions near the Suez, and that most of
            the SAM sites near the Suez Canal are now manned by
            Egyptians.

16   CEYLON - A state of emergency is declared. On 23 March
            the government announces it has uncovered a plot by
            the People's Liberation Front (PLF), that is led by
            Moscow-trained Rohana Wijeweera, to overthrow the
            government.

16   SYRIA - President Assad reports the formation of a
            joint Egyptian-Syrian military command to control all
            of the two nations' armed forces.

18   MEXICO - Five Soviet diplomats are expelled for their
            part in the plot to overthrow the government of
            Mexico.

21   NORTH VIET NAM - US aircraft attack NVA missile sites
            in retaliation for NVA attacks against US aircraft
            flying over Laos.

22   ZAMBIA - President Kenneth Kuanda accuses Portugal of
            imposing an economic blockade on his country when
            Portuguese authorities delay shipments of supplies in
            reprisal for the deaths of a number of people killed
            after being kidnapped from Mozambique.

22-23   ARGENTINA - The government of President Levingston is
            overthrown in a bloodless military coup led by General
            Alejandro Agustin Lanusse. Lanusse assumes the
            presidency on 25 March.

23   SIERRA LEONE - A military coup, this time led by the
            Army's commander, fails for the second time in three
            months. Prime Minister Siaka Stevens asks Guinea for
            assistance and signs a mutual defense pact (26 March).
            Guinean troops enter Sierra Leone to restore order (28
            March).

24   PAKISTAN - Martial law is declared following President Yahya Khan's visit to East Pakistan where a revolt against the West Pakistani-oriented central government is in progress.

24   SOUTH VIET NAM - The government announces that its 44-day old operation in Laos has come to a close. All but about 500 of the 20,000 troops involved have been withdrawn.

25   EAST PAKISTAN - Full scale fighting breaks out in East Pakistan after predominantly West Pakistan army troops attempt to enforce the martial law order.

26   EAST PAKISTAN - Sheikh Mujibur Rahman declares East Pakistan independent as the State of Bangladesh. Mujibur is later arrested by Pakistani authorities.

26   JORDAN - More heavy fighting is reported between Jordanian and Palestinian guerrilla forces.

28   UNITED STATES - Intelligence sources reveal a massive Soviet airlift in Egypt over the last two weeks.

28   SOUTH VIET NAM - NVA forces attack Fire Base Mary Ann south of Da Nang, killing 33 and wounding 76 US personnel. An investigation later reveals gross incompetence on the part of five US officers.

29   UNITED STATES - The Army court martial of Lieutenant William H. Calley, who is accused of leading the platoon that massacred the inhabitants of the Vietnamese village of My Lai, ends in his conviction. He is subsequently released after serving only a few months of his life sentence.

30   UNITED NATIONS - The USSR reverses its position at the Geneva Conference and supports a ban only on biological weapons.

31   INDIA - The government accuses Pakistan of committing genocide in East Pakistan.

APRIL

1   MALAGASY REPUBLIC - Government forces crush a leftist uprising in Tulear Province in the southern part of the country.

1   EGYPT - President Sadat offers to extend the Suez cease-fire if Israel will agree to a partial withdrawal of forces from the canal's east bank.

1   SOUTH VIET NAM - The US Navy formally ends its river-
           ine mission and its role in SVN.

1   WEST GERMANY - Members of the Bolivian terrorist or-
           ganization Ejercito Liberacion Nacional (ELN) assas-
           sinate a former Bolivian Secret Police official,
           Roberto Quintanilla, in Hamburg.

2   JORDAN - Palestinian guerrillas announce a military
           campaign within Jordan to force King Hussein to re-
           lieve Prime Minister Wasfi al-Tal and army commanders
           hostile to the PLO.

2   PAKISTAN - The government formally protests Indian
           support of East Pakistan.

2   EGYPT - Western intelligence sources report heavy
           shipments of Soviet military equipment, especially
           surface-to-air missiles, to Egypt.

4   JORDAN - The PLO announces it will adhere to the 1970
           peace agreement.

5   CEYLON - A PLF uprising begins against the leftist-
           controlled government of Prime Minister Madame Siri-
           mavo Bandaranaike. The PLF fails in an attempt to
           assassinate the Prime Minister. During an amnesty
           period that expired on 4 March, about 4,000 PLF mem-
           bers had turned themselves in. It is the hard core
           remainder that begins the uprising on 5 April.

6   CEYLON - The government imposes a nationwide curfew to
           help control the violence.

7   MALI - There is an unsuccessful coup attempt against
           the government of Moussa Traore.

7   UNITED STATES - The Defense Department announces a
           substantial increase in military aid to Jordan.

7   SOUTH VIET NAM - USMACV announces that President Nixon
           has ordered another 100,000 US troops out of SVN by
           December 1971. The new ceiling authorization is to be
           184,000.

7   SWEDEN - Two Croatian terrorists enter the Yugoslavian
           Embassy in Stockholm on the pretext of applying for
           passports and shoot the Yugoslav Ambassador Vladimir
           Rolovic and another Yugoslav. The Ambassador dies of
           his wounds on 15 April.

8   EAST PAKISTAN - Pakistani troops open an offensive
           against independence forces in the western region of
           the country.

9   JORDAN - Syrian mediators are able to arrange a truce
           between the Jordanian army and Palestinian guerrillas.

12   SOUTH VIET NAM - Allied naval and air units engage and
           sink a NVN infiltration trawler in SVN territorial
           waters off southern MR 4.

12   PAKISTAN - A major military offensive begins against
           the breakaway factions in East Pakistan.

13   CEYLON - Fighting in the cities has generally subsided
           but continues throughout the countryside.

13   SOUTH VIET NAM - The two-week-long siege of Fire Base
           6 in the Central Highlands is lifted by an ARVN relief
           column.

13   JORDAN - PLO forces withdraw from Amman.

14   SOUTH VIET NAM - Headquarters, III Marine Amphibious
           Force leaves SVN with the 1st Marine Division and the
           1st Marine Air Wing. The US Marines formally end their
           role in SVN.

17   MIDDLE EAST - Egypt, Libya, and Syria agree to form a
           Federation of Arab Republics.

17   NORTH VIET NAM - US aircraft begin a new campaign of
           attacking NVA antiaircraft missile sites.

19   FRANCE - The government warns Libya not to attempt to
           sell any of its Mirage fighters to the newly organized
           federation of Libya, Syria, and the UAR.

19   SIERRA LEONE - The former British dominion is declared
           a republic, but remains in the British Commonwealth.

19-24   UNITED STATES - A series of mass demonstrations pro-
           testing the war in SEA takes place in Washington and
           San Francisco. An estimated 200,000 rally in Washing-
           ton, 156,000 in San Francisco.

20   CEYLON - The government announces that the Soviet
           Union is supplying it with helicopters and MiG-17
           fighters. Intelligence reports indicate Soviet pilots
           attend the aircraft. Other reports indicate the gov-
           ernment is also receiving aid from Great Britain,
           India, the UAR, the US, and Yugoslavia.

20   CAMBODIA - A government crisis follows Premier Lon
           Nol's announcement of his resignation for health
           reasons.

21   HAITI - President Francois "Papa Doc" Duvalier dies.
            His son, Jean-Claude "Baby Doc," succeeds him.

22   VENEZUELA - The closure of the University of Caracus
            causes a wave of violence at other universities around
            the country.

23   BULGARIA - The government offers to sign nonaggression
            treaties with all of its Balkan neighbors and with all
            European countries.

23   SOUTH VIET NAM - Phase VI of the US withdrawal is com-
            pleted a week ahead of schedule. Phase VII begins im-
            mediately.

26   EL SALVADOR - The government resumes diplomatic re-
            lations with Honduras.

29   UNITED STATES - The number of US troops killed in com-
            bat in SVN now exceeds 45,000.

MAY

1   EGYPT - President Sadat reiterates his demand that
            Israeli forces pull back from the east bank of the
            Suez Canal as a precondition for a meaningful peace
            settlement.

2   EGYPT - The Vice President, Ali Sabri, is dismissed
            from office.

3   UNITED STATES - A massive anti-war demonstration in
            Washington, DC, fails in its goal to close down the
            federal government. More than 7,000 are arrested.

4   CEYLON - The government reports that more than 1,700
            rebels have surrendered during a four-day amnesty
            period.

5   PAKISTAN - Central government forces complete the
            bloody repression of the revolt in East Pakistan,
            although they had announced the uprising had been
            crushed on 30 March. Some estimates show more than
            100,000 killed. Six million East Pakistanis and
            Bengalis flee into India.

5   SOMALIA - An apparently foiled coup attempt, led by
            Vice-President Muhammad Ainanshe Guleid, leads to
            Guleid's arrest and the arrest of a number of his
            associates.

6   GREECE - The government resumes diplomatic relations,
            that were broken in 1941, with Albania.

6   UNITED STATES - A major crackdown begins on all US personnel and mail leaving SVN as the US Customs Service looks for hard narcotics entering the US from SEA.

8   UNITED STATES - A pro-war demonstration is held in Washington, DC.

10   PAKISTAN - Most opposition to the Pakistani military campaign in East Pakistan is ended.

11   SUDAN - The Communist Party is ordered dissolved.

12   UNITED STATES - The US endorses the Denuclearization of Latin America Treaty proposed by the UN.

12   ARGENTINA - There is an attempt to overthrow the government of President Lanusse.

13   EGYPT - President Sadat, sensing a plot against his leadership, purges anti-moderate and pro-Russian elements in the government and in the military, jailing many in the process.

13   SOUTH VIET NAM - The NVA opens a new offensive in the A Shau Valley.

14   EGYPT - President Sadat reports he has foiled a coup against his government.

14   USSR - General Secretary Leonid Brezhnev asks the West to begin negotiations leading to troop reductions in Europe.

14   CEYLON - A Soviet military mission signs an agreement to supply aircraft and military equipment to Ceylon.

17   LAOS - The government reports that NVA forces have captured the last strategic position in the Bolovens (Bolevon) Plateau region of the country.

17   TURKEY - Terrorists of the Turkish People's Liberation Party (TPLP/F) kidnap the Israeli Consul General, Ephraim Elrom, in Istanbul and demand the release of political prisoners as ransom.

19   UNITED STATES - The Senate defeats (61-36) an amendment put forward by Senator Michael Mansfield that would have reduced US troop strength in Europe by 50% (150,000 troops) by the end of the year.

21   SOUTH VIET NAM - Fire Base Charlie-2, southeast of Hue, sustains a rocket attack that kills 30 US servicemen and wounds 50 others.

22   URUGUAY – The government offers a $50,000 reward for information on the whereabouts of the kidnapped British Ambassador.

23   SOUTH VIET NAM – VC sappers blow up the aviation fuel dump at US air base at Cam Ranh Bay. Almost two million gallons of aviation fuel are lost.

23   TURKEY – The murdered body of kidnapped Israeli diplomat, Ephriam Elrom, is found in Istanbul in an apartment less than a quarter-mile from the building housing the Israeli Consulate.

23   ARGENTINA – The Honorary British Consul in Rosario is kidnapped by members of the Ejercito Revolucionario del Pueblo (ERP). He is released when $100,000 is given to the poor.

25   SOMALIA – There is an unsuccessful coup attempt.

28   EGYPT – A 15-year Treaty of Friendship and Cooperation is signed by President Sadat and the Soviet Union's president, Nikolai Podgorny.

31   CAMBODIA – NVA forces drive elements of the ARVN 5th Division out of Snoul, at the junction of Routes 1 and 13, with heavy loss of life and equipment. The ARVN division commander is relieved on 9 June. Snoul is a major control point for the movement of supplies through the country and a vitally important objective for both sides.

31   MALAGASY – President Philibert Tsiranana announces his government has foiled a plot to overthrow him.

JUNE

1   JORDAN – Palestinian refugees claim Jordanian police opened fire on demonstrators in a refugee camp killing ten people.

1   UNITED STATES – President Nixon announces that the highest priority is being given to a national offensive to counter drug addiction among US service personnel.

2   CAMBODIA – US furnishes close air support to ARVN forces operating in Cambodia.

2   ARGENTINA – ERP terrorists fail in an attempt to kidnap the Honorary Uruguayan Consul in Cordoba.

4   NORTH VIET NAM - When only 13 of 660 NVA prisoners of
        war held in SVN tell the International Red Cross that
        they are willing to go home, the NVN government can-
        cels the repatriation agreement, and refuses to accept
        the return of the 13 desirous of being freed.

5   CONGO-KINSHASA - Luvanium University is closed follow-
        ing serious student unrest and violence. All of the
        students are immediately drafted into the armed
        forces.

7   NIGERIA - The government announces it has resumed dip-
        lomatic relations with Tanzania. Relations were broken
        when Tanzania recognized the breakaway government in
        Biafra.

8   CHILE - President Allende imposes a state of emergency
        in Santiago following the assassination of a cabinet
        minister.

9   CEYLON - The government declares the rebellion to be
        over.

9   ISRAEL - The government asks the US for more aircraft
        to offset the impact of the new Soviet-UAR treaty of
        friendship.

11   LIBYA - The last US forces leave Wheelus Air Force
        Base.

11   MIDDLE EAST - Palestinian commandos attack an Israeli
        tanker in the Bab al-Mandeb Strait, which links the
        Gulf of Aden with the Red Sea.

11   SYRIA - The government of President Assad foils a coup
        attempt sponsored by the followers of former President
        Ahmed al-Khatib who was overthrown in 1970.

12   SOUTH KOREA - To lessen tensions, the United Nations
        Command recommends that both sides clear all military
        installations out of the DMZ.

13   UNITED STATES - The New York Times releases the text
        of the "Pentagon Papers," which discuss US involvement
        in SEA.

17   UNITED STATES - The government signs the Okinawa
        Reversion Treaty with Japan, which will return Okinawa
        to Japanese control in one year. A simultaneous docu-
        ment signing ceremony takes place in Tokyo.

22   BOLIVIA - A state of emergency is declared following a
        right-wing coup attempt against the Torres government.

22   SOUTH VIET NAM - VC/NVA sappers blow up 605 tons of
            ammunition in Quang Tri City.

25   MALAGASY - The US ambassador is expelled on charges of
            interference in the internal affairs of the country.

25   FRANCE - A Pathet Lao proposal to end the fighting in
            Laos is presented at the Paris peace talks.

26   CAMBODIA - Government troops report the capture of a
            vital command post used to protect infiltration routes
            from NVN through Cambodia.

26   SOUTH VIET NAM - Phase VII of the US redeployment ends
            five days early. Phase VIII begins immediately.

26   ARGENTINA - Members of the "Eva Peron Commando" free
            four prisoners held by the police in Buenos Aires.

27   SOUTH VIET NAM - Intelligence sources report that at
            least two NVA regiments have infiltrated into SVN
            across the DMZ and are contributing to the stepped-up
            activity in the northern provinces.

28   MALAYSIA - Prime Minister Tun Abdul Razak announces
            the discovery of guerrilla bases on Malaysian
            territory near Ipoh.

29-30   SOUTH VIET NAM - The ARVN ammunition dump in Qui Nhon
            is attacked by mortar fire. This time 2,775 tons of
            ammunition are lost. The next day, on 30 June, a
            second attack destroys an additional 10,000 tons of
            munitions.

30   VENEZUELA - A cache of weapons is discoverd by the
            authorities on the campus of Caracus University.

30   SOUTH VIET NAM - US strength in SVN is reported at
            239,528. There are, in addition, 66,842 Allied per-
            sonnel, while RVNAF figures reflect 1,060,129.

JULY

1   GREAT BRITAIN - The British and Argentine governments
            announce they will settle the Falkland Islands issue
            by negotiation.

1   FRANCE - NVN and VC representatives offer a
            seven-point peace plan which includes release of all
            American PWs if the US pulls out of Indochina by the
            end of 1971. The US rejects the offer (8 July), but
            private negotiations begin on the basis of the
            proposal.

4   ARGENTINA - Hijackers of a plane bound from Mexico surrender to Argentine authorities when they are refused refueling for a flight to Algeria.

5   USSR - In a joint communique issued in Moscow, Egypt and the Soviet Union state the only way the Suez Canal will reopen is for the Israelis to withdraw from all occupied territory.

5   BURUNDI - There is an unsuccessful coup attempt to overthrow the government of Michel Micombero.

6   MALAWI - Hastings Kamuzu Banda is sworn in as "President for Life."

7   UNITED STATES - The US Army begins destroying its stockpile of BW weapons, most of which are said to be stored at Pine Bluff, Arkansas.

7   ISRAEL - Four persons are killed in an Arab terrorist rocket attack in Tel Aviv.

7   UGANDA - President Idi Amin closes the border with Tanzania.

8   CAMBODIA - ARVN forces are airlifted into the area known as the "Parrot's Beak," in Svay Rieng Province, to attack NVA units and supply dumps.

8   UGANDA - President Idi Amin orders that any plane crossing the Ugandan border from Tanzania be shot down.

8   FINLAND - The fifth round of SALT talks opens in Helsinki.

8   THAILAND - Thailand begins withdrawing its forces from SVN. About 5,000 depart by the end of August.

9   SOUTH VIET NAM - Passage of responsibility for the protection of Quang Tri Province and the DMZ is completed when ARVN forces take over Fire Base Charlie-2.

10-11   MOROCCO - An attempted right-wing army coup against King Hassan II is suppressed with much bloodshed. A group of disgruntled generals induces trainees from the Ahermoumou Training Center to attack the guests at the royal birthday party at the seaside palace at Skhirat. A number of dignitaries, including three Moroccan generals and the Belgium Ambassador, are among those killed. Four generals and a number of junior officers are executed in the coup's aftermath.

11   UNITED STATES - The US Congressional Research Service
            reports that the war in SVN has caused at least one
            million civilian casualties, with 325,000 of that num-
            ber being killed.

11   UGANDA - A coup attempt against the government of Idi
            Amin by troops of the northeast garrison fails. (News
            of the coup is suppressed until 17 October.)

12   SOUTH KOREA - As a means of lessening tensions, the UN
            Command suggests the removal of all military installa-
            tions in the DMZ.

13   LAOS - Within the past week Meo tribesmen, with US CIA
            support, take control of the Plaine des Jarres.

13-19   JORDAN - Following numerous Palestinian violations of
            the terms of the 1970 cease-fire, the Jordanian army
            moves to crush further resistance in north Jordan. The
            bulk of the Palestinians are driven out of the country
            into Syria while some 2,000 of their military person-
            nel are captured. Syria threatens war but, other than
            cross-border artillery fire, does not act.

14   ICELAND - The government announces it will move to
            renegotiate its defense treaty with the US with the
            view of closing the NATO base at Keflavik.

14   URUGUAY - Tupamaro terrorists kidnap Jorge Berembau,
            an Argentinian industrialist, in Montevideo. He is
            released unharmed (26 November) when an exorbitant
            ransom demand is refused.

18   UNITED ARAB EMIRATES - In advance of a planned British
            withdrawal, six of the seven (Ras al-Khaimah refusing
            to join) Persian Gulf emirs unite their principalities
            (formerly known as the Truncial States) and proclaim
            their new status at a meeting at Dubai, Oman.

18   IRAQ - The government closes its border with Jordan
            and asks Amman to recall the Jordanian Ambassador in
            Baghdad.

19-21   SUDAN - In bloody fighting in which the control of the
            country changed hands several times, forces loyal to
            President Mohammed Gafaar al-Nimeiry, with help from
            Egypt and Libya, crush a Soviet-supported coup
            attempt.

23   EGYPT - President Sadat warns he will take decisive
            action if Israel does not withdraw from the occupied
            territory by the end of the year.

26   SOUTH VIET NAM - A major narcotics ring that has been
      supplying Allied servicemen in SVN with drugs is bro-
      ken up by US, Thai, and SVN agents.

26   LIBYA - Libyan fighters force down a British airliner,
      enroute from London to Khartoum, at Benghazi and ar-
      rest Colonel Babakr an-Nur Osman, an alleged leader in
      the coup attempt against Sudan's President Nimeiry.
      The prisoner is then transported to Khartoum where he
      is executed.

28   CYPRUS - A new flair-up of violence between Greek and
      Turkish Cypriots is reported. It is the first report
      of an exchange of gunfire in years.

30   LIBYA - A meeting of Arab leaders condemns Jordan for
      its treatment of the Palestinians and pledges more
      support for the PLO.

30   URUGUAY - Thirty-eight women prisoners are released
      from the Montevideo jail by Tupamaro guerrillas.

AUGUST

1   SUDAN - The government recalls its Ambassador in Mos-
      cow following Soviet protests in the wake of the post-
      coup-attempt crackdown on the Sudanese Communist Party
      (SCP).

5   UNITED NATIONS - The US and USSR present to the Geneva
      Disarmament Conference a joint draft of a treaty ban-
      ning BW weapons.

6   PERU - The government recognizes Communist China.

8   MALAYSIA - Government forces launch an offensive to
      eliminate the guerrilla threat in Sarawak.

9   INDIA - A 20-year friendship treaty is concluded with
      the USSR.

9   NORTHERN IRELAND - At least 12 people are killed in
      rioting. The government invokes emergency powers and
      begins arresting suspected IRA leaders.

11   SOUTH VIET NAM - The responsibility for all ground
      combat is passed to ARVN. Phase One of the
      Vietnamization Program is complete.

11   PAKISTAN - East Pakistani leader Mujibur Rahmen is put
      on trial for his life.

12   UNITED STATES - The Defense Department reports 66 US
            service personnel were killed in SVN in July. This is
            the lowest casualty figure for one month since May
            1965.

12   SOUTH VIET NAM - USMACV begins shipping excess mili-
            tary equipment back to the US (Project HOME RUN
            EXTENDED).

12   SYRIA - The government breaks diplomatic relations
            with Jordan because of its crackdown on Palestinian
            guerrillas.

13   NATO - NATO announces its Mediterranean headquarters
            will be moved from Malta in compliance with Maltese
            demands.

14   BAHREIN - The former British colony declares itself
            independent.

18   BOLIVIA - An uprising begins against the Torres
            government.

18   UNITED STATES - The Defense Department acknowledges
            that B-52 strikes have been used against NVA buildups
            in the southern portion of the DMZ.

18   USSR - The Kremlin signs a new military aid agreement
            with NVN.

20   NATO - The headquarters of the NATO forces in the Med-
            iterranean is transferred from Malta to Naples.

20   EGYPT - An agreement for the union of Egypt, Libya,
            and Syria, which was reached on 17 April 1971, is
            signed. The union is to be put into effect on 1
            September.

21   BOLIVIA - A right-wing military coup, led by Colonel
            Hugo Banzer Saurez, ousts the government of President
            Torres.

21   GREAT BRITAIN - An investigation is begun into charges
            of brutality by UK troops in Northern Ireland.

21   THE PHILIPPINES - Ten civilians are killed during a
            grenade attack on an opposition Liberal Party meeting
            in Manila. The Marcos regime is charged with organ-
            izing the mass assassination attempt.

22   BOLIVIA - Colonel Hugo Banzer Suarez is sworn in as
            President ending the four days of civil war.

23   BERLIN - France, Great Britain, the US, and the   USSR
            sign a Four-Power Agreement on access to Berlin.   East
            and West Germany both endorse the agreement   even
            though its terms forbid access to West Berlin or West
            Germany by East Germans.

23   THE PHILIPPINES - President Marcos suspends a number
            of civil liberties in a crackdown on leftist groups.

24-30   TANZANIA - Regular Ugandan forces attack Tanzanian
            positions along the border in retaliation for alleged
            Tanzanian support of Ugandan rebels.

25   SOUTH VIET NAM - Approximately 6,000 tons of ammuni-
            tion are blown up by VC/NVA sappers at the Tri-Service
            ammo dump at Cam Ranh Bay.

27   CHAD - A Libyan-supported coup attempt fails. Chad
            breaks diplomatic relations with Libya.

31   SOUTH VIET NAM - The eighth phase of the US deployment
            out of SVN is completed.

SEPTEMBER

1   LIBYA - The government announces its formal approval
            of the impotent agreement of union with Syria and
            Egypt. Referenda in Syria and Egypt also approve the
            merger.

1   FRANCE - The government announces it is cancelling
            further nuclear testing at its Mururoa Test Site in
            the Pacific after Peru threatens to break diplomatic
            relations.

2   MALAYSIA - Malaysia and Singapore integrate their air
            defense systems. The combined headquarters is located
            at Butterworth.

3   QATAR - The former British colony declares its inde-
            pendence and signs a treaty of frienship with Great
            Britain.

5   SOUTH VIET NAM - ARVN begins a new division-sized op-
            eration (Operation LAM SON 810) against suspected NVA
            logistical bases in northwestern MR 1 near the Laotian
            border.

6   URUGUAY - Tupamaro terrorists open the Punta Carretas
            maximum security prison and free 111 inmates.

6   AGENTINA - Members of ERP free 17 prisoners held in
            Tucuman.

6   COMMUNIST CHINA - The government agrees to supply North Korea with free military equipment and arms.

9   URUGUAY - Tupamaro terrorists release the kidnapped British Ambassador, Geoffrey Jackson, unharmed in Montevideo.

11-13   COMMUNIST CHINA - Lin Piao is killed in an airplane crash in Mongolia as he flees (13 September) a failed coup attempt against Mao Tse-tung (11 September).

18   EGYPT - Egyptian and Israeli forces exchange rocket fire across the Suez Canal.

18   LIBYA - The government repudiates charges of its complicity in the attempted coup against the government of Chad, and then turns around and recognizes the rebel movement in Chad.

18   SOUTH VIET NAM - Anti-government student riots break out in Saigon.

18   THE PHILIPPINES - The martial law edict imposed on 23 August is lifted.

19   SOUTH VIET NAM - "Operation LAM SON 810" is completed.

20   SAUDI ARABIA - Jordanian and Palestinian representatives open truce negotiations.

22   UNITED STATES - An Army court martial finds Captain Medina not guilty of all charges connected with the My Lai Massacre.

22   GREAT BRITAIN - The government states it has reached an agreement-in-principle with the Maltese government for the continued use of naval facilities on the Mediterranean island.

23   FINLAND - The fifth round of Salt talks is concluded in Helsinki.

25   SOUTH VIET NAM - Veterans' groups join students in massive protests against the government's election policies. Anti-American sentiments are expressed by the demonstrators.

26   SOUTH VIET NAM - The NVA launches a series of heavy attacks on ARVN positions near the Cambodian border.

26   ISRAEL - In defiance of the UN, Israel announces it will continue the development of occupied Jerusalem.

27   COMMUNIST CHINA - The government signs a one-year
            agreement for the supply of military and economic aid
            to NVN.

27   MEXICO - In the first kidnapping of a government of-
            ficial in Mexico in modern times, MAR terrorists kid-
            nap Julio Hirschfield, the head of the Civil Aviation
            Service. He is released on 29 September after payment
            of a $250,000 ransom.

29   COMMUNIST CHINA - A treaty is signed with Japan that
            ends the state of war that has existed since 1937.

29   JAPAN - At the same time that the peace treaty is
            signed with Communist China, Japan severs diplomatic
            relations with Nationalist China.

29   IRAQ - There is an unsuccessful attempt to assassinate
            Mullah Barzani, the leader of the Kurdistan Democratic
            Party.

30   UNITED STATES - The US enters into a nuclear accidents
            pact with the USSR. Both sides pledge to notify the
            other of a nuclear accident, a planned launch in the
            other's direction, or other activities that might
            accidently trigger a confrontation.

OCTOBER

1   GREAT BRITAIN - The War Office authorizes the use of
            automatic weapons against terrorists in Northern
            Ireland.

1   RHODESIA - ZANU and ZAPU join to form the United Front
            for the Liberation of Zimbabwe.

4   EGYPT - Egypt's Anwar Sadat is selected to be the
            first president of the Federation of Arab Republics.

6   MIDDLE EAST - There is an unsuccessful attempt to as-
            sassinate PLO leader Yasser Arafat.

7   GREAT BRITAIN - Three additional army battalions are
            ordered to Northern Ireland.

8   ARGENTINA - Two army regiments revolt. President
            Alejandro Agustin Lanusse orders the Army to crush the
            rebellion.

8   NORTH VIET NAM - Soviet President Podgorny signs a new
            military and economic aid agreement with the North
            Vietnamese.

11-13   USSR - Egyptian President Anwar Sadat, on a state visit in Moscow, is promised additional military aid.

12   SOUTH VIET NAM - A US military convoy with 14 American soldiers on board is kidnapped and held for ransom by SVN veterans. This act of violence is in retaliation for an accident in which a bus loaded of veterans was hit by a US Army truck.

13   USSR - After three days of discussion, Egypt's President Sadat and Soviet officials announce a new arms agreement.

13   NORTHERN IRELAND - Working to stop arms traffic into Northern Ireland from the Irish Free State, British troops destroy roads near the border.

15   SOUTH VIET NAM - US and SVN undercover agents uncover a large quantity of heroin in a raid near the huge US Army installation at Long Binh.

20   CAMBODIA - Titular head of state Lon Nol declares a state of emergency and announces rule by "ordinance."

20   TANZANIA - A Tanzanian army base is attacked and destroyed by Ugandan military aircraft. Uganda claims the base is used by supporters of former President (Apollo) Milton Obote.

21   UNITED STATES - The US Court of Appeals in Boston upholds the constitutionality of the war in SVN.

24   SOUTH AFRICA - Police search 115 dwellings in a predawn raid designed to intimidate critics of apartheid.

25   UNITED NATIONS - The General Assembly votes 76-35, with 17 abstentions, to seat Communist China and expel Nationalist China (Taiwan).

25   EAST PAKISTAN - Some 500 "Indians and Indian agents" are reported killed by Pakistani security forces.

27   ZAIRE - The new state of Zaire comes into being when President Mobutu renames the Democratic Republic of Congo (Kinshasa).

27   PAKISTAN - Following weeks of shelling by Pakistani forces, Indian forces cross the border into East Pakistan. A week-long battle ensues at Kamalpur.

27   INDIA - India invokes a mutual-assistance clause in its treaty with the USSR and asks for Soviet aid.

28   NORTHERN IRELAND - British troops are challenged by Irish Free State forces as the British attempt to destroy a bridge on the border.

28   SOUTH VIET NAM - Of 2,938 VC prisoners released on the occasion of President Thieu's inauguration, 2,297 refuse to be sent back and ask to enter the "Chieu Hoi" program.

28   UNITED STATES - The Senate defeats an amendment to the foreign aid bill that would have halted all military activity in SEA not directly associated with the withdrawal of American forces. The following day, 29 October, the Senate votes to kill the entire SVN aid program.

29   INDIA - A Soviet military team arrives to study Indian defense needs against Pakistan.

31   SINGAPORE - The British presence in Singapore comes to an end after 152 years. On 1 November, a Five-Power force composed of Great Britain, Australia, New Zealand, Malaysia, and Singapore jointly assumes the defense of the republic.

NOVEMBER

1   SINGAPORE - The British garrison in Singapore is replaced by one composed of Australian, New Zealand, and United Kingdom (ANZUK) forces.

1   UNITED STATES - The government signs an agreement-in-principle to furnish industrial aid to Israel. The terms of the agreement are not made public until 13 January 1972.

1   EGYPT - President Sadat takes personal command of Egypt's armed forces.

3   NORTHERN IRELAND - British authorities arm the Royal Ulster Constabulary Reserve in the face of growing terrorist attacks.

3   LEBANON - The government announces it has concluded its first arms deal with the Soviet Union.

5   UNITED STATES - On a state visit to the US, India's Prime Minister Indira Gandhi refuses to consider moving Indian troops away from border areas or to allowing UN observer teams on Indian territory.

6   UNITED STATES - The US conducts a hydrogen bomb test on Amchitka Island in the Aleutians.

6   SOUTH KOREA - The government announces its decision to withdraw 10,000 of its troops in SVN.

7   SOUTH VIET NAM - Australian forces turn over their base at Nui Dat, Phouc Tuy Province to ARVN and begin their nation's withdrawal from the war in SVN. This action also ends New Zealand's role in the war.

8   UNITED STATES - The government announces it has cancelled future arms shipments to Pakistan because of that government's repressive conduct in East Pakistan and Bengal.

9   NORTHERN IRELAND - British forces capture 43 IRA suspects in a sweep of a Roman Catholic enclave in Belfast.

12   UNITED STATES - President Nixon announces that an additional 45,000 will be withdrawn from SVN by February 1972. This sets the new ceiling at 139,000.

12   NORTH VIET NAM - A survey indicates the USSR has supplied about $500 million to Hanoi this year. The high point was $720 million in 1967.

13   SOUTH VIET NAM - Intelligence reports indicate the NVA is massing supplies for a major offensive in the south. At the same time, the government complains to the ICC that NVN forces have kidnapped 30 children during September and October in a drive for children as young as ten years old to be trained in NVN.

15   AUSTRIA - Round six of the SALT talks opens in Vienna.

16   SOUTH VIET NAM - A new redeployment schedule announces the further reduction of US troop strength by 130,000 to 150,000 men by 30 June 1972. This plan will leave 30,000-55,000 American troops in SVN.

17   THAILAND - A bloodless palace coup takes place in which Prime Minister Thanom Kittikachorn seizes full power, abrogates the constitution, and declares martial law.

18   COMMUNIST CHINA - The Chinese conduct their first nuclear test of the year when they detonate a 20 KT device in the atmosphere at Lop Nor.

19   MEXICO - The Rector of the State University at Guerrero, Doctor Jaime Castrejon Diez, is kidnapped by terrorists. A ransom of $500,000 is paid and nine political prisoners are released and sent to Cuba to gain his release on 1 December.

20   CAMBODIA - The Cambodian military command asks for SVN
            to help relieve Communist military pressure north of
            Phnom Penh.

20   EGYPT - President Sadat notifies the armed forces that
            war with Israel is "at hand."

21   UGANDA - President Amin reopens the border with
            Tanzania.

22   EAST PAKISTAN - Pakistani sources claim four columns
            of Indian Army troops are carrying out an invasion of
            East Pakistan.

22   CAMBODIA - RVNAF units open a major offensive into
            Cambodia.

23   UNITED STATES - Another move in the US Senate to
            reduce US troop strength in Europe is defeated.

23   PAKISTAN - President Yahya Khan declares a state of
            emergency following the Indian attacks along the
            frontier.

23   BRUNEI - Great Britain signs a new defense agreement
            with Brunei that limits the British role in internal
            struggles.

24   INDIA - Prime Minister Gandhi acknowledges that India
            has been supporting rebel forces in East Pakistan.

24   MOZAMBIQUE - Guerrillas blow up a train near the
            Malawi border.

27   SOUTH VIET NAM - The major US base at Chu Lai is
            turned over the ARVN.

28   EGYPT - The Jordanian Prime Minister, Wasfi Tal, is
            assassinated by Palestinian "Black September" ter-
            rorists while attending an Arab League meeting in
            Cairo.

29   GUATEMALA - The state of emergency in force since
            November 1970 is lifted.

30   IRAN - Rejecting the claims of Ras al-Khaimah, Iranian
            troops seize the British protectorate of the Greater
            and Lesser Tunb (Tomb-e-Bozorg & Tomb-e-Kuchak)
            Islands at the northern end of the Straits of Hormuz.
            The Iranians also take the island of Abu Musa, but
            return it to the Persian Gulf Emirate of Shahjah, in
            return for basing rights.

30   IRAQ - The government breaks diplomatic relations with
          Iran and Great Britain; the former for carrying out
          seizure of the British protectorate islands in the
          Staits of Hormuz, and; latter for not reacting to the
          seizure.

30   SOUTH VIET NAM - ARVN opens a new offensive in the
          Central Highlands. Over 15,000 ARVN troops are engaged
          in the fighting. Also, USMACV reports that, with the
          completion of Phase IX of the US redeployment, US
          strength in SVN is 184,000.

DECEMBER

1   UNITED STATES - The US cancels a $2 million arms
          shipment to India and suspends all future arms sales
          to that country.

1   CHILE - Serious rioting breaks out in Santiago as pro-
          and anti-Allende forces take to the streets. A state
          of emergency is declared on 2 December.

2   CAMBODIA - The defenses around Phnom Penh are reported
          to be collapsing in the face of heavy NVA ground
          action.

3   INDIA - Pakistani aircraft carry out a massive air
          strike against Indian military air bases at Agra,
          Amritsar, Pathankot, Srinagar, and other locations in
          northern India.

3-4   PAKISTAN - Indian forces, numbering about 250,000, in-
          vade East Pakistan and Bengal.

4   INDIA - Pakistani forces invade Kashmir penetrating
          about 15 kilometers before being stopped by Indian
          troops. India proclaims that a full-scale war has
          begun.

4   SOUTH VIET NAM - The departure of the ROK Marines
          marks the beginning of the South Korean withdrawal
          from the war in SVN.

5-6   UNITED NATIONS - The USSR vetoes a Security Council
          Indo-Pakistani cease-fire order so as to allow its
          Indian allies time to gain and consolidate all their
          objectives. Pakistan immediately petitions the General
          Assembly for action.

6   INDIA - The government recognizes the existence of
          Bangladesh.

7   EAST PAKISTAN - Indian forces capture the strategi-
        cally important city of Jessore, thereby taking
        control of the western half of the country.

8   SOUTH VIET NAM - The last Australian military person-
        nel depart SVN when the 4th Battalion, Royal Austral-
        ian Regiment departs.

9   EGYPT - Former Vice-President Ali Sabri and three
        others are sentenced to death for treason. President
        Sadat commutes the sentences to life imprisonment.

10   UNITED STATES - The State Department announces a bas-
        ing agreement with Portugal which gives the US contin-
        ued use of naval and air bases in the Azores.

10   EAST PAKISTAN - India forces cross the Meghna River.

11-12   EAST PAKISTAN - The capital city of Dacca is placed
        under siege.

12   UNITED STATES - The US increases its naval strength in
        the Indian Ocean to counter a Soviet naval buildup in
        that region.

12   NORTHERN IRELAND - Terrorists kill Trade Unionist John
        Barnhill and blow up his home.

14   PORTUGAL - The government announces it has signed an
        agreement with the US for continued American use of
        the air base at Terceira in the Azores.

14-16   PAKISTAN - Heavy fighting continues as Indian forces
        approach Dacca, the capital of East Pakistan. The East
        Pakistani government flees to a safe haven established
        by the International Red Cross and disavows any fur-
        ther connection with the central Pakistani government.

15   UNITED NATIONS - The General Assembly orders a
        cease-fire in the Indo-Pakistani War. Having no means
        of enforcement, the war continues, especially in the
        western theater, where Indian troops cross into West
        Pakistani territory in the Hyderabad and Punjab Suba
        areas.

15   BAHAMAS - A Cuban gunboat shells, rams, and sinks a US
        freighter in Bahamian waters.

15   GREAT BRITAIN - There is an unsuccessful attempt on
        the life of the Jordanian Ambassador to London by
        "Black September" terrorists.

15   SAUDI ARABIA - The government reestablishes diplomatic
        relations with Oman after a long period of feuding.

15   SUDAN - A major clash takes place between Sudan Army forces and Sudanese guerrillas along the country's southern border with Uganda. After 24 hours of fighting, the guerrillas force the army troops to withdraw.

16   PAKISTAN - About 90,000 Pakistani troops under the command of Lieutenant General A.A.K. Niazi in East Pakistan are forced to surrender to Indian forces. This marks the end of the fighting.

16   UNITED NATIONS - The General Assembly approves the Convention on Biological Weapons. Individual nations are requested to ratify it.

16   COMMUNIST CHINA - The government files an official protest claiming Indian incursions into Tibet.

16   SWITZERLAND - There is another unsuccessful attempt on the life of a Jordanian Ambassador in Geneva by "Black September" terrorists.

17   INDIA - Both the Indian and the Pakistani governments accept the UN cease-fire order.

17   BANGLADESH - The already proclaimed declaration of independence becomes effective.

18   NORTH VIET NAM - The Foreign Ministry claims three US aircraft were shot down in raids over NVN.

20   PAKISTAN - President Yahya Khan resigns. Zulfikar Ali Bhutto is named president. Yahya Khan and the country's senior military officers are arrested.

20   LAOS - NVA forces have apparently recaptured all of the Plaine des Jarres in northern Laos.

22   YUGOSLAVIA - Following an outbreak of violence in Croatia, Marshal Tito warns his people that he will use the army against "internal enemies."

22   URUGUAY - Tupamaro terrorists break the truce by blowing up a golf course at Punta Carretas, Montevideo.

23   BAHREIN - The government announces it has signed an agreement authorizing permanent US naval facilities on the island.

26-31   NORTH VIET NAM - Heavy air raids are carried out in retaliation for Communist attacks in the south.

28   LAOS - NVA and Pathet Lao forces capture almost all of
        the Boloven Plateau in southern Laos.

29   MALTA - Prime Minister Dominic Mintoff issues an ulti-
        matum to Great Britain demanding it leave the island
        by 31 December or pay an additional $11 million. The
        British order an immediately withdrawal of all their
        forces.

30   SOUTH VIET NAM - The US Command announces a halt to
        the intensive bombing of NVN that has gone on for five
        days. The RVNAF Command announces it has ended the
        campaign in eastern Cambodia.

31   SOUTH VIET NAM - US strength in SVN is 158,119. There
        are still 54,497 Allied forces in country, along with
        1,046,254 RVNAF personnel. US losses in 1971 are
        1,298. The total US losses in SVN since 1961 are
        45,388.

                              Notes

1972

JANUARY

2   SOUTH VIET NAM - US military sources confirm that intensive US air raids over NVN during the last week of 1971 were not as effective because of bad weather.

2   UNITED STATES - President Nixon states final US withdrawal from SVN is contingent only on the release of American prisoners of war by NVN.

7   SOUTH VIET NAM - Sources report ARVN forces crossed into northern Cambodia for the fourth time in two months.

7   LAOS - Laotian forces, supported by US aircraft, open a month-long offensive to recapture the Plaine des Jarres.

7   COLOMBIA - Rebel forces attack the town of San Pablo.

8   PAKISTAN - Bangladesh President Mujibur Rahman is released from jail. Former Pakistani President Ayub Mohammed Yahya Khan is held under house arrest.

8   SOUTH VIET NAM - A terrorist's hand grenade thrown into a youth rally bonfire in Qui Nhon kills 15 and injures 212 students.

8   MALTA - The British forces begin the removal of families from Malta in the face of demands by the Maltese Prime Minister for an exorbitant increase in base-leasing fees.

10   UNITED STATES - The government announces the with-
        drawal of the naval task force sent into the Indian
        Ocean during the Indo-Pakistani War.

10   THAILAND - Three multi-million dollar American B-52
        bombers are destroyed at U Tapao Air Base in Thailand
        in a predawn sapper attack.

10   INDIA - The government decides to establish an embassy
        in North Viet Nam.

11   LAOS - North Vietnamese troops rout a Laotian force
        after a fierce battle on the Boloven Plateau in
        southern Laos.

11   IRAQ - Fighting breaks out between Iraqi forces and
        Kurdish tribesmen following Kurdish protests against
        Iraq's expulsion to Iran of alleged infiltrators. At
        least 86 are killed.

12   PORTUGAL - A Lisbon warehouse containing French arms
        for Portuguese troops in Africa is blown up by ARA
        terrorists.

13   GHANA - Prime Minister Kofi Busia is in London for
        medical treatment when he is deposed by a military
        coup led by Colonel Ignatius Kutu Acheampong. The
        Military Redemption Council is established to rule by
        decree.

13   EGYPT - President Anwar Sadat explains in a national
        address that 1971 passed without war with Israel
        because the Indo-Pakistani War confused the issues.

13   UNITED STATES - President Nixon announces the with-
        drawal of an additional 70,000 US troops from SVN over
        the next three months (Phase XI). This will leave
        69,000 troops in SVN on 1 May.

14   YUGOSLAVIA - The Republic of Croatia's government is
        purged of nationalist elements as a new crackdown on
        dissidence begins.

15   UNITED STATES - The government announces an agreement
        whereby Israel is authorized to manufacture American
        military equipment. This plan was first initialed in
        November 1971.

15   GHANA - Colonel Acheampong maintains his newly won
        power by suppressing a counter-coup.

15   MALTA - Prime Minister Dominic Mintoff orders all
        British forces out of Malta but later cancels the
        order.

17   EGYPT - The government is reorganized on a wartime
          footing with Aziz Sidky replacing Mahmoud Fawzi as
          prime minister.

19   NORTH VIET NAM - For the first time in almost two
          years, a NVAF MiG-21 is shot down over NVN by a US
          fighter.

19   EGYPT - Serious rioting breaks out among Cairo stu-
          dents protesting the government's policies toward
          Israel.

21   CAMBODIA - The largest supply convoy in two years be-
          gins arriving at Phnom Penh after a trip up the Mekong
          River.

22   SOUTH VIET NAM - President Thieu offers the NLF repre-
          sentation in the GVN if they will renounce violence.

24   USSR - The government recognizes Bangladesh.

24   UNITED ARAB EMIRATES - Sheikh Khalid bin Mohammed al-
          Qasmi, the ruler of Sharjah, is killed in a coup led
          by his cousin, Sheikh Saqr bin Mohammed al-Qasmi, who
          had been deposed in 1965. Khalid's younger brother,
          Sheikh Sultan bin Mohammed al-Qasmi, the Minister of
          Education, replaces Khalid.

25   SOUTH VIET NAM - Two Soviet-built PT-76 tanks are
          reported in MR 3. This is the first report of NVA
          armor in SVN since May 1971.

26   WARSAW PACT - Ending a two-day conference in Prague,
          Czechoslovakia, the leaders of the Warsaw Pact call
          for a troop and arms reduction in Europe.

26   SOUTH VIET NAM - President Thieu announces that he has
          agreed to a secret peace proposal that requires he
          resign and that the Communists participate in an in-
          ternationally supervised election.

26   SOUTH AFRICA - Military forces are sent to Ovamboland,
          near the Angolan border, to quell a major disturbance.
          Eight black demonstrators are reported killed.

29   SOUTH VIET NAM - Defense Secretary Melvin Laird states
          the US will not send troops back into SVN in case of
          an emergency.

30   NORTHERN IRELAND - British troops kill 13 unarmed
          Roman Catholics during rioting in Londonderry. The day
          becomes known as "Bloody Sunday."

30   UNITED STATES - Defense Secretary Melvin Laird an-
          nounces that there will be no additional draft calls
          before April.

30   PAKISTAN - The government withdraws from the Common-
          wealth of Nations after it is announced that Great
          Britain and other   member   states will   recognize
          Bangladesh.

31   NORTHERN IRELAND - The Irish Republican Army (IRA)
          calls for a general strike to protest the "Bloody
          Sunday" incident.

31   FRANCE - The North Vietnamese delegation at the Paris
          peace talks reveals the US has made a secret peace
          proposal.

31   SOUTH VIET NAM - The US strength in SVN is reported to
          be 136,505.

FEBRUARY

1   UNITED STATES - The Department of State confirms it
          has suggested to the USSR mutual restraints on naval
          activities in the Indian Ocean.

2   REPUBLIC OF IRELAND - A mob attacks and burns down the
          British Embassy in Dublin in retaliation for the
          "Bloody Sunday" incident in Londonderry.

4   SOUTH VIET NAM - Thailand announces the withdrawal of
          the last of its contingent from the forces fighting
          the Communists.

4   ZAMBIA - The government bans the United Progressive
          Party after a long period of violence. More than 100
          of its members are arrested including its leader,
          Simon Kapepwe.

6   GREECE - The government announces it has reached an
          agreement with the US to provide port facilities for
          units of the US Sixth Fleet.

8   INDIA - The government agrees to withdraw its troops
          from Bangladesh by 25 March.

9   SOUTH VIET NAM - Twenty-four rockets hit the air base
          at Da Nang. Ten US servicemen are wounded.

10   UNITED ARAB EMIRATES - Ras al-Khaimah is the seventh
          Trucial State to become a member of the confeder-
          ation.

10   MOZAMBIQUE - FRELIMO guerrillas attack an outpost near
the Cabora Bassa Dam. Five soldiers and four civilians
are killed.

11   GREECE - The government demands Cyprus turn over recently acquired Czech weapons to the UN and form a
government of national unity. On 14 March, President
Makarios agrees to the UN inspection of the Czech arms
but rejects all other Greek demands.

13   SOUTH VIET NAM - US forces go on alert for the Tet
holidays.

14   UNITED STATES - The US places Communist China on the
same commercial footing as the USSR when the government lifts the extraordinary trade restrictions that
have been in effect on China.

15   ECUADOR - The government of President Jose Maria
Velasco Ibarra is overthrown by a military coup.
General Guillermo Rodriguez Lara assumes the Presi-
dency. Ibarra is ordered into exile.

15   FRANCE - The government signs an agreement to reim-
burse Israel for 50 Mirage fighters that were paid for
but not delivered.

15   ICELAND - The Parliament extends the national fishing
boundaries from 12 to 50 miles and abrogates fishing
treaties with Great Britain and West Germany.

16   SUDAN - Peace talks begin between the government and
rebellious Anyanya tribesmen of southern Sudan.
Agreement is reached on 28 February, and ratified on
27 March, to end the 16-year-old war. An amnesty and
lifting of the 1955 state of emergency occurs 19-20
March.

17   NORTH VIET NAM - The US concludes 29 hours of intensive bombing of artillery positions in southern NVN
and in the DMZ.

17   UNITED STATES - The US resumes military aid to Greece.

19   EGYPT - Marshal of the Soviet Union Andrei A. Grechko
begins talks in Cairo on increasing military aid to
Egypt.

20   COMMUNIST CHINA - United States President Richard M.
Nixon meets with Mao Tse-tung and Chou En-lai to end
the emnity that has existed between the two nations
since 1949.

21   YEMEN (ADEN) - People's Democratic Republic of Yemen forces repel an attack by the Saudi Arabian-based "Army of Deliverance" in the Bayhan region.

22   QATAR - During its first year of independence, the nation's ruler, Emir Ahmad bin Ali al-Thani, is overthrown in a bloodless coup, led by his cousin, Prime Minister Sheikh Khalifa bin Hammad ath-Thani.

22   LAOS - The Communists open a counteroffensive in the Plaine des Jarres.

22   GREAT BRITAIN - The Irish Republican Army (IRA) claims responsibility for the bomb blast at the Aldershot military base that killed 7 and injured 19. This is the first IRA bombing in Great Britain since WWII.

22   REPUBLIC OF CONGO - A coup attempt is thwarted in Brazzaville. Former Premier Ambroise Noumazalay is arrested along with scores of others. President Marien Ngouabi's opponents claim the coup was a government trap to allow for a purge.

23   DAHOMEY - Army units mutiny in Ouidah.

23-24   ISRAEL - An Arab guerrilla attack on an Israeli settlement in Upper Galilee brings immediate air strikes on guerrilla bases inside Syria.

24   LEBANON - Israeli forces enter Lebanon in a major operation aimed at the destruction of Palestinian guerrilla bases.

24   FRANCE - NVN and VC delegates walk out of the SEA peace talks in protest to recent US bombings of the north.

25   ZAMBIA - President Kenneth Kaunda takes steps to make Zambia a one-party state.

26   ETHIOPIA - An agreement reached in Addis Ababa ends 16 years of war in Sudan.

26   SYRIA - A Soviet military delegation promises Syria additional military aid.

27   UNITED NATIONS - The Security Council condemns Israel for its raid-in-force in Lebanon.

28   LEBANON - Israeli forces begin their withdrawal after a four-day operation against Palestinian base camps.

29   SOUTH VIET NAM - US troop strength in SVN is 119,606.

MARCH

1   SYRIA - An Israeli ground force raiding party crosses the Syrian border and attacks a guerrilla base as a part of the retaliation for the Galilee attack of 23 February.

3   UNITED NATIONS - The Chinese Communist representative announces his nation's claim over Hong Kong and Macao. He also claims the Japanese-claimed Senkalu Islands and charges Japan with imperialism.

5   SOUTH VIET NAM - Three barges loaded with 300 tons of ammunition blow up in Saigon harbor.

6   LAOS - The government's forces break off their month-long operation to recapture the Plaine des Jarres.

7   SOUTH VIET NAM - The last Australian forces leave SVN.

10   CAMBODIA - Cheng Heng announces his resignation and turns the Presidency over to Lon Nol.

11   TURKEY - The government dismisses 68 army officers and enlisted personnel and arrests scores of others on charges of complicity in the November 1971 release of a group of imprisoned terrorists.

11   LAOS - Communist forces capture Sam Thong after more than a month of fighting.

12   BANGLADESH - The last Indian troops withdraw.

12   CAMBODIA - Lon Nol dissolves the government.

13   GREAT BRITAIN - The government recognizes Communist China as the only legitimate Chinese state.

13   MALAYSIA - The government announces an intensification of the campaign to drive Communist rebel forces out of Sarawak.

15   JORDAN - King Hussein announces a plan for the establishment of a Palestinian state on the West Bank and Gaza as a part of the United Arab Kingdom. Israel, the PLO, and other Arab states immediately reject the plan.

17   ZAIRE - An attempt is made by ELNA members to assassinate the head of the Angolan Revolutionary Government in Exile (GRAE) during an uprising at his base camp at Kinkuzu. Zaire army forces put an end to the disturbance.

19   INDIA - The government announces the signing of a
            25-year treaty of friendship and mutual defense with
            Bangladesh.

21   CAMBODIA - Khmer Rouge forces begin the rocket bom-
            bardment of Phnom Penh.

21   ARGENTINA - The Director of the Fiat plant, Doctor
            Oberdan Sallustro, is kidnapped by ERP terrorists and
            later murdered. His body is discovered on 10 April in
            a Buenos Aires suburb.

22   UGANDA - President Amin accuses Israel of subversion
            and says he will not renew his military aid pact with
            them.

23   FRANCE - US Ambassador William Porter announces the US
            has indefinitely suspended the Paris peace talks on
            SEA.

24   GREAT BRITAIN - The government suspends the Northern
            Ireland Parliament and assumes direct rule over the
            province.

25   EL SALVADOR - An attempted military coup is suppressed
            by troops loyal to President Fidel Sanchez Hernandez.

26   MALTA - After threats by Prime Minister Dom Mintoff
            that he will give the USSR military bases, the
            government announces it has signed a seven-year basing
            agreement with Great Britain in return for $260
            million.

26   FRANCE - The US breaks off the Paris peace talks
            because the NVN delegation refuses to bargain in good
            faith.

26   MALAYSIA - Communist guerrillas kill 15 government
            troops in a fierce battle in Sarawak.

27   SUDAN - An agreement is reached between Arab Muslim
            and Black Christian factions bringing an end to a
            17-year struggle.

27   UGANDA - Israeli military advisors are ordered out of
            the country by the Israeli government.

28   FINLAND - The SALT discussions reconvene in Helsinki.

28   SWITZERLAND - The USSR presents a draft treaty outlaw-
            ing chemical weapons to the UN Disarmament Conference
            being held in Geneva.

29   BOLIVIA - The government   orders 119 Soviet   diplomats out of the country.

30   SOUTH VIET NAM - The Communist "Easter Offensive" begins. Some 20,000 NVA troops (three divisions)   attack across the DMZ into Quang Tri Province with the objective of taking the capital city. It is a   four-pronged attack with the   immediate objective   of clearing   out the 15 firebases   occupied by   the recently   organized 3rd ARNV Division.   The US retaliates   by bombing   and shelling Hanoi and Haiphong.

30   UGANDA - President Idi Amin orders the Israeli Embassy in Kampala closed.

31   SOUTH VIET NAM - US   military strength in SVN is   down to 95,500.

APRIL

1   SOUTH VIET NAM - The US Navy gives up its active   role in the war in SVN. Only about 5,000 US naval personnel remain in advisory capacities.

2   SOUTH VIET NAM - ARVN forces give up the northern half of Quang Tri Province as   more than 30,000 NVA   troops invade MR 1. The enemy   also opens heavy attacks   into Tay Ninh Province north of Saigon in MR 3.

4   INDIA - The government announces it has   reestablished direct diplomatic contact with Pakistan.

5   SOUTH VIET NAM - In a continuation of the "Easter   Offensive," about 50,000 NVA   in Cambodia, supported   by armor, attack through   Binh Long Province   in the   III CTZ toward Saigon. Near   the provincial capital of   An Loc (Hon Quan), they cut the principal road to the SVN capital.

5   GUATEMALA - Count Karl   von Spreti, the German   Ambassador, is kidnapped and killed by terrorists demanding a "political prisoner" exchange for 22 rebels held   in jail. Spreti is murdered   when the government   refuses to negotiate   as it   did for   the release   of   Foreign Minister Alberto Fuentes Mohr, and US Embassy official Sean M. Holly, who had been also kidnapped.

6   NORTH VIET NAM - The US begins a new campaign of heavy bombardment of NVN.

6   MAYALSIA - The   government signs   an   agreement   with Indonesia   for   closer   cooperation   in   antiguerrilla operations in border areas.

7   EGYPT - The government announces it has broken
           diplomatic relations with Jordan in protest to the
           Hussein plan for a Palestinian state.

7   SOUTH VIET NAM - The district capital town of Loc Ninh
           in Binh Long Province is taken by the NVA.

7   SOUTH VIET NAM - General John Lavelle, the Commander,
           US Seventh Air Force, is relieved (March 1972), de-
           moted, and retired for having approved the bombing of
           at least 20 unauthorized North Vietnamese targets be-
           tween November 1971 and March 1972.

7   TANZANIA - Sheikh Abeid Amani Karume, the chairman of
           the Zanzibar Revolutionary Council and First Vice-
           President of Tanzania, is assassinated by members of
           the army. A number of people are arrested including
           the head of the Umma Party, Abdul Rahman Muhammad
           Bubu.

9   IRAQ - The government announces it has signed a 15-
           year treaty of friendship with the USSR.

10   NORTH VIET NAM - US B-52 bombers attack in NVN, 145
           miles north of the DMZ near Vinh.

10   THE WORLD - A treaty banning the production, develop-
           ment, stockpiling, or use of biological warfare is
           signed in London, Moscow, and Washington by more than
           70 nations.

10   ARGENTINA - The commander of the II Army Corps, Major
           General Juan Carlos Sanchez, is assassinated in the
           town of Rosario. His death is linked to the kidnap-
           murder of Oberdan Sallustro, and a leftist-terrorist
           group is accused of both.

10   IRAQ - Soviet Premier Alexei Kosygin signs a friend-
           ship and cooperation treaty with Iraq. Upon announce-
           ment of the treaty, Libya withdraws its ambassador
           from Baghdad in protest.

11   CAMBODIA - NVA forces surround the town of Kompong
           Trabek closing Route 17.

12   CHAD - The government announces it has resumed
           diplomatic relations with Libya.

12   URUGUAY - Sixteen Tupamaro rebels escape from the
           Punta Carretas prison in Montevideo.

12   UNITED STATES - The Senate passes a bill severely
           limiting the President's ability to commit troops to
           hostile action.

13   SOUTH VIET NAM - NVA troops enter the Binh Long Province capital town of An Loc (Hon Quai) and declare it the Viet Cong capital (for less than one week). RVNAF reports at least 18 Soviet-built tanks were destroyed in the battle.

14   IRAQ - Baghdad Radio reports heavy fighting between Iranian and Iraqi forces.

14   TANZANIA - Tanzanian air defense units shoot down a Portuguese aircraft patrolling the Mozambique border area.

15   URUGUAY - The government declares a "state of war" against the Tupamaro guerrillas after they assassinate four people on 14 April. Eight Tupamaros are killed in the incident.

15   NORTH VIET NAM - US warplanes bomb Hanoi and Haiphong for the first time in four years.

16   USSR - The government protests the damage caused to four Soviet ships in Haiphong harbor by US warplanes.

16   NORTH VIET NAM - US naval vessels attack targets on the Din Sol Peninsula near Haiphong. This is the first surface attack of the war in this area. In another engagement, three North Vietnamese MiGs are shot down over NVN.

17   UNITED STATES - Secretary of State William P. Rogers states President Nixon will use any means short of nuclear weapons or the recommitment of ground forces to halt an NVN invasion of SVN.

17   URUGUAY - Seven people are killed in Montevideo when a military patrol opens fire on a Communist club.

17   TURKEY - Prime Minister Nihat Erim resigns. A caretaker government is formed by Defense Minister Ferit Melen.

18   SOUTH VIET NAM - Communist forces attack across Binh Dinh Province in the II CTZ with the objective of cutting SVN in half. A major NVA tank attack at An Loc is repulsed.

19   NORTH VIET NAM - Soviet-built MiG aircraft attack US destroyers shelling North Vietnamese military installations along the coast. The USS Higbee is damaged by a MiG attack and NVA shore batteries damage the destroyer USS Buchanan on station in the Bay of Tonkin.

19   SOUTH VIET NAM - NVA forces cut Route 19 between Qui
            Nhon on the coast in Binh Dinh Province and Pleiku in
            the Central Highlands and capture the district capital
            town of Hoai An. In MR 3, NVA forces attack An Loc
            following a 2,000 round artillery preparation.

20   NORTH VIET NAM - North Vietnamese ships and aircraft
            attack US naval units in the Gulf of Tonkin. Two NVN
            gunboats are sunk.

22   SOUTH VIET NAM - Four NVA divisions attack into Kontum
            Province. Route 14 is blocked in the Kontim Pass
            between Kontum and Pleiku City.

23   SOUTH VIET NAM - Enemy armor attacks force the evacu-
            ation of Dak To and Tan Canh in MR 2.

24   SOUTH VIET NAM - The Kontum Province town of Dak To is
            captured by the NVA. In a separate incident, a NVN
            trawler carrying munitions is sunk by South Vietnamese
            naval units near Phu Quoc Island in the Gulf of
            Thailand.

25   THE PHILIPPINES - Seventeen people are killed in a
            terrorist grenade attack on the Governor of Ilocos Sur
            Province who is a member of the Liberal Party. Presi-
            dent Marcos accuses the Liberals of cooperation with
            the Communist New People's Army (NPA) and sends the
            army to disarm them.

26   UNITED STATES - President Nixon announces that 20,000
            additional troops will be withdrawn from SVN in the
            next 60 days.

26   SOUTH VIET NAM - Route 1 is cut in Binh Dinh Province
            when the Bong Son Pass is catured by the NVA. This
            isolates much of the province from SVN control.

27   SOUTH VIET NAM - Dong Ha falls as the NVA resume their
            offensive in Quang Tri Province in MR 1.

28   SOUTH VIET NAM - The South Vietnamese are forced to
            give up Fire Bases Bastogne and Checkmate, thereby
            jeopardizing the defense of Hue.

29   BURUNDI - A bloody civil war begins after an attempt
            is made to free former King Mwami Ntare V, who is
            killed in the fighting. (It is later discovered that
            he is executed the night of the attack on orders from
            President Michel Micombero.) Over 100,000 of the Tutsi
            Tribe are killed by Hutu tribesmen serving in the
            Burundi army (with the support of Zaire) in the two
            months of butchery that followed.

29   SOUTH VIET NAM - The province capital of Kontum Province is captured. In Quang Tri Province, all ARVN north of the Thach Han River are ordered to withdraw south to defend Quang Tri City.

29   USSR - Egyptian President Anwar Sadat is promised additional military aid during a formal visit to Moscow.

30   CAMBODIA - The important town of Kompong Trach falls to the Communists.

30   SOUTH VIET NAM - There are 68,100 US troops in SVN.

MAY

1   SOUTH VIET NAM - The capital city of Quang Tri Province is captured by the NVA. Hue is looted by ARVN deserters while 150,000 flee south. NVA forces surround Kontum and Pleiku cities. US aircraft mine Haiphong harbor.

1   NICARAGUA - President Anastasio Samoza Debayle hands over power to a three-man junta which is to rule until the December 1974 elections.

3   ZAIRE - The government announces it is dispatching troops to Burundi to help quell the fighting there.

4   FRANCE - The US and SVN call an indefinite halt to the Paris peace talks.

4   UNITED STATES - The US increases its fighter-bomber and carrier strengths in SEA and begins replacing armor lost in Quang Tri with M-48 tanks flown into to SEA aboard C-5A transports.

5   YEMEN (ADEN) - Omani jets attack South Yemeni (Aden) gun sites after the Omani military post at Habrut is shelled from across the border. This action is part of the ongoing struggle between the British-officered Omani army and the Marxist-led Dhofari rebels who operate in southwestern Oman.

6   KASHMIR - A truce ends two days of renewed Indo-Pakistani fighting.

8   UNITED STATES - President Nixon announces that the mining of NVN harbors has begun.

9   ISRAEL - Paratroopers assault and recapture a hijacked airliner at Lod International Airport. Two of four Palestinian Arab terrorists are killed.

9   UNITED STATES - President Nixon announces the mining of NVN ports, to include Haiphong. He also reports other lines of supply will be cut by air strikes. He then sets terms to end the operation: release of US prisoners and an internationally supervised cease-fire.

10   SOUTH VIET NAM - President Thieu declares martial law and replaces the senior ARVN commander in the Central Highlands. A curfew goes into effect in Saigon.

10   NORTH VIET NAM - The "Operation LINEBACKER," a bombing campaign, starts over NVN. The first targets are the Paul Doumer Bridge and the Yen Vien railroad yards near Hanoi.

11   SOUTH VIET NAM - NVA forces, supported with armor, enter An Loc. They are immediately attacked by 70 B-52s loaded with 1,700 tons of bombs. This is the heaviest bombing strike of the war.

12   CAMBODIA - The government reports the loss of 11 important military positions since the beginning of the month.

13   SOUTH VIET NAM - RVNAF begins an offensive operation to regain control of the Central Highlands. In MR 1 SVN Marines open "Operation NGUYEN HUE."

13   NORTH VIET NAM - The Thanh Hoa (Dragon's Jaw) Bridge, 80 miles south of Hanoi, is destroyed by USAF F-4 aircraft. In addition, the Paul Doumer Bridge to the north of Hanoi is attacked and seriously damaged.

13   MALAGASY REPUBLIC - Fighting erupts between security forces and students following the closing of the medical school, the scene of earlier disturbances. The security forces open fire killing scores of demonstrators. A state of emergency is declared and a curfew imposed to restore order. On 14 May, the Tananarive town hall is burned down, which prompts more killing.

14   USSR - Rioting breaks out following the self-immolation of a young worker in Kaunas, Lithuania. Police and army forces finally restore order on 19 May.

14   SYRIA - Soviet Defense Minister Marshal Andrei A. Grechko signs a new military aid agreement with the Syrians during a visit to Damascus.

15   EGYPT - Marshal Andrei A. Grechko visits Cairo to "coordinate practical steps" on further Soviet military aid to Egypt.

15   UNITED STATES - The treaty of 17 June 1971 takes ef-
          fect, and Okinawa is returned to Japanese administra-
          tive control.

15   URUGUAY - The government extends, for another 45 days,
          its "internal war" against the Tupamaros.

15   SOUTH VIET NAM - The last US units leave Cam Ranh Bay.

17   SOUTH VIET NAM - US Vice-President Spiro T. Agnew con-
          sults with President Thieu in Saigon.

18   MALAGASY REPUBLIC - Following a week of student vio-
          lence, the government of President Philibert Tsiranana
          is overthrown in a bloodless military coup led by
          General Gabriel Ramanantsoa.

18   SOUTH VIET NAM - A sixth US aircraft carrier, USS
          Saratoga, joins US naval units off the coast of SVN. A
          total of 60 ships are now on station in these waters.
          There are 46,000 naval personnel involved.

18   NORTH VIET NAM - USAF aircraft destroy 5.5 million
          gallons of fuel north of Hanoi.

19   COMMUNIST CHINA - Representatives of Communist China,
          the USSR, North Viet Nam, and Mongolia meet in Peking
          to arrange aid for the North Vietnamese following the
          US mining of Haiphong harbor.

19   UNITED STATES - A bomb explodes on the concourse in
          the Pentagon causing considerable damage.

19   WEST GERMANY - Two terrorist-placed bombs explode in
          the Axel Springer publishing house in Hamburg.

20   USSR - There are reports that Soviet KGB troops and
          paratroopers have been sent into Kaunas in   the
          Lithuanian SSR to put down riots stemming from the
          death of a student who set himself on fire.

22   CEYLON - Ceylon is proclaimed independent as the
          Republic of Sri Lanka.

23   UNITED STATES - The Defense Department announces it is
          stepping up the air war against NVN.

25   SOUTH VIET NAM - Special NVA sapper units enter Kontum
          city.

25   NORTH VIET NAM - The Lang Ghia Bridge, located 65
          miles northeast of Hanoi, is destroyed by US aircraft
          dropping "smart" bombs.

26   USSR - President Richard Nixon and Soviet Party leader
            Leonid Brezhnev sign the SALT I Agreement.

27   UNITED STATES - After the summit agreement between
            Nixon and Brezhnev, the US stops developmental work on
            the "Safeguard" anti-ballistic missile system.

28   URUGUAY - Security forces find and capture the Tupa-
            maro "People's Prison" in Montevideo.

29   NORTHERN IRELAND - The official wing of the Irish
            Republican Army announces it has suspended "guerrilla
            activity" in Northern Ireland.

30   ISRAEL - Lod Airport near Tel Aviv is shot up by three
            Japanese terrorists hired by the Palestinians. Twenty-
            five are killed, 76 wounded.

30   SOUTH VIET NAM - Elements of the NVA 7th and 9th Div-
            isions are reported to have abandoned An Loc and to be
            pulling back into Cambodia.

31   TANZANIA - An unidentified aircraft drops anti-govern-
            ment leaflets on a number of Tanzanian towns.

31   SOUTH VIET NAM - US strength in SVN stands at 63,000.

JUNE

            CHAD - France begins withdrawing its military forces
            from Chad.

            UNITED ARAB EMIRATES - Tribal warfare breaks out
            between Shahjah and Fujairah.

1   WEST GERMANY - The leader of the Baader-Meinhof Gang,
            Andreas Baader, is captured along with two others
            following a gun battle in Frankfurt.

2   SOUTH AFRICA - White students demonstrate in protest
            to apartheid. They are dispersed by police. By 5 June,
            the demonstrations have grown in size and a number of
            clashes with police are reported. About 600, many of
            them children, are reported arrested.

5   UNITED STATES - Defense Secretary Melvin Laird informs
            Congress that an additional $5 billion would be needed
            to continue the war in SEA.

5   SOUTH VIET NAM - NVA forces begin pulling back at Phu
            My in Binh Dinh Province.

6   FRANCE - US and NVN representatives meeting in Paris
            agree to hold secret discussion on ending the war.

6-7   SOUTH VIET NAM - ARVN drives out NVA troops who have
            held Kontum for two weeks.

8   NORTH VIET NAM - The government charges that the US is
            deliberately bombing dams and dikes.

8   SOUTH VIET NAM - Route 1 is cut by the VC/NVA at Trang
            Banh, 38 miles northwest of Saigon.

9   SOUTH VIET NAM - The anti-submarine warfare (ASW) car-
            rier USS Ticonderoga becomes the seventh US carrier to
            join the US Seventh Fleet off Viet Nam.

9-10   UNITED ARAB EMIRATES - United Defense Force troops are
            employed to break up tribal fighting along the border
            between Fujairah and Shahjah.

11   SOUTH VIET NAM - A spokeman announces that B-52 bomb-
            ers using Laser-guided "smart" bombs have destroyed
            the Lang Chi hydroelectric power plant 63 miles north-
            west of Hanoi. This facility has the capacity to pro-
            duce 75% of NVN electricity.

12   SOUTH VIET NAM - The road from Saigon to An Loc, Binh
            Long Province, is opened by ARVN. More than 10,000
            refugees flee toward Saigon.

12   UNITED STATES - General John D. Lavelle, USAF, ret.
            admits to the House Armed Services Committee that he
            ordered more than 25 air strikes into NVN in violation
            of Congressional rules prohibiting all but protective
            attacks against the north.

13   EGYPT - Both sides claim to have shot down two of the
            opponents aircraft in the first Arab-Israeli dogfight
            over the Suez Canal since the 1970 cease-fire went
            into effect.

15   SOUTH VIET NAM - The US command announces that Hanoi
            will not be bombed during the visit of Soviet Presi-
            dent Nikolai V. Podgorny. A four-day halt is ordered.
            Bombing is resumed on 19 June.

18   SOUTH VIET NAM - The siege of An Loc ends.

19   SOUTH VIET NAM - The US command announces that more
            than 150 aircraft and 2,000 Air Force personnel have
            been shifted from SVN to Thailand.

20   SWITZERLAND - The UN Disarmament Conference reopens in
            Geneva after a seven-month recess.

21   LEBANON - Israeli forces carry out a raid in force
            into southern Lebanon. There they capture five Syrian
            officers while attacking a guerrilla base. The attack
            is in reprisal for the resumption of Arab guerrilla
            raids into Israel after a four-month lull.

22   NORTHERN IRELAND - The Provisional Wing of the IRA
            proposes a truce. Violence increases in response.

23   SOUTH VIET NAM - The government rejects any notion of
            an in-place cease-fire and demands that North Viet-
            namese forces be withdrawn from SVN as a prelude to
            any truce.

23   LEBANON - Israeli forces renew their attacks on
            Palestinian guerrilla bases in southern Lebanon.

24   NORTH VIET NAM - The government claims the US is
            bombing the Red River dike system.

25   SOUTH PACIFIC - French atmospheric nuclear testing
            begins at Mururoa Atoll in the face of worldwide
            protests.

26   NORTHERN IRELAND - The IRA-sponsored truce goes into
            effect.

27   SOUTH VIET NAM - President Thieu is given the power to
            rule by decree after opposition party members walk out
            of the Senate.

28   SOUTH VIET NAM - General Frederick C. Weyand replaces
            General Creighton W. Abrams as COMUSMACV. Also on this
            date the Second Battle of Quang Tri City begins. ARVN
            forces, with heavy US air support, move to retake the
            Quang Tri Province capital which has been in NVA hands
            since 1 May.

28   UNITED STATES - President Nixon announces the with-
            drawal of an additional 10,000 troops from SVN by 1
            September. He also announces that draftees will no
            longer be sent to SVN unless they volunteer.

28   LEBANON - President Suleiman Franjieh announces that
            Palestinian commando forces in southern Lebanon will
            suspend operations against Israel and move their bases
            away from the border.

28   ARGENTINA - Widespread violence marks the anniversary
            of the 1966 military coup that overthrew the Peron
            regime. Six cities, including Buenos Aires, are put
            under military control.

30   SOUTH VIET NAM - ARVN forces reopen Route 14 in Kontum
            Province. Also, US troop strength stands at 48,000   as
            Phase 12 of the redeployment is completed.

JULY

1   CHAD - France formally hands over responsibility for
            internal security to the Chad army.

2   YUGOSLAVIA - Security forces clash with 19   Croatian
            rebels in western Bosnia after they cross into Yugo-
            slavia from Austria. Thirteen Yugoslav soldiers are
            killed in the ensuing month-long search, before the
            rebel force is destroyed.

3   INDIA - An interim peace agreement is signed with
            Pakistan at Simla after five days of difficult
            negotiation. Yet to be settled are the issues of
            Kashmir and prisoner exchange.

3   SOUTH VIET NAM - A South Vietnamese Marine   reconnais-
            sance unit enters Quang Tri City.

3   PERU - The government declares a state of emergency in
            Puno following violence by left-wing extremists.

4   SOUTH KOREA - The government announces it has agreed
            to hold reunification meetings with North Korea.

6   THE PHILIPPINES - Government forces move against Mus-
            lim guerrillas who have been raiding Christian settle-
            ments in Zamboango del Sur.

7   INDIA - A Kashmir truce line is established and both
            sides begin withdrawing their forces.

7   SOUTH VIET NAM - RVNAF headquarters announces that the
            drive to recapture Quang Tri has stalled.

8   INDIA - The government announces a formula for the re-
            lease of the 93,000 Pakistan prisoners of war it is
            holding. The repatriation will not be completed before
            April 1974.

8   PERU - The government restores diplomatic relations
            with Cuba.

10   THE PHILIPPINES - Government air and naval forces
            launch attacks against Maoist enclaves in Isabela
            Province.

11   URUGUAY - The government ends its state of "internal
            war" that has existed since 15 April.

13   NORTHERN IRELAND - The IRA announces that its truce
            has ended and orders a resumption of terrorist ac-
            tivity. There are now 17,000 British troops in Ulster.

14   ICELAND - The government unilaterally extends its
            coastal fishing rights from 12 to 50 miles thereby
            impeding British commercial fishing.

15   PAKISTAN - The government announces that a compromise
            has been reached that should end the rioting in Sind
            Province that developed over the use of the Urdu and
            Sindhi languages. Fifty people die before the settle-
            ment is reached.

18   EGYPT - Apparently concerned about the possibility of
            a Communist-inspired coup d'etat, President Sadat
            orders the withdrawal of Soviet military and civilian
            advisors. Sadat claims the Soviets have failed to fur-
            nish military aid necessary to conduct a war against
            Israel. Egypt also assumes control of all Soviet bases
            and equipment on Egyptian soil.

18   USSR - The government announces it has reached a "mut-
            ual agreement" with Egypt regarding the withdrawal of
            some of the large contingent of Soviet advisors in
            that country.

19   FRANCE - The North Vietnamese and the US resume secret
            peace talks for the first time since Novbember 1971.

19   SOUTH VIET NAM - Troops of the 22nd ARVN Division open
            an offensive to clear enemy forces from Bihn Dinh
            Province.

21   NORTHERN IRELAND - Twenty-two IRA terrorist bombs ex-
            plode in Belfast in less than two hours. Thirteen
            people are killed and 130 injured.

22   SPAIN - Juan Peron announces that, even though he has
            been nominated for the presidency of Argentina by the
            Juristialista Party, for "security reasons" he would
            not leave Spain until after he is reelected.

24   UNITED NATIONS - Secretary General Kurt Waldheim
            states he has evidence that the US is deliberately
            bombing dikes in NVN.

25   SOUTH VIET NAM - ARVN airborne troops breech the wall
            of the Quang Tri Citadel but are driven back after
            fierce fighting. Also, troops of the ARVN 1st Division
            are required to once again give up Fire Bases Bastogne
            and Checkmate west of Hue.

26   SOUTH VIET NAM - The US and SVN air forces have flown 10,000 missions against enemy targets in the Quang Tri offensive.

26   ARGENTINA - A series of terrorist incidents across the country mark the 20th aniversary of the death of Eva Peron.

27   EGYPT - President Sadat rejects an offer for peace talks made by Israeli Prime Minister Golda Meir.

27   SOUTH VIET NAM - Troops of the NVA 711th Division capture Fire Base Ross in the Que Son Valley in Quang Nam Province.

28   UNITED STATES - The government admits that Air Force fighter-bombers unintentionally struck the Red River dike system in NVN while attacking military targets that were deliberately placed close to the dikes.

28   NORTHERN IRELAND - The British army begins a three-day operation that culminates in the removal of barricades blocking entrances into, and occupation of heretofore inaccessible, Roman Catholic and Protestant enclaves in Londonderry and Belfast.

28   SOUTH VIET NAM - ARVN forces recapture Hoai An, a district town in Binh Dinh Province. The town, the third district town retaken, is recaptured without a fight.

29   COMMUNIST CHINA - The death of Lin Piao in September is finally confirmed. He is accused of participation in the plot to overthrow Mao Tse-tung.

31   SOUTH VIET NAM - US troop strength is 46,000 with only one ground combat battalion left in country.

AUGUST

1   SOUTH VIET NAM - MACV reports that there are seven NVA regiments in Dinh Tuong Province in the Delta. MACV also announces that for the first time US fighter-bombers have attacked the shipyards at Haiphong in NVN.

2   LIBYA - At meetings held in both Bengazi and Tobruk, Libya's Muammar Qaddafi and Egypt's Anwar Sadat agree upon a union of their two countries by 1 September 1973.

3   UNITED STATES - The Senate approves the US-USSR Anti-Ballistic Missile Treaty.

3   SOUTH VIET NAM - Fire Base Bastogne is retaken by ARVN after a one-week occupation by the NVA.

4   SOUTH VIET NAM - Fire Base Checkmate is reoccupied by the 1st ARVN Division.

4   UGANDA - President Amin orders all noncitizens of Asian descent out of the country within 90 days.

5   ITALY - Palestinian terrorists blow up the storage facilities at the Trieste terminal of the Trans-Alpine Pipeline.

5   SOUTH VIET NAM - President Thieu severly limits press activity in SVN.

5   UGANDA - President Amin orders the expulsion of all Asians holding British pasports.

6   CAMBODIA - Heavy fighting is reported as NVA forces attack Kompong Trabek north of Phnom Penh.

6   EGYPT - Most Soviet advisors have departed Egypt by this deadline.

7   NORTHERN IRELAND - A Protestant member of the Ulster Constabulary is shot down outside his home in Amagh; he becomes the 500th victim of terrorism in the last three years. This incident effectively ends the cease-fire.

9   SOUTH VIET NAM - More than 900,000 refugees have been created by the current offensive.

9   NORTH VIET NAM - The newly repaired Thanh Hoa Bridge is destroyed, for the second time in three months, by the use of laser-guided bombs.

10   UNITED STATES - The House of Representatives defeats a Senate-passed amendment to the military appropriations bill that would have forced an end to US involvement in SEA by 1 October. At the same time, the President formally presents the Convention on Biological Warfare to the US Senate for ratification.

10   OMAN - A major battle takes place between Omani forces under British command and Dhofari rebels near the coastal town of Mirbat.

11   SOUTH VIET NAM - The end of the US ground combat role in SVN occurs when the 3rd Battalion, 21st US Infantry is withdrawn from Da Nang.

16   NORTH VIET NAM – US aircraft conduct the heaviest
            raids of the war. Over 400 sorties are flown against
            NVN targets.

16   MOROCCO – King Hassan II escapes an assassination at-
            tempt when Moroccan jets strafe his plane as he is re-
            turning to Rabat from a visit in France. The coup
            leader, Defense Minister General Muhammad Oufkir,
            commits suicide.

17   GREAT BRITAIN – The government's formal protests
            against Iceland's extention of its territorial fishing
            rights are upheld by the Internalional Court of
            Justice. Iceland refuses to accept the judgement and
            sends its warships to drive off British fishing
            trawlers.

17   ISRAEL – The Israeli Defense Minister Moshe Dayan
            suggests an interim truce line which divides the Sinai
            Peninsula.

19   SOUTH VIET NAM – NVA forces capture the district town
            of Que Son in Quang Nam Province.

21   CHILE – President Allende declares a state of emer-
            gency in Santiago Province when violence breaks out
            during a 24-hour strike by local merchants.

22   ARGENTINA – Widespread demonstrations follow the kill-
            ing of 16 of 19 jailed terrorists who were allegedly
            breaking out of Rawson Prison.

24   NORTH VIET NAM – The government rejects a South Viet-
            namese offer (made 22 August in Paris) to repatriate
            600 disabled NVA POWs.

25   UNITED NATIONS – Communist China casts its first
            Security Council veto to bar the membership appli-
            cation of Bangladesh.

27   NORTH VIET NAM – Intelligence sources detect a Com-
            munist Chinese minesweeper in Haiphong Harbor.

28   UNITED STATES – President Nixon announces he will end
            the draft in July 1973.

29   UNITED STATES – The President announces an additional
            troop reduction of 12,000 men from SVN that will bring
            the actual strength down to the authorized level of
            27,000 by 1 December.

29   INDIA – At the end of a five-day meeting, the govern-
            ment announces an Indo-Pakistani settlement on a "line
            of control" for Kashmir.

31   CHILE - The army takes control of the city of Concepcion following clashes between opposing political factions and the police.

31   SOUTH VIET NAM - US troop strength is now 36,800.

SEPTEMBER

1   URUGUAY - Uruguayan police wound and capture Raul Sendic, the founder of the Tupamaros, in Montevideo.

1   ICELAND - In defiance of the International Court ruling barring its imposition of a 50-mile no fishing zone around Iceland, the government orders the zone put into place.

2   EGYPT - The government confirms it is seeking military arms from the West.

2   NORTH VIET NAM - The government announces it will release three American POWs (accomplished 28 September).

5   WEST GERMANY - Palestinian Arab terrorists from the "Black September" organization break into and barricade themselves in the Israeli dormitory at the Olympic Village in Munich and demand the release of 200 Arabs held in Israeli jails. They kill two Israelis who resist and hold nine others hostage. Later, when they attempt to fly out of Munich's Furstenfeldbruch Airport, where they and their hostages had been flown by helicopter, West German police carry out a crudely organized assault in which five terrorists are killed. Before the end, however, a terrorist grenade kills all nine Israeli hostages. A West German policeman is also killed in the exchange of gunfire. Three more terrorists are subsequently captured.

7   SOUTH VIET NAM - About 1,000 NVA troops attack the district town of Tien Phouc near Da Nang in Quang Nam Province.

7   SOUTH KOREA - The government announces it will withdraw all of its remaining forces (some 37,000) from SVN by December.

7   SWITZERLAND - The UN Disarmament Conference adjourns without any accomplishments.

8   CAMBODIA - Severe food shortages bring clashes between police and civilian and military looters in Phnom Penh.

8   MIDDLE EAST - Israeli jets attack ten Arab guerrilla bases in Syria and Lebanon in retaliation for the Olympic Massacre.

9   SYRIA - A major battle between Israeli and Syrian jets takes place. This is the first such battle since 1970. No results are reported.

11   NORTH VIET NAM - US warplanes destroy the Paul Doumer Bridge over the Red River in Hanoi just as its re-building is completed.

11   PANAMA - The government refuses to accept the annual US payment for canal rights claiming the canal is "occupied arbitrarily."

14   UNITED STATES - The Senate approves the US-USSR Offensive Nuclear Weapons Agreement with some stipulated reservations about weapons parity.

15   SOUTH VIET NAM - The nearly destroyed city of Quang Tri is recaptured by South Vietnamese Marines. Fighting continues elsewhere in the province.

16   SOUTH VIET NAM - NVA forces open a new offensive in southern Quang Ngai Province.

16   AUSTRALIA - Croatian terrorists bomb a Yugoslav business in Sydney wounding 16 people.

16   SPAIN - Spanish police arrest nine Croatians, three of whom had hijacked an airliner in a successful bid to force Sweden to release the other six.

16-17   LEBANON - Israeli forces attack Palestinian bases in southern Lebanon.

17   UGANDA - The government claims the country has been invaded by Ugandan rebel "People's Army" forces supported by regular Tanzanian army units. Ugandan forces drive the invaders into a swamp near the border.

18   UNITED STATES - President Nixon announces the US will cut all aid to any country protecting or participating in the narcotics trade.

18   TANZANIA - The government claims a Ugandan military aircraft bombed the border town of Bukoba and denies its forces participated in the invasion of Uganda.

18   UGANDA - A number of foreign journalists are reported as having been arrested.

18   GREAT BRITAIN - The first group of Asians expelled
            from Uganda arrives in England.

19   GREAT BRITAIN - An Israeli diplomat is killed in Lon-
            don when he opens a letter bomb.

19   SOUTH VIET NAM - ARVN forces recapture Quang Tri City.

20-22   SUDAN - Five Libyan C-130 transports carrying 399 com-
            bat troops and military equipment are forced to land
            at Khartoum by the Sudanese government. On 21 Septem-
            ber, they are allowed to fly to Cairo but, on 22 Sep-
            tember, land at Entebbe Airbase in Uganda.

21   SOMALIA - A cease-fire agreement for the Tanzania-
            Uganda conflict is worked out at Mogadishu.

23   THE PHILIPPINES - After several bombings in Manila,
            including an attack on the Constitutional Convention
            (19 September), and an unsuccessful attempt (22 Sep-
            tember) on the life of the Defense Minister, Juan
            Ponce Enrile, President Ferdnand Marcos declares
            martial law and the arrest of a number of his critics
            to protect his regime against a "Communist rebellion."

25   LEBANON - Prime Minister Saeb Salam claims to have won
            agreement with Palestinian guerrillas based in south-
            ern Lebanon to abide by the government's movement
            restrictions.

26   SOUTH VIET NAM - RVNAF sources state that fighting in
            SVN is at its lowest point since the offensive began.

26   YEMEN (ADEN) - A major escalation in the border war
            takes place when South Yemeni rebels (FLOSY) and mem-
            bers of the South Arab League supported by tribesmen
            from North Yemen (San'a) attack al-Dali (Dhala) in the
            North-South Yemen border area.

29   CAMBODIA - The government announces its troops were
            unsuccessful in dislodging enemy forces from Angkor
            Wat.

29   COMMUNIST CHINA - Japanese Prime Minister Kakuei
            Tanaka and Chinese officials sign a communique in
            which the two countries agree to end the war that has
            existed between them since 1937 and to establish
            diplomatic relations.

29   NATIONALIST CHINA - The government breaks diplomatic
            relations with Japan following the announcement of the
            agreements with Communist China.

29   SOUTH VIET NAM - The Indian ICC representative goes
          home.   The ICC headquarters is officially moved to
          Hanoi, but the Canadian and Polish representatives
          stay in Saigon.

30   SOUTH VIET NAM - US troop strength in SVN is 35,500.

30   INDIA - Indian and Pakistani troops clash along the
          Kashmir border.

OCTOBER

1   INDIA - A cease-fire is arranged in Kashmir.

1   SOUTH VIET NAM - After a short lull, MACV reports 100
          Communist attacks in SVN, the largest surge of activ-
          ity in two months.

2   YEMEN (SAN'A) - The North Yemeni town of Qa'tabah is
          occupied by South Yemeni (PDRY) forces. North Yemen
          accuses the South Yemens of using foreign pilots to
          attack their towns.

3   LEBANON - Palestinian commando leaders again agree to
          Lebanese demands that they withdraw from the region
          near the Israeli border.

8   NORTH VIET NAM - US B-52s bomb a supply buildup near
          Vinh in the deepest raids into NVN in six months.

8   YEMEN (SAN'A) - North Yemeni forces occupy Kamaran
          Island which is off the North Yemeni coast but belongs
          to South Yemen.

9   EGYPT - Following a demand to do so from the Egyptian
          government, Sudan begins withdrawing its forces from
          the Suez Canal.

12   UNITED STATES - A racially motivated disorder breaks
          out aboard the aircraft carrier USS Kitty Hawk on
          station in the South China Sea.

12   CHILE - President Allende extends the martial law
          edict to 13 additional provinces because of worsening
          conditions brought about by a trucker's strike.

12   SOUTH VIET NAM - The Ben Het Ranger Camp in Kontum
          Province is captured by Communist forces.

12   SENEGAL - Portuguese troops attack the Senagalese
          military post at Nianao.

13   ARAB LEAGUE - A cease-fire is arranged between the two
          Yemens. Sporadic fighting continues, however, until a
          formal agreement is signed in Cairo on 28 October.

13   USSR - The Shah of Iran signs a 15-year economic co-
          operation and trade agreement with the Soviet Union.

14   SOUTH VIET NAM - ARVN evacuates the Minh Thanh Base
          Camp in Binh Long Province. The camp has been under
          siege since April.

17   SOUTH KOREA - President Park Chung Hee declares mar-
          tial law, suspends constitutional guarantees, and
          closes the National Assembly.

17   THE PHILIPPINES - The government announces the arrest
          of four persons implicated in a plot to kill President
          Marcos.

22   THE PHILIPPINES - Government troops defeat a major
          rebel attack on the island of Mindanao.

23   NORTH VIET NAM - "Operation LINEBACKER I," the bombing
          campaign designed to impose a penalty on NVN and to
          lend indirect support to SVN, ends.

23   UNITED NATIONS - The Security Council condemns Portu-
          gal for its attack on Senegal.

24   SOUTH VIET NAM - President Thieu announces that his
          government finds the peace terms, reportedly worked
          out in secret by Henry Kissinger and the North Viet-
          namese, unacceptable as they do not call for the with-
          drawal of NVA forces from SVN.

26   UNITED STATES - US peace negotiator Henry Kissinger
          optimistically announces that "Peace is at hand,"
          after NVN disclosed the nine-point peace plan agreed
          upon in secret negotiations.

26   FRANCE - NVN and VC delegates at the peace talks claim
          the US has "backed down" on a cease-fire agreement,
          and then demand that the peace agreement be signed by
          31 October.

26   SOUTH VIET NAM - The USMACV announces the largest num-
          ber of NVA and VC ground attacks in any one day since
          the 1968 "Tet" offensive.

26   DAHOMEY - A military coup overthrows the government of
          President Justin Timotin Ahomadegbe and puts Major
          Mathieu Kerekou in the presidency.

26   EGYPT - General Muhammad Sadek, Egypt's Minister of War and military Commander in Chief, resigns in protest of President Sadat's attempts at reconciliation with the USSR. General Ahmed Ismail replaces him as defense minister.

27   SOUTH VIET NAM - A halt to the bombing of NVN above the 20th Parallel is announced. The bombing pause has been in effect since 23 October.

27   SOUTH KOREA - President Park promulgates a new constitution that grants him extended powers.

28   EGYPT - Egypt's naval commander, Rear Admiral Mahmoud Abdel Rahman Fahmy, resigns in protest of President Sadat's attempts at reconciliation with the USSR.

28   YEMEN - North and South Yemen sign an agreement ending fighting along the border separating the two states and pledge to reunite within one year.

29   WEST GERMANY - The government decides to release three terrorists jailed in connection with the Munich Olympic Massacre in order to obtain the release of a group of hostages held on a Lufthansa airliner hijacked by Black September terrorists.

30   UNITED STATES - Naval bombardment north of the 20th Parallel is halted.

31   FRANCE - The NVN deadline passes without any movement in the peace talks.

31   NORTH VIET NAM - US B-52 bombers carry out the heaviest raid of the war below the 20th Parallel.

31   SOUTH VIET NAM - ARVN airborne forces recapture Fire Support Base Barbara in Quang Tri Province. US troop strength is reduced to 32,200.

NOVEMBER

EGYPT - President Sadat decides to once again go to war with Israel.

USSR - A border clash on the Sino-Soviet border takes a number of casualties on both sides.

1   UNITED STATES - President Nixon announces that the Viet Nam cease-fire will not be signed until "the agreement is right."

1   UNITED STATES - American Indians seize the Bureau of
            Indian Affairs in Washington, DC, to demonstrate their
            demands for reform.

3   SOUTH VIET NAM - US intelligence sources indicate the
            NVA is moving heavy reinforcements into SVN.

4   NORTH VIET NAM - The area known as the "Panhandle" is
            subjected to the heaviest raids of the war in an at-
            tempt to disrupt movement of more NVA forces into SVN.

5   SOUTH VIET NAM - Fire Base Ross in the Que Son Valley
            in Quang Nam Province is retaken by ARVN.

9   ISRAEL - The government announces a major clash with
            Syrian armor, artillery, and jet aircraft in the Golan
            Heights region.

9   MOZAMBIQUE - FRELIMO forces open new offensives in
            Manica Sofala and Tete Provinces.

12   NORWAY - A Soviet "Whiskey"-class submarine is de-
            tected in Sognefjord but manages to escape about 24
            November without having surfaced.

14   SOUTH VIET NAM - Fire Base Anne in Quang Tri Province
            is reoccupied by ARVN forces.

15   NORTH VIET NAM - US B-52s carry out the heaviest raid
            of the war in a campaign designed to constantly in-
            crease pressure on NVN.

15   UNITED STATES - The Department of State announces that
            Canada, Hungary, Indonesia, and Poland have agreed to
            serve as the International Control and Supervisory
            Commission to oversee the cease-fire in SVN.

16   NATO - Seven members of NATO invite four Warsaw Pact
            members to a conference to be held on 31 January 1973,
            to seek reductions in armed force levels in Central
            Europe.

19   IRELAND - The reputed leader of the Provisional Wing
            of the IRA, Sean MacStiofain, is arrested in Dublin.

20   FRANCE - Henry Kissinger and NVN's Le Duc Tho begin a
            new round of private peace negotiations in Paris.

21   SWITZERLAND - SALT II talks open in Geneva.

21   ISRAEL - Following three weeks of sporadic fighting,
            an eight-hour battle is fought in the Golan Heights
            between Israeli and Syrian forces.

22   NORTH VIET NAM - A US B-52 bomber is seriously damaged by an Soviet-built SA-2 surface-to-air missile near Vinh. The aircraft limps back to Thailand where the crew ejects and is rescued.

23   BOLIVIA - President Hugo Banzer Suarez declares a state of siege to thwart what are called "leftist plots."

25   FRANCE - The Southeast Asia peace talks break off once again without agreement.

25   USSR - A clash is reported on the Soviet Kazakhstan-Sinkiang-Chinese border. Five Soviet border guards are reported dead.

27   JORDAN - King Hussein reports a Libyan-backed plot to assassinate him had been thwarted in early November.

28   LIBYA - An agreement is signed in Tripoli by the Presidents of North Yemen (San'a) and South Yemen (Aden) to merge the two countries.

30   SOUTH VIET NAM - US troop strength in SVN is 25,500.

DECEMBER

1   INDIA - The long-awaited prisoner exchange with Pakistan begins. The first POWs captured during the 1971 war are exchanged.

4   HONDURAS - The government of President Ramon Ernesto Cruz is ousted by a military coup led by former President General Osvaldo Lopez Arellano.

5   AUSTRALIA - The newly elected government of Prime Minister Gough Whitlam orders an end to the draft and promises the withdrawal of troops committed to the fighting in Viet Nam.

6   FRANCE - SEA peace talks once again resume.

6   SOUTH VIET NAM - One American is killed and two wounded when Tan Son Nhut Air Base in Saigon is hit by 43 Soviet-made 122mm rockets. Eight Vietnamese are killed and 52 wounded in the attack.

7   INDIA - In a joint announcement with Pakistan it is announced that a line of demarcation has been agreed upon in Kashmir.

7   THE PHILIPPINES - Imelda Marcos is attacked in public and stabbed. Her would-be assassin is killed.

9   USSR - The government signs a new military aid agreement with NVN.

10   NORTH VIET NAM - Heavy US B-52 raids along the demilitarized zone continue for the fourth straight day even though NVA and VC activity has declined.

11   KASHMIR - India and Pakistan sign an agreement that defines the demarcation line between the two sides in Kashmir.

12   SOUTH VIET NAM - President Thieu proposes a Christmas cease-fire that will continue as long as the peace talks continue.

12   MALAGASY REPUBLIC - Serious rioting breaks out in Tamatave causing a mass exodus from the city.

13   FRANCE - Private peace talks in Paris between US and NVN representatives break off because of lack of agreement.

14   ARGENTINA - Juan Peron leaves the country for Paraguay after rejecting an offer to run for President.

14   UNITED STATES - The administration rejects the SVN cease-fire proposal of 12 December, stating the Paris negotiations are the only creditable means of seeking peace.

14   SOUTH KOREA - The martial law order is rescinded.

14   NEW ZEALAND - The government announces the last of its troops have departed South Viet Nam.

14   MALAGASY REPUBLIC - A state of siege is proclaimed throughout the country.

15   UNITED STATES - The Department of State announces that high-level negotiations will open soon with Chile to resolve the tensions that have developed between the two countries.

18   NORTH VIET NAM - The NVN negotiators at Paris refuse to negotiate in good faith. President Nixon reinstitutes the massive bombing of NVN, especially in and around Hanoi and Haiphong. The US Air Force carries out the heaviest B-52 raid of the war as "Operation LINEBACKER II" begins.

18   SOUTH VIET NAM - The last Australian troops leave the country.

19   EGYPT - Anti-government demonstrations at Cairo University erupt into violence. By the end of the month, most universities in Egypt have been struck by serious rioting.

20   NORTHERN IRELAND - At least eight people are killed in terrorist attacks in Belfast and Londonderry.

21   GERMANY - A treaty is signed between East and West Germany that effectively recognizes the sovereignty of East Germany.

21   RHODESIA - FROLIZI rebels attack a white-owned farm in the first such incident since 1966.

21   AUSTRALIA - The government establishes diplomatic relations with Communist China. The next day New Zealand does the same thing.

23   NICARAGUA - Following a major earthquake, President Anastasio Samoza resumes personal leadership of the country.

26   NORTH VIET NAM - After a 36-hour Christmas break US bombers again attack NVN. By 28 December the air defenses around Hanoi are overwhelmed and offer no further resistance.

27   SOUTH VIET NAM - MACV announces that the air campaign against NVN has not been without a price. From 18-25 December the US flew 147 B-52 missions and more than 1,000 tactical fighter strikes against 68 specific targets in NVN north of the 20th Parallel. Twelve B-52 bombers were lost, primarily to SAMs of which more than 600 were launched against the aircraft.

27   AUSTRALIA - The government terminates all military aid to SVN.

28   GREAT BRITAIN - The government rejects a Maltese demand for a ten percent increase in rent on its installations on the island. Premier Mintoff states if the increase is not paid, British troops will have to leave Malta by 31 March 1973.

28   EGYPT - President Anwar Sadat announces his government is drawing up plans for another war with Israel.

28-29   THAILAND - Four Arab terrorists seize the Israeli Embassy in Bangkok taking 19 hostages. All are released unharmed after 19 hours in captivity when the terrorists, members of "Black September," are given safe passage to Egypt.

30   NORTH VIET NAM - Bombing in the north is once again
            halted by President Nixon. Peace talks are scheduled
            to resume in Paris.

31   SOUTH VIET NAM - US strength in SVN is 24,000. (This
            is 1,000 less than President Nixon stated would remain
            until all prisoners were repatriated.) Losses in 1972
            are 531. During "Operation LINEBACKER II" 15 B-52s and
            13 other US aircraft were lost.

                              Notes

1973

JANUARY

2   FRANCE - Viet Nam peace talks resume in Paris after
the US halts bombing NVN above the 20th Parallel.

2-5   AFRICA - In rapid succession, Congo, Mali, and Niger
break diplomatic relations with Israel.

3   EGYPT - The government closes all of the nation's institutions of higher education following month-long
student violence.

3   THE PHILIPPINES - President Marcos offers amnesty to
some Mindanao Muslim rebels and orders a halt to military operations on the island.

6   NORTH VIET NAM - The government orders a state of emergency to help cope with the effects of the heavy and
persistant US bombing effort of last month (December
1972).

7-12   MIDDLE EAST - At a meeting of the Palestine National
Council, Yasser Arafat is elected the chairman of the
Supreme Military Council.

8   SOUTH VIET NAM - The US Command admits it accidently
hit the ARVN air base at Danang in air strikes that
destroyed a fuel dump and caused a number of casualties.

8   FRANCE - Serious private negotiations resume between
Doctor Henry Kissinger and Le Duc Tho in Paris.

8   ISRAEL - Heavy fighting is reported between Israeli and Syrian forces in the Golan Heights. Israeli jets strike Syrian and Palestinian camps.

8   GREECE - An agreement is signed granting the US Sixth Fleet home port privileges in the Athens area.

8   LIBYA - The Libyans begin the training of 300 Ugandan soldiers and airmen.

9   RHODESIA - The government closes its border with Zambia after two South African policemen are killed (8 January) by an anti-personnel mine.

9   AUSTRALIA - The Australian Maritime Union ends its two-week boycott of US ships, which was called to protest the bombing of North Viet Nam.

10   THAILAND - The government announces the US will be allowed to keep its bases in Thailand after a Viet Nam cease-fire.

13   MALAGASY - The government lifts the state of siege imposed on 14 December 1972.

15   UNITED STATES - Citing the progress being made at the Paris peace talks, the President orders US forces to halt all offensive action against NVN above the 17th parallel.

15   GREECE - The government announces it will no longer accept direct US aid but will continue to purchase US military equipment.

17   THE PHILIPPINES - President Marcos, using what he calls "constitutional authoritarianism," declares his much-debated new constitution ratified.

18   INDIA - Prime Minister Indira Gandhi puts the state of Andhra Pradesh under central government authority in the wake of separatist rioting.

20   GUINEA - Amilcar Cabral, the leader of the African Party for the Independence of Guinea and Cape Verde (PAIGC), is assassinated in front of his house in Conakry.

20   ECUADOR - Government naval patrol craft seize a US fishing trawler in international waters off the Galapagos Islands.

21   NEW ZEALAND - The Prime Ministers of Australia and New Zealand reaffirm their nations' commitment to SEATO at a meeting in Wellington.

21   PERU - The Peruvian navy releases the American fishing
            boat _Apollo_ after a fine in excess of $100,000 for
            allegedly entering the Peruvian 200-mile limit on 20
            January was paid.

23   FRANCE - Henry Kissinger announces a cease-fire agree-
            ment has been reached which is to go into effect at
            0800 hours (Saigon Time), 28 January. All prisoners of
            war are to be released, and the last 23,700 troops in
            SVN are to be withdrawn within 60 days.

23   HAITI - Three Haitian terrorists kidnap the US Ambas-
            sador to Haiti, Clifton Knox. He is ransomed after 20
            hours for $70,000, safe conduct to Mexico for the
            three kidnappers, and the release of 16 political pri-
            soners. Mexico confiscates the ransom money, refuses
            to accept the kidnappers, and forces them to proceed
            to Chile.

26   PAKISTAN - An armed rebellion breaks out in Baluchi-
            stan following the government's promulgation of its
            new draft constitution. Government troops finally re-
            store order on 30 January.

27   FRANCE - The formal signing of the cease-fire agree-
            ment and protocols ending the fighting in SVN takes
            place in Paris.

27   PORTUGAL - The government reports guerrilla forces in
            Mozambique have   begun using   Soviet-built 122mm
            rockets.

27   UNITED STATES - Secretary of Defense Melvin Laird an-
            nounces that the use of the draft to fill the mili-
            tary's ranks has come to an end.

27-31   EGYPT - At a meeting of the Arab Defense Council a
            unified 18-nation plan is drawn up for military and
            political action against Israel. Jordan   accepts
            reactivation of the Jordanian front and all bow to a
            PLO demand for a resumption of fighting against
            Israel.

28   SOUTH VIET NAM - A cease-fire begins in South Viet Nam
            effective 2400 hours (Midnight, GMT), 27 January. US
            forces are ordered to disengage. The US death toll
            stands at 45,958 killed in action.

29   CAMBODIA - Pol Pot declares a test truce for his
            country.

31   NATO - NATO representatives meet with Warsaw Pact
            counterparts to look for paths to mutual and balanced
            force reductions (MBFR) in Europe.

31   SOUTH VIET NAM - US troop strength in SVN is 21,821.

FEBRUARY

2   THE PHILIPPINES - President Marcos offers amnesty to
            Communist rebels but not to their leaders.

4   ZAMBIA - The government announces it will keep its
            border with Rhodesia closed despite a Rhodesian claim
            that it has been reopened (3 February).

5   NORTH VIET NAM - US personnel meet with NVN counter-
            parts at Haiphong to discuss minesweeping operations.

5   AUSTRALIA - The government pledges to honor its mili-
            tary commitments to Malaysia and Singapore even though
            the new Labor government promised to withdraw all
            combat forces stationed in SEA.

5   DOMINICAN REPUBLIC - Troops are sent to find a small
            band of rebels thought to have landed on the southern
            coast on 4 February. As a result of the perceived in-
            vasion, the government orders the arrest of a number
            of opposition leaders including former President Juan
            Bosch and closes all schools and radio stations.

6   SOUTH VIET NAM - US strength in SVN is now less than
            20,000.

8   NORTH VIET NAM - Four US minesweepers begin clearing
            an anchorage 35 miles out of Haiphong Harbor to serve
            as base for vessels sweeping US-mines from NVN ports.

9   EAST GERMANY - The government establishes diplomatic
            relations with Great Britain and France.

9   SOUTH VIET NAM - The ICC reports that the cease-fire
            is not working effectively, and that there are numer-
            ous violations of its provisions as heavy fighting
            continues in several areas.

10   URUGUAY - The military presents a list of 19 demands
            to the government. Although he continues in office,
            President Juan Maria Bordaberry is forced to yield
            power to a military junta (14 February) in a move
            designed to halt Tupamaro guerrilla activity. Mili-
            tary forces then conduct a campaign of extermination
            to remove the Tupamaro threat.

10   USSR - Secretary Brezhnev tells Egypt his country will
            help the Egyptian armed forces but will not supply any
            new weapons.

11   EGYPT - Prime Minister Aziz Sidki announces his coun-
            try has adopted a "war budget."

11-15   PAKISTAN - A cache of arms is discovered in the Iraqi
            Chancellery in Islamabad. Investigation proves these
            weapons are destined for Baluchi rebels in Iran (12
            February). A number of government officials in the
            North West Frontier and Baluchistan are dismissed (15
            February). The Iraqi Ambassador is expelled.

12   NORTH VIET NAM - As a part of the cease-fire agree-
            ment, NVN begins releasing US POWs. This is the start
            of "Operation HOMECOMING." The first group consists of
            143 Americans; eight American civilians and 19 mili-
            tary personnel are released at Loc Ninh, and 116 more
            Americans are released in Hanoi.

13   USSR - The government announces it has delivered its
            first postwar shipment of aid to NVN.

13   NORTH VIET NAM - The government authorizes the Inter-
            national Red Cross to begin a search for 1,328 missing
            US service personnel.

15   UNITED STATES - The government announces it has signed
            a five-year pact with Cuba that is designed to curb
            hijacking.

15   RWANDA - Hutu tribesmen open a campaign of destruction
            against the minority Tutsi tribe. Many Tutsi begin
            leaving the region.

16   GREECE - Students from Athens University and police
            clash.

16   SOUTH VIET NAM - ARVN forces recapture the coastal
            town of Sa Huynh, denying the NVA a port of entry for
            war materiel.

17   SOUTH VIET NAM - The Four-Power Joint Military Commis-
            sion (FPJMC) urgently appeals for a cease-fire between
            South Vietnamese and Communist forces. Also, US mili-
            tary strength in SVN is reported as less than 15,000
            personnel.

17   IRAQ - The execution of 17 army officers, convicted of
            participating in a coup attempt against the Baathist
            government, is reported.

21   IRAN - The press reports that Iran has purchased $2
            billion in military equipment from the US, including
            70 F-4 and 111 F-5E aircraft.

21   SINAI - Israeli jets shoot down an unarmed Boeing 727
            belonging to Libya's Aran Airlines, killing all 113
            passengers and crew on board.

21   LEBANON - Israeli forces destroy seven Palestinian
            bases in raids designed to thwart terrorist attacks on
            Israel.

21   LAOS - The Laotian government and the Communist Pathet
            Lao announce a cease-fire agreement to take effect at
            1200 hours (Vientiane Time), 22 February. All foreign
            troops are to be withdrawn within 60 days of the for-
            mation of a coalition government.

21   UNITED STATES - In response to the Laotian cease-fire,
            the US asks the Pathet Lao for the release of American
            POWs known to be in their hands.

21   SOUTH VIET NAM - ARVN reopens Route 1 from the MR 2
            border to Quang Tri.

23   LAOS - When the Pathet Lao break the treaty, the Royal
            Laotian Army asks for and receives American B-52
            support in attacking a number of targets in Laos.

26   FRANCE - An international conference on Viet Nam opens
            in Paris.

27   UNITED STATES - When NVN officials announce there will
            be no further prisoner release until the US meets cer-
            tain truce agreements, President Nixon orders a halt
            to all minesweeping in Haiphong Harbor, stops the US
            troop withdrawal, and suspends US participation in all
            international conferences dealing with Viet Nam.

MARCH

            CAMBODIA - As Khmer Rouge forces cut all of the roads
            into the city, Phnom Penh comes under virtual siege.

1   RWANDA - Civil war breaks out between Hutu and Tutsi
            tribesmen.

1   NATIONALIST CHINA - The Taiwan government refuses
            direct negotiations with Peking.

1-4   SUDAN - The Saudi Embassy in Khartoum is captured by a
            group of eight, "Black September" terrorists during an
            evening reception. The terrorists demand the release
            of prisoners held in three countries: the US (includ-
            ing Sirhan Sirhan, Robert Kennedy's killer), Jordan
            (60 Palestinians), and West Germany (the Baader-
            Meinhof Gang). They also demand the release of all the

1-4   SUDAN (Cont'd) - Arab women detained in Israel. During the confusion many of the diplomats in attendance are able to escape. Apparently, on 2 March, the newly appointed US Ambassador, Cleo Noel, Jr., the outgoing US Charge d'Affaires, George C. Moore, along with the Belgian Charge d'Affaires, Guy Eid, are murdered. The terrorists surrender on 4 March, and are held for a trial that is several times delayed. They are then deported to Egypt, where President Sadat apparently releases them to the PLO.

2   MOROCCO - A Libyan-supported "invasion" fails. About 100 rebels are killed or captured.

2   FRANCE - An agreement guaranteeing the settlement of the war in Viet Nam is initialed by the 12 nations attending the Paris Conference.

2   SOUTH VIET NAM - The last elements of the Thai and Filipino military contingents leave SVN.

3   NIGERIA - The government signs a treaty of friendship and cooperation with Mali.

4   SOUTH VIET NAM - The withdrawal of US forces resumes as a group of 106 American PWs is released by Hanoi.

5   SOUTH VIET NAM - US troop strength in SVN is less than 10,000.

6   SUDAN - The government blames al-Fatah for the attack on the Saudi Embassy in Khartoum. President Numeiry bans all Palestinian guerrilla activities in Sudan.

10   BERMUDA - Sir Richard Sharples, the Governor of Bermuda, is assassinated at the Government House in Hamilton by unknown assailants. His aide is also killed. A state of emergency is declared (11 March). Six months earlier, the island's Police Commissioner was also assassinated.

12   SWITZERLAND - The second round of SALT II talks begins in Geneva.

14   UNITED STATES - The government partially lifts the arms embargo that was imposed on India and Pakistan during the 1971 war.

15   UNITED NATIONS - During the course of a 14-day meeting of the Security Council in Panama City, Panama, the US vetoes a resolution calling for the immediate turnover of the Canal Zone to the Panamanian government.

17   CAMBODIA - Prime Minister Lon Nol declares a state of
            emergency and suspends civil liberties after a lone
            Cambodian Air Force pilot, flying a stolen plane,
            bombs the Presidential Palace in Phnom Penh, killing
            43 and injuring another 50.

19   ZAMBIA - At a four-day meeting between rival Rhodesian
            ZAPU and ZANU insurgent leaders a decision is reached
            to set up a joint military command and a political
            council.

19   FRANCE - South Vietnamese officials and representa-
            tives of the Viet Cong open full-scale talks in Paris.

20   KUWAIT - The government accuses Iraq of attacking its
            border police post at Sameta, 2.5 miles inside the
            border near the Iraqi Persian Gulf port of Umn Qasr.
            Although the Iraqis withdraw on 26 March and Saudi
            Arabia reinforces the Kuwaiti border, the issue is not
            resolved. Iran and Jordan offer forces to further
            secure its border with Iraq on 31 March.

20   CAMBODIA - An eight-ship convoy with US air cover
            arrives at Phnom Penh with food, fuel, and ammunition.

20-21   IRAQ - The government beats a hasty retreat from its
            belligerent stance over border clashes with Kuwait
            when Saudi Arabia sends a force of at least 20,000
            troops to reinforce the Kuwait army.

21   LIBYA - Two Libyan fighter aircraft shoot at, but
            miss, a USAF C-130 cargo plane over the Mediterranean
            83 miles off the Libyan coast.

21   ARGENTINA - Government troops are used to quell a
            police revolt in La Plata.

23   SOUTH VIET NAM - The final elements of the ROK mili-
            tary forces in SVN depart for home.

26   EGYPT - Anwar Sadat removes Aziz Sidky and assumes the
            duties of Prime Minister.

26   THE PHILIPPINES - The government announces its forces
            have killed 200 Muslim rebels in Mindanao.

27   UNITED STATES - The White House announces that the
            bombing of Cambodia will continue until Cambodia
            agrees to a cease-fire and the Communists end their
            offensive operations. US troop strength in SVN is
            reported to be less than 5,000.

28   EGYPT - Anwar Sadat declares himself Governor-General
            of Egypt with the power to declare martial law.

29   SOUTH VIET NAM - The last US troops are withdrawn from South Viet Nam. A group of about 8,500 American civilians, plus a few Marine Security Guards at the US Embassy in Saigon, are all that remain in SVN. Revised figures put the death toll at 46,397 Americans killed in action since 1961 with 10,300 dead of other causes and over 305,000 total casualties. At least 6.5 million tons of bombs have been dropped, much of it along the Ho Chi Minh Trail. More than 5.7 million Vietnamese are listed as casualties, with about 1.9 million killed. For the US, however, the war in Viet Nam is over.

29   NORTH VIET NAM - The North Vietnamese government releases the last 62 of the 587 American PWs it claims is all it has held during the war.

APRIL

3   SPAIN - Police fire into a crowd of about 1,500 demonstrators in Barcelona.

4   CAMBODIA - Khmer Rouge forces cut Highway 5 north of Phnom Penh, the last remaining resupply route into the capital.

5   ITALY - The US Embassy's Marine Security Guards' living quarters in Rome are severely damaged by a bomb. There are no casualties.

5   ATLANTIC OCEAN - A Soviet freighter flees after ramming a French trawler; six fishermen are killed. Having given chase, a French destroyer stops the Soviet freighter in international waters, puts an armed boarding party aboard the ship, and compels the freighter's return to a French port.

6   UNITED STATES - Intelligence reports indicate the USSR has moved about 1,200 additional tanks into Central Europe.

7   SOUTH VIET NAM - A UN Peacekeeping Force helicopter is shot down by the Communists in Quang Tri Province while on its way to investigate one of the numerous truce violations reported in SVN. The nine-man crew is killed.

8   SIKKIM - Administrative control of the tiny principality is assumed by India at the request of Chogyal (King) Palden Thonup Namgyal following a two-week period of antigovernment unrest.

8-9   CAMBODIA - Heavily protected river convoys coming up the Mekong River break through the siege line and bring supplies to Phnom Penh. In one convoy, only five of 18 ships get through.

9   PORTUGUESE GUINEA - PAIGC rebels are reported to have shot down a Portuguese Fiat G-91 fighter-bomber with a Soviet-built SA-7 missile.

9-10   CYPRUS - The Israeli ambassadorial residence in the city of Nicosia is unsuccessfully attacked by Arab terrorists who then attempt to hijack an airplane at Nicosia Airport.

10   CAMBODIA - The USAF reinstitues an airlift to deliver fuel to Phnom Penh from bases in Thailand.

10   LEBANON - Three Palestinian leaders are killed in Israeli commando reprisal raids in Beirut and Saida. At least 40 other Palestinians are killed or injured.

11   CAMBODIA - A strong road convoy uses the recently opened road from Kampong Som (Route 4) to bring supplies to Phnom Penh.

12   SWAZILAND - King Sobhuza II abrogates the constitution and assumes personal leadership of the country.

14   LEBANON - Twenty members of a little-known terrorist group, the "Lebanese Revolutionary Guard," blow up the US-owned Caltex-Mobil oil facility near Saida. Some damage is done but the raid falls far short of total success. The group claims the raid was carried out to protest American support of Israel.

16-17 LAOS - US B-52s and FB-111s attack Communist targets at the recently overrun village of Tha Vieng in the Plaine des Jarres.

17   THE PHILIPPINES - The government announces that the amnesty promised Muslim rebels on Mindanao has been cancelled.

19   NORTH VIET NAM - Because of repeated truce violations on the part of the North Vietnamese, the US again halts minesweeping operations in Haiphong Harbor.

20   PAKISTAN - President Zulikar Ali Bhutto rejects three-way talks with India and Bangladesh that were to be aimed at settling the prisoner exchange question.

22   ISRAEL - The government accuses Libya of transferring to Egypt Mirage jet fighters it had received from France.

28   UNITED STATES - A Senate Foreign Relations sub-commit-
            tee releases sensitive Defense Department data indi-
            cating a shift in the bombing program from NVA lines
            of communication to support of Cambodian forces
            against the rebels.

30   ARGENTINA - Terrorists of the People's Revolutionary
            Army blow up a Goodyear-owned building in Cordoba.
            There is much damage, but no injuries.

MAY

1   ARGENTINA - A state of emergency is declared when the
            military takes power following the leftist assassina-
            tion of Rear Admiral Hermes Quijada.

1-17   LEBANON - Following the kidnapping of two Lebanese
            officers by PFLP soldiers, the Lebanese Army attacks a
            number of guerrilla bases. This triggers an invasion
            by Palestinian forces based in Syria (9 May). Lebanese
            forces quickly disperse this force driving it back
            into Syria (11 May). Syria then closes its border with
            Lebanon. Finally, on 17 May, an agreement is reached
            to curb Palestinian activities in Lebanon.

4   MEXICO - The US Consul in Guadalajara, Terence
            Leahardy, is kidnapped by members of the Fuerzas
            Revolucionarias Armadas Populare (FRAP). The
            terrorists demand $80,000 (1 million pesos) and the
            release of 30 political prisoners. When the demands
            are met, Leahardy is released (7 May).

10-11   BURUNDI - As a part of the ongoing Hutu-Tutsi con-
            flict, the country is invaded from Rwanda and Tanzania
            by Hutu tribesmen .

13   THE PHILIPPINES - Conscription into the armed forces
            is imposed as a means of dealing with the insurgency
            in the Sulu Islands.

14   UNITED STATES - The US successfully mans an orbiting
            space laboratory (Skylab). The mission continues until
            22 June when the crew is returned safely to earth.

14   AUSTRIA - NATO and Warsaw Pact representatives open
            mutual force reduction talks in Vienna.

14   BOLIVIA - Former Defense Minister Colonel Andres
            Selich is arrested for his part in plotting a right-
            wing military overthrow of President Hugo Banzer
            Suarez's government.

17   LEBANON - The government and the PLO reach a cease-
            fire agreement following 16 days of fighting after two
            Lebanese officers are kidnapped.

17   NORTHERN IRELAND - IRA terrorists bomb Aldergrove
            Airport near Belfast.

17   RHODESIA - The government implements a program of
            forcibly removing natives from "restricted areas" and
            confiscating or destroying all items that might be of
            use to guerrilla forces.

19   JAPAN - The government announces the establishment of
            a permanent airbase on Iwo Jima for antisubmarine pat-
            rol operations and pilot training.

19   ARGENTINA - The government ends the state of emergency
            that has been in effect since 1 May.

20   ICELAND - In retaliation for British warships protect-
            ing British fishing trawlers that are working the
            Icelandic waters, Premier Johannesson bans all British
            military flights from landing at the NATO airbase at
            Keflavik.

21   GREECE - A coup attempt led by a group of naval offi-
            cers, including Vice Admiral Constantine Margaritis,
            the Chief of Naval Operations, fails. Margaritis is
            dismissed and the ruling military junta remains in
            power.

21   ARGENTINA - Two Ford Motor Company executives are
            wounded in an unsuccessful kidnapping attempt by the
            People's Revolutionary Army. One of the two Ford
            employees, Luis Giovanelli, dies of his injury on 25
            June.

22   INDIA - A revolt by the Provincial Armed Constabulary
            in Uttar Pradesh is categorized as a part of the
            general economic discontent throughout the country.

23   GUAM - In a pact announced at Agana, the US grants
            commonwealth status to the Mariana Islands.

23   AUSTRALIA - The government grants Papua New Guinea
            independence effective in 1975.

24   GREECE - The government announces it has broken up a
            royalist coup attempt planned by a group of both
            active and retired naval officers.

25   INDIA - Labor disputes in Uttar Pradesh culminate in a
            police revolt in which more than 40 die before govern-
            ment troops can restore order.

26   ICELAND - An Icelandic gunboat opens fire on a British trawler fishing inside the 50-mile limit.

28   NATO - The NATO Council receives a note from Iceland demanding that Great Britain be ordered to remove its warships from Icelandic waters.

28   BOLIVIA - President Suarez assumes command of the armed forces following a right-wing attempt to overthrow the government.

28   ARGENTINA - The government resumes diplomatic relations with Cuba.

29   CANADA - Claiming interference in the team's ability to do its job, the government orders home the 200-man Canadian contingent to the International Commission on Control and Supervision (ICC) operating in Vietnam.

30   YEMEN (SAN'A) - The third member of the North Yemen Presidential Council (along with the President and Premier), Sheikh Muhammad Ali Othman, is assassinated by South Yemeni Marxist terrorists.

JUNE

1   GREECE - The cabinet abolishes the monarchy, and the nation is proclaimed a republic with Georgios Papadopoulos as its President.

1   BELIZE - The former colony of British Honduras changes its name to Belize.

1   FINLAND - At the close of Franco-American talks in Helsinki, France's President Georges Pompidou stresses the need for a continued US military presence in Europe.

2   IRAN - An American military advisor, Lieutenant Colonel Lewis Hawkins, is shot to death by two assassins believed to be members of a left-wing radical group.

4   FRANCE - An agreement is reached with Malagasy whereby the French government agrees to withdraw 4,000 troops from Madagascar by 1 September and from the Diego Suarez naval base within two years.

6   UNITED NATIONS - The Security Council opens general debate on the Middle East amid renewed Egyptian demands that Israel abandon the occupied territories.

7   ICELAND - The government accuses Great Britain of al-
           lowing its warships to behave in an "unlawful manner"
           when one of them collides with an Icelandic Coast
           Guard cutter within the disputed zone. Great Britain
           claims it was their vessel that was rammed.

8   SPAIN - Generalissimo Francisco Franco Bahamonde re-
           signs as Premier but retains the title of Chief of
           State.

11   LIBYA - In retaliation for US support of Israel, Libya
           nationalizes a US-owned oil firm.

12   ICELAND - The government asks the US for a revision of
           the 1951 Defense Treaty that allows the US and NATO to
           station forces at Keflavik.

13   FRANCE - A supplemental cease-fire agreement is signed
           by the US, SVN, NVN, and the VC. This agreement is de-
           signed to end further truce violations. In spite of
           this, fighting continues throughout SVN as the Com-
           munists refuse to abide by the treaty.

14   CAMBODIA - The US carries out the 100th day of bombing
           Khmer Rouge positions.

14   SOUTH VIET NAM - SVN and VC headquarters order their
           troops to cease the fighting in compliance with a new
           Paris agreement.

18   NORTH VIET NAM - The US reinstitutes the minesweeping
           of Haiphong Harbor which was halted on 19 April be-
           cause of Communist truce violations.

18   ARGENTINA - The president of the Firestone Rubber Com-
           pany subsidiary in Buenos Aires, John R. Thompson, is
           kidnapped by terrorists of the People's Revolutionary
           Army. Thompson is released unharmed on 6 July after a
           substantial ransom is paid.

20   ARGENTINA - Rioting erupts when exiled ex-President
           Juan Peron visits the country.

21   UNITED NATIONS - The US rejects Libyan charges that
           the presence of the Sixth Fleet in the Mediterranean
           constitutes an immediate threat to security and peace.

21   UNITED STATES - The second phase of the SALT Agreement
           (SALT II) is signed between the US and Soviet Union in
           Washington.

21   UNITED STATES - The Defense Department declares that
           Haiphong harbor in North Viet Nam is clear of mines
           and is safe for shipping.

22   UNITED STATES - The Prevention of Nuclear War Agreement is signed in Washington by Richard Nixon and Leonid Brezhnev. By its terms, the two sides agree that if there is a risk of nuclear war, the US and the USSR will "immediately enter into urgent consultations . . . to make every effort to avert this risk."

22   FRANCE - The government refuses to accept an International Court of Justice injuction against further nuclear testing at the Mururoa Test Facility in the Pacific Ocean. Australia and New Zealand had sought the injunction, but France claims the Court has no competence in the matter.

23   AUSTRALIA - Along with New Zealand, the two nations indicate they will send naval vessels into the waters around the Mururoa Atoll to prevent further French atmospheric nuclear testing.

25   UNITED STATES - A joint US-USSR communique announces mutual force reduction talks for Europe will begin in Vienna on 30 October.

26   LIBYA - Two Greek ships hit mines in the harbor at Tripoli. One ship sinks. The harbor is reported to have been mined to protect against Israeli raids.

27   COMMUNIST CHINA - An atmospheric test shot becomes the 15th nuclear device detonated at Lop Nor. It is a hydrogen device with a yield of about 2-3 megatons.

27   UNITED STATES - The President vetoes a bill ordering an immediate halt of the bombing of Communist targets in Cambodia.

27-30   URUGUAY - Parliamentary government is suspended when President Juan Maria Bordaberry dismisses Congress and establishes rule by a Council of State. A general strike is called by the National Confederation of Labor (CNT) on 29 June. Bordaberry abolishes the CNT on 30 June.

28   ICELAND - An Icelandic gunboat fires on a West German trawler which it said was fishing inside the 50-mile Icelandic fishing area.

29   CHILE - The government of President Salvador Allende Gossens survives a coup attempt when loyal troops crush an army revolt.

29   BURUNDI - Government troops cross into Tanzania and kill ten persons following a series of Hutu raids into Burundi from Tanzania and Rwanda.

30   CAMBODIA - Khmer Rouge forces open a major   offensive
            aimed at the provincial capital town of Kompong Speu.
            Heavy fighting is also reported in several   locations
            around Phnom Penh.

30   UNITED STATES - President Nixon agrees with a Congres-
            sional requirement to end   all US military   operations
            in Indochina by 15 August.

JULY

1   IRAQ - Government forces, under strongman Vice-Presi-
            dent Saddam Takriti, crush a coup attempt led by
            Colonel Nazem Kazzar, the Chief of Internal Security.
            The plot called for the assassination of President
            Ahmed Hassan al-Bakr. While this failed, one minister
            was killed and another injured. Kazzar and 35 of his
            associates are subsequently executed (7-8 July).

1   PORTUGAL - The government announces that the major
            military communications center at Estima was attacked
            by rebels using Soviet-made 122mm rockets. The Estima
            base controls the strategically vital Cabora Bassa
            Dam.

5   RWANDA - President Gregoire Kayibanda is overthrown in
            a bloodless coup led   by Major General   Juvenal
            Habyalimana, the commander of the National Guard.

7   UGANDA - President Idi Amin orders 112 US Peace Corps
            volunteers detained while he determines if they are
            "mercenaries." They are released unharmed on 9 July.

9   URUGUAY - On orders from the President, army troops
            occupy Montevideo.

10   THE BAHAMAS - The former British island colony becomes
            independent.

10   MOZAMBIQUE - There are reports published in leading
            European newspapers about a massacre by Portuguese
            troops of 406 people in Wiriyamu in Tete Province. The
            Portuguese government immediately denies the reports
            and arrests (26 July) two missionaries on charges of
            aiding and abetting the Frelimo.

11   LIBYA - Muammar Qaddafi offers to resign as Chairman
            of the Revolutionary Council to clear the way for his
            nation's merger with Egypt.

13   ARGENTINA - Juan Peron is elected President.

17   AFGHANISTAN - The forty-year reign of King Mohammed
          Zahir Khan is ended by a coup led by his brother-
          in-law, Lieutenant General Prince Mohammed Daud Khan.
          The country is declared a republic. The former king
          remains in Italy where he was undergoing medical
          treatment at the time of his ouster.

17   JORDAN - The government severs diplomatic relations
          with Tunisia after President Habib Bourguiba calls for
          King Hussein's abdication and the establishment of a
          Palestinian state on both banks of the Jordan.

17   CAMBODIA - The government orders the call-up of all
          men 18 to 35 as the Khmer Rouge intensifies its drive
          on Phnom Penh.

18   UNITED STATES - The Navy Department announces it has
          completed "Operation END SWEEP," the minesweeping
          operation in North Vietnamese waters.

18-23   LIBYA - About 40,000 Libyans begin the "Tripoli to
          Cairo March" designed by Qaddafi to force the union of
          Egypt and Libya. (Qaddafi was rebuffed in his drive to
          get this plan into effect during his visit to Cairo on
          29 June-9 July.) Egyptian troops stop the procession
          at the border (20 July). Qaddafi resigns his leader-
          ship in Libya to "pave the way" for unification (20
          July). When the marchers return to Tripoli, Qaddafi
          withdraws his resignation (23 July).

21   NEW ZEALAND - As a protest against French testing of
          nuclear weapons at Mururoa Atoll near Tahiti, a New
          Zealand naval frigate is ordered into the test area.
          The vessel is withdrawn on 5 August because of
          resupply difficulties.

22   FRANCE - The government announces a continuation of
          its nuclear weapons testing program at Mururoa Atoll
          in the Pacific and detonates the first weapon in the
          series: a miniturized warhead for a submarine mis-
          sile. There are four more tests before the series ends
          on 28 August.

23   LIBYA - Muammar Qaddafi withdraws his offer to resign.

24   LIBYA - A Japan Air Lines airliner, which was hijacked
          at Amsterdam, the Netherlands, is blown up when it ar-
          rives at Bengazi after a stop at Dubai. All the pas-
          sengers and crew had been released.

26   CHILE - Chilean truckers begin a nationwide strike.

27   CHILE - Captain Arturo Arroyo (Araya?), President Sal-
          vador Allende Gossens' naval aide, is assassinated.

27   CYPRUS - The Minister of Justice, Christos Vakis, is kidnapped by followers of General Georgios Grivas who is dedicated to uniting Cyprus with Greece.

29   FRANCE - The government detonates, above Mururoa Atoll, the second weapon in the new series, a small low-yield bomb.

29   LAOS - A political and military settlement between the government and the Pathet Lao is reported.

31   CANADA - The government announces its formal withdrawal from the ICC in Viet Nam. Iran is scheduled to take Canada's place in the three-nation team.

AUGUST

2   CAMBODIA - A series of roadblocks is put out around Phnom Penh in a last-ditch effort to stop the Khmer Rouge offensive.

5   GREECE - Two Arab terrorists, claiming to be members of the "Seventh Suicide Squad," surrender to police after mistakenly attacking a group of passengers going to New York who they thought to be Israelis going to Tel Aviv. Five passengers (including three Americans) were killed and 55 injured in the assault. Thirty-five others were held hostage for a short time. The terrorists are sentenced to death by a Greek court, but their sentences are later commuted to life imprisonment. They are expelled to Libya in May 1974 where they are freed.

6   CAMBODIA - In an operation designed to support government forces defending Phnom Penh, US B-52s bomb the friendly village of Neak Luong by mistake killing or wounding 387 civilians.

7   COMMUNIST CHINA - The government-controlled press calls the Soviet Union a "nuclear tyrant."

8   JAPAN - The exiled former South Korean presidential candidate and opponent of Korean President Park Chung Hee, Kim Dae Jung, is kidnapped from a Tokyo hotel by five ROK CIA agents. On 13 August Kim is located under house arrest in South Korea. The Japanese government protests the incident to Seoul on 14 August. The Korean government expresses its regrets for the incident on 20 August but does not release Kim.

8   EGYPT - Libya and Egypt agree to a gradual merging.

10 LEBANON - A Middle East airliner thought to be carrying PLO guerrilla leader George Hadash and his deputy, Salah Salah, is intercepted by Israeli jets and forced down while enroute from Beirut to Baghdad, Iraq. The Israelis claim Hadash is responsible for the Athens Airport attack.

12 HAITI - Marie Denise Duvalier, the President's sister, is forced to leave the country when an overthrow plot is discovered in which she was an active participant.

13 GREECE - A court-martial is ordered for 56 Greek naval officers following an attempt by the group to seize the fleet and overthrow the government.

13 ICELAND - Icelandic gunboats chase a British trawler for more than 100 miles outside Iceland waters.

14 ISRAEL - Israeli and UAR naval vessels exchange fire in the Gulf of Suez.

14 UNITED STATES - The White House announces that, based on a Congressional decision, US bombing in support of Cambodia has stopped. The President accuses the Congress of undermining chances for "world peace."

15 ISRAEL - Intelligence sources state that 10-20 North Korean pilots are flying combat missions for the Egyptians.

17 SYRIA - The government reopens its border with Lebanon which has been closed since 8 May.

18 GREAT BRITAIN - IRA terrorists of the Provisional Wing begin a campaign of mailing letter bombs to persons in London.

19 GREECE - The last vestiges of the 1967 edict of martial law are lifted.

20 BOLIVIA - The government announces it has crushed a right-wing coup attempt led by the former Minister of Health, Carlos Valverde Barbery.

20 LAOS - The government crushes a right-wing military coup attempt.

20 CAMBODIA - The Khmer Rouge break a five-day lull in the fighting by attacking two provincial capitals.

21 CHILE - A number of people die as antigovernment rioting spreads throughout the country.

28   INDIA - An Indo-Pakistani accord is signed in New
Delhi that completes all details of the final settlement of the 1971 war. About 90,000 Pakistani prisoners
are to be exchanged for 160,000 Bengalis and an unde-
termined number of Biharis held in Bangladesh.

29   LIBYA - Although Qaddafi had hoped for a quick union
of his country with Egypt, a joint communique announces that the process will be a slow and deliberate
affair.

30   SAUDI ARABIA - King Faisal issues a warning to the US
that "...complete support of Zionism against the
Arabs..." would make future deliveries of oil to the
US "extremely difficult."

30   MOROCCO - The trial of 157 people accused of plotting
the overthrow of the government of King Hassan begins
in Kenitra. Sixteen will be sentenced to death.

SEPTEMBER

1   THAILAND - The last squadron of Marine F-4 fighter
jets leaves Thailand. This move of about 3,500 men and
more than 100 aircraft ends an 11-year Marine commitment in SEA.

4   ITALY - Police arrest five Arab terrorists and seize
two Soviet-built SA-7 "Grail" shoulder-fired surface-
to-air missiles. The arrests are made the day before
the terrorists had planned to attack an airliner at
Rome's airport.

5   UNITED STATES - The Defense Department reports the apparent collision of a Soviet ECHO-II submarine and a
Soviet cruiser in the Caribbean.

5   SUDAN - A state of siege is declared by President
Gaafar Numeiry following a period of student and labor
unrest.

5   FRANCE - Five Jordanian terrorists capture the Saudi
Arabian Embassy in Paris and take 13 hostages. The
terrorists demand the release of al-Fatah leader Abu
Da'ud. Along with four hostages, they are transported
to Kuwait (6 September), where they release the hos-
tages and surrender (8 September). In October, the
Kuwaiti government allows the terrorists to go to
Syria.

7   KUWAIT - Five Arab terrorists surrender to Kuwaiti
authorities after landing with the hostages they took
at the Saudi Arabian Embassy in Paris.

10   ICELAND - A British frigate and an Icelandic gunboat
            collide off the coast of Iceland in the continuing
            "Cod War."

11   GREAT BRITAIN - Terrorists bomb two railway stations
            in London in reprisal for placing other terrorists on
            trial for earlier bombings.

11   CHILE - A military coup ousts the Marxist government
            of Salvador Allende Gossens. Allende is reported to
            have allegedly committed suicide in the palace after
            refusing to yield power. A military junta, headed by
            General Augusto Pinochet Ugarte, takes power, and a
            program of terror aimed at eradicating "Marxism" be-
            gins. At least 6,000 are arrested in Santiago in the
            first stages of the purge.

11   ICELAND - The government threatens to break diplomatic
            relations with Great Britain if the British "ram" any
            more Icelandic naval vessels.

11   SOUTH AFRICA - Eleven blacks are killed in rioting in
            Carltonville, Transvaal.

12   EGYPT - At a secret meeting in Cairo, Egyptian Presi-
            dent Anwar Sadat and Syria's Hafez Assad select 6 Oct-
            ober as the day to attack Israel. The Egyptian War
            Minister, Ahmad Ismail Ali, is also present at the
            meeting. Also, Egypt resumes diplomatic relations with
            Jordan.

12   SOUTH AFRICA - Eleven blacks are killed by police dur-
            ing a demonstration at the Western Deep Levels gold
            mine.

12   CAMBODIA - The government claims it has won the battle
            for Kompong Cham.

12   USSR - A five-megaton underground nuclear detonation
            is detected in the USSR.

13   ISRAEL - Israeli jets are reported to have downed 13
            Syrian aircraft in a dogfight off Syria's northern
            Mediterranean coast. One Israeli Mirage fighter is
            reported lost. Syria reports it lost eight aircraft
            and that five Israeli aircraft were shot down.

14   LAOS - A new cease-fire goes into effect after 20
            years of war.

15   SWEDEN - King Gustaf VI Adolf dies at age 90. Carl XVI
            Gustaf, his grandson, becomes king.

15   CAMBODIA - Government forces reopen Route 4 between
            Phnom Penh and the seaport of Kompong Som.

18   JORDAN - King Hussein grants amnesty to 1,500 politi-
            cal prisoners.

18   SENEGAL - The government breaks diplomatic relations
            with Guinea following incessant verbal attacks on
            Senegal by Guinean President Sekou Toure.

19   INDIA - The exchange of some 250,000 persons isolated
            since the 1971 Indo-Pakistani War begins.

21   RHODESIA - Prime Minister Ian Smith reports that more
            than 130 rebels have been killed since December 1972.
            There have been 35 incidents in which casualties have
            been reported. Nine whites and 19 blacks have been
            killed and 366 people kidnapped, of which at least 40
            are presumed dead.

25   SWITZERLAND - SALT II talks resume in Geneva after a
            three month recess.

26   ISRAEL - Even though there are no real indications of
            impending war the Israelis are alerted by Egyptian and
            Syrian troop movements, which are reported to be
            nothing more than maneuvers. The Israelis increase
            their military readiness posture.

27   PORTUGUESE GUINEA - The rebel PAIGC declares the inde-
            pendence of Guinea-Bissau.

28   AUSTRIA - Palestinian terrorists hijack the Moscow-
            Vienna train and take three Jewish passengers and an
            Austrian customs agent hostage at Vienna's airport.
            They demand the Schonau Jewish transit point be closed
            and that Austria restrict Jewish emigrant travel.

29   ISRAEL - The Israelis reinforce their troop strength
            in the Golan Heights with a second armored brigade.

29   AUSTRIA - The government accedes to Palestinian ter-
            rorist demands and promises to halt Jewish emigration
            to Israel through Austria and to close the Schonau
            Castle transit facility in return for the release of
            their hostages.

OCTOBER

            SAUDI ARABIA - In support of the expected Arab attack
            on Israel, King Faisal leads an oil embargo against
            those in the West who support the Israelis.

1   COMMUNIST CHINA - A number of newspapers carry editor-
     ials warning of a surprise attack by the Soviet Union.

2   GREAT BRITAIN - Defense Minister Lord Carrington warns
     that the Soviet Union's naval buildup could give them
     dominance at sea.

4   EGYPT - President Sadat informs Soviet Ambassador
     Vladimir Vinogradov of Arab plans to attack Israel. At
     the same moment, President Assad is informing the
     Soviet Ambassador in Damascus of the Syrian decision
     to go to war. Later in the day the chief of the Soviet
     military mission informs General Ismail that, while
     the Soviets had been aware that an attack on Israel
     was planned, they were not aware of the date. He then
     asks permission for Soviet transport aircraft to fly
     into Egyptian airspace to evacuate all civilians and
     the dependents of military personnel. Ismail approves
     this request.

4   AUSTRIA - Chancellor Bruno Kreisky, reacting to criti-
     cism of recent dealings with Palestinian terrorists,
     promises to expedite the transfer of Jewish emigrants
     through Austria.

4   COLOMBIA - Fifty National Liberation Army guerrillas
     attack an American-owned gold mine and kidnap two
     Americans. A 4-million peso ransom is demanded. When
     the company attempts to pay the ransom, the Colombian
     army steps in and seizes the money. The two Americans
     are rescued at a terrorist hideout by army troops on 7
     March 1974.

4-5 EGYPT - The Soviet Union orders the departure of all
     dependents and most of its military advisors. These
     movements are noted by both Israeli and American in-
     telligence.

5   UNITED STATES - Intelligence sources assure the gov-
     ernment there will be no war in the Middle East.

5   ISRAEL - Intelligence sources assure their governments
     there will be no war.

6   ISRAEL - Intelligence informs the government that an
     Arab attack may be expected by 6 PM (1800 hours).
     During the feast of Yom Kippur (Day of Atonement),
     Israel is attacked on two broad fronts. Most of the
     populace is in the synagogues or at home when mobili-
     zation is ordered at 9:30 AM (0930 hours). Full mobi-
     lization is accomplished in a matter of hours, well
     ahead of schedule. Many active duty units were not
     immediately alerted, however, and this causes later
     problems. At 2:05 PM (1405 hours), Egyptian military

6   ISRAEL (Cont'd) - aircraft begin a series of air
           strikes against Israeli positions in the Sinai.
           Egyptian artillery opens preparatory fires against the
           surprised lightly held Israeli Bar Lev Line on the
           east bank of the Suez Canal. The assault crossing of
           the canal begins 30 minutes later (1435 hours) follow-
           ing days of careful preparation of the west-bank dike
           to allow for the rapid erection of bridges. The as-
           sault is led by heliborne commandos who are put down
           in four general locations: near Baluza in the north,
           Bir Gifgafa deep in the center, at a strategic cross-
           roads west of the Mitla Pass, and near Suder on the
           Gulf of Suez. The Egyptian Second Army, composed of
           about 25,000 troops and 200-300 tanks, attacks in a
           zone from north of the Great Bitter Lake (el Buheirat
           el Murrat el Kubra) to Kantara (al-Qantarah). The
           Third Army, with about 20,000 troops and 200 tanks,
           attacks in the southern zone that runs south from
           Little Bitter Lake (el Buheirat el Murrat el Sughra)
           to Suez. On the Syrian front, at 2:05 PM (1405 hours),
           Syrian forces carry out a massive air and artillery
           attack on Israeli positions in the Golan Heights. This
           is followed by a heliborne commando attack which cap-
           tures the tactically important Israeli observation
           post on Mount Hermon (Hill 2814 - Jabal esh Sheikh).
           This is then followed by the major ground attack car-
           ried out by two infantry divisions supported by about
           500 tanks along an axis generally following the
           Damascus-Quneitra (al-Qunaytirah, Kuneitra) road.

6   EGYPT - The government declares the waters off the
           coast of Israel a "War Zone" and blockades the Bab al
           Mandeb Strait, which leads from the Gulf of Aden into
           the Red Sea, to stop supplies from reaching Eilat. In
           a number of engagements over the next few days, the
           Egyptians withdraw before there is a chance for either
           side to inflict casualties.

6   SYRIA - Israeli "Saar"-class missile boats attack a
           Syrian naval squadron after dark outside Latakia (Al
           Ladhiqiyah) Harbor on Syria's short Mediterranean
           coast. Four Syrian ships are sunk before the Syrians
           break off the action by entering the harbor. There are
           no Israeli casualties. A second engagement the follow-
           ing night proves inconclusive.

7   UNITED STATES - The Congress severely limits the power
           of the President to commit military forces into for-
           eign conflicts without prior approval.

7   SINAI - Bridging the Suez Canal is completed before
           midnight in the Egyptian Second Army area. The bridg-
           ing of the Canal in the Third Army area is delayed and
           will not be completed until the 8th.

7   GOLAN HEIGHTS - North of Quneitra, Israeli tank forces (7th Armored Brigade) defeat an attack by the 7th Syrian Infantry Division destroying most of the Syrian armor (Battle of Amadiya). The Syrian 3rd Tank Division is rendered ineffective in the continuing tank battle in the Ahmadiya (Amadiye) sector as it attempts to pass through the Syrian 7th Division along an axis Samdaniya-Ahmadiya-Merom Golan. Also, in an action south of Quneitra, the Syrian 5th Mechanized Division overruns the Israeli 188th Armored Brigade, which after the fierce two-day battle (Battle of Rafid) is all but annihilated. Crossing the Raqqad River the Syrians, reinforced by the 1st Tank Division, drive deep into Israeli territory stopping only when Israeli pressure and a shortage of resupply prevents their decent into the Ha-Galil region.

8   SINAI - Nearly 500 Soviet-built Egyptian tanks and armored vehicles have already crossed the Canal into the Sinai.

8   ISRAEL - Two reserve armored divisions are dispatched into the Sinai along two axes: Abraham Adan's division moves along the northern littoral toward Romani, and Ariel Sharon's division goes toward Tasa, an important town 10 miles east of the Canal at Ismailiya and 20 miles south of Romani. Elements of both divisions begin a counterattack only to be thrown back with heavy losses. Thereafter, Israeli forces consolidate their positions and dig in. At the same time, in the Golan, newly arrived Israeli units reinforce elements of the 7th Armored Brigade, which has moved south from the Ahmadiya sector, and counterattack against the Syrian 5th Mechanized and 1st Tank penetration west of Khushniya (Al Khushniyah). At Khushniya, the main Israeli command post (Hill 929) has been surrounded for more than 36 hours. The Israeli attack restores most of the pre-war line of contact. An Israeli attempt to retake Mount Hermon is repulsed.

8   EGYPT - Egyptian naval vessels engage several Israeli fast-attack craft outside the harbor at Damietta and suffer severe losses before withdrawing.

8   UNITED STATES - Israeli El Al aircraft begin flying needed military supplies from Oceana Naval Air Station in Virginia to Israel.

9   GOLAN - A Syrian counterattack north of Quneitra is repulsed by the remaining elements of the Israeli 7th Armored Brigade. Heavy losses are reported on both sides.

9   SYRIA - Israeli naval vessels carry out unopposed attacks on a number of coastal towns in Syria (Banias, Tartus, and Latakia).

9   EGYPT - Israeli naval units attack Egyptian naval vessels off Port Said and sink three before the Egyptians withdraw into the harbors at Damietta and Alexandria (Al Iskandariyah).

9   USSR - The Soviet Union begins air lifting large quantities of military supplies to Egypt and Syria. The bulk of the shipments are sent to Syria. Circuitous routes through Hungary and Yugoslavia are used to reach Egypt to avoid NATO territories and interception by Israeli fighters. These shipments continue until the end of the war.

10   GOLAN - The Israeli Army opens a counteroffensive against Syria in the sector north of Quneitra. Three Israeli divisions begin a drive toward Damascus by breaking through a series of Syrian defensive lines. At a point near Sa'sa' (Saassaa), on the Damascus Plain about half the distance to Damascus, the Israeli forces halt and dig in.

11   EGYPT - Plans are prepared for a new Egyptian offensive aimed primarily at relieving pressure on the Syrians in the east.

11   SYRIA - Iraqi forces who, along with the Jordanians, have joined the Syrians, counterattack (Iraqi 3rd Armored Division) against the southern flank of the Israeli salient, but are repulsed the next day.

12   SYRIA - Israeli forces begin shifting units to the Sinai front. At the same time, Israeli naval units bombard Latakia and Tartus with only minor interference from the Syrian navy.

12   UNITED STATES - President Nixon announces the nomination of House Republican leader Gerald Ford to fill the unexpired term of Vice-President Spiro T. Agnew. Agnew is forced to resign (10 October) in the face of a growing number of income tax evasion charges.

13   UNITED STATES - The US Air Force begins airlifting military supplies to Israel. The first shipments arrive in Israel aboard C-5A aircraft routed through the Azores. These shipments continue until the end of the war. A massive US sealift of supplies into Israel is also begun.

14   SINAI - The Egyptian offensive is repulsed with heavy losses in men and equipment.

14-16   THAILAND - The military dictatorship of Thanon Kitti-
         kachorn is ended by a coup following a long period of
         civil unrest and violence. Kittikachorn and a group of
         his followers flee the country (15 October). The King
         appoints (16 October) a civilian educator, Sanya
         Dhamasakti (Thammasak), to be the new Prime Minister.

15   SYRIA - A second counterattack by the Iraqi 3rd
         Armored Division is repulsed by the Israelis. The
         Jordanian 40th Armored Brigade, which counterattacked
         on the Iraqi flank, is also thrown back the next day.

15-16   SINAI - Israeli forces, led by paratroopers, cross the
         Suez Canal into Egyptian territory. The initial pene-
         tration is near the Deversoir Military Base north of
         Great Bitter Lake (near Abu Sultan) and is roughly at
         the boundary between the Second and Third Armies. The
         Third Army is eventually encircled and completely cut
         off, while the Second Army, to the south of Ismailiya,
         is confined to a narrow strip of land.

16   EGYPT - Sailing into the Nile Delta, Israeli fast-
         attack boats damage a number of Egyptian landing
         craft.

16-18   SINAI - After heavy fighting in which elements of the
         Egyptian Second and Third Armies participate, Adan's
         division breaks through and relieves Sharon's nearly
         surrounded forces holding the bridgeheads across the
         Canal. Adan's division, with some 15,000 troops and
         200 mostly American-built tanks, then crosses the
         Canal (17-18 October).

17   KUWAIT - The Arab oil-producing nations agree to cut
         oil production by 5% a month until the US is forced to
         change its Middle East policies favorable to Israel.

18-19   SINAI - In a continuation of the Battle of the
         "Chinese Farm," so named because the Israelis had
         earlier (1967) thought a Japanese-operated experi-
         mental station was Chinese, the Israeli bridgeheads
         are still threatened.

18-19   EGYPT - Adan's forces continue westward raising havoc
         in the Egyptian rear areas. The destruction of
         Soviet-built surface-to-air missile sites allows
         Israeli aircraft to more easily attack ground targets.

19   SINAI - Sharon's forces drive northwestward where an
         attempt to capture Ismailiya is repulsed.

19   SYRIA - Another counterattack, led by the Jordanians,
         is repulsed.

19   LEBANON - Arab terrorists seize the Bank of America in Beirut and threaten to blow it up along with a number of hostages if their demands are not met. Army and police units storm the bank building killing two terrorists and one hostage in the process.

19   LIBYA - The government orders an oil boycott against the US.

20   BAHREIN - The Emirate cancels US fleet anchorage privileges because of US support of Israel in the recent fighting.

20   SOUTH VIET NAM - VC headquarters orders its forces to step up the campaign against the government.

20   SAUDI ARABIA - The government orders a boycott on oil shipment to the US.

20-23   SINAI - Sharon continues his attempts at capturing Ismailiya whose garrison has been reinforced from across the Canal. The road between Ismailiya and Suez is cut by Israeli forces.

21   GOLAN - Another Israeli attempt to retake Mount Hermon is repulsed.

21   EGYPT - Israeli naval craft attack Alexandria Harbor and Aboukir Bay sinking two Egyptian patrol craft.

21   UNITED ARAB EMIRATES - Bahrein, Dubai, and Qatar order a boycott on oil to the US.

22   UNITED NATIONS - The Security Council issues an order (Resolution 338) calling for an immediate cease-fire in the Middle East.

22   EGYPT - Adan's forces cut the Suez-Cairo road near Suez. Israeli forces are within 50 miles of Cairo.

22   GOLAN - Israeli forces recapture Mount Hermon after taking the surrounding high ground.

22   COMMUNIST CHINA - The government reports that forces of the Soviet Far East Command are holding maneuvers along the Sino-Soviet border. About 45 divisions, including 10,000 tanks, are involved.

23   SINAI - A UN-mandated cease-fire goes into effect, but attempts by the Egyptian Third Army to break out of its impending encirclement cause a renewal of the fighting. The Third Army is completely encircled east of the Suez Canal by the time a US-USSR sponsored cease-fire goes into effect.

23 ETHIOPIA - The government breaks diplomatic relations with Israel, the ninth African state to do so since the outbreak of hostilities in the Middle East.

24 USSR - The Soviet government alerts its airborne forces for possible action in Egypt, if the Israelis do not remove their forces surrounding the Egyptian Third Army, and if the Israelis do not accept the cease-fire. As a part of these preparations, the Soviet resupply airlift is curtailed as the aircraft are marshalled for a possible airborne operation.

24 SYRIA - The government accepts the UN cease-fire proposal and fighting ceases on that front.

25 UNITED STATES - Following the President's receipt of a Soviet note threatening the "destruction of the State of Israel," the Joint Chiefs of Staff order a precautionary alert, an advanced readiness condition (DEFCON-3). Intelligence sources point to signs that the Soviet Union is about to intervene in the Middle East.

25 UNITED NATIONS - With US and USSR support, the Security Council passes Resolution 340 providing for UNEF to supervise the Middle East cease-fire.

26 UNITED STATES - The Defense Department begins relaxation of the alert status. At the same time, the government criticizes a number of its NATO allies for failing to support US policies in the Middle East.

26 NORTHERN IRELAND - At least 17 bombs go off in a number of locations in Northern Ireland as a wave of violence spreads across the countryside.

27 UNITED NATIONS - The Security Council agrees to place a 7,000-man UNEF in the Sinai and Golan Heights areas to keep the peace. The arrangement includes a provision that neither the US nor the USSR will participate. At the same time, in order to allow non-military supplies to be sent to the surrounded Egyptian Third Army, a UN Truce Supervision Organization Team (UNTSO), meeting at the cease-fire line, arranges an agreement between Egyptian and Israeli representatives.

29 UGANDA - President Amin orders the immediate removal of the US Marine Security Guard detachment protecting the US Embassy in Kampala after charging them with "subversive activities."

30 AUSTRIA - Mutual Bilateral Arms Reduction talks open in Vienna.

30   UNITED STATES - The US protests continued NVA infil-
            tration of forces into SVN in violation of the cease-
            fire agreement.

31   UNITED STATES - All military forces, except the US
            Sixth Fleet in the Mediterranean, are ordered off
            alert (DEFCON 5). Intelligence sources report that all
            USSR and East European forces appear to have ended
            their alerts.

NOVEMBER

1   ISRAEL - Prime Minister Golda Meir declares her nation
            will not withdraw to the 22 October cease-fire line.

2   UNITED NATIONS - The General Assembly recognizes the
            independence of Guinea-Bissau.

4   SOUTH VIET NAM - Heavy fighting is reported between
            ARVN and NVA forces near the Cambodian border.

7   UNITED STATES - The Congress overrides a Presidential
            veto of a bill severely limiting Executive war-making
            authority. On the same date, the Department of State
            announces the US will resume diplomatic relations with
            Egypt after a six-year break.

7   PAKISTAN - The government announces its departure from
            SEATO.

8   UNITED STATES - The Department of State announces the
            US is closing its Embassy in Uganda and is withdrawing
            US representation in that country after Ugandan Presi-
            dent Idi Amin ordered the members of the Embassy's
            Marine Security Guard detachment out of the country.

11   MIDDLE EAST - Israel and Egypt sign a six-point,
            cease-fire agreement.

13   SINGAPORE - The government orders a halt to sales of
            oil to those countries under the Arab embargo.

13   ICELAND - An interim agreement is reached with Great
            Britain to bring an end to the on-going conflict over
            fishing rights in the waters surrounding Iceland.

14   SINAI - At Kilometer 101, a point on the Egyptian-
            Israeli cease-fire line 101 kilometers from Cairo, an
            impasse over the implementation of the terms of the
            cease-fire is broken with an agreement for a prisoner
            of war exchange. Upon acceptance of the terms, 241
            Israeli and 8,031 Egyptian PWs are returned to their
            homelands. The exchange is completed by 22 November.

14-16   GREECE - Students riot in Athens following the arrest of five people. The violence soon spreads to Patras and Salonica (15 November). Eleven are killed when tanks are used to dislodge demonstrators holding Athens Polytechnic Institute (16 November). That day, five more are killed and at least 200 injured when the rioting spreads throughout Athens.

19   UNITED STATES - The US Sixth Fleet is taken off alert and returned to normal training duties in the Mediterranean.

19   CAMBODIA - A lone aircraft again bombs the Presidential Palace in Phnom Penh. Lon Nol again escapes injury.

19   ARGENTINA - The government signs a treaty with Uruguay ending a long-standing dispute over navigation on the Plate River.

25   GREECE - A military coup, led by Brigadier General Demetrios Ioannides, ousts President Papadopoulos. He is arrested and replaced as President by Lieutenant General Phaidon Gizikis.

29   MIDDLE EAST - Egyptian-Israeli peace talks break off when a disengagement formula cannot be agreed upon.

29   INDIA - A 15-year treaty of friendship and cooperation with the USSR is signed in New Delhi.

DECEMBER

1   LIBYA - The government orders its Embassy in Cairo to close in retaliation for Egypt's poor showing in the war.

1   URUGUAY - All Marxist political activity is banned.

2   PAKISTAN - Rioting breaks out anew in Baluchistan following the murder of Abdus Samad Khan Achakzai, the leader of the National Awami Party.

3   SOUTH VIET NAM - About 30-45% of SVN's oil reserves are destroyed in a VC rocket attack on an oil storage area in the Rung Sat (the Saigon River estuary) 30 miles southeast of Saigon.

4   SOUTH VIET NAM - A major battle develops in Chang Doc Province between ARVN and NVA forces.

6   UNITED STATES - Gerald R. Ford is sworn in as the 40th Vice-President of the United States.

6   ARGENTINA - The manager of the Esso Oil Refinery at
           Campana, Victor E. Samuelson, is kidnapped by the
           People's Revolutionary Army. He is ransomed for $14.2
           million on 11 March 1974. The amount is said to be
           enough to equip and maintain 1,500 guerrillas for one
           year.

11   WEST GERMANY - The government announces the resumption
           of diplomatic relations with Czechoslovakia. They were
           originally interrupted by the 1938 Munich Agreement.

17   ITALY - Five Palestinian terrorists kill 31 people in
           Rome's Fiumicino Airport. They then take a number of
           hostages, including 14 Americans, and throw grenades
           into a Pan Am 707 readying for a flight to Beirut.
           Next, they hijack a Lufthansa airplane to Athens where
           they demand the release of a group of PLO terrorists
           being held by Greek authorities. They then fly to
           Kuwait and surrender. On 2 March 1974 the terrorists
           are flown to Cairo where they are to be tried by the
           PLO, but Egyptian authorities refuse to release them.
           On 22 November 1974 they are flown to Tunis to be
           exchanged for hostages aboard a hijacked British air-
           liner. The entire group then goes to Libya.

20   WEST GERMANY - The government establishes diplomatic
           relations with Bulgaria.

21-22   SWITZERLAND - At a preliminary meeting in Geneva, re-
           presentatives of Egypt, Israel, the US, and the USSR
           agree to open peace talks on 29 December

28   SOUTH KOREA - The government imposes new press re-
           strictions after a month of demonstrations.

29   SWITZERLAND - Middle East peace talks begin.

1974

IRAQ - The Kurds, supported by Iran, renew their war against the central government.

THE PHILIPPINES - The government is finally able to end the Hukbalahap insurgency.

JANUARY

3 THAILAND - The government announces that 3,700 US troops have been withdrawn from Thailand since September 1973, and that less than 35,000 still remain in country.

6 UNITED STATES - The Secretary of Defense, Arthur Schlesinger, warns the oil producing nations of military reprisals should they attempt to cripple the West's industrial base.

7 LESOTHO - A coup attempt leads to the death of five members of the opposition Congress Party. An armed uprising follows in which police posts are attacked and many deaths reported.

7 UNITED STATES - The US and Panama sign a "declaration of principles" dealing with future sovereignty over the Panama Canal.

8 SOUTH KOREA - President Park Chung Hee proclaims two new emergency measures aimed at suppressing dissent. It becomes a crime, punishable by 15-years' imprisonment, to criticize the government.

9   GREAT BRITAIN - The government extends its state of
            emergency into its third month in the face of the on-
            going labor crisis.

11-16   INDONESIA - Violent demonstrations attend the formal
            visit of Japanese Prime Minister Tanaka to Jakarta.
            Indonesian troops open fire on one group of demon-
            strators killing 11 and injuring 137.

11-17   MIDDLE EAST - US Secretary of State Henry Kissinger
            engages in shuttle diplomacy to arrange a separation-
            of-forces (disengagement) agreement.

12   LIBYA - The government announces a union with Tunisia.

15   TUNISIA - The government announces that the union with
            Libya is indefinitely postponed. President Bourguiba
            dismisses his foreign minister for his part in the
            affair.

15   CYPRUS - General George Grivas, the leader of a Greek
            Cypriot underground movement (EOKA-B), is reported
            dead.

15   MALAYSIA - Malaysian jets attack Communist hideouts in
            Pahany State.

18   MIDDLE EAST - A disengagement agreement is arranged in
            which Israeli forces are to be withdrawn to a line
            about 20 kilometers east of the Suez Canal. The
            Egyptians are to occupy a strip about 8 kilometers
            deep east of the Canal with the UNEF controlling the
            space in between.

18   INDIA - Food price riots break out among students in
            the state of Gujurat. Similar rioting occurs in
            Maharashtra earlier in the month. At least 29 are
            reported killed.

18-20   SOUTHEAST ASIA - A series of naval and land engage-
            ments is fought between SVN and Communist Chinese
            forces over the sovereignty of the Paracel Islands
            southeast of Chinese-held Hainan Island. The South
            Vietnamese are driven out of the island group.

21   GREAT BRITAIN - The government announces it is lifting
            its embargo on arms shipments to the Middle East.

24   SINAI - Israeli forces begin their withdrawal from the
            west bank of the Suez Canal to the agreed-upon line
            following a final meeting with Egypt commanders at
            Kilometer 101 on the Cairo-Suez road.

26   ARGENTINA -, Nineteen bombings aimed at leftist leaders and organizations follow by one day the passage of a tough antiterrorism law. These attacks come about as the result of President Peron's urging of strong action against terrorists.

27   ISRAEL - Fighting continues between Israeli and Syrian forces in the Golan Heights region. The Syrians claim to have inflicted heavy casualties on the Israelis.

28   COLOMBIA - President Hugo Banzer Suarez declares a state of emergency in the face of peasant violence over the soaring cost of living.

30   CAMBODIA - The Lon Nol government declares a six-month state of emergency in the face of heavy fighting between the Khmer Rouge and government forces. Nearly 100 civilians are reported dead in Phnom Penh in the last week as a result of Khmer Rouge attacks.

FEBRUARY

            SYRIA - The Syrians begin a campaign of shellings and small arms attacks against Israeli positions along the cease-fire line. These attacks will continue until May as a tactic to receive better treatment at the conference table.

1   SOUTH CHINA SEA - South Vietnamese forces occupy Spratley (Spratly) Island in the South China Sea, about 450 miles east southeast of Saigon. The Philippines, Nationalist, and Communist China all protest the move.

2   COMMUNIST CHINA - An ideological campaign begins that is called a new Cultural Revolution. It focusses largely on the denigration of the writings of Confucius and Lin Piao. This campaign is directly associated with a shake-up in the Army that is reported to have occurred in January.

2-3   EAST GERMANY - The government imposes vehicular traffic controls on road movement between Berlin and the West. The Western Allies protest this violation of the Four-Power Agreements.

6   LAOS - Communist Pathet Lao and neutralist Royal Laotian representatives sign an agreement for a joint police force in the twin capitals of Vientiane and Luang Prabang. This settles the last major issue in the implementation of the January 1973 cease-fire agreement.

6   KUWAIT - Five members claiming to represent the PFLP
         and the Japanese Red Army attack the Japanese Embassy
         and take 12 hostages, including the Ambassador. The
         terrorists demand the release of two PFLP and two
         Japanese Red Army members held in Singapore. Singapore
         complies and the terrorists are given safe passage to
         South Yemen.

7   GRENADA - The Caribbean island of Grenada becomes in-
         dependent after 200 years of British rule. It immedi-
         ately joins the British Commonwealth of Nations. The
         island is in a state of emergency and has been swept
         with violence and disorder since November 1973, mostly
         aimed at the rule of Prime Minister Eric Gairy.

8   EGYPT - The job of clearing the Suez Canal begins.

8   SOUTH VIET NAM - The SVN-VC prisoner exchange resumes
         after a seven-month suspension.

8   UPPER VOLTA - An army coup overthrows the government
         of Premier Gerard Kango Ouedraogo. President Sangoule
         Lamizana names a new cabinet and appoints himself
         Premier on 11 February. The constitution is suspended
         and the National Assembly dissolved.

9   FRANCE - The government agrees to build five nuclear
         power plants for Iran as a part of an $8 billion in-
         dustrial modernization agreement.

10   MIDDLE EAST - Armed clashes between Iranian and Iraqi
         forces are reported in the Persian Gulf and along the
         frontier.

11   CAMBODIA - Nearly 200 civilians are reported dead in
         Phnom Penh as a result of the Khmer Rouge shelling the
         city.

11   SOUTH VIET NAM - About 118 VC are reported killed in a
         battle south of Pleiku.

13   SOUTH AMERICA - Four left-wing guerrilla groups from
         Argentina, Bolivia, Chile, and Uruguay announce the
         formation of a "junta of revolutionary coordination."

15   NORTH KOREA - North Korean gunboats, operating in
         their home waters, sink a South Korean fishing boat.
         The government claims the craft was a "spy boat."

20   SOUTH AFRICA - Week-long tribal clashes account for
         the deaths of 19 black miners and the injuring of 287
         others.

22   GREECE - People's Resistance Army terrorists blow up the Dow Chemical Plant at Lavrion, 40 miles from Athens. Considerable damage is caused by the four bombs that explode. Two Greek demolitions men are killed attempting to disarm another bomb.

26-28   ETHIOPIA - An army mutiny breaks out in Asmara in Eritrea and soon spreads to Addis Ababa. Emperor Haile Selassie attempts some reforms but without success. The government resigns (27 February) and Endalkatchen Makonnen is appointed the new Prime Minister.

28   UNITED STATES - The Department of State announces a resumption of diplomatic relations with Egypt.

MARCH

            THAILAND - The US and Thailand reach agreement that an additional 10,000 US troops will be withdrawn in the next several months.

2   KUWAIT - The government releases the five Palestinian hijackers who shot up the Fiumicino Airport in Rome on 17 December. They are flown to Cairo where they are to be tried by the PLO but are released instead by the Egyptian government who sends them to Tunis in response to a 22 November hijack demand from those who hold a British airliner.

4   SINAI - The Israelis complete their withdrawal to the disengagement line.

4-5   MIDDLE EAST - More clashes between Iranian and Iraqi forces are reported. One report indicates at least 56 Iraqi soldiers are killed.

7   WEST GERMANY - The Bonn government announces an exchange of diplomatic missions with East Germany.

7   GREAT BRITAIN - The Foreign Secretary announces a halt to arms shipments and aid to Chile.

11   IRAQ - The government gives the Kurdish tribes limited autonomy. This concession falls far short of Kurdish expectations.

14   IRAQ - Kurdish rebels, under the leadership of General Mustafa al-Barzani, seize a large area of Iraqi Kurdistan along the border with Turkey.

15   CAMBODIA - The US supplies the Cambodian government with ammunition to assist in a planned campaign against rebel forces.

16   PORTUGAL - A military revolt, based upon opposition to
            government policies in Africa, fails when more mili-
            tary units do not join the uprising. The leaders,
            about 20, who were loyal to the recently dismissed (14
            March) Deputy Chief of Staff, General Antonio de
            Spinola, are arrested.

18   UNITED STATES - The government announces that the Arab
            oil embargo against the US has been lifted.

18   SOUTH VIET NAM - Fighting intensifies in the Central
            Highlands with over 400 NVA and 100 ARVN reported
            killed.

19   INDIA - Food price riots are reported in Bihar State.

20   GREAT BRITAIN - The government reimposes its arms em-
            bargo on South Africa.

22   MEXICO - In Hermosillo, the US Vice-Consul, John S.
            Patterson, is kidnapped by a group allegedly calling
            itself the "People's Liberation Army of Mexico". It
            demands $500,000 ransom. The Mexican authorities come
            to believe the kidnapping was the work of American
            criminals.

24   YUGOSLAVIA - The government reinforces its frontier
            garrison in Koper northwest of Trieste when Italy
            renews its claims to parts (Zone B) of Trieste.

24   UGANDA - An army mutiny is put down after six hours of
            bitter fighting with loyal troops. Two days later (26
            March) President Amin begins the systematic execution
            of all officers involved in the uprising.

24   SWEDEN - The government announces it will triple its
            aid to FRELIMO guerrillas fighting the Portuguese in
            Mozambique.

28   GREECE - Turkish attack aircraft penetrate Greek air-
            space during a NATO exercise. Greece immediately with-
            draws from the exercise.

28   IRAQ - The government grants autonomous rule to the
            Kurds.

29   UNITED STATES - With US Secretary of State Henry
            Kissinger acting as the intermediary, Israel and Syria
            begin indirect peace talks in Washington.

29   FRANCE - The government announces an agreement with
            Senegal under which French military strength will be
            reduced from 2,250 to 1,300 men, and the French base
            at Dakar returned to Senegalese control by April 1975.

APRIL

ISRAEL - The Palestine Liberation Organization (PLO) carries out intensive raids inside Israel from bases in Lebanon. These attacks last until May when Israel retaliates with heavy bombing of suspected PLO targets, causing heavy civilian casualties.

2   FRANCE - President Georges Pompidou dies suddenly of natural causes in Paris.

5   LAOS - A coalition government including right-wing, neutralist, and Communist Pathet Lao representatives is formed to run the country. Prince Souvanna Phouma continues as Premier.

5   UNITED STATES - The Congress rejects a proposal for $474 million increase in military aid to SVN.

6   LIBYA - There are reports that Muammar al-Qaddafi has been relieved of "political, administrative, and traditional duties." It is said the real power is in the hands of Prime Minister Abdul Salam Jalloud.

7   EASTERN MEDITERRANEAN - Both Greece and Turkey place their military forces on alert due to a dispute over oil rights in the Aegean Sea.

7   ETHIOPIA - Rebel troops seize the government radio station. The government is forced to make a number of concessions. The next day, many senior civilian government and military officials are arrested and charged with crimes against the people.

11   ISRAEL - Three Palestinian terrorists attack the northern Israeli village of Qiryat Shemona killing 18 inhabitants. The terrorists then kill themselves before Israeli forces can take them.

12   LEBANON - Israeli forces attack six villages in southern Lebanon in retaliation for the raid on Qiryat Shemona.

12   IRAQ - Iraqi jets attack Kurdish military positions in the northern part of the country.

13   THE PHILIPPINES - Unknown assailants shoot and kill three American Naval officers on the perimeter of the US Naval Base at Subic Bay.

13   UNITED STATES - US Secretary of State Kissinger concludes the first round of his Washington-based Middle East diplomacy when he receives the Syrian plan for disengagement in the Golan Heights.

14   SAUDI ARABIA - The government signs a $335 million
            economic and military aid agreement with the US.

15   NIGERIA - The government of President Diori Hamani is
            overthrown in a military coup led by Lieutenant Colo-
            nel Seyni Kountie.

16   UNITED NATIONS - The stalled (8 months) UN Disarmament
            Conference reopens in Geneva.

18   EGYPT - The government announces that, since the USSR
            has failed to resupply military needs as requested,
            Egypt will no longer rely upon Soviet arms and equip-
            ment. The announcement goes on to say the Soviet de-
            mands that must be met for a resupply are totally un-
            acceptable.

19   ISRAEL - Israel and Syria fight a major air battle
            over the Golan Heights. Artillery engagements continue
            in the Golan-Mount Hermon area.

25   PORTUGAL - The Portuguese Army rebels and overthrows
            the government of President Americo Tomas and Premier
            Marcello Caetano. A military junta led by ex-General
            Antonio de Spinola takes power.

MAY

1   MOZAMBIQUE - The Portuguese military command releases
            hundreds of captured FRELIMO guerrillas.

6   UNITED STATES - The Senate rejects an administration
            request for an additional $266 million in military aid
            for SVN.

6   WEST GERMANY - Chancellor Willy Brandt is forced to
            resign after the disclosure that his personal aide,
            Gunther Guillaume, is an East German spy.

14   UNITED NATIONS - The Security Council begins hearings
            on alleged Portuguese atrocities in Mozambique.

15   PORTUGAL - Antonio de Spinola becomes Provisional
            President.

15   ISRAEL - Three terrorists from the Popular Democratic
            Front for the Liberation of Palestine (PDFLP) cross
            into Israel from Lebanon and take 90 school children
            hostage in the town of Ma'alot. They demand the re-
            lease of 20 Arab terrorists in Israeli prisons. In a
            confusion of orders, Israeli forces attack the school
            killing all the terrorists and 20-22 of the children.

16   LEBANON - In the heaviest air raids in the history of
            the Arab-Israeli struggle, Israeli jets attack seven
            Palestinian targets in southern Lebanon killing at
            least 50 and injuring at least 170 more. In Lebanon,
            the head of the PDFLP, Nayef Hawatmeh, claims the
            Ma'alot raid was ordered to sabotage the Kissinger
            peace mission.

18   INDIA - The government announces it has detonated, in
            an underground test in the Rajasthan Desert, its first
            nuclear device.

18   ARGENTINA - Police and security forces begin an opera-
            tion in Tucuman Province designed to eradicate the
            left-wing People's Revolutionary Party (ERP).

19   NORTHERN IRELAND - A state of emergency is declared in
            the wake of violence precipitated by the 15 May gen-
            eral strike called by Protestant factions to demand a
            repeal of the 1973 Sunningdale Agreement that linked
            Northern Ireland with the Catholic Irish Republic. The
            next day (20 May) an additional 500 British troops are
            airlifted into Northern Ireland, bringing the total
            force to 16,500 men.

21-22   ISRAEL - Many areas in Israel are put under security
            alert when reports of Palestinian-terrorist infiltra-
            tors are confirmed. At the same time, Israeli jets
            continue their relentless attacks on Palestinian tar-
            gets in southern Lebanon in retaliation for the
            Ma'alot massacre.

22   NORTHERN IRELAND - Implementation of the Sunningdale
            Agreement is delayed. Direct British rule is extended
            an additional four months.

25   GREAT BRITAIN - Cease-fire talks between the Portu-
            guese government and Guinea-Bissau nationalists begin
            in London.

28   LEBANON - A small bomb goes off at the John F. Kennedy
            Center (USIS Library) in Beirut. The Revolutionary
            Arab Youth Organization claims responsibility for the
            blast that injures three.

31   UNITED STATES - US Secretary of State Henry Kissinger
            completes a month-long shuttle diplomacy effort and
            announces an Israeli-Syrian disengagement agreement
            has been reached. The Israelis are to withdraw to pre-
            war lines. A buffer strip is established, including
            the town of Quneitra, that will be patrolled by the
            UNEF.

31   UNITED NATIONS - The Security Council approves the
            establishment of a UN force to patrol the Israeli-
            Syrian border.

31   COMMUNIST CHINA - The government and the Malaysian
            Prime Minister, Tun Abdul Razak, sign an agreement
            establishing diplomatic relations between their two
            countries.

JUNE

            UNITED STATES - The US withdraws its Ambassador to
            Sudan after that government frees the terrorists con-
            victed of killing an American diplomat in 1973. The
            terrorists are released to the PLO.

1   MIDDLE EAST - An exchange of prisoners of war begins
            between Syria and Israel, and Israel begins an evacu-
            ation of Syrian territory captured during the 1973
            war.

3   LAOS - The last US advisors leave Laos under the terms
            of the 1973 peace agreement.

5   SYRIA - The first 500 troops of the 1,250-man UN Dis-
            engagement Observation Group arrive in Quneitra
            (Qunaytirah).

5   BOLIVIA - A military coup attempt fails to overthrow
            the right-wing government of President Hugo Banzer
            Suarez.

9   PORTUGAL - The new government announces it has estab-
            lished diplomatic relations with the Soviet Union.

13   NORTH YEMEN - A successful coup overthrows the gov-
            ernment of President Abdul Rahman al-Iryani and places
            a pro-Saudi Arabian, Colonel Ibrahim al-Hamidi, in
            power.

13   ISRAEL - Four Arab terrorists and three Israeli women
            are killed in a firefight in an Israeli kibbutz in the
            Huleh Valley. The PDFLP claims responsibility and
            states the attack was aimed at protesting the Nixon
            visit to the Middle East.

16   OAU - Somalia calls for the immediate independence of
            all Portuguese colonies in Africa.

17   UNITED STATES - The US and Syria reestablish diplo-
            matic relations which were broken off in 1967.

17   GREAT BRITAIN - London's House of Parliament is bombed
            by terrorists of the Provisional Wing of the IRA.
            Eleven persons are injured in the blast.

18-20   LEBANON - Israeli jet fighter-bombers carry out a
            series of air strikes in reprisal for recent Arab
            terrorist activities in Israel.

23   SYRIA - Israeli forces complete their withdrawal from
            Syrian territory occupied during the 1973 war.

24   ISRAEL - Three Arab terrorists of al-Fatah kill three
            Israeli civilians and one soldier in a raid on the
            coastal city of Nahariyya.

24   ETHIOPIA - The army seizes control of the country,
            including all of the private and government radio
            stations. Haile Selassie remains Emperor but without
            much power.

27   EASTERN MEDITERRANEAN - Greek and Turkish leaders meet
            in an attempt to settle the Aegean dispute. The effort
            fails.

28   SOUTH KOREA - North Korean gunboats attack and sink a
            South Korean gunboat nine miles south of the 38th
            Parallel.

30   ETHIOPIA - The army begins arresting national leaders
            accusing them of corruption. A Supreme Military
            Council is formed which appears to be autonomous of
            government rule.

JULY

1   ARGENTINA - President Juan Peron dies in Buenos Aires
            and is replaced by the Vice-President, Isabel Peron.
            The new president becomes the first women chief of
            state in the western hemisphere.

3   SOUTH KOREA - The government reports that a ROK naval
            patrol boat has sunk a North Korean naval vessel in
            the second engagement in four days.

3   ETHIOPIA - Haile Selassie grants additional conces-
            sions to the army, including amnesty for all political
            prisoners.

5   ARAB LEAGUE - The Arab League Defense Council, meeting
            in Cairo, decides to give financial aid to Lebanon and
            the PLO to assist them in their defense against
            Israel.

7   MEXICO - The body of US diplomat John S. Patterson who was kidnapped on 22 March, is found in a creek bed near Hermosillo. This follows the arrest of an American in San Diego on 28 May on charges of conspiracy to kidnap a US diplomat. Another man is also charged.

8   LEBANON - Israeli naval units carry out reprisal raids on Palestinian ports along the Lebanese coast sinking at least 30 fishing boats. These raids are in retaliation for the 24 June Palestinian terrorist raid on the coastal town of Nahariyya.

8   BOLIVIA - The part-civilian cabinet resigns to make way for an all-military cabinet.

9   CAMBODIA - Lon Nol annnounces his offer to negotiate with the rebels after government forces capture Phsar Ouden. Prince Sihanouk refuses the offer.

10   WEST GERMANY - The government announces a normalization of relations with Czechoslovakia.

11   SOMALIA - The government signs a treaty of friendship and cooperation with the Soviet Union.

15   CYPRUS - President Makarios is forced to take refuge at a British military base when a National Guard coup, led by Greek Cypriot officers and abetted by the Greek military government, seizes power. A Greek Cypriot, newspaper publisher and former rebel leader Nikos Sampson, is sworn in to replace Makarios. Fighting breaks out in Nicosia between Greek and Turkish Cypriots.

16   CYPRUS - A Royal Air Force plane flies Makarios to safety in Malta, thence to London.

17   NATO - Heavy pressure from NATO forces Cyprus to replace the 650 Greek officers involved in the plot to overthrow the Makarios governmment.

18   CYPRUS - Over 1,000 Makarios supporters are arrested by the new Greek Cypriot government.

19   ICELAND - The Icelandic gunboat _Thor_ attacks and captures the British trawler _C.S. Forester_ for allegedly fishing in Icelandic waters.

20   CYPRUS - Moving to thwart a Greek Cypriot plan for the unification the island under Greece, Turkish forces land at sunrise along the northern coast. The Turks quickly open a 16-mile corridor from the northern port of Kyrenia to the capital of Nicosia. Fighting breaks out in the capital at the "Green Line" separating the

20   CYPRUS (Cont'd) - Greek and Turkish sections of the city. Although the Greek government issues an ultimatum to Turkey, and mobilizes its armed forces, their relative weakness becomes immediately apparent. Greece also sends troops to reinforce its common border with Turkey in Thrace.

20   SOUTH KOREA - The government claims the sinking of the second North Korean spy vessel this month.

21   USSR - Leonid Brezhnev proposes the withdrawal of all Soviet and US nuclear weapons-carrying ships from the Mediterranean.

22   CYPRUS - US Marine and British Naval helicopters evacuate more than 400 civilian personnel from the British base at Dhekelia in southern Cyprus to the USS Coronado (LPD-11). The civilian personnel are then put ashore at Beirut.

22   UNITED NATIONS - Both Greece and Turkey accept a Security Council cease-fire order. Despite this action, fighting continues.

22   ETHIOPIA - Prime Minister Endalkachew Makonnen resigns after serving only five months in office. He is then arrested, along with a number of his colleagues, by the army.

23   CYPRUS - Nikos Sampson resigns as President and is succeeded by Glafkos Clerides.

24   ANGOLA - A Portuguese military junta is established to rule the country.

24   GREECE - The military junta relinquishes authority to former Premier Konstantin Karamanlis who returns from exile.

24   CYPRUS - British forces evacuate foreign personnel from Kyrenia on Cyprus.

24   TURKEY - Turkish jets accidently bomb and sink the Turkish training-destroyer Kocatepe. An Israeli maritime training vessel, Mevuot Yam, rescues 42 of the Turkish sailors. Eighty are reported killed.

24   UNITED STATES - Four US Air Force C-130 transports carry 400 Finnish troops to Cyprus to reinforce the UNEF there.

25   WORLD COURT - The World Court rules against Iceland's claim to 50-mile territorial water rights.

25   MOZAMBIQUE - Governor-General Doctor Henrique Soares
            de Melo and all of the members of the provisional gov-
            ernment of Mozambique resign when it is learned a Por-
            tuguese military junta is about to be put into place
            to rule the country.

26   FRANCE - The French conduct an atmospheric nuclear
            test at Mururoa Atoll in the South Pacific.

26   EAST GERMANY - The government imposes travel
            restrictions between Berlin and the West.

27   PORTUGAL - The government announces the decolonization
            of its African possessions.

27   GUINEA-BISSAU - The former Portuguese colony (Portu-
            guese Guinea) is declared independent.

28   CYPRUS - Turkish forces continue to land on Cyprus and
            consolidate their positions in a 200-mile area between
            Nicosia and Kyrenia. Renewed fighting between the
            Turkish forces and Greek Cypriots is reported in
            several sectors.

28   UNITED NATIONS - Greece asks for an emergency session
            of the Security Council to discuss the Cyprus crisis.

29   CYPRUS - Turkisk forces continue to expand their occu-
            pation zone eastward from the landing area at Kyrenia.

30   INDIA - Communist members of the Indian Parliament ac-
            cuse the US of using the World Health Organization for
            biological weapons development. The Indian government
            denies the allegations.

30   CYPRUS - A new cease-fire is signed by Turkey, Greece,
            and Great Britain.

30   CHILE - A military tribunal sentences four former
            Allende aides to death for treason.

31   CYPRUS - The government charges Turkey with repeated
            truce violations.

31   AUSTRALIA - The government establishes diplomatic re-
            lations with North Korea.

AUGUST

            CYPRUS - Although the threat of war has diminished,
            the Turkish force that invaded the island continues to
            expand its area of control and to consolidate its
            gains.

1   GREECE - The government reinstates the constitution that was abolished in 1967.

1   USSR - During a visit by Yassir Arafat an agreement is reached by which the PLO will be able to open an office in Moscow. The Kremlin pledges support to the PLO.

1   UGANDA - The government accuses neighboring Tanzania of spying. Military forces are moved to the border.

4   CYPRUS - Turkish authorities expel 20,000 Greek Cypriots from the Turkish section of the island.

7   UNITED STATES - The House of Representatives cuts aid to SVN by $300 million.

8   SWITZERLAND - Cyprus cease-fire talks resume in Geneva.

9   UNITED STATES - Facing certain impeachment proceedings, Richard M. Nixon resigns the presidency. Gerald R. Ford becomes the 38th President of the United States. One of Ford's first acts is to reiterate the policy of his five predecessors and inform the RVN that they can "count on us."

10   ANGOLA - Leaders of the FNLA rebel organization reject the Portuguese plan for Angolan independence.

13   GREAT BRITAIN - The British reinforce their garrison on Cyprus and order the necessary preparations in case war breaks out on the island.

14   CAMBODIA - The US conducts its last air raid on Cambodian territory.

14   SYRIA - A bomb explodes near the US pavilion at the Damascus International Fair. The Arab Communist Organization claims responsibility.

14   SWITZERLAND - Cyprus cease-fire talks, being held in Geneva, break down when Turkey refuses to allow time for Greek consultations.

14   CYPRUS - Within hours of the breakdown of cease-fire talks in Geneva, Turkish forces conduct heavy ground and air attacks to achieve their political as well as military objectives.

15   GREECE - Greece withdraws its forces from NATO claiming the organization failed to stop the Turkish attack on Cyprus.

15   SOUTH KOREA - There is an unsuccessful attempt on the life of President Park Chung Hee. Park's wife is killed when a gunman of an anti-Park youth group opens fire on the President. The would-be assassin is arrested.

15   CYPRUS - Great Britain begins reinforcing its garrison on Cyprus.

16   ETHIOPIA - That power remaining in Haile Selassie's hands is revoked by the military junta.

16   TURKEY - The government announces a unilateral cease-fire in Cyprus after completing its military operation aimed at partitioning the island into Turkish and Greek sections.

18   UNITED STATES - The government warns Turkey not to attempt extending its control in Cyprus too far.

19   CYPRUS - The US Ambassador, Rodger P. Davies, and a Foreign Service National employee of the US Embassy are assassinated during a Greek Cypriot anti-American demonstration at the US Embassy in Nicosia. Although a number of persons are arrested, tried, and found guilty of charges arising from the killings, none are seriously punished.

21   PANAMA - The government announces it has restored diplomatic relations with Cuba.

25   FRANCE - The French detonate another nuclear device in the atmosphere in their current test series at Mururoa Atoll in the South Pacific.

27   UNITED NATIONS - Turkey rejects a Soviet-sponsored proposal for a UN-sponsored peace conference on Cyprus.

29   ICELAND - The newly-installed government announces it has reversed the former government's policy and will allow continued NATO use of its base in Iceland.

30   GREECE - The government notifies its Western Allies that it will begin reassessing the value of foreign military bases on its soil.

30   ISRAEL - The government announces it will cooperate with Soviet minesweeping operations in the Gulf of Suez.

31   USSR - The government denies US President Ford's charge that the Soviets have three naval bases in the Indian Ocean.

SEPTEMBER

SOUTH VIET NAM - Intelligence estimates place at least 300,000 NVA in SVN.

4   UNITED STATES - The government establishes diplomatic relations with East Germany.

7   ZAMBIA - Portuguese and FRELIMO leaders sign an agreement whereby Mozambique will be granted full independence on 25 June 1975. An interim provisional government is established to rule until that date.

8   UNITED STATES - President Ford pardons Richard Nixon for all crimes he may have committed while in the White House.

8   GREECE - A TWA jetliner bound from Tel Aviv to New York crashes into the Ionian Sea when a member of the Arab National Youth for the Liberation of Palestine detonates an explosive device he is carrying. Of the 88 people on board, all whom are killed, 17 are known to be Americans.

12   ETHIOPIA - Emperor Haile Selassie I is deposed in a bloodless coup after 44 years as ruler. His son, the 57-year-old Crown Prince Asfa Wossen, is named his successor by the army, but he refuses to return to Addis Ababa from Switzerland where he has lived since suffering a stroke in 1972. The junta then names General Aman Michael Andom head of state. Selassie and most of his ministers are charged with corruption in office.

13   THE NETHERLANDS - Japanese Red Army terrorists seize the French Embassy in The Hague. Ambassador Jacques Senard and ten others are taken hostage. The terrorists demand the release of a Red Army member imprisoned in France and $1 million.

14   UNITED STATES - President Ford vetoes a military appropriation for Turkey in order to allow further mediation of the Cyprus question.

15   FRANCE - The eighth nuclear device in three months is detonated by the French at Mururoa Atoll in the South Pacific.

16   UNITED STATES - President Gerald Ford signs an amnesty proclamaton offering conditional clemency to the thousands of deserters and draft dodgers who fled to avoid service in the Viet Nam War.

17   THE NETHERLANDS - When their demands are met by the
            French government, and their colleague is flown to The
            Hague, the Japanese Red Army terrorists release their
            hostages and leave the country in an airliner provided
            by France.

22   EGYPT - The government recognizes the PLO as the   "le-
            gitimate representative of the Palestinian people."

23   CYPRUS - The exchange of Greek and Turkish prisoners
            of war begins and is completed on 1 October with a
            total of 3,308 Turkish Cypriots and 2,479 Greek
            Cypriots being repatriated.

27   DOMINICAN REPUBLIC - In two coordinated attacks, mem-
            bers of the 12th of January Liberation Movement
            capture the local USIS Director when they seize the
            Venezuelan Consulate in Santo Domingo. The terrorists
            demand $1 million and the release of 38 political
            prisoners. The government refuses to negotiate with
            the terrorists.

30   PORTUGAL - Leftist elements in the government of Pre-
            mier Vasco Goncalves force the resignation of Presi-
            dent Spinola. A new Provisional President, General
            Francisco de Costa Gomes, reappoints Goncalves as
            Premier.

OCTOBER

1   NIGERIA - The military government headed by General
            Yakubu Gowon announces its decision to   postpone
            indefinitely any plans for a return to civilian
            government.

9   DOMINICAN REPUBLIC - Seven hostages, including the
            local Director of the USIS, are finally released by
            left-wing terrorists after being held for nearly two
            weeks in the Venezuelan Consulate in Santo Domingo.
            This occurs only after the Dominican government
            changes its position and negotiates with the ter-
            rorists. The terrorists are then granted safe passage
            to Panama.

10   SYRIA - A bomb kills two Syrian personnel in the
            offices of the National Cash Register Company in
            Damascus. The following day the NCR offices in Aleppo
            are bombed. The Arab Communist Organization claims re-
            sponsibility for both bombings.

14   UNITED NATIONS - The General Assembly recognizes the
            PLO.

15   ANGOLA - A cease-fire is agreed upon among the rival groups vying for power in the newly autonomous former Portuguese colony.

15   UNITED STATES - Four hundred fifty members of the Massachusetts National Guard are mobilized in the face of racial violence sparked by court-ordered bussing in the Boston school system.

16   ETHIOPIA - Heavy fighting breaks out between Ethiopian forces and separatist rebel forces of the Eritrean Liberation Front (ELF).

20   ISRAEL - The government says it will not withdraw from the captured Egyptian oil fields at Abu Rudeis until it has guarantees of future oil supplies from Egypt.

21   JAPAN - Massive leftist anti-American demonstrations take place protesting the forthcoming visit of US President Gerald Ford.

23   UNITED NATIONS - The mandate for the UNEF patrolling the Israeli-Syrian border is extended an additional six months by the Security Council.

29   MOROCCO - A four-day Arab summit conference held in Rabat closes with a unanimous statement that the PLO is the "sole legitimate representative of the Palestinian people on any Palestinian land that is liberated." A fund of $2.35 billion is established to help defend those Arab states (Egypt, Syria, and Jordan) that face Israel.

30   UNITED NATIONS - The US, Great Britain, and France veto a Security Council resolution aimed at the expulsion of South Africa from the UNO because of its apartheid policies.

NOVEMBER

1   UNITED NATIONS - A Security Council resolution calls for the immediate withdrawal of all foreign troops in Cyprus.

1   LEBANON - Israeli jets carry out an overnight attack on Palestinian positions. Six persons are reported killed.

5   ISRAEL - The government rejects the Arab summit's recognition of the PLO and announces an enlargement of the Israeli Defense Forces.

6   ARGENTINA - President Isabel Peron places the nation in a state of siege as political unrest continues and grows in intensity.

8   UNITED STATES - The US Court in Cleveland, Ohio, acquits eight Ohio National Guardsmen of charges stemming from the Kent State University riots in which four students were killed when the Guard opened fire on the demonstrators.

12   UNITED NATIONS - The General Assembly votes to suspend South Africa from Assembly activities.

12   OAS - The Foreign Minister's conference being held in Quito, Ecuador fails by two votes to overthrow the sanctions placed on Cuba.

16-17 MIDDLE EAST - Syrian and Israeli forces are put on alert as tensions mount in the Middle East.

19   ISRAEL - Three Arab terrorists attack the village of Beit Shean in the Jordan Valley, killing four and injuring 23.

21   GREAT BRITAIN - Twenty-one persons are killed and about 120 injured in IRA terrorist bombings in Birmingham.

22   PERU - Revolutionary Vanguard terrorists blow up the Sears Roebuck store in Lima. Eleven people are injured.

22   ETHIOPIA - Lieutenant General Aman Michael Andom is ousted by a coup. He is murdered the next day along with 60 other former officials and members of Haile Selassie's family. The government claims all 60 were tried and executed.

24   USSR - At a summit meeting in Vladivostok, US President Gerald Ford and Soviet General Secretary Brezhnev sign an accord limiting offensive weapons to a combined ICBM, SLBM, and manned long-range bomber total of 2,400 for each side, including 1,320 with MIRV warheads.

24   GREAT BRITAIN - The police capture six men from Northern Ireland and charge them with the bombings of two pubs in Birmingham in which 19 were killed and more than 100 injured.

25   UNITED NATIONS - The General Assembly votes to suspend the UNO membership of South Africa.

26   USSR - Moscow rejects a Chinese Communist demand that
            Soviet troops be withdrawn from the Sino-Soviet border
            as a precondition to any normalization discussions.

27   MEXICO - The government breaks diplomatic relations
            with Chile.

29   GREAT BRITAIN - The government outlaws the Irish Re-
            publican Army.

DECEMBER

2   WEST GERMANY - The government bans all Icelandic fish-
            ing vessels from West German ports following the sei-
            zure of a West German fishing trawler off the Ice-
            landic coast.

2   ISRAEL - President Ephraim Katzir announces that
            Israel has the capability of manufacturing nuclear
            weapons.

3   GREAT BRITAIN - The government announces it plans to
            withdraw all military forces in the Far East in the
            next ten years.

3   RHODESIA - The government temporarily releases Joshua
            Nkomo and the Reverend Ndabaningi Sithole to allow
            their participation in talks in Lusaka on Rhodesia's
            future.

4   FRANCE - The government announces it has signed an
            agreement to sell $800 million in military equipment
            to Saudi Arabia.

7   UNITED NATIONS - The General Assembly approves a
            Soviet proposal that the five nuclear powers cut their
            defense budgets by 10 percent.

8   GREECE - The Greeks vote the return of the monarchy
            and King Constantine.

9   PERU - The Declaration of Ayacucho, which, among other
            things, limits the importation of offensive military
            equipment into Latin America, is signed by eight
            nations in Lima.

9   SOUTH VIET NAM - The government reports the heaviest
            fighting since the cease-fire went into effect.

9   PAKISTAN - A bomb explodes in the USIS Center in
            Peshawar causing extensive damage. Two Pakistani
            employees of the center are injured in the blast.

11   BURMA - A major student protest in Rangoon begins when
            police and troops forcibly remove the remains of for-
            mer UN Secretary General U Thant from a mausoleum the
            students had built on their campus. Martial law is
            declared. U Thant died in New York on 25 November.

15   FRANCE - An extreme right-wing organization known as
            the Youth Action Group detonates bombs outside the TWA
            and the Coca Cola offices in Paris. No one in the
            building is injured in the attacks aimed at protesting
            a Franco-American summit in Martinique. The next day
            the group attacks the Minnesota Mining Company
            offices.

16   UNITED STATES - After a nearly 50-year delay the
            Senate ratifies the 1925 Geneva Protocol on Chemical
            Warfare and the more recently approved 1972 Convention
            on Biological Warfare.

16   IRAQ - The government accuses Iran of shooting down
            two Iraqi aircraft operating in the border area in
            connection with the Kurdish uprising.

17   LEBANON - The government asks the Arab states for help
            in defending itself against Israel.

20   RHODESIA - After weeks of difficult negotiations,
            Prime Minister Ian Smith announces a cease-fire in the
            guerrilla war and the release of political prisoners
            as the first step toward a constitutional convention.

22   COMORO ISLANDS - The French-owned Indian Ocean pro-
            tectorate votes for full independence.

28   BANGLADESH - A state of emergency is declared and all
            constitutional rights suspended in the wake of sub-
            versive activities and violence that are tied to the
            economic situation.

27   NICARAGUA - Sandinista terrorists kill two policemen
            and a civilian and take a number of prominent poli-
            ticans and businessmen hostage in Managua when they
            invade a private party held in honor of US Ambassador
            Turner B. Shelton. Shelton had already departed the
            party when the terrorists arrive. Thirteen hostages
            are released on 29 December after the government ac-
            cedes to demands. The terrorists and the 14 released
            political prisoners, along with $1 million in ransom,
            are allowed to fly to Cuba on 30 December.

30   UNITED NATIONS - Venezuela announces it will establish
            diplomatic relations with Cuba.

1975

1   CAMBODIA - The Communist Khmer Rouge open their annual dry season offensive with attacks around the capital city of Phnom Penh.

3   UNITED STATES - Secretary of State Henry Kissinger refuses to rule out the use of force should the OPEC nations attempt to "strangle" the US.

5   EGYPT - At a Cairo reconciliation meeting also attended by Egypt and Syria, both Jordan and the PLO pledge mutual constraint in the future.

7   SOUTH VIET NAM - After a week-long siege, NVA regulars capture the province town of Phouc Binh (Song Be) in Phouc Long Province, about 75 miles north of Saigon.

8   CYPRUS - Greek and Turkish Cypriot leaders agree to resume negotiations to form a federal government for the island nation.

8   EGYPT - President Anwar Sadat announces that the USSR has failed to meet Egyptian arms requirements in the wake of the 1973 war.

9   UNITED STATES - The government agrees to sell $756 million worth of F-5 fighters to Saudi Arabia.

12-16   LEBANON - Israeli forces carry out two attacks against the town of Kfar Shouba clashing with Palestinian and Lebanese troops.

13   UNITED STATES - Warning of the dangers inherent in
            North Viet Nam's continued and flagrant violations,
            the Department of State dispatches a note to the eight
            nations who guaranteed South Viet Nam sovereignty in
            the 1973 Paris Accords.

15-17   USSR - Talks between the Soviet Union and Japan fail
            to resolve the dispute over the Kurile Islands.

16   NORTHERN IRELAND - The Provisional Wing of the IRA an-
            nounces it will not extend the 25-day-old cease-fire
            when it expires at midnight.

19   PAPUA NEW GUINEA - A female House of Assembly member,
            Josephine Abaijah, and a civil servant, Simon Kaumi,
            declare a Papuan republic and threaten to seize the
            government.

22   UNITED STATES - President Ford signs the protocol ban-
            ning the manufacture, storage, or use of biological
            weapons.

23   CAMBODIA - Twenty-three US ships carrying ammunition
            arrive at the beleaguered city of Phnom Penh. At the
            same time, Communist Khmer Rouge forces are closing
            the ring around the capital and are driving on the
            naval station and the important Mekong River ferry
            crossing site at Neak Luong.

25-26   PORTUGAL - Leftists surround a meeting of the Social
            Democratic Party in Oporto. When police and local mil-
            itary forces are unable to disperse them, the govern-
            ment sends airborne troops from Lisbon to lift the
            siege.

28   ETHIOPIA - The government declares an all-out war
            against Eritrean rebels seeking independence for the
            province.

29   FRANCE - Ending a state visit to France, Egypt's Pres-
            ident Sadat announces the purchase of $2.2 billion in
            French arms and equipment.

31   ETHIOPIA - Eritrean secessionist rebels surround the
            provincial capital of Asmara.

FEBRUARY

3   CAMBODIA - Khmer Rouge mines in the Mekong River sink
            a number of ships returning down river having dis-
            charged their cargoes at Phnom Penh. The capital is
            now surrounded with Communist rockets set within range
            of the center of the city.

5   UNITED STATES - Abiding by the law passed in December
         1974, the US is forced to cut off military aid to Tur-
         key because of the lack of "substantial progress"
         toward settlement of the Cyprus question. Both the
         President and the Secretary of State strongly criti-
         cize the Congressional action in this case.

5   TURKEY - The government withdraws from the Cyprus
         peace talks because of the US arms embargo.

5   MALAGASY REPUBLIC - An 11-day government crisis ends
         as Colonel Richard Ratsimandrava, the former Minister
         of Interior, takes over control from General Gabriel
         Ramanantsoa.

5-6   PERU - Army troops are called in when Lima police go
         on strike demanding higher wages. A national state of
         emergency is declared as rioting and excessive vio-
         lence accompany the strike. At least 100 are killed in
         the capital.

8   BOLIVIA - The government announces it has restored
         diplomatic relations with Chile after 12 years of in-
         activity.

8   SPAIN - The government dispatches warships to the
         Spanish enclaves of Ceuta and Melilla on the Medi-
         terranean coast, after the Moroccan government lays
         claims to them.

9   NORTHERN IRELAND - The IRA announces that "hostilities
         against crown forces" will cease for an indefinite
         period on 10 February.

11   MALAGASY REPUBLIC - President Richard Ratsimandrava,
         who had just assumed power on 5 February, is assassi-
         nated in the capital city of Tananarive. General
         Gilles Andriamahazo assumes power at the head of a
         military junta.

12   UNITED STATES - The government doubles its airlift of
         supplies to Cambodia as the rebel Khmer Rouge inten-
         sify their efforts to block resupply from the sea up
         the Mekong River.

12   ARGENTINA - The army is ordered to crush the insur-
         gent left-wing People's Revolutionary Army (ERP).

13   CYPRUS - Turkish Cypriot leader Rauf Denktash pro-
         claims an independent Turkish Cypriot state which
         encompasses about 40% of the northern part of the
         island.

15   ETHIOPIA - The government declares a state of
            emergency in the northern province of Eritrea in the
            wake of continued heavy fighting. At least 1,200 are
            reported dead in Asmara, the province capital, since
            31 January.

18   EGYPT - New shipments of Soviet war materiel begin to
            arrive in Egypt. At least 50 aircraft, including
            MiG-23 fighters, along with tanks and surface-to-air
            missiles are among the expected items.

18   SYRIA - The USSR sends 45 MiG-23 fighters to Syria.

18   IRAQ - At least 40 Soviet aircraft are reported to
            have been shipped to Iraq.

21   ETHIOPIA - A government offensive designed to cripple
            the rebels in Eritrea begins.

24   GREECE - A right-wing military coup fails. At least 37
            officers are arrested.

24   UNITED STATES - The government lifts its embargo on
            the sale of arms to India and Pakistan.

25   CAMBODIA - Communist Khmer Rouge forces capture Oudong
            (Odong), 21 miles north of Phnom Penh at the junction
            of Routes 6 and 26, and Peam Reang (Phum Peam Reang),
            37 miles southwest of the capital in Takev Province.

26   COLOMBIA - Twelve leftist urban guerrillas, belonging
            to the Montoneros group, abduct the US Consul Agent,
            John P. Egan, from his home in Cordoba. When the
            government refuses to negotiate his release, he is
            murdered (28 February [?]) and his body, draped in a
            Montoneros flag, is left by the side of the road
            outside Cordoba.

MARCH

1   USSR - The government withdraws its recognition of the
            Lon Nol government in Cambodia and recognizes Prince
            Sihanouk as that nation's leader.

4   RHODESIA - The government begins arresting opposition
            leaders. A Methodist minister, Ndabaningi Sithole, the
            President of the Zimbabwe African National Union, is
            arrested on charges of plotting murders of other black
            leaders.

4   UNITED STATES - The government concludes a $21 billion
            deal with Iran for its purchase of nuclear reactors
            and conventional weapons over a five-year period.

5   ISRAEL - Eight Palestinian terrorists of the Al-Fatah group land on the beach near Tel Aviv and shoot their way into the Savoy Hotel. In the ensuing battle 18 are killed, seven of the eight terrorists among them.

5   ALGERIA - Representatives of Iraq and Iran meet in Algiers to conclude a settlement of the recent border clashes. Iran agrees to closing its Kurdistan border with Iraq.

6   ISRAEL - The government announces that its navy has captured the ship that transported the eight Al-Fatah Palestinian terrorists who attacked the Savoy Hotel.

7   CAMBODIA - Fire Base "Sierra II," a vital position on the Mekong River south of Phnom Penh in the vicinity of Phum Prek Toch, is captured by Communist rebels. Survivors of the garrison are evacuated by watercraft and transported upriver to Neak Luong.

7   IRAQ - The central government opens an offensive against Kurdish positions in the Mount Serti and Mount Handran areas.

10   SOUTH VIET NAM - The capital of Darlac Province, Ban Me Thuot (Lac Giao) in the Central Highlands in MR2 is stormed and captured by NVA forces. President Thieu orders the ARVN Airborne Division into Saigon.

11   PORTUGAL - A right-wing military coup attempt by supporters of General Antonio de Spinola is thwarted by troops loyal to the government. Spinola flees to Spain, thence to Brazil where he is granted political asylum.

13   SOUTH VIET NAM - The commanding general of MR1 receives orders to withdraw to the coast near Danang.

14   SOUTH VIET NAM - The commanding general of MR2 receives orders to evacuate his forces in Pleiku and Kontum provinces and make for the coast.

18   SOUTH VIET NAM - More than 100,000 South Vietnamese flee the Central Highlands after the fall of Ban Me Thuot and two weeks of mounting defeats for the Saigon forces.

22   IRAQ - In the wake of the Iraq-Iran border agreement, Kurdish leader General Mustafa al-Barzani states the fighting between his forces and those of the Iraqi central government "is over." Many of the Kurds are said to flee into Iran.

23   SOUTH VIET NAM - The ancient capital city of Hue (the
            capital of Thua Thien Province) is surrounded by NVA
            forces. Refugees from the area flee south toward Da
            Nang along with others from the northern provinces of
            Tam Ky and Quang Ngai.

24   CAMBODIA - The US airlift of military supplies into
            Phnom Penh's Pochentong Airport resumes after a 48-
            hour stoppage caused by damage from enemy ground fire
            while aircraft attempted to land at the field.

25   SAUDI ARABIA - King Faisal is assassinated in Riyadh
            by his nephew Prince Faisal ibn Musad ibn Abdul Aziz.
            Prince Khalid ibn Abdul Aziz is crowned, succeeding
            his brother Faisal.

26   UNITED STATES - The Biological Weapons Convention
            comes into force. The treaty was signed in Washington,
            London, and Moscow in 1972.

27   ANGOLA - Fifty die in fighting between rival factions
            in the capital city of Luanda. A truce is declared the
            following day, 28 March.

30   SOUTH VIET NAM - Danang, the strategically vital city,
            with its huge military base, is taken by the NVA. The
            ARVN defenses simply crumble, and a general route
            begins. Thousands of refugees flee south.   The
            situation in South Viet Nam appears to be hopeless.

APRIL

1   CAMBODIA - General Lon Nol leaves Cambodia for Indo-
            nesia in a move calculated to enable the conflict
            between the government and Communist Khmer Rouge
            rebels to be resolved.

1   SOUTH VIET NAM - The third largest city in SVN, Qui
            Nhon in Binh Dinh province, is abandoned by South
            Vietnamese forces and occupied by the NVA. There are
            reports that an American evacuation has begun.

4   NATIONALIST CHINA - Chiang Kai-shek dies at 87.

10   TANZANIA - A four-day ministerial meeting of the OAU
            ends with a call for stronger military action against
            the white government in Rhodesia.

11-12   CAMBODIA - Because of the deteriorating military situ-
            ation in the country, the US closes its Embassy in
            Phnom Penh and begins the evacuation (Operation GOLDEN
            PULL) of the several hundred Americans in the capital.

13   CAMBODIA - The new military government formed after
            the departure of Lon Nol vows to fight on.

13   CHAD - President N'Garta Tombalbaye is assassinated by
            a group of soldiers who storm the presidential palace
            in N'Djamena. General Noel Ordingar takes over control
            of the country on 16 April.

15   LEBANON - More than 100 are reported killed in Beirut
            after three days of fighting between Palestinian and
            Christian forces.

17   CAMBODIA - The government of Premier Long Boret sur-
            renders to the Communist Khmer Rouge. Immediately
            after the surrender the Communists begin a massive
            program designed to return millions of Cambodians to
            the countryside.

21   SOUTH VIET NAM - President Nguyen Van Thieu resigns
            and is replaced by Vice-President Tran Van Houng.

22   SOUTH VIET NAM - The provincial capital of Long Khanh
            Province, Xuan Loc (Xa Xuan Loc), is evacuated by
            South Vietnamese forces after two weeks of heavy
            fighting.

22   HONDURAS - The government of President Oswaldo Lopez
            Arellano is ousted in a bloodless military coup.

24   SWEDEN - Six terrorists of the West German Red Army
            Faction attack the West German Embassy killing the
            military attache and taking 12 hostages. The terror-
            ists demand the release of 26 anarchists held in West
            German jails even though the West German government
            had previously refused to release them. The terrorists
            then kill the Economics Attache. At midnight, the ex-
            plosion of a hand grenade within the Embassy causes
            the terrorists and their hostages to flee the build-
            ing. Swedish police capture five (one seriously
            wounded, dies later in West Germany) of the terrorists
            and find the sixth dead in the Embassy. The five are
            extradited to West Germany where the four survivers
            are each given two life terms in prison.

25   CAMBODIA - Prince Norodom Sihanouk is named the head
            of the newly formed Khmer Rouge Royal Government of
            National Union of Cambodia.

27   SOUTH VIET NAM - Communist forces cut the vital High-
            way 1A between Saigon and Bien Hoa. The Communists are
            reported to be within five miles of the city. The 18th
            ARVN Division makes a heroic stand at Xuan Loc in Long
            Khanh Province but is defeated. President Tran Van
            Huong resigns in favor of Duong Van Minh.

29   GREECE - As a result of US-Greek negotiations that be-
            gan on 7 April, the US naval facility at Elefis and
            the US air base at Athens Airport are closed. The
            overall US military strength in Greece is also cut
            drastically.

29   SOUTH VIET NAM - All remaining US personnel are or-
            dered out of SVN. By 7:52 PM (1952 hours) the evacua-
            tion is complete and US presence in SVN ceases.

30   SOUTH VIET NAM - President Minh surrenders to repre-
            sentatives of the Provisional Revolutionary Government
            of South Viet Nam (PRG). NVA tanks enter Saigon. Sai-
            gon is immediately renamed Ho Chi Minh City.

30   SOUTH KOREA - President Park Chung Hee informs his
            people that an attack by North Korea is imminent and
            puts his army on alert.

MAY

2   IRAQ - Kurdish resistence to the central government
            ends after Kurd leader General Mustafa al-Barzani
            states that further struggle is futile.

7   LEBANON - Seven cabinet officers resign over govern-
            ment inaction in stopping the fighting between Mus-
            lim and Christian militiamen.

12   CAMBODIA - A Cambodian naval vessel seizes the 10,000-
            ton American merchant freighter SS Mayaguez in in-
            ternational waters about 60 miles off the Cambodian
            coast in the Gulf of Siam (Thailand). The ship and its
            crew of 39 are taken to the island of Koh Tang (Kaoh
            Tang) about 25 miles southeast of the port city of
            Kompong Som (Sihanoukville).

14   CAMBODIA - A US naval task force arrives in the vicin-
            ity of Koh Tang Island, and a Marine landing party of
            250 with the support of 11 helicopters recapture the
            Mayaguez after a major firefight with Cambodian
            troops. The landing party fails to find the crew.
            Three Cambodian gunboats are sunk during the raid. In
            the meantime, US naval fighter-bombers from the USS
            Coral Sea attack Ream airfield, 200 miles from Koh
            Tang, where they destroy 17 Cambodian Air Force air-
            craft. The operation was poorly prepared and executed
            as attested by the loss of 15 US service personnel
            killed, 50 wounded, and three missing. Twenty-three
            more are killed in an associated helicopter crash in
            Thailand. The operation is also a diplomatic failure
            as the Cambodian government had already announced the
            release of the ship and crew when the attack began.

14   CAMBODIA (Cont'd) - The staging of the operation through bases in Thailand without that government's permission also brings a Thai protest.

14   LAOS - A major anti-American, student demonstration takes place in Savannaket. The US Aid for International Development (USAID) office is occupied by the demonstrators and the USAID officials and their dependents detained. Other American buildings in Savannaket and Luang Prabang are attacked and ransacked.

15   LAOS - The US Embassy announces the immediate evacuation of all US citizens from the country.

15   PORTUGAL - The government orders its troops to take control of the situation in Angola and to halt the factional fighting.

16   LEBANON - Prime Minister Rashid-al-Solh resigns his office and blames the Christian Phalangists for the continuing violence.

19   UNITED STATES - Although the Senate votes to end the prohibition on the sale of arms to Turkey, the House of Representatives refuses to go along, and the embargo continues. In a separate action, Defense Secretary Schlesinger warns North Korea against any miscalculation of America's intention to defend South Korea in light of the recent collapse in South Viet Nam.

20   LAOS - Communist Pathet Lao troops occupy Savannaket and complete a takeover of almost all of the southern half of the country.

20-21   LEBANON - Fighting in Beirut intensifies between Muslim and Christian militiamen.

21   UNITED NATIONS - Syria and Israel agree to a six-month extension of the UN mandate in the Golan Heights.

21   IRAN - Iranian terrorists assassinate two US Air Force officers in Tehran. Ten members of the People's Strugglers are arrested and tried for the murders. Nine are executed on 24 January 1976.

22   LEBANON - The army is ordered to enforce a cease-fire.

23   LAOS - As a means of preventing a civil war, Premier Souvanna Phouma orders the Royal Laotian Army to cease its resistence. US authorities begin an immediate evacuation of USAID and Embassy personnel in country.

23   LEBANON - An eight-man military government is established to restore order to the country.

25   LEBANON - Israeli forces engage Lebanese army troops
            on the southern border of the country.

26   LEBANON - Muslim opposition brings about the collapse
            of the military government.

JUNE

1-2   RHODESIA - Fighting breaks out between two factions of
            the African National Congress in Salisbury. At least
            13 blacks are killed and more than 25 wounded.

5   EGYPT - The Suez Canal is reopened for the first time
            in eight years.

5   FRANCE - France conducts the first in a series of un-
            derground nuclear tests held in the Pacific.

5   UNITED STATES - Intelligence sources reveal the USSR
            is building a missile storage facility in Berbera,
            Somalia. The Soviets deny the report.

8   UNITED STATES - The government announces the with-
            drawal of the last US fighter aircraft stationed in
            Nationalist China (Taiwan). Only 4,000 US service
            personnel remain there after the aircrews depart.

9   COMMUNIST CHINA - The government announces that diplo-
            matic relations have been established with the Philip-
            pines during a state visit in Peking by President
            Marcos.

12   BELGIUM - The government approves a $2 billion deal to
            purchase 102 F-16 fighters from the US.

13   GULF OF THAILAND - Cambodian and Vietnamese naval and
            land forces clash in a dispute over the Poulo Wai
            Islands about 60 miles off the coast and claimed by
            both.

24-29   LEBANON - Heavy fighting breaks out again in Beirut
            between Palestinian and Lebanese factions. A cease-
            fire is arranged on 25 June. The truce lasts until 29
            June when fighting resumes.

25   MOZAMBIQUE - The former Portuguese colony is granted
            its independence under FRELIMO leadership after 470
            years of colonial rule.

26   INDIA - The government of Prime Minister Indira Gandhi
            declares a state of emergency after ordering the ar-
            rest of hundreds of opposition leaders.

JULY

1   THAILAND - After establishing diplomatic relations with Communist China, the Thai government breaks diplomatic relations with Nationalist China.

3   LEBANON - A truce between Christian and Muslim factions in Beirut goes into effect.

3   IRAN - Terrorists from the People's Strugglers assassinate a Foreign Service National employee of the US Embassy in Tehran.

4   ISRAEL - Fourteen Israelis are killed when a bomb, hidden in an old refrigerator in Jerusalem's Zion Square, explodes.

4   BALKANS - Greece and Bulgaria call for a conference of the Balkan States to be convened in 1976.

6   UNITED STATES - Congressmen returning from a junket to Somalia confirm that the Soviets are building missile facilities in that country.

6   COMORO ISLANDS - The native government of the islands declares its unilateral independence from France.

7   LEBANON - Israel launches a series of air and land attacks in retaliation for the 4 July terrorist bombing in Jerusalem.

9-11   ANGOLA - Fighting breaks out in Luanda between rival black factions. The Communist-backed Popular Movement for the Liberation of Angola and the National Front for the Liberation of Angola forces attack each other's positions in very heavy fighting. At least 200 are killed on both sides.

12   WEST AFRICA - The islands of Sao Tome and Principe gain their independence after 500 years of Portuguese rule.

16   ICELAND - The government declares its intention to extend its fishing rights from 50 to 200 nautical miles.

16   SAUDI ARABIA - A meeting of the Islamic foreign ministers calls for the expulsion of Israel from the UN.

16   SOUTH AFRICA - The expiration of the Simonstown Agreement officially ends 20 years of naval cooperation with Great Britain.

16   ANGOLA - MPLA forces defeat the FNLA and take control
            of Luanda.

17   PORTUGAL - When the fourth coalition government falls,
            the Armed Forces Movement (AFM) triumvirate assumes
            full control of the country.

20   SINAI - Israeli forces are put on alert after Egyptian
            President Sadat (15 June) threatens to refuse the
            renewal of the UN peacekeeping force mandate due to
            expire on 24 June.

21   COMORO ISLANDS - Amid charges of intervention in the
            internal affairs of the newly independent nation,
            French forces begin their evacuation of the islands.
            Two hundred French troops are left on Mayotte, where
            the inhabitants reject the independence movement.

22   EGYPT - President Sadat renews the UN mandate in the
            Sinai.

22-23   INDIA - The Indian Parliament authorizes the govern-
            ment of Indira Gandhi to rule under the emergency
            powers invoked on 26 June. Most of the opposition
            members of the bicameral body do not attend the
            sessions.

23   ANGOLA - A cease-fire fails to work.

24   UNITED STATES - The House of Representatives hands
            President Ford a resounding defeat when it rejects a
            move to restore arms sales to Turkey.

25   TURKEY - The government orders all US bases on Tur-
            kish soil closed within 24 hours. Only the NATO base
            at Incirlik in southern Turkey is exempted.

28   ANGOLA - The FNLA mounts a counterattack to retake
            Luanda.

29   NIGERIA - The government of General Yakubu Gowon, the
            leader of the ruling provisional military council, is
            ousted while Gowon attends the OAU meeting in Kampala,
            Uganda. Leadership in Nigeria is given to Brigadier
            Murtala Ramat Mohammed.

29   OAS - The Organization of American States lifts its
            11-year-old embargo on Cuba.

31   TURKEY - The government rejects an offer of $50 mil-
            lion in US arms if Turkey will allow the reopening of
            US bases.

AUGUST

3   COMORO ISLANDS - A pro-French coup, led by four opposition parties under the banner of the National United Front, overthrows the government of President Ahmed Abdullah.

4   MALAYSIA - Five Japanese Red Army terrorists seize the consular sections of the US and Swedish Embassies in Kuala Lumpur and take 52 hostages. They demand the release of five JRA members held in Japan. All ten JRA members are then flown to Libya (8 August).

5   LEBANON - Israeli forces carry out amphibious and air attacks on Palestinian and Lebanese targets in and around Tyre. At least 16 Arabs are killed and at least 30 wounded. The raid centered on an attack on a Syrian operated base used by the al-Saiqah guerrilla force and shared by the Popular Front for the Liberation of Palestine.

5   ANGOLA - UNITA begins mobilizing its forces.

8   MALAYSIA - After having released all but 15 hostages, the terrorists holding the US Embassy in Kuala Lumpur exchange those 15 for two Japanese and two Malay volunteer hostages, and the five JRA prisoners they demanded, and fly to Libya on a Japan Airlines aircraft.

9   ZAIRE - While on a state visit, French President Valery Giscard d'Estaing announces an arms embargo against all future arms sales to South Africa.

10   ANGOLA - The MPLA defeats the combined FNLA-UNITA force and drives it out of Luanda.

10   TIMOR - A coup led by the Democratic Union of Timor, takes control of the former Portuguese island colony which was proceeding toward independence.

13   ANGOLA - UNITA declares war on the MPLA. The MPLA threatens to declare unilateral independence.

14   ANGOLA - The Portuguese government resumes control of Angola "in the absence of a functioning government." At the same time, thousands of white settlers begin a mass exodus from the country as the spectre of all-out civil war looms on the horizon.

15   BANGLADESH - President Sheikh Mujibur Rahman is assassinated in an army coup. He is replaced as President by Khandakar Mushtaque Ahmed.

21   UNITED STATES - The government announces it is lifting
      the ban on exports to Cuba.

21   TIMOR - As the Portuguese are evacuating their person-
      nel, a civil war erupts between the various factions
      intent upon taking over control of the former Portu-
      guese island possession in the Malay Archipelago.

21-22 LEBANON - A series of clashes takes place between
      Palestinian commandos and Israeli forces along the
      border. Israeli jets retaliate by raiding a PLO set-
      tlement close to the Syrian border.

22   SYRIA - President Assad and Jordan's King Hussein
      announce the formation of a supreme command to coor-
      dinate political and military policy.

22   SPAIN - A US Marine Security Guard at the US Consulate
      in Valencia is shot from a passing car. The Anti-
      Fascist Patriotic Front claims responsibility for the
      attack.

23   LAOS - The Pathet Lao capture the administrative capi-
      tal of Vientiane.

27   ETHIOPIA - Former Emperor Haile Selassie dies at age
      83 as a result of complications growing out of recent
      surgery.

29   LEBANON - Lebanese army force move to intervene in the
      factional fighting in Zahle (Zahlah) on the road from
      Beirut to Damascus.

29   PERU - President Juan Velasco and Premier Vasco dos
      Santos Goncalves are ousted in a bloodless coup, led
      by the military, because of their leftist leanings.

SEPTEMBER

1   ECUADOR - A right-wing coup attempt, led by General
      Raul Gonzalez Alvear, is crushed by troops loyal to
      President Guillermo Rodriguez Lara. About 18 are
      killed and 80 injured in the fighting around the
      government palace in Quito.

4   SWITZERLAND - In Geneva, Egyptian and Israeli offi-
      cials initial a US-mediated peace agreement.

5   UNITED STATES - An attempt is made upon the life of
      President Gerald Ford by a former member of the
      "Manson Family," Lynette "Squeaky" Fromme. The in-
      cident takes place in Sacramento, California.

5   SUDAN - Rebellious army personnel seize the radio station in Omdurman and attempt to overthrow the government of President Gaafar Nimeiry. The coup attempt is crushed by loyal troops within hours of its inception.

8   SOUTH AFRICA - The government confirms that its forces conducted a combat patrol into Angola.

9   TIMOR - The left-wing Revolutionary Front for the Independence of East Timor (Fretilin) claims total control of the island.

10   LEBANON - Lebanese army units are alerted when Muslim militiamen lay siege to the Christian stronghold of Zegharta.

11   THE PHILIPPINES - Members of the Moro National Liberation Front deny that they have signed a cease-fire accord with the government of President Marcos and vow to continue to fight for full autonomy.

12   TURKEY - The government gives US-built F-5 "Freedom" fighter aircraft to Libya as part of a military aid package.

15   SPAIN - Four "Black September" terrorists seize the Egyptian Embassy in Madrid and threaten to murder their hostages unless the Egyptian government renounces the Sinai Agreement with Israel. After a paper is signed, which is later repudiated, the four terrorists, accompanied by the Algerian and Iraqi Ambassadors, fly to Algiers where the terrorists are freed.

16   PAPUA NEW GUINEA - The former Australian colony becomes independent.

17   UNITED STATES - The House of Representatives votes to lift the arms embargo on Turkey.

18   INDONESIA - The government orders its naval forces around the island of Timor reinforced.

18-26   LEBANON - Heavy fighting continues in Lebanon despite the cease-fire. A Syrian-mediated truce is put into effect on 25 September, but it too fails on 26 September when new fighting erupts in Beirut.

22   UNITED STATES - Another attempt is made on the life of President Ford. This time in San Francisco, where Sara Jane Moore fires at the President. Her aim is deflected, however, by an alert ex-Marine, Oliver Sipple, who grapples with the women until she is taken into custody.

24   MIDDLE EAST - Egypt and Israel sign an accord imple-
          menting the Sinai Agreement.

24   SEATO - The SEATO Council agrees to disband the organ-
          ization but to retain the treaty.

25   TIMOR - Clashes are reported between Timorese and
          Indonesian forces.

30   BAHREIN - The government requests the US remove its
          naval facility at Jufair by mid-1977. In the meantime,
          the rent on the base is increased 600 percent.

OCTOBER

1   ITALY - Italy and Yugoslavia settle the Trieste dis-
          pute and agree to recognize the existing border.

3   UNITED STATES - The Congress approves a relaxation on
          the arms embargo imposed on Turkey.

5   UNITED STATES - The government announces it has
          reached an agreement with Spain to extend US basing
          rights on Spanish soil for five more years. In return,
          the US increases its military aid to Spain.

6   SOUTH KOREA - South Korean jets sink a North Korean
          intelligence collection ship operating in South Korean
          waters.

7   USSR - A new treaty of friendship and cooperation that
          eliminates all reference to the reunification of the
          two Germanys is signed with East Germany.

7   ARGENTINA - Guerrillas attack an army base at Formosa,
          in Chaco Province near the Paraguayan border.

10   ISRAEL - The government announces its timetable for
          the withdrawal from the Sinai.

12   NIGERIA - The government confirms the delivery of a
          number of Soviet-built MiG-21 fighters.

17   SOUTH YEMEN - Omani aircraft attack insurgent supply
          lines in South Yemen. These supply routes are used to
          aid the Dhofar rebels who are led by the Communist-
          controlled Popular Front for the Liberation of Oman
          (PFLO).

23   UNITED NATIONS - The Security Council extends the UN
          peace-keeping mandate in the Sinai for an additional
          year.

23   GREAT BRITAIN - The government opens talks with Iceland over the new Icelandic fishing restrictions. After two days, Iceland rejects British proposals for quotas and breaks off the talks.

23   ANGOLA - Cuban military advisors and troop units are reported in country.

24   PORTUGAL - A full military alert is ordered in Portugal in the face of a possible left-wing coup attempt.

24   FRANCE - The Turkish Ambassador and his chauffeur are assassinated while driving to their Embassy in Paris. ASALA takes credit for the killings.

27   COMMUNIST CHINA - The Chinese carry out an underground nuclear test at their test facility at Lop Nor.

28   LEBANON - Terrorists shoot up the Chamber of Deputies in Beirut after condemning politicans for attempting to find a solution to the Christian-Muslim fighting. At least one minor official is killed and one policeman wounded.

NOVEMBER

2   SPAIN - The government announces its intention to intervene directly in Spanish Sahara. This signals a stiffening of Spain's position toward Moroccan claims on the territory.

2   SOUTHEAST ASIA - Thailand and Cambodia establish diplomatic relations.

2   ANGOLA - A new cease-fire goes into effect, but heavy fighting continues. The UNITA and FNLA establish a joint military headquarters to coordinate their forces.

3-7   BANGLADESH - The army takes control of the government in the wake of violence and murder following the assassination of President Sheikh Mujibur Rahman and members of his immediate family on 15 August. He is replaced by Khandakar Mushtaque Ahmed, the former Minister of Trade and Commerce, as President.

5   BELIZE - The Belize garrison is reinforced by 250 British paratroopers who are flown in after Guatemala threatens to annex the former colony of British Honduras. The Guatemalan claim is supported by most of the Latin-American states.

6-7   MOROCCO - A flood of Moroccan civilians, numbering nearly 50,000, march into Spanish Sahara in a peaceful demonstration of their determination to have the territory. This group is eventually joined by 300,000 more. On 9 November, King Hassan II of Morocco declares an end to the "Green March" and orders his people back into home territory.

10   YUGOSLAVIA - The government formally recognizes the agreement with Italy that settled the Trieste dispute.

10   UNITED NATIONS - The General Assembly adopts a resolution calling Zionism a form of racism.

10   ANGOLA - With the country gripped in a bitter civil war and no organized government in existence, Portugal relinquishes sovereignty over the colony it has ruled since 1485.

11   ANGOLA - The principal forces vying for control of Angola proclaim two distinct governments. The Communist-controlled MPLA establishes the People's Republic of Angola in Luanda, while the People's Democratic Republic of Angola is founded in Nova Lisboa (Huambo) by a coalition of the FNLA and UNITA.

12   YUGOSLAVIA - The government accuses the Soviet Union of numerous violations of existing agreements and charges Moscow with meddling in internal Yugoslav affairs.

13-25   GREAT BRITAIN - A British warship is ordered into Icelandic waters after a second round of talks (13-17 November) fails to achieve any positive results, and after Icelandic gunboats cut a British fishing trawler's net lines (18 November).

14   PORTUGAL - A mob attacks the Parliament building in Lisbon.

14   SPAIN - The government agrees to hand over administration of Spanish Sahara to Morocco and Mauritania.

14   SINAI - Israeli forces evacuate the Abu Rudeis oil fields as a part of the disengagement agreement.

16   ANGOLA - At least 400 Soviet advisors and technicans are reported to have arrived in Luanda to aid the Communist-led MPLA.

20   UNITED NATIONS - Objecting to the recently announced Spanish plan to turn Spanish Sahara over to Morocco and Mauritania, Algeria demands it be put under UN administration.

20   SPAIN - At age 82, Generalissimo Francisco Franco
            Bahamonde dies of natural causes following a heart
            attack suffered on 21 October. On 22 November Juan
            Carlos is proclaimed King of Spain.

20   UNITED STATES - Intelligence sources state that 3,000
            Cuban combat troops are presently deployed in Angola.

21   PORTUGAL - The provisional (AFM) government suspends
            operations as violent demostrations grow and spread
            through Lisbon.

24   UNITED STATES - Secretary of State Henry Kissinger
            warns the USSR and Cuba against further interference
            in the affairs of Angola.

24   NORWAY - The government reopens discussions with the
            Soviet Union over the control of the Barents Sea.

25   SURINAM - The former Dutch colony in South America
            becomes independent.

25-28   PORTUGAL - A state of emergency is declared in the
            Lisbon Military District by President Francisco da
            Costa Gomes after fighting breaks out between Commu-
            nist rebels and government troops. On 27 November,
            after the revolt has been crushed by loyal troops, a
            number of senior military officers, including Army
            Chief of Staff General Carlos Fabiao and Admiral
            Antonio Rosa Coutinho, are dismissed. Coutinho's
            ouster sparks new violence and left-wing military
            units capture four air bases in northern and central
            Portugal. Order is not restored until 28 November.

27   ANGOLA - The Communist Chinese withdraw the advisors
            that were supporting the FNLA.

30   DAHOMEY - The West African republic of Dahomey changes
            its name to the People's Republic of Benin on the
            first anniversary of the Marxist takeover of the
            government.

DECEMBER

1   UNITED NATIONS - When the Security Council announces
            it will invite the PLO to attend the Middle East
            debates planned for January 1976, Israel announces it
            will not attend.

2   LEBANON - Israeli fighters attack a number of Pales-
            tinian guerrilla bases across Lebanon. About 60 are
            killed as a result of the most devastating raid of the
            year.

2   THE NETHERLANDS - A group of South Moluccan terrorists
         hijack a train near Beilen in the northern part of the
         country. Two civilians are killed and 50 are taken
         hostage.

4   THE NETHERLANDS - Another group of South Moluccan ter-
         rorists seizes the Indonesian Embassy in The Hague and
         takes 25 people hostage. The two incidents are planned
         to force The Netherlands into helping the people of
         the South Moluccan Islands gain independence.

7   ICELAND - As a third Royal Navy frigate is dispatched
         to the waters around Iceland, the government threatens
         to break diplomatic relations with Great Britain and
         to reexamine its NATO commitments.

7   TIMOR - Indonesian troops supported by pro-Indonesian
         Timorese capture the capital city of Dili.

8-9   LEBANON - Leftist Muslim militiamen attack the Holiday
         Inn in Beirut which has become a Christian Phalangist
         headquarters. Lebanese army forces are able to disen-
         gage the two factions, but not before at least 100 are
         killed in action or murdered.

11   SPANISH SAHARA - Moroccan troops occupy the capital
         city of El Aiun.

11   OMAN - The Sultan of Oman announces that the ten-year
         war with Dhofar rebels is over. Oman's British-led
         army has forced the PFLO into an isolated area near
         the Yemeni border.

14   THE NETHERLANDS - The South Moluccan terrorists kill
         one hostage who is trying to escape, then surrender to
         Dutch police. The remaining hostages are released
         unharmed.

14   THAILAND - Cambodian forces operating out of Ta Phraya
         District clash with Thai border security forces.

15   LEBANON - Government forces begin taking control of
         the contested sections of Beirut.

17   SPANISH SAHARA - Mauritanian troops and Algerian-
         supported rebels clash along the territories southern
         border.

18   PORTUGAL - As a result of the invasion of Timor, Port-
         ugal breaks diplomatic relations with Indonesia.

18   MOZAMBIQUE - The FRELIMO government crushes a military
         revolt led by rebellious soldiers and police.

18-22   ARGENTINA - Right-wing Air Force officers revolt and seize two air bases near Buenos Aires in an attempt to overthrow the government of President Isabel Peron. On 21 December, after the base at Moron is attacked by jets flown by loyal pilots, the rebels surrender.

19   THE NETHERLANDS - The siege at the Indonesian Embassy ends when the South Moluccan terrorists release their hostages and surrender without having achieved their goals.

19   UNITED STATES - The Senate votes to end military aid to the FNLA and UNITA factions in Angola.

19   THAILAND - The last US combat aircraft on the SEA mainland fly out of Thailand.

21-23   AUSTRIA - Palestinian terrorists kill two persons and take 60 hostages when they attack an OPEC meeting in Vienna. On 22 December the terrorists are allowed to fly out of Austria with ten of their hostages, most of whom are freed in Algiers. The Algerian government subsequently refuses to extradite the terrorists to Austria and grants them political asylum.

23   GREECE - Richard Welch, the Special Assistant to the US Ambassador and CIA Station Chief in Athens, is assassinated by three unknown assailants in front of his home.

29   UNITED STATES - A bomb explodes in a locker at New York's LaGuardia Airport killing 11 persons and injuring 80 more. There is no immediate identification of the culprits.

29   TURKEY - The government announces it has signed a treaty of friendship and cooperation with the Soviet Union.

Notes

1976

CAMBODIA - Reports from refugees indicate that at least 300 former members of the Royal Cambodian Army who had been captured in the fighting in 1975 have been executed.

OAU - The OAU fails to produce a unified policy on Angola.

2   VIET NAM - In a last ditch stand, remnants of ARVN open a major battle with NVA forces in Darlac Province in the Central Highlands.

4   ISRAEL - The government announces it will boycott the upcoming Geneva peace talks and the UN Security Council debates on the Middle East if the PLO is invited to participate.

5   NORTHERN IRELAND - In retaliation for the murder of five Roman Catholics on 4 January, ten Protestant workmen are shot to death near Belfast. At least sixteen people have been killed in the first five days of the year. In response, the British government orders more troops into Northern Ireland.

5   LEBANON - The continuing civil war causes a cancellation of the general elections scheduled for April.

5   ANGOLA - Forces of the Soviet-backed Popular Movement for the Liberation of Angola (MPLA) capture the National Front for the Liberation of Angola (FLNA) airbase at Negage and the FLNA capital at Carmona.

6   NORTHERN IRELAND - An additional 600 British troops
         are sent into Ulster to help quell the recent wave of
         violence.

6   MALTA - British Defense Minister Mason announces an
         end to British basing rights on Malta when the current
         agreement expires in March 1979.

7   PORTUGAL - The wave of attacks on left-wing organi-
         zations intensifies with bombings in Oporto (7 Janu-
         ary) and Braga (29 January).

7   SOMALIA - The government receives two missile boats
         outfitted with anti-ship missiles from the USSR.

8   INDIA - The government suspends constitutional freedom
         throughout the country.

11   ICELAND - In an attempt to force NATO into curtailing
         British fishing in Icelandic waters, Icelandic fisher-
         men begin a campaign of blocking the entrances to out-
         lying US radar and communications sites attached to
         the NATO base at Keflavik.

11   ECUADOR - The government of President Guillermo
         Rodriguez Lara is replaced by one led by Vice Admiral
         Poveda Burbano, following a bloodless coup.

12   UNITED NATIONS - Although the US attempts to block the
         session, the Security Council meets to debate the Mid-
         dle East with the PLO in attendance.

13   LEBANON - Druze militia lay siege to the Christian
         militia positions at Al Darmhour.

15   KUWAIT - The government announces it has an agreement
         with the USSR to purchase arms and military equipment.

18   LEBANON - The 22nd cease-fire arranged in the last
         nine months breaks down and renewed fighting is re-
         ported. The government of Prime Minister Rashid Karami
         resigns.

19   LEBANON - Intelligence reports indicate that units of
         the Syrian-backed Palestine Liberation Army are in
         Lebanon.

19   CAMBODIA - The government continues the forced relo-
         cation of hundreds of thousands of civilians which
         began in October 1975.

21   SOUTH AFRICA - The government announces plans to
         double the size of the standing army.

22   LEBANON - A cease-fire goes into effect that is under-
            written by Syria.

22   SWITZERLAND - The government lifts a 1975 arms sale
            ban on Spain.

23   SOUTH AFRICA - The government orders its troops with-
            drawn from the fighting in Angola.

24   SPAIN - A five-year Treaty of Friendship and Coopera-
            tion is signed in Madrid between the US and Spain
            (ratified by the US Congress 21 June). The treaty
            extends US basing rights in Spain until 1979 and
            extends $1.2 billion in military sales credits to
            Spain.

25   COMMUNIST CHINA - The government announces it has
            begun a new series of nuclear tests at Lop Nor. The
            series is completed on 17 November.

25   MOROCCO - A US-built Moroccan F-5 fighter is shot down
            by a Soviet-built surface-to-air missile belonging to
            the Popular Front for the Liberation of Saquia el
            Hamra and Rio de Oro (Polisario).

26   SINAI - Egyptian troops begin the occupation of posi-
            tions in the UN buffer zone under the 1975 Sinai
            Agreement.

27   UNITED NATIONS - The US vetoes a Security Council re-
            solution calling for the establishment of a Pales-
            tinian state.

27   UNITED STATES - The Congressional House of Representa-
            tives refuses President Ford's request for aid to the
            pro-Western factions in Angola despite solid evidence
            that the Soviet Union is pouring massive amounts of
            military aid into the country in support of the MPLA.

28   MOROCCO - Fighting is reported between Moroccan and
            Algerian forces near the strategically important town
            of Amgala. Algerian forces capture the town but later
            lose it.

28   SOUTH AFRICA - Legislation is introduced that would
            allow the South African Army to operate beyond its own
            borders.

28   SWITZERLAND - SALT III negotiations resume in Geneva.

30   BANGLADESH - There is a report that Indian-supported
            rebels have clashed with troops on the Indian border.

30   WARSAW PACT - The Warsaw Pact rejects the latest NATO
            Mutual Balanced Force Reduction (MBFR) proposal as
            "insufficient."

FEBRUARY

2   INDIA - Hundreds of members of parties in opposition
            to Indira Gandhi's Congress Party are arrested.

4   UNITED STATES - The government carries out two under-
            ground nuclear tests in Nevada.

4   MOZAMBIQUE - The right of privately owned property is
            abolished.

5   SOUTH ATLANTIC - An Argentinian destroyer fires on a
            British research vessel south of the Falkland Islands.

5   GREAT BRITAIN - After Iceland rejects a British offer
            to reduce the size of its fishing fleet in waters
            claimed by Iceland, the government orders British
            naval patrol vessels back into those waters to protect
            its fishermen.

5   EGYPT - The government announces that a cease-fire has
            been arranged in the Algeria-Morocco conflict of
            Spanish Sahara.

9   ANGOLA - Soviet-backed MPLA forces, led by Cuban
            advisors, capture the capital town of Huambo (Nova
            Lisboa) Province, the seat of the National Union for
            the Total Independence of Angola (UNITA), in the
            central part of the country.

10   RHODESIA - The government suspends rail traffic with
            the Mozambique port city of Maputo (Lourenco Marques).

10   ANGOLA - The MPLA gains control of the important rail-
            road that runs inland from the seaport of Benguela.

11   OAU - The Organization of African Unity announces it
            is recognizing the MPLA as the rightful government in
            Angola.

11   ANGOLA - The FLNA and UNITA announce the beginning of
            a guerrilla struggle to free their country of the
            Soviet-backed MPLA.

11   UNITED STATES - The government announces it has agreed
            to a $1.2 billion sale of arms and equipment to Saudi
            Arabia.

12   COMMUNIST CHINA - The government reports armed clashes
        along the Soviet border. The USSR denies any part in
        the activity.

12   ALGERIA - The government reports that the Egyptian-
        mediated negotiations with Morocco have broken down.

13   NIGERIA - A military coup attempt, led by Lieutenant
        Colonel Bukar S. Dimka, fails. Murtala Ramat Mohammed,
        the head of state, is killed during the fighting.
        Lieutenant General Olusegan Obasanjo, a supporter of
        Mohammed, takes control of the country.

16   VIET NAM - The Communists announce they have defeated
        the ARVN force operating in Dar Lac Province in the
        Central Highlands.

18   SINAI - United Nations' forces occupy their new posi-
        tions as directed by the Interim Agreement.

19   ICELAND - The government breaks diplomatic relations
        with Great Britain because London refuses to stop ex-
        tensive commercial fishing in Icelandic waters.

19   KENYA - President Jomo Kenyatta threatens war on
        Uganda over Ugandan claims of territory along the
        common border.

21   ISRAEL - The government announces its forces have
        withdrawn to new positions in the Sinai to affect the
        separation ordered by the UN disengagement agreement.
        Three US-manned surveillance outposts are activated in
        the Mitla and Giddi (Gidi) passes to ensure the peace.

23-24   SOUTHEAST ASIA - At Bali, Indonesia, a summit meeting
        of Southeast Asian leaders is held. It is decided to
        establish an Association of Southeast Asian Nations
        with a seretariat at Jakarta. Indonesia, Malaya, The
        Philippines, Singapore, and Thailand join the group.

26   SPAIN - The government formally hands over control of
        Spanish Sahara to Mauritania and Morocco.

27   EGYPT - President Sadat urges an immediate resumption
        of the Geneva conference on the Middle East with PLO
        participation.

27   UGANDA - President Idi Amin withdraws his claim to
        Kenyan territory near the common border.

29   EGYPT - The government warns Syria that if it goes to
        war with Israel it may not have Egyptian support.

MARCH

3   MOZAMBIQUE - In a move supported by the British government, President Samora Macel closes his country's border with Rhodesia, thereby depriving the Rhodesians of access to the sea. The government also mobilizes its armed forces to prevent any overt Rhodesian military action.

3   SPAIN - Violence erupts in the Basque region. Two demonstrators are killed.

4   UNITED STATES - The administration announces a plan to lift the military sales embargo on Egypt.

8   ISRAEL - Violence erupts over charges of brutality by Israeli troops toward Arabs in Nablus in the West Bank area. The resignation of the city council follows the rioting.

9   LEBANON - Fighting breaks out again in Beirut.

11   LEBANON - The military commander of Beirut, Brigadier General Abdul Aziz al-Ahdab, faced with dissension and mutiny in the army's ranks, declares a state of emergency and demands the government resign.

11   NIGERIA - The government executes 30 people, including the former Minister of Defense; all were allegedly involved in the assassination of Murtala Mohammed on 13 February. Colonel Dimka, the leader of the abortive coup, and seven others are executed on 15 May.

11   LIBYA - In response to Egypt's arrest of 27 Libyans accused of subversion, the government expels 3,000 Egyptians.

12   LEBANON - President Suleiman Franjieh rejects the demand to resign and barricades himself in the Presidential Palace at Baabda. Syrian troops prevent leftist troops (generally loyal to Kamal Jumblatt) from attacking Baabda. There is renewed fighting in Beirut (13-14 March).

14   EGYPT - President Sadat abrogates the 1971 Treaty of Friendship and Cooperation with the Soviet Union. This is approved by the People's Assembly the next day (15 March).

16   UNITED STATES - Because of Soviet activities in Angola, the Department of State notifies the Kremlin that the US will not participate in a number of scheduled conferences (energy, housing, commercial cooperation) with the USSR.

17   ISRAEL - Rioting spreads after an Arab boy is shot by an Israeli soldier.

19   RHODESIA - Prime Minister Ian D. Smith and black leader Joshua Nkomo break off their majority rule negotiations.

20   THAILAND - The government orders the US to remove its forces from Thai territory. The order exempts about 270 US military advisors to the Thai Armed Forces.

21   ISRAEL - The government orders Israeli troops to leave Hebron (Hevron, Al Khali), south of Jerusalem, after severe rioting by the city's populace.

22   UNITED STATES - Secretary of State Henry Kissinger warns that the US "will not accept further Cuban military interventions abroad."

24   ARGENTINA - In a bloodless coup, a military junta overthrows the government of President Maria Estela Martinez de Peron. On 29 March Lieutenant General Jorge Raphael Videla, a member of the ruling junta, is sworn in as the country's new President. Madame Peron will later be indicted on charges of fraud and malfeasance.

25   LEBANON - With his palace at Baabda under bombardment, President Franjieh flees to Christian positions on the coast at Juniyah.

25   ZAMBIA - Rhodesian rebel leader Joshua Nkomo meets with the presidents of Botswana, Mozambique, Tanznia, and Zambia and endorses a full-scale guerrilla war against the white government of Ian Smith.

26   UNITED STATES - The government signs a military aid agreement with Turkey including $1 billion in US aid in return for the reopening of 26 US bases.

26   SYRIA - Syrian troops in large numbers are observed massing along the Lebanese border.

26   EGYPT - The government withdraws permission for Soviet naval vessels to use Egyptian port facilities.

27   ANGOLA - The last South African troops leave the country, thereby ending their protection of the refugee camps in southern Angola.

29   ZAMBIA - President Kenneth Kuanda prophesies that the breakdown in talks between white and black factions in Rhodesia will lead to civil war.

29   MALDIVES REPUBLIC - Great Britain relinquishes to the
            government control of the Royal Air Force Base on Gan
            Island.

31   SINGAPORE - Great Britain completes the withdrawal of
            its armed forces from its former Crown Colony.

APRIL

1   LEBANON - A truce is arranged under threat of large-
            scale Syrian intervention.

2   FRANCE - The French detonate their third nuclear de-
            vice in the present series of tests at Mururoa Atoll
            in the South Pacific.

5   COMMUNIST CHINA - Violent demonstrations, apparently
            aimed at the anti-rightist movement that sprang up
            after the death of Chou En-lai, take place in Peking
            and a number of other cities.

5   CAMBODIA - Prince Sihanouk resigns as head of state.

5   COMMUNIST CHINA - Antigovernment rioting breaks out in
            Peking against Teng Hsiao-ping. He is dismissed and
            stripped of his Party positions on 6 April.

7   UNITED NATIONS - The Security Council broadens its
            economic sanctions against Rhodesia.

7   AUSTRIA - A proposal to end the long violent dispute
            over rule in Cyprus is rejected by Greek Cypriots in
            Vienna.

7   RHODESIA - Rebel leader Joshua Nkomo rejects the Smith
            plan for gradual black assumption of power and demands
            immediate majority rule.

11   ZAMBIA - The government agrees to open another front
            in the guerrilla war against Rhodesia.

14   MALAYSIA - Fighter-bombers attack guerrilla bases on
            the border with Thailand.

15   INDIA - After a 15-year disruption, the government
            announces it is resuming diplomatic relations with
            Communist China.

15   UNITED STATES - The government reaches agreement with
            Greece for four years of basing privileges in return
            for $700 million in US aid.

16   LEBANON - A Syrian-backed cease-fire is accepted by the PLO.

20   LEBANON - Fighting breaks out in Beirut. At least 125 are killed.

20   COMMUNIST CHINA - In a protocol signed in Peking the government promises Egypt military aid.

21   USSR - The Soviets begin a new series of underground nuclear tests at their Central Asian test facility at Semipalatinsk.

22   UNITED NATIONS - Although Malaysia (20 April) has sided with Indonesia in the debate over the latter's military intervention against leftist separatists on Portuguese Timor, the Security Council orders an immediate withdrawal of all Indonesian forces.

23   TURKEY - A bomb explodes at the entrance to the American Language and Trade Institute, a private girls' school operated by the American Board Mission and the YMCA in Istanbul. Damage is negligible. No one claims responsibility for the bombing.

24   LEBANON - President Franjieh is forced to sign a constitutional amendment authorizing new elections.

25   MALAYSIA - Rebels blow up a section of the country's main northern railroad in Perak Province.

27   NATIONALIST CHINA - The government establishes diplomatic relations with South Africa.

29   LEBANON - The planned election is postponed as Syrian forces enter Beirut.

MAY

2   FRANCE - The government extends the 12-month conscription law for an additional five years.

3   LIBYA - The hostages aboard a Philippine Air Lines plane hijacked by Muslim terrorists are released. The anti-Marcos hijackers surrender to Libyan authorities.

4   GREAT BRITAIN - Six hundred British troops are withdrawn from Northern Ireland.

5   THE PHILIPPINES - The government establishes diplomatic relations with Cambodia.

5   ANGOLA - Western intelligence agencies report the presence of Soviet-built surface-to-air missiles and MiG-21 jet fighters in the country.

5   RHODESIA - Rebel guerrillas attack the railway from Botswana into Bulawayo.

6   SINGAPORE - The government establishes diplomatic relations with Cambodia.

8   LEBANON - Following much political maneuvering, Elias Sarkis replaces Suleiman Franjieh as president. Sarkis is backed by Syria. General fighting rages throughout the country.

9   IRAN - Iran buys two nuclear reactors from France. The French government will announce (7 September) that it will build eight nuclear power plants in Iran for almost $10 billion.

13   LEBANON - A week-long period of intensified fighting between Christian and Muslim militias begins. Hundreds will die.

14   INDIA - The government announces an agreement with Pakistan to resume diplomatic relations (in July) that were interrupted by the 1971 war.

14   SOUTH AFRICA - The government pledges not to intervene militarily in Rhodesia.

17   ISRAEL - Widespread rioting breaks out in a number of places after Israel decides to eject settlers in the northern half of the West Bank (Samaria) (9 May).

18   ETHIOPIA - The government begins the mobilization of 20,000 peasant troops into militia units along the Eritrean border.

19   TONGA - The USSR requests the right to build a fishing facility in the Polynesian Kingdom of Tonga in return for the authority to construct an airfield.

21   NATO - The NATO Foreign Ministers warn of increasing Soviet military strength in Central Europe.

23   THE PHILIPPINES - Filipino troops storm a hijacked aircraft at Manila Airport. Thirteen people are killed including the Muslim terrorists.

24   ALBANIA - A widespread purge of government officials is reported.

25   CUBA - In an announcement made through Swedish Prime Minister Olof Palme, Fidel Castro states his intention to withdraw Cuban troops from Angola.

28   UNITED STATES - A nuclear testing treaty which limits the size of underground nuclear tests is signed with the USSR.

30   GREAT BRITAIN - Following some success in negotiations with Icelandic representatives meeting in Oslo, Norway, the British government orders its frigates out of Icelandic waters.

30   CYPRUS - President Makarios rejects a Turkish Cypriot proposal that would have established autonomous Greek and Turkish states on Cyprus.

31   SYRIA - The government orders additional troops into Lebanon to help curtail the violence of the civil war.

JUNE

1   ICELAND - Upon reaching a negotiated settlement of the "Cod War," the government restores diplomatic relations with Great Britain.

1   LEBANON - Syrian troops enter the country in force and occupy the Beqaa Valley. Heavy fighting is reported against leftist forces around Mount Lebanon.

1   WEST GERMANY - Two bombs explode at the headquarters of the US Army V Corps. Sixteen people are injured and there is extensive damage to the building. The "Revolutionary Cells Group" (RZ) claims responsibility.

2   THE PHILIPPINES - The Filipino government establishes diplomatic relations with the Soviet Union.

3   GREECE - When Turkish forces begin naval maneuvers in the Aegian, the government orders a partial mobilization.

4   ETHIOPIA - The government halts its campaign against the Eritrean sessionists.

4   USSR - The government agrees to furnish a nuclear reactor to Cuba.

6   THAILAND - The Malaysian troops that pursued Malaysian rebels into Betong on Route 15 in Thailand are withdrawn at Thailand's request.

6   VIET NAM - The government claims the Spratley and
           Paracel islands currently held by Communist China.

7   OAS - The Organization of American States accuses
           Chile of carrying on a campaign of terror against its
           citizens.

8   MAURITANIA - Polisario guerrillas attack the capital
           of Nouakchott. Morocco immediately pledges to extend
           its defense against Polisario attacks to include the
           Islamic Republic of Mauritania.

10   RHODESIA - The government reports an increase in guer-
           rilla warfare along its border with Mozambique. At
           least 40 Rhodesian troops and 295 guerrillas have been
           killed since the beginning of the year.

10   EGYPT - At a meeting in Cairo twenty members of the
           Arab League agree to establish a peacekeeping force in
           Lebanon. This force will replace the 12,000 Syrian
           troops now in Lebanon who have drawn much criticism in
           the Arab world.

10   UGANDA - An attempt to assassinate Idi Amin Dada
           fails.

12   URUGUAY - President Juan Maria Bordaberry is removed
           from office in a bloodless coup led by the army.
           Alberto Demicheli is appointed as temporary president
           until Aparicio Mendez is elected on 1 September.

13   SYRIA - Syria accuses Iraq of moving 8,000 troops and
           armor up to their common border.

16   LEBANON - The US Ambassador, Francis E. Meloy, Jr.,
           the US Economic Counselor, Robert O. Waring, and a
           Lebanese driver are assassinated as the Ambassador's
           sedan crosses the "Green Line" from West to East
           Beirut. The three are first detained by PFLP members
           at a checkpoint and then shot and killed. Their bodies
           are found in a garbage dump near the beach at Ramlat
           al-Bayda.

16   UNITED STATES - The government announces it is pre-
           pared to sell arms and materiel to Kenya and Zaire to
           offset the Soviet arming of neighboring Angola,
           Somalia, and Uganda.

16   SOUTH AFRICA - Rioting in Soweto Township kills at
           least 175 people.

17   NORTH YEMEN - Under heavy pressure from Saudi Arabia,
           the government severs its links with the USSR.

18   SOUTH AFRICA - Rioting erupts in Natal, Pretoria, and
            Transvaal.

19   ETHIOPIA - The government halts (14 June) the mobili-
            zation of thousands of Christian natives along the
            border of the predominantly Muslim province of
            Eritrea. The peasant army of 20,000 is disbanded. Ne-
            gotiations with Eritrean guerrilla leaders is cited as
            the reason for the cancellation order.

20   SWITZERLAND - Negotiations held in Berne between
            Greece and Turkey over who controls the Aegian Sea end
            in failure.

20   LEBANON - A large number of American and other Western
            civilian personnel are evacuated from the country by
            ship.

21   CANADA - At a price of $1 billion, the government pur-
            chases 18 Lockheed P-3 Orion maritime patrol aircraft.

23   LEBANON - Christian militia surround the Palestinian
            refugee camp at Tel al-Zaatar (Tall Zaatar).

23   EGYPT - The Arab League meets in emergency session.

23   UNITED NATIONS - The US vetoes Angola's application
            for membership in the UNO.

23   NATIONALIST CHINA - The US withdraws its advisors from
            Quemoy and Matsu islands.

24   SAUDI ARABIA - At a meeting in Riyadh, Egypt and Syria
            settle a number of long-standing differences.

24   UGANDA - Idi Amin is appointed President-for-Life.

25   POLAND - Polish workers demonstrate against increased
            food prices in a number of cities throughout the
            country.

27   GREECE - Pro-Palestinian terrorists hijack an Air
            France jetliner after it leaves Athens enroute from
            Tel Aviv, Israel, to Paris and take 216 passengers,
            including 80 Israelis, plus the crew, hostage. The
            plane is ordered to fly to Entebbe Airport in Uganda.
            The terrorists demand the release of 53 prisoners in
            five countries.

30   FRANCE - The government announces the establishment of
            a "Hot Line" with the Soviet Union as a means of pre-
            venting accidental war.

30   UGANDA - Forty-seven hostages are released from   among
          those taken in the 27 June Air France hijacking.

JULY

2   VIET NAM - The two parts of the country are   reunified
          under a   Communist government with the capital   in
          Hanoi.

2   LEBANON - An Arab League-sponsored cease-fire is
          ordered.

2   SUDAN - An attempted coup, led by former Prime
          Minister Sadik al-Mahdi and backed by Libya against
          the government of President Gaafar Nimeiry, fails.

2   ARGENTINA - Political violence breaks out in Buenos
          Aires. Twenty-five policemen are killed in a bomb
          blast.

2   PERU - The government declares a state of emergency
          after rioting breaks out following an increase in food
          prices.

3-4   UGANDA - Between 100 and 200 Israeli commandos, led by
          Brigadier General Dan Shomron, attack the Entebbe
          Airport to   rescue 103 hostages taken aboard an Air
          France jetliner out of Athens. Seven of the ten hi-
          jackers are killed along with 20 Ugandan soldiers.
          Seven Soviet-built Ugandan MiG-21s and four MiG-17s
          also are destroyed. One Israeli officer is killed. One
          hostage in a Ugandan hospital is killed in retali-
          ation for the rescue mission.

4   LEBANON - Christian militamen seize the Palestinian
          refugee camp at Tel al-Zaatar.

8   THAILAND - Rebels attack and destroy an army post in
          central Thailand.

8   KENYA - The government orders Uganda to pay, in Kenyan
          currency, for all goods and passengers transiting
          Kenya because of Uganda's growing indebtedness.

10   ANGOLA - The government executes three British and one
          American mercenary who had fought against the MPLA in
          the civil war.

11   KENYA - Large numbers of Kenyans flee Uganda claiming
          a bloodbath is in progress.

12   LEBANON - Christian militia forces open a drive toward
          Tripoli.

16   KENYA - Kenyan truck drivers and railway personnel re-
        fuse to enter Uganda.

17   INDONESIA - With the Portuguese government's approval,
        Indonesia formally annexes Portuguese Timor.

19   SUDAN - In the wake of the recent Libyan-inspired coup
        attempt, Egypt and Sudan sign a mutual defense agree-
        ment.

20   THAILAND - The last US serviceman leaves Thailand.

21   REPUBLIC OF IRELAND - The new British Ambassador,
        Christopher T.E. Ewart-Biggs, is killed by an IRA bomb
        placed under his car at his residence in Dublin. Sev-
        eral other Embassy personnel are killed or injured in
        the blast.

22   HONDURAS - The government reports an attack along its
        border with El Salvador.

24   ANGOLA - Intelligence sources indicate an increase in
        Cuban troop strength in Angola as a result   of
        increased UNITA guerrilla activity.

25   INDIA - Diplomatic relations with Pakistan are re-
        stored.

25   KENYA - The government cuts the flow of oil to Uganda.

25   UGANDA - Idi Amin threatens Kenya with war.

27   RHODESIA - The government claims its soldiers have en-
        gaged Mozambique troops on Rhodesian territory.

28   LEBANON - An additional 308 American and Western civ-
        ilians are evacuated from Beirut by US naval vessels.

28   GREAT BRITAIN - The government breaks diplomatic re-
        lations with Uganda (which is a Commonwealth member).

29   TURKEY - After talks once again break down, the gov-
        ernment orders a military alert as the result of a
        Greek threat to use military force to protect the
        Aegian Sea from Turkish penetration.

30   UGANDA - Uganda agrees to open negotiations with Kenya
        in Nairobi.

AUGUST

1   HONDURAS - The government reports the country has been
        invaded by El Salvador.

2   THE PHILIPPINES - The government announces its inten-
           tion of taking control of the two major US installa-
           tions at Clark Air Force Base and the naval base at
           Subic Bay.

2   ISRAEL - The government charges Egypt with breaking
           the Sinai Agreement by introducing new forces east of
           the Suez Canal.

4-12   SOUTH AFRICA - New rioting breaks out in the black
           township of Soweto, near Johhannesburg. The violence
           eventually spreads to Cape Town where 27 die in two
           days.

4   COLOMBIA - In a series of bomb attacks in Bogota,
           aimed chiefly at US corporations, an explosion at the
           Summer Institute of Linguistics injures five Americans
           who have just arrived in country.

6   THAILAND - The government establishes diplomatic rela-
           tions with Viet Nam.

7   IRAN - The government announces it will purchase $10
           billion worth of US military hardware by 1980.

7   UGANDA - President Idi Amin signs a peace agreement
           with Kenya's Jomo Kenyatta ending a long period of
           hostility between the two countries.

8   MOZAMBIQUE - A Rhodesian raiding force wipes out a
           guerrilla base inside Mozambique killing at least 300
           (some soures say 600) black rebels. The attack is
           carried out in retaliation for cross-border mortar
           attacks from Mozambique.

9   UNITED NATIONS - Greece request UN action to settle
           its dispute with Turkey over who controls the Aegian
           Sea.

11   SOUTH AFRICA - Black rioting spreads to a number of
           villages around Cape Town.

11   TURKEY - Security officials spot a group of would-be
           hijackers about to board an Israeli El Al airliner
           bound for Tel Aviv. The two terrorists open fire on
           the passengers killing four of them, including one
           American, and wounding 17. The terrorists are captured
           in the ensuing firefight with Turkish security forces.
           They are members of the PFLP.

11   HONDURAS - The government announces that an agreement
           has been reached with El Salvador in which each side
           will withdraw its military forces from their common
           border.

12   LEBANON - Following a 52-day siege the Muslim Pales-
            tinian enclave of Tel al-Zaatar in the predominantly
            Christian sector of Beirut is captured by Christian
            militia.

12   EGYPT - In the wake of Libyan threats Egyptian mili-
            tary forces are mobilized along the common border.

15   TURKEY - The government offers to resume negotiations
            with Greece over the Aegian crisis.

18   SOUTH KOREA - North Korean soldiers attack a work par-
            ty of US and ROK soldiers working in the demilitarized
            zone at Panmunjom. Two US officers are killed as work
            is being completed on pruning a tree that obstructs a
            clear view of the area. In a show of force, the United
            Nations Command and the ROKA go to an advanced state
            of readiness while US and ROK soldiers cut down the
            tree (21 August). The UN alert continues until 8 Sep-
            tember when a decision is made to partition the Pan-
            munjom joint security area.

19   EGYPT - The government orders the Libyan diplomatic
            mission in Alexandria closed.

20   UNITED NATIONS - The US fends off an attempt by Viet
            Nam to gain membership to the UNO.

20   ARGENTINA - Violence continues in the country as
            right-wing extremists kill 46 in retaliation for left-
            wing raids on police and military outposts. More than
            600 have died since the ouster of Isabel Peron.

22   TURKEY - The government ends the military alert begun
            on 29 July.

23   AUSTRALIA - Violent student demonstrations at Monash
            University in Melbourne follow cuts in educational and
            medical allowances.

23-25   SOUTH AFRICA - Unrest leads to violence among blacks
            in Soweto. Twenty-one are killed by Zulu tribesmen, 19
            others by police.

26   UNITED STATES - A British nuclear device is tested un-
            derground in Nevada.

27   UNITED STATES - The government announces it will sell
            Iran 160 F-16 fighters.

27   LEBANON - Christian leaders accept an Arab League pro-
            posal for cease-fire negotiations with the Muslims as
            fighting continues in various parts of the country.

28   IRAN - Three American officials of Rockwell Inter-
            national are assassinated in Tehran by terrorists of
            the People's Strugglers group.

31   MALTA - The government announces that it will become a
            neutral after the basing agreement with Great Britain
            ends in 1979.

31   RHODESIA - Black guerrillas attack a Rhodesian mili-
            tary outpost near the Mozambique border.

SEPTEMBER

1   REPUBLIC OF IRELAND - The government declares a state
            of emergency to help thwart the growing terrorist
            threat.

1   GREECE - The government puts its Aegian naval forces
            on alert after Turkey announces it is sending an
            oceanographic vessel into the region on an oil ex-
            ploration mission.

1   SINAI - The number of Egyptian troops in the Sinai is
            reduced to bring the force within the limits set by
            the Sinai Agreement.

2   SOUTH AFRICA - Police clash with black rioters in Cape
            Town.

5   YUGOSLAVIA - The government rejects a Soviet request
            for naval basing rights on the Adriatic.

6   JAPAN - A Soviet Air Force officer, Lieutenant Victor
            I. Belenko, defects with his MiG-25 aircraft, the
            USSR's most advanced operational fighter, and lands at
            Hakodate civil airport on the northern island of
            Hokkaido. Belenko is later granted asylum in the US by
            President Ford (9 September). The aircraft is dismant-
            led by US and Japanese intelligence experts and, fol-
            lowing Soviet demands for its return, is turned over
            to Soviet officials in pieces (12 November).

6   ARAB LEAGUE - The PLO is admitted to full membership.

6   TANZANIA - Called to consider the Rhodesian question,
            a meeting of the leaders of Angola, Botswana,
            Mozambique, Tanzania, and Zambia, ends with a call for
            more fighting.

9   COMMUNIST CHINA - Mao Tse-tung dies in Peking at age
            82.

9-15   SOUTH AFRICA - Violence breaks out in Johannesburg and Cape Town. At least 33 blacks are killed.

10-12   UNITED STATES - Five Croatian terrorists, brandishing fake weapons, hijack a New York-to-Chicago flight and force the crew to fly to Paris. They demand that Croatian freedom pamphlets be air dropped over a number of cities. The four men and one women then surrender to police.

11   USSR - Leonid Brezhnev requests the Syrian government withdraw its forces from Lebanon. Syrian President Assad refuses.

12   WORLD COURT - The court rejects the Greek request for an injunction to halt Turkish exploration in the Aegian Sea.

14   COMMUNIST CHINA - The government rejects the Soviet Union's official message of condolence marking the death of Mao Tse-tung.

14   RHODESIA - Following a visit of US Secretary of State Henry Kissinger, Prime Minister Ian Smith announces his government's acceptance of an American proposal for the immediate establishment of a biracial government, and black rule in two years.

15   VIET NAM - The country is admitted into the International Monetary Fund.

21   UNITED STATES - Former leftist Chilean Cabinet Minister, Orlando Letelier, and an associate, Ronni Karpen Moffitt, are assassinated in Washington, DC, by a bomb placed in Letelier's car. Letelier served a number of posts in the Allende government that was overthrown in Chile in 1973.

21   CUBA - The government announces it has withdrawn 3,000 of its troops from Angola.

23   LEBANON - The PLO announces a unilateral cease-fire.

26   SYRIA - Four Palestinian terrorist seize a hotel in Damascus and hold 90 people hostage. Syrian security forces overpower the PLO terrorists killing one of them (and four hostages). The other three terrorists are hanged in the street across from the hotel the next day (27 September).

30   LEBANON - Heavy fighting is reported between Syrian and PLO forces east of Beirut.

OCTOBER

1   UNITED NATIONS - The United States, France, and Great
           Britain veto a resolution imposing sanctions on South
           Africa.

2   ARGENTINA - President Jorge Rafael Videla narrowly
           escapes an assassination attempt in Buenos Aires.

3   GREECE - The government announces it has reached
           agreement with Turkey on the establishment of a demar-
           cation line in the Aegian.

6   THAILAND - After a number of violent clashes between
           police and ultra-rightist students belonging to a
           group known as the Red Gaur (Red Bull), a military
           coup overthrows the civilian government of Prime Min-
           ister Seni Pramoj and assumes power under the leader-
           ship of Defense Minister Admiral Sa-ngad Chaloryu.

8   FRANCE - The government announces the withdrawal of
           10,000 of its troops from West Germany as a result of
           a major reorganization of its armed forces.

8   SOVIET UNION - A friendship and cooperation treaty is
           signed with Angola during a state visit of Angola's
           President Antonio Agostinho Neto.

10   ISRAEL - The government rejects a Soviet-sponsored
           plan (1 September) to reconvene the Geneva conference
           on the Middle East.

12   COMMUNIST CHINA - The newly-seated government of Hua
           Kuo-feng orders the arrest (18 October) of the so-
           called "Gang of Four," which includes Mao's wife,
           Chiang Ch'ing, on charges of plotting a military
           takeover.

15   UNITED STATES - The Defense Department announces that
           84 F-111 bombers are being sent to Great Britain to
           reinforce the NATO defenses.

17   SAUDI ARABIA - The leaders of Egypt, Syria, the PLO,
           and three other Arab countries meet in Riyadh to agree
           upon a new cease-fire for Lebanon and the formation of
           a 30,000-man peacekeeping force.

22   UNITED NATIONS - The Security Council extends its man-
           date in the Sinai for an additional 12 months.

25-26   EGYPT - The Arab League meets and approves the Riyadh
           cease-fire plan for Lebanon.

26   TRANSKEI – The new nation is declared independent by
      Pretoria although its independence is controlled by
      South Africa along strickly racial lines.

26   UNITED NATIONS – With the US abstaining, the General
      Assembly votes not to recognize Transkei as an inde-
      pendent nation.

28   LEBANON – PLO forces reoccupy the border area adjacent
      to Israel.

NOVEMBER

1   BURUNDI – The army overthrows the government of Presi-
      dent Michel Micambero in a bloodless coup led by Lieu-
      tenant Colonel Jean-Baptiste Bagaza.

2   IRAQ – The border with Syria is closed. The Iraqi Am-
      bassador in Damascus is called home.

2   LEBANON – Arab League peacekeeping forces begin the
      occupation of Christian-held areas.

2   PERU – The government announces the purchase of 36
      Soviet-built Sukhoi (Su-22 "Fitter") jet fighters.

3   ANGOLA – UNITA bases are attacked in southern Angola
      by Angolan forces led by Cuban officers.

10   LEBANON – Syrian troops, operating as a part of the
      Arab League's multinational force, occupy Beirut with-
      out encountering serious opposition.

10   MALAYSIA – The government reaches an accord with the
      Thai government for conducting combined operations
      against guerrilla activity along the common border.

15   UNITED NATIONS – The US vetoes Viet Nam's application
      for membership.

19   CHILE – The government rejects a Peruvian proposal to
      develop a corridor to the sea for Bolivia.

21   ISRAEL – Israel begins reinforcing its garrisons along
      the Lebanese border as Syrian forces take up positions
      on the other side.

23   USSR – The Soviet Union ends its series of nuclear
      tests at Semipalatinsk.

24   COMMUNIST CHINA – There are reports that the govern-
      ment is sending troops into Fukien Province in the
      wake of violence in the region.

25   IRAQ - Troops on both sides of the Iraqi-Syrian border
            are withdrawn.

25   SOUTH YEMEN - The government claims to have shot down
            an Iranian F-4 jet.

26   SYRIA - The government calls upon the PLO to halt its
            operations in southern Lebanon against Israel.

26   WARSAW PACT - At a Warsaw Pact meeting in Bucharest,
            Romania, the Soviet Union proposes a no-first-use
            treaty for nuclear weapons.

DECEMBER

1   UNITED NATIONS - Angola is admitted to membership in
            the world organization.

1   LEBANON - Arab League peacekeeping forces order Muslim
            and Christian militias to turn in their weapons.

1   WEST GERMANY - The Officers' Club at the US Rhein-Main
            Air Force Base is bombed. The Revolutionary Cells (RZ)
            claims responsibility. Eighteen, including nine Ameri-
            cans, are injured in the explosion.

5   THE PHILIPPINES - President Marcos rejects a US offer
            to increase its payments in return for retention of
            its Clark Field and Subic Bay bases.

8   CANADA - The government suspends nuclear cooperation
            with Pakistan.

9   NATO - The NATO Council of Foreign Ministers formally
            rejects a Warsaw Pact proposal calling for a mutual
            no-first-use of nuclear weapons and endorses a freeze
            on memberships.

9   UNITED NATIONS - The General Assembly approves an Arab
            resolution to reconvene the Geneva conference on the
            Middle East early in 1977.

10   FRANCE - The government detonates a nuclear device in
            an underground test at Mururoa Atoll in the South
            Pacific.

10   ISRAEL - The first 25 US-built F-15 fighters are de-
            livered.

19   SOVIET UNION - There are reports that the USSR has
            successfully launched and recovered what are best
            described as two "attack" satellites.

20   BOTSWANA - The government   accuses Rhodesia of   having
            allowed its troops to attack a police barracks   inside
            the Botswanan border.

22   THE PHILIPPINES - The government announces agreement
            with the Muslim separatist rebels, which ends the   re-
            bellion in the southern Philippines.

31   COMMUNIST CHINA - Reports reach the free world of
            armed unrest in at least three areas on the Chinese
            mainland, one of which is Pao Ting, 110 miles south of
            Peking. It is generally considered that this   trouble
            stems from a government order aimed at purging from
            the party pro-Mao supporters the government claims
            collaborated with the "Gang of Four."

Notes

1977

JANUARY

1 CANADA - The government extends its offshore fishing limits from 12 to 200 miles.

11 FRANCE - Just four days after he is apprehended by French authorities, a French court releases Abu Daoud, a known member of the Palestinian Revolutionary Council and the suspected leader of the terrorists who murdered 11 Israeli athletes during the 1972 Munich Olympics.

12 SOUTH KOREA - The government states it will not oppose the withdrawal of US forces, if North Korea will sign a mutual non-aggression pact.

13 LEBANON - President Elias Sarkis orders the PLO to remove its regular troops from Lebanon by 13 January. The Arab League's peacekeeping force orders all heavy weapons not in the hands of the Lebanese Army turned in by 12 January.

13 IRAN - The Shah decides to withdraw a 3,500-man Iranian force that has been assisting Sultan Qaboos (Qabus ibn Sa'id) against Dhofari rebels in Oman. On 20 January, the withdrawal begins.

14-17 CZECHOSLOVAKIA - At least 16 dissidents are arrested in connection with the publication (6 January) of the "Charter 77" manifesto on human rights bearing the signatures of 300 prominent Czechs.

16   BENIN - A group of about 100 mercenaries lands at
            Cotonou Airport and attempts the overthrow of the
            government of President Mathieu Kerekou. The attempt
            is defeated. The mercenaries are apparently in the pay
            of opposition leaders, including former President
            Emile Zinsou. A number of neighboring states send
            military assistance to help restore order. Later it is
            charged that the mercenary force was trained in
            Morocco.

17   EGYPT - At least 79 persons die in Cairo in rioting
            sparked by substantial increases in food and gasoline
            prices. The government calms the situation by lowering
            the prices.

20   UNITED STATES - James Earl "Jimmy" Carter becomes the
            39th President of the United States. As one of his
            first acts in office he issues a pardon to all Viet
            Nam War draft dodgers.

21   LEBANON - Arab League peacekeeping forces begin a
            series of raids to collect contraband weapons that
            were not surrendered as ordered.

24   RHODESIA - Prime Minister Ian Smith rejects the latest
            British proposals for an interim government as a basis
            for further negotiations.

27   UNITED STATES - Detailed studies on the reduction of
            the US nuclear stockpile are ordered by President
            Carter.

27   EUROPE - The European Convention for the Repression of
            Terrorism is signed by 17 members of the Council of
            Ministers. Ireland and Malta refuse to sign it, while
            France refuses to ratify it.

31   USSR - During a visit to Moscow the Vice-Chairman of
            the Iraqi Revolutionary Council, Saddam Hussein, re-
            ceives Soviet assurances of increased military support
            for his country.

FEBRUARY

3   ETHIOPIA - Brigadier General Teferi Benti, the Chief
            of State and Chairman of the Provisional Military Ad-
            ministrative Council, is shot and killed when a gun
            fight breaks out during a ruling military council
            meeting. At least six others also are killed. Lieuten-
            ant Colonel Mengistu Haile Mariam becomes the new head
            of state.

6   RHODESIA - Black guerrillas murder seven Catholic mis-
        sionaries at Saint Paul's Mission, 35 miles from
        Salisbury.

7   UNITED STATES - The government rejects Israel's pro-
        posal to sell 24 Kfir fighter-bombers with US-built
        engines to Ecuador.

9   SPAIN - The government reestablishes diplomatic re-
        lations with the USSR, Hungary, and Czechoslovakia.
        Diplomatic relations were resumed with Bulgaria,
        Romania, Poland, and Yugoslavia in January. The Madrid
        government broke relations with all seven countries in
        1939 following the Spanish Civil War in which the
        Soviet Union and its followers backed the losing side.

10   LEBANON - Renewed fighting is reported between Syrian
        peacekeeping forces and Palestinian guerrillas.

13   LEBANON - Fearing an Israeli reaction a Syrian bat-
        talion in Nabatiya, nine miles from the border with
        Israel, is withdrawn to a new position. At the same
        time, the Arab League imposes strict curbs on PLO
        military and political activities in Lebanon.

15   SRI LANKA - The state of emergency imposed in 1971 is
        lifted by Prime Minister (Mrs.) Sirimavo Bandaranaike.

15   MALI - French President Giscard confirms that France
        will continue its ban on weapons sales to South
        Africa.

16   RHODESIA - The government establishes a military
        border area on the Botswana border, paralleling the
        one already in place along the Mozambique border.

17   UGANDA - There are persistent reports that President
        Idi Amin Dada has had three opposition leaders, the
        Anglican Archbishop of Uganda, Janani Luwum, and two
        former cabinet ministers, murdered while in the
        custody of Amin's notorious State Research Unit.

18   ANGOLA - South African troops operating out of Namibia
        clash with MPLA forces based in Angola.

20   SOUTH KOREA - Foreign Minister Park Tong Jiu states
        his country has no intention of acquiring nuclear
        weapons to offset the expected withdrawal of US
        forces.

21   ETHIOPIA - Somali and Ethiopian forces clash over
        Somalia's claim in the Ogaden region.

22   UNITED STATES - The Carter defense budget for 1978 in-
            cludes a $2.8 billion reduction of former President
            Ford's program.

22   FRANCE - The government conducts a nuclear test at its
            Mururoa test facility in the Pacific.

25   UNITED STATES - Secretary of State Cyrus Vance an-
            nounces the US will cut off all aid to Argentina,
            Ethiopia, and Uruguay because of human-rights vio-
            lations.

25   ANGOLA - Western diplomatic sources claim Angola is
            actively assisting in the buildup of guerrilla forces
            for the rebel campaign against Rhodesia. This assis-
            tance includes the training of guerrillas at coastal
            town of Mossamedes (Mocamedes).

27   MOROCCO - The government suspends its association with
            the OAU following accusations that Morocco participa-
            ted in a coup attempt in Benin on 16 January.

28   COMMUNIST CHINA - Three months of discussions over the
            long-standing Sino-Soviet border dispute end in Peking
            without results.

28   ARGENTINA - The government rejects all US military aid
            after being accused of repeatedly committing human-
            rights violations.

28   URUGUAY - The government rejects all US military aid
            after being accused of repeatedly committing human-
            rights violations.

MARCH

1   UNITED STATES - The US introduces a 200-mile fishing
            limit.

6-11   BRAZIL - The government announces it is cancelling a
            25-year US military aid treaty and refuses to accept
            $50 million in US military sales credits. Brazil also
            charges the US has interfered in Brazilian internal
            affairs. This is the result of earlier US Department
            of State criticism of human rights violations in
            Brazil.

9   UNITED STATES - Terrorists belonging to the Hanafi
            Muslim sect seize three buildings in Washington, DC.
            One person is killed and a number wounded during the
            takeovers of the Islamic Center, the headquarters of
            B'nai B'rith, and the District (of Columbia) Building.

10   ZAIRE - The government reports its territory has been invaded from Angola and that three cities in the important copper-producing Shaba Province have been captured. The next day, the Congolese National Liberation Front claims responsibility for the invasion.

11   UNITED STATES - The 12 Hanafi Muslim terrorists holding three buildings and 134 hostages in Washington, DC, surrender. None of the hostages was injured after the initial shootings on 9 March.

12   CHILE - The government announces stringent new rules designed to crack down on dissidence against the rule of President Augusto Pinochet Ugarte.

14   ITALY - Left-wing students, disenchanted with the Italian Communist Party's recent cooperation with the government, riot in Rome, Bologna, Florence, Milan, Naples, and Turin.

14   PAKISTAN - Demonstrations protesting the results of the 6 March elections in which the People's Party of Zulfikar Ali Bhutto won 154 seats lead to violence throughout the country.

14   ZAIRE - The government asks the US for additional military assistance to help thwart the invasion from Angola. The US quickly agrees to furnish additional military aid.

16   LEBANON - The leftist Druze leader Kamal Jumblatt is assassinated by unknown gunmen. A wave of retaliatory attacks on Christian villages follows.

17   EL SALVADOR - The government rejects US military assistance.

18   CONGO - President Marien Ngouabi is assassinated at his residence in Brazzaville.

18   UNITED STATES - President Carter signs an order imposing a ban on the importation of Rhodesian chrome.

20   ZAIRE - President Mobutu claims the forces invading his country are led by Cubans.

22   UNITED STATES - In a joint communique issued in Washington, Japanese Prime Minister Takeo Fukuda and President Carter confirm the US' intention to withdraw all its troops in South Korea. They further agree that a US presence in the Pacific is desirable.

25   PAKISTAN - Twenty-four opposition leaders are arrested by the Bhutto government.

26   THAILAND - A military coup against the ruling junta
            fails.

26   ARGENTINA - Six bombs go off in Buenos Aires; one of
            them in the Sheraton Hotel. Nine persons are injured.
            No one claims responsibility.

27   AFGHANISTAN - Nearly four years of military rule ends
            when President Sadar Mohammad Daud Khan appoints a
            17-member civilian cabinet.

27   ARAB LEAGUE - The mandate of the Lebanon peacekeeping
            force is extended six months.

27   ETHIOPIA - A band of unidentified terrorists kills an
            American missionary as he is preparing to leave the
            country. Others in the house are spared.

28   MEXICO - The government restores diplomatic relations
            with Spain after a 38-year break.

29   TURKEY - Terrorists of the Acilciler Faction of the
            Turkish People's Liberation Party attack the US Con-
            sul's residence with automatic weapons and a pipe
            bomb. Considerable damage is done but no one is in-
            jured. Several suspects are arrested by Turkish
            authorities.

30   ANGOLA - Cuban troops operating in the southern part
            of the country open an offensive against UNITA forces.

31   MOZAMBIQUE - The government signs a friendship treaty
            with the USSR.

APRIL

1   CHAD - In N'Djamena the government of President Felix
            Malloum is able to withstand a coup attempt led by
            members of the Nomad Guards.

2   FRANCE - The government authorizes military aid to
            Zaire to help thwart the rebel invasion from neigh-
            boring Angola.

4   LEBANON - Syrian forces support Palestinian attacks on
            Christian villages in southern Lebanon.

4   ZAIRE - The government suspends diplomatic relations
            with Cuba.

6   USSR - During a visit to Moscow, PLO leader Yassir
            Arafat receives Soviet backing for PLO participation
            in any Middle East talks.

6   RHODESIA - The government announces that 2,338 guerrillas have been killed since December 1972. Three hundred one government troops were killed during the same period. There are at least 2,500 guerrillas still operating in Rhodesia.

8-10   ZAIRE - The government is promised aid by Morocco and Communist China in its fight against the rebel forces in Shaba Province. About 1,500 Moroccan troops aboard ten military transport aircraft sent by the French are prepared for airlift into the area. An Egyptian military team arrives in Kinshasa to discuss military assistance.

9   LAOS - Rightist rebel forces based in Thailand capture two small islands in the Mekong River. The Laotian government protests to Thailand.

11   ETHIOPIA - The government claims Sudanese forces are attacking towns inside the northwest Ethiopian border. The Sudanese govenment denies the allegation.

11   LAOS - Government troops repossess the Mekong River islands and claim they have killed most of the rebels involved.

12   USSR - Talks with Japan over fishing rights break down when the Soviet Union insists Japan recognize Soviet jurisdiction over the coastal waters of the Kurile Islands.

17   ETHIOPIA - About 200 Cuban commandos arrive in the country.

18   TANZANIA - The government announces it has "permanently" closed its border with Kenya.

21   PAKISTAN - After six weeks of unrest in which 230 persons have lost their lives, the government declares martial law in six cities.

21   ZAIRE - Government troops and Moroccan reinforcements open an offensive against the rebel forces in Shaba Province.

24   ETHIOPIA - The government announces it is closing most US military installations in the country. This includes the Military Assistance Advisory Group headquarters. The government also indicates that it is closing the US, British, French, Belgium, Sudanese, and Italian Consulates in Asmara, the capital city of Eritrea.

24   MOZAMBIQUE - US intelligence sources reveal that the USSR has recently shipped antiaircraft weapons to Mozambique.

25   VIET NAM - Prime Minister Pham Van Dong signs an economic and cultural treaty with France. France grants a long term loan worth about $100 million.

28   WEST GERMANY - Andreas Baader and two other members of the Baader-Meinhof terrorist gang are sentenced to life in prison.

28   ETHIOPIA - The Department of State confirms that shipments of military arms and equipment to Ethiopia have been suspended.

28   UNITED STATES - Two US newspapers report that a 200-ton shipment of uranium disappeared in 1968 while in transit from Belgium to Italy. Most intelligence services believe the shipment was taken by the Israelis.

29   UNITED ARAB EMIRATES - The Emirates sign an agreement with France for French military equipment, weapons, and training facilities.

MAY

1   TURKEY - A huge May Day rally in Istanbul is disrupted by gunfire from leftist terrorists on nearby rooftops. Thirty are killed and more than 200 injured.

1   SOMALIA - The government announces that Somalia is extending naval basing facilities to the Soviet Navy.

1   EGYPT - The government announces that air force pilots are being sent to Zaire to reinforce the Zaire Air Force.

2   JAPAN - The government establishes a 12-mile territorial limit on its coastal waters and a 200-mile fishing limit.

2   COMMUNIST CHINA - The government announces it supports Japan's claim of rights to four islands in the Kuriles which are currently held by the USSR.

3-12 FRANCE - Negotiations on normalizing relations between the US and Viet Nam take place in Paris. Viet Nam refuses to resume normal relations unless the US pays NVN reconstruction costs. The US refuses.

4   UNITED STATES - Intelligence reports indicate the USSR has delivered MiG-21 fighters to Syria.

4-6	USSR - While on a visit to Moscow, Ethiopia's head of state, Mengistu Haile Mariam, signs a series of cooperative agreements with the Soviet Union. These economic and political accords draw Ethiopia into the Soviet sphere.
5	UNITED STATES - A Congressional committee blocks a Carter proposal to sell F-4 jet fighters to Turkey.
9-13	THAILAND - Thai border police fight Cambodian Khmer Rouge forces in three separate raids into Thailand. The country is put on a war alert.
11	SWITZERLAND - The US and USSR open SALT II talks in Geneva.
15	BAHREIN - The government announces that it is closing the US Navy's docking and port facilities as of 30 June.
16	SUDAN - After negotiating an arms deal with French President Giscard, the government expels all Soviet advisors on 18 May.
22	MOROCCO - The government announces that its role in Zaire has been successfully concluded.
23	THE NETHERLANDS - In the northern province of Drenthe, two groups of South Moluccan terrorists seize a train and a school and take 165 hostages, including 100 school children. The action is taken to dramatize their demands for the independence of their formally Dutch-ruled island in Indonesia. On 24 May, the 13 terrorists demand an airplane and the release of 21 of their countrymen held in Dutch jails. The government refuses to negotiate until the children are released.
24	USSR - Without any explanation, President Nicholai V. Podgorny is removed from the Politburo. He will resign as President on 16 June. Leonid Brezhnev will immediately assume the post.
24	EGYPT - The government announces it is withdrawing its pilots from Zaire as a need for their services no longer exists.
26	ZAIRE - The government announces that it has taken the last rebel position in Shaba Province, and that the invasion is crushed.
27	THE NETHERLANDS - A flu epidemic forces the terrorists to release the 100 school children they are holding hostage near Groningen.

27   DENMARK - The government reports that the USSR has raised to six the number of its operational nuclear submarines in the Baltic.

27   ANGOLA - An uprising among dissident troops in Luanda is crushed by forces loyal to pro-Soviet Agostinho Neto. Five members of the ruling Revolutionary Council, along with five other senior government officials, are killed in the coup attempt. There is some evidence that the uprising began among extremists in the MPLA itself.

29-31   MOZAMBIQUE - Rhodesian forces carry out a raid in force into southern Mozambique and attack a number of guerrilla bases. On 31 May, they capture Mapai on the Limpopo River, about 100 miles inland from the border. The Rhodesian forces then withdraw on 2 June reporting they have killed 20 guerrillas.

JUNE

2   LEBANON - Palestinian forces and right-wing Lebanese Christian militiamen fight a pitched battle near the Israeli border in southern Lebanon.

5   UNITED STATES - The Defense Department announces that 5,000 US troops will be withdrawn from South Korea by the end of 1978. In all, 33,000 troops are projected for redeployment.

5   SEYCHELLES - The coalition government of President James R. Mancham is overthrown in an apparently Soviet-aided coup. Mancham is in London at a Commonwealth meeting when the overthrow takes place. Although denying any part in the coup or any Soviet inspiration, former Prime Minister Albert Rene assumes the Presidency. A cabinet is formed exclusively from the Seychelles People's United Party, and a new constitution is promised.

6   COMMUNIST CHINA - The government attacks Soviet activities in Africa.

6   CUBA - Fidel Castro acknowledges that he ordered a halt to the withdrawal of Cuban troops from Angola in April, and that Cuban military forces are still in Angola.

8   UNITED STATES - The Carter Administration blocks the sale of 250 F-18L advanced fighters by the Northrop Company to Iran.

11   THE NETHERLANDS - Royal Dutch Marines attack the train
            and the school held by South Moluccan terrorists. Six
            terrorists and two of the 51 hostages are killed   at
            the train site. In the attack on the school, the   four
            remaining hostages were freed without incident and the
            six terrorists there are captured.

13   FRANCE - The government announces its intention to
            withdraw 12 of its non-NATO regiments from West Ger-
            many in 1978. This will leave about 53,000 French
            troops on Germany soil.

16   UNITED NATIONS - The Security Council renews its man-
            date to maintain peace-keeping forces in Cyprus for
            another six months.

20   FRANCE - On a formal visit to Paris, Leonid Brezhnev
            is assured by President Giscard that French forces are
            not under NATO control.

24-27   DJIBOUTI - After having voted overwhelmingly for in-
            dependence on 8 May, the former French Territory of
            Afars and Issas becomes the Republic of Djibouti. Up-
            on the inauguration of Hassan Gouled Aptidon as the
            nation's first President (24 June), Djibouti signs a
            military alliance with France (27 June).

26   SPAIN - Following criticism of the Spanish Party Sec-
            retary, Santiago Carrillo, in the Soviet New Times
            weekly, the Spanish Communist Party tells the Soviet
            Union to stay out of its affairs.

29   MOZAMBIQUE - The government appeals to the United
            Nations for assistance against further Rhodesian
            aggression.

30   UNITED NATIONS - The Security Council votes "material"
            aid to Mozambique.

30   SEATO - After 23 years of existence, the South East
            Asia Treaty Organization (SEATO) dissolves.

30   UNITED STATES - The President halts production of the
            B-1 bomber, citing the effectiveness of cruise mis-
            siles as a less-costly alternative.

JULY

3   LEBANON - Right-wing Lebanese militia forces, sup-
            ported by the Israeli Army, attack Palestinian posi-
            tions in southern Lebanon.

4   PAKISTAN – Even though Premier Bhutto promises (14 June) new elections, the state of affairs in Pakistan brings about a military coup. Army Chief of Staff Mohammed Zia-ul-Haq seizes power and dissolves the Parliament.

5   GABON – The leaders of 48 African nations meet but fail to resolve any of the fundamental issues that face them. They do agree to endorse the Patriotic Front which is conducting the campaign for black power in Rhodesia.

7   UNITED STATES – The government announces it has tested a neutron bomb.

10   LEBANON – Palestinian forces counterattack to retake lost positions in southern Lebanon. The fighting continues for two weeks before the Palestinians agree to withdraw from the border area.

10   ALBANIA – The government criticizes Communist China for developing contacts with the West.

12   SOMALIA – Diplomatic sources in Mogadishu report the Somali government has ordered Soviet military advisors out of the country.

14   NORTH KOREA – A US CH-47 helicopter strays into North Korean air space and is shot down killing three of the four crewmen on board. The North Koreans release the captured crewman and the three bodies on 16 July.

15   ITALY – A three-day meeting held in Rome between representatives of Argentina and Great Britain ends without resolution of the Falkland Islands dispute.

17   ETHIOPIA – Heavy fighting is reported between government troops and forces of the West Somali Liberation Front near the town of Dire Dawe on the Addis Ababa-Djibouti road.

20   MIDDLE EAST – Iraq and Kuwait agree to pull back their forces and create a buffer zone along their common border. Kuwait opens its border (24 July) for the first time since 1972.

20   UNITED NATIONS – When the US does not object, Viet Nam is accepted for membership in the UNO.

20   FRANCE – The government acknowledges that it is furnishing logistic support to Chad in its ongoing border clashes with Libya.

21   THAILAND - A major battle between Thai and Cambodian border units occurs near Aranyaprathet. Tanks and air support are used by the Thais to regain control of the territory. Thirteen Thais and about 50 Cambodians are killed in the fight.

21   EGYPT - Several weeks of border clashes along the Libyan border culminates in a major battle employing armor and air strikes. During the next four days Egyptian jets attack deep into Libya. On 24 July Egypt declares a unilateral cease-fire which Libya accepts.

24   LAOS - At the end of a four-day visit Vietnamese Premier Pham Van Dong announces agreement on military and economic cooperation.

25   ALBANIA - There are reports in Yugosalvia that Albania is expelling its Communist Chinese advisors.

26   ISRAEL - The government grants permanent status to three villages in the West Bank.

28   NATO - NATO sources report the Soviet Union has deployed 100 submarines into the Atlantic in a show of naval power.

28   NORTH AFRICA - A plan is agreed upon to end the border dispute between Egypt and Libya.

AUGUST

1   NORTH KOREA - The government announces the establishment of a 50-mile military sea boundary along its east and west coasts. The US immediately states it will not abide by the boundary (2 August).

3   UNITED STATES - President Carter reaffirms the US determination to use nuclear weapons if the Communists attack Western Europe.

3-9   ETHIOPIA - West Somali Liberation Front forces launch a final offensive against Ethiopian positions in Ogaden Province. On 9 June the Ethiopian government admits Ogaden has fallen to the rebels.

11   ETHIOPIA - Reports circulating in Addis Ababa indicate tens of thousands have died in the fighting between the Ethiopian armed forces and troops of the West Somalia Liberation Front. The Ethiopian government accuses the Somolia Democratic Republic of aiding the rebels.

16   IRAQ - The government announces it has pledged support
            to the rebels fighting in Eritrea and in Ogaden.

17   EGYPT - The government announces it has suspended all
            trade with the USSR and Czechoslovakia. In doing so,
            the Egyptians cite   numerous deliberate violations of
            recent agreements.

19   USSR - A joint communique issued by Yugoslav President
            Tito and the Kremlin reiterates the Yugoslavs' right
            to determine their own course.

23   SOUTH AFRICA - The government denies French reports
            that it is about to test a nuclear device.

25   THE PHILIPPINES - A human rights march in Manila,
            which violates the 1972 martial law order, is forcibly
            dispersed by police. More than 100 demonstrators are
            injured.

27   THE PHILIPPINES - The government announces the release
            of 500 prisoners arrested and imprisoned for various
            violations of the 1972 martial law order. At least
            4,700 have been arrested since the law went into
            effect. To date, only 1,500 in all have been released.

29   SRI LANKA - Two weeks of nationwide Sinhalese vio-
            lence, aimed primarily at the Tamil minority, begins
            to subside. More than 100 are reported killed during
            the period as the Sinhalese burned and looted Tamil
            stores and homes.

29   USSR - Visiting Moscow a second time, Yassir Arafat
            extracts a Soviet acknowledgement of the Palestinian
            right to a homeland.

29   PERU - President Francisco Morales Bermudez lifts the
            14-month state of emergency.

30   FRANCE - The government agrees to supply arms to
            Somalia.

SEPTEMBER

1   RHODESIA - A series of Anglo-American proposals, aimed
            at settling the crisis, is published. By 14 June most
            parties involved have either accepted or rejected the
            proposals.

1   SOMALIA - In a turnabout, France refuses arms sales to
            Somalia as long as fighting in Ogaden continues. The
            US also refuses to supply arms.

2   SOUTHEAST ASIA - A number of sources, including refugees, report heavy fighting along the Cambodian-Vietnamese border in May and June. Other reports indicate Viet Nam mounted a major artillery and air attack on Cambodian border positions at the end of August.

2   USSR - The government agrees to supply Ethiopia with 48 MiG-21 fighters, about 200 T-54/55 tanks, SA-3 and SA-7 SAMs, and "Sagger" antitank missiles.

5   WEST GERMANY - Doctor Hanns-Martin Schleyer, the head of the West German Industries Federation, is kidnapped in Cologne by terrorists who demand the release of Baader-Meinhof Gang members held in prison. Several bodyguards and Schleyer's chauffeur are killed in the firefight that accompanies the kidnapping.

5   ARAB LEAGUE - At a Foreign Ministers conference in Cairo the members refuse support to Somalia in its war with Ethiopia.

7   UNITED STATES - The US and Panama sign the Panama Canal Treaty, which will transfer the canal to Panama by the year 2000. At the same time, President Carter asks Congress for the authority to sell seven AWACS aircraft to Iran for $1.2 billion.

10   NEW ZEALAND - The government announces that a 200-mile economic zone will go into effect around the island nation effective 1 October.

15   SOUTH AFRICA - Citing the Riotous Assemblies Act as grounds for the arrests, the police arrest 1,200 students attending a peaceful commemorative service for Steven Biko at the University of Fort Hare in Alice. Biko died of brain injuries while in police custody in Pretoria. The police will later be absolved of responsibility for his death.

15   PAKISTAN - President Mohammed Zia-ul-Haq declares an end to the state of emergency imposed in his country in November 1971.

17   COMMUNIST CHINA - The government announces the detonation of its 22nd nuclear device at its test site at Lop Nor. This is the first test in nearly a year.

20   UNITED NATIONS - The UNO admits Viet Nam and Djibouti to full membership.

20   UGANDA - President Idi Amin bans most Christian church activities in his country claiming they are security risks.

21   BRAZIL - The government cancels four treaties with the
            US effectively ending all military ties with that
            country.

26   LEBANON - A cease-fire is ordered along the Israeli-
            Lebanon border after ten days of bitter fighting be-
            tween Palestinians and Lebanese Christian militiamen
            supported by Israelis. When the cease-fire goes into
            effect the Israelis withdraw their forces back into
            Israel.

28   INDIA - Eleven members of the Japanese Red Army, a
            left-wing terrorist group, hijack a Japan Air Lines
            DC-8 in Indian airspace and order it to fly to Dacca,
            in Bangladesh. There are 151 passengers on board. Upon
            arrival at Dacca, 115 hostages are released in return
            for $6 million in ransom and the release of six Red
            Army members held in Japanese jails.

28   COMMUNIST CHINA - Cambodian Communist leader Pol Pot
            receives a warm welcome in Peking on his first visit
            outside his country since the end of the war in
            Southeast Asia.

29   ETHIOPIA - The West Somali Liberation Front claims the
            capture of the Gara Marda Pass in northern Ogaden.

29   UNITED STATES - The government rejects a request that
            it resume arms shipments to Ethiopia.

OCTOBER

1   UNITED STATES - The US and USSR issue a joint state-
            ment calling for a new Middle East peace conference
            that will consider the "legitimate rights of the
            Palestinian people."

1   PAKISTAN - Head of State General Mohammad Zia-ul-Haq,
            citing the preparation of criminal charges against
            deposed Prime Minister Zulfikar Ali Bhutto as the
            dominant factor, indefinitely extends the martial law
            edict and cancels plans for the expected 18 October
            national elections.

2   BANGLADESH - At the height of the negotiations with
            the airline hijackers at Dacca airport, an attempted
            coup by a group of military personnel takes place. At
            least 200 are killed, including 11 senior Air Force
            officers. President Rahmen then outlaws three politi-
            cal parties for their alleged parts in the affair (14
            October). On 19 October, 37 military personnel are
            executed and, on 27 October, 55 more are sentenced to
            death for complicity in the affair.

3　　　ALGERIA - The eleven members of the Japanese Red Army hijack group surrender to authorities in Algiers. The last 19 hostages are released unharmed. Others were released at stops in Kuwait and Damascus.

10　　THE PHILIPPINES - Terrorists ambush and kill all 34 members of a Filipino military team sent to Jolo Island to discuss amnesty with the insurgents of the Moro National Liberation Front.

11　　YEMEN ARAB REPUBLIC - President Ibrahim al-Hamdi is assassinated in the capital city of San'a'. His brother, Colonel Abdullah Mohammed al-Hamdi, is also killed in the machine-gun attack.

13-18　SPAIN - A Lufthansa 737 airliner enroute to Frankfurt am Main from Palma de Majorca is hijacked by Palestinian terrorists in retaliation for the West German government's refusal to deal for the release of imprisoned Baader-Meinhof Gang members for the return of kidnapped industrialist Hanns-Martin Schleyer. The ransom demand includes a huge sum of money, the Baader-Meinhof prisoners, and other terrorists held in Turkish jails. In the ensuing travels around the Mediterranean and Middle East, the aircraft's captain is murdered in Aden for his refusal to cooperate. Finally, at Mogadishu, Somalia, West German anti-terrorist commandos attack the aircraft, free the 86 hostages and kill (3) or capture (1) all of the terrorists. Within hours of the incident, on 18 October, Baader and his two fellow gang members allegedly commit suicide in their West German prison.

19　　FRANCE - The body of Doctor Hanns-Martin Schleyer, aged 62, who was kidnapped in Cologne, West Germany on 5 September, is found in a car near Mulhouse in northeastern France.

19　　GREAT BRITAIN - Her Majesty's government establishes diplomatic relations with Angola.

19　　USSR - The government announces it has halted arms shipments to Somalia.

20　　THAILAND - A military coup ousts the civilian government of Prime Minister Thanin Kraivichien. A military junta takes control.

21　　SOMALIA - President Muhammad Siyad Barrah states the Soviet arms buildup in Ethiopia could jeopardize Soviet-Somali relations.

23　　MIDDLE EAST - The PLO rejects Western moves to reconvene the Middle East peace conference.

NOVEMBER

4   UNITED NATIONS - The Security Council unanimously orders an arms embargo against South Africa.

9   EGYPT - President Anwar Sadat states he is ready to overcome all obstacles blocking peace with Israel. On 11 November, Prime Minister Menahem Begin reciprocates and offers peace with Egypt.

9   LEBANON - Israeli jets launch a massive attack on a number of PLO targets in southern Lebanon following the shelling of the northern Israeli town of Nahariyya by PLO artillery on 6 and 8 November.

9   UNITED STATES - President Carter rejects an Israeli request to allow them to manufacture the F-16 fighter.

13   SOMALIA - The government expels several thousand Soviet and Cuban advisors from the country. Somalia also breaks diplomatic relations with Cuba, and abrogates its 1974 friendship treaty with the USSR. These actions are taken in retaliation for Soviet and Cuban support of Ethiopia in the ongoing war.

16   UNITED STATES - The President agrees to place US bases in the Philippines under Filipino control.

16   NATO - In the only territorial dispute between NATO and Warsaw Pact nations, Norway and the USSR agree to partition the Barents Sea with Norway receiving 23,000 square miles and the USSR, 3,000 square miles.

19   LIBYA - The government breaks diplomatic relations with Egypt after Egyptian President Sadat accepts an invitation to visit Israel.

23-30   ETHIOPIA - Somali forces mount a major offensive in the area near Harar. An Ethiopian counterattack, led by Cuban officers, begins on 27 November. Somali forces begin a general withdrawal on 30 November.

24   USSR - The Soviet Union begins a major airlift of men and equipment into Ethiopia to supplement its already extensive sealift of military aid.

26   EGYPT - President Sadat calls for a summit meeting of confrontation states and a number of others involved in the Middle East situation. The UN and US accept; the USSR rejects the proposal. Most Arab states reject the meeting instead proposing (28 November) a rejectionist conference in Baghdad.

30   USSR - An underground nuclear test is conducted at the
            Soviet Semipalatinsk test facility. The estimated
            yield of the detonation is 150 kilotons.

DECEMBER

2-7   BERMUDA - The execution of two blacks for the murder
            of a white man touches off three days of rioting. A
            curfew is ordered and the Governor requests British
            troops (2 December). The arrival of 250 British
            soldiers (5 December) helps restore order, and the
            troops are withdrawn on 7 December.

5   LIBYA - Leaders of several Arab nations close a stormy
            four-day meeting in Tripoli by issuing a declaration
            condemning Egypt for its conciliatory policy toward
            Israel.

5   EGYPT - President Sadat breaks diplomatic relations
            with Algeria, Iraq, Libya, Yemen (Aden), and Syria in
            retaliation for the Tripoli Declaration and orders 270
            of their diplomats out of the country. He also orders
            a number of Soviet consulates and cultural centers
            closed.

5   SOUTH AFRICA - The government grants independence to
            Bophuthatswana. The new black "homeland" stays within
            the South African realm.

7   EGYPT - President Sadat orders all consulates and
            cultural agencies belonging to the USSR, Czecho-
            slovakia, East Germany, Hungary, and Poland closed in
            retaliation for their support of Arabs aligned against
            Egypt.

16   UNITED STATES - The government accuses Cuba of
            doubling its military strength in Ethiopia since 10
            December.

16   UNITED STATES - At the latest round of Anglo-Argentine
            talks on the Falklands held in New York City, Britain
            states it will not transfer sovereignty without the
            consent of the islands' inhabitants. Another round of
            talks is scheduled for mid-1978.

18-23   SPANISH SAHARA - Polisario accuses France of using
            Jaguar fighter-bombers to attack one of its columns.
            On 19 December Polisario forces attack a Mauritanean
            troop position killing 30 but losing 82 of their own
            personnel. On 23 December Polisario releases eight
            French hostages held since May.

20   INDONESIA - The government announces it has freed
            10,000 political prisoners arrested in 1965 and held
            twelve years without trial. Outside sources, such as
            Amnesty International, accuse the Indonesian govern-
            ment of lying; they claim that no one has been re-
            leased, and that nearly 100,000 are held without due
            process.

28   IRAN - A bomb destroys the Iran-American Society Cen-
            ter in Tehran. A group calling itself the People's
            Sacrifice Guerrillas claims responsibility.

28-29   THAILAND - There are numerous foreign diplomatic
            reports out of Bangkok that heavy fighting is in
            progress between Vietnamese and Cambodian forces in
            the Cambodian border province of Svay Rieng.

31   CAMBODIA - The government severs diplomatic relations
            with Viet Nam in what some observers call a test of
            wills between Communist China and the USSR.

31   CANADA - Prime Minister Pierre Trudeau warns that he
            will use troops to prevent a unilateral separation of
            Quebec Province from the confederation.

Notes

1978

1   INDIA - Shortly after taking off from Bombay Airport, an Air India Boeing 747 explodes over the Arabian Sea. All 213 on board are killed. The bomb that causes the blast is probably the work of terrorists belonging to the International Proutist Organization of the Hindu Ananda Marga Sect.

3   CAMBODIA - The government again refuses to negotiate a peace treaty with Viet Nam until all Vietnamese forces are withdrawn from Cambodian soil.

5   NATO - US President Carter announces that 8,000 additional troops will be made available to NATO within 18 months.

6   UNITED STATES - US intelligence sources indicate that the Soviet Union has stopped arms shipments to Ethiopia.

6   CHAD - President Felix Malloum announces a cease-fire agreement with Frolinat. He also breaks diplomatic relations with Libya for supporting the rebels. Malloum also agrees to meet with other African leaders to draft a peace treaty.

8   SYRIA - The USSR furnishes Syria with new MiG-23 aircraft, T-62 tanks, and SA-6 air defense missiles.

9   INDIA - Premier Desai states his country will allow nuclear safeguards only if the US, USSR, and Great Britain sign a nuclear test-ban treaty.

10   NICARAGUA - The assassination of Pedro Joaquin
        Chamorro Cardenal, the editor of anti-Somoza news-
        paper La Prensa, sparks a major riot in Managua. The
        rioting continues for days.

11   EGYPT - Military talks begin with the Israelis. The
        talks, along with those aimed at political issues,
        soon break down, however, and are halted.

12   SOUTH AFRICA - Foreign Minister Botha returns home
        from New York after breaking off UN discussions of the
        South African problem.

12   MALTA - Talks on the Rhodesian situation end in a
        deadlock.

16   LEBANON - New fighting erupts between the PLO and
        Lebanese Christian forces in southern Lebanon.

16   ITALY - The government of Giulio Andreotti falls fol-
        lowing his rejection of a Communist demand for more
        power.

16   ETHIOPIA - The Soviet and Cuban Ministers of Defense
        meet in Addis Ababa.

18   ETHIOPIA - The government denies foreign troops are
        being used in Ogaden Province.

18   UNITED STATES - US intelligence reports indicate at
        least 2,000 Cuban and 1,000 Soviet military advisors
        are in the Ogaden region in Ethiopia.

20   INDONESIA - Without explanation, President Suharto
        bans four major newspapers.

22   ETHIOPIA - The government expels the Ambassador from
        West Germany after it is announced that West Germany
        has given Somalia $20 million in credit.

22   TRANSKEI - The first black homeland granted indepen-
        dence by South Africa orders all South African mili-
        tary advisors out of the country.

23   UNITED STATES - The government imposes a military em-
        bargo on South Africa.

23   USSR - Leonid Brezhnev warns the West that deployment
        of the neutron bomb could destroy detente.

23   NICARAGUA - The country is paralyzed by a general
        strike.

26   TUNISIA - President Habib Bourguiba declares a state
        of emergency following a nation-wide strike that
        spawns the worst violence in decades.

27   USSR - The Soviet Union deploys more than 300 SS-20
        medium-range ballistic missiles (MRBM) near the Polish
        border.

27   NICARAGUA - The murder of opposition publisher Pedro
        Chamorro Cardenal (10 January) leads to a general
        strike (23 January), which evolves into a massive de-
        monstration demanding the resignation of President
        Anastasio Somoza Debayle. Somoza rejects the demand.

FEBRUARY

1   UNITED STATES - Intelligence sources estimate 5,000
        Cuban reservists have been called up to fight in
        Ethiopia.

2   ALGERIA - A high-level meeting of leaders of the radi-
        cal Arab bloc (Algeria, Libya, PLO, South Yemen, and
        Syria) meet in Algiers to plan strategy against Egypt.
        Iraq refuses to attend because it feels the group is
        not radical enough.

3   NICARAGUA - Following a 12-day general strike in the
        city, leftist Sandinista rebels attack Granada in
        force.

5   VIET NAM - The government puts forward a three-point
        proposal to settle the border dispute with Kampuchea.

6   ISRAEL - The government acknowledges it has given mil-
        itary assistance to Ethiopia.

6   ETHIOPIA - Central government forces launch an attack
        into Ogaden Province.

6   UNITED STATES - As the Ethiopia-Somalia War intensi-
        fies in the Horn of Africa, additional naval units are
        dispatched to reinforce the task force of the US Sixth
        Fleet operating in the Red Sea.

7   LEBANON - Lebanese army units clash with Syrian peace-
        keeping forces in East Beirut.

7   NICARAGUA - The nationwide strike that began on 23
        January ends after demands are made for Somoza's
        resignation.

10   UNITED STATES - The Secretary of State declares
        Israeli settlements in the Sinai illegal.

10   CYPRUS - The Greek Cypriot terrorist organization
            known as EOKA-B disbands after 23 years devoted
            primarily to driving the British out of Cyprus.

11   SOMALIA - The government orders a general mobilization
            of its armed forces.

12   NICARAGUA - The leftist Sandanista National Liberation
            Front declares it is ready to begin a civil war to
            overthrow the Somoza government.

13   UNITED STATES - Intelligence sources indicate Soviet
            Air Defense Force (PVOIA) fighter pilots are flying
            for the Cuban air defense system.

15   RHODESIA - An agreement is reached on a plan to estab-
            lish black-majority rule in the country.

16   SPAIN - The government refuses a Soviet request for
            basing rights at Algeciras near Gibraltar.

18   CYPRUS - Two Palestinian terrorists assassinate Yusuf
            as-Sibai, the editor of the Egyptian newspaper Al-
            Ahram, in the Hilton Hotel in Nicosia. In addition,
            they take 30 hostages and then demand passage to
            Larnaca Airport. In exchange for transport, they
            release 12 of the hostages, then seven more when they
            are allowed to board a DC-8 airliner. After taking
            off, the terrorists are refused landing rights in
            Algeria, Ethiopia, Greece, Kuwait, Libya, Somalia, and
            Yemen (Aden). The aircraft then returns to Nicosia
            after refueling at Djibouti.

19   ETHIOPIA - After two days of meetings, US representa-
            tives pledge not to supply arms to Somalia.

19   CYPRUS - About three hours after its return to Larnaca
            Airport, Nicosia, the plane carrying its crew, the
            Palestinian terrorists, and their 11 hostages is at-
            tacked by a 74-man Egyptian commando force. In the
            ensuing firefight, which probably involves members of
            the Cypriot National Guard and a 12-man PLO unit oper-
            ating in Cyprus, 15 of the Egyptian commandos are
            killed. Even though their Egyptian Air Force C-130
            transport is parked more the one-half mile from the
            hijacked airliner, it is destroyed by ground fire
            adding to the speculation of Cypriot complicity in the
            terrorists' activities. The remaining hostages are
            finally released when the two terrorists surrender to
            the Cypriot police.

21   ETHIOPIA - Ethiopian leader Mengistu Haile Mariam
            assures the US his country will not invade Somalia.

22   EGYPT - The government breaks diplomatic relations with Cyprus.

22   THE NETHERLANDS - The government announces it is halting aid to Cuba because of Cuban involvement in Africa.

23   UNITED STATES - Military supplies bound for Ethiopia, held up since the 1977 abrogation of the arms agreement, are released.

24   USSR - During a state visit in Moscow, Syrian President Assad is promised increased military aid for his country.

25   INDIA - The government gives Viet Nam $50 million in reconstruction funds.

27   NICARAGUA - Police clash with opposition demonstrators leaving ten dead.

27   EAST GERMANY - Iranian students attack the Iranian Embassy in East Berlin.

28   VIET NAM - The government orders the closure of 30,000 mostly Chinese-owned businesses.

MARCH

1   WEST GERMANY - The government approves the sale of warships worth 250 million pounds sterling to Iran.

2   IRAN - The government breaks relations with East Germany for its part in supporting Iranian student demonstrations in East Berlin. All commercial activities are halted on 5 March.

3   RHODESIA - Leaders of the various internal factions agree upon a plan to set up a transitional multiracial government by the end of the year.

8   THE NETHERLANDS - The government goes on record as being opposed to the deployment of the neutron bomb.

8   NICARAGUA - Anti-Somoza demonstrations become more widespread.

9   SOMALIA - The government begins the withdrawal of its regular forces from Ethiopia's Ogaden Province after the Somalis are badly beaten by Ethiopian forces supported by Cuban troops and Soviet equipment.

10   UNITED STATES - The government refuses to accept an
            Israeli request for more weapons.

10   GUYANA - Along with Jamaica, Guyana agrees to partici-
            pate in a multinational security force designed to
            guarantee the territorial integrity of Belize.

11   CHILE - President Augusto Pinochet Ugarte ends four
            and one-half years of martial law.

11   ISRAEL - An 11-man PLO terrorist group, operating out
            of southern Lebanon, attacks a bus and several vehi-
            cles on the road between Haifa and Tel Aviv killing
            between 30 and 37 Israeli civilians and one US citi-
            zen. At least 82 other Israelis are injured in the
            attack. Nine of the terrorists are killed in the
            ensuing firefight with Israeli security forces.

14   UNITED NATIONS - The Security Council declares illegal
            any settlements reached by the present regime in
            Rhodesia.

14   ISRAEL - Israeli forces carry out large-scale retali-
            ation raids against PLO bases in southern Lebanon.
            They also establish a "security zone" 4-6 miles wide
            along the Lebanese-Israeli border.

14   FRANCE - The government signs an arms package with
            Egypt, Qatar, Saudi Arabia, and the United Arab
            Emirates.

14   CUBA - The government admits it has ground and air
            forces in Ethiopia giving direct combat support to
            that government's fight against Somalia.

15   SOMALIA - Somalia completes its military withdrawal
            from Ogaden Province in Ethiopia.

16   UNITED STATES - The Senate ratifies the Panama Canal
            Treaty declaring the permanent neutrality of the
            waterway. The Senate ratifies a second Panama Canal
            treaty on 18 April.

16   ITALY - Former Premier Aldo Moro is kidnapped by 12
            Red Brigade terrorists. Five bodyguards are slain in
            the incident.

17   BOLIVIA - The government severs diplomatic relations
            with Chile when an accord cannot be reached over ac-
            cess to the Pacific Ocean.

18   IRELAND - Prime Minister John Lynch claims foreign
            aid, especially from the US, helps keep the fighting
            going in Northern Ireland.

18   PAKISTAN - Former Prime Minister Zulfikar Ali Bhutto
            is sentenced to death by the Lahore High Court after
            being found guilty of charges of murder. Four others
            are also sentenced to death.

19   UNITED NATIONS - The Security Council calls for an im-
            mediate Israeli withdrawal from Lebanon.

21   ISRAEL - The government announces a unilateral cease-
            fire in its operational area in southern Lebanon.

22   LEBANON - A UN emergency force arrives in southern
            Lebanon.

24   ETHIOPIA - The government announces its forces have
            cleared southeastern Ogaden of all rebels and have
            secured the region.

24   ERITREA - Two rival groups, the EPLF and the ELF, join
            forces.

27   SOUTH AFRICA - King Kapuuo, the government's choice to
            be leader of Namibia, is assassinated.

28   LEBANON - PLO leader Yasser Arafat accepts a UN cease-
            fire call.

31   IRAN - Violence breaks out in several cities following
            a week of strike and political demonstrations.

31   AUSTRALIA - Along with other members of the South
            Pacific Forum (New Zealand, Papua New Guinea, and a
            number of island states) the government imposes the
            200-miles fishing limit which was voted 31 August
            1977.

APRIL

4   ANGOLA - Government forces, heavily reinforced by
            Cuban ground troops and Soviet jets and helicopter
            gunships, open an attack against rebel UNITA forces.
            Hundreds of Angolan refugees flee to neighboring
            Namibia.

6   UNITED STATES - President Carter asks the Congress to
            lift the 1975 arms embargo on Turkey.

8   LEBANON - The government demands an immediate Israeli
            withdrawal.

9   ISRAEL - The government admits using US-made cluster
            bombs in Lebanon in mid-March.

10   TRANSKEI - The government breaks diplomatic relations with South Africa.

11   LEBANON - Israel begins withdrawing its forces from southern Lebanon.

12   UNITED STATES - Micronesia is granted self-rule by the government although the right to build military bases on the islands is retained.

13   UNITED STATES - The government demands an end to the use of special US munitions by the Israelis against terrorist targets.

18   UNITED STATES - The Senate ratifies the second of two treaties (Basic Panama Canal Treaty), which gives Panama sovereignty over the canal and the Canal Zone. The US will continue operation of the canal until 1999.

19   NATO - A new MBFR proposal is handed to the Warsaw Pact who consider it to be a "major new initiative."

19   CYPRUS - The government rejects as inadequate a Turkish plan for the settlement of the Cyprus situation.

20   NATO - In the face of growing opposition from some of its members, the NATO Nuclear Planning Group retains the option of deploying neutron weapons in Europe.

20   USSR - On a flight from Paris to Seoul a South Korean Air Lines (KAL) Boeing 707 jet airliner is forced down by Soviet fighters 280 miles from Murmansk. Of the 110 passengers who are released on 23 April, 13 are injured (two were killed when the plane crash landed on a frozen lake). The crew is released on 29 April after questioning.

21   UNITED STATES - President Carter announces significant reductions in troop strength in South Korea during 1978 and 1979.

25   USSR - The Soviet Union signs the Tlatelolco Treaty (1969) that bans nuclear weapons in Latin America.

27   LEBANON - The Parliament votes to prohibit all military forces in Lebanon except the Lebanese Army.

27-28   AFGHANISTAN - The government of President Sardar Mohammed Daoud Khan is overthrown by a pro-Soviet military coup. Daoud, the Vice President, a number of ministers, and the chiefs of the armed forces all are killed. Thousands of others are probably killed in the fighting.

30   AFGHANISTAN - A revolutionary council, headed by Nur
            Mohammad Taraki, assumes control of the government.
            Taraki is a known Communist.

MAY

3   UNITED NATIONS - The General Assembly orders an uncon-
            ditional withdrawal of all foreign forces in Namibia.

3   ARGENTINA - The ruling military junta appoints General
            Jorge Videla President.

4   ANGOLA - South African paratroopers attack the South
            West Africa People's Organization (SWAPO) base at
            Cassinga, more than 150 miles from the border, and two
            other suspected bases.

6   UNITED NATIONS - The Security Council condemns South
            Africa for its raid into Angola.

9   ITALY - Aldo Moro's bullet-riddled body is found in
            the trunk of a car in central Rome.

10   AFGHANISTAN - The government announces a program to
            improve relations with the Soviet Union.

10   TRANSKEI - Transkei abrogates the non-aggression pact
            it has with South Africa.

11   COMMUNIST CHINA - Soviet MVD border troops cross the
            Ussuri River south of Kharboarovsk into the Yueh Ya-
            pao District of China ostensibly in "hot pursuit" of
            an escaping criminal. The government rejects (14 May)
            the Soviet apology (12 May).

11   ETHIOPIA - The Soviet Union supplies 224 MiG fighters
            to the Ethiopian government.

11   ZAIRE - Some 4,000 Katangan rebels of the Congolese
            National Liberation Front (FNLC), generally suspected
            of being supported by Soviet, Libyan, and Algerian
            interests, capture the important copper-mining town of
            Kolwezi and the railroad center at Mutshatsha in their
            attack into Shaba Province.

11   IRAN - Widespread rioting has continued for three
            days. In Tehran, rioters demand the ouster of the
            Shah.

13   COMORO ISLANDS - President Ali Soilih is overthrown in
            a coup organized by Robert Denard, a French mercenary.
            Former President Ahmed Abdallah is reinstalled and
            becomes co-President with Mohammed Ahmed (24 May).

15   KAMPUCHEA - The government makes a counter-proposal to Viet Nam to settle the border crisis.

15   UNITED STATES - The Congress approves a massive military aircraft sale to a group of Middle Eastern countries. Egypt is to receive 50 F-5Es, Israel is to get 15 F-15s and 75 F-16s, and Saudi Arabia, 60 F-15s.

15   ETHIOPIA - A new offensive is lauched into Eritrea.

15   PERU - Rioting breaks out in the wake of a government austerity program that has caused food prices to double.

17   CUBA - Fidel Castro assures the US that Cuban troops are not participating in the Katangan rebel invasion of Zaire.

18-19   ZAIRE - Six hundred French Foreign Legion and 700 Belgian paratroopers are airlifted into Shaba Province by US and British military transports to rescue 2,500 foreigners trapped there by the fighting between government troops and Katanganese rebels of the FNLC who had crossed into Zaire from bases in Angola.

19   PERU - Widespread rioting following the announcement of an IMF-mandated austerity program causes President Francisco Morales Bermudez to declare a state of emergency.

19   UNITED STATES - The President gives $17.5 million in non-lethal military and medical aid to Zaire.

19   ISRAEL - The government announces an agreement with Syria to renew the UN mandate on the Golan Heights for another six months.

20   ZAIRE - The important town of Kolwezi is recaptured by government troops.

22   ZAIRE - The rescue mission completed, the Belgian airborne force begins its withdrawal from Shaba Province.

25   ZAIRE - French forces begin their withdrawal.

25   COMMUNIST CHINA - The government warns Viet Nam to stop harassing its ethnic Chinese population.

26   CANADA - The Prime Minister announces that Canadian military aircraft will no longer carry nuclear weapons.

JUNE

1   EGYPT - President Sadat receives permission from the People's Assembly to restrict criticism of government policies.

2   ISRAEL - A group of Al-Fatah terrorists blow up a bus in Jerusalem killing six people, including one American.

2   SPAIN - Armenian terrorists attack the limousine of the Turkish Ambassador in Madrid. The Ambassador's wife, brother-in-law, and chauffeur are killed.

3   ZAIRE - US aircraft transport Moroccan and Senegalese forces into Shaba Province.

5   FRANCE - At an emergency meeting in Paris, held to discuss the invasion of Zaire's Shaba Province, Belgium, France, Great Britain, the US, and West Germany agree to aid Zaire but cannot agree upon a formula for the formation of a pan-African force.

5   COMMUNIST CHINA - Some 110,000 persons have regained their liberty as the government moves to release political prisoners held since the 1957 Cultural Revolution.

6   SOUTH AFRICA - The government stipulates a list of conditions before it will sign the Nuclear Non-Proliferation Treaty.

6   VIET NAM - The government rejects the Kampuchean proposals and instead offers a cease-fire to allow establishment of a demilitarized zone along the border.

7   IRAN - A general strike follows the death of anti-Shah demonstrators in Tehran.

7   USSR - Despite Japanese protests, the Soviets carry out military exercises near the Kurile Islands.

7   ETHIOPIA - The government offers amnesty to Eritrean rebels.

8   EGYPT - Anwar Sadat reveals he rejected an Israeli offer to return the Sinai in exchange for a separate peace.

8   WARSAW PACT - The Warsaw Pact submits an MBFR counter-proposal to NATO.

8   FINLAND - US-USSR talks on limiting anti-satellite weapons begin in Helsinki.

9   PERU - Martial law is lifted.

9   CHILE - The Pinochet government consents to a UN investigation of alleged human rights violations.

13   ISRAEL - The Israeli Army completes its withdrawal from southern Lebanon.

16-19   COMMUNIST CHINA - The government recalls its Ambassador in Hanoi and orders the Vietnamese government to close its three consulates in southern China.

17   ZAIRE - Belgian forces complete their withdrawal from Shaba Province.

20   UNITED STATES - The President orders US intelligence satellites protected from attack.

20   JAPAN - The government buys 50 F-15 and 45 P-3C aircraft from the US.

24   UNITED STATES - The US recalls its Ambassador to Chile and halts all future arms shipments to that country in reprisal for Chile's failure to properly support the US investigation into the 1976 Letelier assassination in Washington, DC.

24   LEBANON - While meeting in Beirut with an envoy of South Yemen President Salem Ali Rubayyi, North Yemeni President Ahmad al-Ghasmi is killed by a bomb concealed in an attache case.

26   FRANCE - The south wing of the 17th century Palace of Versailles is severely damaged by a bomb planted by French terrorists, most likely from the radical Breton Republican Army, the military wing of the Breton Liberation Front.

26   SOUTH YEMEN - A pro-Soviet coup, led by the National Liberation Front, overthrows President Salem Ali Rubayyi. He is then executed.

29   ERITREA - Rebel forces offer Ethiopia an opportunity for unconditional talks to end the 17 years of fighting.

29   ZAMBIA - The Western Powers give Zambia $1 billion in aid.

JULY

2   ARAB LEAGUE - The Council votes to boycott South Yemen and its pro-Marxist government.

3   COMMUNIST CHINA - The government suspends all economic and technical assistance to Viet Nam following Viet Nam's acceptance into full membership in the Council for Mutual Economic Assistance (Comecon) (29 June).

5   FRANCE - The government announces the sale of 170 military aircraft engines to Argentina.

7   SOLOMON ISLANDS - The former British colony becomes independent.

9   ISRAEL - The government rejects an Egyptian plan for transitional rule in the Gaza Strip and in the West Bank.

9   BOLIVIA - Juan Pereda Asbun wins the election for President.

10   MAURITANIA - The government of Moktar Ould Daddah is overthrown. Lieutenant Colonel Mustafa Ould Salek takes over the nation's leadership. At the time, POLISARIO, which is carrying on a guerrilla campaign for the independence of West Sahara, decides to call a unilateral cease-fire in Mauritania.

10   ZAIRE - The last Belgian forces leave the country.

11   UNITED STATES - Press reports indicate there has been US naval support for US Drug Enforcement Agency operations. Navy ocean surviellance satellites are credited with assisting in the capture of 40 ships and boats involved in attempting to smuggle about $400 million (one million pounds) worth of marijuana into the US between December 1977 and April 1978.

11-12   NAMIBIA - SWAPO agrees to a plan for black majority rule.

11-14   COMMUNIST CHINA - In retaliation for Albanian criticism of Sino-American relations, Peking recalls its technicians and cuts all aid to the Tirana government.

13   LEBANON - Syria warns Christian militiamen that continued skirmishing will lead to an armed crackdown.

18   OAU - The organization approves the Western plan for an all-party conference on the Rhodesian question.

19   NICARAGUA - Another general strike is called to protest the Somoza regime.

19   BOLIVIA - The National Electoral Court voids the election as having been totally dishonest.

20   CHAD - President Malloum demands an immediate with-
            drawal of Libyan forces in his country.

21   BOLIVIA - The government of Hugo Banzer Suarez is
            ousted in a military coup led by Juan Pereda Asbun who
            declares himself President.

23   ISRAEL - The Cabinet rejects a plan formed in the
            Sadat-Weizman meeting in Austria that would have re-
            turned Mount Sinai and El Arish to Egypt as good will
            gestures.

24-30   YUGOSLAVIA - A non-aligned nation conference criti-
            cizes Cuba's intervention in Ethiopia.

25   YUGOSLAVIA - President Tito criticizes Cuban military
            intervention in Africa as a Soviet-backed ploy.

26   EGYPT - The government requests Israel to withdraw the
            Israeli military mission stationed in Egypt.

27   UNITED NATIONS - The Security Council approves the
            Western-backed plan for the independence of Namibia.

28   JAPAN - The government warns the Soviet Union against
            attempting to establish a sphere of influence in the
            islands surrounding the Japanese home islands.

28   UNITED NATIONS - Secretary General Kurt Waldheim urges
            Lebanon to deploy troops along the Israeli-Lebanese
            border to assist the UNEF in carrying out its mandate.

28   ETHIOPIA - The ten-month-long siege around Asmara is
            broken when Ethiopian forces penetrate the ELF lines.

31   COMMUNIST CHINA - The government promises military
            support to Kampuchea in case of a Vietnamese invasion.

31   LEBANON - Regular forces are sent to the Israeli bor-
            der but dissuaded from deploying by firefights between
            Syrian and Lebanese Christian forces.

31   FRANCE - Two Al Fatah terrorists attack the Iraqi Em-
            bassy in Paris. In the confusion, one of the two
            flees. Then the lone terrorist shoots his way into the
            Embassy and seizes nine hostages. He demands the
            release of an Arab woman held in connection with an
            attempt on the life of the Iraqi Ambassador in London.
            After he surrenders nine hours later, the Embassy's
            security guards open fire on the crowd outside. A
            French policeman and one security guard are killed.
            Three Embassy personnel are arrested but are released
            and ordered out of France because they hold diplomatic
            immunity.

AUGUST

1 KAMPUCHEA - Heavy fighting erupts at four points along the border with Viet Nam. Vietnamese aircraft attack targets 35 miles inside the Kampuchean border.

1 UNITED STATES - Congress lifts the four-year-old arms embargo on Turkey.

4 MALTA - Libyan military personnel fly into the former RAF base at Hal Far and begin converting it into a helicopter base.

7 HONDURAS - President Juan Alberto Melgar Castro is ousted in a bloodless military coup. A three-man military junta, led by General Policarpo Paz Garcia, takes over the country's rule.

8 MIDDLE EAST - Egypt and Israel agree to an American proposal for September peace talks to be held at Camp David, the US President's retreat in Maryland.

9 LIBYA - The government opens diplomatic relations with Communist China.

10 LEBANON - A cease-fire between Syrian and Christian militia forces goes into effect.

11 LEBANON - The cease-fire is broken.

11 BOLIVIA - The state of siege which was imposed on 21 July is lifted by President Juan Pereda Asbun.

12 COMMUNIST CHINA - A treaty of peace and friendship is signed with Japan in Peking.

12 IRAN - Martial law is declared in four more cities as the violence spreads in the wake of the appointment of Jafaar Sharif-Emami as Prime Minister.

13 VIET NAM - Government gunboats capture six Chinese fishing boats inside territorial waters.

13 LEBANON - A violent explosion destroys an apartment house and kills 150 Palestinian guerrillas of the Palestine Liberation Front (PLF). The headquarters of the rival Al Fatah is also located in the building. No one claims credit for the attack although many, including the US, are accused.

18 ICELAND - The recently-installed Communist government fails to close the vitally important NATO air base at Keflavik.

21   ANGOLA - A joint commission is formed with Zaire to
            increase security along the border.

21   VIET NAM - The government lays claim to the Chinese-
            held Poulo Wai Islands.

22   KENYA - President Jomo Kenyatta (Kamau wa Ngengi) dies
            at 84. His Vice-President, Daniel Torotich arap Moi,
            becomes acting President.

22   NICARAGUA - Eden Pastora Gomez, called "Zero," leads
            24 Sandanista rebels in an attempt to seize and hold
            the National Palace in Managua; they fail after two
            days to gain all of their demands. Six are killed and
            more than 1,000 held hostage during the siege.

24   NICARAGUA - Having met some of their demands (release
            of 59 political prisoners and a $500,000 ransom),
            Gomez, the Sandanista guerrillas, the prisoners, and
            the money are allowed to fly to Panama.

25   COMMUNIST CHINA - The government reports a heavy bor-
            der clash with the Vietnamese. Casualties are reported
            on both sides.

25   LEBANON - Syrian forces attack a number of Christian
            villages north of Beirut.

27   COMMUNIST CHINA - The government warns Viet Nam that
            it must evacuate Chinese territory or face the conse-
            quences.

30   UNITED NATIONS - The plan for Namibian peace and inde-
            pendence is announced.

SEPTEMBER

1   VIET NAM - The government denies it has any forces on
            Chinese territory.

1-17   UNITED STATES - Egyptian and Israeli leaders meet at
            the Presidential retreat at Camp David. Middle East
            talks begin on 5 September.

3   RHODESIA - Rebels of Joshua Nkomo's rebel faction
            shoot down a Rhodesian Viscount airliner near Lake
            Kariba. Thirty-eight on board are killed and the
            guerrillas murder ten of the 18 survivors.

4   NICARAGUA - Seven hundred are arrested in an attempt
            to break a general strike which has paralyzed the
            country.

5	COMMUNIST CHINA - The government accuses the Vietnamese of occupying the railway right-of-way where the fighting took place on 25 August.
6	COMMUNIST CHINA - The government announces it will not renew the 1950 Sino-Soviet Defense Treaty when it expires in 1980.
6	COLOMBIA - The government adopts a "get tough" policy in its war on crime and subversion.
6-12	IRAN - All opposition rallies are banned. Mullahs (clergymen), newspapermen, and anti-Shah politicans are arrested.
8	GHANA - The government expels a number of East German and Soviet diplomatic personnel for aiding and abetting unrest among students and unionists.
8	IRAN - Martial law is imposed by the Shah in Tehran and 11 other cities after troops fire on demonstrators who refuse to disperse. As many as 1,000 are killed.
8	DOMINICAN REPUBLIC - The government announces an amnesty, which will affect several hundred political prisoners.
9	NICARAGUA - Guerrilla forces seize a number of cities including Chinandega, Esteli, and Leon.
10	RHODESIA - The Smith government imposes martial law to strengthen its hand in dealing with the rebels.
10	NAMIBIA - The UN plan is accepted by SWAPO.
11	VIET NAM - The country mobilizes its armed forces and announces the formation of a paramilitary five-million man "National Task Force."
12	SOUTH AFRICA - The government rejects the UN's plan for Namibia.
12	COSTA RICA - Nicaraguan forces cross into Costa Rica in pursuit of about 50 insurgents.
13	NICARAGUA - President Somoza declares martial law.
16	PAKISTAN - Mohammed Zia-ul-Haq, who seized power in July 1977, becomes President.
16	NICARAGUA - Leon is liberated by National Guard forces.

17 UNITED STATES - President Carter announces an Israeli-Egyptian peace accord at Camp David.

17 NICARAGUA - The government accuses Venezuela of carrying out air strikes against Nicaraguan positions in support of rebel forces attacking from bases in Costa Rica.

17 FRANCE - An agreement is signed with an Arab consortium to allow assembly of French-made Dassault Alfa-Jets in Egypt.

18 UNITED NATIONS - The mandate for the emergency force in Lebanon is extended an additional four months.

18 NICARAGUA - Chinandega is recaptured from the guerrilla forces who have held it since 9 September.

20 USSR - In retaliation for the signing of the Sino-Japanese Treaty, the Soviets reinforce their garrisons on two of the Kurile Islands.

20 MIDDLE EAST - A so-called "rejectionist" summit establishes a $1-billion fund to support Arab nations that boycott Egypt in response to the settlement with Israel. A joint military command is established to coordinate Arab efforts against Israel.

22 NIGERIA - The martial law decree that has been in effect since 1966 is revoked by Lieutenant General Olusegun Obasanjo, the head of state.

22 NICARAGUA - Federal National Guardsmen regain control of Esteli. The city is virtually destroyed in the process.

22-25 MOZAMBIQUE - The Rhodesian Air Force attacks 25 ZAPU bases inside Mozambique.

23 OAS - The organization refuses to accept a US motion to mediate the Nicaraguan crisis.

24 UNITED STATES - During a visit by Yugoslav Defense Minister Nikola Ljubicic, the US announces the sale of 400 jet engines to his country.

24 MIDDLE EAST - During his five day visit in the Middle East, US Secretary of State Cyrus Vance is told Saudi Arabia and Jordan will not abide by the Camp David agreement.

25 UNITED STATES - President Carter sends a personal envoy to Nicaragua.

25   VIET NAM - A major military clash takes place follow-
        ing Vietnamese accusations of a heavy Chinese buildup
        along the border.

25   KAMPUCHEA - The government acknowledges it has been
        invaded by Vietnamese forces. Reports indicate the
        Vietnamese have already penetrated 5 miles into the
        country.

26   NICARAGUA - President Somoza accepts the US offer of
        mediation and grants amnesty to all political prison-
        ers except the Sandanistas.

26   UNITED STATES - The government lifts the embargo on
        arms shipments to Turkey, an action approved earlier
        by Congress, when the $2.8 billion International
        Security Assistance Act is signed.

27   COMMUNIST CHINA - The government accuses Viet Nam of
        preparing for war.

27   INDONESIA - The government frees 1,324 political pri-
        soners who have been imprisoned since the Communist
        coup attempt in 1965. About 16,000 are still in jail
        although the government claims many have been freed.

28   ISRAEL - The government gives only qualified approval
        to the Camp David agreement.

28   SOUTH AFRICA - Foreign Minister Pieter Botha succeeds
        Johannes Vorster as premier.

28   AUSTRIA - A new round of MBFR talks begins in Vienna.

29   UNITED NATIONS - The Nicaraguan Ambassador denounces
        his own country's policy of "genocide" and demands
        President Somoza's resignation.

30   NICARAGUA - President Somoza accepts a multi-national
        mediation plan.

30   MOROCCO - The US closes its last military base in
        Africa when the US Naval Communication Station at
        Kenitra (25 miles north of Rabat) is returned to
        Moroccan government control.

OCTOBER

1   IRAN - The Shah declares an amnesty to all those, in-
        cluding the Ayatollah Khomeini, who have been involved
        in anti-government activities.

2   VIET NAM - Declining the Kampuchean offer to negotiate
           the border crisis, Vietnamese forces continue their
           drive into the country.

2   LEBANON - Heavy fighting is reported between Syrian
           and Christian militia forces.

2   MOROCCO - The government accepts Nigerian mediation
           for the settlement of the West Sahara crisis.

3   USSR - The government announces it has agreed to fur-
           nish Libya with a nuclear power complex and research
           center.

5   UNITED STATES - The Federal Bureau of Investigation
           reveals it has broken up a plot to steal a US Navy
           nuclear attack submarine and sell it to an undisclosed
           foreign power.

6   ZAMBIA - The border with Rhodesia is reopened for eco-
           nomic reasons.

9   TURKEY - The government allows the reopening of four
           important US intelligence collection stations which
           have been closed since the arms embargo went into
           effect.

10   RHODESIA - The transitional government moves to end
           segregation.

11   LEBANON - The Syrian command allows PLO forces to
           begin operations near Christian positions.

11   IRAN - A pipe bomb explodes in Isfahan after being
           thrown through the window of a bus owned by Bell
           Helicopter International. No one claims responsi-
           bility for the attack. Three Americans are slightly
           injured.

12   UNITED NATIONS - The UN puts into effect a treaty
           against "weather warfare."

12   UNITED STATES - Formal Egypt-Israel peace talks open
           in Washington.

12   CHILE - President Pinochet announces his plan to stay
           in office until 1985 when a civil-military government
           will assume power.

12   UGANDA - The government claims Tanzanian troops have
           invaded its territory. Tanzania calls the Idi Amin's
           claims "complete lies."

17   UNITED STATES - The Defense Department announces the
            redeployment of some US forces in Western Europe to
            counter a Soviet buildup in Central Europe.

17   MIDDLE EAST - At least seven Arab nations condemn
            Syrian activities in Lebanon.

18   ZAMBIA - The Rhodesian Air Force attacks ZAPU targets
            in Zambia.

20   UNITED STATES - The Washington peace talks between
            Israel and Egypt stall because of the PLO issue.

20   LEBANON - Saudi Arabian troops are used to replace
            Syrian forces in East Beirut.

20   MOROCCO - Polisario forces attack El Aiun.

20   RHODESIA - The transitional government adopts the
            US-Great Britain plan for an all-party conference.

22   RHODESIA - ZAPU leader Nkomo rejects the all-party
            conference plan.

22   SYRIA - The border with Iraq is reopened.

24   IRAQ - A National Charter of Joint Action is init-
            ialed by Syria and Iraq at the close of a meeting de-
            signed to end the bickering between the two countries.

24   NAMIBIA - SWAPO rejects a South African counter-
            proposal for Namibian independence.

25   IRAN - Two universities are closed as violence con-
            tinues and spreads through at least a dozen cities.

26   UNITED NATIONS - A coalition of Black African nations
            asks the Security Council for economic sanctions
            against South Africa because of its continued refusal
            to abide by the UN decision on Namibia.

26   UNITED STATES - President Carter signs a bill author-
            izing the production of neutron-warhead components.

26   ARAB LEAGUE - The Arab peacekeeping force mandate in
            Lebanon is extended six months.

27   IRAN - Major anti-Shah demonstrations take place in 13
            cities.

27   YUGOSLAVIA - Western intelligence sources show that
            Yugoslavia is servicing Soviet submarines.

27   GREAT BRITAIN - The government announces it is ship-
            ping air defense weapons to Zambia.

27   TANZANIA - The government declares the country has
            been invaded by Uganda.

27   SOUTH KOREA - The United Nations Command reports the
            discovery of the third North Korean tunnel found since
            1974. This one is large enough to allow for the pas-
            sage of about 30,000 troops an hour. The tunnel exits
            into South Korea about one-quarter mile below the DMZ
            boundary.

29   IRAN - A number of Iranian secret police (Savak) of-
            ficials are dismissed in a government attempt to pla-
            cate the populace.

30   UNITED STATES - The Washington peace talks between
            Israel and Egypt resume after an exchange of notes.

31   IRAN - A general strike is more than 50% effective.

31   UNITED NATIONS - The Security Council opens debate on
            Namibia amid a wide range of divergent opinions as to
            what course of action should be taken against South
            Africa.

31   TANZANIA - The government claims Ugandan military
            forces have penetrated some 20 miles into Tanzanian
            territory.

NOVEMBER

1   UGANDA - The government announces it has annexed about
            700 square miles of Tanzanian territory known as the
            Kagera Salient.

1   RHODESIA - The government postpones implementation of
            majority rule until 20 April 1979.

3   USSR - The government announces it has signed a 25-
            year treaty of friendship and cooperation with Viet
            Nam.

3   ARAB LEAGUE - At a meeting in Damascus the League
            establishes a $3.5 billion fund to support Arab states
            opposed to the Egypt-Israel peace treaty. It is also
            decided that Egypt's signature on the peace treaty
            will cause immediate expulsion from the League and
            future boycotts the same as those imposed on Israeli
            firms.

4   EGYPT - President Sadat refuses to meet with Arab League representatives who are in Egypt to offer $50 billion in aid if Egypt will break off peace talks with Israel.

4   UGANDA - President Idi Amin claims he has ordered a withdrawal of his forces from Tanzania. Other reports contradict him, however, and fighting is reported to be continuing.

5   IRAN - A major anti-Shah demonstration takes place in Tehran. Prime Minister Sharif-Emami resigns and is replaced by a military officer, General Gholam Reza Azhari.

5   UNITED STATES - The government cancels an enriched uranium contract with South Africa because South Africa refuses to sign the Nuclear Nonproliferation Treaty.

6   UNITED STATES - The Department of State announces its support of the new Azhari government in Iran.

7   TANZANIA - The government moves about 8,000-10,000 troops to the border of the territory annexed by Uganda.

9   UNITED NATIONS - The General Assembly votes to oust Turkey from Cyprus.

9   UNITED STATES - President Carter agrees with Egypt's President Sadat that the Egypt-Israel peace settlement should be linked to the larger question of peace in the Middle East.

10   TANZANIA - Casualties in the war with Uganda are reported to be as high as 10,000 killed or wounded.

11   IRAN - Opposition leader Karin Sanjabi is arrested.

12   ISRAEL - The Knesset rejects the Sadat linkage proposal.

13   UNITED NATIONS - The Security Council directs South Africa to cancel plans for December elections in Namibia or face full economic sanctions.

13   IRAN - The government receives a 60% response to its back-to-work order issued to oil workers.

15   UNITED STATES - Intelligence reports indicate the presence of Soviet-built MiG-23 fighter-bombers in Cuba.

16   UNITED STATES - President Carter orders reconnaissance overflights of Cuba to determine whether the MiG-23 aircraft located there have a nuclear capability.

17   FINLAND - The government approves a $75 million purchase of Soviet-built SA-3 surface-to-air missiles.

18   USSR - The government confirms it has transferred a number of MiG-23 aircraft to Cuba.

19   USSR - Brezhnev warns the US against intervening in Iran.

19   GUYANA - Members of the People's Temple cult ambush a group of US officials who are investigating the cult's activities. Congressman Leo Ryan is killed along with an NBC reporter and a California-based photographer. Eleven others are wounded. One cult member is killed in the attack. Shortly after the attack most of the cult's members commit suicide.

20   ETHIOPIA - The government signs a 20-year treaty of friendship and cooperation with the Soviet Union.

21   EGYPT - When Israel states it is ready to sign the peace proposal but refuses to establish a timetable for free elections leading to autonomy in the occupied territories, the Egyptians recall their negotiator.

22   UNITED NATIONS - The Security Council declares the Rhodesian settlement "null and void."

22   COSTA RICA - Following clear indications that President Somoza of Nicaragua might be willing to make concessions but will not step down, the government breaks diplomatic relations with Nicaragua and demands its ouster from the UNO.

22   VIET NAM - The government accuses Kampuchea of raiding across its border in the latest episode of the ongoing crisis.

23   KAMPUCHEA - Employing Soviet-built MiG-23 fighter-bombers, the Vietnamese carry out heavy air attacks against Kampuchea.

23   ETHIOPIA - Federal forces cut the Asmara-Massawa road.

24   RHODESIA - Rule by martial law is extended to more than three-quarters of the country.

24   BOLIVIA - President Juan Pereda Asbun is ousted in a bloodless military coup. He is replaced by General David Padilla Aranciba.

25   RHODESIA - The government announces that a UN-sanc-
            tioned election will be held in Namibia after the
            December elections.

25   WARSAW PACT - Romania refuses to allow any further
            integration of its armed forces into the Warsaw Pact
            or to increase its payment to the Pact.

25-28   JORDAN - In Amman, the government holds the first
            talks with the PLO in six years.

27   UGANDA - Tanzanian troops invade Uganda and penetrate
            up to 25 miles into the country.

30   IRAN - A pipe bomb is thrown into the apartment of a
            member of the US Military Mission in Tehran. Two
            people are injured.

DECEMBER

1   COMMUNIST CHINA - The government delivers the first in
            a shipment of fighter planes to Kampuchea.

1   THAILAND - Intelligence sources place 40,000 Vietnam-
            ese troops on the Laos-Kampuchea border.

3   LEBANON - Christian forces confirm the building of
            military airfields and of harbor construction outside
            the UN emergency force sphere of authority.

3   SOUTH AFRICA - Under a number of pretexts, the govern-
            ment controls the elections in Namibia. The Turnhalle
            Alliance wins 82% of the votes cast.

3   CAMBODIA - The Kampuchean United Front for National
            Salvation comes into being with the avowed purpose of
            ousting the Pol Pot government.

4   ISRAEL - The government rejects the latest Egyptian
            peace proposal.

4-6   NATO - The NATO defense ministers approve the $1.8-
            billion purchase of 18 AWACS aircraft.

5   MAURITANIA - The government breaks off peace talks
            with Polisario.

5   CAMBODIA - Vietnamese troops cut the vitally important
            Highway 4 between Kompong Som on the Gulf of Siam and
            Phnom Penh. Chinese advisors with the Cambodian Army
            advise a reversion to guerrilla tactics to defeat the
            numerically superior and better-equipped Vietnamese.

5   USSR - While in Moscow, Afghan President Nur Mohammed
           Taraki signs a 20-year treaty of friendship with the
           Soviet Union.

7   NICARAGUA - President Somoza lifts the decree of
           martial law and abolishes censorship. The Broad Front
           Opposition still refuses to meet with him.

9   CUBA - In an attempt to improve relations with the US,
           Fidel Castro orders the release of more than 1,000
           political prisoners.

10   THAILAND - The government alerts its forces against
           possible Vietnamese moves into Kampuchea.

10   TANZANIA - The government claims Uganda continues to
           attack into Tanzania.

14   UNITED NATIONS - The UN renews its mandate to maintain
           a UNEF in Cyprus.

15   UNITED STATES - The US announces it will normalize
           diplomatic relations with Communist China beginning on
           1 January 1979, and that relations with Nationalist
           China will end at the same time. The security treaty
           with Nationalist China will end at the beginning of
           1980.

15   NICARAGUA - President Somoza grants amnesty to all
           political prisoners.

16   ALGERIA - The government accuses Morocco of airlifting
           weapons to Algerian rebels.

17   MIDDLE EAST - The self-imposed deadline for signing a
           peace treaty, which was agreed to at Camp David,
           passes without the treaty being signed.

20   LEBANON - Palestinian bases are attacked by Israeli
           aircraft in retaliation for bomb attacks against
           Israeli targets.

20   GREAT BRITAIN - The government announces that the
           UK-Argentinian discussions over the Falkland
           (Malvinas) Islands have concluded with agreement only
           insofar as scientific research is concerned. The two
           nations agree to meet again in 1979 to continue
           discussions.

21   LEBANON - Rockets fired into Israel by PLO forces
           bring an immediate Israeli reaction in the form of
           heavy artillery bombardments.

26 TURKEY - Heavy polito-religious rioting between Sunni and Shi'ite (Alevis) Muslims in southeastern Turkey, which takes more than 100 lives, forces the government to declare martial law in 13 districts.

27 KAMPUCHEA - Vietnamese forces invade Kampuchea.

27 ALGERIA - President Houari Boumedienne dies in a coma at 52. He is replaced by Rabah Bitat as interim President.

27 NICARAGUA - President Somoza rejects a proposal for an internationally supervised election to determine the nation's leadership.

29 ISRAEL - Prime Minister Begin rejects any Egyptian plan to establish a Palestinian State but promises to follow the Camp David agreement and establish autono- mous regions for the Palestinians in the West Bank and in the Gaza Strip.

30 IRAN - Shahpour Bakhtiar, an outspoken critic of the Shah, is named Prime Minister, heading a new civilian government at a point in time when chaos grips the country.

31 THE PHILIPPINES - The government agrees to extend US basing rights in the Philippines in return for $500 million in aid.

31 KAMPUCHEA - Vietnamese forces supported by Kampuchean rebels capture Kratie on Highway 13 at the Mekong River.

31 NATIONALIST CHINA - The Communist Chinese halt the shelling of the off-shore islands.

31 COMMUNIST CHINA - Military forces located along the coast are redeployed along the borders with the Soviet Union in the north and Viet Nam in the south.

31 ISRAEL - Begin accepts two of four Egyptian proposals and announces that Israel is ready to continue peace talks.

1979

AFGHANISTAN - Reports circulate that the Taraki regime has instituted a widespread program of repression in which some 72,000 are reported killed.

1   UNITED STATES - The US and Communist China establish full diplomatic relations. At the same time, and in accordance with the 1976 Treaty of Cooperation and Friendship with Spain, the US Navy begins moving its submarine base out of Rota. Submarine Squadron 16 is redeployed to Kings Bay, Georgia.

2   KAMPUCHEA - The government asks the UN for support against Vietnamese and Soviet aggression.

3   KAMPUCHEA - Vietnamese-backed rebel forces capture the provincial capital town of Stung Treng on the upper Mekong River near the Laotian border and the town of Lomphat in Ratanakiri Province.

5   COMMUNIST CHINA - The government indicates it will not send advisors to assist the Cambodians in the defense of Kampuchea.

6   IRAN - The Shah replaces the two-month-old military government and appoints Shahpour Bakhtiar to be the new civilian government's Prime Minister.

6   PERU - The government orders a state of emergency to halt a threatened 72-hour general strike. At least 120 union officials are arrested in Lima on the first day.

7   UNITED STATES - Additional naval units are sent to the
         Indian Ocean, but the government refuses to tie the
         movements to the Iranian situation. Also, the govern-
         ment announces that after two years of negotiations it
         has reached an agreement which grants the US unencum-
         bered use of its military bases in the Philippines. At
         the same time, US intelligence sources report that
         Communist China has begun massing large numbers of
         military forces on the Vietnamese border.

7   KAMPUCHEA - The   Communist-backed Kampuchean National
         United Front, reinforced with NVA units, takes Phnom
         Penh.

7   GREAT BRITAIN - The government signs an agreement
         granting Brunei independence in 1985.

7   IRAN - Street violence erupts in Tehran following the
         still-exiled Ayatollah Khomeini's demand that the de-
         posed Shah be tried.

8   UNITED STATES - Favoring the construction of smaller
         naval vessels instead, President Carter refuses a
         Pentagon request for authority to build   another
         90,000-ton "Nimitz"-class aircraft carrier.

8   FRANCE - The government reaffirms its support for an
         independent Kampuchea.

8   KAMPUCHEA - An eight-man revolutionary council is
         formed under the leadership of Heng Samrin, a Khmer
         Rouge military leader who rose to power under Pol Pot
         before he defected to Viet Nam.

8   IRAN - Iran's new Prime Minister, Shahpour Bakhtiar,
         states that the nation's $10 billion in military
         contracts will be revised.

9   USSR - The government recognizes the government of
         Heng Samrin in Kampuchea.

10   UNITED NATIONS - Greek- and Turkish-Cypriots accept a
         UN proposal for the resumption of peace talks.

10   ZIMBABWE - The first call-up of black Rhodesians for
         military service fails when only 300 of the 1,554
         ordered to report show up.

10   NICARAGUA - At least 10,000 demonstrate peacefully
         against the Somoza government.

14   ISRAEL - The government expresses its determination to
         build three new settlements in the West Bank and Gaza
         Strip.

15   UNITED NATIONS - The USSR vetoes a Security Council resolution calling for the withdrawal of all foreign forces in Kampuchea.

16   EL SALVADOR - The Mexican Embassy and the Offices of the OAS and the Red Cross are seized by about 30 members of the United Popular Front. More than 120 hostages are taken and ransom, including the release of political prisoners, is demanded. The siege ends after 48 hours, when the terrorists are given safe passage to Mexico.

18   TURKEY - Turkish and US representatives meet in Ankara to discuss a new military treaty alliance.

19   ZIMBABWE - ZAPU forces shell Salisbury for the first time in seven years.

20   UGANDA - The government accuses Tanzania of invading its territory.

24   VATICAN - At the request of Argentina and Chile, the Pope agrees to mediate the Beagle Channel conflict.

25   SOUTH KOREA - The government accepts a North Korean proposal to open preliminary reunification talks.

26   HONG KONG - Numerous sources report the Chinese have moved two divisions to within striking distance of Viet Nam.

26   TANZANIA - The government admits its troops crossed the Ugandan border.

26   IRAN - Military authorities ban all demonstrations throughout the country.

27   ETHIOPIA - The two main Eritrean liberation fronts, ELF and EPLF, create a joint political organ to help settle the war.

28   IRAN - An unknown terrorist attempts to assassinate the US Naval Attache in Tehran by shooting at the officer through the front door of his residence.

30   THE PHILIPPINES - President Marcos revokes his promise of local elections this year and threatens to reinstitute rule by edict.

30   MIDDLE EAST - Iraq and Syria sign a mutual defense pact and declare their intention to create a unified state.

30   ETHIOPIA - The town of Afabet in the subprovince of
            Sahel is captured by Eritrean sessionists. The towns
            of Nakfa and Karora are also in the hands of the
            rebels.

FEBRUARY

1   IRAN - The Ayatollah Khomeini returns to Iran after 14
            years in exile. His first act is to tell the Bakhtiar
            government to resign or he will have them arrested.

3   PAKISTAN - The military government orders the arrest
            of hundreds of members of the former Prime Minister
            Bhutto's Pakistan People's Party.

6   IRAN - The government cancels an order for nearly $7
            billion worth of military equipment from the US.

7   CONGO - The government of President Joachim Yhombi-
            Opango is overthrown in a bloodless coup led by the
            pro-Soviet former Defense Minister, Colonel Denis
            Sassou-Nguesso.

7   CUBA - The government takes possession of a Soviet
            "Foxtrot"-class, diesel-powered, attack submarine. The
            Soviets also give the Cubans two torpedo boats.

8   UNITED STATES - The government recalls 47 of its dip-
            lomats from Nicaragua and orders an end to all mili-
            tary assistance to the Somoza government.

10   UNITED STATES - President Carter announces that the US
            Seventh Fleet will continue to protect Taiwan against
            any Communist Chinese aggression. In a different
            statement, he announces that the withdrawal of US
            forces from South Korea will be halted in light of the
            North Korean military buildup across the DMZ.

11   IRAN - The Bakhtiar government collapses allowing
            Khomeini to take over. Two days later (13 February)
            Bakhtiar is arrested.

12   CHAD - Fighting breaks out in N'Djamena between the
            forces (ANT) of Christian President Felix Malloum and
            those (FAN) of Muslim Premier Hissen Habre. The fight-
            ing soon spreads into the countryside where it in-
            volves the segmented Frolinat rebels. When four French
            civilians are killed, the 2,000-man French garrison
            (plus 400 French advisors with ANT) is reinforced by
            additional French airborne units. President Malloum is
            forced to take refuge in the French garrison and hands

12   CHAD (Cont'd) - over the instruments of power to the Chief of the National Police. On 19 February a cease-fire is arranged between ANT and FAN forces.

12   ZIMBABWE - A Viscount airliner on an internal flight is shot down 29 miles east of Karibe by Joshua Nkomo's ZIPRA forces using two Soviet-built SA-7 "Grail" anti-aircraft missiles. All 59 people on board are killed. The following day (13 February) Nkomo claims responsibility for the attack.

13   TURKEY - The government refuses to allow US Marines stationed at a NATO base at Adana to participate in the evacuation of Americans stranded in Iran.

13   EGYPT - A bomb explodes in the Cairo Sheraton Hotel. Seven people are injured.

14   IRAN - Armed Iranian militants shoot their way into the US Embassy in Tehran wounding two Marine Security Guards and killing one Iranian employee. The US Ambassador and about 100 Embassy employees are taken hostage. The militants leave the Embassy under the supervision of the Deputy Prime Minister of the Provisional Government.

14   AFGHANISTAN - US Ambassador Adolph Dubs is killed in the cross-fire of a Soviet-engineered attempt to rescue a group of hostages held in a Kabul hotel. Dubs had been kidnapped from his car by four right-wing Muslim terrorists and was being held in the hotel when police storm the building.

17   SOUTH KOREA - North and South Korean representatives meet for the first time in six years. Future meetings are planned.

17   VIET NAM - Communist Chinese troops cross the border in force into Viet Nam. Viet Nam immediately declares China is waging a "war of aggression."

18   UNITED NATIONS - The Vietnamese government asks the UN to order the Chinese to withdraw from its territory.

20   VIET NAM - On 18 February Chinese forces capture military positions on the Hong (Red) River just inside the Vietnamese border.

20   NICARAGUA - The Sandanista guerrillas open an all-out offensive against the Somoza regime.

21   IRAN - US naval units evacuate 440 people from the ports of Bandar Abbas and Char Bahar. Two hundred Americans are among the group rescued.

22   UNITED STATES - Intelligence sources report eight
            Soviet naval vessels have moved into the South China
            Sea, apparently in reaction to the Communist Chinese
            attack on Viet Nam of 17 February. Other intelligence
            reports indicate the USSR has begun a massive airlift
            of military supplies to Viet Nam.

22   MIDDLE EAST - More than 100 are killed along the Iraq-
            Iran border in clashes between Kurds and Khomeini sup-
            porters.

23   ZAMBIA - Rhodesian (Zimbabwe) jets attack a national-
            ist guerrilla base near Livingstone to disrupt rebel
            plans to interfere with the upcoming elections.

25   TURKEY - The martial law edict is extended an addi-
            tional two months.

25   MIDDLE EAST - Fighting breaks out along the border
            between North and South Yemen. The US immediately
            announces that it is accelerating the shipment of
            military supplies to the North Yemeni government at
            Sana.

25   UGANDA - Tanzanian military forces supporting Ugandan
            rebels take Masaka on Lake Victoria about 75 miles
            south of Kampala. The Ugandan government admits its
            military forces are being beaten and asks for aid from
            friendly countries.

26   UNITED NATIONS - Secretary General Kurt Waldheim asks
            for a 15 March cease-fire in Namibia.

27   COMMUNIST CHINA - The government asks Viet Nam to en-
            ter into negotiations to end the border war.

28   SAUDI ARABIA - Because of developments in Yemen, the
            Saudi government cancels all military leaves.

MARCH

            AFGHANISTAN - A report indicates that between 20 and
            50 Soviet advisors and technicians are massacred in
            the provincial town of Herat in eastern Afghanistan.

            UGANDA - Libyan reinforcements are sent to Uganda.

1   NORTH YEMEN - Troops of South Yemen (Aden) drive deep
            into North Yemen (San'a) territory.

2   MIDDLE EAST - Iraq and Syria mediate a cease-fire in
            the Yemeni war. Both sides agree to the terms.

4	CHAD - Fresh fighting breaks out and more than 800 casualties are reported.
4	IRAN - The government breaks diplomatic relations with South Africa and refuses to export any more oil to them.
5	UNITED STATES - The US sells $99.8 million in F-5E/F fighter aircraft to Thailand.
5	COMMUNIST CHINA - Claiming it has met all of its military objectives, the government announces it is beginning the withdrawal of its forces from Viet Nam.
5	VIET NAM - The government orders a general mobilization of its armed forces.
6	NORTH YEMEN - Despite the cease-fire, South Yemen aircraft attack targets in North Yemen. The Arab League steps in and establishes a mediation committee to settle the dispute.
7	VIET NAM - The government claims they are still fighting Chinese forces in northern Viet Nam.
7	GHANA - An end to military rule is proclaimed. Parliamentary elections are scheduled for 18 June.
8	VIET NAM - Western sources indicate the Chinese are withdrawing, and that they are destroying everything of value as they go.
8	UNITED NATIONS - The Security Council states the upcoming elections in Rhodesia-Zimbabwe will not be recognized.
9	CHILE - The government extends for six months the state of emergency that has been in effect since 1973.
11	COMMUNIST CHINA - The government announces that Laos has asked it to withdraw its advisors and to close down all of its projects.
12	PAKISTAN - The government announces its decision to withdraw from CENTO.
12	AFGHANISTAN - The Muslim National Liberation Front declares a holy war (jihad) against the regime of Premier Nur Mohammed Taraki.
13	MIDDLE EAST - Both sides in the Yemeni war accept the terms of the Arab League truce and begin disengaging their forces.

13   GRENADA - The government of Prime Minister Sir Eric
            Gairy is ousted in a bloodless coup. The New Revo-
            lutionary Government takes power with Maurice Bishop
            as the leader.

14   AFGHANISTAN - Clashes between government troops and
            rebel Muslims are reported in Paktia Province.

14   MIDDLE EAST - PLO leader Yasser Arafat calls for an
            oil embargo against Egypt if it signs a peace treaty
            with Israel.

14   NICARAGUA - Sandanista guerrillas attack the National
            Guard posts at Chichigalpa, Grenada, and Ticuantepe.

15   TURKEY - Turkey joins Iran and Pakistan by withdrawing
            from CENTO.

15   COMMUNIST CHINA - The government announces its forces
            have completed their withdrawal from Viet Nam.

15   EGYPT - The Cabinet unanimously approves the peace
            treaty with Israel.

16   UNITED STATES - Intelligence sources report a massive
            Soviet buildup ostensibly to conduct maneuvers along
            the Afghan border in the Turkmen Soviet Socialist Re-
            public (SSR) and in the Tadzhik SSR.

16   NIGERIA - At a meeting in Kano a new cease-fire is
            worked out among the 11 Chad factions and a number of
            African states. A Nigerian peacekeeping force is
            established. Accepting Frolinat demands France agrees
            on 20 March, to withdraw its forces stationed in Chad.

19   MIDDLE EAST - A cease-fire is arranged between Iran
            and the Kurdish rebels.

19   UNITED ARAB EMIRATES - More than 3,000 demonstrate in
            favor of President Sheikh Zaid ibn Sultan an-Nahayan's
            proposal for doing away with borders within the Emir-
            ates and unifying the armed forces.

19   USSR - The government verbally attacks Communist
            China, Egypt, and Pakistan for aiding the rebels
            fighting the Taraki regime in Afghanistan.

21   AFGHANISTAN - Fighting has spread to at least five
            provinces. All army leaves are cancelled.

22   THE NETHERLANDS - Terrorists from the Provisional Wing
            of the IRA shoot and kill the British Ambassador, Sir
            Richard Sykes, and his valet as they are entering the
            Ambassador's limousine.

23   UNITED STATES - President Carter warns the USSR on external involvement in the internal affairs of Afghanistan and rejects the Soviet claim that the rebel uprising is US instigated.

23   CHAD - A new government is formed under the leadership of Goukouni Oueddei after both Malloum and Habre resign in accordance with the Kano cease-fire agreement. On 21 August Goukouni Oueddei is reconfirmed as President.

25   GUATEMALA - Unidentified right-wing gunmen assassinate Manuel Colom Argueta, the leader of the Opposition United Front of the Revolutionary Party of Guatemala.

26   UNITED STATES - Egypt's President Sadat and Israel's Menachim Begin sign a peace treaty in Washington, DC.

26   UGANDA - President Amin claims his estate at Entebbe is besieged by Tanzanian troops and tanks.

27   LIBYA - Muammar Qadaffi threatens war on Tanzania if it does not halt its invasion of Uganda.

28   MIDDLE EAST - Israeli forces begin withdrawing from occupied Egyptian territory.

29   UNITED STATES - The House of Representatives halts any further military sales to Jordan until King Hussein begins cooperating with Middle East peace efforts.

29   AFGHANISTAN - Hafizullah Amin is appointed Prime Minister and is placed in charge of the armed forces and the security police.

30   GREAT BRITAIN - The Secretary of State for Northern Ireland, Airey Middleton Neave, is assassinated by Irish extremists when a bomb planted in his car, parked in the underground garage of the House of Commons in London, explodes.

31   MALTA - The British and NATO links with Malta end.

APRIL

AFGHANISTAN - There are reports of widespread defections in the armed forces. Other reports, predominantly Soviet in origin, state that President Taraki requested Soviet military aid to restore order in his country. Lastly, Afghan troops are reported to have killed between 640 and 1,000 civilians (mostly males over seven years of age) in retaliation for rebel activities near the village Kerala.

USSR - General of the Army A. A. Yepishev, the Director of the Main Political Directorate of the Soviet Armed Forces, is reported to be on an official visit to Afghanistan.

1   MALTA - The British give up their naval base after a 179-year presence on the island.

1   IRAN - The Ayatollah Khomeini declares his country an Islamic Republic.

1   CONGO - Former President Yhombi-Opango is tried for treason.

3   COMMUNIST CHINA - The government announces it will not renew the friendship treaty with the Soviet Union that is due to expire in 1980.

5   UGANDA - The airfield at Entebbe is captured by Tanzanian forces.

6   PAKISTAN - Following the execution (in Rawalpindi on 4 April) of former Prime Minister Bhutto, President Zia lifts the martial law edict that has been in effect since 1975. There are massive demonstrations in Karachi protesting the execution.

6   COMMUNIST CHINA - The government accepts a Vietnamese invitation to discuss the border problem.

6   PERU - The government extends the state of emergency a fourth month.

9   IRAN - All new orders for military arms and equipment that were made by the deposed Shah's regime are cancelled by the new government.

10   ZAMBIA - Rhodesian jets attack Joshua Nkomo's ZIPRA military headquarters base near Lusaka.

11   UGANDA - Tanzanian forces capture the capital city of Kampala.

12   TURKEY - Two US servicemen are shot as they walk on a street in Izmir. One is killed and the other seriously wounded. The Turkish People's Liberation Party/Front (TPLP/F) claims credit for the attack. In 1981 four Turks are arrested and accused of the crime.

13   UGANDA - Yusefu Lule becomes the new president. Idi Amin Dada is expelled from the country and travels first to Iraq seeking assistance. Amin finally arrives in Libya where he begins his exile.

13   NICARAGUA - Sandanista forces capture Esteli. Two days later, on 15 April, the National Guard retakes the town.

15   BELGIUM - Alert Belgian and Israeli security personnel thwart an attempted hijacking of an El Al airliner at Brussels Airport.

20   NICARAGUA - Heavy fighting is reported near the Costa Rican border.

22   LEBANON - Fighting breaks out between Syrian forces and the Christian militia.

22   UGANDA - The town of Jinja is captured by Tanzanian forces who also take the important Owens Falls hydro-electric station. Tanzanian forces later arrest former Vice-President Mustafa Adrisi (25 April). At the same time forces still loyal to Idi Amin, disguised as Tanzanian troops, massacre the population of Tororo in eastern Uganda.

24   TURKEY - The government again extends its proclamation of martial law.

24   NICARAGUA - Opposition rebel force leaders meet to coordinate their campaign against the Somoza regime.

25   LEBANON - Israel enters the new fighting by furnishing artillery support to the Christian militia forces. The UN emergency force is able to negotiate a truce.

25   KENYA - Kenyan forces turn back more than 1,000 Ugandan troops who are attempting to flee their own country.

26   NATIONALIST CHINA - The last US military forces leave Taiwan.

30   NICARAGUA - Sandanista forces attack Leon near the west coast.

MAY

1   UNITED NATIONS - The Security Council condemns the Rhodesian elections calling the results null and void.

1   TURKEY - Some Turkish troops are withdrawn from Cyprus to develop a better atmosphere for the pending Summit Talks with Greece.

1   NICARAGUA - National Guard forces reestablish control over Leon.

3   COMMUNIST CHINA - The Chinese admit they took 20,000 casualties, killed and wounded, in the recent war with Viet Nam.

4   ISRAEL - The government informs Egypt that nothing in the Camp David Accords requires an Israeli withdrawal from the West Bank, Golan Heights, or Gaza Strip.

4-24   EL SALVADOR - Antigovernment coalitions of peasants, students, and labor unionists seize the French and Costa Rican Embassies and invade the Cathedral of San Salvador to protest economic and political conditions in the country. On 8 May the hostage held at the Costa Rican Embassy manages to escape. On 9 May, National Guardsmen kill 23 and wound 38 Popular Revolutionary Bloc members demonstrating in support of those holding the cathedral. The Venezuelan Embassy is seized on 11 May by the same coalition. The capital city of San Salvador is paralyzed by an electrical workers strike on 19-20 May. On 22 May, 14 students are killed when police open fire on a group of demonstrators marching to the Venezuelan Embassy in support of those holding the building. Terrorists assassinate the Minister of Education on 23 May (the Swiss Charge d'Affaires is also killed). President Romero imposes a state of siege on 24 May.

11   TURKEY - A group of US service personnel are fired on by unidentified gunmen as they wait for a bus in Istanbul. The Marxist-Leninist Armed Propaganda Unit (MLAPU) takes credit for the attack.

14   USSR - The government acknowledges that its naval forces are using the former US naval facilities at Cam Ranh Bay in Viet Nam as a part of its friendship agreement with the Vietnamese.

15   UNITED STATES - The Senate votes to lift sanctions against Rhodesia. In an unrelated matter the US orders its Ambassador home from Chile after the Chilean government refuses to extradite three secret police officials, including the head of DINA, General Manuel Contreras Sepulveda, accused of planning and ordering the assassination of Orlando Letelier in Washington, DC, in 1976.

15   LIBYA - The government agrees to pay $40 million in ransom for its troops captured by the Tanzanians in Uganda.

15   GHANA - A coup attempt, led by Flight Lieutenant Jerry Rawlings against the military government of Lieutenant General Fred Akuffo, fails. Rawlings is thrown into prison.

16   NATO - The NATO defense ministers express support for SALT II.

18   VIET NAM - When Communist China breaks off peace talks after the fifth session, the Vietnamese accuse China of massing 500,000 troops on the Vietnamese border.

22   CENTRAL AFRICAN REPUBLIC - There are reports that more than 100 children were massacred by Emperor Bokassa I for their participation in demonstrations (19-20 January) against a new order forcing them to wear uniforms purchased from Bokassa's own factory. Later reports, circulated in part by the Central African Republic's Ambassador in France, (c.18 August) assert that Bokassa took a personal hand in the killings.

25   SINAI - El Arish is returned to Egyptian control after 12 years of Israeli occupation.

29   ZIMBABWE - Bishop Muzorrewa is installed as the first black Prime Minister of his country. He immediately appoints himself Minister of Defense (30 May).

JUNE

      AFGHANISTAN - There are reports that at least 2,000 Soviet advisors are in country.

1   UNITED NATIONS - The General Assembly votes economic sanctions against South Africa to force it to comply with the UN-mandated independence of Namibia.

1   EL SALVADOR - The rebels holding the French and Venezuelan Embassies evacuate the buildings.

1   NICARAGUA - Heavy fighting is reported throughout the country. A two-day general strike grips Managua.

4   UGANGA - Tanzanian and Ugandan rebel forces complete their consolidation and announce they hold the entire country.

4   GHANA - A coup overthrows the government of President Fred W. K. Akuffo. Lieutenant Rawlings is released from imprisonment. Shortly afterward, Rawlings has Akuffo and a number of other former leaders and senior gov- ernment officials executed.

5   EGYPT - The government announces it has consummated an arms deal with Communist China.

6   NICARAGUA - Sandanista forces capture Leon. President Somoza declares a state of siege.

7   UNITED STATES - President Carter announces the US will not lift its economic sanctions against Rhodesia.

12   PORTUGAL - The government agrees to a continuation of US use of its air base in the Azores.

16   SOUTH CHINA SEA - A heavily reinforced Soviet naval task force enters the South China Sea.

18   LEBANON - The government sends Lebanese army units into Beirut to halt the fighting in the Christian sector.

18   SWITZERLAND - The US and USSR sign the SALT II Agreement in Berne.

23   OAS - The OAS calls for the ouster of the Somoza government in Nicaragua.

24   TURKEY - The government refuses to allow the US to launch SALT verification flights over the USSR from bases in Turkey or to overfly Turkey on such flights.

25   BELGIUM - An assassination attempt is made on the life of the Commander-in-Chief of NATO Forces, US General Alexander Haig, in Mons. A command-detonated mine, hidden in a culvert, fails to detonate under Haig's car but badly damages a security car following behind. No one is seriously injured. The Red Army Faction's "Commando Andreas Baader" claims responsibility for the attack.

27   LEBANON - Israeli and Syrian jets clash over Lebanon.

JULY

        AFGHANISTAN - Babrak Karmal is appointed Ambassador to Czechoslovakia.

3   ISRAEL - The government announces its decision to suspend arms shipments to Nicaragua.

11   NICARAGUA - A major Sandanista drive aimed at Managua begins.

12   GRENADA - The government signs a two-year technical assistance pact with Cuba.

13   TURKEY - Four Palestinian terrorists belonging to the Syrian-controlled al Saiqa group storm the Egyptian Embassy in Istanbul. A police officer on duty outside the Embassy is killed. Two security personnel inside the Embassy are also killed and 20 people, including

13   TURKEY (Cont'd) - the Ambassador, are taken hostage.
            The terrorists demand that two Palestinians held in
            Egypt be freed, that Turkey break relations with
            Egypt, and that Palestine be recognized. One hostage
            is freed and four others escape during the negotia-
            tions. The terrorists surrender two days later.

15   CZECHOSLOVAKIA - The government arrests ten members of
            the "Charter 77 Human-Rights Movement.'

16   IRAQ - Saddam Hussein at-Takriti becomes President
            following the resignation of Ahmad Hassan al-Bakr.

17   NICARAGUA - President Anastasios Somoza Debayle flees
            the country. The government continues to operate with
            Francisco Urcuyo as head of state. Urcuyo refuses any
            dealings with the Sandanistas.

17   UNITED STATES - US naval units, including the helicop-
            ter landing ship USS Saipan, are on stand-by off the
            coast of Nicaragua in case it becomes necessary to
            evacuate Americans in that country in the wake of
            the fall of the Somoza government.

19   NICARAGUA - Urcuyo flees the country. The National
            Guard surrenders and the Sandanistas take Managua.

20   UNITED NATIONS - The Security Council condemns Israel
            for its establishment of new settlements in the
            occupied territories.

24   FRANCE - The government sells 16 Mirage-50 fighters to
            Chile.

25   SINAI - Israel evacuates its forces from 2,500 square
            miles of the Sinai. Egyptian forces begin filling the
            void thus created.

27   NORTHERN IRELAND - Eighteen British soldiers and a
            civilian are killed in an IRA ambush.

AUGUST

            USSR - The Soviets hold practice exercises airlifting
            about 10,000 troops and their equipment to South Yemen
            and Ethiopia.

3   EQUATORIAL GUINEA - The government of Francisco Macius
            Nguema is deposed by a coup led by a relative, Lieu-
            tenant Colonel Teodoro Obiang Nguema. Macius is subse-
            quently tried and executed for treason, embezzlement,
            and genocide.

4   UNITED STATES - All arms sales to Northern Ireland's Royal Ulster Constabulary are halted by the US.

5   AFGHANISTAN - There is an Army uprising in Kabul which prompts a greater Soviet presence in the country. Loyal government troops, using modern Soviet equipment, crush the rebellion. In the wake of the uprising, General of the Army I.G. Pavlovski, the Deputy Minister of Defense and Commander-in-Chief of the Soviet Ground Forces, visits Kabul and stays until October. (Pavlovski commanded the 1968 Soviet invasion of Czechoslovakia.) There are now about 4,000 Soviet advisors in country. There are also early reports of the Soviets using chemical weapons on suspected rebel villages.

5   UGANDA - President Godfrey L. Binaisa announces the offer of a large reward for the capture and return to Uganda of former President Idi Amin Dada.

6   MAURITANIA - The government signs a peace treaty with Polisario and renounces all claims to Spanish Sahara.

10   MOROCCO - The government announces it is withdrawing its forces from Mauritania.

15   MOROCCO - The government announces the annexation of West Sahara.

17   IRAN - Kurdish forces overrun the border town of Paveh (Pawe) northwest of Kermanshah.

18   FRANCE - The government cuts off aid to the Bokassa government in the Central African Republic when the Emperor is personally implicated in the massacre of school children.

22   CHAD - Rival leaders reach an agreement to end the 16-year-old civil war.

24   UNITED NATIONS - The Security Council opens debate on a resolution calling for the creation of a Palestinian state.

27   IRAN - Heavy fighting is reported between the Kurds and Iranian forces.

27   GREAT BRITAIN - The Crown announces that Fleet Admiral Lord Louis (Francis Albert Victor Nicholas) Mountbatten of Burma had been killed when a bomb placed by terrorists of the Provisional Wing of the IRA blew up the fishing boat of the WWII Supreme Allied Commander in Southeast Asia off the coast of Sligo, Ireland. The IRA later claims credit for the attack.

30   CANADA - Canadian Coast Guard units seize six American
            tuna boats that are fishing without the license re-
            quired by Canada's recently imposed 200-mile coastal
            limit. Two more American tuna boats are captured the
            next day (31 August). They all are released on 1 Sep-
            tember after paying a $5,000 bond each against a court
            appearance.

SEPTEMBER

            AFGHANISTAN - The Soviets begin pressuring President
            Taraki to rid himself of Prime Minister Amin.

1   UNITED STATES - Revised intelligence estimates place
            between 2,000 and 3,000 Soviet combat troops (a bri-
            gade-size unit) in Cuba.

3   EGYPT - President Sadat offers military aid to Morocco
            in its fight against Polisario.

4   SYRIA - Serious religious rioting breaks out in
            Latakia. The government sends in 1,400 army troops to
            restore order.

5   CANADA - Eleven more American tuna boats are charged
            with illegal fishing in Canadian waters.

6   UNITED STATES - The government warns the USSR it will
            not tolerate Soviet troops in Cuba.

7   MOZAMBIQUE - Rhodesian forces carry out an attack on a
            guerrilla base 50 miles inside the Mozambique border.
            The forces withdraw after three days.

10   ANGOLA - President Antonio Agostinho Neto dies follow-
            ing cancer surgery in Moscow. He was 57. He is re-
            placed by acting President Jose Eduardo dos Santos on
            20 September.

11   SAUDI ARABIA - Kenya's President Daniel Torotich arap
            Moi and Somalia's Siyad Barrah (Siad Barre) meet to
            draw up a treaty of friendship and mutual defense.

11   USSR - The government denies it has any combat forces
            in Cuba.

11-13   USSR - Afghanistan's President Taraki visits Moscow
            and is assured of Soviet military support if needed.
            Soviet leaders also warn Taraki about the intrigues of
            his deputy, Hafizullah Amin. Taraki meets with Babrak
            Karmal during his stay.

14-15   AFGHANISTAN - A Soviet-organized coup attempt, in which Soviet Ambassador A. Puzanov is involved, takes place in Kabul. This is apparently a move to assassinate Amin and establish a Taraki-Karmal coalition government. A 400-man Soviet Spetsnaz (Special Forces) unit is sent to Bagram Airport, 40 miles from Kabul. The coup attempt fails and Amin seizes power. Taraki is killed instead, but his death is not announced until 9 October.

14-15   USSR - Soviet units are deployed along the Afghanistan border.

16   USSR - Soviet airborne forces are put on alert.

19   AFGHANISTAN - A general amnesty is declared in an attempt to placate the Muslim population.

19   THE PHILIPPINES - The government refuses a Soviet request to grant visitation rights for all its warships in Filipino ports-of-call.

22   UNITED STATES - The President demands the USSR remove some of its combat forces in Cuba.

23   EL SALVADOR - An American is among the three persons killed when gunmen attack the Armed Forces Instruction Center on the grounds of the Presidential Palace in San Salvador.

24   GHANA - Hilla Limann is elected President.

25   KAMPUCHEA - A Vietnamese-led offensive is launched against Pol Pot forces operating north and northeast of Phnom Penh.

28   CENTO - The Baghdad Treaty organization goes out of existence and its headquarters in Ankara, Turkey closes.

28-29   USSR - After the US and USSR end talks on the issue of Soviet troops in Cuba, the Soviet press attacks the US for threatening intervention into Cuba.

29   EQUATORIAL GUINEA - After being convicted of mass-murder, fraud, and treason, deposed President Francisco Macias Nguema is executed.

OCTOBER

USSR - During this period, the style of Soviet broadcasts into Afghanistan changes in an apparent attempt to pander the country's Muslim clergy.

1   UNITED STATES - President Carter announces the US will
         take additional military steps to counter the Soviet
         military presence in Cuba. The list of steps includes
         the establishment of a permanent Caribbean Joint Task
         Force Headquarters at Key West, Florida. Rear Admiral
         Thomas Replogle is placed in command of the new task
         force (2 October).

2   UNITED STATES - The US turns over control of the Canal
         Zone to Panama after 76 years of occupation.

9   AFGHANISTAN - At this time, when Taraki's death is an-
         nounced, 22 of the 28 Afghan provinces are in rebel
         hands.

9   COMMUNIST CHINA - The government states that talks
         with the USSR have reached an impasse, especially on
         points dealing with the border situation.

10   IRAN - The government reinforces military units en-
         gaged in the fight against the Kurds along the Iraqi
         border.

13   UNITED STATES - The US Senate votes to cut foreign aid
         by 3% in 1981.

15   IRAN - The governor of the province of West Azerbaijan
         states that government forces no longer control the
         city of Mehabad (Mahabad), and that it is in Kurdish
         hands.

17   PAKISTAN - President Zia cancels upcoming general
         elections, institutes censorship, and bans all
         political parties.

17   EL SALVADOR - The government of Carlos Humberto Romero
         is overthrown by a military junta led by Colonels
         Jaime Abdul Gutierrez and Adolfo Arnoldo Majano.
         Romero is exiled. Unrest and violence continue.

18   UNITED STATES - The aircraft carrier USS Midway and
         six other US naval vessels are ordered into the Indian
         Ocean because of a buildup of tensions in the Middle
         East.

20   USSR - As Syria's President Assad departs Moscow after
         a state visit, he receives a pledge of increased mili-
         tary aid.

22   UNITED STATES - The Defense Department announces the
         sale of reconnaissance aircraft and helicopter gun-
         ships to Morocco.

22   SOUTH KOREA - Following student demonstrations, President Park declares the industrial cities of Masan and Pusan military areas.

22   IRAN - Despite earlier government reports that their forces had lost Mehabad to the Kurds, fighting still persists in the city.

24   MAURITANIA - A token force of 150 French troops arrives in Mauritania as a warning to Morocco and the Polisario.

24   EL SALVADOR - The martial law edict is lifted.

25   UNITED STATES - The US gives $12 million in immediate aid to Kampuchea.

25   USSR - The government signs a 20-year friendship and cooperation treaty with South Yemen.

26   SOUTH KOREA - President Park Chung Hee is murdered by the Chief of South Korea's CIA, Kim Jae Kyu. Five others also are killed in the dinnertime incident at a special KCIA restaurant. Kim is arrested later in the evening at the Korean Army's headquarters. Prime Minister Choi Kyu Hah becomes acting President (27 October).

27   UNITED STATES - The US announces detection of a low-yield nuclear explosion in the Indian Ocean near the South African coast on 22 September. The South African government denies all knowledge of any such test or incident.

28   UNITED STATES - The government announces the deployment of a large naval task force into Korean waters in the wake of the assassination of South Korean President Park Chung Hee.

28   SAINT VINCENT - The group of islands in the Lesser Antilles known as Saint Vincent and the Grenadines is given its independence as a constitutional monarchy with the British Commonwealth of Nations.

29   UNITED STATES - In light of South Korean President Park's murder and apprehension over the possibility of anarchy, the US orders military forces on the alert and moves an aircraft carrier into the area as a protective reaction.

29   ZIMBABWE - The Muzorewa government accepts British proposals for a transition of power to a freely elected government.

30-31   EL SALVADOR - Two Marine Security Guards are injured when about 200 leftist demonstrators attempt to storm the US Embassy in San Salvador. The two Marines are wounded when the demonstrators open fire on the Embassy. The demonstrators are finally repulsed when Salvadoran government troops open fire. Twenty-four are killed during these two days in this and other incidents.

NOVEMBER

AFGHANISTAN - There are reports that President Amin is urgently seeking a meeting with Pakistan's Mohammed Zia-ul-Haq.

1-4   BOLIVIA - The government of Walter Guevara Arze is overthrown after less than four months in power. The military coup, led by Colonel Alberto Natusch Busch, seizes power within hours of the close of the General Assembly of the OAS in La Paz. Busch appoints himself president, dissolves Congress, and declares a state of siege. On 2 November, the country is paralyzed by a general strike. At least 200 demonstrators are killed when government troops use tanks and aircraft to disperse a crowd on 4 November.

2   UNITED STATES - The government suspends all military and economic aid to Bolivia.

4   IRAN - Iranian "students" seize the US Embassy in Tehran taking 63 of its American personnel and visitors hostage. They demand that the former Shah of Iran, who is in a New York hospital, be returned for trial.

4   AFGHANISTAN - President Amin refuses an invitation to Moscow to discuss the Muslim uprising.

4   ZIMBABWE - The government reports the lose of 22 soldiers, while claiming to have killed 60 guerrillas in a two-day raid into Zambia.

5   ZIMBABWE - The government halts shipments of maize to Zambia as a means of forcing that government to stop allowing guerrilla operations into Zimbabwe. The Zambian government refuses to yield.

6   IRAN - The Ayatollah Khomeini replaces the government with a revolutionary council.

7   GREAT BRITAIN - The government announces its sanction against Rhodesia (Zimbabwe) will end on 15 November.

9   UNITED STATES - A computer error puts the US on a six-minute nuclear war alert.

9   UNITED NATIONS - The Security Council orders Iran to release the American hostages.

10   UNITED STATES - President Carter orders the deportation of all Iranian students in the US.

12-15   UNITED STATES - The US cuts off all oil imports from Iran and freezes that country's assets in America.

15   UNITED NATIONS - The General Assembly votes to order Viet Nam to remove its military forces from Kampuchea.

15-25   BOLIVIA - More than 250 of the nation's top military personnel issue a proclamation demanding the resignation of President Alberto Natusch Busch. The following day Natusch resigns. On 17 November Lydia Gueiler, the President of the Senate, is sworn in as President. On 24 November there is a short-lived military revolt led by the replaced Army Chief of Staff. The matter is settled the following day.

16   AFGHANISTAN - President Amin demands and gets the removal of Soviet Ambassador Puzanov. Pushanov is replaced by F. Tabaiev, a Soviet Tatar Muslim.

17   UNITED NATIONS - The General Assembly condemns Iran because of the American hostage situation.

18   ZAMBIA - Rhodesian forces blow up three bridges south of Lusaka cutting the principal road links into neighboring Zimbabwe.

19   IRAN - Three Americans (two black male Marines and one female) are freed from captivity at the US Embassy in Tehran on the orders of the Ayatollah.

20   IRAN - Ten more Americans are freed by the Iranians holding the US Embassy in Tehran. All are black or female.

20   UNITED STATES - The government orders a large US naval task force into the Indian Ocean.

20   SAUDI ARABIA - The Grand Mosque in Mecca is seized by a group of Sunni Muslims.

20   ZAMBIA - The government puts the country on full war alert in light of the recent attacks by Zimbabwe and violent demonstrations against the British High Commissioner.

21   PAKISTAN - A mob of students and townspeople attacks
        and destroys the US Embassy in Islamabad after rumors
        are spread that the US has seized the Grand Mosque in
        Mecca. Pakistani troops finally rescue 100 Americans
        stranded in the Chancery. Two US military personnel
        assigned to the Embassy and two Foreign Service
        National employees are killed in the incident.

23   UNITED NATIONS - The Security Council condemns the
        Rhodesian attacks on Zambia.

25   UNITED NATIONS - The Security Council is ordered into
        emergency session over the Iranian situation.

25   MIDDLE EAST - In Phase Four of the Israeli withdrawals
        from the occupied territories, the Alma oil fields on
        the Gulf of Suez are evacuated.

25   NORTH YEMEN - There are reports that the government
        has concluded an arms deal with the USSR that includes
        MiG-21 fighters, antitank weapons, and tanks.

25   ZAMBIA - Rhodesian aircraft bomb a guerrilla base near
        Lusaka.

26   ZIMBABWE - All parties agreeing, the government ac-
        cepts the British cease-fire plan.

26   PAKISTAN - More than 300,000 Afghani refugees have
        arrived in Pakistan after fleeing the civil war raging
        in Afghanistan. Most tell of Soviet personnel being
        actually engaged in the fighting.

27   UNITED STATES - The Department of State warns US citi-
        zens about visiting 11 Islamic states and begins the
        withdrawal of non-essential personnel from the troub-
        led areas.

28   EL SALVADOR - Rebels of the Popular Liberation Front
        kidnap South African Ambassador Gardner Dunn. They
        demand $20 million in ransom and the publication of a
        manifesto denouncing the Salvadoran government.

28   UNITED STATES - The aircraft carrier USS Forrestal is
        ordered to reinforce the US Sixth Fleet in the Med-
        iterranean. The USS Kitty Hawk and five warships are
        deployed to join the USS Midway in the Arabian Sea.

28   SAUDI ARABIA - Pro-Iranian Shi'ite Muslims rebel in
        the oil-rich Eastern Province. The government employs
        20,000 troops to restore order.

29   AFGHANISTAN - Lieutenant General Viktor Patutin, the Soviet First Deputy Minister of Internal Affairs (MVD), arrives in Kabul ostensibly to help the government. His real purpose is to engineer a coup following an earlier decision in Moscow to replace the Amin government.

30   USSR - Month-long Sino-Soviet normalization talks end with no progress reported.

30   UNITED STATES - The Carter Administration imposes sanctions on Chile for refusing to extradite to the US secret police personnel to stand trial for the 1976 murder of Orlando Letelier.

DECEMBER

CZECHOSLOVAKIA - Soviet agents apparently tell Babrak Karmal to be prepared to return to Afghanistan.

AFGHANISTAN - There are reports that the USSR has been contracted to build three new airbases in Afghanistan.

UNITED STATES - Soviet Ambassador Anatoli Dobrinin meets with the Secretary of State to discuss East-West relations before going to Moscow.

1   AFGHANISTAN - The Soviet Ambassador attempts to convince President Amin to accept Soviet troops in Afghanistan. The offer is refused.

1   ETHIOPIA - The government signs a treaty of friendship and cooperation with South Yemen (Aden).

2   LIBYA - The US Embassy in Tripoli is attacked and set on fire by a mob of Libyan demonstrators which includes army personnel. All 14 American and six Foreign Service National (FSN) personnel assigned to the Embassy escape without injury.

3   ETHIOPIA - The Eritrean People's Liberation Movement declares an all-out war against Ethiopian domination in the northwestern province.

3   PUERTO RICO - US naval personnel aboard a bus enroute to a naval communications site are attacked by terrorists. Two naval personnel are killed and ten wounded by gunfire from the terrorists.

4   UNITED NATIONS - A Security Council resolution calls for the immediate release of the American hostages held by Iran.

5   UNITED STATES - The aircraft carrier <u>USS Kitty Hawk</u>
           arrives to reinforce the growing US naval presence (in
           all, 21 ships) in the Arabian Sea.

5   USSR - The government warns the US against taking any
           action in Iran to free the American hostages. At the
           same time, Soviet diplomats in Tehran are instructed
           to   assure   the Khomeini government of unspecified
           support in case of US intervention. During the early
           days of the month, there are a number of Warsaw Pact
           meetings which are attended by the commanders of the
           Soviet Military Districts facing Iran and Afghanistan.
           The government closes the Central Asian region to all
           travel by foreign diplomats and military attaches.

5   SOUTH AFRICA - The government accepts a demilitarized
           zone between Namibia and Angola.

6   SOUTH KOREA - Newly-elected President Choi Kyu Hah
           revokes the emergency decree outlawing all forms of
           political dissent.

6   UNITED STATES - The Senate agrees to lift US sanctions
           against Zimbabwe as soon as the interim British gover-
           nor arrives in Salisbury.

7   IRELAND - Following the unexpected resignation of John
           Lynch (5 December), the former Minister of Health
           Charles J. Haughey is elected Prime Minister by the
           ruling Fianna Fair Party.

8   ANGOLA - A 35-man Soviet military mission arrives in
           Luanda.

8-9   AFGHANISTAN - About 1,000 Soviet airborne troops land
           at Bagram Airport outside Kabul where they join the
           detachment deployed there since September. Control of
           the airbase is now in Soviet hands. A number of other
           small Soviet military units are landed at Kabul Mun-
           icipal Airport.

8-20   AFGHANISTAN - The Soviet forces at Bagram begin clear-
           ing the highway from Kabul west to Termez.

9   IRAN - Fighting breaks out in the northwestern city of
           Tabriz as followers of the Ayatollah Seyed Shariat-
           Madari, one of Khomeini's chief opponents, battle gov-
           ernment troops for control of television and radio
           stations.

11   LIBYA - The government cuts off all financial support
           to the PLO.

11-13   IRAN - Opposition leader Ayatollah Shariat-Madari warns Khomeini that the mishandling of the revolt in Azerbaijan could mean civil war. On 13 December several hundred thousand demonstrators march in Tabriz to support Shariat-Madari.

11-15   USSR - The Ministry of Defense begins mustering transport aircraft in the Moscow area and at military fields near the Afghan border. This is followed by reports (19 December) of massive logistics buildups in the same areas.

12   UNITED STATES - President Carter orders 183 of 218 Iranian diplomats out of the US.

12   SOUTH AFRICA - The South African Air Force opens its ranks for the first time to black cadet pilots.

13   UNITED STATES - The US formally protests the Soviet buildup in Afghanistan.

13   SOUTH KOREA - A group of generals seize a group of buildings in Seoul in an attempt to take power.

13   TANZANIA - The government signs a two-year agreement to train the Ugandan army and police.

14   SOUTH KOREA - Prime Minister Shin Hyon Hwak orders the arrest of a number of individuals charged with conspiracy in the death of Park Chung Hee.

14   TURKEY - Four Americans are killed by terrorists from the Turkish People's Liberation Party/Front (TPLP/F) as they are returning from work at the NATO base in Istanbul.

16   UNITED STATES - The government lifts its sanctions against Rhodesia.

16   SAUDI ARABIA - Saudi troops are finally able to dislodge the Muslim fanatics holding the Grand Mosque.

19   AFGHANISTAN - An abortive attempt is made on President Amin's life. He is wounded, his nephew killed. The operation is apparently run by the Soviet KGB.

21   LIBYA - The PLO offices in Libya are ordered closed by the government.

21   UNITED NATIONS - The UN lifts its 13-year-old sanctions against Rhodesia (Zimbabwe).

22   SOMALIA - The government offers the US access to the former Soviet naval facility at Berbera.

23	UNITED STATES - The US accuses the USSR of threatening Afghanistan by the dispatch of 1,500 troops to Kabul and by a military buildup along the Soviet-Afghan border.
23	USSR - The government calls Western allegations of Soviet interference in Afghanistan "lies."
24-26	AFGHANISTAN - About 200 sorties by Soviet military air transports lift 10,000 troops of the Soviet 105th Guards Airborne Division into a landing area near Kabul.
27	AFGHANISTAN - President Amin is overthrown, captured at the Darulaman Palace outside Kabul, and shot, along with members of his family, in a coup led by Soviet special purpose (Spetsnaz) forces. The Soviet-run Radio Kabul makes the announcement of Amin's ouster. Upon his return to Afghanistan, Babrak Karmal becomes President with Soviet backing. MVD General Patutin is reported killed "near Kabul" and may have died in the attack on the Presidential Palace. Most senior Afghan officers who refuse to "cooperate" with the Soviets are taken out and summarily executed.
28	AFGHANISTAN - Soviet airborne forces are in complete control of Kabul.
28	USSR - Moscow justifies its actions in Afghanistan as a response to an urgent request from the Kabul government under the terms of a 20-year treaty of friendship.
28	UNITED STATES - President Carter condemns the Soviet invasion of Afghanistan.
29	AFGHANISTAN - The lead elements of at least two Soviet motorized rifle divisions (MRD) cross the border into Afghanistan.
29	UNITED STATES - President Carter warns Soviet leader Leonid Brezhnev that the invasion of Afghanistan will "severely and adversely affect Soviet-American relations." The President further castigates Brezhnev for not telling him the truth and for not responding candidly to his questions about the situation. Carter goes on to intimate that the US and its Allies are contemplating retaliatory action.
30	UNITED STATES - The US warns the USSR that it will use force to defend Pakistan under the terms of a 1959 defense agreement.

30   EGYPT - President Sadat announces that he will provide military facilities for US forces engaged in defending Arab countries in the Middle East.

30   AFGHANISTAN - Soviet strength in Afghanistan is estimated at 25,000 troops.

30   ZIMBABWE - The British governor, Lord Soames, orders Rhodesian troops into Mozambique to halt guerrillas operating in violation of the cease-fire.

31   UNITED STATES - The defense treaty with Nationalist China (Taiwan) expires.

31   UNITED NATIONS - The Security Council gives Iran one week to release the American hostages.

Notes

1980

UNITED STATES - A special group of soldiers, airmen, Marines, and Navy personnel is selected to participate in a rescue mission designed to free the American hostages in Iran.

1   UNITED NATIONS - Pakistan and a number of other nations put forward a Security Council resolution condemning the USSR for the invasion of Afghanistan.

1   IRAN - Heavy fighting between Iranian troops and Kurdish rebels is reported in Sanandaj in northwestern Iran.

1   RHODESIA - Rhodesian troops clash with guerrilla forces at the time when the British Governor, Lord Soames, is pleading with the rebels to turn themselves in to assembly points as stipulated in the peace agreement.

2   AFGHANISTAN - The new regime criticizes the US for meddling in Afghan internal affairs and says the Soviets were invited to help protect the country against its enemies. As soon as the crisis is past, the Soviets will go home.

3   UNITED STATES - The government orders its Ambassador in Moscow, Thomas J. Watson, Jr., home for consultations in the wake of the Soviet invasion of Afghanistan. The US also approaches Communist China in a bid to get that country's assistance in helping Pakistan build up its defense against a possible Soviet attack.

3   AFGHANISTAN - Reports from a number of diplomatic sources indicate Soviet troops are engaged with Afghan rebels about 100 miles from Kabul in Bamian Province. Pakistan sources indicate fighting between Soviet and rebel forces is widespread throughout the country especially in Badakhshan Province and in the cities of Kunar and Nuristan near the Pakistani border.

3   IRAN - Mohammed Hojatolislan, an Iranian religious leader, states that thousands of Iranians will travel to South Lebanon to fight the Israelis.

3   INDIA - Afghani students occupy the Afghanistani Embassy in New Delhi and hold several Afghan diplomats hostage in a protest against the Soviet invasion of their country.

4   UNITED STATES - President Carter orders a grain embargo on the USSR in reprisal for the Afghanistan invasion and wins Congressional support to lift the arms embargo on Pakistan.

4   MAURITANIA - Head of state Lieutenant Colonel Mohamed Mahmoud Ould Louly is ousted from office and replaced by Lieutenant Colonel Mohamed Khouna Ould Haidalla.

4   AFGHANISTAN - Afghan rebels claim to have ambushed a Soviet column on the road from Kabul northwest into Bamian Province. Several tanks and armored vehicles are reported to have been destroyed before the column withdrew. Also, a number of Soviet trucks in Afghanistan are noted to have been built in the USSR at the Kama River truck plant with American-supplied technology.

4   PANAMA - National Guard troops injure 25 students demonstrating against the presence in their country of the deposed Shah of Iran.

4   EL SALVADOR - Leftist rebels of the Popular Liberation Force seize five radio stations in San Salvador.

5   PAKISTAN - At least 400,000 Afghan refugees are said to have crossed into Pakistan to avoid Soviet attacks on their towns. There are also reports that the leaders of the five Afghan rebel factions have met to form a unified front against the Soviet invaders.

5   AFGHANISTAN - Soviet forces occupy Kandahar, Ghazni and Jalalabad.

5   FRANCE - The French sell 24 Mirage F-1 fighters to Iraq.

5   EGYPT - President Anwar Sadat renews his offer of fa-
     cilities, but not bases, should the US come to the aid
     of any Arab nations asking for help.

5   EL SALVADOR - Leftist rebels of the February 28
     Popular League attack a National Guard headquarters in
     San Salvador.

6   UNITED NATIONS - Pakistan and Egypt denounce the
     Soviet invasion of Afghanistan in the continuing
     Security Council debate over the problem.

6   AFGHANISTAN - Mutinies are reported in Afghan army
     units with at least one report of a unit defecting to
     the rebels at Urgun. There are further reports of
     Soviet troops looting homes and shops. Most Soviet
     troops have left Kabul and occupied positions on the
     environs of the city.

6   INDIA - The government warns that if the US continues
     giving military aid to Pakistan India will step up its
     nuclear weapons program.

6   LIBYA - The government severs relations with Al Fatah,
     the Palestinian commando group, and halts all financ-
     ial support because of alleged deviation from the
     principles of armed struggle against Israel.

7   USSR - The government states that proposed US sanc-
     tions against the Soviet Union will hurt America more
     than it will the USSR.

7   NORTHERN IRELAND - A landmine kills three members of
     the Ulster Defense Regiment in County Down.

8   UNITED NATIONS - The USSR vetoes a Security Council
     resolution calling for the immediate withdrawal of
     Soviet forces from Afghanistan.

8   AFGHANISTAN - At least 24 Soviet soldiers have been
     killed by Afghan snipers in the Kabul area in the last
     two weeks.

8   UNITED STATES - Intelligence sources indicate that
     there are at least 85,000 Soviet troops in Afghani-
     stan, and that the number will soon exceed 100,000.
     The Department of State accuses the Soviet Union of
     preparing a permanent operating base in Afghanistan.

9   SAUDI ARABIA - The government publicly beheads 63
     participants in the November 1979 raid on the Grand
     Mosque at Mecca.

9   NATO - Under the terms of a new agreement, NATO has 24 bases available for its use on Turkish soil.

9   UNITED STATES - US intelligence reports indicate that it is the Afghan army that is primarily engaged with the rebels. This tends to contradict State Department and press reports. The DOD sources claim the Soviets are spending their time rebuilding the Afghan armed forces and strengthening positions around major towns, highways, and airfields. It is the consensus that the Soviets are preparing for a long stay.

10   AFGHANISTAN - Soviet units are patrolling Kabul at night. Western diplomats in Kabul say the evidence is overwhelming that the Karmal government is summarily executing all political prisoners. At least 45 Soviet and Afghan soldiers are killed in five separate clashes around Kabul.

11   UNITED NATIONS - The General Assembly takes up the question of Afghanistan.

11   UNITED STATES - The government announces it does not contemplate any punitive actions against the USSR because of the Afghanistan invasion.

11   AFGHANISTAN - Western diplomatic and press sources claim the Soviet's principle effort appears to be clearing and securing the road network toward the Iranian border. Analysts will eventually claim that the Soviet's long-term goal is the establishment of military bases on the Persian Gulf which would mean the invasion of Iran.

12   USSR - The government warns the US about the effects of any reprisal measures in the Afghanistan situation, such as cutting off of grain sales as ordered by the White House. Moscow goes on to state that the decision to intervene in Afghanistan was a difficult one.

12   AFGHANISTAN - About 800 Afghans attack the prison in Pul-i-Charkhi to force the release of political prisoners held there. At least 12 prisoners are freed before Afghan and Soviet troops arrive to restore order.

12   UNITED STATES - Intelligence sources indicate that between 900 to 1,200 Soviet troops have been killed in Afghanistan since the invasion began December 1979. The sources also indicate that Soviet troops have taken part in the execution of at least 300 Afghan political prisoners.

12   EL SALVADOR - Leftist rebels of the February 28 Popular League seize the Panamanian Embassy in San Salvador. They take as hostages, among others, the Panamanian and Costa Rican Ambassadors and demand the immediate release of three of their jailed compatriots.

13   UNITED NATIONS - The USSR vetoes a US proposal for sanctions against Iran where a group of US citizens are still held hostage.

13   EGYPT - In a show of displeasure over the Soviet invasion of Afghanistan, the government orders the USSR to reduce its diplomatic staff in Cairo by more than one-third.

14   UNITED NATIONS - The General Assembly votes 104-18 (with 30 abstentions) to condemn the USSR for its invasion of Afghanistan and orders an "immediate, unconditional, and total withdrawal of foreign troops" from that country.

14   UNITED STATES - The US offers Pakistan $400 million to be distributed over the next two years. The funds are to be used for military and economic aid to help the country strengthen its defenses against further Soviet expansion.

15   ETHIOPIA - The Eritrean Peoples' Liberation Front claims 5,000 government troops have been killed, wounded, or captured in a five-day battle at the Mahimet army base.

15   REPUBLIC OF IRELAND - Police carrying out an anti-terrorist raid seize more than a ton of explosives and bombs found in an abandoned farmhouse near the town of Dundalk, on the border with Northern Ireland.

15   EL SALVADOR - The siege at the Panamanian Embassy ends when the ruling junta releases seven jailed members of the February 28 Popular League group. All hostages are released unharmed.

16   IRAN - Western sources in Tehran report that Afghan rebels have been receiving substantial military aid from Iranian tribesmen in the Baluchistan region of West Pakistan.

18   NORTHERN IRELAND - IRA terrorists explode a bomb on a crowded commuter train in a tunnel near Belfast. Three are killed. There are two other explosions in the province within minutes of the first blast.

19   MIDDLE EAST - A teen-age Lebanese Shi'ite Muslim hi-
            jacks a Lebanese airliner over the Mediterranean and
            demands to know the whereabouts of his spiritual
            leader, Imam Musa Sadr, who disappeared in 1978. The
            incident ends with the hijacker's arrest at Beirut
            airport.

20   CENTRAL AFRICAN REPUBLIC - The government breaks dip-
            lomatic relations with the Soviet Union.

21   UNITED STATES - President Carter says the US will use
            force, if necessary, to protect Pakistan against
            Soviet attack.

22   COLOMBIA - Fifty urban guerrillas attack a police
            station in El Paraiso killing three policemen.

22   MIDDLE EAST - President Carter orders US B-52 bombers
            to overfly Soviet naval vessels in the Arabian Sea as
            a demonstration of American military power.

22   USSR - Nobel Peace Prize winner Andrei D. Sakharov is
            deprived of his Soviet honors by the Presidium of the
            Supreme Soviet and exiled to the city of Gorky. The
            action is taken in retaliation for his outspoken
            condemnation of Soviet intervention in Afghanistan.

23   AFGHANISTAN - Figures indicate that the USSR has had
            2,000 soldiers killed, wounded, or missing since the
            invasion began.

23   UNITED STATES - President Carter announces the US will
            protect the Persian Gulf area from Soviet encroach-
            ment.

23   EL SALVADOR - At least 20 civilians are killed when
            100,000 antigovernment leftist demonstrators are fired
            on by civilians.

24   EL SALVADOR - Leftist rebels attack a police station
            in San Salvador; three are killed, the remainder flee
            back into the city where they take refuge at the
            National University which is under student control.

25   UNITED STATES - In a major policy shift, the Carter
            Administration announces it will sell arms to Com-
            munist China. The shift is related to the growing
            Afghanistan crisis.

25   LEBANON - Several persons are injured when uniden-
            tified gunmen attempt to break into an army barracks
            in Sidon.

25   SINAI - In compliance with the first two phases of the
      Camp David withdrawal agreement, Israeli forces evacu-
      ate (Operation RAMON) the strategically important,
      5,560-square-mile area generally located along a line
      Al-Arish to Ras Muhammad. Egyptian forces subsequently
      occupy the territory.

26   PAKISTAN - In an interview in Islamabad, Afghan rebel
      leader Zia Khan Nassry claims his forces control the
      provinces of Ghazni, Logar, and Paktia in eastern
      Afghanistan. The "Free Islamic Republic" is proclaimed
      as the rightful government in Afghanistan.

27   UNITED STATES - US officials express concern that Viet
      Nam may be preparing for an operation inside Thailand
      to disperse Cambodian refugees camped along the
      border. At least 200,000 Vietnamese troops are known
      to be in Cambodia supporting the Communist government
      of Heng Samrin. About 50,000 of them are deployed
      along the Thai border.

28   AFGHANISTAN - Evidence continues to mount that Soviet
      forces are employing chemical warfare against the
      Afghan rebels.

28   GUATEMALA - The Guatemalan insurgent Guerrilla Army of
      the Poor is reported to have begun recruiting native
      Indians into its ranks in the populated mountainous
      region in the northwestern part of the country.

29   IRAN - Six US citizens who had been trapped in Iran
      and who took refuge in the Canadian Embassy at the
      time of the takeover of the US Embassy are spirited
      out of the country with the help of the Canadian
      Embassy and forged exit visas.

29   EL SALVADOR - A group of more than 30 terrorists seize
      the headquarters of the Christian Democratic Party in
      San Salvador. At least 17 are taken hostage. In a
      separate incident, leftist rebels of the Unified
      Popular Action Front seize a church in Ilobasco in
      retaliation for the killing of 22 demonstrators on 23
      January. Army forces attack the church killing three
      rebels.

30   LEBANON - Israeli and Lebanese Christian artillery
      bombards Tyre causing heavy damage.

30   FRANCE - A bomb explosion at the Syrian Embassy in
      Paris kills one and injures eight. The Syrian gov-
      ernment accuses the US and Israel of committing the
      act of terrorism, but three unknown Arab groups claim
      responsibility.

30   RHODESIA - At least 17,300 guerrillas turn themselves
            in to Rhodesian and British authorities at the check
            points.

31   AFGHANISTAN - A slackening in the pace of Soviet
            operations against the rebels is noted, but scattered
            and effective rebel resistance continues.

31   GUATELMALA - The Spanish Embassy in Guatemala City is
            seized by a group of 39 Quiche Indians who claim to be
            members of a leftist organization. They take hostage
            the Ambassador, Maximo Cajal y Lopez, and a number of
            others. After the police storm the building it burns
            down in a fire probably caused by a gasoline bomb
            carried by one of the terrorists. Thirty-eight of the
            terrorists and all the hostages except the Ambassador
            are killed. The Ambassador is kidnapped from the
            hospital bed in which he is recuperating from the
            ordeal and murdered the following day (1 February).

FEBRUARY

            UNITED STATES - Intensive and highly secret training
            for the Iran rescue mission begins.

2   UNITED STATES - The US announces it would be willing
            to sell sophisticated military equipment to India if
            Delhi will defer its plans to increase nuclear weapons
            production.

2   SPAIN - The government breaks diplomatic relations
            with Guatemala over its handling of the hostage
            situation which killed 36 people.

2   PAKISTAN - Afghan refugees claim that Soviet reserve
            troops entering Afghanistan are being told they are
            going to fight American and Chinese forces who have
            invaded the Soviet Union. Many reservists are being
            returned to the USSR because they are too friendly
            with the Afghans or because they are themselves
            Muslims.

3   IRAQ - The government denounces the Soviet invasion of
            Afghanistan.

4   LIBYA - The French Embassy in Tripoli is destroyed and
            the French Consulate in Benghazi wrecked by Libyan
            demonstrators, probably organized by the government,
            protesting French support of Tunisia.

4   ISRAEL - A terrorist bomb kills six in the Tel Aviv
            suburb of Rehovot. The Democratic Front for the
            Liberation of Palestine claims credit for the blast.

4   EL SALVADOR - Rosario Church in San Salvador is at-
         tacked by rightists who machine-gun the mostly leftist
         congregation. Only one person is killed, but 17 are
         injured.

5   IRAN - The Ayatollah Khomeini condemns the Soviet
         invasion of Afghanistan and pledges full support for
         the rebels.

5   EL SALVADOR - The Spanish Embassy in San Salvador is
         seized by 50 terrorists representing the February 28
         Popular League. The Spanish Ambassador is among those
         taken hostage and held for the release of 13 political
         prisoners and a visit by an OAS inspection team. A
         newly formed rightist group, the Central American
         Liberation Front, threatens to burn down the embassy
         if the leftists do not evacuate immediately. Another
         group, calling themselves the Revolutionary Salvadoran
         Student Movement, seizes the Ministry of Education and
         takes a number of hostages.

5   SYRIA - The government announces it will withdraw its
         peacekeeping force in Lebanon in the next few days and
         move the remainder of its forces out of Beirut.

6   SYRIA - President Hafez al-Assad tells Lebanon he will
         not withdraw Syrian peacekeeping forces until the
         Lebanese have an effective government or an effective
         security force.

6   CAMBODIA - Heavy fighting is reported between Viet-
         namese forces and Pol Pot troops at Phnom Chat.

8   CUBA - Fidel Castro admits there are 36,000 Cuban
         troops in Angola and another 12,000 in Ethiopia.

10   IRAN - The government issues a statement that it is
         convinced that recent Soviet troop movements near the
         Iranian border are designed to silence Iranian criti-
         cism of Soviet actions in Afghanistan.

10   AFGHANISTAN - Heavy fighting is reported in eastern
         Afghanistan. Large numbers of Soviet reinforcements
         are moving into the area.

10   KUWAIT - The government says the nation will take part
         in the liberation of Arab lands held by Israel.

11   AFGHANISTAN - Afghan rebels capture two towns in
         Badakhshan Province and have the Soviet garrison at
         Faizabad near the Soviet border surrounded and under
         siege.

11   BANGLADESH - Two demonstrators are killed and 50
           wounded protesting last week's killing of three and
           wounding of 37 in the earlier demonstration.

12   SOMALIA - The government agrees to furnish the US with
           military bases in return for military aid.

12   KENYA - The government agrees to furnish the US with
           military bases in return for military aid.

12   EL SALVADOR - The terrorists holding the Ministry of
           Education leave the building. They are then engaged by
           the police; three are killed. Police also attack the
           group holding the Christian Democratic Party head-
           quarters and kill seven terrorists (23 are wounded and
           captured).

12   UNITED STATES - The Department of State estimates that
           95,000 Soviet troops are in Afghanistan.

13   ISRAEL - The government accuses the USSR of supplying
           the PLO with 60 World War II T-34 tanks and other
           armored vehicles.

14   EGYPT - Defense Minister Kamal Hassan Ali discloses
           that Egypt is training Afghan rebels.

14   COMMUNIST CHINA - There are reports of a major shakeup
           in the Chinese armed forces as a part of efforts to
           modernize the military structure of the country.

15   AFGHANISTAN - A gun battle is reported to have broken
           out among members of the Soviet-backed Karmal govern-
           ment in Kabul. At least one minister is killed and
           several wounded including Karmal's deputy Asadolla
           Sarvari. Rumors persist that Karmal is under house
           arrest.

17   INDIA - Prime Minister Indira Gandhi dissolves the
           assemblies in nine states and places their admini-
           stration under the central government.

17   LEBANON - Heavy fighting continues in northern
           Lebanon. Following a six-day artillery duel between
           Christian Phalangist and Syrian forces, at least 60
           are reported dead in Gnat. The Christians are also
           reported to be fighting among themselves.

17   ISRAEL - Two terrorist bombings in the Gaza Strip kill
           two and injure eleven persons.

18   EL SALVADOR - When the government releases 11
           political prisoners the siege at the Spanish Embassy
           ends.

19   EUROPE - The European Community offers to guarantee Afghanistan's neutrality if the Soviet Union will withdraw it forces from that country. The note is delivered to the Soviet Ambassador in London on 28 February.

21   AFGHANISTAN - The capital city of Kabul is gripped by a general strike to protest the presence of Soviet troops. At least 300 are killed in the violence that accompanies the strike.

22   AFGHANISTAN - Martial law is declared in Kabul, and all Afghan forces are brought under a "joint" command headed by Soviet officers.

22   UNITED STATES - The State Department estimates that the Soviets will have to commit an additional 400,000 troops into Afghanistan to gain effective control of the entire country.

23   UNITED STATES - The government announces it will furnish military aid to El Salvador as part of a plan to thwart a Marxist takeover of Honduras.

24   USSR - Official Soviet sources acknowledge that Afghan rebels are offering serious resistance in Kabul and a number of other cities.

24   AFGHANISTAN - The road between Kabul and Peshawar, Pakistan is closed by the Afghan army.

24   LEBANON - Eight persons are killed and 20 injured in Beirut by a bomb set off to assassinate Bashir Gemayle, the Lebanese, right-wing Christian militia commander. Gemayle's daughter, his driver and two bodyguards are killed in the blast. Gemayle was not in the car.

25   SURINAM - A group of noncommissioned officers overthrow the government of Prime Minister Henck Arron. A new military-controlled government is set up with Hendrick R. Chin A Sen as Prime Minister (15 March).

25   SYRIA - The government indefinitely postpones the withdrawal of its 8,000-man peacekeeping force from Beirut in view of a possible Israeli sweep into southern Lebanon.

26   AFGHANISTAN - A number of Shi'ite Muslims are arrested on charges of fomenting trouble.

26   MIDDLE EAST - In formal ceremonies Israel and Egypt exchange ambassadors.

27   COLOMBIA - About 20 terrorists of the leftist April 19
            Movement (M-19) seize the Embassy of the Dominican
            Republic in Bogota. Fifty-seven members of the diplo-
            matic community, including the ambassadors of Austria,
            Brazil, Costa Rica, Dominican Republic, Egypt, Guate-
            mala, Haiti, Israel, Mexico, Switzerland, United
            States, Uruguay (later escapes), and Venezuela are
            taken hostage. Five are wounded in the attack. The
            terrorists demand the release of 311 political
            prisoners and $50 million in ransom. By 27 April all
            the hostages have been released, a $2.5 million ransom
            has been paid, and the terrorists get safe passage to
            Cuba.

27   AFGHANISTAN - Mass arrests are reported in Kabul where
            authorities are seeking ways of ending the strikes
            that have paralyzed the city.

27   UNITED STATES - President Carter says the US is ready
            to join other nations in guaranteeing Afghan neutral-
            ity if the Soviet Union withdraws from that country.

27   EL SALVADOR - Fifteen leftist rebels are killed in a
            clash with government security forces in Sonsonate.

MARCH

1   UNITED NATIONS - All 15 members of the UN Security
            Council, including the US, vote to order the Israeli
            government to dismantle its new settlements in the
            Gaza Strip and in the West Bank.

2   AFGHANISTAN - Soviet forces are reportedly building
            permanent structures such as barracks and radio
            stations. This tends to reinforce the prediction that
            the USSR intends to maintain a presence in Afghanistan
            for quite some time.

2   LEBANON - Fighting breaks out between Palestinians and
            government forces in Beirut.

2   EL SALVADOR - A bomb levels the city hall in Caluco.
            Three police officers are killed by unidentified
            assailants in Ilobasco.

3   AFGHANISTAN - Heavy fighting is reported in Kunar
            Province on the Pakistani border where Soviet and
            Afghan army forces are attacking rebel strongholds.

5   PAKISTAN - Foreign Minister Agha Shahi announces that
            his government has found the US offer of $400 in aid
            is too little and therefore "unacceptable," as it
            would hinder rather than assist Pakistani security.

5   AFGHANISTAN - Rebel sources report a Soviet and Afghan victory in Kunar Province where a large number of villages between Chagasarei and Asmar have been destroyed. Rebels of the Jamiati Islami group accuse the Soviets of using napalm and poison gas. Some reports claim the gas used was an incapacitating agent and not lethal.

5   CAMBODIA - Pol Pot rebels attack a bridge construction site at Phnom Melai where Vietnamese forces are upgrading the road for the movement of armor and heavy equipment.

6   UNITED STATES - The government authorizes $5 million in military aid to Honduras.

7   UNITED STATES - Military analysts feel the Soviet Union is about to send an additional 40,000 troops into Afghanistan. The unexpectedly stubborn rebel resistance is causing about 400-600 casualties a week.

7   AFGHANISTAN - The rebel leader of the Hizbe Islami, Gulbadin Hekmatyar, claims Kunar Province has not been overrun by the Soviets, but that resistance continues in this area near the Pakistani border. He claims the Soviets lost 300 killed and 1,100 wounded in the Kunar operation, and that at least 110,000 Afghans on all sides have been killed in the last 20 months of fighting.

8   LEBANON - Fifteen hundred Syrian troops are withdrawn from Beirut in a planned turnover of responsibility by the Christian sector to the Lebanese Army. The Syrians are relocated in the Bekaa Valley in eastern Lebanon.

9   USSR - Reports of heavy casualties in Afghanistan ignite rumors all over the Soviet Union. The government and the press remain silent on the question of casualties but Western diplomats claim at least 3,000 to 5,000 have been killed.

12   PAKISTAN - Military sources in Pakistan report that Soviet forces are pressing their attacks in Kunar Province but have not as yet been completely successful in eliminating rebel resistance. Refugees claim Soviet forces are razing their villages so they will not be able to return to Afghanistan.

13   PERU - The government accepts delivery of two squadrons of Soviet-built Su-22 "Fitter" jet fighters.

14   USSR - The government rejects the European Community offer on Afghanistan.

14   LEBANON - Palestinian guerrillas and leftist Lebanese militiamen clash in Beirut.

15   SYRIA - The government sends 10,000 troops into Aleppo as a show of force against the opponents of President Hafez al-Assad.

16   SCOTLAND - Police arrest 40 rightest demonstrators in a banned protest march against Irish terrorists.

16   UGANDA - At least 10,000 Tanzanian troops are reported as remaining in Uganda one year after helping the Ugandan army oust Idi Amin.

18   EL SALVADOR - At least 41 leftist student demonstrators are killed in a clash with police near the National University.

18   PUERTO RICO - On the busy Las Americas Expressway, terrorists, favoring Puerto Rican independence, ambush a vehicle carrying three uniformed US Army Reserve Officers Training Corps instuctors. One soldier is wounded.

19   THAILAND - Intelligence sources indicate that at least 45 refugees are killed in fighting between rival factions of the Cambodian National Liberation Movement at a camp near the Thai border.

19   SYRIA - There are reports that President Assad has authorized Palestinian raids into Israel from the Golan Heights, which has been out of bounds to guerrillas since Syria concluded the disengagement agreement with Israel in 1974.

21   THAILAND - Fighting continues between rival anti-Communist factions in a number of refugee villages along the Thai-Cambodia border. In the Sisophon Distict Thai troops enter the fight after armed Cambodians cross into Thailand. Vietnamese artillery fires into Thailand from Cambodian firing positions. More than 100 are reported dead.

22   UNITED STATES - President Carter is briefed on a plan to free the hostages held in Iran.

22   LEBANON - Most of the Syrian Army forces remaining in Beirut are withdrawn to positions in the Bekaa Valley.

23   PANAMA - After President Anwar Sadat offers him permanent asylum, the deposed Shah of Iran, Mohammad Reza Pahlavi, leaves Panama with his family for Egypt.

24   COMMUNIST CHINA - Reacting to the Afghanistan crisis, Great Britain sends Defense Minister Francis Pym to Peking to discuss the sale of British military arms.

24   EL SALVADOR - Catholic Archbishop Oscar Arnulfo Romero y Galdamez, an outspoken critic of repression, is assassinated while saying Mass in San Salvador.

24   CHAD - Foreigners fleeing the country report that several days of street fighting between troops loyal to President Goukouni Oueddei, and those supporting his rival Hissen Habre, have caused the deaths of more than 700 persons in N'Djamena in the last three days.

25   CHAD - French military forces evacuate nearly half of the 900 whites in N'Djamena as the heavy fighting continues.

26   CHAD - Although there is movement toward a cease-fire, a new element is added as the sector of the city controlled by Habre's forces is shelled by troops loyal to Vice-President Wadal Abdel Kader Kamougue. Fighting later erupts between the two principal contenders for power, Hissen Habre and President Goukouni Oueddei. Truce talks are halted.

29   INDIA - The government puchases $1.6 billion in military equipment from the Soviet Union.

30   EL SALVADOR - At least 30 mourners are killed and more than 400 injured in a stampede started by gunfire and grenades at the funeral of Archbishop Romero. About 75,000 are forced to flee when the firing and bombing start. The terrorist attack is most likely the work of a right-wing faction.

30   AFGHANISTAN - Soviet forces are said to have virtually wiped out Afghan rebel resistance in the Kunar Valley and Badakshan Province.

30   IRAQ - The government announces that an Iranian attack on one of its border outposts has been repulsed.

30   UNITED STATES - The US signs an agreement with Turkey authorizing continued American use of military bases in Turkey in exchange for economic and military aid.

31   CHAD - A cease-fire is put into effect.

APRIL

        UNITED STATES - President Carter approves the plan for the rescue of the American hostages held in Iran.

1   AFGHANISTAN - Rebels kill 75 government troops in Samangan and capture the towns of Roidoab and Saf.

1   CHAD - Fighting breaks out again in Chad as troops loyal to Foreign Minister Abmat Acyl join Oueddei's forces.

2   CHAD - A new battle for control of N'Djamena begins and will last for at least ten days without any sign of victory or defeat for either side. At least 1,500 are killed.

4   UNITED STATES - Police in Evanston, Illinois, arrest 11 members of the Armed Forces of National Liberation (FALN), a terrorist organization advocating independence for Puerto Rico. All are subsequently convicted of a number of various state and federal statute violations, including 28 bombings.

4   SOUTH AFRICA - Black urban guerrillas attack a police station in Johannesburg causing considerable damage but no deaths.

5   AFGHANISTAN - An apparent stalemate sets in as Soviet forces control the cities and lines of communications while the rebels control the countryside. Western sources report heavy casualties among the rebels and tend to discount exaggerated claims by rebel leaders as to the number of Soviet casualties.

7   UNITED STATES - After learning that the Ayatollah Khomeini intended to hold the US hostages until after the election of the Parliament (Majlis) in the late spring, President Carter severs diplomatic relations with Iran and orders all Iranian diplomats to leave the US within 24 hours. The President also imposes an embargo on all US exports to Iran.

7   ISRAEL - A squad of Palestinian terrorists infiltrates the Israeli border from Lebanon and attacks the Misgav Am Kibbutz where it takes a number of children as hostages. Four Israelis are killed in the ensuing fight. Israeli army troops storm the children's dormitory in the kibbutz, killing five of the terrorists.

8   LEBANON - A force of about 300-350 Israeli troops crosses into southern Lebanon and digs into positions five miles inland from the border in the Kunin-Atiri area. This operation is aimed at screening Israel's northern frontier from Palestinian attacks such as the one yesterday (7 April) in which five PLO terrorists killed three Israelis, one of them a child, in Misgav Am Kibbutz. There are reports that Israeli troops are

8   LEBANON (Cont'd) - patrolling the territory under the jurisdiction of the UN Irish Battalion that has had recent clashes with Christian militia units.

10   COLOMBIA - The terrorists holding US Ambassador Diego C. Asencio and other hostages scale down their demands and are willing to accept the release of seven, rather than 28, political prisoners.

11   GREAT BRITAIN - Libyan assassins kill a political opponent of Muammar Qaddafi. Two Libyan students studying in England are arrested and charged with the crime.

11   CAMBODIA - At least 45 persons are killed in fighting between rival anti-Communist groups in refugee villages along the Thai-Cambodia border.

11   LEBANON - Further clashes are reported between Christian militiamen and Irish soldiers in southern Lebanon.

12   LIBERIA - President William R. Tolbert, Jr., and 27 others are killed in a coup led by Master Sergeant Samuel K. Doe. Doe takes power as the head of state.

12   UGANDA - There is a report that the Tanzanian troops that have been in Uganda since the ouster of Idi Amin are withdrawing.

13   UNITED STATES - The Defense Department announces the US Navy will withdraw its Polaris submarines from Guam in July.

13   LEBANON - In the second incident in less than a week, Israeli-backed Christian militiamen kill a UN soldier from Fiji and destroy two UN helicopters in a clash near the Israeli border. In the first incident nine Irish UN soldiers were kidnapped and then released on 9 April.

13   ISRAEL - The government announces the withdrawal of its small force in Lebanon.

14   LEBANON - The UN peacekeeping force commander General Emmanuel Erskine and Israeli commander Major General Avigdor Ben-Gal demand the immediate removal of the Irish Battalion from the peacekeeping force after evidence implicates the Irish in aiding Palestinian terrorists in crossing into Israel.

15   CENTRAL AFRICAN REPUBLIC - The government breaks diplomatic relations with Libya.

15   COLOMBIA - Terrorists of the leftist M-19 Group attack the Uruguayan Embassy in hopes of capturing Acting Ambassador Raul Lira. They flee empty-handed. The attack is probably in retaliation for the fact that Ambassador Fernando Gomez was able to escape from the Dominican Republic residence after it was taken by other members of their group in February.

16   LEBANON - Muslim Shi'ite militiamen clash with pro-Iraqi guerrillas in Beirut. Five persons are killed and 24 wounded.

17   UNITED STATES - The government imposes additional sanctions on Iran.

17   IRAN - Unofficial sources state a US C-130 "Hercules" aircraft flies into Iran undetected, lands in the Kabir Desert, and remains for several hours while intelligence specialists collect soil samples and implant special gear for an impending American hostage rescue attempt.

18   ZIMBABWE - The former British colony of Southern Rhodesia becomes independent as Zimbabwe. The Reverend Canaan Banana is sworn in as President. Robert Mugabe is appointed Prime Minister.

18   LEBANON - Israeli troops raid a guerrilla base in Tyre killing at least six Palestinians.

19   LEBANON - Two Irish soldiers are killed by armed Lebanese after being kidnapped, along with two journalists, in reprisal for the recent deaths of two Arab youths. The journalists are released. The assassins are reported to be members of the dead youths' families who have declared a blood feud against the Irish.

21   REPUBLIC OF IRELAND - The government refuses to consider withdrawing its forces from the UN peace-keeping force in Lebanon despite criticism about the conduct of its troops and the recent murders of two Irish soldiers.

22   UNITED STATES - The government concludes military and economic accords with Oman and Kenya that give US forces access to air and naval bases in return for military aid.

23   SOUTH AFRICA - Police fire tear gas to disperse 3,000 school children marching in Cape Town protesting segregated schools.

24   IRAN - Eight US "Sea Stallion" helicopters are
            launched from the USS Nimitz in the Gulf of Oman,
            while six C-130 "Hercules" cargo aircraft take off in
            Egypt and head for the Desert of Salt (Kabir Desert)
            east of Tehran in Iran as the first phase of an ill-
            conceived, poorly planned, and ineptly led rescue
            attempt to free the American hostages. The aircraft
            land at Posht-a-Badam (Desert 1). Mechanical failures
            cause three of the helicopters to abort their mis-
            sions. There are no backups available. A timid Pres-
            ident then orders the 180-member rescue force to abort
            its mission. A subsequent crash between one of the
            helicopters and one of the cargo aircraft at the
            desert site kills eight men and injures four others.

25   UNITED NATIONS - The Security Council condemns Israel
            for its recent raid into Lebanon.

25   UNITED STATES - The government announces that a rescue
            mission planned to bring about the release of the
            hostages held in the US Embassy in Tehran, Iran, has
            failed.

25   GREAT BRITAIN - Libyan assassins kill a second polit-
            ical opponent of Muammar Qaddafi.

26   LIBYA - Muammar Qaddafi orders all Libyans to return
            home or face certain "liquidation."

27   COLOMBIA - The siege at the Embassy of the Dominican
            Republic in Bogota ends when $2.5 million is paid in
            ransom and a promise given that the Inter-American
            Human Rights Commission will investigate charges
            against the Colombian government. Sixteen terrorists
            and 12 hostages, including six ambassadors and the
            Papal Nuncio, are flown to Havana where all of the
            hostages are released.

29   CHAD - France begins withdrawing its forces from Chad.

29   AFGHANISTAN - Anti-Marxist students and teachers set
            off a new series of anti-Soviet riots in Kabul. The
            police repeatedly open fire on the demonstrators to
            stop the rioting. Soviet helicopter gunships arrive
            and fire on demonstrators at Kabul University. At
            least 16 are reported dead and scores more injured.
            About 200 are believed dead in the disorders in Kabul
            in April.

30   GREAT BRITAIN - The Iranian Embassy in London is at-
            tacked by six Arabic-speaking Khuzestan Iranians.
            After taking 26 hostages they threaten to blow up the

30   GREAT BRITAIN (Cont'd) - building if 91 political prisoners held in Khuzestan jails are not released and the province given autonomy. Five of the hostages are released over the next few days.

MAY

1   WARSAW PACT - Warsaw Pact leaders meet in Warsaw to coordinate positions on Iran and Afghanistan.

3   ISRAEL - Palestinian terrorists kill five Israeli settlers and injure 16 others in Hebron.

3   SOUTH AFRICA - Bombings and major fires at two synthetic petroleum plants and one of the country's largest oil refineries are blamed on the African National Congress.

4   YUGOSLAVIA - Josef Broz (Tito) dies in a Ljubljana hospital after a long illness.

4   GUATEMALA - Police report that at least 12 kidnap victims, most of them leftists, have been found tortured and killed in the last three days.

5   GREAT BRITAIN - Specially trained British SAS forces attack the Iranian Embassy after one of the hostages is killed by the Khuzestani terrorists. Three terrorists are killed and the others are captured. The body of a second murdered hostage is found, but the other 19 are released unharmed. Much of the embassy building is destroyed by fire.

8   LEBANON - Israeli commandos successfully ambush two groups of Palestinian guerrillas near the Israeli border and kill a number of them.

11   USSR - Soviet newspapers report that Afghan government troops are facing heavy resistance from rebels in the Hindu Kush region of Afghanistan.

12   AFGHANISTAN - Rebel snipers have driven almost all Soviet and East European civilian advisors out of the country. The government appeals to India not to withdraw its advisors who are apparently the last ones remaining.

12   UGANDA - Army troops take over the radio station and central post office in Kampala as military pressure grows against the government of President Godfrey L. Binaisa. Binaisa remains in Entebbe under Tanzanian protection.

13   THE BAHAMAS - Five Cuban jets buzz a small village on
          Ragged Island. They turn for home when US fighters
          arrive.

13   LEBANON - Fighting breaks out between rightist and
          leftist groups in Beirut.

13   UGANDA - A six-man military commission assumes the
          powers of the presidency.

15   NATO - At a special NATO meeting in Brussels the US
          and 12 of its allies agree upon military measures to
          strengthen Western defenses because of the Soviet
          invasion of Afghanistan.

16   LEBANON - Israeli forces cross into Lebanon and attack
          Palestinian bases near the border.

17   UNITED STATES - Racial violence breaks out in Miami,
          Florida, after an all-white jury acquits four former
          police officers of the fatal beating of a black man.
          At least 14 people are killed and more than 300 in-
          jured in the 72 hours of rioting.

18   SOUTH KOREA - Following antigovernment rioting in
          Seoul and five other cities the government imposes
          total martial law.

19   COMMUNIST CHINA - The government announces it has
          successfully launched its first intercontinental
          ballistic missile (ICBM).

19   PAKISTAN - In a move seen as an indication of major
          support by Iran for anti-Soviet resistance in Afghani-
          stan, nine Afghan rebel leaders are seated with the
          Iranian delegation at the Islamic Foreign Ministers
          conference in Islamabad.

19   EL SALVADOR - Ten government soldiers and about 100
          leftist rebels are killed in a clash in northern
          Chalatenango Province near the Honduran border.

21   SOUTH KOREA - Antigovernment rioters seize control of
          the southern city of Kwangju.

22   SOUTH KOREA - Opposition leader Kim Dae Jung is
          accused of plotting the overthrow of the government.

22   IRAN - Two Soviet-built helicopters are reported to
          have penetrated Iranian air space for the second time
          in as many days.

24   LEBANON - Christian militiamen shell Palestinian
          positions in Sidon.

25   AFGHANISTAN - Thousands take to the streets of Kabul
      to protest the presence of Soviet troops in their
      country. At least four high school girls and three
      policemen are reported dead in incidents during the
      previous week.

25   SOUTH AFRICA - Police break up a demonstration by
      4,000 students of mixed ancestry who demand equal
      education.

26   LEBANON - Christian militiamen shell the predominantly
      Muslim port city of Sidon killing five and wounding 12
      others.

27   SOUTH KOREA - The government orders the army to retake
      Kwangju. After four days of fighting the city is
      secured. One hundred seventy are dead, 144 of whom are
      civilians. (Other estimates claim the death toll is
      much higher.)

29   PAKISTAN - Over 900,000 Afghan refugees are reported
      to have crossed the border into Pakistan since the war
      began.

29   LEBANON - Nineteen are killed in clashes between rival
      Muslim and leftist factions in southern Lebanon.

29   COLOMBIA - Colombian police and special army units
      ambush an M-19 Group team as it attempts to pick up
      ransom money. Two of the rebels are killed and five
      captured.

29   SOUTH AFRICA - Police open fire on stone-throwing
      teen-agers in a racially mixed area outside Cape Town.
      Two students are killed and three injured.

30   AFGHANISTAN - Anti-Soviet demonstrations in Kabul now
      include elementary school children. Many of them are
      arrested by Afghan police. Teachers are being drafted
      into the military as punishment for their roles in
      demonstrations.

30   JAMAICA - Government troops kill one person while
      restoring order in a Kingston slum.

JUNE

1   UNITED STATES - About 300 Cuban refugees riot at the
      relocation center in Fort Chaffee, Arkansas. After two
      attempts to break out of the compound are twarted by
      military forces and police, the trouble subsides but
      continues to simmer due to what the Cubans perceive as
      unjustified delays in their processing.

2   ISRAEL - Two pro-Palestinian West Bank mayors are severely injured in separate car-bombing incidents. A third mayor narrowly escapes when he is warned away from his automobile. More people are injured by a hand grenade tossed into a crowd. Previously unknown Jewish underground terrorist groups claim responsibility for the incidents.

2   SOUTH AFRICA - Guerrillas attack three fuel storage facilities outside Johannesburg, setting off explosions and fires in seven storage tanks.

4   ARAB LEAGUE - Of the total of 22 Arab nations in the Arab League only Somalia, Oman, and Sudan retain their diplomatic relations with Egypt after Egypt signs its peace treaty with Israel.

6   LEBANON - Israeli forces kill a number of Palestinian guerrillas in a raid on Sidon.

6   EL SALVADOR - Two days of strikes by 20,000 teachers end in the death of two teachers protesting the continued violence in the country.

8   INDIA - At least 378 immigrants are massacred in Mandai, Tripura State, in the northeastern corner of India. The perpetrators are local tribesmen intent on maintaining the ethnic quality of their region.

8   AFGHANISTAN - Heavy fighting is reported between Soviet forces and rebels in Charikar and Qarabagh. The Soviet command is said to expect a rebel offensive in the near future.

9   AFGHANISTAN - The government executes ten supporters and aides of the late President Hafizullah Amin. Included are Amin's brother and nephew, and rebel leader Abdul Majid Kalakhani.

10   GUATEMALA - Since the beginning of May at least seven right-wing lawyers, professors, and politicans have been assassinated in Guatemala.

10   IRAN - Ayatollah Khomeini warns his people that internal dissention is driving Iran toward chaos.

10   AFGHANISTAN - Soviet bombers are now being used to destroy rebel-held villages. More than 1,000 rebels are reported to have been killed in recent fighting.

10   MIDDLE EAST - An Al Fatah Central Committee member, Majed Abu Shrar, says his organization intends to reestablish a major base in Jordan for military operations against Israel.

10   SOUTH YEMEN - Intelligence reports indicate at least
            1,000 Soviet advisors are in South Yemen and that the
            USSR has, since March, been delivering military
            hardware to that country.

11   AFGHANISTAN - Foreign diplomats report that the
            capital city of Kabul is ringed by Soviet troops and
            that the city is sealed off from the rest of the
            country.

12   EL SALVADOR - At least eighteen persons are reported
            dead in fighting between leftist rebels and government
            forces in the northwestern part of the country.

13   CAMBODIA - Rebel forces are reported to have ambushed
            a train and killed at least 150 people in northwestern
            Phnom Pehn.

13   GREAT BRITAIN - The government orders the immediate
            departure of Musa Kusa, the head of the Libyan dip-
            lomatic mission, for his part in supporting Libyan
            murder squads operating in Great Britain.

15   AFGHANISTAN - Heavy fighting is reported in eastern
            Paktia Province after a large Soviet armored column is
            ambushed near the garrison town of Urgun.

15   WESTERN EUROPE - Intelligence sources report that
            about 1,000 East German paratroopers are stationed in
            Angola.

19   EL SALVADOR - Leftist rebels ambush a government
            convoy in northern El Salvador killing six soldiers
            and wounding at least ten more.

22   THAILAND - At least 50 Thai fishermen are reported
            drowned when a Vietnamese gunboat sinks three trawlers
            in the Gulf of Thailand.

22   AFGHANISTAN - Most western analysts agree that Soviet
            troop strength in Afghanistan is currently about
            100,000 and that the Soviet Union is now stuck in a
            quagmire of its own invention.

24   THAILAND - Vietnamese forces engaged in a battle with
            Cambodian rebel forces cross into Thailand near Non
            Mak Mun.

26   FRANCE - The government announces it has developed its
            own neutron bomb.

26   COMMUNIST CHINA - The government warns Viet Nam
            against any further encroachments into Thailand.

26   THAILAND - More than 8,000 Vietnamese infantry troops are observed digging in along the border with Thailand. It is assumed the purpose of this is to prevent Pol Pot forces, known to have bases in Thailand, from crossing back into Cambodia. A number of Vietnamese patrol members are captured in Thailand. Most of the 2,000 Vietnamese forces who crossed into Thailand on the 24th of June are thought to have retired back into Cambodia.

29   AFGHANISTAN - A mutiny among Afghan troops is reported in a troop compound near Kabul. At least ten Soviet soldiers are reported killed and a number of tanks destroyed in the fighting that followed.

30   LEBANON - Israeli forces kill a number of Palestinian guerrillas in an operation in southern Lebanon.

JULY

2   GREAT BRITAIN - The government announces it has a new plan that will lead to eventual home rule in Northern Ireland. Home rule was suspended in March 1972 because of the growing violence in the province.

2   UGANDA - Opponents of the military junta form the Uganda Struggling Joint Front and demand the immediate withdrawal of the Tanzanian forces and the holding of free elections.

3   UNITED STATES - The Department of State reports that recent Soviet troop withdrawals from Afghanistan are merely organizational readjustments, and that troops being withdrawn are being replaced with specially trained antiguerrilla forces.

4   ZIMBABWE - Prime Minister Robert Mugabe orders the South African diplomatic mission in Salisbury closed after it is disclosed that it was being used for the recruitment of troops to help in destabilizing black governments in Africa.

4   EL SALVADOR - The state of siege imposed four months ago by the ruling junta to help quell the violence in the country is extended for another 30 days.

4-5   AFGHANISTAN - At least 50 planeloads of new Soviet equipment and fresh troops are landed in Kabul despite claims of a troop reduction. Supplies include light tanks, armored personnel carriers, and containers of otherwise unidentified liquid.

5   UNITED STATES - A massive airlift of arms and equipment for Thailand begins. The purpose of the airlift is to assist the Thais in maintaining their positions along the Cambodian border in the face of repeated incursions by Vietnamese forces operating in Cambodia.

5-8   AFGHANISTAN - Rebels attack a Soviet military camp north of Kabul inflicting heavy casualties. Soviet forces retaliate with attacks using more than 400 tanks and armored personnel carriers.

8   LEBANON - Christian Phalangist militiamen decisively defeat rival Christian National Liberal Party (NLP) forces in two days of fighting around Beirut.

8   SOUTH AFRICA - The government orders home all of its senior diplomats in Zimbabwe.

8   LEBANON - Heavy fighting erupts between Christian Phalangist forces and those of President Camille Chamoun's rightist forces in the Maronite Catholic section of Beirut.

8   UNITED STATES - The Senate announces it will reject a Saudi Arabian request to buy F-15 fighters.

10   IRAN - A military coup is foiled by the government. Eventually 36 are executed for their parts in the plot.

10   LEBANON - An attempt is made to consolidate all Christian forces in east Beirut into what is to be called the "National Home Guard of Lebanon."

11   MOZAMBIQUE - Government forces attack and occupy the main insurgent base camp of the National Resistance Movement, killing 272 rebels and capturing at least 300 more.

11   POLAND - A new wave of strikes is reported following an announcement by Communist Party chief Edward Gierek telling workers they will have to accept higher prices and hold back demands for higher wages.

12   EL SALVADOR - One hundred peasants storm the Costa Rican Embassy in San Salvador and demand political asylum. A police officer is shot during the breakin. The Ambassador then refuses a request of Salvador police to enter the building and eject the peasants.

13   BOTSWANA - President Sir Seretse Khama dies of cancer in the capital city of Gaborone. Vice-President Quett Masire succeeds him (18 July).

13   THAILAND - Fighting between rival Cambodian guerrilla groups moves into its third day at a refugee camp in eastern Thailand. At least 30 civilians are reported killed and more than 100 injured.

14   UGANDA - Milton Obote is elected President.

15   POLAND - Seventeen thousand workers strike the Lenin Shipyard in Gdansk. Bus drivers and others join the strike on succeeding days. Within 24 hours the number of strikers exceeds 50,000.

16   CHILE - Four terrorists of the Revolutionary Left Movement assassinate the director of the Chilean Army Intelligence School, Lieutenant Colonel Roger Vergara Campos, and his driver near Santiago.

17   BOLIVIA - A military coup led by General Luis Garcia Meza Tejada takes over control of the country to prevent the election of leftist Hernan Siles Zuaro by the Bolivian Congress on 4 August.

17   GUATEMALA - Unidentified gunmen machine-gun the headquarters of the Municipal Workers' Union. Two are killed and several wounded.

18   JAMAICA - A dark-to-dawn curfew is put into effect in parts of Kingston to help halt the string of murders committed by roving gangs that have claimed 70 lives since 1 July.

26   UNITED STATES - The government orders its military mission out of Bolivia and cuts economic aid to that country following the military takeover of the government on 17 July.

27   EGYPT - The Shah of Iran dies of cancer while in exile in Cairo.

30   EL SALVADOR - Six leftist rebels are killed when government security forces storm their hideout in San Salvador.

31   ISRAEL - The Israeli Knesset (Parliament) enacts a law making Jerusalem the capital of Israel.

AUGUST

CAMBODIA - Periods of heavy fighting are reported throughout western Cambodia as the Vietnamese Army attempts to dislodge both Pol Pot and anti-Communist guerrilla forces. This fighting goes on until the end of the year.

1   AFGHANISTAN - There are reports that Soviet troops were able to foil a coup attempt against the Karmal government sometime in the past two weeks.

2   ITALY - A bomb placed in the main waiting room in Bologna's central railway station kills 76 and injures more than 200. Neo-Fascist terrorists are blamed for the incident. Eventually police in several countries in Europe will arrest 23 persons accused of the crime.

4   AFGHANISTAN - More than 4,500 Afghan troops desert their base at Ghazni and join the rebels. Soviet forces are required to fight to regain control of the military base. In another action at Tangi Wardak, 200 Soviet troops and 300 rebels are reported killed.

10   SOMALIA - Ethiopian troops ambush a Somali military convoy in the disputed border area on the Ogaden Plateau. At least 1,500 are killed and 2,000 wounded.

13   SURINAM - A new military coup takes place in which Sergeant Major Daysi Bouterse emerges as the strongman. President Johan Ferrier is arrested and a number of members of the ruling junta are imprisoned. Prime Minister Chin a Sen is also named president.

14   POLAND - Seventeen thousand workers go on strike and seize the Lenin Shipyards in Gdansk. Within days, nearly 120,000 workers in northern Poland have joined the strike.

14   GUATEMALA - An army convoy is ambushed in Alta Verapaz by leftist guerrillas. Twelve soldiers are killed and four wounded. Mazatenanga's mayor is assassinated by three unidentified gunmen in a separate incident. A week earlier, on 6 August, two gunmen assassinated a newspaper reporter in Guatemala City.

15   EL SALVADOR - An American diplomat, Brian Woo, is wounded by Salvadoran troops during three days of bitter fighting against leftist rebels in the streets of San Salvador.

17   AFGHANISTAN - Near Kabul, Soviet aircraft are reported to have attacked Muslim worshipers celebrating the end of Ramadan. About 1,200 are killed. In separate incidents, 13 Soviet soldiers are reported killed and four captured in a rebel attack on a base near Kabul, and at least 22 Afghan pilots and mechanics are reported captured and being held for ransom.

18   ETHIOPIA - Between 12,000 and 13,000 Cuban troops are reported to be in Ethiopia.

19   IRAN - The government breaks diplomatic relations with
            Chile over alleged acts of suppression by the military
            junta.

20   UNITED NATIONS - The Security Council approves a
            resolution urging   the   member   nations   to   disregard
            Israeli claims to Jerusalem.

20   LEBANON - A force of about 500 Israelis crosses into
            southern Lebanon and attacks a number of Palestinian
            bases. More than 100 Palestinians are killed or
            wounded. Three prisoners are taken back to Israel.
            Three Israelis are killed and 12 wounded.

21   UNITED STATES - The government announces it has signed
            a defense agreement with Somalia. The terms of the
            agreement give US military forces use of the airfields
            and port facilities at Mogadishu and Berbera in return
            for $25 million in US aid in 1981 and more later.

21   GREECE - The government warns that it will close all
            US bases in Greece if Greece is not readmitted to NATO
            by the end of 1980.

22   THE PHILIPPINES - A series of bombings damages public
            buildings and businesses in Manila. A group calling
            itself the April 6 Liberation Movement claims re-
            sponsibility and condemns the Marcos regime.

22   NORTHERN IRELAND - A bomb explosion damages the
            Belfast headquarters of Sinn Fein, the political wing
            of the Provisional IRA.

23   GUATEMALA - At least 36 are known dead in the latest
            round of political killings. The Police Chief in the
            town of Joyabaj is the latest victim.

24   AFGHANISTAN - Heavy fighting is reported between the
            Afghan rebels and Soviet forces in the mountains
            around the city of Paghman northeast of Kabul in the
            Hindu Kush.

25   UNITED NATIONS - Zimbabwe is admitted to membership in
            the UNO.

25   LEBANON - Strong Israeli forces attack Beaumont Castle
            in Arnun in southern Lebanon to dislodge Palestinian
            guerrillas who use the 12th-century Crusader fortress
            to shell Christian positions.

25   ISRAEL - The government reports its fighters have shot
            down a Soviet-built Syrian MiG-21 over southern
            Lebanon.

26   THAILAND - A land mine placed by Communist rebels kills 12 policemen and 3 civilians in Krabi Province.

27   AFGHANISTAN - Reports originating in Kabul claim that Soviet troops have successfully reopened the highway from the capital into Pakistan. The highway was cut at Sarobi and in Laghman Province by rebel forces.

28   POLAND - Strikes continue to spread across Poland as teams of workers from Gdansk seek support in industrial centers around the nation.

30   POLAND - The strikes that have paralyzed northern Poland now spread into the south as 20,000 copper miners walk out near Wroclaw. Eventually 150,000 miners will enter the dispute.

31   SOUTH AFRICA - The government reports its forces have killed or wounded nearly 50 Angola rebels in three recent raids.

SEPTEMBER

1   LIBYA - Muammar Qadaffi announces that following secret negotiations, Libya and Syria will be merged so that Israel can be opposed more effectively. Syria agrees to the plan. A previous attempt at merger failed in 1973.

1   POLAND - Labor leaders end the strike that has paralyzed Poland for 17 days.

2   LEBANON - Palestinian guerrillas clash with Muslim Shi'ite militiamen in Ghaziye.

6   GUATEMALA - A bomb planted by leftist terrorists explodes outside the National Palace. Eight are killed and more than 150 injured. Police disarm at least three other bombs in Guatemala City.

6   POLAND - Edward Gierek is dismissed and is replaced by Stanislaw Kania as the head of the Communist Party.

6   SWITZERLAND - About 600 youths riot in Zurich after the youth center is closed because of drug dealing.

9   GUATEMALA - Leftist insurgents attack the army base at Quiche. At least nine are killed on both sides.

9   SWITZERLAND - The Swiss Federal President is asked to send troops into Zurich to quell the rioting by about 6,000 youths demanding the reopening of the youth center.

11   AFGHANISTAN - Soviet troops are reported to be using
            "Dum Dum" bullets in violation of international
            conventions. Foreign diplomats stationed in Kabul also
            report that at least 50% of the Afghan armed forces
            have deserted or are dead. The city of Herat in
            northeastern Afghanistan is reported to be in rebel
            hands. In the Lake Tiga region villagers kill Faiz
            Mohammed, the Afghan Minister for Frontier Affairs,
            and several aides when Faiz tries to enlist the towns-
            people's support for the Soviet-backed government in
            Kabul.

11   SOUTH AFRICA - Police in Cape Town open fire on
            stone-throwing youths, killing one.

12   IRAN - The Ayatollah Khomeini stipulates four con-
            ditions for the release of the American hostages. The
            US has to: cancel all claims against Iran; return to
            Iran all property belonging to the late Shah; release
            Iran's frozen assets; and promise no political or mil-
            itary reprisals against Iran.

12   TURKEY - A bloodless military coup, led by Armed
            Forces Chief of Staff General Kenan Evran, overthrows
            the government. Parliament is dissolved and the con-
            stitution suspended. Evran becomes head of state (18
            September).

12   THE PHILIPPINES - More bombings, attributed to the
            April 6 Liberation Movement, take place in Manila. One
            person is killed and 60 wounded.

14   IRAQ - Two oil installations near Kirkuk in north-
            eastern Iraq are destroyed by saboteurs. Renewed
            fighting is also reported along the border with Iran.

15   IRAN - Majlis (Parliament) Speaker Ayatollah Hasheimi
            Rafsanjani states the Ayatollah Khomeini inadvertently
            forgot to mention that the US also has to apologize to
            the Iranian people for all its past interferences in
            Iranian affairs.

16   EL SALVADOR - The leftist Popular Liberation Front
            assumes responsibility for four bombings in San Sal-
            vador over the past weekend.

17   IRAQ - The government abrogates the Algiers Agreement
            and claims the Shatt al-Arab waterway as Iraqi
            territory.

17   BANGLADESH - Rebel tribesmen kill 17 and injure 23 in
            attacks on a number of villages.

17   PARAGUAY - Deposed Nicaraguan dictator Anastasio
            Somoza Debayle is assassinated in Ascuncion in an
            ambush attack which also kills an aide and a driver.

18   EL SALVADOR - Leftist rebels seize the OAS offices in
            San Salvador. Five persons are wounded and six taken
            hostage. The rebels demand an end to repression in El
            Salvador.

19   PARAGUAY - Paraguayan police shoot and kill Hugo
            Alfredo Irurzun, a known Argentine terrorist and
            suspected assassin of Anastasio Somoza.

22   IRAN - Iraqi forces, having already entered Kurdistan,
            push into Khuzestan in the latest phase of the unde-
            clared Gulf (Iran-Iraq) War. Iraqi aircraft attack at
            least ten Iranian airfields, including Tehran, and an
            oil refinery at Kermanshah. Iran calls up several
            thousand reservists. Artillery and rocket fire are
            reported around Khorramshahr (Khurramshahr) and Abadan
            on the Shatt Al-Arab.

22   IRAQ - The government claims its forces have occupied
            about 90 square miles of territory which it claims was
            taken from it by the terms of the 1975 accords. It
            also claims to have shot down a US-built Iranian F-4
            Phantom jet and to have sunk eight Iranian gunboats.
            Artillery and rocket fire are reported around Basra
            (Al Basrah). Iraq also claims Iranian gunners fired on
            the British freighter SS Orient Star and the Singa-
            pore-registered SS Lucille in the Shatt Al-Arab.

23   IRAN - Iraqi air strikes start huge fires in oil and
            gas storage areas in the Abadan refinery complex.
            Naval units exchange fire in the Shatt al-Arab.

23   IRAQ - Retaliatory Iranian air raids take place around
            Baghdad and the oil refineries at Kirkuk and Mosul.
            The petrochemical plants at Basra and Zubair are also
            hit. A number of Americans and Britons are reported
            killed in Basra.

24   COMMUNIST CHINA - The government states that growing
            tension along its border with Viet Nam and the deteri-
            orating situation in Southeast Asia make it impossible
            to resume peace talks with the Vietnamese government.

26   WEST GERMANY - A terrorist bomb blast at the entrance
            to Munich's Oktoberfest grounds kills 12 and injures
            at least 200. The Defense Sports Group, an outlawed
            German organization, is charged with the bombing. A
            number of suspects are eventually arrested.

26   FRANCE - A number of Jewish centers in Paris, including a synagogue, school, daycare center, and a
memorial, are damaged when they are machine-gunned by
unknown terrorists.

26   IRAQ - Iraqi forces claim they have captured the
Iranian port city of Khorramshahr and have cut the
rail line to Tehran. Heavy fighting is reported in
Qasr-i-Shirin on the border near Kermanshah.

27   PAKISTAN - Six Soviet-built helicopter gunships with
Afghan markings attack a Pakistani border post killing
two soldiers and wounding a third.

28   FRANCE - A second synagogue is machine-gunned by unknown terrorists. An attempt by a group known as
National European Fascists to take credit for the
attacks is discounted by the police.

28   LEBANON - A bomb explodes at a bus stop in Christian
east Beirut killing three civilians and injuring 15
more.

28   TURKEY - Kurdish rebels blow up an important pipeline
carrying oil from Iraq.

30   SAUDI ARABIA - US AWACS early warning aircraft arrive
in Saudi Arabia to help protect the country's eastern
oil fields against Iranian air attacks. The US Department of Defense announces the dispatch of the aircraft
to Saudi Arabia on 1 October.

OCTOBER

1   IRAN - The Iraqi advance into Khuzistan Province
stalls.

3   IRAQ - Iranian aircraft again bomb the oil refineries
at Basra and Kirkuk.

4   IRAN - A week after Iraqi forces claimed to have captured Khorramshahr, heavy fighting still continues for
the city.

5   AFGHANISTAN - Intelligence sources, supported by eye-
witness reports from rebel leaders, claim that the
Soviets have taken over the combat role and are carrying out harsh measures in their attempt to gain control of the Kunar Valley. The reports go on to say
that the Soviets now look upon the Afghan armed forces
as a liability.

6   IRAN - Iraqi aircraft hit targets at Tehran, Tabriz, Kermanshah and Ahwaz. The city of Khorramshahr is virtually destroyed by two weeks of constant Iraqi shelling. Most of its 150,000 population have fled north.

7   JORDAN - The government begins transporting food and supplies to Iraq.

7   IRAN - At least 20 seamen are killed when Iranian artillery, exchanging fire with advancing Iraqi forces, sinks three and damages two other foreign-registry freighters at anchor in the harbor at Khorramshahr. At the same time, Iraqi planes attack Tehran and Iraqi artillery shells Dizful and Ahwaz.

8   IRAN - Iraqi forces bombard Abadan.

8   IRAQ - Iranian jets attack the oil refineries at Kirkuk and Sulaimaniya.

9   IRAN - Iranian gunners sink three of five ships they attack with artillery fire in the Shatt Al-Arab.

9   AFGHANISTAN - Intelligence sources indicate that between 20 and 25 Soviet soldiers are being killed each week. This number may be higher as it is based upon the number of caskets returned to the Soviet Union every seven days and does not include those whose bodies are not recovered.

10   IRAN - Iraqi forces begin using surface-to-surface missiles in their attacks on Iranian cities.

10   EL SALVADOR - The Popular Liberation Front claims to have executed South African Ambassador Gardner Dunn, who was kidnapped on 28 November 1979.

10   LEBANON - A bomb is defused on the lawn of the Swiss Embassy in Beirut.

13   UNITED NATIONS - In a 74-35 vote (32 abstentions) the General Assembly votes down a resolution to unseat the Cambodian Pol Pot delegation even though the former expresses its abhorrence of the past human rights violations of the latter. The alternative considered was the seating of the delegation of the puppet government of Heng Samrin that is kept in power by the presence of 200,000 Vietnamese troops.

13   IRAN - Heavy fighting is reported between Iranian and Iraqi forces in Ahwaz and Dizful.

13   GREAT BRITAIN - Armenian terrorists of the October 3 Organization bomb the Turkish Airlines' office and the Swiss Center in London. Another group calling itself the Armenian Secret Army also claims credit for the blast at the Turkish Airlines' office.

13   FRANCE - A bomb goes off outside the Swiss Tourist Office in Paris. The Armenian October 3 Organizations claims responsibility.

15   IRAN - Government forces suppress a Kurdish uprising in northwestern Iran.

15   EAST GERMANY - As labor unrest continues in Poland, East German leader Erich Honecker warns of possible Soviet bloc military action to stop any threat to the Communist government in Poland.

15   COMMUNIST CHINA - The government reports that Vietnamese troops crossed into Chinese territory and attacked a commune killing or injuring an unspecified number of civilians.

16   COMMUNIST CHINA - The Chinese detonate a nuclear device in the atmosphere at the Lop Nor test facility in northwestern China.

16   AFGHANISTAN - Clashes between Soviet troops and Afghan army forces are reported in Kabul.

17   INDIAN OCEAN - Over 60 US, British, French, and Australian warships are gathered in the Indian Ocean and Arabian Sea to insure Iran does not interfere with the world's oil supply out of the Middle East. About 29 Soviet warships are also in the Indian Ocean, but the USSR is not dependent on the oil from the region.

17   IRAN - The final battle for Abadan appears to be beginning. Iraqi forces are within one mile of the city, while Iranian forces are digging in for the final struggle. Heavy Iraqi shelling of the city is reported.

17   LEBANON - Israeli forces conduct a series of raids on Palestinian staging areas in southern Lebanon.

19   THE PHILIPPINES - A bomb injures at least 20 persons shortly after President Marcos concludes an address given to a convention of American travel agents. The April 6 Liberation Movement claims responsibility.

20   THE PHILIPPINES - Thirty persons are ordered arrested in connection with the recent wave of bombings. Most of the suspects reside in the United States.

20   GREECE - Greece rejoins NATO after the Planning Committee unanimously votes in favor of its return to the alliance.

20   IRAN - Iraqi infantry supported by heavy tanks enters the outskirts of Abadan cutting the city off from the rest of Iran.

21   EL SALVADOR - At least 15,000 civilians are displaced in northeastern El Salvador because of heavy fighting between leftist rebels and government forces.

23   IRAN - Iraqi forces claim they have isolated the oil-rich Khuzistan Province from the rest of the country.

24   IRAN - The city of Khorramshahr is finally captured by Iraqi forces. In one week it will be secured and no Iranian presence found within the city.

25   EL SALVADOR - Government forces open a major campaign in a remote mountainous zone near the Honduran border. At least 150 rebels are killed as the government troops sweep through several training camps. They also capture a Swedish journalist, Piter Turbuison, who is subsequently held for questioning.

26   IRAN - Iranian jets attack Iraqi positions in Khuzistan Province and Iraqi aircraft attack the Iraqi cities of Basra and Kirkuk.

27   ISRAEL - A wave of terrorist bomb attacks rocks Tel Aviv.

28   SAUDI ARABIA - The government breaks diplomatic relations with Libya following Muammar Qadaffi's criticism of Saudi relations with the US. The move is also seen as designed to emphasize the growing division in the Arab world over the Iran-Iraq conflict.

28   IRAN - A two-pronged Iraqi ground assault on Abadan is stopped by stiff Iranian resistance.

29   COMMUNIST CHINA - A bomb explodes in the main Peking railway station. Nine are killed and more than 80 injured. It is suspected that one of the dead is the bomber. No group claims responsibility for the violence.

30   IRAN - In conflicting reports Iraq claims to have sent its Soviet-built medium bombers deep into Iran without loss. Iran claims it has shot down two bombers over Qum and Isfahan.

30   LEBANON - After three days of fighting Phalangist
        militiamen occupy positions held by rival Christian
        militia groups in east Beirut.

31   IRAN - The Iranian Minister of Petroleum Mohammad
        Jawad Baqir Tunguyan is captured by Iraqi troops near
        the Abadan oil refinery complex. Five other high-
        ranking ministry personnel are also captured. The
        prisoners are removed to Baghdad. Tunguyan is appar-
        ently wounded and requires medical treatment.

NOVEMBER

2   IRAN - The Majlis (Parliament) approves the terms set
        forth on 12 September for the release of the US
        hostages.

6   PAKISTAN - At least 200,000 Afghan refugees are re-
        ported to be camped around Peshawar near the border.

6   LEBANON - Heavy fighting breaks out between rival
        Muslim militia groups following an argument over a
        minor traffic accident in Beirut.

6   CHAD - About 3,000 heavily armed Libyan troops, ap-
        parently under the direct control of Colonel Qadaffi,
        enter northern Chad and occupy a 125-mile area near
        the Libyan border.

7   ISRAEL - Rockets, known to have been fired from
        Lebanon, injure five Israelis in Kiryat Shemona.

11   LEBANON - Two car-bomb explosions kill 15 and injure
        40 in Christian east Beirut.

12   EGYPT - An advance party of about 1,400 US para-
        troopers arrives at Cairo-West Airbase to participate
        in joint tactical exercises with Egyptian forces.

13   IRAN - About 100 civilians are reported killed when
        Iraqi warplanes attack Sanandaj.

14   CAMBODIA - Two Soviet advisors are killed in a rebel
        ambush near Kompong Som.

14   GUINEA-BISSAU - A socialist-inspired coup, led by Pre-
        mier Joao Bernardo Vieira, overthrows the government
        of President Luis de Almeida Cabral.

15   IRAN - In fierce fighting near Susangird (Susangerd)
        northwest of Ahwaz, 100 Iranian and 250 Iraqi soldiers
        are killed. In all, 282 Iranian soldiers are killed in
        all of the day's actions.

16   IRAN - Susangird is entered by Iraqi troops. Heavy fighting will continue for a week.

16   AFGHANISTAN - Soviet troops are reported to have seized the Wakhan Corridor. Heavy fighting in Herat and Kandahar leaves thousands dead after the Soviets bombard both cities.

17   KUWAIT - For the second time in five days Iranian warplanes attack Kuwaiti border posts with rocket fire.

17   THAILAND - Sabotage is not ruled out in an explosion at the main military ammunition depot in Bangkok which kills 21 and injures more than 200.

19   UNITED STATES - Although the threat of Soviet intervention in Poland has receded, Western intelligence sources doubt it has disappeared.

21   SAUDI ARABIA - The government is quietly allowing war material bound for Iraq to pass through its territory.

22   IRAQ - Iranian jets attack the Dokan Dam and Kurdish villages around Erbil in northeastern Iraq.

23   IRAN - Iraqi forces are reported to have attacked Gilan and to have increased the shelling of Ahwaz.

25   UPPER VOLTA - A military coup led by Colonel Saye Zerbo overthrows the government of President Sangoule Lamizana.

27   IRAQ - Iranian aircraft attack the oil refinery at Kirkuk in hopes of disrupting Iraqi oil distribution through Turkey.

27   JORDAN - The government voices concern because Syria has deployed 20,000 troops and 400 tanks along the common border.

28   HAITI - The government orders the arrest of 200 persons charged with criticizing the government of Jean-Claude Duvalier.

28   EL SALVADOR - About 200 persons in army and police uniforms storm the Jesuit-run San Jose High School in San Salvador. They drag away eight leaders of the leftist coalition that is meeting there (and at least 20 other persons) and murder at least four of them. The ruling junta denies any knowledge of the affair, but the right-wing Maximiliano Hernandez Group is suspected of carrying out the raid.

29   AFGHANISTAN – Soviet aircraft bomb villages in Logar and Parwan provinces as the latest move of a new campaign to dislodge Afghan rebels active in the region.

30   IRAQ – A major naval engagement is reported near the oil terminal of Mina al-Bakr and the port city of Fao. There are conflicting reports as to the outcome with both sides claiming victory.

DECEMBER

2   EAST GERMANY – The Commander, Group Soviet Forces Germany (GSFG), General Yevgeny F. Ivanovsky, informs Western alliances that the area along the East German-Polish border has been established as a "restricted area" and all observers are prohibited to enter it.

2   SYRIA – Intelligence reports indicate nearly 30,000 Syrian troops are deployed along the Jordanian border.

3   EUROPE – Nine European Community members warn the USSR against intervening in Poland.

4   CHAD – Libyan forces are reported within 35 miles of the capital city of N'Djamena.

4   TUNISIA – In light of the worsening situation in Chad, Tunisia puts its military forces on full alert.

4   GAMBIA – The government breaks diplomatic relations with Libya because of its intervention in Chad.

5   WARSAW PACT – A meeting of the Warsaw Pact held in Moscow adjourns without a statement condemning activities in Poland or an announcement of military action against the Polish state.

5   EL SALVADOR – Three Catholic nuns and a women volunteer worker driving from San Salvador's airport to their mission at La Libertad are kidnapped and murdered (4 December) by Salvadoran security force personnel. Their bodies are discovered in a crude grave 25 miles southeast of San Salvador.

6   UNITED STATES – The government suspends all aid to El Salvador pending a complete investigation of the murder of the four American missionary women two days ago.

6   AFGHANISTAN – US official sources confirm earlier reports that the Soviet Union is preparing for a long stay in Afghanistan.

6   IRAN - Iraqi aircraft destroy the main oil pipeline at
           the port city of Bandar Khomeini.

6   IRAQ - The cities of Sulaimaniya and Darbandikhan in
           northeastern Iraq are attacked by Iranian jets in an
           attempt to cut off supplies to Kurdish insurgents.

6   SWITZERLAND - Six gasoline bombs are thrown into army
           barracks in Zurich causing thousands of dollars worth
           of damage.

9   UNITED STATES - The White House confirms that there
           have been some reservists called up in the USSR, East
           Germany, and Czechoslovakia in possible preparation
           for intervention in Poland.

10   UNITED STATES - Intelligence sources indicate the
           Soviet Union is fully prepared to intervene in Poland,
           but there is no firm information as to a possible
           timetable. The US also informs NATO that it will sup-
           ply the command with surveillance (AWACS) aircraft to
           counter any possible surprise air attack on Western
           Europe.

12   NATO - The leaders of NATO signal their readiness to
           join the US in economic, political, and military
           measures against the USSR if the Soviets move into
           Poland.

12   ITALY - Red Brigade terrorists kidnap Giovanni D'Urso,
           a Director General in the nation's Ministry of
           Justice. D'Urso is a key government figure in Italy's
           campaign against terrorism. The closure of a maximum
           security prison on the island of Asinara is demanded
           by the terrorists for his release.

12   MIDDLE EAST - Both Jordan and Syria are reported to be
           withdrawing their forces deployed along their common
           border.

13   CHAD - Soviet-equipped Libyan forces join in the bat-
           tle against Habre's troops.

13   NATO - NATO formally warns the USSR that intervention
           in Poland would bring about basic changes in the in-
           ternational situation and effectively end any East-
           West cooperation.

14   FRANCE - France warns Libya against further military
           intervention in Chad.

15   EL SALVADOR - Jose Napoleon Duarte is named the first
           civilian president in 40 years.

15   COLOMBIA - A domestic flight with 65 passengers on
        board is hijacked by leftist terrorists and flown to
        Havana, Cuba.

15   AFGHANISTAN - Afghan rebels report that Vietnamese
        troops have joined the Soviets in fighting in the
        Panjshir Valley. About 1,500 Soviet and Vietnamese
        troops are reported killed.

16   CHAD - President Goukouni Oueddei requests that Libyan
        troops drive forces loyal to Premier Hissen Habre out
        of the capital city of N'Djamena. Following a heavy
        artillery and air preparation, the Libyan forces take
        the city. Harbe flees to Cameroon. A cease-fire is
        then arranged by the OAU.

19   AFGHANISTAN - Afghan rebels attack the important
        Soviet airbase at Jalalabad.

20   GUATEMALA - Leftist guerrillas ambush an army convoy
        near Quezaltenango killing ten soldiers.

21   IRAN - The government demands the US turn over $24
        billion for the release of the 52 American hostages.
        Part of this amount is to serve as a bond until all of
        the former Shah's assets were returned to Iran.

21   LEBANON - Syrian peacekeeping forces shell Christian
        militia bases in southern Lebanon causing heavy damage
        and many casualties.

22   CUBA - Fidel Castro announces his unconditional
        support of the Soviet intervention in Afghanistan.

27   IRAN - A demonstration by about 5,000 Afghans in front
        of the Soviet Embassy in Tehran marks the anniversary
        of the Soviet invasion of Afghanistan. A second demon-
        stration follows at the Afghan Embassy where more
        thousands of Afghans demonstrate. One is killed in the
        ensuing battle with police at this location.

27   IRAQ - President Saddam Hussein claims Iraqi troops
        have opened a new offensive in the past week by in-
        vading Iran's northwestern province of Kurdistan and
        that the war front now extends the length of the Iraq-
        Iran border.

27   AFGHANISTAN - Three members of President Karmal's
        family are reported killed as they attempt to flee the
        country. Other reports indicate about 1,000 Cuban
        troops stationed at two airfields outside Kabul have
        engaged in fighting rebel raiding parties.

27   LEBANON - Syrian and Christian militia trade artillery
            fire in Zahle. The Syrians later try to storm the
            town.

28   CHAD - President Gourkouni Oueddei asks France to
            withdraw the remainder of its forces in Chad charging
            the French have been supporting Hissen Habre's forces.
            Libyan forces are now in firm control of the capital
            and, apparently, the country as well.

29   EL SALVADOR - Thousands of leftist rebels open a major
            attack against government forces in Chalatenango Pro-
            vince near the Honduran border. Intelligence reports
            indicate it may be a leftist move to establish a zone
            of occupation where a Marxist revolutionary government
            may be established.

29   AFGHANISTAN - Violent anti-Soviet and antigovernment
            demonstrations take place in Kabul. Soviet forces
            finally restore order after moving armor into the city
            and surrounding the presidential palace. Afghan police
            are reported to be taking part in the rioting as they
            protest the extension of their drafted service by two
            years.

31   IRAN - Fighting breaks out in northwest Iran between
            government forces and Iraqi-backed Kurdish rebels.

Notes

1981

JANUARY

5   IRAN - Army forces launch a counteroffensive against advancing Iraqi forces in the Khuzestan region.

6   LIBYA - Colonel Muammar Qaddafi announces that his country will merge with Chad.

6   IRAN - The government accepts the Algerian offer to act as guarantor of an agreement to release the American hostages.

6   SOUTH AFRICA - The government reports its forces have killed 81 SWAPO guerrillas during a two-week offensive in Angola.

10   EL SALVADOR - The Farabundo Marti National Liberation Front (FMNLF) launches a campaign to overthrow the government.

12   EL SALVADOR - The FMNLF claim to be fighting in 50 towns and to hold four of them, including the important city of Santa Ana in the northern part of the country. The government imposes a nationwide curfew.

14   UNITED NATIONS - Special Envoy Olaf Palme begins four days of fruitless negotiations trying to gain a cease-fire in the Iraq-Iran War.

15   ECUADOR - Ecuadorian naval units seize a US tuna boat 65 miles off the coast claiming it violated their territorial waters.

15   ITALY - In Rome, Red Brigade terrorists release the
            kidnapped Director General of the Ministry of Justice,
            Giovanni D'Urso, who has been held in captivity since
            12 December 1980.

16   UNITED STATES - The US and Norway announce an agree-
            ment to store in Norway heavy equipment for a 10,000-
            man US Marine brigade.

16   THE NETHERLANDS - Despite Communist Chinese threats,
            the government decides to sell Nationalist China
            (Taiwan) two submarines. Communist China retaliates on
            19 January by reducing its diplomatic representation
            in The Hague.

17   THE PHILIPPINES - President Marcos lifts the martial
            law edict that has been in effect since September,
            1972.

17   IRAQ - President Hussein claims the Iranian counter-
            offensive is crushed.

20   IRAN - The Iranian government frees 52 American hos-
            tages following US acceptance of an agreement worked
            out by Algeria. The group released, including nine
            Marines and three Naval personnel, was taken prisoner
            in the attack on the US Embassy in Tehran on 29
            November 1979. They have been held hostage for 444
            days.

22   UNITED STATES - The government halts the sale of the
            destroyer USS Southerland to Ecuador following Con-
            gressional protests arising from the recent seizure of
            an American fishing vessel in international waters by
            the Ecuadorian Navy.

24   SOUTH KOREA - The martial law edict is lifted by Pre-
            sident Chun Doo Hwan.

25   COMMUNIST CHINA - Chiang Ch'ing, Mao Tse-tung's widow
            and an alleged leader of the "Gang of Four," is sen-
            tenced to death for treason by a Peking court. She is
            given a two-year suspension to atone her crimes and
            confess her treason. One other defendent, Chang
            Ch'un-ch'iao, the former Mayor of Shanghai, receives a
            similar sentence; the other defendents receive less
            severe sentences.

25-28   SAUDI ARABIA - An Islamic summit conference at Taif,
            near Mecca, calls for a jihad to recover lands held by
            Israel, condemns the Soviet invasion of Afghanistan,
            and forms a commission to mediate the Iraq-Iran War.

28   UNITED STATES - The Secretary of State, Alexander
        Haig, announces that there will be no further military
        sales to Iran. All present orders are cancelled and
        the $550 million in hand will be returned.

28   PERU - Ecuadorian troops take up positions eight miles
        inside the Peruvian border as fighting breaks out in
        several areas along the border.

28   ECUADOR - President Jaime Roldos Aguilera declares a
        state of emergency because of the border fighting with
        Peru.

29   SPAIN - Basque separatists of ETA (Euzkadi za Azkata
        -suna [Homeland and Liberty]) kidnap Jose Maria Ryan,
        a nuclear engineer.

29   LEBANON - Israeli aircraft attack Palestinian bases in
        southern Labanon following the shelling of the Israeli
        settlement at Quiryat Shemona.

FEBRUARY

1   FRANCE - France begins the delivery of 60 F-1 "Mirage"
        bombers to Iraq.

1   IRAN - President Bani-Sadr accuses his rivals among
        the clergy of attempting to impose a "new despotism"
        on Iran.

2   OAS - At a meeting in Washington, DC, Ecuador and Peru
        agree to a cease-fire. It does not hold.

4   UNITED STATES - Air National Guard F-106 fighters in-
        tercept two Soviet naval Tu-20 "Bear" long-range air-
        craft 150 miles off Cape Cod, Massachusetts, in the
        latest incident of Soviet attempts to penetrate US air
        space illegally. The two bombers are escorted south
        toward Cuba.

6   SPAIN - Jose Maria Ryan is murdered by his Basque
        terrorist kidnappers. A general strike is called in
        Spain on 9 February to protest his death.

6   UNITED STATES - The State Department announces the
        first large-scale military arms sale to Somalia in
        exchange for naval-basing rights at the Red Sea port
        of Berbera.

7   THAILAND - Using nearly $2 million in US military aid,
        the Thai armed forces begin an air-sea campaign aimed
        at destroying the pirates who prey on South Vietnamese
        refugees fleeing their Communist-controlled homeland.

8 THAILAND - The government closes its border with Laos after a number of skirmishes with Laotian forces.

8 KAMPUCHEA - Prince Sihanouk joins in the fight against Vietnamese aggression in his country.

9 POLAND - Upon the dismissal of Jozef Pinkowski as Premier, Defense Minister General Wojciech Jaruzelski is appointed to replace him.

9 ISRAEL - The government expropriates an additional 4,000 acres of land in the West Bank for new settlements.

9-17 ZIMBABWE - Army forces clash with forces loyal to President Mugabe (ZANLA) and those loyal to Minister Nkomo (ZIPRA). More than 300 deaths are reported.

10 JORDAN - Jordanian forces withdraw from the joint border post with Syria near Naharayim. The government calls its Ambassador in Damascus home for consultations and abrogates the six-year-old customs and trade agreement with Syria.

11 FRANCE - The Corsican National Liberation Front is responsible for at least 46 bombings that occur during the night on the island of Corsica.

11 IRAN - The government claims its forces have crushed an Iraqi offensive in Ilam Province. It goes on to claim that Iran is now on the offensive and will fight until all Iraqi forces are driven or withdraw from Iranian soil.

16 SPAIN - A second general strike in a week hits Spain, this time over the death of Jose Ignacio Arregui Izaguirre, an ETA member suspected of killing Civil Guards (Federal Police). He had been arrested on 4 February and allegedly was tortured and died in a prison hospital. Two days of rioting accompany the strike.

16 LEBANON - A high-ranking PLO leader in Lebanon declares that PLO officers are being trained at military academies in the Soviet Union and are prepared to command large military formations. He goes on to state that at least 2,000 PLO civilians are also being trained in the sciences in the USSR.

16 COMMUNIST CHINA - The government accuses the USSR of annexing the Wakhan Corridor which links Afghanistan to China in the Hindu Kush region.

19	SPAIN - The Uruguayan Consul in Pamploma is kidnapped from his home by Basque ETA terrorists. Representatives of Austria and El Salvador are also kidnapped in Bilbao. Attempts to take the West German and Portuguese Consuls in San Sebastian fail.
20	SPAIN - An ETA broadcast demands independence from Spain for the Basque homeland and release of over 300 Basque political prisoners in return for the kidnapped foreign diplomats.
20	THE NETHERLANDS - The government announces the sale of two Dutch-built submarines to the Nationalist Chinese on Taiwan. Communist China immediately denounces the sale.
21	USSR - The Kremlin informs Mozambique that it will come to its aid if it is invaded by South Africa.
21	ZIMBABWE - The government establishes diplomatic relations with the USSR.
23	UNITED STATES - Secretary of State Alexander Haig accuses Nicaragua of supplying arms to the FMNLF in El Salvador.
23	SPAIN - A right-wing coup, led by the Civil Guard, fails. The group, led by Lieutenant Colonel Antonio Tejero Molina, storms into a session of the Spanish Cortes (Parliament) taking the cabinet and about 350 legislators as hostages. The group then declares a new government. By midday 24 February, Tejero's attempt to seize the government is an obvious failure, and Tejero and his followers are taken under arrest.
24	SOUTH AMERICA - The border between Peru and Ecuador is sealed.
25	PAKISTAN - Scores of political opponents of President Zia's government are arrested in various parts of the country after they demand an end to a martial law edict.
27	COMMUNIST CHINA - The government requests the Dutch Ambassador to leave the country and recalls its own representative in The Hague over the Dutch sale of two submarines to the Nationalist Chinese.
28	UNITED STATES - The Department of State announces that a six-man Navy training team has been sent to El Salvador to help with the repair of naval craft.
28	SPAIN - The Basque ETA terrorists release their three kidnap victims without having their demands met.

MARCH

1-11   MIDDLE EAST - An Islamic peace mission, led by Guinea
        President Ahmed Sekou-Toure, begins negotiations to
        end the Iraq-Iran War. On 6 March Iran rejects the
        peace proposals put forward by the group. Iraq also
        rejects them on 11 March.

2   UNITED NATIONS - The General Assembly votes 112-22
        against allowing South Africa to reoccupy its seat in
        the world organization.

2   FRANCE - The government halts the delivery of ten mis-
        sile-carrying patrol craft to Libya because of Libyan
        activity in Chad.

2   PAKISTAN - Three Pakistani terrorists hijack a Boeing
        727 domestic airliner and order it flown to Kabul, Af-
        ghanistan, where it is believed they receive automatic
        weapons and explosives. One hundred forty-eight
        hostages are being held.

4   AFGHANISTAN - The terrorist hijackers holding the
        Pakistani airliner release 29 of their hostages.

6   AFGHANISTAN - The hijackers holding the Pakistani
        airliner murder a passenger, a Pakistani diplomat
        stationed in Iran, and dump his body onto the runway.

6   UNITED NATIONS - The General Assembly adopts ten reso-
        lutions all of which condemn South Africa for its
        policies toward Namibia and call for mandatory sanc-
        tions against South Africa.

6   SOUTH AMERICA - Peru and Ecuador agree to withdraw
        their troops from the disputed region along their com-
        mon border.

8   IRAN - An Iranian judge demands President Bani-Sadr be
        tried for treason.

9   AFGHANISTAN - The terrorist hijackers order the Paki-
        stani airliner to be flown to Damascus, Syria.

11   YUGOSLAVIA - Rioting over the cost of living breaks
        out at the University of Pristina.

12   SYRIA - After the terrorists hijackers threaten to
        blow up the hijacked airliner, including the passen-
        gers, crew, and themselves, the Pakistani government
        agrees to release 54 of the prisoners demanded. The
        released prisoners are delivered to Syria.

14   SYRIA - When the released prisoners arrive in Syria from Pakistan, the terrorists release their remaining hostages. The hijackers are then taken into custody by Syrian authorities.

16-17   MAURITANIA - A coup attempt led by two army officer deserters fails to overthrow the government. The government accuses Morocco of complicity in the affair and severs diplomatic relations.

16   IRAN - The Ayatollah Khomeini forbids public speeches by political figures.

16   EGYPT - The government confirms it is supplying arms to rebels fighting in Chad.

17   COSTA RICA - In San Jose a bomb is thrown at a US Embassy vehicle carrying US Marine Corp personnel. Three US Marines are injured.

19   SYRIA - The government refuses a Pakistani request for extradition of the hijack terrorists and the return of the released prisoners.

19   POLAND - Special riot police injure several workers in Bydgoszcz when an unauthorized assembly refuses to disperse. The next day, 20 March, 500,000 Solidarity workers conduct a two-hour "warning strike."

20   CENTRAL AFRICAN REPUBLIC - A state of siege is proclaimed following a week of violence sparked by what is termed a rigged election.

22   EL SALVADOR - A team of 12 US Army Special Forces personnel arrive in El Salvador, increasing the number of advisors in the country to 54.

22   CENTRAL AFRICAN REPUBLIC - In a show of support for the newly elected President David Dacko, the French reinforce their garrison at Bangui.

25   EL SALVADOR - The US Embassy in San Salvador is attacked for the third time in three weeks. There is extensive damage but no casualties. The Popular Liberation Front (FPL) claims responsibility for the attack.

26   UNITED STATES - The government confirms the sale of 60 F-16 fighters to South Korea.

27   POLAND - Millions of Polish workers participate in an orderly four-hour general strike.

28   INDONESIA - Five Indonesian terrorists hijack a do-
          mestic DC-9 Garuda Airlines' flight. Fifty-five hos-
          tages are held in exchange for the demanded release of
          80 political prisoners in Indonesia, the punishment of
          certain government officials, and the expulsion "of
          all Jewish officials and Israeli militarists."

30   UNITED STATES - President Ronald Reagan is shot in the
          chest by a deranged gunman, John W. Hinckley, Jr.,
          outside a hotel in downtown Washington, DC. Three
          other people around the President are also wounded by
          the gunman.

31   THAILAND - Operating with the approval of the Thai
          government, Indonesian commandos storm the 28 March
          hijacked airliner killing four of the five terrorists
          and safely freeing all of the hostages.

31   EGYPT - The government announces it is selling ad-
          vanced weapons to Iraq to replace its war losses.

APRIL

1-3   THAILAND - A military coup attempt against the
          government of Prime Minister Prem Tinsulanond, led by
          the Deputy Commander of the Army General Sant
          Chipatima, fails when loyal troops crush the uprising.

1   UNITED STATES - The US ends financial aid to Nicaragua
          because of its support of Salvadoran guerrillas.

1   IRAN - The Ayatollah Khomeimi calls for a purge of the
          judiciary and the Revolutionary Guard.

2   LEBANON - A new wave of violence begins in which hun-
          dreds are killed. Fighting is especially heavy in
          Beirut and in the Christian city of Zahle, 30 miles to
          the east of the capital, where Syrian forces clash
          with Phalangist militia.

2-6   YUGOSLAVIA - The predominantly Albanian district of
          Kosovo is put under a state of emergency because of
          month-long student unrest. By 6 April, 11 are dead and
          57 injured.

3   UNITED STATES - In a letter to Leonid Brezhnev,
          President Reagan expresses concern over the Soviet
          buildup around Poland.

4   ITALY - The leader of the outlawed Red Brigade, Mario
          Moretti, is arrested in Milan.

8	LEBANON - President Elias Sarkis orders a cease-fire that is to be enforced throughout the country.
10	POLAND - All strikes are banned by the government.
10	UGANDA - Antigovernment violence breaks out in Kampala as members of the Uganda Freedom Movement (UFM) carry out a terrorist bomb attack.
10	INDIA - Informed sources in New Delhi report Soviet and Afghan forces are engaged against the rebels in 23 of Afghanistan's 29 provinces. Rebel forces are reported to have captured Kandahar in the south-central part of the country.
10	NICARAGUA - The government announces it has signed a ten-year $100-million cooperation package with Libya, and a $64-million technical-aid package with Cuba.
11-12	GREAT BRITAIN - The Brixton area in London is beset with two days of violence in which 150 police and 60 civilians are injured. The cause of the rioting is thought to be more social than racial, although the Brixton population is predominantly West Indian.
13	LEBANON - Syrian forces occupy the high ground around Zahle thereby cutting off Israeli supplies to the Christian city.
13	UNITED STATES - The Department of State announces the US will sell 15 F-4E "Phantom" jets to Turkey.
14	ISRAEL - The government admits it is supplying Christian forces in northern Lebanon. At the same time, the Israelis keep up their attacks on Palestinian bases in the south.
19	THE PHILIPPINES - Filipino terrorists of the New People's Army, the militant branch of the Filipino Communist Party, hurl hand grenades into a Catholic Cathedral during Easter services in Davao City on the island of Mindinao.
23	AFGHANISTAN - Heavy fighting is reported as Soviet forces attempt the recapture of Kandahar.
28	TANZANIA - The government confirms it has sent 10,000 troops into Uganda to support the Obote government in Kampala.
29	ARGENTINA - The government closes its border with Chile after Chile arrests (25 April) two Argentine army officers as spies.

30   UNITED NATIONS - Great Britain, France, and the US ve-
            to a Security Council resolution imposing mandatory
            sanctions against South Africa.

MAY

3   IRAN - While on a contract mission for Kuwait the
            seismographic research ship <u>Western Sea</u>, with a
            British crew of 19, is seized in the Persian Gulf by
            an Iranian naval vessel. The government claims the
            American-owned ship entered the Iraq-Iran declared war
            zone.

3   AFGHANISTAN - Rebel forces withdraw from Kandahar
            after the Soviets resort to bombing in an attempt to
            recapture the city.

4-24   SPAIN - Left-wing terrorists carry out a series of as-
            sassinations, bombings, and bank robberies in Madrid
            and Barcelona.

6   UNITED STATES - The Department of State orders the
            Libyan Embassy closed and all its diplomats out of the
            country within five days because of Libya's support of
            international terrorism.

7   UNITED STATES - The House Foreign Affairs Committee
            votes to lift the US embargo on arms sales to
            Argentina.

8   USSR - Muammar Qadaffi, during a state visit in Mos-
            cow, disappoints the Soviets by refusing to agree to
            their building bases in Libya.

12   UNITED STATES - The House Foreign Affairs Committee
            votes to maintain the ban on aid to friendly factions
            in Angola.

13   VATICAN - Pope John Paul II is shot by Mehmet Ali-
            Agca (a Turkish terrorist possibly in the pay of
            Bulgaria) during a ceremony in Saint Peter's Square,
            Rome.

18   LEBANON - Syrian forces move a number of Soviet-built
            SA-6 surface-to-air missiles into eastern Lebanon.

19   MEDITERRANEAN SEA - The US naval buildup in the East-
            ern Mediterranean, following the crisis raised by the
            Syrian deployment of antiaircraft missiles in Eastern
            Lebanon, includes two carrier groups headed by the <u>USS
            Forrestal</u> (CV-59) and the <u>USS Independence</u> (CV-62).
            The helicopter-cruiser <u>Moskva</u> leads a Soviet task
            group in the same area.

19   YUGOSLAVIA - The University of Pristina in the Kosovo
            district is closed   after new ethnic-motivated disor-
            ders break out.

21   USSR - The government warns Japan not to allow US nav-
            al vessels carrying nuclear weapons to dock at Japan-
            ese ports. The Japanese government rejects the Soviet
            demand (25 May).

21   ISRAEL - Israel demands Syria remove its surface-to-
            air missiles presently deployed in Lebanon and along
            the Syrian side of its border with Israel.

21   IRAN - Iraqi jets attack the Panamanian bulk carrier
            SS Louise I outside the port of Bandar Khomeimi.
            Slight damage is reported. The government also reports
            its forces have recaptured the strategic heights above
            Susangird in Khuzestan Province. Heavy fighting con-
            tinues.

24   ECUADOR - President Jaime Roldos Aguilera, his wife,
            and his defense minister are killed in an air crash in
            the Andes.

24   TURKEY - A Turkish domestic flight is hijacked by four
            Turkish-Marxist terrorists while enroute from Istanbul
            to Ankara and is flown to Bulgaria. The hijackers
            demand $500,000 and the release of 47 people held in
            Turkish prisons.

25   BULGARIA - The Turkish-Marxist hijackers are over-
            powered by their hostages at the airport at Burgas.

25   SOUTH AFRICA - Guerrillas of the ANC carry out five
            attacks to mark the 20th anniversary of the South
            African Republic.

28   LEBANON - Israeli jets attack and destroy Libyan-sup-
            plied Soviet-built SA-9 surface-to-air sites south of
            Beirut.

29   LEBANON - Israeli forces resume their attacks on
            Palestinian bases in southern Lebanon.

30   BANGLADESH - President Ziaur Rahman is assassinated in
            his sleep during a military uprising in the port city
            of Chittagong. Many others are also slain in the
            attempted military coup led by Major General Manzur
            Ahmed.

31   IRAN - Iranian forces beat off an Iraqi armored attack
            on Dehloran.

JUNE

1   BANGLADESH - The government announces the arrest of Major General Mohammed Abdul Manzoor and several other senior officers for their parts in the coup attempt.

4   SINAI - Egypt's President Sadat and Israel's Menachem Begin meet to exchange views on the on-going Lebanese situation.

7   IRAQ - Eight US-built Israeli F-16s and six F-15s attack and destroy the Osirak nuclear reactor facility near Bagdhad.

8   LEBANON - An Arab negotiated cease-fire goes into effect in Beirut and Zahle.

10   UNITED STATES - The government announces it will hold up the sale of 4 F-16 jet aircraft to Israel as a result of Israel's use of US-built aircraft on the Iraq raid.

10   IRAN - The Ayatollah Khomeini dismisses President Bani-Sadr as CinC of the Iranian Armed Forces.

16   UNITED STATES - The government announces that a decision has been made to sell certain classes of weapons to Communist China.

19   EGYPT - Three days of religious rioting in Cairo between members of the Christian Coptic sect and Muslims leaves ten dead and 55 injured.

19   UNITED NATIONS - The Security Council unanimously condemns Israel for its recent attack on Iraq.

20   WEST GERMANY - More than 100,000 march in Hamburg in protest of West German nuclear policies.

21   WEST GERMANY - Chancellor Helmut Schmidt reaffirms the West German government's decision to allow US nuclear missiles on its soil.

21   IRAN - The Majlis (Parliament) votes to impeach President Bani-Sadr and his arrest is ordered.

25   SUDAN - An explosion at the Embassy of Chad in Khartoum is blamed on Libya. All Libyan diplomats are ordered to leave the country. Sudan recalls its diplomats in Benghazi.

27   TANZANIA - The government announces it has withdrawn its 10,000 troops from Uganda.

28   IRAN - A number of important leaders of the country's present regime are killed when a bomb detonates at a rally in Tehran. In all, 72 are killed including Chief Justice Ayatollah Mohammad Beheshti, four cabinet officers, eight deputy ministers, and at least 20 members of the Majlis (Parliament).

28   OAU - The 50-nation OAU conference held in Nairobi, Kenya, calls for a peacekeeping force in Chad.

30   LEBANON - The Syrian blockade around Zahle is lifted when Lebanese police replace the Christian militiamen guarding the city.

JULY

3   GREAT BRITAIN - A wave of racially motivated rioting spreads across England in the wake of one that starts in the West London district of Southall. At least 30 cities are involved in the next ten days.

5   MEDITERRANEAN SEA - A total of 53 Soviet naval vessels are deployed in the Mediterranean.

5   IRAN - More than 100 are executed as the result of a two-week purge of opponents of the Khomeini regime.

9   UNITED STATES - The government announces the sale of 54 M-60A3 tanks to Tunisia to help its military build-up against Libyan aggression.

11-14   KASHMIR - A border clash between Indian and Pakistani troops occurs in the disputed border area in Kashmir. Five Pakistani soldiers are killed in the initial engagement. The clashes continue for three more days; at least ten more Pakistanis and four Indian soldiers are killed.

12   LEBANON - The Israelis bomb Palestinian targets in Lebanon for the second time in three days.

14   LEBANON - A Soviet-built Syrian MiG is shot down in a dogfight over Lebanese territory.

15   ISRAEL - A series of Palestinian rocket attacks are carried out against northern Israeli border settlements.

16   SOUTH AFRICA - Police use tear gas to disperse 1,000 black demonstrators who are protesting against recent mass arrests for alleged pass-law violations.

17   LEBANON - Israeli jets bomb Beirut for the first time in seven years. The main targets are the offices of Al Fatah, the militant wing of the PLO, and the offices of the Democratic Front for the Liberation of Palestine. More than 350 civilians are killed and 1,000 injured as a result of the deliberate placement of military targets in crowded civilian population centers.

17   UNITED NATIONS - At the close of a three-day conference on Kampuchea, the UN issues a report calling for the immediate withdrawal of all foreign troops and the insertion of a UN peacekeeping force.

19   KAMPUCHEA - Khmer Rouge guerrilla forces open a new offensive against the Vietnamese. Road traffic into Phnom Penh is disrupted.

22   CENTRAL AFRICAN REPUBLIC - President David Dacko declares a state of emergency following increasingly violent antigovernment demonstrations organized by three opposition parties.

24   IRAN - Mohammad Ali Raja'i replaces Abohassan Bani-Sadr as President in a landslide election victory. Bani-Sadr has already fled the country and is granted political asylum in France.

29   FRANCE - Former Iranian President Bani-Sadr and the leader of the Mujaheddin, Massoud Rajavi, are granted political asylum by France.

29   ISRAEL - The government reports that one of its aircraft has shot down a MiG-25 "Foxbat" as it tried to intercept an Israeli reconnaissance plane.

29   MOROCCO - The government announces it has restored diplomatic relations with Libya.

30   UNITED STATES - The House of Representatives resolves to warn the USSR and the Polish government against the use of force in settling Poland's internal crisis.

30   ANGOLA - The government announces South African forces have invaded its territory and have pushed inland up to 90 miles from the border.

30-31   THE GAMBIA - An attempted coup against the government of Sir Dawda Kairaba Jawara takes place while he is in London. The leftist coup is led by Socialist leader Kukli Samba. Jaswara asks for and gets Senegalese troops who enter the country the following day. Order is restored but not without considerable bloodshed. In their flight, the rebel forces take 135 hostages.

AUGUST

1   PANAMA - The de facto head of the Panamanian government, General Omar Torrijos Herrera, is killed in a airplane crash in western Panama.

2   IRAN - The government reports its aircraft have attacked and destroyed 80% of the Iraqi oil refinery at Tikrit, 100 miles inside Iraq.

3   IRAN - A bomb explodes near the presidential office building in Tehran. Seven people are killed.

3   MIDDLE EAST - The US, Israel, and Egypt sign a peacekeeping agreement for the Sinai.

4-5   THE GAMBIA - The Senegalese rescue force crushes the rebels and rescues the hostages.

5   FRANCE - The government withdraws its ambassador in Tehran and advises French citizens to leave Iran following demonstrations there protesting France's granting political asylum to former Iranian President Abolhassan Bani-Sadr.

5   BOLIVIA - President Luis Garcia Meza is forced to resign in a bloodless military coup.

5-19   POLAND - Civil unrest continues throughout Poland as Solidarity presses its demands upon the government.

10   UNITED STATES - The Defense Department announces that the US is producing neutron weapons, and that they are to be stockpiled in the US.

10   LIBERIA - A coup attempt against the Doe regime is crushed. The plotters will all be put on trial and executed.

14   LIBERIA - Five members of the Liberian People's Redemption Council, including the deputy head of state, Thomas Weh Syen, are executed for their parts in an attempted coup against the regime of Samuel K. Doe.

17   UNITED STATES - The Department of State announces that the US will no longer delay the delivery of F-15 and F-16 aircraft to Israel.

19   LIBYA - Two US Navy F-14 "Tomcat" fighters, operating from the carrier USS Nimitz (CVN-68), shoot down two Soviet-built Libyan Su-22 "Fitter" fighter-aircraft with Sidewinder missiles over the Gulf of Sidra. The Libyan aircraft appeared to have been preparing to attack the Americans.

24   ANGOLA - Two South African armored columns supported
          by aircraft strike into Angola from Namibia and attack
          rebel bases.

25   ANGOLA - Following a major battle with South African
          forces at Lubango, the government orders a general
          mobilization.

25   UNITED NATIONS - The US vetoes a Security Council re-
          solution condemning South Africa for its invasion of
          Angola.

26   NORTH KOREA - A surface-to-air missile is fired at a
          US SR-71 "Blackbird" reconnaissance aircraft operating
          off the Korean coast south of the DMZ.

28   SOUTH AFRICA - The government announces it is with-
          drawing its troops from Angola after successfully
          destroying bases from which rebels operated into
          Namibia.

30   IRAN - President Mohammad Ali Raja'i, Prime Minister
          Mohammad Javad Bahonor (Bahonar), and three other
          members of the Supreme Defense Council are killed in a
          bomb blast in Bahonor's office.

31   USSR - The government announces a new five-year aid
          agreement with Viet Nam.

SEPTEMBER

1   SOUTH AFRICA - The government claims it captured a
          Soviet warrant officer and killed other Soviet
          soldiers on the 24 August raid into Angola.

2   CENTRAL AFRICAN REPUBLIC - The government of President
          David Dacko is replaced in a bloodless coup led by
          General Andre Kolingba. Kolingba, a former Chief of
          Staff, proclaims himself head of state. An all-mili-
          tary government is appointed and the constitution
          suspended.

2   IRAN - Prosecutor General Ayatollah Ali Ghoddusi is
          killed in a bomb explosion.

2   EGYPT - More than 1,500 Muslim fundementalists, Coptic
          Christians, and opposition leaders are arrested by the
          police.

3   IRAQ - The government claims it has repulsed a major
          Iranian offensive.

3   ANGOLA - The government claims at least 10,000 South African troops are occupying southern Kunene Province.

4   LEBANON - The French Ambassador is assassinated by four unidentified gunmen in West Beirut.

6   SINGAPORE - An anti-Vietnamese coalition is formed among Prince Sihanouk, Khieu Samphan, and Son Sann.

7   USSR - Moscow warns Spain not to join NATO.

7   EGYPT - Egyptian security forces take over more than 40,000 mosques and withdraw recognition of the Coptic Patriarch, Shenouda III.

8   USSR - The government announces that 100,000 Soviet military personnel are taking part in maneuvers near the northeastern border of Poland. At the same time, it accuses the Polish labor movement, Solidarity, of planning to take over the government.

8   UNITED STATES - The Department of State declares the Soviet maneuvers are in violation of the 1975 Helsinki Accords which provide for advance notification of any maneuvers involving more than 25,000 troops.

9   SYRIA - The government extends its territorial waters to 35 nautical miles.

9   AFGHANISTAN - A Soviet-Afghan force reports it has recaptured Gulbahar, 42 miles from Kabul. The Soviet offensive is pushing into the Panjshir Valley.

11   CHILE - The government of President Augusto Pinochet Ugarte extends its ban on political activity for eight more years.

11   ZAMBIA - The government accuses South Africa of attacking military and civilian targets in Zambian territory at Sesheke, north of the Caprivi Strip.

12   GREAT BRITAIN - Nine top-level Italian terrorists are arrested by Scotland Yard. Some of them will be charged with the 1970 bombing of the Bologna railway station in Italy in which 80 people died.

13   USSR - The Soviets detonate a large-yield nuclear device or weapon at their test site at Semipalatinsk.

15   WEST GERMANY - Terrorists attack the car carrying General Frederick Kroesen, the Commander in Chief, US Army, Europe. General Kroesen is not injured even though antitank grenades are used in the attack.

15   EGYPT - The government expels 1,500 Soviets, including
            the Ambassador. The principal charge is fomenting
            religious unrest. The majority of the Soviets told to
            leave are technicans and members of the Soviet Mili-
            tary Liaison Mission in Cairo.

17   LEBANON - A car bomb detonates prematurely outside the
            command center of the PLO in Sidon. The PLO leaders
            and leftist Lebanese officials who were due to meet
            there had not yet arrived. At least 20 are killed and
            more than 100 injured. Damage is extensive. The Front
            for the Liberation of Lebanon from Aliens takes credit
            for the bombing.

19   USSR - The government admits it has troops fighting in
            Angola.

21   BELIZE - The former Central American colony of Great
            Britain becomes independent as a member of the Common-
            wealth. Belize was the last British colony on the
            American continent.

24   HONDURAS - Two US military advisors are shot by left-
            wing terrorists.

24   FRANCE - Four Armenian terrorists storm the Turkish
            Consulate and get into a firefight with French police.
            One Turkish security guard is killed and the Vice
            Consul is seriously wounded. Two terrorists are also
            wounded. The terrorists claim to be ASALA, Suicide
            Commando Yeghia Kechichian, Van Operation members.
            They demand the release of all Armenian prisoners in
            Turkish jails plus five Turkish revolutionaries and
            five Kurds. After 15 hours they release their hostages
            and surrender without incident.

26   POLAND - The government begins a crackdown on "law-
            breakers" and all anti-Soviet activity.

27   IRAN - The year-long siege of Abadan is lifted.

OCTOBER

1   KUWAIT - Iranian jets bomb the oil facilities at Um-
            Aish, 25 miles below the Iraqi border. On 4 October
            Kuwait recalls its Ambassador to Tehran.

2   UNITED STATES - The President orders the construction
            of the B-1B bomber and 100 MX ICBMs.

2   POLAND - The Solidarity Congress reelects Lech Walesa
            as its chairman and resolves (9 October) that Poland
            should have a pluralistic political system.

5   EGYPT - President Sadat accuses Libya of planning an invasion of Sudan.

5   SUDAN - President Gaafar Nimeiry dissolves the Parliament as the threat from Libya grows.

6   EGYPT - President Anwar as-Sadat is assassinated by a group of Egyptian Army Muslim fanatics during a military parade in Cairo. Vice-President Muhammad Hosni Mubarak is immediately sworn in as his successor.

6   GUATEMALA - After earlier acquiescence, the government now refuses to acknowledge the independence of Belize.

10   WEST GERMANY - An estimated 250,000 people march in Bonn protesting the NATO decision to deploy nuclear weapons in western Europe.

12   UNITED STATES - The government reaffirms that it will not negotiate with the PLO until that organization recognizes Israel's right to exist.

13   MOROCCO - Polisario forces attack the Moroccan garrison at Guelta Zemmour, 25 miles from Morocco's border with Mauritania. The government immediately accuses Mauritania of harboring the guerrillas.

16   TURKEY - The government abolishes all political parties and confiscates their assets.

17   ROMANIA - Strikes are reported in Jiu Valley, the country's largest coal-producing region. The cause of the strikes appears to be the imposition of bread rationing and a general food shortage.

18   POLAND - The Central Committee of Poland's Communist Party ousts its leader, Stanislaw Kania.

18   SUDAN - More than 10,000 people are detained by the security forces in the crackdown on pro-Libyan elements.

19   IRAN - An Iraqi missile damages the Liberian tanker SS Al Tajdar near the northern port of Bandar Khomeini. A bombing attack seriously damages the Panamanian bulk carrier SS Moira in the same area.

20   POLAND - Police clash with Solidarity marchers in a major outbreak of violence in Katowice.

21   NATO - NATO reaffirms its decision to deploy nuclear weapons in western Europe but indicates it will cancel the plan if the Soviet Union removes the weapons it has targeted on western Europe.

21   UNITED STATES - The Senate passes a foreign aid bill
            that prohibits dealings with any country detonating a
            nuclear device or weapon.

25   IRAN - The Indian tanker SS Rashi Vish Wamitra is hit
            by Iraqi missiles and catches fire outside Bandar
            Khomeini.

26   HONDURAS - The government reports that the towns of
            Mocoron, Auka, Tipia, and Leimas near the border were
            attacked by Nicaraguan forces.

27   SWEDEN - Stockholm reports that a Soviet "Whiskey"
            -class submarine, probably armed with nuclear tor-
            pedos, ran aground inside Swedish territorial waters
            and within a restricted area near the naval base at
            Karlskrona, 300 miles south of Stockholm. The vessel
            is finally released on 6 November.

27   FINLAND - President Urho Kekkonen resigns citing his
            age (he is 81) and poor health as the reasons.

27   POLAND - Military forces take control of much of the
            country "to maintain law and order." The wave of
            strikes continues, however, and builds in intensity.

28   UNITED STATES - The Senate approves the sale of five
            AWACS aircraft to Saudi Arabia.

31   HONDURAS - The government reports Nicaraguan forces
            have crossed the Coco (Segoria) River into Honduras.

NOVEMBER

            POLAND - Labor problems continue throughout the month.

1   ISRAEL - The Israelis reject a Saudi Arabian peace
            plan for the Middle East claiming it would lead to the
            destruction of Israel.

1   ANTIGUA AND BARBUDA - The former British island colony
            of Antigua becomes independent as Antigua and Barbuda.

2   USSR - The government refuses a demand to allow
            Swedish officials to inspect the grounded Soviet
            submarine.

3   CHAD - Libyan forces begin withdrawing from Chad.

4   ISRAEL - The government closes Bir Zeit University,
            the largest Arab university in the occupied West Bank,
            following three days of disturbances.

6   SWEDEN - The Soviet submarine which ran aground is refloated and allowed to depart.

6   ANGOLA - South African military aircraft bomb the city of Cahama, 120 miles inside the border. An Angolan aircraft is shot down.

8   JORDAN - The government announces it is buying $2 million worth of Soviet-built SA-7 missiles.

8   ZIMBABWE - The merger of the former Zimbabwe rebel armies into a single force is completed.

10   UNITED STATES - The Department of State accuses the USSR of using chemical weapons in Afghanistan. The USSR denies the accusation.

10   CHAD - The commander of Libyan forces in Chad, Colonel Radan Salah, states he is convinced that civil war will erupt once his troops are replaced by those of an African peacekeeping force.

11   GREECE - The government announces it wants to ban all nuclear weapons from its territory and wants to negotiate the speedy removal of those already there.

13   CHAD - The OAU peacekeeping force, composed of troops from Nigeria, Senegal, and Zaire, arrives in country.

14   THE GAMBIA - The government announces it has formed a new federation with Senegal to be known as Senegambia.

15   SPAIN - At least 100,000 march in Madrid to protest Spain's possible entry into NATO.

16   ISRAEL - Israeli forces blow up three West Bank Arab houses in reprisal for recent attacks on Israeli citizens.

16   CHAD - Libyan forces complete their withdrawal out of Chad.

17-19   LEBANON - Christian militiamen surround and besiege the UN peacekeeping force headquarters. The siege lasts until 19 November.

21   THE NETHERLANDS - At least 100,000 march in Amsterdam to protest the US deployment of nuclear weapons in Europe.

24   UNITED STATES - The Congress approves the sale of 40 F-16 aircraft to Pakistan.

25   ·ARAB LEAGUE - The preliminary meeting of the Arab League held in Fez, Morocco, collapses after a short debate on the Saudi Arabian peace plan for the Middle East. Further meetings are suspended for six months.

25   SEYCHELLES - A coup attempt by 50 mercenaries, disguised as rugby players, against the rule of President France-Albert Rene fails. After they are engaged by government force, 44 of the mercenaries hijack an Indian airliner and fly to Durban, South Africa, where all but five are set free (2 December). The Seychelles government accuses South Africa of complicity in the abortive coup (28 November).

26   SPAIN - The Cortes (Parliament) approves Spain's entry into NATO.

29   SYRIA - A car bomb explodes in front of a school in Damascus killing 90 persons and wounding scores more. Muslim Brotherhood terrorists are accused of the attack.

29   MIDDLE EAST - Iranian forces open an offensive against Iraqi positions in Khuzestan Province.

30   UNITED STATES - The US and Israel sign a memorandum of understanding on strategic cooperation in the Middle East.

30   ISRAEL - The government authorizes pro-Israeli Palestinian leaders to set up their own armed units for self-protection.

30   ANGOLA - The government accuses South Africa of blowing up its only oil refinery.

DECEMBER

POLAND - Labor troubles continue as the government seeks ways to placate the workers without incurring the wrath of the Soviet Union.

2   SOUTH AFRICA - The government releases 39 of 44 mercenaries accused of hijacking an Air India jetliner after a failed attempt at overthrowing the government of President France-Albert Rene of Seychelles.

3   ISRAEL - The government conditionally accepts a European peacekeeping force in the Sinai. The force will be composed of British, Dutch, French, and Italian troops.

8   CUBA - A Boeing 727 and two Venezuelan DC-9s are hi-
         jacked over Venezuela and flown to Havana after flying
         all over the Caribbean. Eleven hijackers are taken in-
         to custody by Cuban police. The hijackers are a mixed
         bag of Puerto Rican nationalists, Salvadoran leftists,
         and Venezuelans seeking ransom and the release of po-
         litical prisoners.

11   ARGENTINA - A three-man military junta ousts the gov-
         ernment of President Roberto Eduardo Viola. Lieutenant
         General Leopoldo Galtieri takes the presidency.

13   POLAND - Martial law is imposed in Poland in the face
         of growing labor unrest.

14   ISRAEL - The Golan Heights are annexed after the
         Knesset approves the act.

14   UNITED STATES - The US halts food shipments to Poland
         in light of the recent martial law edict.

15   LEBANON - The Iraqi Embassy is completely destroyed by
         a car bomb driven into the building. About 55 people
         are killed and some 100 injured when the building
         collapses. The Iraqi government blames Iran and Syria
         for the attack. A group calling itself the Iraqi
         Liberation Army-General Command claims credit for the
         attack.

16   BAHREIN - Government forces crush an Iranian-sponsored
         revolution.

17   ITALY - Brigadier General James L. Dozier, a senior US
         officer serving as Deputy Chief of Staff for Logistics
         at Headquarters, Land Forces Southern Europe, in
         Verona, Italy, is kidnapped by the Red Brigade.

18   UNITED NATIONS - The Security Council unanimously
         declares Israel's annexation of the Golan Heights
         illegal.

18   UNITED STATES - In retaliation for Irsael's annex-
         ation of the Golan Heights, the government suspends a
         recently signed memorandum of understanding with
         Israel that deals with a unified position against
         Soviet threats in the Middle East.

23   UNITED STATES - President Reagan warns the USSR and
         Poland of possible sanctions if the "outrages" against
         the Polish people continue.

28   UNITED STATES - The government announces it is selling
         $97 million in military spare parts to Nationalist
         China (Taiwan).

29   UNITED STATES - The government imposes a list of
            sanctions against the USSR for its activities in
            Poland.

31   GHANA - The government of President Hilla Limann is
            overthrown in a bloody coup led by Jerry J. Rawlings,
            a former flight lieutenant who had previously led a
            coup against Lieutenant General Fred Akuffo's military
            regime in 1979.

31   SAUDI ARABIA - The government announces it is reestab-
            lishing diplomatic relations with Libya after a 14-
            month break.

Notes

1982

KAMPUCHEA - Heavy fighting is reported between Vietnamese-led government forces and Khmer Rouge guerrillas near the Thai border. This fighting lasts into February.

1   GHANA - A new Provisional National Defense Council is set up to rule with Jerry Rawlings as its leader. The constitution is suspended. Former President Hilla Limann is arrested.

1   THAILAND - Thai naval vessels sink a Kampuchean gun-boat that was discovered inside Thai territorial waters. Eight persons aboard the Kampuchean vessel are killed.

1   ITALY - Red Brigade terrorists issue a picture of US Brigadier General James L. Dozier who was kidnapped in Verona on 17 December 1981. The picture was left in a Rome bar.

2   UNITED STATES - Intelligence sources report that the USSR is moving an additional 10,000 combat troops into Afghanistan. This will raise the total Soviet strength there to 95,000.

3   HONDURAS - The government claims Nicaraguan troops have twice, since the beginning of the year, crossed the border into Honduras in the east coast region of Mosquitia. About 200 Nicaraguan refugees are reported to have been killed during the raids.

3   EL SALVADOR - Rebel bombing of electrical installations knocks out power in San Salvador for two
hours. Most other cities in the country are also
affected. Later, a firefight between rebels and
government forces breaks out at a telegraph office in
San Salvador.

3   SOUTH KOREA - The government lifts the 36-year-old
curfew that has been in effect since the end of WWII.

3   EGYPT - The government signs an agreement with France
to purchase 20 Mirage 2000 fighter aircraft.

3-7   MIDDLE EAST - Oil pipelines carrying crude oil to
Mediterranean ports are blown up in two separate
incidents by an anti-Iraqi group calling itself the
Iraqi Mujahedeen Movement. The 3 January blast knocks
out the Iraqi line to Tripoli, Lebanon, while the 7
January attack is on the Iraqi pipeline to Turkey.

11   HAITI - The island of Tortuga is taken by Haitian
rebels. Government forces immediately recapture the
island.

12   SAUDI ARABIA - Sixty of the US-built F-15s purchased
for the Saudi Air Force are delivered.

13   LIBYA - Muammar Qaddafi is wounded by a bullet fired
by a Libyan army officer.

15   SPAIN - Prior to its entrance into NATO, the Spanish
government replaces its four top military leaders amid
speculation that the relief is tied to an alleged 1981
plot to overthrow the government.

15   THE PHILIPPINES - Two Philippine Air Force planes
strafe a Japanese methyl-alcohol carrying chemical
tanker when it strays into territorial waters south of
Mindinao. Allegedly flying no flag and refusing to
answer radio calls, the ship is suspected of running
guns to the rebels on Mindinao when it is taken under
attack.

17   VIET NAM - The government offers a partial withdrawal
of its forces in Kampuchea if the Thai government
stops giving sanctuary and arms to the Khmer Rouge
rebels.

17   SRI LANKA - The government ends the state of emergency
that has been in effect since August 1981.

18   THE PHILIPPINES - The government accepts responsibility for the attack on an unarmed Japanese chemical
tanker on 15 January.

18   FRANCE - An Assistant Military Attache at the US Embassy, Paris, Lieutenant Colonel Charles R. Ray, is shot and killed while walking to his car. His assailant is reported to be of "Middle Eastern appearance." The Lebanese Armed Revolutionary Faction claims credit for the murder.

19   KAMPUCHEA - Vietnamese forces operating near the Thai border call in air strikes for the first time against Khmer Rouge targets.

22   ARGENTINA - The government abrogates the 1972 border treaty with Chile.

24   USSR - The Soviets report the death of Lieutenant General P. I. Shkidchenko in Afghanistan in January as a result of the rebels shooting down his helicopter.

27   EL SALVADOR - Leftist rebels using artillery and placed explosive charges seriously damage a number of US-supplied Salvadoran military aircraft (6 of 14 helicopters, six fighters, one trainer, and five C-47 transports) at the Ilopango Air Base outside San Salvador.

27   HONDURAS - Nine years of military rule end with the installation of Roberto Suazo Cordova as President.

28   ITALY - Italian antiterrorist units raid an apartment in Padua and free US Brigadier General James Dozier after 42 days of captivity. Three male and two female members of the Red Brigade are apprehended along with arms, ammunition, and dossiers of a number of prominent people whom the police suspect of being targeted as future kidnap victims. Dozier is unhurt.

28   JORDAN - King Hussein calls upon the nation's youth to volunteer to fight alongside the Iraqis against Iran. A volunteer organization called the Yarmouk Brigade is formed in what Hussein calls an "arabization" of the war.

28   UNITED STATES - The Turkish Consul General in Los Angelos is assassinated while driving in his automobile. The group known as Justice Commandos for the Armenian Genocide claims credit for the attack.

30   POLAND - Clashes between workers and police in Gdansk result in the arrest of more than 200.

31   EL SALVADOR - A force estimated at about five hundred rebels enters a village northeast of San Salvador and kills 200 civilians.

FEBRUARY

1   LIBYA - The government claims that it has opened its
           borders with Egypt for the first time in three years.
           The next day (2 February) Egypt denies that the border
           is open.

1   SENEGAMBIA - The confederation of Senegal and Gambia
           comes into being.

2   EL SALVADOR - Leftist rebels carry out a daylight
           attack on the province capital of Usulutan near the
           southern coast of the country.

2   SYRIA - In Hama (Hamah) an antigovernment uprising
           stemming from the ongoing struggle between the gov-
           ernment and the Sunni Muslim Brotherhood begins. The
           call to overthrow the government goes out from the
           temples following reports that a Muslim Brotherhood
           center was attacked and leveled by government forces.
           Before the uprising is quelled (after 19 January) many
           hundreds are killed on both sides.

5   UNITED STATES - The Israeli Ambassador to the US,
           Moshe Arens, states that an Israeli invasion into
           Lebanon to punish the PLO is just "a matter of time."

6   SYRIA - The Foreign Ministry reports that there is no
           truth to reports that there was a coup attempt against
           President Hafez al-Assad.

10   ZIMBABWE - The government says it has uncovered a
           cache of weapons in Matabeleland that is large enough
           to equip a 5,000-man force.

10   COLOMBIA - Five persons posing as Colombian National
           Police break into the rooms of two US Drug Enforcement
           Agents in Cartagena. The two DEA are kidnapped, shot,
           and left for dead. Both survive the attack.

11   OAU - The OAU warns Chad's President Goukouni Oueddei
           that if he continues in his refusal to negotiate with
           the rebels in his country the OAU will withdraw its
           peacekeeping force.

13   EGYPT - A court orders the release of more than 1,000
           political prisoners many of whom have been held since
           the declaration of a state of emergency in September
           1981. The court also removes a number of prohibitions
           against publishers.

17   THAILAND - A Thai patrol engages a Vietnamese force
           that has crossed into Thailand in pursuit of Khmer
           Rouge guerrillas.

17   ZIMBABWE - Prime Minister Robert Mugabe dismisses
          Joshua Nkomo from the coalition government after
          evidence implicates Nkomo in a plot to overthrow the
          government.

18   EGYPT - The government announces it has acquired two
          Communist Chinese submarines.

18   UNITED STATES - President Reagan denies the US has
          plans to send combat troops into El Salvador.

22   UNITED NATIONS - An official announces plans to send
          1,000 more peacekeeping troops to southern Lebanon to
          reinforce the 6,000 already there. This decision is
          apparently reached in light of Israeli threats to
          enter the country if PLO raids into Israel do not
          cease.

23   UGANDA - Armed rebels of the Uganda Freedom Movement
          (UFM) attack the main army barracks in Kampala. In the
          ensuing 8-hour firefight at least 67 rebels are
          killed.

26   UNITED NATIONS - The Security Council orders the UNEF
          in Lebanon increased from 6,000 to 7,000.

26   UNITED STATES - The US relaxes its trade restrictions
          with South Africa.

MARCH

1   IRAN - A number of reports indicate Iranian forces
          have dislodged the Iraqis and are pushing them back
          across the border into Iraqi territory in heavy
          fighting in the north.

2   EL SALVADOR - The government suddenly halts a major
          offensive against rebel forces operating near
          Suchitoto 30 miles east of the northern city of Santa
          Ana. That most of the rebels have fled north in
          advance of the government troops is the reason given
          for stopping the operation.

3   JORDAN - Jordan Radio announces that the first group
          of Jordanian "volunteers" has left to join the Iraqis
          in their war against Iran.

3   ARGENTINA - The government reasserts its claim to
          sovereignty over the Falkland Islands which the
          Argentines call the Islas Malvinas. The Falklands have
          been British possessions since 1833. The issue of
          their ownership has been before the UN for the past 15

3   ARGENTINA (Cont'd) - years. Argentina has stated (1 March) that "other means" would be sought to end the situation if it could not be settled politically.

8   EL SALVADOR - Heavy fighting breaks out as a rebel offensive designed to disrupt the 28 March elections begins.

10   UNITED STATES - The government orders an embargo on all oil products imported from Libya and bans the export of all high technology items to that country.

11-12   SURINAM - Right-wing elements begin an uprising during the hiatus following the resignation of the old government (4 February) and before a new government can be formed. Sergeant Major Willem Hawker is released from the prison he has been in since he led an abortive coup attempt in 1981. On 12 March, forces loyal to the ruling National Military Council regain control and capture Hawker. He is immediately executed.

13   ANGOLA - South African forces conduct a raid into Angola. They claim to have captured a large quantity of weapons at a SWAPO camp and to have killed 210 rebels.

15   AFGHANISTAN - Rebels kill five officials of the ruling People's Democratic Party (PDP) during a party conference in Kabul.

17   SINAI - The first contingent of 670 US troops arrives at Ophira, on the Red Sea coast of the Sinai Peninsula, 10 miles north of Sharm esh Sheikh, preparatory to the planned withdrawal of Israeli forces.

18   GUATEMALA - An army helicopter spots a group of terrorists after they have shot and killed an American plantation owner 33 miles north of Guatemala City in San Christobal. The government lays the blame for the incident on a group known as the Guerrilla Army of the Poor.

19-20   THE FALKLANDS - A group of 50-60 Argentinian civilian scrap merchants lands on South Georgia Island ostensibly to dismantle an unused whaling station. They immediately hoist the Argentine flag and inform the British authorities that they (the British) are illegally on the island. This is immediately reported to England and to the British Parliament. Other sources report both Great Britain and Argentina are dispatching naval units to the area.

22   IRAN - A new Iranian offensive begins and is described as highly successful, with penetrations of up to 24 miles into Iraqi positions being reported. By 24 March, 3,000 Iraqi prisoners are reported to have been taken.

23   GUATEMALA - The government of President Fernando Romeo Lucas Garcia is toppled by a junta led by General Efrain Rios Montt. Montt assumes the Presidency, suspends the constitution, and bans all political parties.

24   BANGLADESH - The government of President Abdus Sattar is overthrown by a military coup led by Lieutenant General Hossain Mohammad Ershad. Ershad imposes martial law and suspends the constitution.

28   IRAQ - President Hussein calls for a cease-fire in the Gulf War. On 30 March the Iraqi Fourth Army is withdrawn from Iranian territory.

29   ARGENTINA - All leaves for the nation's naval personnel are cancelled.

30   IRAN - The government claims its latest offensive has regained 800 square miles of territory.

30   GREAT BRITAIN - The government informs Argentina that it will not tolerate further interference with British sovereignty in the Falklands.

31   UNITED STATES - The government recognizes the new regime in Guatemala.

APRIL

1   THE FALKLANDS - At 9 PM local time 70 Argentinian commandos land from the destroyer Santisima Trinidad on East Falkland (Soledad) Island where they go into hiding. "Operation ROSARIO," the Argentine invasion of the Malvinas (Falkland) Islands, has begun.

1   PANAMA - The Panamanian government takes over control of the Panama Canal on the basis of the agreement signed with the US in 1978.

2   THE FALKLANDS - At 3 AM (0300 hours) local time the Soledad force splits into two elements and moves to capture the Marine barracks at Moody Point and the Government House. The first patrol reaches the Government House at 5 AM (0500) and, after attempting to convince the Royal Marines to surrender, opens fire.

2   THE FALKLANDS (Cont'd) – Upon arrival at the barracks at 5:30 AM (0530), the second patrol finds them empty. Simultaneously, to theinitial landing, at about 3:45 AM (0345), ten Argentinian frogmen are put ashore by the submarine _Santa Fe_ near Pembroke Light at Port Stanley on East Falkland to secure the main entrance to the harbor. Then, at 6:45 AM (0645), approximately 600 Argentinian Marines are embarked in amphibious vehicles under the protection of the _Santisima Trinidad_ from the LST _Cabo San Antonio._ The landing force, under the command of Argentine Marine Rear Admiral Carlos Busser then enters York Harbor where it meets minimal resistance from the 68 British Marines stationed at Port Stanley. The Argentine force is supported by an old-model aircraft carrier, landing craft, and several destroyers and is under the command of Vice Admiral Juan Jose Lombardo. The 80-man British Royal Marine garrison holds out for three hours equipped only with small arms. The airport is then secured and C-130 transports begin flying in reinforcements from Comodoro Rivadivia Air Force Base on the mainland. At 8 AM (0800) Governor Rex Hunt orders the Royal Marines to lay down their arms and surrender. Argentine casualty figures for the operation are disputed but British losses are zero. At 9:25 AM (0925) Governor Hunt formally surrenders.

2   ARGENTINA – The government claims its invasion of the Falklands is the result of an "interminable succession of British evasions and delays designed to perpetuate their dominion over the islands and their zone of influence."

2   GREAT BRITAIN – The government severs diplomatic relations with Argentina.

3   UNITED NATIONS – Resolution 502 passes the Security Council. This resolution calls for the immediate cessation of hostilities in the Falklands.

3   GREAT BRITAIN – Prime Minister Margaret Thatcher informs Parliament that a strong naval task force is being dispatched to the Falklands to restore the British hegemony.

3   THE FALKLANDS – At 12 noon the Argentine frigate _Guerrico_ lands troops by helicopter at Grytviken on South Georgia Island. The British garrison of 23 Royal Marines engages the Agentinians and shoots down at least two, possibly three, aircraft and severely damages the Argentine frigate, which is forced to retire. After two hours of heavy fighting, the Royal Marines are forced to surrender. About 15 Argentinian

3   THE FALKLANDS (Cont'd) - Marines are dead, 20 wounded. Only one British Marine is wounded. This same day the total of 86 Royal Marines and British civilians captured in the Falklands are released in Montevideo, Uruguay.

4   FRANCE - An Israeli diplomat is shot and killed in the lobby of a Paris apartment house by an unidentified woman. The Lebanese Armed Revolutionary Faction claims responsibility for the assassination.

5   GREAT BRITAIN - A naval task force, with the carrier HMS Hermes as flagship, sails for the Falklands after Queen Elizabeth II approves (4 April) the requisition of a fleet of merchant ships. Among the forces embarked (on the liner Canberra) is the 3rd Parachute Battalion of 1,950 men. "Operation CORPORATE" begins.

5   THE FALKLANDS - The Argentinian Marine raiding force that took the islands is withdrawn back to the main- land. They are replaced by troops who are reported to be conscripts with less than two months service.

6   EUROPE - The European Economic Community (EEC) votes an embargo against Argentina.

6   CHILE - The government alerts its forces and reinforces its southern garrisons in response to the Argentinian invasion of the Falklands.

6   PERU - The government sends a number of its Mirage fighters to reinforce the Argentine air force. The Peruvian aircraft will not see action in the fighting that lies ahead.

6   USSR - The government offers direct military aid to Argentina. The Argentine government declares it will refuse Soviet aid "until the last possible moment."

7   AFGHANISTAN - The end of winter brings reports of renewed fighting. Two rocket attacks on Kabul are noted along with reports of fighting in three other areas including the second most important city of Kandahar.

7   UGANDA - Authorities arrest nearly 10,000 people sus- pected of having knowledge of rebels operating around Kampala.

7   GREAT BRITAIN - Defense Minister John Nott announces a 200 nautical mile exclusion area around the Falklands effective 11 PM (1100) EDT, 11 April, and declares that any Argentine vessel found inside that area will be considered hostile.

7   CHILE - The Chilean navy begins to deploy southward in anticipation of some sort of Argentine action in the Beagle Channel.

7   IRAN - Former Foreign Minister Sadegh Ghotbzadeh is arrested for plotting the assassination of the Ayatollah Khomeini.

9   ARGENTINA - The government announces it has installed a governor (Major General Mario Benjamin Menendez) and a group of governmental experts in the Falklands. Martial law is declared there and severe punishments are announced for those breaking the law. Port Stanley and Darwin are renamed Puerto Argentino and Belgrano, respectively.

9   GREAT BRITAIN - The government exercises deception by reporting that a number of Royal Navy surface combatants are sailing for the Falklands.

11-14   ISRAEL - A deranged Jewish immigrant soldier, Alan Harry Goodman, opens fire on Muslim worshipers at the Dome of the Rock in Jerusalem killing two and wounding 20. He is subdued by the police. Later in the day Israeli security troops are forced to use tear gas to disperse an angry Muslim crowd on the Temple Mount. Within days the violence spreads throughout the city, and protest demonstrations take place throughout the Arab world (12 April). On 13 April Goodman is charged with murder. On 14 April a one-day general strike takes place throughout the Muslim Middle East. On 20 April the UN Security Council condemns Israel for the attack.

12   THE FALKLANDS - The 200-nautical-mile exclusion imposed by the British goes into effect.

14   THE FALKLANDS - Intelligence reports indicate about 10,000 Argentinian troops are now in the Falklands.

15   EGYPT - Five assassins of Anwar Sadat are executed in Cairo.

15   ARGENTINA - Argentine naval forces move to sea, but stay in shallow water to prevent attack by British submarines. The Argentine press announces the arrival of two Soviet electronic warfare ships at Ushusia.

17   LEBANON - An Assistant US Military Attache, Major Frederick C. Hof, is wounded on a Beirut street by an unknown assailant.

18   SYRIA - The government breaks relations with Iraq.

18   NORTH AFRICA - Polisario says it will get weapons from the Soviets if the US deals with Morocco.

21   LEBANON - Israeli jets attack Palestinian refugee camps in southern Lebanon.

21   ATLANTIC OCEAN - An Argentine Air Force Boeing 707 attempts to reconnoiter the British task force steaming for the Falklands, but is intercepted and turned back by a British vertical takeoff and landing (VTOL) "Harrier" fighter.

21-23   SOUTH GEORGIA ISLAND - A dozen British heliborne commandos from the Special Boat Service (SBS) reconnoiter South Georgia Island. Two Wessex helicopters crash in a blizzard with 70-knot winds. There are no British casualties. The force withdraws in 24 hours. A second reconnaissance is performed on 23 April.

25   UNITED STATES - The government announces it is contributing 1,200 troops to the 3,000 peacekeeping force on the Sinai Peninsula.

25   SINAI - The eastern portion of the Sinai Desert is returned to Egypt under the terms of the 1979 peace treaty signed with Israel.

25   GREAT BRITAIN - The government announces that the Falklands exclusion area includes any vessel or aircraft threatening its fleet.

25-26   SOUTH GEORGIA ISLAND - As British forces prepare to land on South Georgia Island, the Argentine submarine Santa Fe is sighted at 6:30 AM (0630) as it proceeds toward the island with 50 reinforcements for the 44-man Argentine garrison. (One report has it leaving Grytviken Harbor.) It is attacked at 10 AM (1000) by two "Lynx" antisubmarine helicopters. The submarine is badly damaged and has to be abandoned in King Edward Harbor; she settles in shallow water. At 4 PM (1600), about 100 men from Company M, 42d Royal Marine Commando, land and recapture the island by 10 AM (1000), 26 April. In all, 156 Argentine military personnel plus the 83-man crew of the Santa Fe and 39 civilians are captured. There are no casualties on either side.

27   THE FALKLANDS - Special Air Service (SAS) and Special Boat Service (SBS) teams are landed on East and West Falkland to prepare for an invasion.

30   ARGENTINA - Foreign Minister Nicanor Costa Mendez states that the issue of sovereignty over the Falklands is "non-negotiable."

30   GREAT BRITAIN - The government extends the blockade of
            the Falklands to include aircraft.

30   UNITED STATES - The US announces its support for the
            British claims in the Falklands.

MAY

1   THE FALKLANDS - Flying from Ascension Island just
            below the Equator in the South Atlantic, a lone
            British "Vulcan" bomber drops 21 1,000-pound bombs on
            the Port Stanley airport. The bomber is refueled three
            times enroute. Air strikes from carrier-based VTOL
            "Harrier" aircraft hit the airfields at Port Stanley
            and Goose Green. Helicopters then attack Goose Green
            with rockets. British naval vessels begin a bombard-
            ment of shore installations at Port Stanley. In an-
            other action, six Argentinian Mirages and Skyhawks
            attack the British fleet. In the ensuing dogfight with
            "Harriers," one Mirage is shot down. Another Argentine
            Mirage is shot down by Argentine ground fire from the
            Falklands. A second attack by Argentine "Canberra"
            bombers results in one "Canberra" lost and another
            damaged by "Harriers." Two British fast frigates (FF)
            (HMS Glamorgan & HMS Arrow) are slightly damaged in
            the action. The British task force also attacks an
            unidentified submarine (Argentine sub San Luis) and
            drives it off. HMS Onyx puts SAS and SBS teams ashore
            to begin ground operations.

1   ARGENTINA - The government calls up 80,000 reservists.

1   POLAND - More than 30,000 demonstrate in Warsaw for
            the release of Lech Walesa. Riot police break up a
            second Solidarity-sponsored demonstration on 3 May. A
            curfew is reestablished in Warsaw.

2   THE FALKLANDS - When three Argentine squadrons set out
            to engage the British fleet, the Argentinian cruiser
            General Balgrano (ex-USS Phoenix[CL-46]) in the
            company of two destroyers is sunk by the British
            nuclear submarine, HMS Conqueror. Of the ship's crew
            of 1,024, 368 are lost. In another engagement two
            Argentine small craft are attacked by British "Sea
            King" helicopters after the ships had fired on and
            damaged a third "Sea King." One vessel is sunk, the
            other damaged. The damaged ship limps back to Puerto
            Deseado on 6 May.

3   ISRAEL - Prime Minister Menachem Begin announces that
            Israel claims sovereignty over the West Bank and would
            assert that claim when the five-year transitional
            period stipulated in the Camp David Accords expires.

3   IRAN - On the fourth day of the new Iranian offensive
        fighting continues eight miles from the border.

4   THE FALKLANDS - About 70 miles northeast of Port
        Stanley the British destroyer HMS Sheffield is lost
        while serving as a radar picket station. The ship is
        hit by a French-built AM-39 "Exocet" air-to-ground
        missile fired by one of six Argentinian attack
        aircraft (two are French-built "Super Entendards").
        Twenty British crewmen are killed and 30 are wounded.
        The ship burns to the hull and is taken in tow. (It is
        scuttled on 10 May.) During the rescue HMS Yarmouth
        engages and probably sinks an unidentified submarine
        near the burning ship. In another action British
        aircraft carry out two raids on the airport at Port
        Stanley. One British "Harrier" is destroyed by a
        Argentine "Tigercat" missile.

4   IRAN - Iranian gunners shoot down a plane carrying
        Algerian Foreign Minister Muhammad Seddik Benyahia on
        a peace mission to the Gulf War. Benyahia is killed in
        the crash.

5   THE FALKLANDS - The British bomb Port Stanley Airport.

6   THE FALKLANDS - Two British "Harrier" aircraft are
        declared missing, probably due to a mid-air collision
        while on combat air patrol (CAP) in bad weather.

7   GREAT BRITAIN - The government extends its exclusion
        area to include any ship outside Argentine territorial
        waters.

7   IRAN - Iranian troops reach the Iraq-Iran border in
        their latest offensive.

9   LEBANON - Israeli jets attack Palestinian bases in
        southern Lebanon. In retaliation, Jewish settlements
        in Galilee are shelled by Palestinian artillery.

9   ARGENTINA - The government restates its conditions for
        negotiations on the Falklands in somewhat more concil-
        iatory tones. A British declaration of Argentine
        sovereignty is no longer a precondition. In a separate
        incident an Argentinian intelligence collection ship
        (AGI) is sunk inside the exclusion zone. Twenty-five
        on board are rescued. Also, British naval vessels
        shell Port Stanley Airport and shoot down an Argentine
        Puma helicopter. At the same time "Harrier" jets chase
        off an inbound Argentine C-130 transport. Twenty
        "Harrier" jets land at Ascension Island, refuel, and
        depart to meet the converted helicopter carrier SS
        Atlantic Conveyor in the South Atlantic.

10   GREAT BRITAIN - Additional naval units, including <u>HMS Bristol</u> and two Exocet missile frigates, depart for the South Atlantic. At the same time, the government establishes a 100-nautical-mile control zone around Ascension Island.

10   THE FALKLANDS - A ferryboat, <u>Isla de los Estados</u>, is mistaken for a tanker on radar and is sunk by naval gun fire in the Falkland Sound.

10   NICARAGUA - The government signs an agreement with the USSR for $166.8 million in aid over the next five years.

11   THE FALKLANDS - Eight British Special Air Service (SAS) personnel are put ashore opposite Pebble Island to carry out reconnaissance and sabotage missions.

12   THE FALKLANDS - A flight of 12 Argentinian A-4 "Sky-hawks"s flying from the mainland attack a group of British warships in thick fog near the Falklands. There is some damage to one British frigate; three Argentine aircraft are lost.

12   GREAT BRITAIN - The <u>MS Queen Elizabeth II</u> sails from England with the Fifth Brigade embarked. It later makes a rendezvous with the carriers <u>HMS Invincible</u> and <u>HMS Hermes</u>. Upon arriving at South Georgia Island, the brigade tranfers to attack transports.

12   GUATEMALA - The Brazilian Embassy in Guatemala City is seized by 13 terrorists of the January 31 Popular Front. The Brazilian Ambassador and eight others are taken hostage. The next day (13 May) the hostages are released unharmed. On 14 May the terrorists are flown to Merida, Mexico, where they are granted political asylum.

13   POLAND - Police arrest 650 in demonstrations pro-testing six months of martial law.

14   ISRAEL - The Israeli General Staff confirms the move-ment of 30,000 troops to the Lebanese border.

14   SYRIA - In response to announcements of Israeli troop movements, the Syrian government begins shifting its forces into southern Lebanon.

14   USSR - The government declares the exclusion zone around the Falklands "illegal."

14   THE FALKLANDS - "Harriers" attack Port Stanley Air-port. In another action, four 12-man SAS teams attack the air field on Pebble Island. The teams had been put

14   THE FALKLANDS (Cont'd) - ashore by helicopter at a
            landing zone cleared by the SAS team which landed
            across from Pebble Island on 11 May. The action is
            supported by naval gunfire. The Argentinians on the
            island suffer heavy casualties. A mobile radar site
            and an ammunition dump are destroyed. British
            casualties are two wounded.

15   THE FALKLANDS - "Harriers" attack military targets
            around Port Stanley.

16   THE FALKLANDS - In addition to attacking Port Stanley,
            "Harrier" aircraft carry out an air strike on the
            4,000-ton Argentine naval auxiliary vessel Rio
            Carcarania near Darwin on the East Falkland Island
            coast. The ship is badly damaged but not sunk. In a
            second attack in Fox Bay off West Falkland Island two
            "Harriers" hit the 3,100-ton Bahia Buen Suceso. One
            aircraft is damaged by ground fire but returns to its
            base.

17   EUROPE - The EEC extends its sanctions against Argen-
            tina for an additional seven days.

18   SOUTH ATLANTIC - The SS Atlantic Conveyor, with 20
            "Harriers" embarked, makes a rendevous with the
            British task force which now moves into a battle
            formation.

19   THE FALKLANDS - A British destroyer bombards targets
            around Port Stanley. Other targets on East Falkland
            Island are attacked by "Harriers."

20   UNITED STATES - The Defense Department transfers a
            number of KC-135 tanker aircraft to NATO control to
            allow for British Vickers aerial resupply tankers to
            support operations in the Falklands.

21   ISRAEL - Israeli military forces continue to mass
            along the Lebanese border.

21   THE FALKLANDS - Following a heavy air and naval
            bombardment British forces land on East Falkland
            Island at 6:30 AM. About 2,500 Royal Marines and
            Airborne Brigade (Red Devil) personnel assault four
            separate points around Port San Carlos on the island's
            west coast (on the Falkland Sound side between the two
            main islands). These forces are immediately reinforced
            by engineers, armor, artillery, and air defense
            missile units and associated radars. Diversionary
            raids are carried out by SAS and SBS teams at Goose
            Green, Darwin, and Fanning Head. Additional reinforce-
            ments are put ashore over the next four days. On West
            Falkland Island heavy air strikes are concentrated on

21   THE FALKLANDS (Cont'd) – the only large Argentine
            troop concentration near Fox Bay. In another engage-
            ment approximately 70 Argentinian aircraft, flying
            from the mainland, counterattack the landing force and
            its escort ships but avoid challenging the main
            British task force, under the command of Rear Admiral
            John Woodward, north of Falkland Sound. One ship is
            sunk (HMS Ardent), four damaged. Twenty Argentine
            aircraft are shot down (9 "Mirage/Daggers," 5 A-4Q
            "Skyhawks," 2 "Pucaras," and 4 helicopters).

22   THE FALKLANDS – At least 5,000 British troops are now
            ashore and the beachhead covers approximately ten
            square miles. An airstrip is completed and "Harriers"
            and transport aircraft begin operating between the
            shore and the carriers.

23   THE FALKLANDS – Argentinian aircraft ("Mirages" and
            "Skyhawks") attack the task force. Six to eight
            aircraft are destroyed; one British frigate sustains
            moderate damage. At the same time British naval units
            challenge the Argentine steamer SS Monsunen, which is
            ferrying reinforcements, and force it to run aground
            where it is abandoned. Argentine air strikes are
            carried out against Goose Green. Argentine aircraft
            losses from this attack and other incidents are heavy.

24   IRAN – The government announces its forces have recap-
            tured the important seaport of Khorramshahr on the
            Shatt-al-Arab. An estimated 30,000 Iraqi troops are
            taken prisoner.

24   LEBANON – A bomb planted in the automobile driven by a
            secretary at the French Embassy explodes by remote
            control as the car enters the compound. Eighteen are
            killed and 25 injured. France blames Syria for the
            incident.

24   THE FALKLANDS – HMS Antelope, one of the ships damaged
            in the air attack on 22 May, explodes and sinks when a
            500-pound unexploded bomb goes off while being
            defused. The ship was anchored in San Carlos Bay and
            the crew safely ashore. One British demolition
            specialist is killed, seven injured in the explosion.
            In another incident Argentinian aircraft again attack
            the British task force. Seven are shot down.

24   EUROPE – The European Economic Community (EEC) extends
            its sanctions against Argentina until 24 June.

25   THE FALKLANDS – Following another air attack on the
            task force HMS Coventry capsizes and sinks after
            sustaining damage from 1,000 pound bombs. Following
            the first attack by one hour (about 4:30 PM), a second

25   THE FALKLANDS (Cont'd) - wave of Exocet-armed "Super
        Entendards" attack <u>HMS Ambuscade</u> which fires chaff to
        defend itself. The Exocet misses its target and locks
        on to the converted VTOL/helicopter carrier <u>SS</u>
        <u>Atlantic Conveyor</u> which is hit and catches fire. More
        than 30 crewmen are killed and the ship is aban-
        doned. Although no "Harriers" are aboard, the ship
        carries numerous helicopters and spare parts. <u>HMS</u>
        <u>Broadsword</u> is also hit in the attack and is slightly
        damaged. (To offset these losses, at least ten ves-
        sels, including eight additional surface combattants,
        have joined the task force in the last ten days.) On
        shore an Argentine patrol from Goose Green makes
        contact with British positions around the beachhead
        and is driven off by artillery and mortar fire.

25   GUATEMALA - The government grants amnesty to all left-
        wing guerrillas who turn themselves in within 30 days.

26   THE FALKLANDS - British "Harriers" carry out a number
        of air strikes around Port Stanley.

27   THE FALKLANDS - The British Navy captures an Argentine
        oil rig support ship, the <u>Stenta Prospector</u>. Moving
        out of Port San Carlos beachhead British forces open a
        two-pronged attack on Goose Green and Darwin and on
        Port Stanley. The 2nd Battalion, Paratroop Regiment,
        attacks toward Darwin (1,600 Argentine defenders). Two
        Royal Marine Commando battalions, reinforced by armor,
        attack along an axis San Carlos-Stanley where four
        Argentine battalions are located. The 3rd Battalion,
        Paratroop Regiment, and one Royal Marine Commando
        battalion cut the Darwin-Stanley road and move along
        it toward Stanley. Also, Argentine antiaircraft
        defenses at Port Stanley shoot down a "Harrier" on
        reconnaissance. The pilot is rescued three days later
        by a British helicopter. Argentine "Mirages" and
        "Skyhawks" attack the British task force. Two "Sky-
        hawks" are shot down. Argentine "Canberra" bombers
        attack the British beachhead around Port San Carlos
        after dark. Damage is minimal.

27   UNITED STATES - The government announces an agreement
        with Morocco that will allow US use of Moroccan air
        bases in case of a crisis in the Middle East.

28   THE FALKLANDS - The 2nd Battalion, Paratroop Regiment
        attacks its two objectives at Goose Green and Darwin
        before dawn (2 AM/0200). The attack is supported by
        naval gunfire and "Harrier" air strikes. After twelve
        hours of bitter fighting, both objectives are secured.
        British losses 17 killed, including the Battalion Com-
        mander, Lieutenant Colonel Herbert Jones, and 34 more

28   THE FALKLANDS (Cont'd) - wounded. The Argentines lose
          234 killed, 120 wounded, 1,400 captured, and masses of
          materiel captured or destroyed. The heavy Argentine
          casualties are the result of their showing the white
          flag of surrender and then opening fire on the ad-
          vancing British troops killing at least one officer.

29   THE FALKLANDS - Argentine "Mirages" and "Skyhawks"
          carry out the sixth attack of the San Carlos beach-
          head. One "Skyhawk" is destroyed.

30   THE FALKLANDS - Argentine "Skyhawks" and "Super En-
          tendards" attack the British task force aiming to sink
          or damage HMS Invincible. There is no damage to the
          fleet but two "Skyhawks" are destroyed. In another
          action the towns of Douglas Settlement and Teal Inlet
          on East Falkland Island are taken by the British, thus
          protecting the northern flank of their forces moving
          on Stanley. Heavy air and naval bombardment is
          directed at Port Stanley.

30   SPAIN - Spain becomes the 16th nation to join the
          North Atlantic Treaty Organization (NATO).

31   THE FALKLANDS - The Fifth Infantry Brigade is landed
          at Port San Carlos. The entire British land force is
          now under the command of Major General Jeremy Moore.
          Repairing the Darwin-Stanley road delays movement for
          several days. In other actions a number of inter-
          mediate objectives are taken, including Mount Kent and
          Mounts Harriet and Two Sisters, which close an invest-
          ment line around Stanley. The heavy bombardment of
          Stanley continues. A 16-man Argentine commando group,
          which had been airdropped into the British rear, is
          taken after a firefight with a Royal Marine patrol.
          Four are killed, 12 captured. There are no British
          casualties. In another incident, after suffering
          irreparable damage from the Argentine attack on 25
          May, the SS Atlantic Conveyor sinks.

JUNE

1   THE FALKLANDS - A US-built Argentine C-130 transport
          is shot down near Pebble Island by a "Harrier." The
          C-130s mission or purpose is not known; the Argentines
          are using the aircraft as a tanker, bomber, and
          reconnaissance aircraft in addition to its normal
          functions. In another incident, British positions near
          Mount Kent are bombed by Argentine "Canberras" (later
          by "Mirages" and "Pucaras"). There is only some minor
          damage reported at what has become the British forward

1   THE FALKLANDS (Cont'd) - operating base. Also, a group
     of Argentine prisoners are killed or wounded in an
     explosion at Goose Green as they attempt to move
     ammunition that apparently had been booby-trapped.

2   THE FALKLANDS - The final artillery preparations begin
     for the attack on Port Stanley. British forces, having
     moved at a snail's pace, are still five-seven miles
     from the town. Commandos from Mount Kent begin to
     probe the Argentine outpost line. The aerial and naval
     bombardment of the town continues.

3   BRAZIL - A fully-armed British "Vulcan" bomber makes
     an emergency landing at Rio de Janiero after it loses
     its fuel probe during mid-air refueling. Brazilian
     fighters react when the aircraft enters their airspace
     and escort it to the field. It is disarmed and allowed
     to return to Ascension Island. Elsewhere, as the naval
     and air bombardment of Port Stanley continues,
     "Harrier" aircraft drop leaflets asking Argentine
     troops to surrender.

3   THE FALKLANDS - British artillery at Mount Kent (12
     miles west) and Argentine artillery exchange fire as
     the tempo of the bombardment of Port Stanley
     increases.

3   GREAT BRITAIN - The Israeli Ambassador to the Court of
     Saint James, Shlomo Argov, is shot and critically
     wounded as he leaves a London hotel following a diplo-
     matic dinner. A PLO splinter group known as Al Ashifa
     (Black June) (BLO) takes the credit for the attack (9
     June).

3   AFGHANISTAN - Both sides claim victory after three
     weeks of heavy fighting in the Panjshir Valley.

4   THE FALKLANDS - The bombardment of Port Stanley goes
     on as the British continue their interminable pre-
     parations for the ground attack.

4   LEBANON - Israeli jets attack Palestinian settlements
     in southern Lebanon in retaliation for the attack on
     the Israeli Ambassador in London. Palestinian forces
     then fire rockets at Israeli settlements in northern
     Israel.

5   THE FALKLANDS - Argentine "Canberra" bombers carry out
     a night attack on British positions amid reports that
     Israel is supplying large amounts of aviation
     materiel, including "Skyhawk" aircraft, to the
     Argentine armed forces. British troops occupy Fitzroy
     and Bluff Cove without opposition and begin ferrying
     supplies and additional personnel into the area.

5   EUROPE - Massive demonstrations against nuclear weapons take place in Paris, London, and Rome.

6   THE FALKLANDS - British Gurkha troops conduct rear-area security sweeps rounding up Argentine stragglers and bypassed pockets of resistance.

6   LEBANON - Israeli forces invade Lebanon by land, sea, and air with the objective of eradicating the PLO in southern Lebanon.

6   CHAD - Forces loyal to Hissen Habre capture the capital city of N'Djamena. On 8 June Habre begins forming a provisional government.

7   THE FALKLANDS - British forces attack and capture the ridge line called Mount Low five miles from Port Stanley. The artillery, naval gunfire, and air bombardment continues. Argentine aircraft attack supply ships in the harbor at San Carlos. There is no damage although one aircraft is shot down.

7   LEBANON - Israeli forces capture the three Palestinian strongholds at Beaufort Castle, Nabatiya, and Tyre.

7   PORTUGAL - A Turkish diplomat is assassinated outside his home in a Lisbon suburb. The JCAG claims responsibility for the incident in which the diplomat's wife is also critically wounded.

8   THE FALKLANDS - When weather over the Falklands clears, Argentine aircraft attack and set afire two British supply ships in Bluff Cove near Fitzroy. HMS Sir Galahad sinks immediately; HMS Sir Tristam sinks some time later. One aircraft is shot down, five are known damaged. About 50 British seamen and soldiers (Welsh Guard Regiment) are killed and more than 60 wounded. In San Carlos harbor HMS Plymouth is attacked by "Mirages" and is damaged. She remains on station, however, and shoots down one attacking aircraft. In Choiseul Sound on the east coast of East Falkland Island Argentine "Mirages" attack a landing craft from HMS Fearless and kill four Royal Marines and two sailors. Two "Harriers" flying combat air patrol (CAP) nearby respond and shoot down four of the "Mirages."

8   SOUTH ATLANTIC - An Argentine maritime radio transmission orders the Liberian supertanker SS Hercules into port. The ship is 480 nautical miles north of the Falklands at the time. When she fails to answer the call she is attacked and bombed by an Argentine C-130. The tanker is damaged and taking on water when it changes course for a safe port.

8   LEBANON - The Palestinian base at Sidon is captured by
           Israeli forces.

9   ARGENTINA - Sources claim Argentina has received about
           25 US-built "Skyhawk" fighters and war materiel, in-
           cluding "Exocet" missiles, from Israel, Iraq, and
           Libya.

9   LEBANON - The important Palestinian base at Damur is
           captured by Israeli forces.

10   LEBANON - Israeli forces engage a 25,000-man Syrian
           force on the outskirts of Beirut. Fierce air battles
           take place over central Lebanon. Syrian surface-to-air
           missile installation in the Bekaa Valley are attacked
           and destroyed.

10   THE FALKLANDS - Argentine aircraft attack the British
           forward base positions around Mount Kent.

11   LEBANON - A cease-fire goes into effect.

11   THE FALKLANDS - British forces launch a night attack
           against Argentine positions on the high ground near
           Mount Longdon, Mount Harriet, and Two Sisters. The
           objectives are taken by dawn. British losses are 25
           killed and 72 wounded. Argentine losses include 40
           killed and 1,800 captured. A shore-based "Exocet"
           missile damages HMS Glamorgan as it bombards Port
           Stanley at night. About 30 crewmen are killed or
           wounded.

12-13   THE FALKLANDS - Argentine aircraft make a number of
           ineffective raids on British positions. One aircraft
           is shot down.

13   SAUDI ARABIA - King Khalid dies of a heart attack.
           Crown Prince Fahd becomes king.

13   THE FALKLANDS - The 2nd and 3rd Battalions, Paratroop
           Regiment, 2nd Battalion, Scots Guards, 1st Battalion
           Welsh Guards, 42 and 45 Marine Commando, and 1st
           Company, 7th Gurkha Battalion, attack Argentine
           positions at Mount Tumbledown, Mount William, and
           Wireless Ridge after dark.

13   LEBANON - Israeli forces complete the investment of
           Beirut.

14   THE FALKLANDS - With the objectives on Mount
           Tumbledown, Wireless Ridge, and Mount William secured,
           the British forces continue their attack and enter the
           outskirts of Port Stanley. The Argentine positions in
           the town are now dominated by the British-held high

14   THE FALKLANDS (Cont'd) - ground. Argentine troops
            begin deserting and surrendering to the British. At 11
            AM (1100) the Argentine commander, General Mario
            Menendez, asks for a cease-fire and terms for
            surrender. At 8 PM (2000) the Argentine forces
            surrender.

14   POLAND - Large-scale clashes take place between police
            and demonstrators in Kracow (Crakow), Gdansk, Nova
            Huta and Wroclaw.

15   THE FALKLANDS - Argentinian forces that had been
            fighting in the islands continue the process of sur-
            rendering. At least 255 British troops and civilians
            have been killed. Argentinian losses are unknown but
            are suspected of being considerably higher (about
            700). At least 11,200 Argentinian troops are prisoners
            although British intelligence estimated only 9,000
            troops were on the islands.

17   ARGENTINA - President Leopoldo Galtieri resigns.

18   LEBANON - Israeli forces encircle a force of about
            6,000 PLO in West Beirut.

18   UNITED STATES - Intelligence sources report the USSR
            has successfully tested a "killer" satellite.

19   THE FALKLANDS - About 4,200 Argentinian prisoners are
            repatriated. The remaining 7,000 are to be sent home
            within a few days.

20   IRAQ - The government announces it has ordered the
            unconditional withdrawal of its forces from Iranian
            territory.

21   IRAN - Ayatollah Khomeini states his country will
            continue the Gulf War.

21   UNITED STATES - During a visit to Washington Israel's
            Premier Begin agrees to the withdrawal of all foreign
            troops from Lebanon.

22   MALAYSIA - Cambodian exiles meet in Kuala Lumpur and
            form a Kampuchean government-in-exile to fight the
            Vietnamese takeover of their country.

22   ARGENTINA - Retired Major General Reynaldo Benito
            Antonio Bignone becomes president.

22   LEBANON - There is a major clash between Israeli and
            Syrian forces.

22   CHAD - Former President Goukouni Oueddei flies into exile in Algeria.

23   LEBANON - An Israeli-imposed cease-fire collapses.

26   LEBANON - Having consolidated their positions around West Beirut, the Israelis affect a cease-fire while negotiations for a PLO withdrawal from Lebanon continue.

26   UNITED NATIONS - The US vetoes a Security Council order for an Israeli withdrawal from Beirut.

27   LEBANON - An Israeli air strike in the Bekaa Valley knocks out Syrian forward surface-to-air missile sites. At the same time, the Israelis insist on tough peace terms for the PLO. They must lay down their arms and withdraw into Syria. Israel promises safe passage along the Beirut-Damascus road.

27   PERU - The British Ambassador's residence on the out-skirts of Lima is seriously damaged by explosions when unidentified persons throw sticks of dynamite at the structure. No injuries are reported.

28   POLAND - Police in Poznan break up a large demon-stration commemorating the 26th anniversary of serious riots in that city.

29   IRAQ - The government announces that the withdrawal of its force from Iranian territory is complete.

30   POLAND - The curfew in lifted in Warsaw.

JULY

1   SOMALIA - The government reports Soviet-built Ethiopian MiG fighters attacked Somali positions in the Mudag region near Ogaden.

3   ETHIOPIA - The government denies its planes struck at Somali positions on 1 July and blames the attacks on the Somali Democratic Salvation Front.

3   LEBANON - Yasser Arafat signs an agreement for the withdrawal of PLO forces from Lebanon. Israeli forces tighten their grip on Beirut sealing off the Muslim section of the city. Electricity, food, water, and medical supplies are stopped from entering West Beirut.

4   DOMINICAN REPUBLIC - President Guzman Fernandez commits suicide. He is 71 years old.

5   SOMALIA - The government claims Ethiopian troops sup-
            ported by tanks have invaded Somalia. At least 200 are
            reported dead in the early fighting.

6   UNITED STATES - President Reagan conditionally agrees
            to the use of US Marines to guard the withdrawal of
            the PLO out of West Beirut. France also agrees to send
            troops into Lebanon (10 July).

7   LEBANON - At the urging of the UN and the US, Israel
            allows one large shipment of food delivered into West
            Beirut.

7   VIET NAM - The government announces plans to withdraw
            its forces from Cambodia.

9   SYRIA - The government rejects the proposal that PLO
            refugees be allowed to enter Syria claiming that the
            PLO should be allowed to remain in place while
            "awaiting the return of their legitimate rights."

10   UNITED NATIONS - The UN Disarmament Conference closes
            its second special session without finding any agree-
            ment on a comprehensive program.

11   LEBANON - Another cease-fire becomes effective al-
            though there is little respite in the exchange of
            artillery fire between the Israelis and Palestinians.

12   PERU - President Fernando Belaunde Terry suspends
            constitutional guarantees in three southern provinces
            and orders special security forces into the area to
            help quell the violence spread by the Maoist-oriented
            "Shining Path" (Sendero Luminoso) organization.

12   POLAND - Another 50,000 members of the Polish Com-
            munist Party are expelled bringing the number thrown
            out of the Party since the imposition of martial law
            to 100,000.

12   GREAT BRITAIN - Whitehall declares that the war with
            Argentina is officially ended and lifts the 200 mile
            exclusion area around the Falklands.

13   IRAQ - Iranian forces invade Iraq. Heavy fighting is
            reported around Basra.

14-21   MIDDLE EAST - As Iranian troops pour across the border
            into Iraq in the latest offensive of the protracted
            Iraq-Iran War, the Ayatollah Khomeini calls upon the
            Iraqi people to overthrow the Iraqi government. At
            least 200,000 Iranian and Iraqi troops battle over the
            Iraqi oil refinery city of Basra (Al Basrah) on the
            Shatt al Arab located at the head of the Persian Gulf.

14-21   MIDDLE EAST (Cont'd) - Three major Iranian pushes toward the city take place (14, 17, & 22 July). Iraq responds with air strikes against the Iran's Kharg Island oil facilities on 14 and 15 July. Other Iraqi air attacks against inland targets take place on 19 July. An Iranian bombing raid on Baghdad takes place on 21 July.

18   VIET NAM - The government announces that between 20,000 and 30,000 troops are in the process of leaving Cambodia.

19   BOLIVIA - The government of President Celso Torrelio Villa resigns under extreme pressure from the military and is replaced by a military junta. On 21 July Brigadier General Guido Vildoso Calderon is appointed Head of State.

23   JAPAN - The government initiates a five-year military expansion program.

25   UNITED STATES - The US begins airlifting arms and munitions into Somalia.

25   ANGOLA - The government rejects a plan calling for the simultaneous withdrawal of Cuban troops from Angola and South African troops from Namibia.

25   ZIMBABWE - A night attack on the nation's main air base at Gwera results in the destruction of 12 fighter aircraft. A number of white and black employees at the air base and some Air Force personnel are arrested as suspects by the security police.

27   LEBANON - Israeli aircraft bomb West Beirut. The Israeli forces circling the city once again cut off water and electricity.

27   UNITED STATES - Military aid is resumed to El Savador when the President certifies improvement in that country's civil rights record.

30   IRAQ - The government claims it has killed 27,000 Iranians during the successful defense of Basra.

AUGUST

1   KENYA - A coup organized by Air Force personnel fails to overthrow the government of President Daniel arap Moi. Loyal Army forces arrest about 3,000 in the wake of the attempt, including all 1,200 members of the Air Force. On 21 August the Air Force is disbanded.

1-4	LEBANON - Israeli aircraft carry out a 14-hour raid against West Beirut. Israeli ground forces bring tanks into the city, thereby nullifying the cease-fire. The Israelis also capture the airport. These actions take place at a crucial point in US-PLO negotiations and severely strain US-Israeli relations. The Israeli attack on West Beirut is designed to dislodge about 6,000 PLO forces located there. Israel also rejects (5 August) a UN-ordered (4 August) cease-fire.
2	AFGHANISTAN - The government extends conscription from two to three years.
4	PANAMA - The Supreme Court overrules a 30 July government order closing eight newspapers.
6	LEBANON - The government announces PLO acceptance of a plan for the withdrawal of its troops. This follows a heavy bombing of central Beirut by Israeli aircraft.
6	UNITED NATIONS - The US vetoes a Soviet-sponsored UN Security Council resolution calling for an arms embargo on Israel.
9	FRANCE - Three unidentified terrorists shoot up a well-known Jewish restaurant in Paris. Six people are killed and 22 wounded in the attack. No one claims credit.
11	ANGOLA - South African forces carry out another raid into Angola. On 13 August the Angola government says South African troops have penetrated 120 miles into the country.
11	PACIFIC OCEAN - A bomb under a seat on a Pan AM jumbo jet bound from Tokyo's Narita Airport to Honolulu, Hawaii, explodes 140 miles from landing. One passenger is killed and 14 others injured in the explosion. The plane lands safely at Honolulu. The group known as the "15 May Arab Organization" is suspected of planting the bomb.
12-13	LEBANON - Even though accepting the US-proposed withdrawal plan (10 August), the Israelis maintain constant pressure on the PLO with incessant bombing and artillery attacks on West Beirut.
13	POLAND - Demonstrators clash with riot police in Gdansk, Warsaw, and other cities.
15	SOMALIA - The government declares a state of emergency along the Ogaden border with Ethiopia.

17   SEYCHELLES - Troops loyal to President France-Albert
            Rene restore order following a military mutiny in
            Victoria in which the mutineers captured the radio
            station.

18-30   IRAN - Iraqi jets carry out a series of raids on the
            Kharg Island oil facility.

20   LEBANON - There is agreement among all participants in
            the Lebanese conflict as to the PLO evacuation plan.

21   KENYA - President Daniel arap Moi dismisses the entire
            Air Force.

21   LEBANON - About 400 PLO fighters form the first con-
            tingent to leave Lebanon when they board a ship at
            Tripoli.

25   LEBANON - Eight hundred Marines from the 32nd MAU land
            in Beirut as a part of a multinational force to assist
            in the evacuation of the PLO. Four hundred French and
            800 Italians are also part of the force.

26   COMMUNIST CHINA - The government rejects a Vietnamese
            proposal for a six-week truce along the border between
            the two countries.

27   LEBANON - As the PLO evacuation goes forward, 800 US
            Marines land, along with British and French forces, to
            participate in the supervision of the withdrawal of
            PLO and Syrian units from Beirut.

30   IRAQ - The fight for the Iraqi city of Basra reaches a
            stalemate.

31   POLAND - Tens of thousands demonstrate against the
            continued state of martial law in cities throughout
            the country. At least 4,000 are arrested.

SEPTEMBER

1   LEBANON - The evacuation of the 15,000 PLO and Syrian
            troops from Beirut is completed two days ahead of
            schedule. Arafat departs vowing to continue the fight.
            Most PLO go to Syria with about 1,000 to Tunisia and
            more to other Arab countries. US forces are withdrawn
            from Beirut.

1   UNITED STATES - President Reagan calls for self-deter-
            mination for Palestinians on the West Bank in assoc-
            iation with Jordan. He also calls for a freeze on new
            Jewish settlements on the West Bank and an undivided
            Jerusalem. Israel immediately rejects the plan.

1   THE PHILIPPINES - The Marcos government begins a roundup of 29 persons, including 23 labor leaders, accused of being Communists.

1   POLAND - A dusk-to-dawn curfew is imposed in at least four provinces. Serious rioting is reported in Lublin. The city is in a state of siege.

6   EL SALVADOR - Salvadoran troops are accused of the massacre of about 300 civilians.

6   SWITZERLAND - A group of Polish dissidents occupies the Polish Embassy in Bern. The terrorists take 13 hostages and demand an end to martial law in Poland. The Swiss police end the siege on 9 September without bloodshed.

7   IRAN - Iraqi planes again attack the Kharg Island oil facility.

7   THE PHILIPPINES - Thirteen persons are charged with instigating the overthrow of the Marcos government.

9   ARAB LEAGUE - At a meeting in Fez, Morocco, the League unanimously adopts an eight-point Middle East peace plan which calls for an independent Palestinian state. This proposal is generated in response to a US peace plan put forward by President Reagan. On 10 September Israel rejects the plan.

10   LEBANON - The multi-national force begins its withdrawal from Beirut.

13   POLAND - Street fighting is reported in at least four major cities in Poland as demonstrators protest the continuing state of martial law.

14   LEBANON - President-elect Bashir Gemayle is killed in a bomb blast in East Beirut. To insure success, the terrorists used a 400-pound bomb to kill him.

15   LEBANON - Israeli forces push deeper into West Beirut.

15   IRAN - Sadegh Ghotbzadeh is executed for allegedly plotting the assassination of the Ayatollah Ruhollah Khomeini and the overthrow of the government. About 70 others are also reported to have been executed in connection with the plot.

15   ARGENTINA - The government signs an agreement with Chile which extends their 1972 non-agression pact and reiterates acceptance of Papal mediation of the Beagle Channel dispute.

16   LEBANON - A massacre of Palestinian refugees in two Beirut camps (Sabra & Shatila) is initially blamed on Israel, but is actually carried out by Christian militiamen. Over 600, including numerous women and children, are reported murdered in the attack. A major scandal erupts in Israel over the handling of the whole affair.

17   HONDURAS - Twelve Salvadoran terrorists sieze the Chamber of Commerce building in San Pedro Sula taking 107 hostages. They demand the release of Salvadoran guerrilla leader Alejandro Montenegro, who was captured by Honduran police on 15 September, and other political prisoners.

17   BOLIVIA - In the wake of a paralyzing general strike, the military decides to return power to the Parliament that was disbanded two years ago.

19   LEBANON - Israel begins withdrawing its troops from Beirut.

20   LEBANON - The multinational force begins returning to Beirut after the Israeli withdrawal leads to chaos.

20   EGYPT - The government recalls its Ambassador in Israel.

25   HONDURAS - The seige at the Chamber of Commerce building in San Pedro Sula ends without any of the demands of the terrorists being met. They are allowed to leave the country going first to Panama thence to Cuba.

26   LEBANON - Israeli forces evacuate West Beirut and are replaced by members of the UN peacekeeping forces (US, French & Italian) in "Operation LEBANON 2."

28   ISRAEL - The government orders an investigation of the Palestinian massacre in Beirut.

29   LEBANON - The 32d MAU returns to Beirut where it joins 2,200 French and Italian forces already in place.

30   COMMUNIST CHINA - The government declares it will take back the British Crown Colony of Hong Kong "when conditions are ripe."

OCTOBER

1   SWEDEN - The government reports a submarine in the restricted area around Musko Island.

2   IRAN - Approximately 350 pounds of explosives hidden
         in a truck parked in the central square in Tehran
         detonates killing 60 and injuring 700 others. The
         government blames "American mercenaries" for the
         attack.

3   SUDAN - The government offers troops to help defend
         Iraq.

4   UNITED NATIONS - The Security Council passes a reso-
         lution calling for the immediate withdrawal of Iranian
         and Iraqi forces from each other's territory and for a
         cease-fire.

5   LEBANON - Lebanese army units reenter Beirut and begin
         a sweep through the city's western (Muslim) sector.

5   BOLIVIA - The leftist Hernan Siles Zuaro is elected
         President.

6   IRAN - The government formally rejects the UN cease-
         fire and withdrawal resolution.

7   ANGOLA - The Angolan government rejects a US proposal
         to settle the Angola-South Africa border conflict.

8-14   POLAND - The Parliament formally disbands the
         Solidarity Movement. A major strike begins (11 Octo-
         ber) in Gdansk, where workers call for the release of
         Lech Walesa. Rioting breaks out in Gdansk's Lenin
         Shipyard (14 October). Martial rule is imposed in the
         shipyard (14 October).

11   INDIA - The Indian House of Parliament in New Delhi is
         attacked by Sikhs of the Akali Dal sect. Four people
         are killed and many more injured in the attack. The
         Sikhs demand an inquiry into the deaths of 30 Sikh
         prisoners in a freak accident in Punjab in September.

12   JORDAN - The PLO says it is ready to accept federation
         with Jordan, but only if it leads to the establish-
         ment of an independent Palestinian state.

12   AFGHANISTAN - The Soviets launch a new military
         offensive against rebel forces near Paghman, north of
         Kabul.

14   LEBANON - The government reports that operations in
         West Beirut have netted tons of arms and ammunition,
         and the arrest of more than 1,440 persons. More than
         23,000 were found to have forged papers.

15   POLAND - The government outlaws the Solidarity Party
         (Solidarnost).

16   GREECE - Prime Minister Papandreou promises that   he
            will not take unilateral action to remove US bases   in
            Greece or to pull out of NATO.

18   INDIA - The government announces the purchase of   40
            Mirage 2000 fighters from France.

19   EL SALVADOR - Leftist rebels claim they control   the
            road network in the northern part of the country.

24   MIDDLE EAST - Guinean President Sekou Toure, the head
            of the peace commission ordered by the Islamic
            Conference Organization to end the Gulf War, says the
            negotiations are deadlocked and the commission will
            not meet again.

26   AUSTRALIA - The Parliament House in Canberra is
            attacked by 50 unemployed workers from Wollongong in
            New South Wales. They are demanding an audience with
            Prime Minister Malcolm Fraser.

26   NIGERIA - Islamic fundamentalists instigate serious
            rioting. Hundreds, including at least 100 police, are
            killed in the violence.

29   LEBANON - The government asks for an increase in the
            size of the 4,100-man UN peace-keeping force.

NOVEMBER

2   IRAN - The government claims to have recaptured 100
            square miles of territory in a single day near Dizful.

2   UNITED STATES - President Reagan admits the CIA is
            training guerrilla groups attacking Nicaragua from
            Honduras.

2   AFGHANISTAN - An explosion occurs following a col-
            lision between an Afghan fuel truck and a Soviet
            convoy vehicle in the Salang Pass Tunnel north of
            Kabul, killing at least 1,000 people. One report
            indicates about 500 of them are Soviet troops.

4   LEBANON - The US Marines stationed in Beirut extend
            their security zone to include patrolling the "Green
            Line" which divides the city into Christian and Muslim
            sectors.

4   UNITED NATIONS - The General Assembly calls upon Great
            Britain and Argentina to renegotiate the sovereignty
            of the Falklands. Great Britain refuses (5 November).

7	UPPER VOLTA - The government of Colonel Saye Zerbo is overthrown in a military coup led by Major Jean-Baptiste Ouedraogo.
9	LEBANON - The Parliament grants President Amin Gemayle special emergency powers for six months.
10	USSR - Leonid I. Brezhnev dies of a heart attack. The official announcement of the death comes on 11 November. Yuri V. Andropov is named to succeed him.
10	POLAND - Riot police are used to disperse groups of demonstrators in Warsaw and other cities.
10	GREAT BRITAIN - The government concludes a multi-million-pound arms deal with Communist China.
11	LEBANON - At least 89 are killed when the Israeli army headquarters in Tyre collapses. Although the PLO is considered the likely culprit in having planted a bomb, an investigation indicates the building may have collapsed under its own weight.
18	COLOMBIA - In an attempt to stop more than 30 years of unrest, the government offers unconditional amnesty to all guerrilla forces.
24	GHANA - A military uprising takes place in a camp outside Accra. Loyal troops suppress the rebellion.
24	ISRAEL - The commission investigating the Beirut massacre (16 September) warns a number of top Israeli officials that they will probably be harmed by the results of the inquiry.
25	OAU - Because of a confrontation over which of two Chadian delegations should be seated, the planned OAU meeting in Tripoli, Libya, ends before it starts.
26	SYRIA - A PLO Central Council meeting in Damascus rejects a US proposal that a Palestinian homeland(s) be established in the West Bank and in the Gaza Strip.
29	TURKEY - The government signs a treaty allowing the US the use of Turkish airfields.

DECEMBER

1	THAILAND - As a part of an amnesty program about 1,000 Communist rebels surrender to the government.
3-10	LEBANON - Tank and artillery units are put ashore as the US Marines strengthen their positions.

4   EGYPT - Two hundred eighty are put on trial in Cairo for plotting the overthrow of the government.

6   ARGENTINA - A general strike paralyzes the country in the most serious challenge to the military junta in six years.

8   SURINAM - The government foils a coup attempt with considerable bloodshed. Opposition leaders are exe- cuted (9 December) and martial law is declared (11 December). Both the US (17 December) and the Nether- lands suspend aid to the country when it becomes clear that the military junta is back in control after a short respite of civilian control.

9   LESOTHO - South African troops attack ANC targets inside the capital city of Maseru. At least 42 are killed.

13   LEBANON - US Marines begin training Lebanese military personnel.

15   UNITED NATIONS - The Security Council unanimously condemns South Africa for its raid into Lesotho.

15   CHILE - Anti-Pinochet demonstrations lead to the arrest of 200 persons.

16   ARGENTINA - Violence breaks out at a massive anti- government demonstration in Buenos Aires.

19   POLAND - The government rescinds the martial law order as of midnight, 30 December 1982.

20   SRI LANKA - The government extends emergency rule for another six months.

Notes

1983

JANUARY

2   PERSIAN GULF - Iraqi jets attack a convoy out of Bandar Khomeini in the Persian Gulf. The Singapore-based freighter _SS Eastern_ and the Liberian freighter _SS Orient Horizon_ are run aground.

5   MOZAMBIQUE - Antigovernment guerrillas blow up the Beira-Mutare pipeline which supplies fuel to Zimbabwe.

5   KAMPUCHEA - The Vietnamese open a major offensive in western Kampuchea.

5   FRANCE - The government declares the Corsican National Liberation Front to be an illegal armed group.

6   WARSAW PACT - At the close of the Warsaw Pact meeting in Prague, Czechoslovakia, the organization proposes a reduction in the number of medium-range ballistic missiles deployed in Europe.

7   UNITED STATES - The government lifts its 1980 arms embargo on Guatemala.

7   ANGOLA - Very heavy fighting is reported in southeast Angola between army forces and UNITA guerrillas.

13   SAUDI ARABIA - The government announces a resumption of diplomatic relations with Libya. The Saudis had broken diplomatic relations with Libya in October 1980 when Muammar Qaddafi called for a holy war (jihad) to "liberate" Mecca, Islam's holiest shrine.

17   NIGERIA - The government orders all illegal aliens to
            leave the country by the end of the month. This af-
            fects nearly two million people. Skilled aliens are
            exempted from the order until 28 February.

18   SOUTH AFRICA - The South African government dissolves
            the Namibian (South West African) National Assembly
            and reasserts direct control over the region.

18   UNITED NATIONS - The Security Council extends the man-
            date of its peacekeeping force in Lebanon for an
            additional six months.

19   ZAIRE - The government signs a five-year military
            agreement with Israel.

23   THAILAND - The government announces that 466 Com-
            munist rebels have taken advantage of the amnesty
            program by surrendering together at a prearranged
            ceremony. More than 1,800 have surrendered since the
            program went into effect in December 1982.

25   USSR - The Kremlin announces it has agreed to UN-
            sponsored talks on Afghanistan.

27   SWITZERLAND - Arms talks between the US and USSR
            resume in Geneva after a two-month recess.

27   USSR - The Soviet newpaper TASS admits at least
            100,000 troops are fighting in Afghanistan.

27   EUROPE - The Council of Europe suspends Turkish voting
            rights until democracy is restored in that country.

28   LEBANON - A bomb levels the PLO Security Headquarters
            in the Syrian-controlled Bekaa Valley. At least 53 are
            killed. The Front for the Liberation of Lebanon from
            Foreigners (FLLF) claims credit for the attack.

FEBRUARY

1   COMMUNIST CHINA - The third round of talks on the
            Sino-Indian border dispute ends without progress in
            Peking.

1   EL SALVADOR - Rebel forces capture the important
            industrial city of Berlin and hold it for 48 hours
            before government forces liberate it.

2   SWITZERLAND - Strategic arms reduction talks (START)
            between the US and USSR begin in Geneva.

2   NORTH KOREA - In reaction to large-scale US-ROK
          military exercises in South Korea involving 118,000
          ROKAF and 73,000 US forces, the North Korean armed
          forces of 800,000 men go on alert.

5   LEBANON - The Palestine Research Center, the site of a
          PLO office, is blown up by the FLLF. Ten are killed
          and 40 injured.

8   IRAN - Government forces open a new major offensive
          against Iraq.

8-10   ISRAEL - A three-man commission investigating the West
          Beirut massacre of September 1982 issues its final
          report. No direct Israeli responsibility is fixed, but
          Defense Minister Ariel Sharon is accused of derelic-
          tion of duty. The report does conclude that Lebanese
          Christian Phalangist militiamen bear the brunt of the
          responsibility for the tragedy. The Cabinet accepts
          the report on 10 February.

13   LESOTHO - A fuel depot is blown up. The government
          accuses South Africa and demands compensation (14
          February).

14-15   INDIA - Election violence between Hindus and Muslims
          breaks out in the state of Assam. (More than 1,300 die
          in Mangaldai and Nellie alone during the ensuing
          several weeks.) The following day (15 February), more
          than 500 Muslim villagers, mostly aliens from
          Bangladesh, are killed by Hindi tribesmen.

15   LEBANON - The government regains control of all of
          Beirut when Christian Phalangist militias withdraw
          from the eastern sector to positions outside the city.

16   EGYPT - On becoming convinced that Libya was about to
          attack Sudan, President Hosni Mubarak asks the US for
          military assistance. Four airborne warning and control
          systems surveillance (AWACS) aircraft are sent to
          Egypt and the nuclear aircraft carrier USS Nimitz is
          ordered into the Egyptian waters.

18   INDIA - Hindus attack 17 Muslim villages near Nellie
          in Assam killing at least 600 people.

21   NAMIBIA - In a campaign that began on 14 February,
          South African forces report killing 96 SWAPO rebels.

22   SUDAN - President Gaafar Nimeiry states that intel-
          ligence information indicates Libya has delayed the
          invasion of his country by one to two months.

22   SPAIN - The "Basque Anticapitalist Autonomous Com-
            mandos" blow up the Michelin Tire Company warehouse in
            the Basque region.

24   INDIA - As many as 3,000 are killed in Assam in three
            weeks of ethnic and political rioting. About 90,000
            security troops are sent into the province by the
            central government but they cannot control the
            situation.

25   SOUTH KOREA - President Chun Doo Hwan releases 250 op-
            position leaders from a ban that prevented them from
            carrying on political activities.

MARCH

2   IRAN - Part of a major off-shore oil facility is de-
            stroyed by an Iraqi air attack.

2   GHANA - A third attempt to overthrow the Rawlings
            regime is crushed.

2   INDIA - Martial law is declared in the state of Assam.

3   GREECE - About 80,000 Greeks in Athens protest US mil-
            itary bases in Greece in a massive rally organized by
            leftist and Communist organizations.

8   UNITED STATES - President Reagan calls the Soviet
            Union an "evil empire."

8   ZIMBABWE - Government troops complete a four-day hunt
            for rebels in Bulawayo, in Matabeleland.

9   YUGOSLAVIA - Two JCAG terrorists shoot and kill the
            Turkish Ambassador in Belgrade. At least three others
            are shot in the melee that follows. One terrorist is
            captured at the scene and a second later arrested
            trying to leave the country.

9   USSR - The Soviet newspaper TASS accuses US President
            Reagan of a "pathological hatred" for Communism and
            Socialism.

9   ZIMBABWE - Opposition leader Joshua Nkomo is forced to
            flee the country for Great Britain. His rebel lieu-
            tenants follow him into exile four days later (12-13
            February).

10   UNITED STATES - The government adopts a 200-mile eco-
            nomic exclusion zone in US coastal waters.

14 ANGOLA - UNITA rebels capture 84 Czech and Portuguese technicans.

15 AFGHANISTAN - Increased fighting is reported as the rebels begin their spring campaign.

15-16 LEBANON - Muslim militia units attack US and other Multi-National Force positions in Beirut. Five US Marines and ten Italians are wounded.

16 LEBANON - A lone member of the Islamic Jihad attacks a US Marine patrol in the Ouzai section of Beirut near Beirut Airport. Five Marines are wounded when Nazmi Mohammed al-Sakka throws a grenade into the patrol. Sakka is arrested and a confederate detained.

17 UNITED NATIONS - Chad asks Security Council intervention in its long-standing border dispute with Libya.

21 GUATEMALA - President Efrain Rios Montt lifts the state of siege imposed in July 1982. At the same time, however, all political activities, strikes, public assemblies, labor organizations, and news about rebel activities are forbidden.

21 NICARAGUA - The government claims US-backed rebels have invaded the country from Honduras and warns of war if Honduras continues its present policies.

21 ISRAEL - The government announces a decision to build 22 new settlements in the West Bank in 1984.

23 UNITED STATES - President Reagan makes the first move in the "Star Wars" strategy when he calls for development of new weapons capable of shooting down incoming Soviet missiles.

28 ANGOLA - UNITA rebels attack a number of towns along the Benguela Railway.

28 GRENADA - The government warns that the island is facing imminent attack from the US and puts its military forces on alert.

31 UNITED STATES - President Reagan refuses to authorize the sale of F-16 fighters to Israel until that country had withdrawn from Lebanon.

31 KAMPUCHEA - Vietnamese forces launch a major offensive against Kampuchea (Cambodian) settlements near the Thai border. At least 25,000 refugees flee into Thailand.

APRIL

1   GREAT BRITAIN - Massive demonstrations protest the deployment of cruise and Pershing II missiles in Europe.

1-3   WEST GERMANY - More than 500,000 participate in demonstrations against NATO deployment of nuclear missiles in Europe.

4   THAILAND - Thai air force fighter-bombers attack Vietnamese troops on Thai territory.

4-5   BRAZIL - Serious rioting breaks out in Sao Paulo over the problem of unemployment.

6   EL SALVADOR - A leading member of El Salvador's rebel alliance, Melida Anaya Montes, known as "Ana Maria," is assassinated in Managua. Later in the month a second guerrilla leader, Salvador Cayetano Carpio, is murdered.

9   UNITED STATES - The US begins an emergency airlift of military supplies including "Redeye" air defense missiles and long-range artillery to Thailand.

12   VIET NAM - The government claims its forces have defeated the Kampuchean rebels in a two-week offensive along the Thai border. Hundreds of civilians are reported to have been killed by Vietnamese troops.

16   BRAZIL - Government authorities halt onward passage of four Libyan air transports loaded with weapons for Nicaragua. After much diplomatic effort the planes are allowed to return to Libya.

18   LEBANON - The US Embassy in Beirut is destroyed by a 2,000 pound bomb on a flatbed truck. The fundamentalist Islamic Jihad, a pro-Iranian Shi'ite organization, takes credit for the blast. Sixty-three are killed, of whom 17 are Americans. At least 100 are injured.

24   TURKEY - The military government announces its intention to allow the formation of political parties within the country.

MAY

1   POLAND - Tens of thousands of Poles observe May Day demonstrating against the government and its martial law edict. At least 20 cities have demonstrations and,

1   POLAND (Cont'd) - although there is some trouble, no real violence breaks out when riot police put an end to the demonstrations. One person is killed.

2   VIET NAM - The government claims it has begun the withdrawal of more than 10,000 of its troops in Kampuchea. The planned withdrawal is to be completed in 30 days.

4   EL SALVADOR - The government (Constituent Assembly) offers amnesty to about 250 political prisoners and to leftist rebels who surrender within 60 days.

4   NICARAGUA - The government claims it has been invaded from the north and the south by forces that total about 2,000 men.

4   IRAN - The government outlaws the Communist (Tudeh) Party and expels 18 Soviet diplomats.

5   SOUTH KOREA - A Chinese civilian airliner lands in South Korea after the first successful hijack of a aircraft from mainland China.

5   LEBANON - Beirut is shelled from villages under Syrian army control.

6   ISRAEL - The government accepts a US-sponsored plan calling for the simultaneous withdrawal of all Israeli and Syrian troops in Lebanon.

7   SYRIA - The government rejects the US peace plan.

11 CHILE - Violence erupts at a massive antigovernment demonstration. At least two people are known dead. Police begin a roundup of suspected anti-Pinochet people. More than 1,000 are taken but most are released immediately.

12 CHILE - Following a "Day of National Protest" against the Pinochet regime, rioting breaks out in Santiago.

15 PERSIAN GULF - The Panamanian tanker SS Pan Oceanic Sane is attacked and set afire by a missile fired from an Iraqi jet.

16 USSR - An arms agreement between the Soviet Union and Angola is signed in Moscow.

17 LEBANON - A Lebanese-Israeli withdrawal agreement is signed. The accord also sets up procedures for bilateral relations between the two contries.

17   UPPER VOLTA - President Jean-Baptiste Ouedraogo orders
            the ouster and arrest of a number of senior officials
            including Premier Thomas Sankara. All are accused of
            plotting the overthrow of the government. The Libyan
            Charge d'Affairs is also ordered out of the country
            for what is called his complicity in the coup plot.

18   SUDAN - Loyal army troops put down a mutiny among
            soldiers stationed in the south who refuse to be
            transferred north into other tribal areas.

18   SRI LANKA - The government declares a state of emer-
            gency to preclude post-elections violence.

18   SOUTH KOREA - For the first time in 30 years Chinese
            and Korean officials meet to discuss the hijacking of
            a Chinese airliner. The plane had ben flown to South
            Korea earlier in the month. The airliner is returned
            after brief negotiations and the six Chinese hijackers
            are sentenced to prison by a South Korean court.

19   PAKISTAN - The Soviet Ambassador states the Afghan
            government is willing to set up a Soviet withdrawal
            schedule if it can be guaranteed protection against
            outside interference.

20   SOUTH AFRICA - A car-bomb blast at the Air Force head-
            quarters in Pretoria kills 18 and injures more than
            200. The outlawed African National Congress (ANC)
            assumes responsibility for the bombing.

20   UNITED STATES - The US lifts its ban on the sale of
            F-16 fighter aircraft to Israel.

23   SOUTH AFRICA - South African aircraft bomb the sus-
            pected headquarters of the ANC in retaliation for the
            Pretoria bombing.

24   FRANCE - Student marches against planned educational
            changes become violent. Police finally restore order.

24   SOUTH AFRICA - The government says it will not with-
            draw from Namibia until Cuban forces are withdrawn
            from Angola.

25   EL SALVADOR - US Navy Lieutenant Commander Albert
            Schaufelberger, the Deputy Commander of the US Mili-
            tary Advisory Group, is shot and killed in his car on
            a university campus. The Farabundo Marti National
            Liberation Front is probably responsible for the
            murder.

26   IRAN - The government rejects a UN-proposed peace
            plan.

26-27   PERU - Rebels black out the capital city of Lima after a state of emergency is declared by the government.

29-30   SYRIA - Anti-Arafat PLO rebels attack PLO administrative centers and seize six PLO supply depots.

30   PERU - The government extends the state of emergency for an additional 60 days to combat widespread acts of terrorism caused by a rebel group known as Shining Path (Sendero Luminoso).

31   PERSIAN GULF - The Indian bulk carrier SS Atj Priti is seriously damaged by Iraqi missiles near Bandar Khomeini.

JUNE

1   UNITED STATES - The government signs an agreement ensuring the continuation of its basing rights in The Philippines.

4-6   LEBANON - Heavy fighting breaks out among the various Palestinian factions over the proper leadership for their campaign against Israel.

6   FINLAND - The government extends its treaty of friendship and cooperation with the Soviet Union for another 20 years.

7   UNITED STATES - The government closes its six consulates in Nicaragua and orders Nicaraguan consulate officials in the US out of the country. This comes about after six US diplomats are expelled (6 June) from Nicaragua on charges that they interferred in the internal affairs of the country.

12   OAU - The organization adopts a peace plan for Western Sahara.

15   UNITED STATES - The Congress refuses a White House request to resume the production of chemical weapons.

16   TURKEY - ASALA terrorists indiscriminately open fire on a crowd in a bazaar in Istanbul. Two are killed and 23 injured in the attack.

19   GHANA - Yet another coup attempt against the Rawlings regime fails as government troops crush the rebels.

24   SYRIA - The government expels Yasser Arafat, the PLO leader.

24   CHAD - The town of Faya Largeau in Borkou Province is
            taken by troops loyal to former President Goukouni
            Oueddei. Goukouni has Libyan backing in his drive to
            recover power.

25   LEBANON - US Marines begin conducting patrols with
            Lebanese Army personnel.

26   FRANCE - The government begins an airlift of 35 tons
            of military equipment to Chad.

28   LEBANON - Heavy fighting breaks out among Palestinian
            factions in the Bekaa Valley.

JULY

3   CHAD - The first contingent of 250 Zaire troops arrive
            to reinforce the army in its fight against Libyan-
            backed rebel forces fighting in the north.

6-7   BRAZIL - A major strike by oil and metal workers pro-
            tests government austerity plans.

7   SYRIA - The US Secretary of State visits Damascus in a
            fruitless attempt to get the Syrians to withdraw their
            forces from Lebanon.

10   MOROCCO - Western Saharan Polisario rebels attack
            Moroccan defensive positions along the border.

11   PERU - Shining Path (Sendero Luminoso) terrorists
            attack the headquarters of the Popular Action Party in
            Lima killing two people and wounding about 30 others.
            The Communist Party joins numerous other political
            groups in denouncing the wave of terror.

14   BELGIUM - Terrorists of the Justice Commandos for the
            Armenian Genocide assassinate a Turkish Administrative
            Attache in Brussels.

15   FRANCE - ASALA terrorists claim responsibility for an
            explosion at Orly Airport outside Paris that kills
            five and injures 50 others. The bomb was hidden in
            luggage deposited at the Turkish Airlines counter.

16   OAU - A nine-member committee of the OAU demands im-
            mediate foreign withdrawal from Chad so that local
            negotiations can begin.

17   MEXICO - The presidents of four Contadora nations call
            upon all those with interests in Central America to
            settle their disputes by negotiations and not by war.

| 20 | LEBANON - Israeli forces in Beirut and in the Shouf Mountains begin withdrawing south across the Awali River. This redeployment is authorized by the Israeli Knesset. |

20   LEBANON - Israeli forces in Beirut and in the Shouf Mountains begin withdrawing south across the Awali River. This redeployment is authorized by the Israeli Knesset.

20   UNITED STATES - Lebanese President Amin Gemayel visits the US as the conditions in his homeland worsen.

21   POLAND - Martial law in effect since December 1981 is ended.

22   LEBANON - Three US personnel are wounded as increasing amounts of indirect artillery, mortar, and rocket fire are placed on Beirut airport. Fire primarily from Druze militia units is also directed against Lebanese Army positions and other members of the multinational force.

23-25   SRI LANKA - A new period of violence begins when Tamil rebels ambush and kill 13 soldiers near Jaffna. By 24 July serious violence against the Tamil minority breaks out in Colombo. The next day (25 July) thirty-seven Tamils are murdered in a Colombo prison by the Sinhalese inmates. In all, about 400 are killed and 100,000 left homeless on both sides in the wave of violence.

25   UNITED STATES - An emergency airlift of military supplies to Chad is begun.

26   ITALY - Twelve members of the Red Brigade terrorist organization are sentenced to life in a Turin courtroom. Forty-eight others are given lesser sentences; one is acquitted.

27   PORTUGAL - Five Armenian terrorists (probably ASALA) shoot their way into the Turkish Embassy in Lisbon, then blow up themselves and the building. Four terrorists, a policeman, and a civilian are killed. The other terrorist is shot and killed before the explosion.

27   GREECE - The government approves US retention of its bases in Greece under certain restrictions as to their use.

30   CHAD - Government forces recapture Faya Largeau, but it is once again taken by Libyan-supported rebel forces loyal to Goukouni Oueddei.

30   ZIMBABWE - The government withdraws its Fifth Brigade from Matabeleland after charges of murder and repression are lodged against its personnel.

AUGUST

2   UNITED NATIONS - The US vetoes a Security Council resolution dealing with conditions in the occupied territories in Israel.

2   ITALY - Two Red Brigade terrorists receive life sentences; 37 others get lesser sentences, and 21 are acquitted by a Sardinian court.

2   LEBANON - Heavy fighting breaks out between Druze and Christian militiamen in the Shouf (Chouf) Mountains above Beirut. This fighting continues through 22 August.

2   IRAN - An Iranian offensive against Iraqi positions in the central sector is stopped with heavy casualties.

3   UNITED STATES - The Defense Department orders two AWACS aircraft to Sudan to monitor events in Chad.

5   SRI LANKA - In an attempt to halt the present upsurge of violence in which more than 400 will die, the government bans all political activity which advocates a separate Tamil state.

5   UPPER VOLTA - Former Premier Thomas Sankara successfully overthrows the government of Major Jean-Baptiste Ouedraogo.

5   LEBANON - A car bomb explodes in front of the Bakkar Mosque in Tripoli. Nineteen are killed, 43 injured. Although no one takes credit for the bombing, bickering between Muslim factions over who is responsible leads to gunfire in the streets.

6   CHAD - The government requests additional French military assistance to fight rebel attacks in the north.

7   SOUTH KOREA - A Communist Chinese air force pilot defects to South Korea in his MiG-21. Earlier in the year, in February, a North Korean pilot defected in his MiG-19.

7   LEBANON - A FLLF bomb blast in a crowded market in the Syrian-controlled town of Baalabakk kills 33 and injures 133.

8   GUATEMALA - The government of President Efrain Rios Montt is overthrown in a military coup that appoints Brigadier General Oscar Humberto Mejia Victores in his place.

9   FRANCE - Following a plea from Chad's President Hissen
           Habre for more military assistance, the government
           orders an additional 500 paratroopers to Chad.

9   IRAN - Iraqi forces begin a withdrawal from Iranian
           territory after heavy fighting and heavy casualties.

10   LEBANON - Druze militia artillery and mortar units at-
           tack Beirut International Airport. One US Marine is
           wounded. Rockets are fired at the Presidential Palace
           and the Lebanese Ministry of Defense building. Attacks
           of this type continue intermittently.

10-12   CHAD - With heavy Libyan military support rebels loyal
           to former President Goukouni Oueddei recapture the
           strategically important, northern town of Faya Largeau
           (Faya) in the Borkou district.

12-13   CHILE - More than 24 are killed and 100 injured in two
           days of demonstrations against the Pinochet govern-
           ment.

13   CHAD - An additional 180 French paratroopers and
           several helicopters arrive in the eastern city of
           Abeche (Abecher) to reinforce the government's
           positions there. French forces are given orders to
           fight if attacked. Rebel forces capture two more
           strategically important towns.

13   LIBERIA - The government announces it has concluded a
           military agreement with Israel which includes a
           resumption of full diplomatic relations.

14   PAKISTAN - More than 50,000 pro- and anti-Zia demon-
           strators clash in the streets of Karachi. Many anti-
           Zia leaders are arrested.

14   CHAD - French and Zairian military forces occupy
           blocking positions to the north and east of the
           capital city of N'Djamena to protect it from Libyan-
           supported rebel attack from the Faya Largeau area.

15   ZIMBABWE - Joshua Nkomo returns from his short-lived
           exile.

17   FRANCE - The government alerts an additional 2,000
           troops for airlift to Chad.

19   ARGENTINA - Tens of thousands demonstrate in Buenos
           Aires against the government's proposed amnesty for
           military personnel accused of committing atrocities
           and other human rights violations in the 1970s.

21   THE PHILIPPINES - Opposition leader Benigno Aquino is assassinated within minutes of deplaning at Manila airport after a three-year exile in the US. Most witnesses claim it is Filipino soldiers who shoot Aquino, and that the entire affair has the Marcos government's blessing.

21   CHAD - A squadron of French fighters is deployed to Chad.

22   PAKISTAN - Police open fire on demonstrators in Sind. Three are killed and 75 injured.

23   UNITED STATES - The US withdraws its AWACS aircraft from Sudan.

24   ISRAEL - The government announces a restoration of diplomatic relations with the Central African Republic.

24   SWITZERLAND - The government announces it has decided to buy the West German "Leopard II" main battle tank instead of the US-built "Abrams" tank which they say is inferior to the German model.

27   AUSTRIA - An Air France flight from Vienna to Paris is hijacked by a group of Lebanese. The plane eventually lands in Tehran, Iran. The hijackers demand a change in French policy in Chad, Lebanon, and Iraq and the release of prisoners in French jails.

28   LEBANON - A combined Lebanese Army-US Marine position in Beirut is subjected to a ground attack. In a firefight that lasts 90 minutes the Marines return fire for the first time.

29   LEBANON - Two US Marines are killed and 14 wounded in action in a heavy rocket and mortar attack on the east side of Beirut airport. Marine artillery joins the Lebanese Army in the action for the first time against Druze militia forces.

30   LEBANON - Attacks on French and Italian positions culminate in four French soldiers killed in action and five Italians wounded.

31   POLAND - Ten thousand Solidarity supporters clash with police in Nowa Huta, near Kracow (Cracow).

31   LEBANON - Muslim artillery shells the US Ambassador's residence. US Marine artillery engages in counter-battery fire.

SEPTEMBER

1   USSR - Soviet fighter aircraft shoot down an unarmed Korean Airlines (KAL 007) Boeing 747 which apparently strays into Soviet air space over Sakhalin Island. All 269 on board are killed.

1   UNITED STATES - President Reagan orders a naval amphibious force to the eastern Mediterranean to support the US Marines ashore in Lebanon.

2   GREECE - In Athens the government signs a defense treaty with Great Britain.

2   CHAD - Government force repulse a Libyan-supported rebel attack on Oum Chalouba.

3-4   EL SALVADOR - Leftist guerrillas attack and temporarily occupy San Miguel, the country's third-largest city.

4   LEBANON - Israeli forces withdraw from the Shouf area to positions along the Awali River creating a vacumn that is quickly filled with forces of a number of factions. Heavy fighting then breaks out in the Shouf Mountains between Muslim and Christian factions as Lebanese army forces attempt to occupy and take control of the area.

5   SRI LANKA - The government eases the restrictions of its state of emergency.

6   USSR - The government admits shooting down KAL 007, but claims the aircraft refused to heed warnings and was actually on a US spy mission.

6   LEBANON - Druze militiamen carry out a rocket attack against Beirut Airport from positions in the Shouf Mountains. Two US Marines are killed and two wounded in this attack.

7   LEBANON - President Amin Gemayle asks for UN assistance in controlling the fighting in the Shouf Mountains.

8   LEBANON - Naval gunfire from the frigate USS Bowen adds to the artillery support available to the Marine amphibious force ashore in Lebanon. Artillery fire from Druze artillery positions in the Shouf Mountains is silenced by the naval supporting fires. Later, more ships, including the battleship USS New Jersey, will join in the naval gunfire support (14 December).

8   GREECE - The government signs a five-year agreement with the US for military basing rights on Greek territory.

8   CHILE - At least four people die in anti-Pinochet rioting.

8-9   NICARAGUA - Managua is bombed by rebels flying two light aircraft over the city. They force the closing of the airport. The next day (9 September) jet fighters attack the major seaport of Corinto.

10   PERU - The government lifts the state of emergency imposed in May, although several Andean Districts (Apurimac, Ayacucho, and Huancavelica) still remain under martial law.

11   CHILE - At least ten civilians are reported dead in the latest round of anti-Pinochet violence.

12   UNITED NATIONS - The Soviet Union vetoes a Security Council resolution comdemning it for shooting down an unarmed KAL airliner.

15   THE PHILIPPINES - Thousands demonstrate in Manila in protest of the Aquino assassination.

16   LEBANON - Yasser Arafat returns to Lebanon after a three-month absence.

16-19 LEBANON - Off the coast of Lebanon, US naval gunfire from the warship USS Virginia (CGN-38) and the destroyer USS John Rodgers support loyal Lebanese army units struggling to retain possession of the strategically important village of Suq-el-Gharb in the Shouf Mountains.

19   SAINT CHRISTOPHER AND NEVIS - The southern Caribbean islands of Saint Kitts and Nevis become independent members of the British Commonwealth.

21   SCOTLAND - A Soviet delegate at a conference in Edinburgh admits the pilot that shot down KAL 007 erred in believing his target was a US spy plane.

21   THE PHILIPPINES - About 500,000 demonstrate against the Marcos government. Violence breaks out after dark when 11 are killed, more than 200 injured.

22   LEBANON - French forces retaliate with air strikes against militia positions following the shelling of French units in the peacekeeping force.

23   ARGENTINA - The ruling military junta grants immunity
        from prosecution to those accused of political crimes
        since 1973.

23   UNITED ARAB EMIRATES - An Omani Gulf Air airliner ex-
        plodes in midair on a flight near Abu Dubai. All 111
        on board are killed. The Arab Revolutionary Brigades
        (an Abu Nidal group) claims credit for the attack and
        says it was in retaliation for the repres- sion of PLO
        activities in the UAE.

25   USSR - The government doubles its fighter strength on
        Etorofu Island off northern Japan, in reaction to the
        furor over the shooting down of KAL 007.

25   URUGUAY - At least 25,000 demonstrators against the
        military government march in Montevideo.

25   NORTHERN IRELAND - Thirty-eight IRA terrorists are
        allowed to escape from the maximum security prison at
        Maze.

26   SYRIA - Syrian and Saudi Arabian officials in Damascus
        announce that a cease-fire has been in effect since
        dawn. To date, five US Marines have been killed, 49
        wounded in action.

27   ARGENTINA - The military-controlled government passes
        an antiterrorism law that grants sweeping powers to
        police, security forces, and the courts.

OCTOBER

        LEBANON - Throughout the month to 23 October harassing
        fire from Arab snipers kills or wounds a number of US
        Marines. Several US Marine helicopters are hit by Arab
        ground fire.

1   UNITED STATES - The 31st MAU is sent from the Mediter-
        ranean into the Indian Ocean in response to the crisis
        in the Strait of Hormuz.

3   LEBANON - Twenty-three Al Fatah officers of Yasser
        Arafat's PLO defect to Syria and the anti-Arafat PLO
        forces there.

6   NIGER - An Army coup attempt aimed at toppling the
        government of President Seyni Kountche fails. Kountche
        is in France at the time.

6   INDIA - The central government assumes direct control
        of the state of Punjab as a means of restoring order
        to the violence-torn region.

9   BURMA - Four South Korean cabinet members, the South
           Korean Ambassador to Burma, and several top advisors
           to President Chun Doo Hwan are among 21 killed by the
           premature detonation of a terrorist bomb at a wreath
           laying ceremony in Rangoon. President Chun escapes
           death because of a traffic jam. North Korea is blamed
           for the incident, and South Korea's armed forces are
           put on alert.

9   IRAQ - France delivers five Super Etendard jet fight-
           ers to Iraq despite the protests of the US, British,
           West German, and several Persian Gulf governments.
           Most feared the Iranians would follow through with
           their threat to close the Strait of Hormuz if Iraq
           used the new aircraft to launch Exocet missiles
           against Iranian targets.

13   GRENADA - Prime Minister Maurice Bishop is overthrown
           and arrested by rebels led by Bernard Coard, the
           Deputy Prime Minister.

17   MIDDLE EAST - The Palestine Liberation Army (PLA)
           withdraws its recognition of Yasser Arafat as its
           leader.

18   ISRAEL - Intelligence sources confirm the arrival of
           Soviet-built SS-21 surface-to-surface missiles in
           Syria.

19   IRAN - Government forces launch an attack on Iraqi
           positions at Panjwin, in the northern sector.

19-20   GRENADA - Prime Minister Maurice Bishop, along with a
           number of his cabinet members, is killed by the radi-
           cal military faction of his own New Jewel Movement
           during a melee following his release by his supporters
           from house arrest. At least 60 are killed in the coup
           and its aftermath. On the following day (20 October)
           General Hudson Austin leads a Revolutionary Military
           Council in assuming control of the former British
           colony. Governor General Sir Paul Scoon asks the OAS
           for help.

21   UNITED STATES - A naval task force, including 1,900
           Marines of the 22nd Marine Amphibious Unit (MAU), is
           diverted from its original destination off the coast·
           of Lebanon and is ordered to close on the Caribbean
           island of Grenada. "Operation URGENT FURY" begins.

22   EUROPE - At least two million demonstrate in protest
           against US deployment of cruise and Pershing II mis-
           siles. Associated antinuclear rallies in the US re-
           sult in the arrest of more than 1,000 protestors.

23   LEBANON - An Arab bent on suicide drives a truck car-
            rying 12,000 pounds of explosives into the poorly
            protected US Embassy in Beirut. The truck's explosives
            detonate in the foyer of the building housing the 1st
            Battalion Landing Team, Eighth Marines (BLT 1/8). Two
            hundred forty-one US Marines are killed, 70 wounded in
            the attack. Simultaneously, a second suicide attack is
            made on the barracks of the French Airborne Battalion
            two miles north of the US attack. Fifty-eight French
            soldiers are killed in the ensuing blast.

24   USSR - The government announces it has begun moves to
            station nuclear missiles in Eastern Europe and will go
            ahead with the plans if the US deploys missiles in
            Western Europe.

25   GRENADA - More than two thousand US Army and Marine
            personnel land on the island of Grenada to restore
            order in the wake of chaos caused by local political
            conditions and to prevent a suspected Cuban takeover
            of the island. Six other Caribbean nations (Antiqua,
            Barbados, Dominica, Jamaica, St. Lucia, and St. Vin-
            cent) participate in the intervention with a 300-man
            multinational force.

27   GRENADA - Resistance on the island is overcome by the
            US and OAS landing forces. The principal source of the
            resistance was a force of Cuban military personnel on
            the island. Bernard Coard and General Hudson Austin
            are arrested.

28   UNITED NATIONS - The US vetoes a Security Council re-
            solution condemning the raid on Grenada.

29   EUROPE - Another series of demonstrations protesting
            deployment of cruise and Pershing II missiles takes
            place. In the Netherlands Princess Irene takes part in
            the demonstration in The Hague where 500,000 march. In
            Denmark nearly 250,000 participate in a demonstration
            in Copenhagen.

29   COMMUNIST CHINA - Sino-Soviet normalization talks
            break off in Peking. The Soviet delegation returns to
            the USSR.

31   UNITED STATES - The Defense Department accepts respon-
            sibility for the accidental bombing of an unmarked
            hospital on Grenada which caused considerable damage
            and loss of life.

31   SWITZERLAND - Representatives of Lebanese political
            and religious factions meet in Geneva in hopes of
            finding a solution to the civil war that is destroying
            their country.

31   PERSIAN GULF - The Greek freighter _SS Avra_ is set
            ablaze by Iraqi missiles while sailing in a convoy
            protected by Iranian naval vessels.

NOVEMBER

1   CARIBBEAN - US Marines from the 22nd MAU carry out a
            coordinated amphibious and heliborne operation on the
            island of Carriacou, 15 miles northeast of Grenada, in
            search of Cuban military installations and personnel.
            Weapons, training areas, and 17 Grenadian soldiers are
            all that are found.

1   INDIA - More than 400 arrests are reported in Punjab
            as the central government moves to quell the ongoing
            disturances.

2   CARRIACOU - The Marines of the 22nd MAU are withdrawn
            from the island and, when reembarked aboard their
            ships, the naval task force sails for Beirut.

3   LEBANON - PLO troops loyal to Yasser Arafat come under
            intense rebel Palestinian mortar and rocket fire at
            their base north of Tripoli. Some reports indicate
            that PLO rebels are reinforced by Libyan and Syrian
            forces.

4   ISRAEL - Israeli jets are sent against Palestinian
            targets along the Beirut-Damascus road within hours of
            a truck-bomb explosion in an Israeli compound in Tyre
            in which at least 60 are killed. The jets attack a
            number of suspected Druze guerrilla bases in the Shouf
            Mountains and the Syrian military base at Sofar.

4   BURMA - The government announces it has broken diplo-
            matic relations with North Korea after the capture of
            two North Korean "commandos" who confessed to and were
            charged with the 9 October bombing in Rangoon that
            killed 21. Another North Korean terrorist agent is
            killed in a gun battle with Burmese police. The two
            captured North Korean officers will be sentenced to
            death by a Burmese court on 9 December.

7   SYRIA - A general mobilization is ordered.

8   LEBANON - PLO forces loyal to Yasser Arafat retreat to
            the refugee camp at Beddawi where Arafat's headquar-
            ters used to be located.

8   ANGOLA - UNITA rebels shoot down an Angolan Boeing 737
            airliner shortly after takeoff from the airport at
            Lubango. There are no survivors among the 126 on
            board.

9   GRENADA - Governor General Sir Paul Scoon establishes a nine-man non-political interim government to rule until elections can be arranged.

10   TURKEY - The National Security Council tightens censorship controls with the passage of new laws.

11   SWITZERLAND - The Lebanese national reconciliation conference, which opened on 31 October, closes without any progress.

15   CYPRUS - Turkish Cypriots declare their part of the island independent.

15   GREECE - Captain George Tsantes, the Chief of the US Naval Mission in Greece is assassinated while driving in downtown Athens. His Greek driver is also killed. The November 17 Organization claims credit for the attack.

16   LEBANON - Rebel PLO forces penetrate the defenses of Arafat's position at Beddawi. Arafat is forced to move his troops into Tripoli where a cease-fire can be arranged.

17   LEBANON - French fighter-bombers twice attack Shi'ite Muslim positions near Baalbek in the Bekaa Valley in retaliation for the bomb attack on French positions in Beirut on 23 October.

17   TANZANIA - The government reopens its land border with Kenya after a six-year closure.

18   UNITED NATIONS - The Security Council orders the Turkish Cypriots to withdraw their declaration of independence.

18   CHILE - More than 100,000 antigovernment demonstrators march in Santiago.

19   LEBANON - The 22nd MAU, which participated in the Grenada operation, arrives in Beirut to replace the 24th MAU.

21   POLAND - The Parliament establishes a National Defense Committee with almost unlimited powers that will allow it to exercise total control when a state of emergency exists.

21   PERSIAN GULF - The 13,000-ton Greek bulk carrier SS Antigoni is sunk by Iraqi jets while sailing in the convoy protected by Iranian naval vessels.

22   UNITED STATES - Secretary of Defense Caspar Weinberger
            states that Iranians, with the support and approval of
            the Syrian government, planned and executed the 23
            October attack on the US Embassy in Beirut.

24   LEBANON - An Israeli-PLO prisoner exchange is arranged
            after several months of negotiation. Six Israelis are
            ex- changed for 4,500 Palestinian and Lebanese Arab
            prisoners.

27   URUGUAY - A massive demonstration takes place in Mon-
            tevideo in which 300,000 demand that the ruling mili-
            tary junta led by General Gregorio Alvarez Armelino
            make the promised return to democracy more quickly.

28-30   BANGLADESH - Renewed rioting breaks out in Dhaka and
            Chittagong. The government immediately reimposes a
            freeze on political activity.

DECEMBER

1   LEBANON - Sheikh Halim Takieddin, the President of the
            Supreme Druze Religious Court, is assassinated by an
            unidentified gunman in West Beirut.

2   SPAIN - Eight US installations in Basque areas are
            bombed. The Basque separatist group, Iraultza, is
            believed to be responsible for the attacks which are
            aimed at showing displeasure over US policies in
            Central America.

3   UNITED NATIONS - The Security Council approves a plan
            for five neutral vessels to evacuate Yasser Arafat's
            army of 4,000 from Tripoli, Lebanon, to Tunisia and
            North Yemen.

4   LEBANON - Marine positions around the Beirut Airport
            are subjected to intense fire. Heavy naval gunfire and
            a 28-plane air strike are employed to reduce the enemy
            artillery and antiaircraft positions. Eight US Marines
            are killed on the ground. Two US naval aircraft are
            shot down by Syrian antiaircraft fire. One US naval
            crewman, Lieutenant Robert O. Goodman, is taken
            prisoner by the Syrians.

4   NICARAGUA - The government offers amnesty to almost
            all emigres who wish to return to Nicaragua.

6   TURKEY - The National Security Council is dissolved. A
            civilian Prime Minister is named.

6   ISRAEL - The PLO blows up a bus in Jerusalem killing
            four and wounding 46.

8   UNITED STATES - The government lifts its ban on arms sales to Argentina.

8   PERSIAN GULF - The 16,000-ton Greek bulk carrier SS Iapetus is attacked by Iraqi jets near Bandar Khomeini and abandoned by her crew.

11   BANGLADESH - Lieutenant General Hossain Mohammad Ershad proclaims himself President. Martial law is extended until the elections planned for 1985.

12   KUWAIT - The US Embassy is subjected to a suicide attack. No Americans are hurt, but five other people are killed and 37 injured. The attack is timed to coincide with similar suicide attacks at the French Embassy, the Kuwait airport control tower, a Raytheon Company compound, and other buildings. Shi'ite Muslim terrorists (Islamic Jihad), possibly sponsored by Iran, are blamed (18 December) for the attack.

15   GRENADA - The last US combat troops depart the island. A 300-man US military support group and a 392-man OAS multinational force remain in Grenada.

15   LEBANON - More than 2,000 Christian militiamen are evacuated by the Israelis from the village of Deir el-Kamar in the Shouf Mountains.

17   GREAT BRITAIN - A car bomb explodes behind Harrods Department Store in London killing five and injuring 91. The Provisional Wing of the IRA claims credit for the attack. Leaders of the IRA claim, however, that the attack was unauthorized and that necessary steps will be taken to ensure that it will not happen again.

20   LEBANON - Greek vessels flying the UN and PLO flags, and apparently financed by Saudi Arabia, evacuate Yasser Arafat and 4,000 of his troops from Tripoli. French naval vessels protect the small fleet of ships as they leave Lebanese waters.

21   LEBANON - A large bomb loaded on a truck explodes outside the French Multinational Force (MNF) headquarters in Beirut killing one French soldier and nine Lebanese civilians. At least 125 are injured. No one claims credit for the attack.

22   LEBANON - An Israeli military spokeman announces that the military headquarters of the Israeli forces in Lebanon will move from Sidon to Kfar Falus, but denies this indicates a withdrawal of Israeli forces south of the Awali River.

22   THAILAND - About 5,000 Communist Thai rebels surrender
        to authorities   in   northern   Nan   Province   near   the
        Laotian border.   The   surrender follows   a   government
        offer of amnesty that effectively ends rebel   activity
        in the north.

26   LEBANON - The   Phalangist radio,   "Voice of   Lebanon,"
        announces that US   Ambassador Reginald Batholomew   has
        stated the   Italian   contingent   in the   MNF   will   be
        reduced from 2,000 to 1,200 men.

26   SOUTH AFRICA - The government announces it has invaded
        Angola to thwart rebel attacks aimed at Namibia.

26   PERU - Sendero Luminoso   terrorists throw five   sticks
        of dynamite in the Chinese Communist Embassy   compound
        in Santiago to celebrate the birthday of Mao Tse-tung.
        This is the third year that this has occurred.

30   EL SALVADOR -   More than 100   government soldiers   are
        killed when leftist guerrillas attack and capture   the
        garrison at   El Paraiso   in Chalatenango   Province   40
        miles north of   San Salvador. After   holding the   base
        for six hours the rebels withdraw. The Farabundo Marti
        Liberation Front takes credit for the raid.

31   NIGERIA - A bloodless   military coup topples the   gov-
        ernment of President Alhaji Shehu Shagari.

                                Notes

1984

LEBANON - Hostile militia forces, especially those of the Druze faction, subject US Marine positions to sporadic but intense fire throughout the month. Some US casualties are reported.

1   NIGERIA - Major General Mohammed Buhari is installed as the new president.

1   BRUNEI - The independence of the former British colony is proclaimed.

1   EL SALVADOR - Leftist guerrillas destroy the Cuscatlan Bridge over the Lempa River on the Pan American Highway after driving off several hundred Salvadoran army troops assigned to guard it. The span was the largest in El Salvador linking San Salvador with the eastern part of the country.

2   TURKEY - The government announces it is withdrawing 1,500 more troops from Cyprus.

2   SPAIN - October First Antifascist Resistance Group (GRAPO) terrorists murder two policemen in retaliation for the police killing of their leader in a shootout in Barcelona in December 1983.

3   TUNISIA - President Habib Bourguiba declares a state of emergency because of rioting over increased food prices. The decree remains in effect three days and is then cancelled (6 January).

3   SYRIA - After a personal appeal to President Assad by
             the Reverend Jesse Jackson, the government releases US
             Navy pilot Lieutenant Robert O. Goodman, who was   shot
             down on 4 December 1983.

3   FRANCE - The government announces it will withdraw 500
             men from the Multinational Force in Lebanon by the end
             of January.

4   LEBANON - Israeli bombers attack Palestinian   targets
             near Baalbek. At least 60 are killed and 300   injured
             as a result of the bombing.

6   UNITED NATIONS - The Security Council condemns South
             Africa for its attacks into Angola.

7   LEBANON - A US Marine helicopter is fired on as it is
             landing at the British Embassy in Beirut.

8   SOUTH AFRICA - The government begins withdrawing   its
             forces in southern Angola.

9   NORTHERN IRELAND - An IRA command-detonated bomb in-
             jures two Royal Ulster Constabulary officers   in
             Londonderry.

10   UNITED STATES - The US reestablishes full diplomatic
             relations with the Vatican after a break lasting
             almost a century.

10   USSR - The Soviet Union suggests NATO-Warsaw Pact
             talks aimed at banning the use of chemical weapons in
             Europe.

11   NORTH KOREA - The government suggests the US and ROK
             join them in tripartite negotiations aimed at reuni-
             fying Korea.

12   SPAIN - The government replaces a number of military
             commanders and puts the armed forces under more direct
             civilian control.

13   ITALY - Prime Minister Craxi reaffirms Italy's role as
             the protector of Malta's neutrality.

14   LEBANON - The leader of the Israeli-supported South
             Lebanon Army, Major Saad Haddad, dies of cancer.

14   FRANCE - France sells $4.5 million in arms to Saudi
             Arabia.

15   SOUTH AFRICA - Two thousand troops are pulled out of
             the battle area 100 miles north of the Namibian
             border.

18   URUGUAY - For the first time in ten years of military
        rule, the country is paralyzed by a politically moti-
        vated general strike.

18   LEBANON - Malcolm Kerr, the President of the American
        University in Beirut is shot and killed in the admin-
        istration building by two or more assailants. The
        Islamic Jihad takes credit for the murder.

19   UNITED STATES - Citing a general improvement in con-
        ditions, the US lifts some of the sanctions imposed
        upon Poland following that country's declaration of
        martial law in December 1981.

19   MOROCCO - The Islamic Conference Organization votes to
        reinstate Egypt into the group. Egypt was expelled in
        1979 after signing the Camp David Accords.

22   MOROCCO - King Hassan II urges calm after rioting
        breaks out in Marrakech and spreads across the coun-
        try. Food prices and higher education costs are the
        proximate causes of the violence that kills 29 or more
        and injures hundreds.

23   INDIA - Serious rioting by Congress Party activists
        causes injury to 300.

23   THE VATICAN - Argentina and Chile initial a Papal-
        negotiated treaty of friendship and cooperation and
        pledge to settle the Beagle Channel dispute.

25   BRAZIL - A major demonstration in Sao Paulo calls for
        greater democracy. Some 200,000 participate in the
        peaceful march.

27   PAKISTAN - Soviet-built Afghan MiG fighters attack
        Pakistani border settlements. About 40 civilians are
        killed.

28   GUATEMALA - The government announces that despite a
        Congressional ban the US will sell them $2 million in
        spare helicopter parts.

30   MIDDLE EAST - Egypt rejoins the Islamic Conference Or-
        ganization after the organization lifts the five-year-
        old quarantine placed on Cairo for dealing with
        Israel.

30   LEBANON - One US Marine is killed and two wounded when
        they are fired on at Beirut Airport. Four civilians
        are also wounded. In the ensuing firefight, two of the
        attackers are allegedly killed and 15 wounded.

FEBRUARY

1   COMMUNIST CHINA - When the Netherlands indicates it has cut off all military sales to the Nationalist Chinese on Taiwan, Peking reestablishes full diplomatic ties with The Hague.

1   ARGENTINA - The government restricts the courts ability to prosecute military personnel for past crimes.

2   LEBANON - Fighting erupts in a Beirut suburb between Shi'ite militiamen and Lebanese army units.

3   ZIMBABWE - The government moves additional troops into Matabeleland Province where rebels, allegedly trained in South Africa, are setting up base camps among the Ndebele tribe. Others claim the military operations are against the Ndebele who politically oppose Prime Minister Robert Mugabe's government.

5   LEBANON - Heavy fighting between the Lebanese Army and militia units is reported in Beirut. The US warns that it will protect Lebanese Army positions with air and naval strikes against antigovernment forces, presumably those of Syria and the Lebanese militias under their control.

6-7   LEBANON - After heavy street fighting in which the Lebanese Army is routed and the forced resignation of Prime Minister Shafiq al-Wazzan and most of the cabinet, Druze and Shi'ite Muslim militiamen take control of most of Beirut. Some reports indicate that as many as 40% of the Lebanese troops desert and join the attacking militias. The Shi'ites again demand the resignation of the Maronite Christian President, Amin Gemayel.

7   UNITED STATES - The President announces the decision to withdraw the Marine landing force currently in Beirut. The main body of the force will be embarked aboard ships that will remain on station off the Lebanese coast (completed 26 February). A small residual force will guard the US Embassy. The Beirut Airport will be abandoned.

7   UNITED NATIONS - A forty-nation UN Disarmament Conference opens in Geneva.

8   LEBANON - The USS New Jersey carries out a devasting attack on Druze positions in the Shouf Mountains. British and Italian peacekeeping contingents begin a withdrawal from positions in Beirut (completed 20 February).

8 WEST GERMANY - The Revolutionary Cells claims respon- sibility for the bombing of the Turkish Consulate in Cologne.

9 USSR - Communist leader Yuri V. Andropov dies in Mos- cow at 69.

10-11 LEBANON - American civilians are ordered out of Lebanon. A number of other Western civilian personnel join them in being airlifted by helicopter out of Beirut to nearby ships.

11 IRAQ - Iraqi aircraft bomb non-military targets in Iran in an escalation of the 40-month-old war. Iran retaliates with similar air strikes of its own.

13 USSR - Konstantin Chernenko is named Communist Party Secretary.

13 IRAN - Iranian forces open a new offensive against Iraq in the Gulf War.

13 PANAMA - Vice President Jorge Illueca assumes the presidency from Ricardo de la Espriella.

15 INDIA - Talks in New Delhi on Sikh autonomy among Premier Indira Gandhi, the opposition parties, and the Sikh Akali Dal party collapse when communal rioting between Hindus and Sikhs in Punjab causes 15 deaths.

15 SOUTH KOREA - The government, in answer to the North Korean proposal of 11 January, responds that bilateral talks should be held first, with US participation at a later time.

15 ITALY - Leamon Hunt, the American Director General of the Multinational Force and Observers in the Sinai, is assassinated by two terrorists while riding in his armored car in Rome. The attack was executed by mem- bers of the Red Brigade, but the LARF also claims credit.

16 UNITED STATES - The government mediates an agreement between South Africa and Angola for the establishment of a joint commission to monitor the truce in southern Angola.

16-23 IRAN - The government opens a new offensive aimed at Basra on the Shatt-al-Arab on the southern front. More than one-half million troops are involved. Both sides claim victory when the fighting abates.

18 UNITED STATES - The government announces it has or- dered a naval task force into the Persian Gulf.

18   IRAN - The government orders a "maximum alert" ostensibly against US naval passage of the Strait of Hormuz.

18   LIBYA - A mob burns the Jordanian Embassy in Tripoli.

20   NEW ZEALAND - The government resumes full diplomatic relations with the USSR.

21   UNITED NATIONS - The USSR offers to allow inspection of its chemical weapons stockpile as a part of a future arms agreement.

22   IRAN - Iranian forces launch an attack against Iraqi positions along the southern front.

22   JORDAN - The government breaks diplomatic relations with Libya after accusing (19 February) the Qaddafi government of direct responsibility for the burning of its embassy in Tripoli.

22   INDIA - Violence again erupts between Sikhs and Hindus in the state of Punjab. More than one hundred are reported dead or injured.

22   GRENADA - Murder charges are placed against members of the overthrown junta for the slaying of Prime Minister Maurice Bishop and others.

25   ZIMBABWE - Government estimates indicate that more than 100,000 refugees have crossed the border from Mozambique to flee the ravages of famine and guerrilla warfare that plague the land.

26   USSR - Konstantin Chernenko is named Chairman of the Soviet Defense Council.

26   LEBANON - The last members of the US 22nd MAU still in Lebanon are withdrawn.

27   IRAQ - Iraqi government sources announce that a blockade of Iran's main oil terminal at Kharq Island in the Persian Gulf is in effect. Iraqi jets are reported to have already attacked an oil cargo ship at the petroleum facility.

28   AFGHANISTAN - Following a year-long cease-fire, Soviet forces launch a major offensive in the Panjshir Valley.

28   CAMEROON - A military court convicts former President Ahmadou Ahidjo of leading an attempt to overthrow the government and sentences him to death. He is not in the country at the time of sentencing.

MARCH

1   SOUTH AFRICA - The government releases SWAPO leader Andimba (Herman) Toivo Ja Toivo who has been in prison on Robbern Island for 16 years.

2   NIGERIA - President Buhari orders the military into the state of Gongola to put an end to the religious violence between traditionalist Muslims and those of the Maitatsine sect. The fighting has claimed the lives of hundreds in Yola City over recent weeks.

2   KENYA - Several senior members of the government charge that as many as 5,000 Degodia tribesmen have been tortured and massacred by the military as a part of a campaign of extermination aimed at breaking the link between the Degodias and the Somali guerrilla forces operating along the Kenya-Somalia border.

4   INDIA - Punjab state (Punjabi Suba) authorities give police and militia units extraordinary powers to deal with rampant violence between Sikh and Hindu extremists.

4   IRAN - The Speaker of Parliament claims at least 400 Iranian soldiers have died as a result of Iraq's use of chemical warfare.

5   UNITED STATES - Intelligence sources indicate Iraq is using outlawed mustard gas as a chemical weapon in its war against Iran.

5   IRAQ - The government denies it is employing chemical weapons in its war with Iran.

5   UNITED STATES - The Senate Appropriations Committee refuses to approve $21 million in military aid for the Contra forces in Nicaragua but does approve $64.5 million in military aid for El Salvador.

5   LEBANON - The government abrogates the May 1983 troop withdrawal agreement with Israel.

7   SOUTH AFRICA - Imprisoned African National Congress (ANC) leader Nelson Mandela refuses a government offer of freedom because he must agree to reside in the Transkei homeland.

9   INDIA - Soviet Defense Minister Ustinov ends a four-day visit by promising sophisticated weaponry to India to assist in strengthening the Indian military posture against Pakistan.

10	COLOMBIA - A police raid on an illegal cocaine pro- cessing factory on the Yari River nets the largest and most valuable drug cache ever taken. The estimated street value of the 27,500 pounds of cocaine is said to be $1.2 billion.
12	SWITZERLAND - Representatives of the various Lebanese religious and political factions begin peace talks.
12	USSR - The fourth round of Sino-Soviet normalization talks opens in Moscow.
14	EL SALVADOR - An unidentified gunman assassinates Hector Flores Larin, a leader of the Salvadoran National Conciliation Party.
15	COLOMBIA - President Betancur declares a state of siege in four districts (departments) following a guerrilla attack on the Caqueta District capital.
16	UNITED STATES - The Defense Department sends two AWACS aircraft to Egypt to assist in preventing air strikes against Sudan from Libya.
16	AUSTRIA - MBFR negotiations resume in Vienna after a three-month suspension called by the Warsaw Pact nations.
16	LEBANON - A US diplomat, William Buckley, is kidnapped is West Beirut by the Islamic Jihad. Buckley will later be identified as the CIA Chief of Station. He will be murdered while in captivity.
16	SUDAN - Omdurman is bombed by a Soviet-built Libyan Tu-22 bomber. Omdurman is the site of an anti-Qadaffi radio transmitter.
17	IRELAND - Dominic "Mad Dog" McGlinchey, the Chief of Staff of the outlawed Irish National Liberation Army, is captured after a 90-minute gun battle with County Clare police. He is immediately extradited to British custody in Northern Ireland to stand trial on murder charges.
17-19	CUBA - Angola President Jose Eduardo dos Santos visits Havana with the aim of getting the Cubans to withdraw their forces from his country. Cuba offers immediate withdrawal if the US and South Africa halt aid to UNITA.
18	SOUTH AFRICA - The government and Mozambique sign a nonagression pact (Accord of Nkomati), each side agreeing to end aid to rebels operating in the other's country.

20   SWITZERLAND - The Lebanese peace talks break down.

20   NICARAGUA - A Soviet oil tanker strikes a mine outside
            the harbor at Puerto Sandino. Contra leaders of the
            US-backed Nicaraguan Democratic Force based in Hon-
            duras take responsibility for this latest in a series
            of similar incidents.

20   SOUTH AFRICA - The government rejects the Cuban offer
            to withdraw its forces from Angola if they halt aid to
            UNITA.

22   LEBANON - Shi'ite and Druze militia˙units tighten
            their control over West Beirut.

24   JORDAN - A bomb explodes in the parking lot of the In-
            tercontinental Hotel in Amman. A second larger bomb is
            discovered before it detonates and is defused. Two
            people are injured.

25-31   LEBANON - The French peacekeeping contingent completes
            its withdrawal.

26   UNITED NATIONS - The UN accuses Iraq of using chemical
            warfare against Iran in the Gulf War.

26   UNITED STATES - The government prohibits the sale of
            certain chemicals to Iraq and Iran.

26   FRANCE - The US Consul in Strasbourg, Robert Homme, is
            shot and wounded by LARF terrorists who accuse him of
            being a CIA agent.

27   GUINEA - President Ahmed Sekou Toure dies after 26
            years of rule. He was 62. President Toure was under-
            going emergency heart surgery in Cleveland, Ohio, at
            the time of his death.

28   GREECE - Terrorists of the Revolutionary Organization
            of Socialist Muslims assassinate a British diplomat,
            Kenneth Whitty, and his driver in Athens.

29   THAILAND - Thai government forces capture 40 Viet-
            namese soldiers in Thai territory. The government
            lodges a formal protest against Viet Nam's unprovoked
            aggression.

30   CHILE - In Santiago a bus carrying 25 national
            policemen is badly damaged by a command-detonated
            bomb. One policeman is killed and 11 wounded. Four
            bystanders are also injured. The Manuel Rodriguez
            Patriotic Front claims credit for the attack.

APRIL

2   SOUTH CHINA SEA - The Soviet helicopter cruiser <u>Minsk</u> fires flares at an American frigate. The US vessel is hit three times but sustains neither damage nor casualties.

2   INDIA - Severe rioting breaks out in Punjab following the assassination of a high-ranking Hindu official. A 48-hour curfew is imposed in Amritsar in the northern part of the state.

3   ITALY - The government announces that the first 16 US cruise missiles emplaced on Italian soil are now operational.

3   SOUTH AFRICA - An ANC terrorist car bomb kills three and injures 16 in Durban.

3   GUINEA - The military seizes power following the death of Sekou Toure.

4   LEBANON - A retired general, Antoine Lahad, is named the new commander of the South Lebanese Army.

4   UNITED NATIONS - The US vetoes a UN Security Council resolution that would have condemned the US for its part in the mining of Nicaragua's harbors.

5   GUINEA - Colonel Lansana Conte is named President by the military junta ruling the country.

5   INDIA - The government introduces detention laws aimed at curbing the increasing Sikh terrorism.

5   FRANCE - The government offers Nicaragua assistance in clearing its harbors that were allegedly mined by the Central Intelligence Agency.

6-8   CAMEROON - The Palace Republican Guard commanded by Colonel Ibrahim Saleh attempts a government overthrow in the capital city of Yaounde. President Paul Biya is able to retain power after two days of intense fighting.

8   UNITED STATES - The government announces it will not be bound by decisions of the World Court regarding Central America.

9   USSR - Communist leader Chernenko states the US must remove Pershing and cruise missiles from Europe before arms talks can resume.

9   NICARAGUA -   At the World Court the Nicaraguan gov-
        ernment charges that the US is conducting illegal
        operations against it.

9   LEBANON - Faction leaders endorse a plan for disen-
        gagement in Beirut.

9   SRI LANKA - Bombs placed by Tamil terrorists in the
        Northern Province capital town of Jaffna wound nine
        soldiers.

10-12   UNITED STATES - Both Houses of Congress pass resolu-
        tions repudiating US mining operations in Nicaragua.
        Reports indicate at least eight ships from six nations
        have been damaged by the mines.

11   USSR - Konstantin U. Chernenko is named President of
        the Supreme Soviet.

12   ISRAEL - Arab terrorists hijack a bus and its 24
        passengers in the Gaza Strip.

13   ISRAEL - Israeli commandos storm the hijacked bus in
        the Gaza Strip killing four terrorists.

13   NICARAGUA - Rebel forces capture the port city of San
        Juan del Norte (Greytown) on the Caribbean coast and
        seize about 30 miles of coastline.

15   UNITED NATIONS - The USSR proposes a naval disarmament
        conference.

15   SPAIN - Three Spanish Army officers are imprisoned for
        their parts in a 1982 coup attempt.

15   INDIA - Sikh terrorists burn 40 railway stations in
        the Punjab.

15   VIET NAM - Government forces attack the headquarters
        of the KPNLF. More than 35,000 refugees flee into
        Thailand.

15   NAMIBIA - US Army Lieutenant Colonel Kenneth Crabtree
        and US diplomat Dennis Keough are killed by a bomb
        blast while stopped in the town of Oshakati in
        northern Namibia. They are there to monitor the with-
        drawal of South African troops from Angola. A civilian
        is also killed and four others injured in the ex-
        plosion. SWAPO is blamed but denies the allegation.

16   INDIA - Two hundred members of the banned All-India
        Sikh Students Federation are arrested.

17   GREAT BRITAIN - During an anti-Qadaffi demonstration outside the Libyan People's Bureau (Embassy) in London, a policewoman is shot and killed by a Libyan firing an automatic weapon from inside the Embassy. Ten demonstrators are wounded. After claiming their diplomatic immunity the building's occupants refuse to turn the killer over to the authorities. British Special Air Service (SAS) and police personnel surround the barricaded building.

17   NICARAGUA - Government forces retake San Juan del Norte.

17   NIGERIA - The government imposes press censorship.

18   UNITED NATIONS - The US delegation at the Geneva Arms Conference proposes a comprehensive chemical weapons ban treaty.

18   HONDURAS - A US Army helicopter is shot down near Colomoncagus on the border with El Salvador. A second helicopter is hit but manages to return to base. Among the passengers on board the two aircraft are the wife of the US Ambassador and two US Senators. No one is injured. No one claims credit for the attack.

18-22   LIBYA - Great Britain breaks diplomatic relations with Libya after Libyan police surround the British Embassy in Tripoli. All British diplomatic personnel are ordered home.

19   EGYPT - The government announces it has agreed to a resumption of diplomatic relations with the USSR after a three-year break.

20   GREAT BRITAIN - A bomb explodes in a baggage area in Terminal 2 at London's Heathrow Airport injuring 25 people. No one takes credit for the bombing.

20   HONG KONG - British Foreign Secretary Sir Geoffrey Howe announces that sovereignty of the colony will pass to Communist China when the current lease expires in 1997.

21   WEST GERMANY - Four days of anti-missile demonstrations begin that are aimed at US deployment of missiles in Western Europe.

23   NIGERIA - The new military government announces that the borders to its country will be closed as a step toward controlling internal corruption.

24   AFGHANISTAN - Soviet forces are reported to have captured the main part of Panjshir Valley.

25 ANGOLA - Representatives meet with a South African delegation at Lusaka, Zambia, to continue discussions on a South African troop withdrawal from Angolan territory.

26 UNITED NATIONS - The USSR rejects the US chemical warfare ban treaty proposed in Geneva.

26 LEBANON - Rashid Karami is named Prime Minister.

27 GREAT BRITAIN - All Libyans with diplomatic immunity, including the killer of the London policewomen, are allowed to leave the country after evacuating the People's Bureau building. Numerous weapons and spent shell casings are found in the vacated building.

29 ISRAEL - Israeli security forces arrest 20 members of a Jewish terrorist organization which was planning retaliatory raids against Arab-owned buses of the Jerusalem-Klandia Bus Co. Officials say this group has been responsible for a number of other attacks on Arabs in Israel.

29 SUDAN - President Numeiri declares a state of emergency and grants special powers to the military.

30 COLOMBIA - Minister of Justice Rodrigo Lara Bonilla is assassinated in Bogota by gunmen working for an illegal drug ring.

MAY

1 SUDAN - The government announces the formation of nine military courts to enforce the new restrictions imposed by President Numeiry as he tightens his control over the nation.

2 SOUTH AFRICA - The government agrees to supply Mozambique with military forces to guard the transmission lines from the Cabora Bassa hydroelectric system from MNR attack.

7 EUROPE - The Warsaw Pact calls upon NATO to join in talks aimed at an East-West nonagression pact that would rule out the use of force in settling disputes.

8 LIBYA - An assassination attempt against Muammar Qaddafi fails when Libyan troops drive off 20 heavily armed men at Qaddafi's compound in Tripoli. All 20 are apparently killed in the fighting.

9 UNITED STATES - The Congress votes to cut military aid to Turkey by $85 million (to $670 million).

10   UNITED STATES - The government announces it has agreed
            to provide $230 million in military sales credits to
            South Korea in 1984.

10   INDIA - The Sikh High Priest of the Amritsar Golden
            Temple in   the   Punjab   is   assassinated by   Sikh
            extremists because he criticized their current terror
            tactics.

10   WORLD COURT - The Court votes unanimously that the US
            should not mine Nicaragua's harbors.

10   DENMARK - The Parliament votes to cut its payments to
            NATO so as to stop deployment of Pershing II and
            cruise missiles in Western Europe.

10   HAITI - The government bans all political activity in
            the country except that supporting "the president's
            party."

14   INDIA - Punjabi Hindus protest the recent killing of
            the High Priest of the Golden Temple with a general
            strike. Amritsar is placed under curfew.

16   MOZAMBIQUE - The government demands a South   African
            assurance that the MNR will be neutralized.

17   MIDDLE EAST - The Gulf Cooperation Council (GCC) goes
            into emergency session after Iranian attacks on Saudi
            Arabian and Kuwaiti ships in the Persian Gulf.

19   INDIA - More than 44 people are   reported dead fol-
            lowing two days of violence between Hindus and Muslims
            in Bombay.

20   USSR - Soviet Defense Minister Ustinov announces that
            the USSR has increased the number of Soviet submarines
            on station along the US coast.

21   INDIA - The Indian Army is ordered to halt the rioting
            in Bombay.

21   SAUDI ARABIA - A meeting of GCC defense ministers
            takes place in Riyadh to coordinate military efforts
            against future Iranian attacks.

22   COLOMBIA - The US Embassy in Bogota, the Ambassadorial
            residence, and the offices of a number of US-owned
            companies are bombed. The Ricardo Franco Front of the
            Revolutionary Armed   Forces   of   Colombia   claims
            responsibility.

23   ISRAEL - Twenty-five Israeli kibbutz settlers   are
            charged with terrorist crimes against Arabs.

27   INDIA - Eleven days of rioting between Hindus and Muslims leaves more than 230 dead.

27   UNITED STATES - The government approves the sale of 400 Stinger surface-to-air missiles to Saudi Arabia.

30   NICARAGUA - Contra leader Eden Pastora Gomez is injured by a bomb blast during a news conference inside his headquarters encampment. Seven others are killed, including two newsmen, and 27 others are injured.

JUNE

1   UNITED NATIONS - The Security Council condemns Iran for its attacks on neutral shipping in the Persian Gulf.

1   THE NETHERLANDS - The government announces it will accept the deployment of cruise missiles on its territory in 1988 if the USSR continues the deployment of SS-20 surface-to-surface missiles in Eastern Europe.

2   INDIA - The Indian Army occupies the Punjab. The border to the neighboring state of Hariana (Haryana) to the southeast is closed.

4-6   INDIA - Indian forces attack the heavily armed defenders of the Amritsar Golden Temple in the Punjabi. In two days of fighting more than 1,000 Sikhs are killed including the Sikh extremist leader Jarnail Singh Bhindranwale.

5   SAUDI ARABIA - Two American-built Saudi F-15 fighters shoot down two Iranian aircraft approaching the Saudi coast.

7   INDIA - At least three Sikh army units (estimated to be 1,200 troops) mutiny in response to the Indian Army attack on their Golden Temple in Amritsar. One senior Hindu officer is killed.

9   NAMIBIA - Almost all of SWAPOs internal leadership is arrested in a raid in Windhoek.

10   UNITED STATES - A US Army missile successfully intercepts and destroys an incoming ballistic missile warhead in a test.

10   MIDDLE EAST - A Kuwaiti tanker is attacked by Iranian aircraft off the coast of Qatar.

11   USSR - The government proposes US-Soviet talks aimed at banning tests of antisatellite systems and the dismantling of presently existing antisatellite systems.

11   SUDAN - Government forces kill more than 165 rebels in a series of encounters in the south.

13   INDIA - The government accuses Pakistan of training Sikh extremists in western Kashmir.

14   THE NETHERLANDS - The Dutch government postpones a decision on the deployment of cruise missiles on its territory until November 1985.

16   PAKISTAN - An Afghan air strike kills 16 Afghan children and injures others in an attack along the Afghan-Pakistani border.

16   URUGUAY - Opposition Blanco Party leader, Wilson Ferreira, and at least 100 supporters are arrested when the Argentinian ferry they were aboard crosses into Uruguayan territory. Ferreira was on his way to Montevideo to attend a rally.

17   PAKISTAN - The government lodges a strong protest against continued incursions into its territory by Soviet-backed Afghan military forces.

20   AUSTRIA - The Turkish Labor Attache in Vienna is killed by a car bomb. The ARA claims credit for the attack.

21   UNITED STATES - A number of sources report that a massive explosion took place in mid-May at the Soviet Northern Fleet main ammunition dump on the Kola Peninsula. About one-third of the fleet's ammunition was destroyed, but no nuclear detonations took place.

23   INDIA - The government declares the Punjab in rebellion and a terrorist-affected region. Special courts are established to deal with terrorist cases arising in that area.

24   SAUDI ARABIA - The GCC chiefs of staff meet in Riyadh to discuss cooperative action against Iran to thwart further attacks on shipping.

27   EUROPE - The Western European Union cancels a 30-year prohibition of West German production of long-range missile and strategic bombers.

28   ISRAEL - Israel and Syria complete a prisoner exchange; the first since 1973.

29   USSR - The Soviet Union proposes talks to start in Vienna in September on the demilitarization of outer space.

29   UNITED STATES - The US counters with a proposal to discuss both tactical and strategic nuclear weapons.

29   EL SALVADOR - Leftist guerrillas seriously damage the country's largest hydroelectric facility at Cerron Grande which they are able to hold for ten hours. More the 120 are killed in the bitter fighting.

30   COLOMBIA - President Hernan Siles Zuaro is kidnapped by some 60 police and army officers in an abortive coup attempt. He is released after ten hours of intense negotiations.

JULY

        RED SEA - The Red Sea is secretly mined by Libya. The Islamic Jihad will eventually claim credit for the incident.

        FRANCE - The terrorist organization known as Action Directe opens a new campaign of bombings.

1   USSR - The government rejects the US counterproposal.

2   INDIA - The Governor of Jammu and Kashmir dismisses his Chief Minister, Farooq Abdullah, and replaces him with his own brother-in-law, G. M. Shah.

2   COLOMBIA - The government announces that 100 additional persons have been arrested in connection with the abortive coup attempt.

3   LEBANON - Lebanese army units reenter Beirut. Druze militia had already begun withdrawing their artillery from the city.

5   LEBANON - The Lebanese Army reopens the Green Line which separates East and West Beirut.

5   GREAT BRITAIN - British authorities foil a Nigerian attempt to smuggle kidnapped former Minister Umaru Dikko out of the country in a packing crate from Stanstead Airport. Two other men are found unconscious in a second crate. Both crates have diplomatic markings. A Nigerian and three Israelis are arrested in the plot (11 July). The Nigerian High Commissioner and two diplomats are expelled for their part in the abduction (13 July).

5   INDIA - Nine Sikh terrorists hijack an Indian Air
            Lines A-300 Airbus on a domestic flight to New Delhi.
            After landing at Lahore, Pakistan, they release 255
            passengers and nine crewmen and surrender.

7   USSR - The government announces a resumption of diplo-
            matic relations with Egypt, which were broken in Sep-
            tember 1981.

10   USSR - The government warns West Germany against the
            production of strategic bombers and missiles.

10   LEBANON - The Beirut airport and seaport are reopened.

12   NIGERIA - The government expels a number of British
            diplomats in retaliation for British actions in the
            Dikko abduction attempt.

13   ALGERIA - Al Fatah and four other PLO factions sign a
            unification agreement in Algiers.

17   PERU - SL terrorists attack high tension towers, the
            country's main hydroelectric station, and a number of
            other commercial targets. The Soviet Aeroflot office
            in Lima is bombed, as are the offices of the Soviet
            Novosti News Agency, and the Soviet-Peruvian Cultural
            Institute in Arequipa.

21   POLAND - The government gives amnesty to 652 political
            prisoners.

26   LIBERIA - President Samuel K. Doe lifts a four-year
            ban on political activities.

31   MIDDLE EAST - Islamic Jihad takes credit for mining
            the Red Sea. They claim to have placed 190 mines to
            "punish the imperialists."

31   IRAN - Three Arabs hijack an Air France jet airliner
            flying from Frankfurt, West Germany, to Tehran. The
            hijackers release their hostages and surrender to
            Iranian authorities on 2 August.

AUGUST

2   INDIA - A bomb explodes at Madras airport in southern
            India. At least 29 are killed and more than 30 in-
            jured. Sri Lanka separatists of the Tamil Eelam Army
            are probably responsible. The bomb was apparently
            meant to be put on an Air Lanka plane to Delhi but
            missed the flight.

3   UNITED STATES - The government announces it is lifting additional sanctions against Poland.

3   URUGUAY - An agreement is reached in which the government of General Gregorio Conrado Alvarez Armelino consents to its replacement by a civilian-controlled one.

4   SRI LANKA - Tamil rebels attack Sri Lankan military outposts. In the ensuing battles more than 100 are killed on both sides.

7   UGANDA - The government suspends its military ties with the US after the US government accuses the Ugandans of commiting numerous atrocities.

9   IRAN - Ayatollah Ruhollah Khomeini condemns those who mined the Red Sea.

13   EGYPT - President Mubarek accuses Libya and Iran of placing the mines in the Red Sea and the Gulf of Suez, which damaged at least 15 ships between 27 July and 11 August. Both Iran and Libya deny the charges (14 August). British, French, and Italian minesweeping forces join (14 August) US minesweepers looking for more mines.

13   MOROCCO - At the border town of Oujda, Morocco joins Libya in signing an agreement aimed at a "union of the states."

15   KUWAIT - The government buys $325 million in Soviet arms. The purchases include surface-to-surface and surface-to-air missiles.

16   NICARAGUA - The government announces it is building a large airfield that should be operational by the end of 1985.

17   UNITED NATIONS - The Security Council votes South Africa's new apartheid constitution "null and void."

17   INDIA - A state-wide general strike takes place in Andhra Pradesh following the dismissal of Chief Minister Rama Rao.

20   SRI LANKA - At least 95 are reported dead as violent confrontations continue between Tamil and Sinhalese tribemen during the last several weeks.

21   THE PHILIPPINES - The anniversary of the assassination of opposition leader Benigno Aquino, Jr., is marked by an anti-Marcos demonstration in Manila. An estimated 450,000 people participate.

21   EGYPT - The Egyptian Chief of Staff claims the mines
            placed in the Red Sea were secretly dropped from the
            Libyan freighter <u>Ghat</u>.

23   COLOMBIA - The Maoist Popular Liberation Army and the
            Workers' Defense Force, two leftist guerrilla organi-
            zations, sign a truce with the central government.

24   INDIA - Sikhs hijack an Indian airliner enroute to
            Lahore and demand passage to the US. They later
            surrender to authorities at Dubai in the UAE.

SEPTEMBER

2   INDIA - In defiance of a government order barring the
            meeting, the "world convention" of Sikhs opens in
            Amritsar.

4   CHILE - A peaceful demonstration against the rule of
            Augusto Pinochet Ugarte turns into a riot when police
            use dogs, water cannon, and small arms fire to dis-
            perse the otherwise inoffensive demonstrators. Nine,
            including a French priest, are killed.

4   NORTHERN IRELAND - An IRA car bomb detonates in Newry,
            a town 33 miles south of Belfast. Seventy-one are
            injured.

6   UNITED NATIONS - The US vetoes a UN Security Council
            resolution calling for the withdrawal of Israeli
            forces from Lebanon.

7   CENTRAL AMERICA - Contadora members agree upon a plan
            for peace in Central America.

10   SRI LANKA - Terrorists ambush a bus killing 14. A
            military convoy is also ambushed with 19 soldiers
            killed.

10   ETHIOPIA - The government officially designated the
            country as a Communist state.

11   SPAIN - Two Lebanese terrorists wound a Libyan Embassy
            employee in Madrid. The Lebanese Shi'ite group Musa
            Sadr Brigade based in Beirut claims credit for the
            attack. A second group, the Libyan exile organization
            Al Burkan (Volcano), also claims responsibility.

12   INDONESIA - A Muslim riot in the port city of
            Tanjungpriok follows the arrest of four Muslims
            accused of interfering with the police. Many are
            killed as the rioters attack a police station.

16   INDIA - Rama Rao is reinstated as the Chief Minister
        of Andhra Pradesh.

20   LEBANON - A suicide attack on the US Embassy Annex in
        East Beirut leaves 14 dead (two Americans) when a
        lorry loaded with the equivalent of about 3,000 pounds
        of   TNT explodes in   the   entrance to the Embassy
        grounds. At least 70 people (20 Americans), including
        US Ambassador Reginald Batholomew, are injured in the
        blast. The Islamic Jihad claims credit for the blast.

21   NATO - The Supreme Commander of NATO, US General
        Bernard Rogers, requests he be supplied with chemical
        weapons for possible employment in case of war.

21   THE PHILIPPINES - Three thousand demonstrate against
        President Marcos. About 2,000 troops and police use
        tear gas and water cannon to disperse the crowd that
        had set up a vigil in front of the Presidential
        Palace.

21   NICARAGUA - The government agrees to the Contadora
        peace plan provided the US agrees to it and to
        additional conditions.

22   UNITED STATES - The government refuses to agree to the
        Contadora peace plan because of what it calls
        Nicaraguan manipulation.

25   CHAD - France and Libya begin a simultaneous with-
        drawal of their forces from Chad.

25   JORDAN - The government restores diplomatic relations
        with Egypt.

26   INDIA - India Army troops evacuate the Sikh Golden
        Temple in Amritsar.

27   AUSTRIA - The 34th round of MBFR discussions opens in
        Vienna.

28   COSTA RICA - Twelve West European foreign ministers
        join in endorsing the Contadora peace plan while
        attending a meeting with nine Latin American dele-
        gations.

29   ITALY - On information supplied by an informant, about
        2,000 police begin a wholesale roundup of Mafia
        members.

29   IRELAND - Irish naval units intercept and capture a
        ship carrying IRA members and five tons of arms and
        ammunition from the US. The capture ends a two-year
        undercover operation involving the FBI and the CIA.

29   IRELAND (Cont'd) -   Evidence indicates   that the   New
            York Irish Aid Committee paid for the weapons.   An
            international search gets under way for a second
            vessel believed to be involved in illegal arms traffic
            between the US and the IRA.

OCTOBER

1   INDIA - Indian Army units reoccupy the Golden Temple
            in Amritsar after Sikh terrorists move into part of
            the structure.

1   KAMPUCHEA - Kampuchean rebels and Vietnamese troops
            exchange artillery and mortar fire in some of the
            heaviest fighting of the year.

1   EGYPT - Defense officials claim a mine retrieved by
            British divers in the Red Sea is a new advanced
            technology device made in the USSR.

2   UNITED NATIONS - Nicaraguan President Ortega accuses
            the US of planning an invasion of his country.

2   AFGHANISTAN - The government denies Pakistani al-
            legations that their aircraft attacked and bombed
            Pakistani border towns.

2   EL SALVADOR - Salvadoran troops overrun a rebel base
            in Chalatenango Province. Five rebels are killed.

2   SOUTH KOREA - The government reports North Korea is
            increasing its troop strength along the DMZ.

2   BELGIUM - The Cellules Communistes Combattante (Com-
            munist Combatant Cells) opens a week-long campaign of
            bombings of offices the group claims are associated
            with the introduction of nuclear weapons into Belgium.

3   MOZAMBIQUE - Government and rebel MNR leaders sign a
            cease-fire agreement and ask South Africa to monitor
            the truce.

3   CHAD - The government releases 121 Sudanese prisoners
            of war.

3   ISRAEL - Police and security forces break up a demon-
            stration by 200 Arabs in front of the US Embassy in
            Jerusalem.

4   AFGHANISTAN - Afghan troops begin concentrating along
            the Pakistani border.

4   UNITED STATES - The State Department announces there
         is sufficient evidence to blame Libya for mining the
         entrances to the Red Sea where at least 19 ships have
         been damaged.

5   UNITED STATES - President Reagan states that US
         intelligence has identified the Arab terrorist group
         responsible for the 20 September bombing of the US
         Embassy in Beirut. Known as Hezballah, or "Party of
         God," and based in Baalbek, Lebanon, it is suspected
         of carrying out previous attacks on US personnel and
         property in Lebanon and Kuwait.

6   UNITED NATIONS - Soviet Foreign Ministry official
         Vladimir Petrovsky, speaking before the General Assem-
         bly, rules out arms limitation negotiations with the
         US until the West removes its new nuclear missiles
         from Europe.

6   EL SALVADOR - Eight Salvadoran army officers are
         exchanged for four rebel leaders plus safe passage for
         60 wounded rebels to travel to hospitals outside the
         country.

7   IRAN - The government denies involvement in the 20
         September bombing of the US Embassy in Beirut,
         Lebanon.

7   KAMPUCHEA - Kampuchean rebels claim they have
         inflicted heavy damage to Vietnamese supply routes and
         transportation. They also claim to have "crushed down"
         more than 10,000 Vietnamese troops between May and
         September of this year.

7   CHAD - French intelligence sources claim Libyan forces
         are withdrawing.

7   ISRAEL - Border forces kill three well-armed Arabs
         attempting to cross the Jordanian border into Israel.

8   SOUTH AFRICA - Army forces support the South African
         police in fighting a wave of unrest in several black
         townships.

8   CUBA - The government announces it has been conducting
         large-scale evacuation and combat drills designed to
         thwart the expected US invasion that can come at any
         time.

8   UNITED NATIONS - In a speech before the General
         Assembly, El Salvadoran President Jose Napoleon Duarte
         offers to hold peace talks with the rebels in his
         country.

9   MIDDLE EAST - In the continuing Iraq-Iran War, Iraqi aircraft reportedly attack the supertanker <u>SS World Knight</u> near Kharg Island killing seven crewman and injuring eight more.

9   EL SALVADOR - Leaders of the rebels accept President Duarte's offer to meet in La Palma to discuss peace.

9   NORTH YEMEN - The government signs a 20-year treaty of friendship and cooperation with the USSR.

9   BELGIUM - In a third incident in a week, believed to be the work of Communist "fighting cells dedicated to attacking NATO equipment suppliers," the Brussels headquarters of Honeywell-Europe is badly damaged by a bomb.

9   GRENADA - Herbert Blaize calls upon the US and other Caribbean nations to leave their troops in Grenada for several years, if necessary, to ensure the country's security.

10   UNITED STATES - The government releases a White Paper listing numerous Soviet arms control agreement violations.

10   AFGHANISTAN - To help crush increasing attacks by Afghan rebels in and around Kabul, the Soviet troop strength is increased by an additional 70,000. One plan is to seal the Iranian and Pakastani borders.

10   INDIA - The last government security forces are withdrawn from the Sikh Golden Temple complex in Amritsar, Punjab.

12   GREAT BRITAIN - IRA terrorists of the Provisional Wing place a bomb in the Grand Hotel in Brighton, the site of the Conservative Party Conference. Prime Minister Margaret Thatcher escapes injury, but four are killed and 30 injured in the blast.

13   MIDDLE EAST - Iranian aircraft attack an Indian oil tanker in the Persian Gulf, apparently in retaliation for recent Iraqi air strikes. One crewman is injured; the ship sustains only minimal damage.

13   NIGERIA - The government buys 12 MiG-21B jet fighters from the Soviet Union.

14   MIDDLE EAST - Unidentified aircraft attack the <u>SS Gaz Fountain</u> in the Persian Gulf. Loaded with 20,000 tons of liquified gas, the tanker is on fire and adrift.

14   PAKISTAN - The government requests the US sell them a
            Grumman E-2C all-weather reconnaissance aircraft to
            help protect against further intrusions by Afghan
            fighters attacking targets inside Pakistan.

15   EL SALVADOR - The first meeting between the two sides
            takes place in La Palma. President Duarte meets with
            six rebel leaders. A second meeting is planned for
            November.

16   INDIA - The government seals the border with Pakistan
            in an effort to prevent the flight of Sikh extremists
            facing prosecution.

16   CHAD - The warring factions in this 20-year-old civil
            war agree to meet in Congo to discuss peace.

17   CHILE - A Communist rebel group takes credit for the
            bomb blast that knocked out power to Santiago for 24
            hours.

17   UNITED STATES - Customs officers seize the 82-foot
            fishing trawler _Valhalla_ which they claim is the
            second vessel involved in the attempt to smuggle
            weapons to the IRA.

18   COMMUNIST CHINA - A new round of Sino-Soviet normal-
            ization talks opens in Peking.

19   EL SALVADOR - At least 6,000 Salvadoran troops open a
            major offensive against the rebels.

19-24   MIDDLE EAST - An eight-month lull in the ground
            fighting in the Iraq-Iran War ends as Iranian forces
            open an offensive in the mountainous central border
            region. Iraq claims to have killed 923 Iranians and to
            have repulsed the attack.

20   MIDDLE EAST - A US-built Iranian F-4 "Phantom" jet
            fighter-bomber attacks a Panamanian tanker in the
            Persian Gulf, killing two crewmen.

22   EL SALVADOR - Rebels attack and seriously damage the
            power station at Las Delicas. Thirteen soldiers are
            killed.

23   SOUTH AFRICA - Security forces carry out predawn raids
            on the townships of Boipatong, Sebokeng, and Sharpe-
            ville and arrest more than 350 blacks.

23   THE PHILIPPINES - A special tribunal investigating the
            assassination of Aquino accuses three senior military
            officers including the Chief of Staff, General Fabian
            C. Ver, of complicity in the murder.

23   ETHIOPIA - Secessionist rebels capture the tourist
          resort of Lalibela in the Wallo District of
          north-central Ethiopia. One hundred thirty people,
          including ten foreigners, are reported captured. The
          rebels claim to have killed or wounded hundreds of
          government troops in capturing the town.

23   EL SALVADOR - Several senior army officers, including
          Lieutenant Colonel Domingo Monterrosa, are killed in a
          helicopter crash caused by mechanical failure.

24   CHILE - The government imposes new censorship rules.

24   AFGHANISTAN - Reports indicate that Soviet troops
          twice looted the city of Kandahar in October while
          searching for Afghan rebels.

24   KAMPUCHEA - Kampuchean rebels attack a Vietnamese
          outpost near the border with Thailand.

24   SPAIN - Prime Minister Felipe Gonzalez states he
          opposes full integration into NATO and demands an
          immediate reduction of US military strength in Spain.

26   CHILE - A car bomb explodes in front of the principal
          government building in Santiago.

26   IRAQ - The government announces its navy engaged an
          Iranian naval convoy in the Persian Gulf, sinking four
          vessels.

26   MIDDLE EAST - The International Red Cross reports that
          Iranian guards killed a number of Iraqi prisoners of
          war and wounded many others during a riot at a PW
          compound near Tehran.

28   NATO - Newspaper reports indicate most Spaniards are
          in favor of their country quitting NATO.

28   SRI LANKA - Parliament endorses a Presidential order
          extending the state of emergency another month.

29   IRAN - The government accuses the International Red
          Cross of inciting the rioting that cost the lives of a
          number of Iraqi prisoners of war.

29   CHILE - The government places 140 dissidents in
          internal exile.

29   CONGO - Negotiations aimed at ending the 20-year-old
          civil war in Chad collapse over a dispute as to which
          of the warring factions legitimately represents the
          government of Chad.

29   PORTUGAL - Two rocket-propelled grenades that are
        ready to be fired are discovered in a field about 75
        feet from the new US Embassy building. They had not
        been launched because of apparent malfunctions.

30   CHILE - One hundred forty people are exiled in a
        crackdown aimed at stopping demonstrations demanding a
        return to civil rule.

31   UNITED NATIONS - The UN Security Council calls upon
        Viet Nam to withdraw its forces from Kampuchea
        (Cambodia).

31   LEBANON - The government reaches agreement with Israel
        on new withdrawal talks.

31   INDIA - Prime Minister Indira Gandhi is assassinated
        in her New Delhi compound by two of her Sikh body-
        guards. Her son, Rajiv Gandhi, is appointed Prime
        Minister.

NOVEMBER

        NICARAGUA - There are persistent reports that
        Nicaragua has received a number of Soviet-built attack
        helicopters.

1   UNITED NATIONS - The Security Council announces that
        Israeli and Lebanese military teams will meet on 5
        November in southern Lebanon to discuss the Israeli
        withdrawal of its forces.

1   UNITED STATES - The government allots $1.2 billion in
        military and economic aid to Israel.

1   ISRAEL - The government orders the closing of Beth-
        lehem University until 5 November after three days of
        intermittent campus rioting.

2   UNITED STATES - The government announces that, fol-
        lowing months of negotiations with Angola and South
        Africa, the Angolan government is ready to reduce
        Cuban military strength from 30,000 to 10,000 and to
        redeploy those remaining away from the southern
        border, if South Africa gives up South West Africa
        (Namibia).

2   SYRIA - While welcoming the news of the planned
        meeting on the withdrawal of Israeli forces from
        Lebanon, the government rejects an Israeli request
        that Syria guarantee the security of its northern
        border.

3   EL SALVADOR - A two-week government drive against
           leftist guerrillas winds down without any significant
           results.

4   INDIA - More than 2,000 Sikhs are killed in widespread
           rioting following the assassination of Indira Gandhi.
           Indian troops finally restore order after entering
           nine cities, including New Delhi, throughout the
           country.

4   NICARAGUA - Sandinista candidates, including Daniel
           Ortega Saavedra, easily win the first national
           elections held in Nicaragua since 1979.

5   SOUTH AFRICA - Hundreds of thousands of black Africans
           strike in protest to apartheid. Dozens are killed
           before the violence abates.

5   LEBANON - Israeli and Lebanese military officers meet
           at Naqura (Naqoura) to discuss the conditions for an
           Israeli withdrawal from southern Lebanon.

5-7   THAILAND - As Vietnamese forces attack Kampuchean
           rebels near the Thai border they cross into Thailand.
           The government orders reinforcement into the area to
           help drive off the invaders.

6   CHILE - President Augusto Pinochet Ugarte declares a
           90-day state of siege following a series of guerrilla
           attacks.

6   POLAND - Premier Jaruzelski assumes personal control
           of the Ministry of State Security and the security
           forces.

7   UNITED STATES - The government announces that intel-
           ligence reports indicate Soviet-built MiG fighters are
           about to be introduced into Nicaragua, and that a
           Soviet freighter heading for Nicaragua may be carrying
           them.

7   SOUTH AFRICA - Army units set up roadblocks around
           black townships following a second day of rioting.

7   NICARAGUA - The government rejects the US denial and
           again claims the US is planning to invade the country.

8   UNITED STATES - The government invokes the Monroe
           Doctrine and warns the USSR that it will not tolerate
           the introduction of advanced fighter aircraft into
           Nicaragua. The US also denies that any US warships are
           in Nicaraguan waters.

9   UNITED STATES - The government announces that 25
        warships are presently in the Caribbean and that the
        24th US Infantry Division, a battalion of airborne
        troops, and a heliborne infantry battalion are exer-
        cising at Fort Stewart, Georgia, but that none of this
        implies a plan to invade Nicaragua. There is also
        heavy air traffic reported in Puerto Rico.

10   UNITED STATES - The White House announces it is satis-
        fied that no advanced tactical fighters have been in-
        troduced into Nicaragua.

10   LEBANON - The Lebanese break off withdrawal negoti-
        ations with Israel.

10   CHAD - Both France and Libya complete the withdrawal
        of their forces.

10-15   CHILE - Government security forces carry out a number
        of raids into the poorer districts of Santiago and
        arrest more than 2,000 people. Most are subsequently
        released.

11   IRAN - Iranian troops move six miles closer to the
        border after dislodging dug-in Iraqi troops and
        recapturing the Meimak Heights.

11   EL SALVADOR - A second round of peace talks begins at
        a Roman Catholic monastery.

12   NIGERIA - The government indicates it will recognize
        the rebels fighting Morocco in the Western Sahara.

12   OAU - Morocco resigns during a summit meeting at which
        a Saharan Arab Democratic Republic (SADR) delegation
        is seated. SADR represents the Western Saharan
        government-in-exile.

12   NICARAGUA - The country is put on full alert awaiting
        the expected US invasion.

13   UNITED STATES - The government denies it has any
        intention of invading Nicaragua.

13   JAPAN - Japanese fighters are scrambled when seven
        Soviet bombers fly into the air space over the Sea of
        Japan.

13   OAS - The OAS asks the US to counter the flow of
        Soviet arms into Nicaragua by providing a "security
        shield" to protect against Soviet aggression.

13   CHILE - Thirteen separate bombing incidents are
        reported.

14   UNITED STATES - Intelligence sources say satellite photography shows Libyan forces are still in Chad.

14   UNITED STATES - The government indicates it will respond with whatever assistance is necessary if Nicaragua invades either Honduras or El Salvador.

15   CHAD - The government confirms that Libyan troops are still on Chad territory.

15   LEBANON - Israeli troop withdrawal talks resume.

16   UNITED NATIONS - The Security Council demands an immediate withdrawal of Soviet troops from Afghanistan.

16   SOUTH AFRICA - The government states that peace in Namibia may be a possibility following further talks with Angola.

16   SOUTH AFRICA - The government rounds up 2,300 black workers in a mass arrest.

16   UGANDA - About 200 North Korean troops arrive in Uganda to assist the government in driving rebel forces from their strongholds.

17   CRETE - After a meeting with Libya's Qaddafi (15 November) at Elounda Bay, French President Mitterand states Libyan troops are still in Chad.

17   LEBANON - Israeli forces release Mahmoud Fakih, a leading Shi'ite activist, who they had under arrest. He is sent to Beirut as a part of the ongoing negotiations for an Israeli troop withdrawal.

17   ZAIRE - Rebels capture the town of Moba but are quickly driven off by paratroopers and other ground forces.

17   EGYPT - The government announces it has foiled a Libyan plot to assassinate former Libyan Prime Minister Bakroush. The four would-be assassins are captured and are forced to send false information to the Libyan Embassy in Malta to the effect that they successfully completed their mission. The Libyan government then announces its suicide squad has liquidated another one of the "enemies of the revolution."

18   SPAIN - Antiterrorist specialists from 13 countries meet secretly in Madrid to coordinate planning against future Middle Eastern terrorist attacks.

18   NIGERIA - News reports published in London indicate that at least 40 soldiers have been executed in Lagos after the discovery of a plot to assassinate President Mohammed Buhari and other members of the ruling junta in October.

18   TURKEY - When Athens approves NATO use of Greek forces based on Lemnos, the Turkish government accuses Greece of using NATO as an instrument of power in the on-going Greco-Turkish squabble.

19-22 KAMPUCHEA - Vietnamese tanks and artillery attack the major rebel base at Nong Chan near the Thai border. Fighting is extremely heavy.

20   SRI LANKA - At least 40 police and civilians are killed in recent rebel violence.

20   FRANCE - The government indicates it is prepared to send its troops back into Chad if Libyan forces are not promptly withdrawn.

22   SRI LANKA - In the wake of the recent violence that has taken scores of lives, the government declares a nation-wide curfew.

23   NICARAGUA - Contra rebels step up raiding in the fertile northern hills, where most of the country's coffee crop is grown, just as workers begin the harvest.

23   LEBANON - Israel's chief negotiator at the withdrawal talks, Brigadier General Amos Gilboa, states that he wants the Israeli-sponsored Southern Lebanese Army to provide security along the border and not the Lebanese Army.

23   SOUTH KOREA - Trade talks which began 15 November between North and South Korea break off after one ROKA and three NKA soldiers are killed in a firefight following the flight of a Soviet defector into the ROK (southern) side of Panmunjom. At least six more ROKA soldiers are wounded in the exchange of gunfire.

24   DENMARK - Representatives of Denmark, Finland, Iceland, Norway, and Sweden meet in Copenhagen to discuss making Scandinavia a nuclear-free zone.

24   SOUTH KOREA - The United Nations Command reports that North Korean and UN forces exchanged gunfire as a Soviet defector, Vasily Yakovlevich, fled south through the DMZ.

25   PORTUGAL - The US Embassy in Lisbon is hit by four
            60mm mortar rounds fired by the Popular Forces of 25
            April. There are no injuries and damage is slight. The
            attack is in celebration of the ninth anniversary of
            an abortive coup.

26   USSR - Communist leader Chernenko tells the British
            Labor Party that if future Labor governments adhere to
            a non-nuclear policy no Soviet nuclear weapons will be
            targeted on Britain.

26   IRAQ - After a 15-year break the government resumes
            full diplomatic relations with the US.

26   COLOMBIA - A car bomb explodes in front of the US
            Embassy in Bogota. A passerby is killed and seven are
            injured. No one claims responsibility for the attack,
            but drug traffickers are suspected of carrying it out.

26   LEBANON - The army is ordered to begin enforcing the
            new security regulations for Beirut to include dis-
            mantling militia barricades and the taking up of
            positions in Muslim West Beirut. In a first incident,
            government forces engage Druze militiamen in Suk al
            Gharb. Two civilians are killed.

26   BELGIUM - Two bombs damage the Beirset Military Air-
            field. The Communist Combatant Cells claims responsi-
            bility for the attack.

27   GIBRALTAR - An agreement is reached which ends the
            15-year Spanish blockade of the British colony. Febru-
            ary 1985 is accepted as the date for negotiations on
            the future of Gibraltar.

27   KUWAIT - The GCC agrees upon the formation of a rapid
            deployment force to defend the region against attack.

27   INDIA - The British Deputy High Commissioner, Percy
            Norris, is assassinated in Bombay by members of the
            Revolutionary Organization of Socialist Muslims.

28   PERU - The government declares a state of emergency as
            a means of ending a general strike. The strikers defy
            the order, however, and the strike continues.

28   UNITED STATES - Reports indicate $280 million in
            covert aid has been earmarked for Afghanistan in 1985.

28   LEBANON - Israeli jets attack Palestinian positions in
            eastern Lebanon.

29   UNITED NATIONS - The Security Council extends the
            mandate of the UN Observer Team in Israel's Golan
            Heights for another six months.

29   UNITED STATES - Intelligence sources indicate six
            Soviet freighters loaded with war materiel are headed
            for Nicaragua.

29   MALTA - The government announces it has signed a
            five-year treaty of military cooperation and security
            with Libya.

29   SRI LANKA - The government imposes strict emergency
            rules, which include the establishment of a prohibited
            zone, in an attempt to curb further violence.

29   UGANDA - The fourth large explosion in Kampala in a
            week sends people fleeing from the city.

29   THE VATICAN - The Vatican-mediated treaty that settles
            the Beagle Channel dispute is formally signed by Chile
            and Argentina. Chile is awarded the channel islands of
            Picton, Lennox, and Nueva it has claimed for more than
            a century.

30   CHAD - At least 3,500 to 4,500 Libyan troops remain in
            country.

30   SRI LANKA - More than 150 soldiers are killed when
            Tamil rebels attack two prison camps in the northern
            section of the island. In another incident, Sri Lankan
            planes and naval units attack eight boats suspected of
            carrying Tamil rebels from India. Sixty are killed in
            this incident.

DECEMBER

1   EL SALVADOR - An army battalion is ambushed by
            guerrillas at El Salto. Forty-five are killed in the
            ensuing battle.

3   THE PHILIPPINES - Government troops kill 23 rebels who
            attack a military outpost in Boyog.

4   GREECE - A bomb attached to an Iraqi diplomat's car in
            Athens detonates killing a Greek bomb disposal expert.
            Two other bombs on Iraqi diplomatic vehicles are found
            and deactivated.

4   MALTA - The government announces that Libyan military
            personnel will train the Maltese forces under the
            terms of a treaty of friendship and cooperation signed
            in November.

4   MIDDLE EAST - Five Arab terrorists hijack a Kuwaiti
           A-300 Airbus and force it to fly to Tehran, Iran. Two
           US government officials who are among the 166 passen-
           gers and crew on board are killed (4 and 6 August) to
           emphasize a demand for the release of Shi'ite
           prisoners held in Kuwaiti prisons. Some of the
           hostages are released over the next four days.

4   EL SALVADOR - At least 43 government soldiers are
           killed in a battle with rebels on the Chichontepec
           Volcano. Thirty-five others are missing in the action.

4   SRI LANKA - About 20 Tamil rebel prisoners are killed
           trying to escape from a prison camp in Vanuniya. In
           another incident, a rebel ambush of a military convoy
           sparks fighting in the village of Murunkan. Fifty-
           three are killed.

5   SRI LANKA - More than 100 Tamils are killed by Sri
           Lankan forces in Mannar after a soldier is killed by a
           rebel mine.

6   SRI LANKA - Seventeen civilians are killed by Tamil
           rebels. A curfew is imposed in the capital city of
           Colombo.

6   IRAQ - The government reaffirms its intent to attack
           any ship stopping at an Iranian port.

7   SRI LANKA - More than 100 soldiers are killed in a
           Tamil ambush of a military convoy about 300 miles
           northwest of Colombo.

7   MIDDLE EAST - Iraqi aircraft attack a Cypriot super-
           tanker in the Persian Gulf.

7   NORTHERN IRELAND - British forces ambush an IRA assas-
           sination team in Londonderry killing two of the
           terrorists.

8   CHILE - Soldiers and police seal off a Santiago slum
           and round up more than 5,000 suspects in a search for
           terrorists.

8   LEBANON - Fighting breaks out between Druze militiamen
           and Lebanese army troops in the mountains overlooking
           Beirut.

9   IRAN - Iranian security forces storm the hijacked
           Kuwaiti airliner capturing the terrorists and freeing
           the remaining hostages. Most claim they have been
           brutalized by their captors.

9   PORTUGAL - The NATO Iberian headquarters at Oeiras is
        attacked with grenades by members of the Popular
        Forces of 25 April group.

10   MIDDLE EAST - Iraqi aircraft fire an "Exocet" missile
        at a Bahamian tanker south of Kharg Island.

10   EL SALVADOR - In separate actions, government forces
        kill 13 rebels in fighting near Nueva Concepcion,
        while rebel forces ambush a government column near El
        Paisnal.

11   UNITED STATES - The government accuses Iran of com-
        plicity in the Kuwaiti airliner incident and demands
        the extradition of the terrorists for the murder of
        the two Americans.

11   EL SALVADOR - Leftist rebels call a unilateral Christ-
        mas truce and release 42 prisoners, mostly Salvadoran
        army personnel. The government had already said it was
        ready to halt military operations if the rebels took
        similar action.

11   SRI LANKA - Fifteen are killed and 700 captured during
        a Tamil rebel roundup in northern Sri Lanka. At least
        375 suspects are detained; the remainder are released.

11   BELGIUM - Six explosions damage the NATO emergency
        pipelines around Belgium. The leftist organization
        Cellules Communistes Combattante claims the respon-
        sibility for the attacks.

12   GREECE - The government announces it will no longer
        follow NATO policies.

12   MAURITANIA - The government of President Mohammed
        Khouna Ould Haidallah is overthrown in a bloodless
        coup. Haidallah is at a conference in Burundi at the
        time. Lieutenant Colonel Maaouya Ould Sidi Ahmed Taya
        proclaims himself president.

12   FRANCE - The government states it has no obligation to
        force Libyan troops out of Chad.

13   LEBANON - A car bomb explodes outside a Druze Muslim
        religious center in West Beirut. Artillery duels rage
        in the mountains southeast and east of the city be-
        tween Druze and Christian militiamen.

15   GREAT BRITAIN - While on an official visit to London,
        Politburo member Mikhail Gorbachev announces there will
        be no arms control agreement with the West unless the
        West agrees to a ban on nuclear weapons in space.

15-31 MIDDLE EAST - Iraqi aircraft attack a number of foreign-owned ships in the Persian Gulf. On occasion, Iranian planes carry out retaliatory strikes against shipping.

16 UNITED NATIONS - The Security Council extends the mandate of the peacekeeping force in Cyprus for another six months.

16 SPAIN - The government votes to remain in NATO.

17 GREECE - The government announces it is shifting its forces stationed along the Bulgarian border to positions facing its border with Turkey.

18 IRAN - The government refuses the US demand for extradition of the four terrorists accused of hijacking the Kuwaiti airliner to Tehran declaring it will try them.

18 ISRAEL - Three people are wounded in a grenade attack in the main market in Tel Aviv.

18 WEST GERMANY - Red Brigade terrorists attack the NATO Officer's School at Oberammergau in Bavaria.

19 ISRAEL - The government requests $4.1 billion in aid from the US in fiscal 1986.

19 COMMUNIST CHINA - A formal agreement is signed in Peking transferring sovereignty of the British Crown Colony of Hong Kong to Communist China in 1997.

21 UNITED STATES - The US rejects the Israeli request for $4.1 billion in aid and suggests stronger austerity measures be imposed by the government in Jerusalem.

21 ISRAEL - The government warns Lebanon to allow a wider UN role in southern Lebanon or face a wider Israeli role in the area.

21 SOMALIA - Ethiopian troops attack several villages in Somalia before being driven out of the country.

21 LEBANON - Lebanese army units push into Tripoli and wrest control of the important port from militiamen.

22 MALTA - Prime Minister Dom Mintoff resigns and is replaced by Carmelo Mifsud Bonici.

22 EL SALVADOR - The government announces a 13-day Christmas truce.

23   ITALY - A time bomb aboard a train bound from Florence to Bologna explodes in a 12-mile-long tunnel killing 29 and injuring nearly 200 passengers. A right-wing organization is suspected.

24   NORTHERN IRELAND - Police clash with Catholic mourners at the Londonderry funeral of a known IRA terrorist who was killed in a firefight with British forces.

25   ANGOLA - Pro-Western guerrillas increase their attacks forcing the Marxist government to rely on Cuban troops and Eastern-bloc weapons.

25-30   KAMPUCHEA - Heavy fighting is reported between Vietnamese and Kampuchean forces located in four base areas. More than 60,000 flee into Thailand. The Kampuchean main camp at Rithisen is taken on 26 December. This victory is followed up by attacks on Obok and the stronghold at Ampil near Hill 1903 on the Thai border.

26   IRAN - A car bomb explodes in Tehran killing four and injuring 50 more.

28   FINLAND - A Soviet cruise missile crashes in Finland after going astray on a test flight over the Barents Sea and passing over Norwegian territory.

29   JORDAN - Fahd Kawasmeh, a senior official in the PLO, is assassinated by two gunmen associated with the "Black September" terrorist organization.

29   ANGOLA - UNITA rebels kidnap 22 people.

31   AFGHANISTAN - Afghan guerrillas attack Kabul with rocket fire.

Notes

1985

JANUARY

1   JAPAN - The government lifts the sanctions it imposed on North Korea for being implicated in the killing of four South Korean officials in Rangoon in 1983. Also on this date, three homemade rockets utilizing a time-delay mechanism are launched at the US Consulate in Kobe. The attack causes no damage. The leftist Chukaku-Ha (Nucleus Faction) group claims credit for the attack.

3   ISRAEL - The government confirms that it has nearly completed "OPERATION MOSES" in which about 10,000 Ethiopian Jews were, since 1977, secretly brought to Israel. The Ethiopian government denounces the re-location as an invasion into Ethiopian internal affairs.

4   USSR - The government apologizes to Finland and Norway for the penetration of their airspace by an out-of-control cruise missile which overflew Norway and crashed in Finland.

5   COLOMBIA - The government turns four major drug dealers over to the US to stand trial on charges of international illegal drug trafficking and money laundering.

7   KAMPUCHEA - About 4,000 Communist Vietnamese troops launch an attack against non-Communist Khmer People's National Liberation Front (KPNLF) positions near Ampil on the Thai border.

8   GREECE - The government announces that its new defense
         policy emphasizes Turkey as its probable enemy rather
         than the Soviet bloc.

9   KAMPUCHEA - Vietnamese forces capture the key guer-
         rilla base at Ampil after two days of hard fighting.

10   SRI LANKA - Government forces wipe out a guerrilla
         base of the Liberation Tigers of Tamil Eelam. Fourteen
         Tamil rebels are killed.

10   NICARAGUA - Daniel Ortega is sworn in as President.

12   GREECE - The Greek-Albanian border which has been
         closed since 1940 is formally reopened.

14   WARSAW PACT - The planned meeting of the leaders of
         the Warsaw Pact nations is cancelled amid speculation
         that Soviet leader Konstantin Chernenko is seriously
         ill.

14   ISRAEL - The government decides to implement the first
         stage of a three-stage withdrawal of Israeli forces
         from southern Lebanon. The actual redeployment is
         expected to begin in about five weeks. The entire
         operation is expected to take six to nine months.

15   BELGIUM - A group identified as the Communist Com-
         batant Cells sets off a car bomb in front of the US
         NATO Support Activity building outside of Brussels.
         One US soldier is injured and the building is heavily
         damaged. No one claims credit for the attack.

18   UNITED STATES - The government announces it will no
         longer participate in any World Court proceedings in
         which it stands accused of charges leveled by
         Nicaragua.

18   INDIA - The government arrests a number of senior
         Indian officials in what is reported to be a
         large-scale spy network. At least one French diplomat
         is ordered out of the country but no direct link is
         reported between the French Embassy and the espionage
         operation.

20   LEBANON - The Israelis begin withdrawing some of their
         heavy equipment back into Israeli territory.

20   SRI LANKA - Tamil Eelam rebels blow up a military
         train killing 33 soldiers.

21   LEBANON - The leader of the Sunni Muslim faction in
         southern Lebanon, Mustafa Saad, is seriously injured
         in a terrorist bomb blast in Sidon.

23   THE PHILIPPINES - Government prosecutors indicate that at least 26 people will be indicted in connection with the August 1983 assassination of opposition leader Benigno Aquino, Jr. Among the accused is General Fabian C. Ver, the Chief of Staff of the Philippine Armed Forces.

25   FRANCE - General Rene Audran, the French official in charge of international arms sales, is assassinated outside his home in Paris. Credit for the murder is claimed by a group calling itself "Commando Elizabeth Van Dyck of Action Directe."

27   ISRAEL - Government representatives meet with Egyptian envoys to discuss the dispute over the Taba, a border settlement south of Elat near the Red Sea. After three days of meetings there is no agreement.

28   IRAQ - Government forces launch a new offensive on the southern front in the Gulf War with Iran.

28   INDIA - A five-continent meeting takes place in which Argentina, Greece, India, Mexico, Sweden, and Tanzania call for a ban on nuclear weapons in outer space and an end to the arms race.

28   PORTUGAL - NATO warships are fired on in Lisbon harbor. None of the ships is damaged in the mortar attack. The insurgent group known as the Popular Forces of 25 April are blamed for the attack.

31   IRAQ - Government forces open a second offensive against Iranian positions on the southern front.

31   AUSTRIA - MBFR talks resume in Vienna.

31   NEW ZEALAND - The government reaffirms its commitment of refusing port facilities to nuclear-armed or -powered vessels.

FEBRUARY

1   WEST GERMANY - Two terrorists force their way into the Munich home of German industrialist Ernst Zimmermann. Zimmermann is tortured and shot in the head, dying 12 hours later. The Red Army Faction claims responsibility for the attack in the name of Commando Patrick O'Hara, a member of the Irish National Liberation Army, who died on a hunger strike in 1981.

2   CHILE - The government extends the state of siege imposed on 6 November 1984.

2   GREECE - A terrorist bomb injures 79 people, including 57 US servicemen, in an attack on a bar near the US Air Base at Glyfada, outside Athens. The Cypriot National Front group claims responsibility.

4   SPAIN - The border with Gibraltar, which has been closed since 1970, is reopened as a precursor to the start of talks over Gibraltar's future status.

4   UNITED STATES - The Defense Department announces that scheduled ANZUS naval exercises had been cancelled because New Zealand refuses to admit US naval vessels to its ports without a certification that they carry no nuclear weapons.

5   LIBYA - Four British subjects, who were taken hostage in Tripoli when Great Britain broke diplomatic relations with Libya in April 1984, are released. In return, Colonel Qaddafi demands a normalization of relations and the release of four Libyan terrorists who were about to stand trial for bombing attacks on anti-Qaddafi residents of England.

7   COLOMBIA - Seven US firms are bombed in Medellin. One policeman is killed and a second wounded. The ELN and FARC groups both take credit for the attacks.

8   GUATEMALA - Diplomatic relations are resumed with Spain after a five-year break.

11   JORDAN - Following a meeting in Amman, Yassir Arafat and King Hussein issue a joint communique stating they have reached agreement on a framework for peace in the Middle East.

14   TURKEY - The government suspends diplomatic relations with Bulgaria and withdraws its Ambassador to Sofia in protest to the imposition of Bulgarian names on citizens of Turkish origin.

14   AUSTRIA - At the MBFR talks, the USSR proposes it reduce its strength in Central Europe by 22,000, while the US take a reduction of 13,000 troops.

14   UNITED STATES - The government informs New Zealand that US naval units will not participate in upcoming maneuvers (28 February) and that the entire issue of defense arrangements with New Zealand is under review.

16   LEBANON - The first phase of the Israeli withdrawal begins as 300 Israeli troops leave Sidon. The redeployment is completed the next day.

17   PAKISTAN - On the eve of the elections, government
            security teams arrest all but one of the opposition
            party's leaders.

18   SOUTH AFRICA - A least ten blacks die in the latest
            violence in the township of Crossroads. In a separate
            incident, government security forces arrest six black
            leaders for treason.

18   LEBANON - Shi'ite Muslim militia move into the vacumn
            created by the withdrawal of Israeli and Southern
            Lebanon Army forces from Sidon and all but occupy the
            city.

19   UNITED STATES - The government announces the comple-
            tion of the first free-flight test of a cruise missile
            over Canada.

20   LEBANON - Israeli forces carry out the first in a
            series of raids on Arab Muslim settlements. The
            operation is designed to dissuade future ambushes of
            Israeli troops.

20   TUNISIA - The PLO Executive Committee headquarters in
            Tunis issues a statement categorically rejecting the
            UN Security Council's Resolution 242.

20   REPUBLIC OF IRELAND - The government seizes about $1.6
            million said to belong to the outlawed Irish Repub-
            lican Army (IRA).

21   USSR - The government signs an agreement which will
            allow the International Atomic Energy Agency (IAEA) to
            inspect Soviet nuclear facilities for the first time.

21   GREECE - A leftist terrorist organization known as 17
            November assassinates a Greek publisher on an Athens
            street. The terrorists escape but leave leaflets
            behind condemning the socialist government in Greece.

24   EGYPT - President Mubarak asks the US to host a
            meeting in Washington where Jordanian, Palestinian,
            and Israeli delegates may discuss peace in the Middle
            East.

26   LEBANON - The Israeli command imposes a strict
            dark-to-dawn curfew to tighten control over Arab
            activities in the occupied zone of southern Lebanon.

27   ISRAEL - Premier Shimon Peres agrees to meet with
            Jordanian and Palestinian representatives in
            Washington.

28   NORTHERN IRELAND - IRA terrorists kill nine policemen
          when they attack a police base at Newry with mortars.

28   KUWAIT - The Assistant Cultural Attache of the Iraqi
          Embassy and his son are assassinated in their home by
          four gunmen. No one claims responsibility.

28   AUSTRIA - The former Libyan Ambassador to Austria is
          severely wounded by unknown assailants outside his
          home in Vienna. The victim broke with Muammar Qadaffi
          in 1980.

MARCH

1   NORTHERN IRELAND - The Royal Ulster Constabulary bar-
          racks at Newry are hit by IRA mortar rounds. Nine con-
          stabulary officers are killed and 37 others injured.

3   ISRAEL - The government approves implementation of the
          second phase of the withdrawal of Israeli forces from
          southern Lebanon.

6   THAILAND - The government reports a border clash with
          Vietnamese forces who pursued Kampuchean rebels into
          Thai territory.

7   PERSIAN GULF - Both sides in the Iraq-Iran War break a
          nine-month pledge and begin attacking each other's
          cities.

8   LEBANON - The Hizballah (Party of God) spiritual
          leader Muhammad Husayn Fadlallah is the target of a
          car bomb attack outside his home in south Beirut.
          Eighty are killed and 250 injured in the attack for
          which no one claims credit.

10   IRAN - Iraqi bombers attack Ishfahan (Eshfahan). At
          least 130 are killed.

11   IRAQ - Irani forces open a major offensive in the
          southern marsh region.

11   USSR - The government announces the death (10 March)
          from emphysema of General Secretary and Chairman
          Konstantin U. Chernenko at age 73. He is replaced by
          54-year-old Mikhail Gorbachev.

11   KAMPUCHEA - The Kampuchean rebel base at Tatum on the
          Thai border is taken by Vietnamese forces after a
          week-long siege.

12	IRAN - Iraqi aircraft attack the capital city of Tehran.
12	UNITED NATIONS - The Security Council votes to condemn Israel for its actions in southern Lebanon. It also orders the immediate withdrawal of all Israeli forces from southern Lebanon. The US vetoes the motion.
12	CANADA - The Turkish Embassy in Ottawa is seized by three members of the Armenian Revolutionary Army. A security guard is killed. The terrorists surrender after four hours.
13	UNITED NATIONS - The Security Council unanimously votes to condemn South Africa for its apartheid policies.
14	BELGIUM - The government authorizes the deployment of 16 of the 48 ground-launched cruise missiles (GLCM) scheduled into the country.
14	SWITZERLAND - US-Soviet arms-control talks open in Geneva.
14	ANGOLA - UNITA rebels release 22 persons kidnapped on 29 December 1984.
14	GUADELOUPE - A crowded restaurant is bombed in Point-a-Pitre. One person is killed and 11 injured, including four Americans. No one claims responsibility, but the evidence points to the separatist Caribbean Revolutionary Alliance.
17	IRAQ - The government warns all airliners to avoid Iranian air space.
18	IRAQ - Jordan's King Hussein and Egypt's President Mubarak arrive in Baghdad in a fruitless attempt to stop the Iraq-Iran War.
21	SOUTH AFRICA - Security police fire on a black funeral procession killing 19 and injuring 25. About 239 people are arrested in the incident near Uitenhage.
23	ISRAEL - As a second "OPERATION MOSES"-type airlift is completed, it is discovered that US military aircraft have participated in the evacuation of almost all Ethiopian Jews from Sudan to Israel.
26	UNITED STATES - Defense Secretary Casper Weinberger issues an invitation to 17 countries to join in the SDI program.
26	SUDAN - Food rioting breaks out in Khartoum.

27   ITALY - Red Brigade terrorists assassinate Rome University Professor Enzo Tarantelli. Tarantelli is an eminent labor economist.

27   IRAQ - Two car bombs explode in Tikrit killing 36 people. Many others are ·injured. No one claims credit for the bombings.

APRIL

1   IRAN - At least 22 people are killed in Tehran as a result of an Iraqi air raid.

1   LIBERIA - President Samuel Doe narrowly escapes an assassination attempt led by the Deputy Commander of the Palace Guard, Colonel Flanzamaton. Flanzamaton is tried, convicted, and executed (7 April).

2   LEBANON - As a part of their planned withdrawal from Lebanese territory, the Israeli armed forces move 1,100 Lebanese POWs, who are considered unmanageable, to prison camps in Israel.

4   UNITED STATES - President Reagan calls for a 60-day cease-fire between the Nicaraguans and the Contras.

6   SUDAN - A military coup overthrows the government of President Nimeiry while he is on an official visit to the US. General 'Abd ar-Rahman Sowar (Siwar) el-Dahab becomes the nation's new leader.

6   WEST GERMANY - Libyan gunmen murder an anti-Qadaffi Libyan student. Two German passers-by are wounded.

7-9   UNITED NATIONS - UN Secretary General Javier Perez de Cuellar meets in Baghdad and Tehran with each nation's leaders in a fruitless attempt to end the fighting.

8   SOMALIA - Diplomatic relations are restored with Libya after a seven-year break.

9   USSR - Communist Chinese and Soviet representatives open the sixth round of talks aimed at improving relations.

11   ALBANIA - Party leader Enver Hoxha dies at 76. He is succeeded by Ramiz Alia (14 April).

12   LEBANON - Israeli forces complete phase two of the withdrawal schedule by evacuating a 200-square-mile area around Nabatiya.

12   ISRAEL - The government approves the implementation of phase three of the withdrawal of its forces setting the beginning of June as the deadline for completion.

12   SPAIN - A terrorist bomb planted by the Islamic Jihad kills 18 and injures 82, including 15 US service personnel, when it explodes in the El Descanso restaurant near a US air base outside Madrid. Several Middle East terrorist groups claim responsibility for the attack.

15   UNITED STATES - The Department of State announces the US will resume the sale of arms to Algeria.

17   INDONESIA - Completing a six-day visit, Vietnamese Defense Minister Van Tien Dung announces that Vietnamese forces will remain in Kampuchea.

18   ANGOLA - South African forces withdraw from a region in southern Angola which they have occupied for five years.

18   NEW ZEALAND - During an official visit to New Zealand, the Communist Chinese Secretary General, Hu Yaobang (Hu Yao-pang), announces a 25% (1-million-man) reduction in his country's armed forces by the end of 1986.

22   LEBANON - Christian Phalangist militia begin withdrawing inland from Sidon after several days of heavy fighting with Muslims and Palestinians.

22   ARGENTINA - The trial of nine former junta members begins. Among the defendents are former presidents Videla and Galtieri.

22   INDIA - Police in Ahmedabad (Ahmadabad) in the State of Gujarat riot to protest the brutal death of a police sergeant.

23   SWITZERLAND - The first round of arms control talks between the US and USSR ends without progress.

23   INDIA - Rival Hindu castes clash in the State of Gujarat. Fifteen are left dead and more the 100 injured. This incident will be blamed in large part on the police who had abandoned their posts to rampage through Ahmedabad the day before (22 April).

24   LEBANON - Israeli forces begin their withdrawal from the Bekaa Valley and from around Tyre (Sour). Lebanese army and Muslim militia units move in to fill the vacuum left by the departing Israelis.

24   SUDAN - The new Sudanese government resumes diplomatic relations with Libya.

26   WARSAW PACT - The Warsaw Pact Treaty is renewed for an additional thirty years.

26   SWEDEN - The government acknowledges it detonated a nuclear device in 1972 but denies it is producing nuclear weapons.

28   LEBANON - Druze and Sunni Muslim militias join forces to control the Sidon area.

30   LEBANON - Continued fighting is found in several areas. Christian and Muslim militiamen battle in the streets of Beirut, while Muslims fight the pro-Israeli South Lebanon Army (SLA) at Kfar Falous.

MAY

1   UNITED STATES - President Reagan imposes economic sanctions on Nicaragua.

4   SOUTH AFRICA - Eleven are killed when five days of fighting erupts among black townspeople and black migrant workers in Tsakane near Johannesburg.

6   LEBANON - The efforts of President Amin Gemayle to effect a cease-fire fail.

8   UNITED STATES - President Reagan criticizes the Soviet Union and makes a number of proposals for improving East-West relations in a speech before the European Parliament.

8   FRANCE - Defense Minister Charles Hernu leaves for New Caledonia where violence has broken out between pro- and anti-independence factions.

9   SRI LANKA - Government troops report killing more than 75 Tamil rebels as fighting continues.

10   FRANCE - The French carry out the latest blast of the current nuclear weapons test series when they detonate a 150 KT device at Mururoa Atoll in the Pacific.

10-12   INDIA - Two days of Sikh terrorist bombings in New Delhi and elsewhere in northern India leave 85 dead and several hundred injured.

11   EL SALVADOR - Leftist rebels single out mayors as their new prime targets.

11   FRANCE - The Corsican National Liberation Front sets off 15 bombs on Corsica. Seventeen more bombs explode on 15 May.

14   SYRIA - Lebanese Vice-President 'Abd al-Halim Khaddam meets in Damascus with Druze, Shi'ite, and Christian representatives in an effort to reduce the fighting in Lebanon.

14   SRI LANKA - Tamil rebels attack the sacred Buddhist city of Anduradhapura, 105 miles north of Colombo, killing at least 145 people. In reprisal, Sinhalese natives kill scores of innocent Tamil men, women, and children.

15   PERU - The residence of the US Ambassador in Lima and a number of other locations are subjected to simultaneous bombings by the Sendero Luminoso (Shining Path) group.

17   EGYPT - Three days of talks in Cairo between Israeli and Egyptian officials end in a deadlock.

17   UNITED STATES - The government signs an agreement authorizing the transfer of high military technology to India.

18   LEBANON - The Christian "Lebanese Forces" militia's new leader, Elie Hobeika (replacing Samir Geagea on 9 May), announces support for Syrian intervention in Lebanon.

20   LEBANON - Shi'ite Amal militia attack the Sabra, Shatila, and Burj al-Brajneh Palestinian refugee camps in and around Beirut. In fighting in the city, the President's Palace takes a number of direct hits.

20   ISRAEL - The government exchanges 1,150 Palestinian and Lebanese prisoners for three Israeli soldiers held by the PFLP since 1982.

21   USSR - Indian Prime Minister Rajiv Gandhi culminates a six-day visit when he and Premier Gorbachev sign a $1.5 billion economic assistance treaty.

21   AFGHANISTAN - Soviet forces open a major offensive into the Kunar Valley in eastern Afghanistan near the Pakistani border.

23   SOUTH AFRICA - The Chief of the South African Defense Forces admits South African troops are still deployed in Angola. Two members of this force were recently killed, and one captured by Angolan troops.

23   LEBANON - More than 200 are reported killed in the recent fighting.

23   AUSTRIA - MBFR talks resume in Vienna.

24   SRI LANKA - President Junius R. Jayawardene announces his intention to declare martial law to stop the Tamil violence.

25   KUWAIT - A car bomb explodes in a motorcade carrying the Emir of Kuwait. Six people are killed and 12 injured, including the Emir. The Islamic Jihad claims responsibility in the name of the Iranian-backed Dawa Party.

26   IRAN - Iraqi aircraft raid Tehran and several other Iranian cities.

29   LEBANON - President Gemayle goes to Syria for talks with President Assad.

30   SWITZERLAND - The second round of arms-control talks opens in Geneva.

31   LEBANON - Shi'ite Muslim militia units capture the Palestinian refugee camps at Sabra and Shatila.

31   COSTA RICA - Two Costa Rican border guards are killed in a firefight on the Nicaraguan border.

JUNE

3   INDIA - Progress is reported in talks sponsored by the Indian government that are aimed at settling the Sri Lanka crisis.

4   SRI LANKA - Singhalese mobs attack Tamil villages in the eastern part of the nation killing 80.

6   LEBANON - The deadline for completion of the third phase of the Israeli withdrawal passes. Israeli forces still occupy significant portions of southern Lebanon.

7   LEBANON - Twenty-one Finnish members of the UNEF are kidnapped by South Lebanese Army troops. The ransom for their release is set as the freeing of 11 SLA members held by the Shi'ite Amal militia.

7   AFGHANISTAN - Soviet and Afghan government forces clear the Kunar Valley and lift the 11-month seige on the garrison at Barikot.

10   ISRAEL - The government announces it has completed its three-phase withdrawal of forces from Lebanon. It states further that a number of Israeli observers and reconnaissance units remain in the security zone on the Lebanese side of the border to "assist" the Christian South Lebanese Army.

11   UNITED STATES - The Senate votes to repeal the 1976 Clark Amendment which banned aid to UNITA.

11   GRENADA - The last US forces who were part of the invasion leave the island.

12   AFGHANISTAN - Rebels destroy 20 Soviet aircraft at the Soviet-controlled Shindand Air Base.

12   UNITED STATES - The House of Representatives votes $27 million in non-military aid for the antigovernment "Contras" in Nicaragua.

13   NICARAGUA - The two principal opposition groups combine their forces into the Nicaraguan Opposition Union.

14   LEBANON - Two Shi'ite Muslims of the Islamic Jihad hijack a TWA airliner (Flight 847) after departure from Athens. After flying first to Beirut, then to Algiers, and then back to Beirut airport, the terrorists kill an American serviceman and hold 152 other passengers hostage for the release of 700 Lebanese Shi'ite prisoners held in Israeli jails. Several American hostages are removed from the plane and moved to other locations. Twelve Amal members board the plane and remain until the remaining hostages (three crew members stay on board) are removed to other locations (17 June). They are held for 13 days by Amal and Hizballah groups until Syria secures their release.

14   IRAQ - President Saddam Hussein orders a 15-day halt to the bombing of Iranian cities to give the Iranian government a chance to accept his five-point peace proposal.

14   BOTSWANA - South African Defense Force (SADF) commandos carry out an attack on suspected ANC guerrilla bases in Gaborone. Sixteen suspected rebels are killed. Both the ANC and the Botswana government deny that the bases ever existed.

15   UNITED STATES - The Department of State orders the US Ambassador in South Africa home for consultations.

15   LEBANON - The 21 Finnish UNEF members are released
            without ransom by SLA commander General Antoine Lahd,
            when it is discovered that the 11 SLA members held by
            Amal are defectors and not prisoners. The 11 Shi'ite
            Muslim defectors are turned over to Amal.

16   LEBANON - Shi'ite leader Nabih Berri negotiates the
            release of the remaining 42 hostages on the TWA
            airliner held at Beirut airport. The hostages are
            moved to secret locations in Beirut.

16   CHILE - The state of siege which has been in effect
            since November 1984 is lifted and is replaced by a
            state of emergency order.

18   SYRIA - Shi'ite Amal and Palestinian representatives
            sign an agreement in Damascus that is designed to end
            the fighting in the Palestinian refugee camps in
            Lebanon.

18   SRI LANKA - The five major Tamil factions all agree to
            a cease-fire.

19   WEST GERMANY - The main terminal at Rhein-Main Airport
            is bombed. Four are killed and 60 injured. At least a
            half-dozen groups claim responsibility for the attack.

19   EL SALVADOR - An armed attack on a cafe in the Zona
            Rosa district in San Salvadoris carried out by six to
            ten men. Thirteen are killed, including six Americans
            (four Marines and two US businessmen). The Mardoquero
            Cruz Urban Commandos of the Central American
            Revolutionary Workers' Party claim responsibility for
            the attack.

20   CHILE - Five electric transmission towers are damaged
            by bombs probably planted by the leftist Manuel
            Rodriguez Patriotic Front.

20-21   NEPAL - Five bombs are set off by terrorists at five
            locations, including the royal palace in Kathmandu and
            in the western city of Pokhara. Seven are reported
            killed and 24 injured in the blasts. On 21 June three
            more bombs go off in the border town of Birgunj. One
            person is killed. Two previously unknown groups claim
            responsibility.

23   LIBYA - A Strategic Alliance Treaty is signed by Libya
            and Iran.

23   IRAQ - The government severs diplomatic relations with
            Libya.

23   ATLANTIC OCEAN - A bomb planted by a terrorist group
       blows up Air India Flight 182 bound from Canada to
       Bombay while the aircraft is flying just south of
       Ireland. All 329 on board are killed. Two Sikh groups
       and a Kashmir separatist group claim credit for the
       attack.

23   JAPAN - A second unidentified terrorist bomb kills two
       when it explodes in baggage being removed from an Air
       India flight from Canada at Tokyo's Narita Airport.
       Two workmen are killed. The bag carrying the bomb is
       determined to have arrived from Canada and was being
       transferred to another Air India flight when it
       explodes. Sikh terrorists are suspected.

24   ISRAEL - The government releases 31 Lebanese Shi'ites
       held in a Haifa prison but denies any connection with
       the ongoing hostage situation in Lebanon.

26   ZAIRE - The government announces it will double the
       size of its armed forces to 100,000.

29   ANGOLA - South African troops pursue SWAPO rebels into
       Angola killing 45.

30   IRAQ - The government announces the bombing moratorium
       has ended without any change in the status of the war.

30   LEBANON - The intervention of Syrian President Assad
       brings the release of the last 39 American hostages
       held by Shi'ite terrorists in Beirut.

JULY

1   SPAIN - A terrorist bomb explodes in the British
       Airways ticket office in Madrid killing one Spanish
       woman and injuring at least 27 others. Within minutes
       of this attack a grenade is thrown into the Royal
       Jordanian Airlines office and the building is raked
       with small-arms fire. At least three Middle East
       terrorist organizations, one of which is a covername
       for Abu Nidal, claim responsibility.

1   ITALY - A terrorist bomb injures 12 at Rome's inter-
       national airport.

3   ISRAEL - The government releases an additional 300
       Lebanese prisoners from its camp at Atlit.

5   UNITED STATES - The Department of State announces that
       a memorandum of understanding for better utilization
       of the "Hot Line" was signed with the USSR at the June
       meeting of the SALT Standing Consultative Commission.

8   UNITED STATES - President Reagan names Cuba, Iran, Libya, Nicaragua, and North Korea as the chief purveyors of terrorism throughout the world and states the US will fight back if attacked.

8   SUDAN - The new government signs a military agreement with Libya which provides for Libyan assistance in logistics, training, and transportation.

8   BHUTAN - Sri Lankan peace talks open in Thimbu (Tashi-Chho Dzang) under Indian auspices.

8   ARGENTINA - The government offers to end its state of hostilities with Great Britain if the British government agrees to bilateral talks within 60 days.

9   SYRIA - At a meeting in Damascus, Lebanese Druze, Shi'ite, and Sunni leaders agree to end the fighting in West Beirut.

10   ANGOLA - As a result of Congressional action to repeal the Clark Amendment banning aid to UNITA, Angola breaks off talks with the US.

10   ISRAEL - An Israeli court in Jerusalem covicts 15 Jews of terrorist attacks on Arabs.

10   NEW ZEALAND - The Greenpeace flagship, <u>Rainbow Warrior</u> is sunk by two bombs attached to the hull while it is moored in Auckland Harbor as it is being readied to sail into the waters` around Mururoa Atoll to protest continued French nuclear testing. One crewman is killed.

11   KUWAIT - Two large bombs detonate within minutes of each other in two crowded outdoor cafes. Eight are killed and 89 injured. The Abu Nidal group claims credit for the attack.

12   PAKISTAN - Rioting among Shi'ite Muslims in Quetta leaves 27 dead, 600 under arrest.

16   LEBANON - With the announcement (15 July) of the establishment of a Muslim Committee (with Syrian ob-servers) to put into effect the new security plan in West Beirut, two Christian factions, the Phalangists and the SLA, agree to merge their forces.

16   SWITZERLAND - The second round of arms control talks ends without apparent progress.

18   ISRAEL - The government rejects the slate of six Palestinians chosen for the forthcoming Israeli-Jordanian/Palestinian meeting in Washington.

19   CHILE - A powerful carbomb explodes in front of the US
          Consulate in Santiago. One   passer-by is killed and
          four injured. The building is damaged. The Manuel
          Rodriguez Patriotic Front claims responsibility for
          the attack.

20   SOUTH AFRICA - The government declares a state of
          emergency in 36 districts following months of violence
          and unrest.

22   ISRAEL - Fifteen Jewish terrorists are sentenced for
          up to life for crimes committed against Palestinian
          Arabs.

22   DENMARK - The Islamic Jihad bombs a Jewish synagogue
          and old people's home and the offices of Northwest
          Orient Airlines in Copenhagen. At least 32 people are
          injured. The attack is claimed to be retaliation for
          an Israeli raid of the southern Lebanese town of
          Kabrikha on 21 July.

24   ISRAEL - An additional 100 prisoners are released from
          Israeli prisons.

24   FRANCE - The government recalls its Ambassador to
          South Africa and announces economic sanctions against
          the Pretoria government.

25   GUADELOUPE - Rioting breaks out in Point-a-Pitre when
          demonstrators seeking the release of the leader of the
          separatist Mouvement Populaire pour le Quadeloupe
          Independente, Georges Faisans, clash with police.

26   GUADALOUPE - Police reinforcements arrive from France.

26   UNITED NATIONS - The Security Council unanimously
          votes to censure South Africa.

27   UGANDA - President Milton Obote is ousted by a mili-
          tary coup and is forced to flee to Kenya.

29   GUADELOUPE - Violence subsides with the release of
          Georges Faisans.

29   SPAIN - The Director General of Defense Policy, Vice
          Admiral Fausto Escrigas Estrada, is gunned down in
          Madrid by terrorists. The Basque Fatherland and
          Liberty-Military Wing both claim responsibility.

30   LEBANON - The Syrian government gives 50 Soviet-built
          T-54 tanks to the Shi'ite Amal militia in Beirut.

30   SOUTH AFRICA - The government recalls its Ambassador-
          designate to the US from Washington.

30   UGANDA - The nine-man ruling military junta appoints
          Lieutenant General Tito Okello to be head of state.

30   USSR - The Soviet Union announces it will halt nuclear
          testing from 6 August to 31 December and invites the
          US to do the same.

AUGUST

1   SOUTH AFRICA - The ambassadors from 11 West European
          nations are called home.

1   UGANDA - A former minister in the Obote government,
          Paulo Muwanga, is sworn in as Premier. Three weeks
          later (25 August) he is fired.

2   LEBANON - Israeli jets attack the Lebanese head-
          quarters of the southern branch of the Syrian
          Nationalist Party in Chtaura in retaliation for the
          recent wave of car bombings in the Israeli security
          zone.

6   USSR - The government authorizes two IAEA visits to
          nuclear power plants.

6   LEBANON - At a Syrian-sponsored meeting at Chtaura,
          Druze, Shi'ite Amal, and several left-wing groups join
          together to establish political reform in Lebanon.

6   GUYANA - President Forbes Burnham dies at 62. He is
          replaced by Prime Minister Desmond Hoyte.

6   MOZAMBIQUE - The Mozambique National Resistance kills
          33 persons in an attack on a funeral procession in
          Tete Province near the Malawi border.

7   MOROCCO - At an emergency summit meeting of the Arab
          League in Casablanca, ten members reaffirm their sup-
          port of Iraq in the current Iraq-Iran War. Algeria,
          Lebanon, Libya, South Yemen, and Syria boycott the
          meeting.

7   COOK ISLANDS - The 13-member South Pacific Forum de-
          clares the South Pacific a nuclear-free zone.

7-8   WEST GERMANY - A US serviceman is shot and killed in
          Wiesbaden by Red Army Faction terrorists, most likely
          to get his military ID card. With the card, the
          terrorists enter the US Airbase at Rhein-Main and
          explode a car bomb on 8 August. Two US service
          personnel are killed and 20 others injured. The
          terrorists send a communique and the ID card to US.

7-8   WEST GERMANY (Cont'd) - military authorities on 13
        August. In addition to the RAF, the French Action
        Directe group claims credit in the name of "Commando
        George Jackson," an American member of the Black
        Panthers who was killed in an attempted prison escape
        in 1971.

8   SOUTH AFRICA - Five days of violence erupt in the
        townships around Durban. At least 60 die as a result
        of the fighting.

8   INDIA - The government announces it can now produce
        its own plutonium.

13   ISRAEL - An additional 101 Lebanese prisoners are
        released from Atlit prison.

14   LEBANON - A car-bomb blast in Christian East Beirut
        kills 15 and injures more than 120. A second bomb
        kills 55 and injures scores of Christian bystanders.

15   IRAN - A series of Iraqi air strikes seriously damages
        Iran's Kharg Island (Khargu Island) oil terminal in
        the Persian Gulf.

15   INDIA - The government settles a long-standing violent
        dispute with Assam over the immigration of refugees
        from Bangladesh.

15   EL SALVADOR - Rebel groups in El Salvador announce a
        merger into a single political and military organi-
        zation.

16   VIET NAM - The government announces all its forces
        will be withdrawn from Kampuchea by 1990.

19   LEBANON - A series of car-bomb blasts in Muslim West
        Beirut kills about 30 Muslims.

20   LEBANON - Heavy fighting breaks out in Beirut.

20   LIBYA - A car-bomb blast in Saddun Square kills 44
        Muslims in Tripoli.

20   INDIA - The leader of the Akali Dal, the moderate Sikh
        Sant Harchand Singh Longowal, is assassinated by fel-
        low Sikhs in Punjab.

20   EGYPT - The Israeli Administrative Attache in Cairo is
        assassinated. His wife and secretary are wounded. The
        previously unknown Egyptian Revolution group takes
        credit for the murder.

21   UNITED STATES - The government accuses the Soviet Union of using special chemicals to allow tracking of the movements of US diplomats in Moscow. A team of scientific investigators is sent to the Soviet Union to study the evidence.

22   USSR - The government denies the US allegation that it is monitoring the movements of American diplomats through the use of chemicals.

22   TUNISIA - The government orders a military alert along its border with Libya following Libya's expulsion of thousands of Tunisian workers.

22   SRI LANKA - As the Bhutan peace talks break down, the government reports more than 200 civilians dead as new violence erupts.

25   CHILE - A coalition of opposition groups calls for a relaxation of the state of emergency and direct presidential and parliamentary elections.

26   FRANCE - The French government is cleared of direct responsibility in the sinking of the Greenpeace Rainbow Warrior in New Zealand. Five French secret service agents are reported being in Auckland at the time of the sinking.

26   NEW ZEALAND - The government rejects the French report on the sinking of the Greenpeace flagship Rainbow Warrior in Auckland Harbor on 10 July.

27   NIGERIA - The government of Major General Mohammed Buhari is ousted in a bloodless coup led by Major General Ibrahim Babangida. The Armed Forces Ruling Council replaces the Supreme Military Council. The new National Council of Ministers retains six members of the old Federal Executive Council.

27   AFGHANISTAN - Soviet and Afghan government forces open a major offensive in the southeastern province of Paktia.

27   SWITZERLAND - The Third Review Conference of the Treaty on the Non-proliferation of Nuclear Weapons (NPT) opens in Geneva.

28   LEBANON - Israeli forces raid several Arab Muslim villages near the Israeli security zone.

28   ISRAEL - One hundred thirteen more Lebanese prisoners are released.

30   SOUTH AFRICA - Rioting breaks out around Johannesburg. More than 25 die.

SEPTEMBER

2   ALGERIA - The government voices its support of Tunisia in its current dispute with Libya.

3   GREECE - Two grenades are thrown into the lobby of a Greek hotel in Glyfada. Nineteen Britons are injured. "Black September," a covername used by the Abu Nidal group, takes the credit for the attack.

4   TUNISIA - The government cuts all trade with Libya and orders home all of its citizens who reside in Libya.

4   INDIA - Sikh terrorists assassinate Arjun Dass, a leading member of Parliament.

6   LEBANON - A confused battle commences that pits Druze militia artillery against Shi'ite artillery and Shi'ite militia against Palestinian guerrillas.

7   CANADA - The government announces it will not join the US in the SDI project.

9   UNITED STATES - The President announces limited economic sanctions against South Africa.

9   GREAT BRITAIN - Serious racial violence breaks out in Birmingham, Britain's second largest city.

9   THAILAND - A military coup attempt by forces loyal to Colonel Manoon Roopkachorn fails in Bangkok.

9   SPAIN - A remote-controlled car bomb detonates in Madrid injuring 18 Spanish Civil Guardsmen and an American who later dies of his wounds. The Basque Fatherland and Liberty-Military Wing claim credit.

10   ISRAEL - The last 119 Lebanese prisoners of war are freed.

10   EL SALVADOR - Terrorists of the Pedro Pablo Castillo Front kidnap President Duarte's eldest daughter, Ines Guadalupe Duarte Duran, and a female companion in a bloody shootout outside the university in San Salvador. One security guard is killed and another mortally wounded. The women will be held for nearly two months before they are released in a swap for 24 political prisoners.

13   MURUROA ATOLL - French President Mitterand announces nuclear testing will continue in spite of worldwide protests.

15   LIBYA - Heavy fighting breaks out in Tripoli among rival Muslim factions. One-quarter million people flee the city.

16   SAUDI ARABIA - Reconciliation talks between Jordan and Syria take place in Jeddah.

16   ANGOLA - South African troops pursue SWAPO rebels into Angola territory.

16   ITALY - Terrorists throw two Soviet-made F1 grenades into the Cafe de Paris 100 yards from the US Embassy in Rome. About 38 tourists are injured. The Revolutionary Organization of Socialist Muslims (an Abu Nidal covername) claims credit for the attack.

18   SOUTH AFRICA - Foreign Minister Roelof F. Botha admits his government is supporting MNR guerrillas in Mozambique even though South Africa signed the 1984 Nkomati Non-Aggression Treaty.

19   IRAN - Iraqi jets hit the Kharg Island oil terminal for the tenth time severely damaging the facility and further cutting the oil flow out of Iran.

19   SWITZERLAND - The third round of the arms control talks opens in Geneva.

19   BOLIVIA - In the face of a two-week-old general strike, the government declares a state of emergency.

20   JORDAN - British Prime Minister Margaret Thatcher is present at the signing of a multimillion pound arms deal with Jordan.

20   FRANCE - The Minister of Defense, Charles Hernu, and the head of the Foreign Intelligence Service, Admiral Pierre Lacoste, are forced to resign in the wake of the investigation into the sinking of the Greenpeace flagship _Rainbow Warrior_ as it lay at anchor in New Zealand.

21   SWITZERLAND - The NPT conference ends with a call for a Comprehensive Test Ban Treaty.

22   UNITED NATIONS - The UN Security Council unanimously condemns South Africa for its latest raid into Angola and orders an immediate withdrawal of all South African forces in Angolan territory. South Africa reports it has complied.

22   FRANCE - The government officially acknowledges that members of the Foreign Intelligence Service (DGSE) were responsible for the sinking of the Rainbow Warrior.

24   UNITED NATIONS - Soviet Foreign Minister Shevardnadze criticizes the US SDI project.

24   SOUTH AFRICA - The state of emergency order is lifted in six districts.

24   COMMUNIST CHINA - The government agrees to IAEA inspection of some of its nuclear power plants.

25   SOUTH AFRICA - A state of emergency is declared in eight new districts in the Capetown area.

25   CYPRUS - PLO terrorists seize three Israelis on a yacht in the harbor of Larnaca. They kill the hostages, then surrender without waiting for acceptance of their demands.

25   ITALY - A bomb detonates in the British Airways office in Rome. An Abu Nidal group Arab terrorist is captured as he attempts to flee the scene.

26   TUNISIA - The government breaks diplomatic relations with Libya after the expulsion of more than 30,000 Tunisians from Libya.

28   GREAT BRITAIN - Racial violence breaks out in Brixton, South London.

29   ANGOLA - A government offensive against a UNITA stronghold in southern Angola is repulsed by South African ground and air forces operating in support of the rebels.

30   LEBANON - Four Soviet diplomats are kidnapped in West Beirut in two separate incidents. The Islamic Liberation Organization, a Sunni Muslim group, claims responsibility.

OCTOBER

1   TUNISIA - Israeli jets attack the PLO headquarters near Tunis. About 60 are killed and the headquarters is destroyed. Yasser Arafat was not present at the time of the attack.

2   LEBANON - One of the kidnapped Soviet diplomats, Arkady Katakov, is found dead in Beirut.

4   USSR - The government orders most of its diplomats and
           citizens out of Lebanon.

7-9   MEDITERRANEAN SEA - The Italian cruise liner Achille
           Lauro, with 454 passengers and crew on board, is hi-
           jacked by four Palestinian terrorists. The terrorists
           demand the release of 50 Palestinians held in Israeli
           jails. One American passenger, Leon Klinghoffer, is
           murdered. The terrorists surrender to authorities at
           Port Said, Egypt, on 9 October.

10   MEDITERRANEAN SEA - US Navy F-14 fighters force down
           an Egyptian airliner carrying to freedom in Tunis the
           Arab terrorists who hijacked the Achille Lauro. The
           aircraft lands at a NATO base in Sicily. Italian
           police take the terrorists into custody, but their
           leader, Abu Abbas, is allowed to go free because of
           the Italian government's bungling of the affair. Abu
           Abbas apparently seeks refuge in Yugoslavia.

10   EL SALVADOR - Rebels attack the government army
           training camp at Palaquina.

10   HONDURAS - At the request of the US, Honduras seizes
           the first of a group of privately purchased arms
           shipments for the Contras in Nicaragua and returns it
           to the US.

11   ECUADOR - The government breaks diplomatic relations
           with Nicaragua.

13   SYRIA - The government announces that a tentative
           agreement has been reached between Christian, Druze,
           and Shi'ite Lebanese factions on a plan to halt the
           fighting.

14   GREAT BRITAIN - The government cancels a meeting with
           two PLO representatives who refuse to accept UN
           Resolution 242.

21   KUWAIT - At a meeting of the Gulf Cooperation Council,
           the member nations' defense ministers announce the
           formation of a joint strategic defense plan for the
           region and the establishment of a rapid deployment
           force.

21   UNITED NATIONS - Israeli Premier Shimon Peres notifies
           the General Assembly that his country is ready to end
           the war with Jordan.

22   JORDAN - Jordan announces a resumption of diplomatic
           relations with Syria after a four-year break.

22   UNITED STATES - Defense Secretary Caspar Weinberger
            accuses the USSR of deploying SS-25 missiles in
            violation of SALT II.

24   EL SALVADOR - President Duarte's daughter is released
            in exchange for 22 political prisoners and nearly 100
            wounded rebels.

24   UNITED STATES - The Senate orders a halt to weapons
            shipments to Jordan until after 1 March 1986.

24   MURUROA ATOLL - French commandos seize a sailboat
            carrying seven members of Greenpeace alleging they
            entered restricted waters.

25   ARGENTINA - President Alfonsin declares a 60-day state
            of emergency following a series of terrorist attacks
            that involve a number of army personnel and civilians.

26   MURUROA ATOLL - France carries out the second test in
            three days of its nuclear arsenal.

30   LEBANON - The three remaining Soviet diplomats held by
            Arab terrorists are released unharmed.

30   COMMUNIST CHINA - The government introduces conscrip-
            tion for its armed forces.

NOVEMBER

1   THE NETHERLANDS - The government announces its
            decision to deploy 48 US cruise missiles on its
            territory.

6   COLOMBIA - Terrorists from a group known as M-19 seize
            the Supreme Court building in Bogota and take a large
            number of hostages.

6   PUERTO RICO - Two unidentified assailants shoot and
            wound US Army Major Michael Snyder on the street in
            San Juan. A passer-by is also wounded. The separatist
            Organization of Volunteers for the Puerto Rican
            Revolution claims credit for the attack.

7   EGYPT - At a meeting with President Mubarak in Cairo,
            Yassir Arafat announces that in the future all PLO
            terrorist activity will be directed at Israeli
            controlled territories.

8   COLOMBIA - Army troops storm the Supreme Court
            building freeing 38 hostages, but killing more than
            100 people including the President of the Supreme
            Court and eleven other justices.

12   LIBERIA - A coup attempt against the government of
          Samuel Doe fails. The coup leader, General Thomas
          Quiwonka (Quiwonkpa), is killed.

15   UNITED ARAB EMIRATES - The emirates establish diplo-
          matic relations with the Soviet Union.

17   LIBERIA - President Doe accuses Sierra Leone of com-
          plicity in the recent coup attempt, closes the border,
          and recalls the Liberian ambassador in Freetown.

19   SWITZERLAND - US President Ronald Reagan meets Soviet
          leader Mikhail Gorbachev at the first summit meeting
          in six years.

21   SOUTH AFRICA - Twelve are killed when police fire on
          black demonstrators in Mamelodi Township.

22   IRAN - Ayatollah Montazeri is named the future suc-
          cessor of Ayatollah Khomeini.

22   NEW ZEALAND - Two French Secret Service agents are
          tried for manslaughter in connection with the Rainbow
          Warrior affair, are convicted, and are sentenced to 10
          years hard labor. One person was killed when the ship
          was blown up in Auckland Harbor as it prepared to sail
          into French waters in an attempt at halting a
          atmospheric nuclear weapon test.

23   IRAQ - The PLO announces it has moved its headquarters
          from Tunis to Baghdad.

23   MIDDLE EAST - An Egyptian airliner with 96 people on
          board is hijacked by Arab terrorists. The aircraft is
          forced to land at Malta. On the ground, the terrorists
          murder several of the passengers. Egyptian commandos
          storm the plane when the terrorists begin shooting the
          passengers. Sixty are killed, including all but one of
          the terrorists. The Arab Revolutionary Brigades (an
          Abu Nidal covername) and the Egyptian Revolution claim
          joint responsibility.

24   EGYPT - The government closes its border with Libya
          after accusing Libya of masterminding the hijacking of
          its airliner.

24   WEST GERMANY - A car bomb explodes near a US military
          shopping center in Frankfurt. About 36 people are
          injured, half of whom are Americans. No one claims
          responsibility for the bombing.

27   UNITED NATIONS - The General Assembly votes for a
          negotiated settlement to the Falkland Islands problem.

29   JAPAN - National Railway communications are cut in at
        least 16 places by terrorists of the Chukaku-Ha group.
        They also firebomb a railway station. Eleven million
        commuters are stranded.

DECEMBER

2   THE PHILIPPINES - A Manila court acquits all 26 de-
        fendents in the Aquino murder case.

3   SOUTH AFRICA - The state of emergency is lifted in
        eight districts.

3   EGYPT - The government orders a relaxation of the high
        state of readiness that has been in effect along the
        border with Libya.

3   THE NETHERLANDS - Although the government states its
        adherence to NATO and to its earlier decision to
        deploy cruise missiles, it announces that Dutch pilots
        will no longer fly nuclear weapons missions.

6   GREAT BRITAIN - The government announces its decision
        to join the US in the Strategic Defense Initiative
        "Star Wars" Project.

9   ARGENTINA - The trial of former junta members ends
        with ex-President Videla receiving a life term. Former
        President Galtieri is acquitted.

10   COLOMBIA - Approximately 60 armed guerrillas of the
        People's   Liberation   Army   attack   the   Bechtel
        Corporation construction site in the northern part of
        the country. Two American engineers are kidnapped and
        held for $6 million ransom. One of the Americans dies
        in captivity in 1986, the other is released unharmed
        shortly thereafter.

15   SYRIA - Syrian surface-to-air missiles are moved up to
        the Lebanese border to hamper Israeli reconnaissance
        flights. Israel complains.

15   SOUTH AFRICA - Six whites are killed by a land mine in
        Transvaal.

17   UGANDA - In a pact signed by General Okello and by
        Yoweri Museveni, the leader of the National Resistance
        Army, the government and the rebels agree to share
        power and to combine the two military forces.

20   LESOTHO - Terrorists, allegedly from South Africa,
        kill nine South African refugees in Maseru.

20   NIGERIA - The government announces it has foiled a
            military plot to overthrow President Ibrahim
            Babangida.

20   SAUDI ARABIA - The Saudis buy $3 billion worth of
            military equipment from Brazil.

21   HAITI - Thousands of demonstrators take to the streets
            to demand an end to the rule of President Jean-Claude
            (Baby Doc) Duvalier.

23   SOUTH AFRICA - A terrorist bomb placed in a shopping
            center in Amanzimatoti, Natal, kills six whites.

24   SOUTH AFRICA - Thousands of Zulu and Pondo tribesmen
            clash in a major battle near Durban. Fifty-three are
            killed in the battle, but the cause of the conflict is
            far from clear.

25   MALI - Fighting breaks out along the border with
            Burkina Faso (formerly Upper Volta).

27   ITALY - Palestinian terrorists attack the El Al check-
            in counter at Rome's Leonardo da Vinci International
            Airport. A simultaneous attack is carried out at
            Schwechat Airport in Vienna, Austria. Nineteen are
            killed and hundreds injured in the two raids. Investi-
            gators link both Iran and Libya to the attacks which
            are said to be in reprisal for the Israeli destruction
            of the PLO headquarters in Tunisia.

28   UNITED STATES - The US conducts an underground detona-
            tion of the hydrogen weapon which is to form a part of
            a nuclear-powered X-ray laser weapon. This is the
            seventh test since the USSR moratorium went into ef-
            fect on 6 August.

28   LEBANON - A peace treaty signed by Druze, Shi'ite
            Amal, and Christian militia leaders temporarily ends
            the fighting in Lebanon.

30   MALI - The cease-fire is arranged in the border
            dispute with Burkina Faso.

30   PAKISTAN - The eight and one half-year-old decree of
            martial law is lifted by President Mohammed Zia-ul-
            Haq.

Glossary of Abbreviations

The following abbreviations are found in the chronological listings and represent both standard acronyms and otherwise acceptable contractions that are used as a means of saving space. There are a few entries marked with an "*" to indicate that more than one meaning may be applied as they are used in this book.

-A-

AA	Antiaircraft
AAA	Antiaircraft Artillery
ABM	Anti-Ballistic Missile
ACR	Armored Cavalry Regiment (US)
AFB	Air Force Base
AFCENT	Armed Forces, Central Europe
AFM	Armed Forces Movement (Portuguese provisional government)
AFPFL	Anti-Fascist Peoples Freedom League (Burma)
AGI	Intelligence Collection Vessel
ALA	Arab Liberation Army (Israel/Syria)
ALN*	National Liberation Alliance (Brazil)
ALN*	Army of National Liberation (Algeria)
"American"	US 23rd Infantry Division
"Ana Maria"	<u>Melida Anaya Montes</u> (El Salvador rebel alliance)
ANC	African National Congress (South Africa)
ANT	Chad National Army
ANZUK	Combined Australian, New Zealand and United Kingdom armed forces
ANZUS Pact	Treaty signed by US, Australia and New Zealand

ARA	Revolutionary Armed Action (Portugal)
ARVN	Army of the Republic of (South) Viet Nam
ASALA	Armenian Secret Army for the Liberation of Armenia
ASW	Anti-Submarine Warfare
AVO	Hungarian Secret Police
AWACS	Airborne Warning and Control Systems

-B-

Baghdad Pact	Central Treaty Organization (CENTO)
BAOR	British Army on the Rhine
BLO	Black June (Al Ashifa) Organization (Great Britain)
BLT	Battalion Landing Team (US Marines)
BW	Biological Warfare

-C-

CAP	Combat Air Patrol
CENTO	Central Treaty Organization: also called the Baghdad Pact
CIA	Central Intelligence Agency (US)
CIDG	Civil Irregular Defense Group (South Viet Nam)
CinC	Commander-in-Chief
CINCPAC	US Commander-in-Chief, Pacific
CINCUSARPAC	Commander-in-Chief, US Army, Pacific
CNT	National Confederation of Labor (Uruguay)
COMECON	Council for Mutual Economic Assistance (Soviet bloc)
COMINFORM	Soviet Committee on Information
COMUSMACV	Commander, US Military Assistance Command, Viet Nam
CORDS	Civil Operations (&) Revolutionary Development Support (A major US force in South Viet Nam)
COSVN	Central Office for South Viet Nam - Communist political and military headquarters in South Viet Nam
CTZ	Corps Tactical Zone (South Viet Nam)

-D-

DEA	Drug Enforcement Agency (US)
DEFCON	Defense Readiness Condition (US)
DGSE	Foreign Intelligence Service (France)
DINA	Chilean Secret Police
DISK	Confederation of Reformist Workers' Unions (Turkey)
DMZ	Demilitarized Zone
DOD	US Department of Defense

-E-

EDC	European Defense Community
EEC	European Economic Community
ELF	Eritrean Liberation Front
ELN	Ejercito de Liberacion Nacional (Che Guevara Faction of the Bolivian National Liberation Army)
ELNA	Angolan National Liberation Army
EOKA-B	Cypriot Greek separatist movement
EPLF	Eritrean People's Liberation Front
ERP	Ejercito Revolucionario del Pueblo (Argentina)
ETA	Euzkadi ta Azkatasuna (Basque separatist terrorist group) (Spain)

-F-

FALN	Armed Forces of National Liberation (A Puerto Rican nationalist terrorist organization)
FAN	Armed Forces of the North (Chad)
FAR	Rebel (or Revolutionary) Armed Forces (Guatemala)
FARC	Revolutionary Armed Forces of Colombia
FBI	Federal Bureau of Investigation (US)
FF	Fast Frigate (Standard NATO ship-class designation)
FLLA	Front for the Liberation of Lebanon from Aliens
FLLF	Front for the Liberation of Lebanon from Foreigners
FLN	Front de Liberation Nationale (Algeria)
FLOSY	Front for the Liberation of South Yemen
FMNLF	Farabundo Marti National Liberation Front (El Salvador)
FNLA	National Front for the Liberation of Angola
FNLC	Congo National Liberation Front
FOBS	Fractional Orbital Bombardment System
FPJMC	Four-Power Joint Military Commission (Viet Nam)
FPL	Popular Liberation Front (El Salvador)
FRAP	Fuerzas Revolucionarias Armadas Populares (Mexico)
FRELIMO	Frente de Liberatacao de Mocambique (Front for the Liberation of Mozambique)
Fretilin	Revolutionary Front for the Independence of East Timor
Frolinat	National Liberation Front (Chad)
FROLIZI	United Front for the Liberation of Zimbabwe (Rhodesia)
FSN	Foreign Service National - A US Department of State foreign national employee
FUNK	Front Uni National du Kampuchea (National United Front of Kampuchea) - Cambodian Prince Sihanouk's movement dedicated to the overthrow of Lon Nol

-G-

GKR	Government of the Khmer Republic (Cambodia)
GLCM	Ground-Launched Cruise Missile
GMT	Greenwich Mean Time
GRAE	Angolan Revolutionary Government in Exile
GRAPO	October First Antifascist Resistance Group (Spain)
GSFG	Group Soviet Forces, Germany
GVN	Government of (South) Viet Nam

-I-

IAEA	International Atomic Energy Agency
ICBM	Intercontinental Ballistic Missile
ICC	International Control and Supervisory Commission
ICR	Independent Congo Republic
ICS	Integrated Communications System
IMF	International Monetary Fund
IRA	Irish Republican Army
IRBM	Intermediate-Range Ballistic Missile
Irgun	_Irgun Zvai Leumi_ (Israeli terrorist organization)

-J-

JCAG	Justice Commandos for the Armenian Genocide (US)
JCS	Joint Chiefs of Staff (US)
JRA	Japanese Red Army (International terrorist group)

-K-

KANU	Kenya African National Movement
Khmer Rouge	Originally members of the Cambodian leftist party "Pracheachon." Subsequently, a name given to all leftist rebels in Cambodia
KIA	Killed in Action
KPNLF	Khmer People's National Liberation Front (Cambodia)
KSCB	Khe Sanh Base (A USMC Fire Base in South Viet Nam)

-L-

Lao Dong	Viet Nam Workers' Party (Marxist-Leninist Party of North Viet Nam)
LARF	Lebanese Armed Revolutionary Faction
LCI	Landing Craft, Infantry
LST	Landing Ship, Tank

-M-

M-19	19th of April Movement (Colombia)
MAAG	US Military Assistance and Advisory Group
MAAGI	US Military Assistance and Advisory Group, Indochina
MACV	US Military Assistance Command, Viet Nam
MAR	<u>Movimiento de Accion Revolucionaria</u> (Mexico)
MAU	Marine Amphibious Unit (US Marines)
MBFR	Mutual Balanced Force Reduction
MiG	Soviet aircraft developed by Mikoyan and Gurevich
MIRV	Multiple Independent Reentry Vehicles
MLAPU	Marxist-Lenist Armed Propaganda Unit (Turkey)
MNF	Multinational Force (A UN peacekeeping force in Lebanon)
MNR	Mozambique National Resistance
MPLA	Popular Movement for the Liberation of Angola
MR	Military Region (Replaces CTZ in 1970 ARVN reorganization in South Viet Nam)
MRC	Armed Forces Council (South Viet Nam)
MRD	Motorized Rifle Division (USSR)
MTB	Motor Torpedo Boat

-N-

NATO	North Atlantic Treaty Organization
NAVFORV	US Naval Forces, Vietnam
NKA	North Korean Army
NLF	National Liberation Front: properly, the National Front for the Liberation of the South (Viet Nam)
NLP	Christian National Liberation Party (Lebanon)
NORAD	North American Defense Command
NPA	New People's Army (Communist) (The Philippines)
NPT	Non-Proliferation Treaty
NSC	National Security Council (US)
NVA	North Vietnamese Army: properly, the People's Army of Viet Nam
NVG	North Vietnamese Government
NVN	North Viet Nam

-O-

OAS	Organization of American States
OAU	Organization of African Unity
OSA	A class of Soviet torpedo boat

-P-

PAIGC	African Party for the Independence of Guinea and Cape Verde
Pathet Lao	Laotian Communist forces

PDC	Christian Democratic Party (Guatemala)
PDFLP	Popular Democratic Front for the Liberation of Palestine
PDP	People's Democratic Party (Afghanistan)
PF	Popular Force (SVN)
PFLO	Popular Front for the Liberation of Oman
PFLP	Popular Front for the Liberation of Palestine
PKI	Communist Party of Indonesia
PLA*	Palestine Liberation Army
PLA*	People's Liberation Army (Communist China)
PLAF	People's Liberation Armed Forces (Military wing of the NLF); also known as VC (Viet Cong)
PLF*	Palestine Liberation Front
PLF*	People's Liberation Front (Ceylon)
PLO	Palestine Liberation Organization
POL	Petroleum, Oil and Lubricants
Polisario	Popular Front for the Liberation of Saguia el Hamra and Rio de Oro.
POW/PW	Prisoner of War
PRC	People's Republic of China (Communist China)
PRG	Provisional Revolutionary Government (as established by the NLF in South Viet Nam)
PRP	People's Revolutionary Party (Communist party dominant in NLF in South Viet Nam)
PSDF	Popular Self-Defense Force (South Viet Nam)
PVOIA	Air Force of the National Air Defense Forces of the USSR
PW/POW	Prisoner of War

-R-

RAF	Red Army Faction (West Germany)
RF	Regional Force (SVN)
RLT	Regimental Landing Team (US Marines)
ROK	Republic of (South) Korea
ROKA	Republic of Korea Army
ROKAF	Republic of Korea Air Force
ROKN	Republic of Korea Navy
RVN	Republic of Viet Nam
RVNAF	Republic of Viet Nam Armed Forces
RZ	Revolutionary Cells (West Germany)

-S-

SADF	South African Defense Forces
SALT	Strategic Arms Limitation Treaty
SAM	Surface-to-air Missile
SAS	Special Air Service (Great Britain)
Savak	Imperial Iranian Secret Police
SBS	Special Boat Service (Great Britain)
SCP	Sudanese Communist Party
SDI	Strategic Defense Initiative (Star Wars)(US)

SDS*	Students for a Democratic Society (US terrorist organization)
SDS*	Socialist Students League (West Berlin)
SEA	Southeast Asia
SEATO	Southeast Asia Treaty Organization
SED	Social Union Party (Germany)
SHAPE	Supreme Headquarters, Allied Powers, Europe
SL	_Sendero Luminoso_ (Shining Path), a Peruvian terrorist organization
SLA	South Lebanese Army
SLBM	Submerged-Launch Ballistic Missile
SNCC	Student National Coordinating Committee (US)
Spetnaz	Soviet Special Purpose Forces
SRV	Socialist Republic of Viet Nam (Name given to reunified nation in 1976)
SSBN	A nuclear powered, ballistic missile submarine
SSR	Soviet Socialist Republic
START	Strategic Arms Reduction Talks
Stern Gang	_Lohamut Herut Israel_ (An Israeli terrorist organization)
SVN	South Viet Nam
SWAPO	South West African People's Organization

-T-

TAOR	Tactical Area of Operations
TERM	Temporary Equipment Recovery Mission (A US operation in SEA)
TPLP/F	Turkish People's Liberation Party/ Front

-U-

UAE	United Arab Emirates
UAR	United Arab Republic
UDI	Unilateral Declaration of Independence (as in Rhodesia)
UFM	Uganda Freedom Movement
UK	United Kingdom/Great Britain
UN	United Nations
UNC	United Nations Command (South Korea)
UNEF	United Nations Emergency Force (One of many UN-sponsored multilateral forces employed throughout the world)
UNITA	National Union for the Total Independence of Angola
UNO	United Nations Organization
UNTSO	United Nations Truce Supervisory Team
USAF	United States Air Force
USAID	US Agency for International Development
USARV	US Army, Viet Nam
USIA	United States Information Agency
USIS	United States Information Service

USMAAG	See MAAG
USMAAGV	See MAAGV
USMACV	See MACV
USSR	Union of Soviet Socialist Republics

-V-

VC	Viet Cong: properly the PLAF
Viet Minh	Party founded by Ho Chi Minh in 1941. Absorbed in Lao Dong in 1951
VTOL	Vertical Take-Off and Landing

-W-

WIA	Wounded in Action
WP/WPO	Warsaw Pact Organization
WSLF	West Somalia Liberation Front

-Z-

ZANLA	Zimbabwe African National Liberation Army (Mugabe) (Rhodesia)
ZANU	Zimbabwe African National Union (Rhodesia)
ZAPU	Zimbabwe African People's Union (Rhodesia)
ZIPRA	Zimbabwe People's Revolutionary Army (Nkomo) (Rhodesia)

Index

This index was set up using the following basic rules. These should be remembered when searching out specific titles.
- Some localities have not been identified with a country because the jurisdiction is under dispute.
- All acronyms, abbreviations, and local names of groups are listed under the full and proper name. (ex.: Stern Gang is listed as Lohamut Herut Israel.) NATO is listed as North Atlantic Treaty Organization. Check the Glossary provided for proper names or when in doubt. Cross referencing has not been used to any degree because of the length of the index.
- Missiles, tanks, and military aircraft are listed under the headings Missiles, Tanks, and Aircraft, respectively. Ships and commercial aircraft are generally under owner-country.
- References for the United States, South Viet Nam, and Great Britain which are divided into Military and Political sections. Military listings are numerical and by unit size.
- All titles, king, general, etc., have been omitted unless necessary for identification.
- Names of Asian origin are, in some cases, not intended to be reversed when indexed. Therefore, consult all of the possibilities. (ex: Ho Chi Minh is indexed as such.)

Argov, Shlomo, 733
Argueta, Manuel Colom, 629
Arias, Arnulfo, 50,69,324
Arif, Abdul Rahman, 269
Arkansas, US, 150,151
Armed Forces, Central Europe (AFCENT), 290
Armed Forces for National Liberation (FALN) (Puerto Rico), 664
Armed Forces Movement (AFM) (Portugal), 538
Armelino, Gregorio Alvarez, 770,791
Armenian, Revolutionary Army, 817; Secret Army, 683; Secret Army
     for the Liberation of Armenia (ASALA), 543,757,758,759;
     Suicide Commando Yeghia Kechichian, Van Operation, 708;
     terrorists, 603,683
Army of Deliverance, (Saudi Arabia), 444
Army of National Liberation (ALN) (Algeria), 132
Arosemena, Carlos, 25,227
Arosemena, Domingo, 69
Arosemena, Florencio, 48
Arron, Henck, 659
Arroyo (Araya?), Arthuro, 489
Arumburu, Pedro, 122
Arze, Walter Guevara, 641
Asbun, Juan Pereda, 605,606,607,616
Ascension Island, 252,726,727,728,733
Ascuncion, Paraguay, 680
Asencio, Diego C., 665
A Shau Valley, Viet Nam, 316,333,335,340,364,419
Ashdod, Israel, 33,38,296
Asia, 121
Asian Foreign Ministers Conference, 384,385
Asinara Island, Italy, 688
Asluj, Israel, 41
Asmara, Eritrea, 509,528,530,579,606
al-Assad, Hafez, 332,401,413,414,421,493,495,540,567,597,639,
     657,662,718,774,822,825
Assam, India, 751,752,829
Association of Southeast Asian Nations, 553
Aswan Dam, Egypt, 131,346
al-Atasi, Hashim, 51,100
Athens, Greece, 111,326,352,474,503,504,509,547,561,752;
     Airport, 534; Polytechnic Institute, 503; University, 477
Atlantic Ocean, 189,481,552,585
Atlas Moutnains, 231
Atlit, Israel, 825,829
Atomic Energy Commission, 20,54
al-Attassi, 322,339,401
Attlee, Clement, 63
Attopeu (Attapu) (Muang Mai), Laos, 382
Auckland Harbor, New Zealand, 826,830
Audran, Rene, 813
Augusta, Georgia, 384
Auka, Honduras, 710
Aures, Algeria, 116
Auriol, Vincent, 44,95

E
East Africa, 235,388
East African High Commission (GB), 5
East Berlin, 35,92,93,183,198,261; Four Power Agreement on
    Berlin, 427. See also Berlin and West Berlin
"Easter Offensive," 447
East Falkland (Soledad) Island, 721,729
East Germany, 34,35,39,57,59,81,91,92,93,95,102,120,126,135,152,
    164,166,177,183,196,198,201,227,238,241,242,246,259,261,
    328,330,343,370,388,400,402,404,471,476,507,509,518,521,
    591,609,672,683,687; forces, 332,688; Four Power Agreement
    on Berlin, 427; invasion of Czechoslovakia, 321,322;
    Iranian Embassy, 597; sovereignty, 120; Soviet Control
    Commission, 50; treaty with USSR, 542; Warsaw Pact, 117.
    See also Germany and West Germany
East Ghor Canal, Jordan, 345
East Pakistan, 329,411,412,413,415,416,417,418,419,425,430,432,
    433,434,435,436. See also Pakistan
Eben, Abba, 411
Ecuador, 25,71,72,202,227,279,342,345,347,389,408,409,443,474,
    540,550,575,691,692,693,695,696,701,834; US Military
    Mission, 409
Eden, Anthony, 105,116,127,143
Effiong, Philip, 368
Egan, John P., 530
Egypt, 2,3,11,19,20,24,32,33,36,38,39,41,43,56,62,72,78,79,81,
    82,83,84,85,87,88,92,99,103,109,115,119,120,121,122,125,
    128,129,130,131,132,133,135,136,137,138,144,147,148,150,
    151,152,155,161,166,169,171,187,200,211,212,215,216,217,
    223,230,255,259,276,277,293,294,295,296,297,301,302,303,
    309,309,311,319,325,326,339,346,348,354,358,365,368,369,
    370,371,372,376,391,395,397,398,399,405,409,410,411,412,
    413,414,416,417,418,419,423,424,426,428,429,431,433,435,
    440,441,443,448,452,455,458,459,460,462,465,467,471,473,
    475,477,479,480,482,485,488,489,490,491,492,493,495-496,
    497,498,500,502,503,504,508,509,512,522,523,527,530,536,
    552,553,554,555,560,561,568,574,580,581,585,586,590,591,
    594,595,597,598,602,603,605,606,607,608,610,612,613,614,
    615,616,617,619,625,628,629,632,633,637,648,651,653,658,
    659,660,662,671,675,697,698,702,706,707,708,709,716,718,
    719,724,725,743,747,751,775,780,784,790,791,792,793,794,
    802,813,815,821,835,837; agreement with Czechoslovakia,
    121; agreement with Saudi Arabia and Syria, 121; agreement
    with Sudan, 563; airliner hijacked, 836; Anglo-Egyptian
    Treaty 1936, 2,71,74; cease-fire with Israel, 392; Col-
    lective Security Pact, 57; disengagement 1974, 506; Embassy
    in Spain, 541; Embassy in Turkey, 634-635; forces, 301,326,
    333,414,431,476,494,551,565,566,579,596,635,655; High
    Command, 296; Fidayun/Fedaheenal, 131; Ibrahim al-Awal,
    137; Israeli Administration Attache, 829; Navy, 295;
    peacekeeping agreement for Sinai, 705; protocol with C.
    China, 557; Second Army, 496,499; Sinai Agreement with
    Israel, 540,541,542,551,564,566; Soviet Military Liaison
    Mission, 708; Third Army, 496,499,500,501; Treaty of

Ford Motor Company (Argentina), 484
Formosa, Argentina, 542
Formosa, 107,109,115,160,172,211. See also Taiwan
Forrestal, James V., 23
Fort Bragg, N. Carolina, 311
Fort Campbell, Kentucky, 305
Fort Caobang, Indochina, 60
Fort Chaffee, Arkansas, 670
Fort Douglas, Utah, 409
Fort Lewis, Washington, 344,347
Fort Stewart, Georgia, 801
Fountainbleau Conference, 12
Four Power, 27,31,79,94,100,108,117,118,163,207,328,335,372,427;
    Agreement, 183,202,213,507; Joint Military Commission
    (FPJMC), 477; Kommandantura, 35,213; Middle East talks,
    329,336,346; test-ban conference, 227,228. See also Allies,
    WWII and Western Allies
Four Power Fox Bay, Falklands, 729,730
Fractional Orbital Bombardment System (FOBS), 304
France, 2,4,5,8,9,11,12,13,14,16,19,22,24,25,31,32,38,44,46,50,
    51,55,56,59,60,61,63,66,70,77,78,80,81,84,85,87,90,91,92,
    93,94,96,97,100,101,103,104,106,107,108,109,110,111,114,
    115,116,117,118,119,122,126,128,129,130,132,135,136,137,
    144,147,149,150,155,157,158,161,162,167,169,171,175,176,
    178,180,181,182,186,189,190,193,194,196,197,198,200,208,
    209,210,211,212,221,222,224,227,228,236,237,238,239,242,
    244,245,246,256,268,271,278,281,290,291,296,298,299,300,
    308,316,317,318,321,322,328,329,334,339,348,349,350,358,
    359,364,365,368,375,378,383,384,396,400,402,403,404,422,
    427,442,443,451,455,457,458,467,468,469,470,473,475,476,
    478,479,480,481,482,485,486,487,489,490,508,510,511,518,
    520,523,526,528,536,543,556,557,558,568,570,573,574,575,
    576,578,579,584,586,589,591,598,604,605,610,622,635,636,
    650,672,681,683,688,693,696,700,704,705,716,717,723,730,
    740,745,749,756,758,760,766,771,774,781,782,789,792,795,
    803,807,813,820,821,826,827,830,832,835; agreement with
    Saudi Arabia, 525; Airborne Battalion, 767; Airforce, 769;
    Air France flight, 561,562,762,790; Atlantic Naval Forces,
    227; Channel Naval Forces, 227; conference on Shaba
    Province, Zaire, 603; Consulate in Libya, 656; Embassy in
    El Salvador, 632,633; Embassy in India, 812; Embassy in
    Kuwait, 771; Embassy in Libya, 656; Embassy in The Nether-
    lands, 521,522; Expeditionary Force, Viet Nam, 129; Fifth
    Republic, 164; forces, 10,120,139,141,151,153,156,165,240,
    305,312,313,398,454,538,583,624,628,640,663,667,690,697,
    712,738,741,743,761,762,764,791,793,801; Iraqi Embassy,
    606; Israeli Embassy, 365; Mid-East security program, 74;
    Military High Command, Viet Nam, 129; Pentalateral Agree-
    ment, 63; Saudi Arabian Embassy, 492; Syrian Embassy, 655;
    trade agreement with USSR, 328; treaty with United Arab
    Emirates, 580; treaty with Viet Nam, 580; Turkish Consul-
    ate, 708; Union, 9,14,15,35,48,64,82,95,96,104,120,121,161,
    162,163,164,180
Franco, Francisco, 22
Franco, Rafael, 22

Israel (cont'd), 485,486,487,490,493,494,495-496,497,498,499,
    500,501,502,503,504,507,510,511,512,513,514,515,516,520,
    523,524,525,526,535,537,545,549,553,554,555,558,561,564,
    568,569,570,573,575,580,585,588,590,591,594,595,598,599,
    600,602,603,604,605,606,607,608,610,611,612,613,614,615,
    616,617,618,619,622,628,629,631,632,633,635,643,650,651,
    656,657,658,659,660,662,664,665,667,668,671,675,677,678,
    684,685,692,694,698,699,701,704,705,709,710,711,712,713,
    718,719,723,724,726,728,729,733,737,738,742,743,745,751,
    753,755,756,757,760,762,766,768,770,771,783,785,786,788,
    794,795,799,800,801,802,803,805,808,811,812,813,816,817,
    819,821,823,825,826,827,829,830,831,833,834,835,837,838;
    Administrative Attache to Egypt, 829; agreement with
    Lebanon, 755, 799; agreement with Liberia, 761; agreement
    with US, 431; agreement with Zaire, 750; Air Force,
    308,334,340,348,350,360,361,363,364,367,369,372,377,393,
    463,491,618,634,693,702,703,725,727,774,804,828,833;
    Airborne, 1st Battalion, 2nd Paratroop Brigade, 136; Army,
    583,746; British Consulate, 332; cease-fire with Egypt,
    392; Central Command, 295; commandos, 346,369,388,482,562,
    668; Defense Forces, 523; disengagement 1974, 506; Eilat,
    303; El Al airliner, 330,564,631, office in Brussels, 353.
    Embassies in: Bonn, 353; Cyprus, 482; France, 365; Thai-
    land, 471; The Hague, 353; Uganda, 447; forces,310,339,354,
    362,363,375,456,478,509,527,536,538,539,540,544,635,655,
    666,669,673,683,701,720,734,735,736,737,739,740,743,759,
    763,792,813,814,815,818,822,830; Gahal, 392; independence,
    32,33; Haganah, Palmach units, 29; memorandum with US,
    712,713; Mevuot Yam, 517; 9th Infantry, 137; Northern
    Command, 295,296,298; 188th Armored Brigade, 497; peace-
    keeping agreement for Sinai, 705; Sinai Agreement with
    Egypt, 540,541,542,551, 564,566; Seventh Armored Brigade,
    496,497; War with Egypt 1956, 131, 136-139; 1965, 295-
    298,311
Issas, 323,583. See also Djibouti
Istanbul, Turkey, 120,330,331,388,420,580,632,646,757
Istiqlal Party (Morocco), 162
Italy,7,11,12,25,27,36,72,79,95,96,97,108,117,146,171,202,222,
    231,306,312,362,363,389,390,398,399,411,460,481,489,492,
    504,510,542,544,577,579,584,594,598,601,676,688,692,698,
    707,713,715,717,753,759,760,774,777,782,793,809,818,825,
    832,833,838; Achille Lauro, 834; agreement with Austria,
    362; agreement with US, 221; Austrian Alliance, 14; Embassy
    in US, 481; forces, 712,741,743,762,772,776,791; treaty
    with US,30; Treaty of Peace, 21,23; treaty with Turkey, 55
Ituzaingo, Argentina, 377
Ivanovsky, Yevgeny F., 687
Ivory Coast, 164,278; independence, 182
Iwo Jima, Japan, 484
Izaguirre, Jose Ignacio Arregui, 694
Izmir, Turkey, 330,331,630

J
Jackson, Geoffrey,408,420,428

Madrid, Spain, 541,551,700
Madura Island, 16
Mafia (Italy), 793
Maga, Hubert, 232
Magloire, Paul, 7,56,141
Magsaysay, Ramon, 145
Maharashtra, India, 506
al-Mahdi, Imam al-Hadi, 377
al-Mahdi, Sadik, 562
Mahendra, bir Bikham, 187
Mahe Province, India, 38,130
Maher, Ali, 78,79,82
Mahgoub, Mohammed Ahmed, 341
Mahimet army base, Ethiopia, 653
Mahsud tribesmen, 26
Mai Huu Xuan, 238
al-Majali, Hazza, 123,183
Majano, Adolfo Arnoldo, 639
Makarios (Archbishop), 127,128,146,173,233,235,238,243,282,374,
    516,559
Makonnen, Endalkatchen, 509,517
Malagasy Republic, The, 191,415,420,422,452,453,470,474,485,529.
    See also Madagascar
Malan, Daniel F., 80,88
Malatar, Pal, 158
Malawi, 247,423,433
Malaya, 29,35,78,181,199,218,226,230,553
Malay Archipelago, 540
Malay Federation, 223
Malaysia, 30,100,201,237,239,240,244,247,248,256,266,280,281,
    300,303,318,322,330,336,340,341,343,402,422,425,427,431,
    445,446,447,476,506,514,556,557,559,569,736; agreement with
    Thailand, 374; Anglo-Malaysian Defense Agreement, 331;
    Confederation of Malaysia, 230; joint command with Thai-
    land, 360; peace with Indonesia, 282; US and Swedish
    Embassies, 539
Maldives Republic, 556
Malenkov, Georgi, 89,94,114,149
Mali, (The Federal State of Mali) (French Sudan), 164,166,179,
    182,184,187,189,207,232,325,416,473,575,838; National
    Military Liberation Committee, 325; treaty with Niger, 479
Malik, Adam, 381
Malik, Jacob A., 70
Malinovsky, Rodion Y., 152
Malkya, Israel, 34
Malloum, Felix, 578,593,606,624,629
Malta, 251,426,428,437,439,440,471,516,550,566,574,594,607,629,
    630,774,805,808,836; agreement with GB, 446; agreement with
    Libya, 805
Malvinas. See Falklands, or specific Island
Mamelodi Township, S. Africa, 836
Managua, Nicaragua, 526,594,633,634,635,764; National Palace,
    608
Manara (Menara), Israel, 39
Mancham, James R., 582

Tanks, 481,496,497,499,500,530,673,674; "Abrams," 762; "Leo-
     pard," 762; M-48 "Patton," 256,451; M-60A3, 703; PT-76,
     310,441; T-34, 658; T-54, 827; T-54/55, 587; T-62, 593
Tan Son Nhut Airbase, SVN, 347,469
Tanzania, 244,303,315,329,360,383,388,421,423,427,430,433,448,
     449,454,463,464,483,487,519,532,555,566,579,614,615,618,
     623,646,668,769,813; forces, 612,617,626,629,630,631,632,
     633,662,665,673,699,702; Umma Party, 448
Ta Phraya District, Thailand, 546
Taraki, Nur Mohammed, 601,621,627,629,637,638; death announced,
     639
Tarantelli, Enzo, 818
Tarshia, Israel, 39
Tartus, Syria, 498
Tasa, Jordan, 497
Task Force Kilo, 314
Tassigny, De Lattre de, 63
Tatarescu, Jorge, 27
Tatum, Kampupchea, 816
Taya, Maaouya Ould Sidi Ahmed, 807
Taylor, Maxwell D., 201,230,245,247,265,267
Taylor-Rostow Report, 202
Tay Ninh, SVN, 238,284,379; Province, 125,283,289,304,338,381,
     447
Tchepone (Xenon), Laos, 410,412
Teal Inlet, Falklands, 732
Tehran, Iran, 100,537,566,592,601,603,609,617,622,680,681,682,
     702,705,744, 817,818,822
Tejada, Luis Garcia Meza, 675
Tel al-Zaatar, Lebanon, 561,562,565
Tel Aviv, 34,296,352,400,423,521,531,561,684,808
Temple Mount, Israel, 724
Teng Hsiao-ping, 556
Terceira, Portugal, 435
Termez, Afghanistan, 645
Terry, Fernando Belaunde, 323,738
Tet, 285,288,305,309,310,331,368,403,423
Tete Province, Mozambique, 468,828
Tet Offensive, 1st, 310-312; 2nd, 331,333,334,335,361,365,466
Tetuan, Morocco, 100
"Texas Towers", 99
Thach Han River, SVN, 451
Thailand, 44,46,71,74,91,104,105,108,115,162,163,192,210,212,
     218,235,241,280,289,290,291,305,308,320,336,341,351,356,
     360,372,374,376,386,387,391,395,401,425,432,440,455,469,
     474,482,492,499,505,509,534,535,537,543,546,547,553,555,
     556,559,562,563,564,568,569,578,579,581,585,589,592,617,
     618,627,655,662,672,673,674,675,678,686,693,694,698,715,
     716,718,746,750,753,754,772,781,783,798,800,809,816,831;
     agreement with Malaysia, 374; agreement with US, 347,348;
     "Black Panther" Division, 320,331; forces, 11,163,238,302,
     308,331,356,365,376,387,395,401,423, last in SVN withdrawn;
     442,479; Israeli Embassy, 471; joint command with Malaysia,
     360; Royal Thai Volunteer Regiment, 302. See also Siam

About the Author

Dr. John E. Jessup holds a Masters and Doctorate in Russian Studies from Georgetown University. He is also a graduate of the U.S. Army Foreign Area Specialist Program in the Russian Area, and did post-Doctoral research in Moscow at the Lenin Library and the Soviet Academy of Sciences.

His last assignment before retiring from the Army in 1974 was Chief, Histories Division, U.S. Army Center of Military History.

Dr. Jessup is the founding president of the United States Commission on Military History and currently serves as its president. He is also the Vice President of the Commission Internationale d'Histoire Militaire.

Dr. Jessup has been a member of the Board of Governors of the American Military Institute and has served on the Editorial Advisory Panel of *Military Affairs*. He has lectured at numerous universities and military academies both here and abroad.

He is the author of a number of works on military history, including the *Balkan Military History: A Bibliography*, and also co-editor of *A Guide to the Study and Use of Military History*. He has also published numerous articles and book reviews in the fields of military arts and sciences, military history, and Russian and Soviet studies.

Dr. Jessup is an Adjunct Professor of History at George Mason University and concurrently serves as a group program director with the Questech Research Corporation.